Peter Norton's

Guide to
Visual Basic® 6

Peter Norton
Michael Groh

A Division of Macmillan Computer Publishing
201 West 103rd Street, Indianapolis, Indiana 46290 USA

Peter Norton's Guide to Visual Basic® 6

Copyright © 1998 by Peter Norton

International Standard Book Number: 0-672-31054-6

Library of Congress Catalog Card Number: 96-72394

Printed in the United States of America

First Printing: September 1998

00 99 98   4   3   2   1

Trademarks

Warning and Disclaimer

Executive Editor
Bryan Gambrel

Aquistions Editor
Bryan Gambrel

Development Editor
Nancy Warner

Managing Editor
Jodi Jensen

Project Editor
Tonya Simpson

Copy Editor
Sydney Jones

Indexer
Kevin Fulcher

Technical Editor
Dallas Releford

Software Development Specialist
John Warriner

Production
Marcia Deboy
Jennifer Earhart
Cynthia Fields
Susan Geiselman

Overview

Introduction   1

Part I Using Visual Basic 6   9

1   Getting Started with Viusal Basic 6   11
2   Understanding Visual Basic Projects   37
3   Visual Basic Code Basics   49
4   Using Visual Basic Variables   85
5   Designing the User Interface   121
6   Putting Your Forms to Work with Controls   165
7   Mastering Menus and Toolbars   197
8   Using the Visual Basic Debugging Tools   213
9   Handling Runtime Errors   241

Part II Object-Oriented Programming   257

10 Creating Objects and Classes   259
11 Advanced Class Concepts   277
12 Working with Objects and Collections   295

Part III Creating Printed Output   325

13 Using the Printer Object   327
14 Using Crystal Reports   337

Part IV Accessing Data   359

15 Reading and Writing Text Files   361
16 Mastering the Visual Basic Data Control   399
17 Creating Queries in Visual Basic   415
18 Mastering Jet DAO   429
19 Using Advanced Data Access Methods   457

Part V Integrating with Other Applications   487

20 Integrating with Microsoft Office 97   489
21 Integrating with Microsoft Outloook 97   507

Part VI Developing for the Internet   537

22 Integrating with Internet Explorer   539
23 Web Development with Visual Basic 6   559
24 Creating Intranet Applications   577

Part VII Advanced Topics   597

  25   Mastering the Windows API   599

  26   INI Files and the System Registry   639

  27   Using the Package and Deployment Wizard   675

  28   Professionsl Visual Basic Development   687

Part VIII Appendixes   713

  A   Glossary   715

  B   The Reddick VBA Naming Convention   725

     Index   743

Contents

Introduction   **1**

Who Should Read This Book?.................1
Why Study Visual Basic?.........................2
Is Visual Basic the Right Choice? 4
How This Book Is Organized...................5
Wrapping Up 7

PART I   **USING VISUAL BASIC 6**   **9**

1   **Getting Started with Visual Basic 6**   **11**

Visual Basic: The Fast Track to Windows
    Development 12
    Improving Technology for
        Developers 12
    Understanding the Advantages
        of Visual Basic 15
Getting Help...16
Visual Basic Development Overview 17
    Designing and Building the User
        Interface 18
    Writing Code That Responds to
        Events 20
    Creating and Calling Other
        Procedures as Needed 22
    Testing and Debugging 23
    Converting to Runtime Version..........24
    Preparing a Distributable Set
        of Files 25
Creating Your First Visual Basic
    Program 26
    A Simple Project...............................26
    Creating the Project 27
    Adding Controls to the Form 28
    Setting Control Properties.................29
    Writing Event-Driven Code 30
    Testing and Debugging the Sample
        Application 32
    Converting Sample Application to
        Runtime 33
Summary 35

2   Understanding Visual Basic Projects   37

Using Different Types of Projects 37
   Choosing a Project 39
   Understanding the Different
      Components of a Project 40
Understanding the Project Explorer
   Window 43
Working with Multiple Projects..............44
Setting Project Options 44
   Using the General Page 44
   Using the Make Page 45
   Using the Compile Page 46
Summary 46

3   Visual Basic Code Basics   49

Understanding Visual Basic
   Procedures 49
   Understanding Subroutines................50
   Understanding Functions 51
   Understanding Comments.................52
Using the Visual Basic Editor 53
   Opening the Code Window...............56
   Understanding Code Window
      Features 57
   Using Keyboard and Mouse
      Shortcuts in the Editor Window......60
   Understanding Editor Options 66
Controlling Program Flow 69
   Using Conditional Branching 70
   Loops...76
   Using Compiler Directives 81
Summary 84

4   Using Visual Basic Variables   85

Taking a Look at an Example 85
Understanding Visual Basic Data
   Types 88
   Byte...89
   Integer 90
   Long 91
   Single 91
   Double..91
   Currency 91
   Boolean 92
   Date..92
   String..94

Object 95
Variant 96
Declaring Variables 97
   Comparing Implicit and Explicit
      Variable Performance.....................98
   Providing Names for Your
      Variables..99
   Forcing Explicit Declaration............100
Using a Naming Convention 101
Understanding Variable Scope and
   Lifetime 102
   Examining Scope 102
   Determining a Variable's
      Lifetime 103
Converting Between Data Types 105
Working with Arrays 107
   Declaring Arrays..............................107
   Array Limitations 108
Understanding the Variant Data
   Type 109
   Variant Storage Requirements 110
   Special Values of Variant
      Variables......................................113
Passing Variables to Procedures............114
   Optional Arguments 116
   Using Named Arguments 117
Using Constants 118
User-Defined Data Types 119
Summary 120

5   Designing the User Interface   121

Understanding the Visual Basic
   Form...121
Getting the Look and Feel of
   Windows 122
Creating Your First Form 123
Adding New Forms 125
Understanding Form Properties 125
Form Appearance Properties 127
   `BorderStyle` 127
   `Name`...129
   `Caption` 129
   `Icon`...129
   `Picture` 130
   `BackColor` 131
   Font Properties 132

Form Control Properties.......................133
   ControlBox 133
   MinButton and MaxButton...............134
Form Size and Positioning Properties ..134
   StartupPosition 134
   Left, Top, Height, and Width 134
   Movable 135
   WindowState 135
   ShowInTaskbar 136
   More Form Properties.....................136
Other Form Properties 136
   Tag...136
   ScaleMode, ScaleTop, ScaleLeft,
     ScaleWidth, ScaleHeight 137
Referencing Form Properties 138
Setting Properties in Code 139
Positioning the Form with Methods......139
   Move 140
   ZOrder 140
Using Form Drawing Methods 140
   Circle 141
   Line 141
   PSet 142
   Point 143
   Cls 143
   Refresh 143
   TextWidth, TextHeight....................143
   SetFocus 144
Showing and Hiding Forms 144
Loading Forms 145
Unloading Forms 146
Understanding Form Events................147
Form Maintenance Events 148
   Initialize 148
   Load...148
   Activate, Deactivate....................149
   QueryUnload, Unload......................149
   Terminate 149
Form Operation Events 149
   GotFocus, LostFocus.......................149
   Paint 150
   Resize 150
Form Mouse Events 150
   Click, DblClick 151
   MouseDown, MouseUp 151
   MouseMove 153

Form Keyboard Events.........................153
   KeyDown, KeyUp 153
   KeyPress 154
Making the Most of Built-In Dialog
   Boxes 154
   The Message Box 155
   Using the InputBox Function 158
Understanding MDI Applications 159
   Creating an MDI Parent Form 160
   Turning Forms Into MDI Child
     Forms 160
   Behavior of MDI Child Forms 160
   Making the MDI Parent the Startup
     Form 161
   Creating Multiple Instances of
     Forms 161
Wrapping Up Forms............................162
Summary 163

**6 Putting Your Forms to Work
   with Controls   165**
Getting to Know the Toolbox...............165
Getting to Know the Visual Basic
   Tools 166
Customizing the Toolbox 167
Adding Controls to Forms 168
Using the Alignment Grid 168
Multiselecting Controls 169
Form Layout Functions 169
Control Properties 170
   Displaying Simple Text 171
   Displaying a Button 172
   Displaying a List.............................173
   Displaying a Drop-Down
     Selection List 175
   Displaying a Check Box 176
   Providing Mutually Exclusive
     Options 177
   Using the Frame Control 178
   Entering Text....................................178
   Drawing Shapes and Displaying
     Pictures 179
Selecting Files, Colors, Fonts,
   Printers, and Help 180
Generating Timed Events.....................181
   OLE Container Control....................182
   Grid and Spreadsheet Controls........183
   Creating Tabbed Displays...............184

Other Controls 185
Naming Controls 186
Copying Controls 187
Control Arrays 187
Referencing Controls 189
Passing a Control as an Argument 189
Determining the Type of Control 190
Using the Controls Collection 191
Control Focus...191
Setting Tab Order 192
Binding Controls 192
Dragging and Dropping 193
Handling Keyboard Events 194
Handling Mouse Events 195
Summary 195

7 Mastering Menus and Toolbars 197
Understanding Menus 197
Using the Menu Editor.........................198
Menu Arrays..200
Applying Menu Conventions 200
    Using Ellipses 201
    Allowing Keyboard Navigation 202
    Using Shortcut Keys 202
Using Pop-Up Menus............................203
Configuring Menus at Runtime 203
Understanding Toolbars 204
Finding the Perfect Icons 205
Adding Toolbars to Your
    Application 205
Customizing the Toolbar 207
    Removing a Button 207
    Changing a ToolTip 207
    Changing an Icon 208
    Adding a Button 209
    Moving a Button 209
    Creating Toggle-Style Buttons 209
    Creating Option-Style Buttons 210
    Adding Captions to Buttons 210
Configuring the Toolbar at
    Runtime 210
Handling Toolbar Events 210
Running the Menu and Toolbar Demo
    Program 211
Summary 211

**8 Using the Visual Basic
Debugging Tools   213**
Finding Errors 214
    Identifying Syntax Errors 214
    Identifying Logical Errors 216
    Dealing with Runtime Errors 217
    Avoiding Errors................................218
Using the Module Options 219
Traditional Debugging Techniques 220
    Using MsgBox....................................220
    Using Debug.Print 223
Using the Visual Basic Debugging
    Tools 224
    Using the Debug Toolbar 225
    Suspending Execution with
        Breakpoints..................................226
    Stepping Through Code 229
    Controlling Program Flow 231
    Getting to Know the Debugging
        Windows.......................................232
    Using the Call Stack 237
Summary 239

9 Handling Runtime Errors   241
Recognizing Runtime Errors 242
Trapping Errors in Visual Basic
    Applications......................................243
    Trapping the Error 243
    Handling the Error 245
    Redirecting the Program Flow 245
Using the Err Object 245
    Using the Err.Description
        Property 245
    Using the Err.Number Property 246
    Displaying More Helpful
        Information...................................246
Knowing Which Errors to Trap 248
Using the Resume Statement.................249
    Resume Label....................................250
    Resume Next......................................250
    Resume 251
Using On Error GoTo 0 252
Handling Errors Locally.......................252
Logging Errors 254
Summary 255

PART II OBJECT-ORIENTED PROGRAMMING 257

10 Creating Objects and Classes 259

Understanding the Benefits of
Object-Oriented Development............260

Understanding the Component
Object Model (COM) 260

Getting Started with Objects 261

Examining Objects 262

Using Objects in Applications 262

Understanding Classes 263

Creating a Simple Class 264

Beginning the Class Module............265

Adding Properties to the Class 266

Creating Methods for the Class 267

Using the Class Module 269

Using Property Procedures 271

Understanding Property Procedure
Types 273

Bulletproofing Property
Procedures 275

Summary 276

11 Advanced Class Concepts 277

Understanding Initialize and
Terminate..277

Looking At Class_Initialize........278

Using Class_Terminate 279

Testing For Existing Class
Objects 280

Creating Special Types Of
Properties...281

Creating a Read-Only
Property 281

Setting Up Write-Only
Properties......................................282

Setting Up a Default Property or
Method 282

Enhancing the Simple Class.................284

Looking at the Class_Initialize
Procedure 284

Adding Simple Property
Procedures 285

Adding the Color Property
Procedures 285

Adding the Year Property
Procedures 286

Adding Simple Methods to
clsCar2 287

Enhancing the Decelerate
Method 288

Enhancing the Accelerate
Method 288

Using the Enhanced Object Class..........289

Filling the Form with Data 290

Creating and Destroying the Car
Object 290

Setting the Car's Color 291

Making the Clean Check Box
Read-Only 292

Using the Object Browser 292

Understanding Collections 294

Summary 294

**12 Working with Objects and
Collections 295**

Using Collections...............................296

Examining Built-In Visual Basic
Collections...296

Looking at the Forms
Collection 296

Understanding the Controls
Collection 300

Surveying Other Built-In
Collections 303

Using the Collection Object.................303

Creating a Collection 305

Adding Objects to the Collection 305

Counting the Number of Items
in the Collection...........................307

Retrieving Objects from the
Collection 308

Removing Items from the
Collection 310

Destroying the Collection 311

Optimizing Object References.............312

Building the Case for Custom
Collections...313

Understanding Wayward Objects 313

Encapsulating Functionality 315

Creating Custom Collections 316
   Beginning the Collection Class 316
   Adding the `Item` Method 318
   Programming the `Add` Method 318
   Implementing the `Remove`
      Method 319
   Implementing the `Paint` Method 320
   Programming the `BlueCount`
      Property 321
   Wrapping Up the Collection
      Class 322
   Summary 323

PART III CREATING PRINTED OUTPUT 325

13   Using the Printer Object   327

Printing Information..............................327
   Following a Simple Print
      Routine 328
   Using the Printer Object's
      Methods 329
   Controlling the Printer 333
Using the Printer Collection.................334
Summary 335

14   Using Crystal Reports   337

Explaining Crystal Reports 337
Taking a Quick Tour.............................338
   Using the Design Window 339
   Using the Preview Window 341
   Working with the Crystal
      Reports Wizards 342
   Adding Custom Formulas to a
      Report...343
   Selecting the Required Records 344
Creating a Report 345
   Starting the Design Process 346
   Selecting the Fields for the
      Report...347
Using the Crystal Reports Custom
   Control...352
   Selecting the Report to Run 354
   Modifying the Optional
      Properties 355
   Activating the Custom Control........356
   Changing the Properties at
      Runtime 356

   Creating a Report Selection
      Interface 357
   Summary 358

PART IV ACCESSING DATA 359

15   Reading and Writing Text Files 361

Understanding Text Files 361
Downloading the Data 363
Reviewing Database Terminology 363
Looking At Text File Formats 365
Understanding Data Access
   Methods 367
   Sequential File Access 367
   Random File Access 367
   Binary File Access 369
Opening Text Files 369
Reading Fixed-Width Text Files 372
Reading Delimited Text Files...............374
Looking at More Complex
   Examples 375
   Reading Complex Fixed-Width
      Files 376
   Reading Complex Delimited
      Files...379
Taking a Closer Look at File
   Commands...382
   `Open` 383
   `Line Input` 383
   `Input` 383
Creating Text Files 386
   Outputting Fixed-Width Data
      to a File..386
   Creating Delimited Text Files..........390
Understanding Visual Basic's String
   Functions 392
Looking at Other File Operations 392
   Deleting Files 393
   Listing the Contents of a Folder......393
   Detecting the End of a File..............394
   Copying a File..................................395
   Determining a File's `TimeStamp` 395
   Determining the Size of a Closed
      File 395
   Determining the Size of an Open
      File 396

Getting a File's Attributes 396
Setting a File's Attributes 397
Summary 398

**16 Mastering the Visual Basic
      Data Control   399**

Introducing the Data Control 399
  Using the Data Control 400
  Understanding the Data Control
    Properties 402
  Knowing the Current Record 402
  Using Data-Bound Controls 403
Manipulating the Data Control at
  Runtime 405
  Programmed Access Using
    Events 405
  Navigating the Data Control in
    Code 408
Summary 414

**17 Creating Queries in Visual
      Basic   415**

Defining SQL 415
  Using the SELECT Statement 417
  Accessing Multiple Tables 418
  Adding Calculated Fields 419
  Specifying the Filter Criteria 421
  Aggregating the Data 423
  Grouping the Data..........................424
  Using SQL Statements with the Data
    Control 425
Testing the SQL 425
Summary 427

18 Mastering Jet DAO   429

Understanding How Jet Began.............429
What Jet Does 430
  Jet Tables.......................................431
  Jet Storage.....................................431
  Jet Indexes.....................................432
  Jet Relations 432
  Jet Queries.....................................432
Using Jet in the World of Database
  Applications....................................433
  Understanding Relational
    Databases 433
  Understanding Normalization..........435
  Understanding DDL and DML........436
  Understanding DAO Collections,
    Classes, and Objects.....................437

Getting Started with Jet and DAO 438
Changing the Data Structure 441
Creating an Application 443
  Starting the Application 447
  Adding a Record 449
  Saving the Record..........................449
Working with SQL 451
  Working with the Data Bound
    Control 452
  Displaying Related Records with a Data
    Grid..453
Summary 456

**19 Using Advanced Data Access
      Methods   457**

Understanding OLE DB.......................457
  Independently Created Objects........458
  Different Cursor Types 458
Using the ADO Library 458
Looking into the ADO Object
  Model...459
  Establishing ADO Connections 461
  Using BeginTrans, CommitTrans,
    and RollbackTrans.......................464
  Using the Error Object 467
Understanding the Basics of the ADO
  Recordset Object...............................469
  Creating a Recordset......................469
  Adding a New Record 471
  Creating Temporary Tables.............473
Accessing Parameter Queries and
  Stored Procedures 477
  Using the Parameter Object 479
  Executing Parameter-Driven
    Stored Procedures.........................481
  Multiple Resultset Stored
    Procedures 483
Summary 485

**PART V INTEGRATING WITH
          OTHER APPLICATIONS   487**

**20 Integrating with Microsoft
      Office 97   489**

Understanding ActiveX 489
Understanding Automation Concepts ..491
Looking at a Short Example 492

Referencing the Automation Server......494
Understanding Object Models 495
Integrating with Word 97 496
    Opening a Document in
        Word 97 497
    Learning the Word Commands
        to Use 498
    Displaying a Word Document in
        Print Preview 501
Creating a New Word Document 503
Saving a Word Document 503
Using Automation in Visual Basic
    Projects 504
Summary 505

**21 Integrating with Microsoft
     Outlook 97   507**
Understanding the Outlook Object
    Model...508
Controlling Outlook 511
Understanding Outlook Folders 512
Creating an Outlook Instance................513
Making Outlook Visible 515
Creating a Mail Message in
    Outlook 516
Attaching an Object to a Mail
    Message 519
Sending the Message 519
Closing Outlook 520
Creating Outlook Items 521
    Looking at Common Properties 521
    Creating Outlook Contact Items......524
    Adding Appointment Items..............526
    Creating Outlook Note Items 528
    Creating a Journal Entry 530
    Creating Outlook Task Items 532
Summary 535

**PART VI DEVELOPING FOR THE
          INTERNET   537**

**22 Integrating with Internet
     Explorer   539**
Using Automation with Internet
    Explorer...539
    Referencing the Internet Explorer
        Automation Server 539
    Referencing an Internet Explorer
        Automation Object........................540

Hiding and Showing Internet
    Explorer 541
Shutting Down Internet Explorer 541
Browsing a Specific Page or
    Document Using the Navigate
    Method 541
Navigating the History List 545
Displaying the User's Home Page
    or Search Page 545
Using the Properties of the Internet
    Explorer Object 546
Using the WebBrowser Control 549
Understanding the WebBrowser
    Events 552
    The BeforeNavigate2 Event............553
    The CommandStateChange
        Event...553
    The DownloadBegin Event 554
    The DownloadComplete Event..........555
    The NavigateComplete2 Event........555
    The NewWindow2 Event 555
    The ProgressChange Event..............555
    The TitleChange Event 556
Summary 558

**23 Web Development with Visual
     Basic 6   559**
Understanding Scripting Versus
    Components 559
Understanding the Difference
    Between ActiveX Controls and
    Visual Basic Documents 560
Creating an ActiveX Control for the
    Web..560
    Creating the New Control................561
    Adding the Code Behind the
        Form 562
    Adding Properties and Methods
        to Your Web Control......................564
    Changing the Code Functionality....566
Deploying Your Web Control 567
    Compiling Your Control 568
    Creating the Setup for Your
        Control 568
Testing Your Control in a Web
    Page 571
    Enabling a Control Through
        Script 571

Interacting with Your Control in
 a Web Page 574
Summary 575

24 Creating Intranet Applications   577

Comparing Client-Side and Server-
 Side Scripting 577
 Understanding Client-Side
  Scripting 578
 Using ASP with Microsoft Web
  Servers 579
 Creating an ASP Page.....................580
Glimpsing at Database Access
 with ADO...580
 Creating the Default Application
  Screens 581
 Listing the Records 583
 Adding a Record 585
 Editing an Existing Record..............588
 Deleting an Existing Record...........592
Summary 595

PART VII ADVANCED TOPICS   597

25 Mastering the Windows API   599

Defining the Windows API 599
Understanding Dynamic Linking..........600
Why Use the Windows API? 602
 Accessing a Common Code
  Base 602
 Using Tested and Proven Code........602
 Gaining Cross-Platform
  Compatibility 603
 Achieving a Smaller Application
  Footprint.......................................603
Using DLL Documentation 603
 Finding Documentation 603
 Deciphering the Documentation......604
 Understanding API Data Types 604
Moving from Windows 3.1 to
 Win32 607
 Taking Advantage of Architectural
  Differences 607
 Finding New Homes for API
  Functions 608
 Learning New API Function
  Names...608

Accounting for Changes to
 API Calls 609
Using the Windows API......................609
 Understanding the `Declare`
  Statement 610
 Understanding Windows
  Handles...614
Taking a Look at `WinAPI.vbp`..............615
Getting Application Information 615
 `GetWindowTextA` 616
 `SetWindowTextA` 618
 `GetParent` 619
 `GetCommandLineA` 620
 `GetClassNameA` 621
Getting Windows Information 622
 `GetWindowsDirectoryA`...................623
 `GetSystemDirectoryA`.....................624
 `GetTempPath` 625
 `GetVersionExA` 626
 `GetUserNameA` 628
Getting Hardware Information..............629
 `GetComputerNameA`..........................630
 `GetDriveTypeA` 631
 `GetDiskFreeSpaceA`........................632
Getting Disk Volume Information
 with `GetVolumeInformationA` 634
Summary 637

**26 INI Files and the System
 Registry   639**

Understanding the Registry 641
Using Regedit....................................642
 Editing Registry Values....................644
 Adding New Registry Values 645
Programming the Registry 647
 Using VBA Calls to Program the
  Registry 648
 Using the Windows API to
  Program the Registry 654
Manipulating INI Files........................665
 `WriteProfileString`........................667
 `GetProfileString`...........................668
 `GetProfileInt` 669
 `WritePrivateProfileString` 669

GetPrivateProfileString 671
GetPrivateProfileInt...................672
Summary 672

**27   Using the Package and
      Deployment Wizard   675**
Using the Distribution Wizard 675
Working with the Wizard 676
Starting the Wizard...............................677
Deploying the Package.......................682
    Floppy Disks 683
    Folders..683
    WebPost 683
Managing Scripts 684
Testing the Installation 685
Summary 685

**28   Professional Visual Basic
      Development   687**
Understanding What Makes a
    Professional Application 687
    Application Types 688
    Picking the Right Application..........688
    Following the Project Life
        Cycle..................................689
Application Performance 695
    Creating the Right Impression 696
    Letting Windows Work 697
    Distracting the User 697
Understanding an Application's
    Components...................................697
    Designing Good Forms....................699
    Using an About Box 704
    Using the System Registry 705
    Supporting the Users......................706
    Owning Your Program 709
    Protecting Your Application
        Name 709
    Copyrighting Your Work.................710
    Making the Final Decision 711
Summary 712

PART VIII APPENDIXES   713

A   Glossary   715

**B   The Reddick VBA Naming
     Conventions   725**

Version 5.0 725
Changes to the Conventions.................726
An Introduction to Hungarian 726
Tags 727
    Variable Tags.....................................727
    Constructing Properties Names 728
    Collection Tags 728
    Constants..728
    Menu Items 729
Creating Data Types.............................729
    Enumerated Types............................729
    Tags for Classes and User-Defined
        Types 730
    Polymorphism 730
Constructing Procedures 731
    Constructing Procedure Names 731
    Naming Parameters...........................731
    Naming Labels 731
Prefixes...731
    Arrays of Objects Prefix 731
    Index Prefix......................................732
    Prefixes for Scope and Lifetime 732
    Other Prefixes 732
Suffixes...733
File Names 733
Host Application and Component
    Extensions to the Conventions 734
    Access 97, Version 8.0 Objects........734
    DAO 3.5 Objects.............................735
    Visual Basic 5.0 Objects..................738
    Microsoft Common Control
        Objects 739
    Other Custom Controls and
        Objects 740
Summary 741

About the Authors

Computer software entrepreneur and writer **Peter Norton** established his technical expertise and accessible style from the earliest days of the PC. His Norton Utilities was the first product of its kind, giving early computer owners control over their hardware and protection against myriad problems. His flagship titles, *Peter Norton's DOS Guide* and *Peter Norton's Inside the PC* (Sams Publishing) have provided the same insight and education to computer users worldwide for nearly two decades. Peter's books, like his many software products, are among the best-selling and most-respected in the history of personal computing.

Peter Norton's former column in *PC Week* was among the highest-regarded in that magazine's history. His expanding series of computer books continues to bring superior education to users, always in Peter's trademark style, which is never condescending nor pedantic. From their earliest days, changing the "black box" into a "glass box," Peter's books, like his software, remain among the most powerful tools available to beginners and experienced users, alike.

In 1990, Peter sold his software development business to Symantec Corporation, allowing him to devote more time to his family, civic affairs, philanthropy, and art collecting. He lives with his wife, Eileen, and two children in Santa Monica, California.

Michael Groh is an author, writer, and consultant specializing in Windows database systems. His company, PC Productivity Solutions, Inc., provides information management applications to companies across the country. He has authored parts of more than 20 different computer books and is a frequent contributor to computer magazines and journals. He frequently speaks at computer conferences around the United States, provides Access and Visual Basic training for Application Developers Training Company, and is technical editor of *Access / Office / Visual Basic Advisor*, a publication of Advisor Publications.

Dedication

My work on this book project is dedicated to Matt Watson, a young boy living in Belleview, a small town here in north-central Florida. On February 24, 1998 three-year-old Matt suffered burns over 77% of his body in a tragic incident in his home. After four months at the Cincinnati Shriner's Hospital for Children in Cincinnati, Matt is back in Florida facing a long regimen of physical and medical therapy. I've never met Matt, but he obviously faces a long, hard road ahead.

You can read Matt's story at
`http://www.starbanner.com/Headliners/Watson060798.html`

Matt and his family need all the help they can get. I'm pledging my share of the royalties and advance from this book to the Matt Watson fund. You can help, too.

Matt Watson Fund
c/o AmSouth Bank
10715 South US Highway 441
Belleview, FL 34420

—Michael Groh

Acknowledgements

This book, like so many others, is the product of a team of people working behind the scenes. I'd like to take a minute to acknowledge and thank those who pitched in to push this project over the finish line.

First of all, thank you to Matt Wagner and Karen Shaheen, my team at Waterside Productions. Without Karen's frequent phone calls and email burning up the lines between Cardiff-by-the-Sea, California and Ocala, Florida I'd probably still be working on the Introduction to this book.

The Sams editorial staff was great to work with. Bryan Gambrel's guidance, suggestions, and supervision set the pace throughout this project. Bryan formulated the original concept and made many suggestions for the topics covered in this book.

As usual, there are too many editors, production staff, and other people involved at Sams to count them all. My special thanks to Tonya Simpson and Jodi Jensen for their hard work on this project.

My new friend Nancy Warner deserves special attention for her ongoing editing, organizing, and reminding tasks. Nancy did a great job of keeping me informed of this project's priorities and due dates.

And, of course, a big thank you to the Visual Basic experts who contributed several chapter elements of this book. First of all, my friend and associate James Foxall pitched in with Chapter 22, "Integrating with Internet Explorer." James dug into his considerable experience working with IE and came with up a terrific chapter.

I don't where Lowell Mauer gets his writing skill, but he produced Chapters 2, 13, 14, 16, 17, 27, and 28 in record time. I appreciate his generosity sharing his considerable Visual Basic experience on this project.

My new friend Tyson Gill did a terrific job on Chapters 5, "Designing the User Interface," 6, "Putting Your Forms to Work with Controls," and 7, "Mastering Menus and Toolbars."

I was lucky to have Michael Carnell available to produce Chapters 23, "Web Development with Visual Basic 6," and 24, "Creating Intranet Applications." The Internet is a fast-moving topic and requires special attention to document properly.

James Ralston (Chapter 18, "Mastering Jet DAO") and Mark Baciak (Chapter 19, "Using Advanced Data Access Methods") share their extensive database experience in their respective chapters. I appreciate all the work my writing team has done on this book!

Further thanks to Visio Corporation (www.visio.com) for its generous gift of a copy of Visio Technical. This product was used to produce many of the drawings you see in this book.

Finally, a special thank you to Peter Norton. I bought his original *Inside the IBM PC* book more than 15 years ago and still have it on my bookshelves. Peter Norton was the first person to explain that complex new computer using words that I could understand. His early book and magazine work formed the basis of much of my enthusiasm and understanding of desktop computers and software. As a long-time fan it has been a thrill to participate in a Peter Norton book project.

Tell Us What You Think!

As the reader of this book, *you* are our most important critic and commentator. We value your opinion and want to know what we're doing right, what we could do better, what areas you'd like to see us publish in, and any other words of wisdom you're willing to pass our way.

As the Executive Editor for the Programming team at Macmillan Computer Publishing, I welcome your comments. You can fax, email, or write me directly to let me know what you did or didn't like about this book— as well as what we can do to make our books stronger.

Please note that I cannot help you with technical problems related to the topic of this book, and that due to the high volume of mail I receive, I might not be able to reply to every message.

When you write, please be sure to include this book's title and author as well as your name and phone or fax number. I will carefully review your comments and share them with the author and editors who worked on the book.

Fax: 317-817-7070

E-mail: `cs_db@mcp.com`

Mail: Bryan Gambrel
          Executive Editor
          Programming Team
          Macmillan Computer Publishing
          201 West 103rd Street
          Indianapolis, IN 46290 USA

Introduction

I've often wondered what possesses certain people to take up dangerous pursuits such as hang gliding or parachuting. After all, there doesn't seem to be much financial gain in jumping out of an airplane or off a cliff, and you can get hurt doing it. Sometimes it seems like the ultimate folly to jump off a cliff or out of a perfectly good airplane and trust that a few pounds of rip-stop nylon cloth will safely waft you back to earth. I understand jumping out of an airplane can be fun, but I'm not sure the fun would offset the particular brand of excitement that must occur if the parachute doesn't open.

Then again, many people don't understand the appeal and excitement of developing Windows applications using tools such as Visual Basic. Writing computer programs, after all, is hard work and doesn't come easily to most people. I'm sure many parachutists think there is something wrong with a person willing to sit staring at a computer screen for hours and hours twiddling programming code this way and that.

Let's face it, there's nothing *easy* about sitting for hours composing a workable Windows application in Visual Basic or any other development system. The bottom line for people like me is that it's *fun* to master a programming language and get the computer to do something it's never done before. And, there is considerable money to be made in performing these feats of magic with programming languages.

There is no question that parachuting and developing Windows applications have certain things in common. They both require mastery of the equipment and tools associated with those endeavors. The parachutist who does not learn to use his altimeter correctly is heading for trouble the same way a Visual Basic developer who does not learn to use the debugging tools is heading for bugs and errant code.

The biggest difference between parachuting and programming in Visual Basic is that there is little chance you'll hurt yourself creating Windows applications with Visual Basic. You might bruise your ego, of course, but it is unlikely you'll break any bones in the process.

Who Should Read This Book?

This book was written with a certain reader in mind. Although much of the material in this book will be of interest to experienced Visual Basic developers, the primary reader is new to Visual Basic but not necessarily new to application development. Therefore, no previous experience with Visual Basic is required to use this book, but your previous experience with programming languages will be a valuable asset as you work your way through this book's chapters.

Visual Basic appeals to a wide variety of developers. First-time Visual Basic developers range from neophyte programmers who've never prepared any type of application with any development system, on through experienced mainframe developers with many years of developing applications with COBOL or RPG. As a programmer new to Visual Basic, you're probably curious about what Visual Basic is, what it's like to develop an application in Visual Basic, and what are the most important things for you to know about Visual Basic as you begin working with this complex, sophisticated development environment.

Why Study Visual Basic?

Ten years ago I was eking out a meager living as a C programmer, writing applications to run under UNIX. C is an incredibly powerful development system. There is virtually nothing that cannot be done with C or C++, the object-oriented successor to C. I am sure, however, that every successful C/C++ developer has had to climb a very steep learning slope. As powerful as C and C++ are, these languages are characterized by a cryptic, arcane, and difficult language syntax. There are hundreds of important C/C++ functions to master and programming conventions to adopt before you become proficient with these languages. Mastering C++ is as much art as it is science and requires considerable dedication to the learning process.

You've probably heard the story about how the BASIC language came about. Back in the 1960s, John Kemeny, an instructor at Dartmouth College, needed a programming language that would be used by students learning to program computers. The programming languages at that time were extremely difficult, professional-level tools that had little to offer the beginner. Kemeny decided to create an entirely new language that would be easy to learn, yet provide many features of the more sophisticated computer languages of the time. The result of his labor was BASIC, the *Beginner's All-Purpose Symbolic Instruction Code*. BASIC was successful because it was a simple yet powerful language that, with very few commands, could perform tasks that would otherwise require dozens or hundreds of lines of code in traditional languages.

A lot of time has passed since the Dartmouth College days, and the old BASIC language has evolved into Visual Basic, a robust object-oriented language syntax ideally suited for producing Windows applications. The Visual Basic syntax forms the core of the scripting languages built into all the Microsoft Office 97 and Office 98 applications. Word, Excel, Access, and PowerPoint all share *Visual Basic for Applications* (more commonly referred to as VBA), the exact same language syntax in Visual Basic 6.

In 1996, Microsoft began to license VBA to third-party software vendors. This meant that applications outside the Microsoft Office family could share the same programming language with Word, Excel, Access, and PowerPoint. AutoCAD, a computer-aided design application produced by Autodesk Corporation, and Visio, an object-oriented graphics package produced by Visio Corporation, were among the first of many third-party products to host VBA.

In addition to products such as Office 97 and Office 98 that support the full VBA syntax, many other applications such as Outlook and Internet Explorer support VBScript, a subset of the VBA language. VBScript is ideally suited to situations in which the full power of VBA is not required or is even dangerous. If Internet Explorer hosted the full VBA syntax, it would be possible to write damaging Trojan Horse applications that could wipe out a hard disk by simply viewing a Web page on a remote HTTP server. Even with certain language elements removed, however, VBScript is a valuable scripting language in situations such as Web pages and Microsoft Outlook. Anyone comfortable with the Visual Basic language will have no problem programming in VBScript.

All this means that you can leverage your Visual Basic skills to program any number of other systems. You needn't resort to learning an entirely new macro or programming language to provide a powerful, tightly integrated system with Word, Excel, Visio, or a number of other products.

A skilled Visual Basic developer is also a skilled Word, Excel, Access, or PowerPoint developer. The only difference between developing in Word or Excel and developing in Visual Basic is how you get to the code behind the application. Writing a custom Word application (perhaps an image or document management tool) requires the same coding conventions you use in Visual Basic.

The ability to migrate your programming skills to an important and successful product such as Microsoft Office is worth the effort required to master this complex development environment.

One of the beautiful things about the BASIC language is that many Visual Basic commands are the verbs and nouns we use every day. For example, to get data from a file, you use the `Get` command. To make a hidden object visible on the screen, you set its `Visible` property to `True`, and so on. If you're not sure of the exact syntax to use, trust your intuition and try whatever seems most logical based on what you already know about Visual Basic.

Visual Basic continues the tradition of a simple, powerful, and easy-to-learn language yet adds enough extended capabilities to satisfy the most jaded developer. For example, Visual Basic 4 was the first version that gave developers the ability to add their own object types to their Visual Basic applications. An *object* is a model of a physical entity such as a customer or employee. An object contains *properties* that describe the object, *events* that tell you what's happening to the object, and *methods* that provide the actions supported by the object. Objects and their properties and methods are discussed throughout this book, with detailed explanations in Part II, "Object-Oriented Programming."

Is Visual Basic the Right Choice?

Can you go wrong choosing Visual Basic as your primary development platform? After all, many other successful development environments are available including Visual C++, Borland Delphi, and PowerSoft's PowerBuilder. There's no question that it's just as easy as it ever was to choose the *wrong* system. There's always the chance that the vendor of a particular development tool will go out of business or fail to keep improving and supporting the product.

Not long ago, the desktop computing environment was very different from what it is today. In 1990, most desktop computers ran only DOS, and popular development systems included FoxPro, Clipper, and dBASE. Serious programming languages were pretty much limited to assembler, C, and Pascal. Microsoft Windows wasn't yet popular or successful. At that time, many developers devoted considerable time and effort acquiring skills in platforms that soon disappeared. Many of these development platforms failed because they were DOS-based and failed to make the migration to Windows. Others failed simply because they did not provide the power necessary for increasingly sophisticated and demanding users. It's a safe assumption that many development systems failed simply because they did not keep up with the rapid changes in desktop computing.

But in the case of Visual Basic, this possibility is remote. Several significant facts contribute to Visual Basic's bright future: First, Visual Basic is a huge product. Millions of developers of all skill levels are producing applications with Visual Basic. Visual Basic is now in its sixth major revision and is undergoing continual development and improvement at Microsoft. Many important new technologies have been introduced in Visual Basic long before appearing in other Microsoft products.

Furthermore, Visual Basic is a powerful development system. The VBA language itself contains built-in functions and subroutines for dozens of different common tasks. In addition to its intrinsic features, Visual Basic provides the capability to produce custom libraries and objects that can be loaded at runtime or bound into the distributable application. Much of this book's content is devoted to building these custom extensions to the built-in Visual Basic capabilities.

Visual Basic is also well supported by third-party products. Computer magazines targeted toward application developers are chock-full of ads promoting Visual Basic add-ons and development tools. Dozens of magazines and newsletters carry up-to-date articles on Visual Basic topics and technologies. Dozens of books on Visual Basic crowd the shelves of bookstores.

Finally, Visual Basic is a Microsoft product. Microsoft is indisputably the largest and most successful software company in the world. Microsoft's commitment to Visual Basic and VBA has only grown stronger over the past several years. Microsoft has cleverly positioned Visual Basic in such a way that it appeals to virtually all skill levels. Visual Basic 6 is available in three editions: Standard, Professional, and Enterprise. Each edition includes capabilities designed to appeal to a certain segment of application developers and is competitively priced with similar environments.

For all these reasons and many more, Visual Basic is indisputably the most attractive development environment currently available. In contrast to the obsolete systems of the past, Visual Basic has an undeniably bright and shining future. You can be part of Visual Basic's success.

How This Book Is Organized

The design of this book follows a typical programming project. You start out early in the book exploring the Visual Basic environment and getting a feel for what it means to develop a Visual Basic application. Later in this book, you go into more details of creating full-blown, professional-quality applications that will be used by people outside the developer environment. In most cases, this means that the application must include significant error handling and sophisticated user interface design.

This book is divided into seven sections. Although the arrangement of these sections is somewhat arbitrary, you'll learn Visual Basic at a gradual, easy-to-assimilate pace. The sections in this book are as follows:

- Part I, "Using Visual Basic 6"
- Part II, "Object-Oriented Programming"
- Part III, "Creating Printed Output"
- Part IV, "Accessing Data"
- Part V, "Integrating with Other Applications"
- Part VI, "Developing for the Internet"
- Part VII, "Advanced Topics"
- Part VIII, "Appendixes"

Part I, "Using Visual Basic 6," includes nine chapters designed to get you comfortable with the Visual Basic programming environment and get you on your way to creating sophisticated applications with Visual Basic. The chapters in this section include a tour of the Visual Basic 6 environment, working with controls and forms, and an introduction to the code found in all Visual Basic applications. Next you look at the complex subject of using Visual Basic variables and building custom toolbars used to enhance the user interface.

Part II, "Object-Oriented Programming," takes on the advanced topic of object-oriented programming with Visual Basic 6. Although you might wonder why an advanced topic appears so early in this book, because Visual Basic 6 is so dependent on objects and object classes, it's important to get this subject out of the way as soon as possible. The three chapters in this section examine the process of creating object classes and working with not only the Visual Basic built-in object classes but also the custom classes that you create for your applications. Finally, you look at the process of creating ActiveX controls and Automation servers for your Visual Basic applications. You quickly discover the power available to you as a Visual Basic developer through the use of classes and custom ActiveX controls.

Part III, "Creating Printed Output," explains how to produce printed output from your Visual Basic applications. Although the Crystal Reports for Visual Basic add-on is your usual route for generating reports and other printed output, you'll see in these chapters that you are not limited to using an add-on for this purpose. In fact, it is possible to directly control the printer attached to your users' computers, or another computer located somewhere on a network, without resorting to a Visual Basic control or other add-on.

Part IV, "Accessing Data," includes five chapters designed to get you up to speed with Visual Basic's superior data management capabilities. Most Visual Basic applications involve considerable data manipulation. Microsoft estimates that the primary purpose of more than 60 percent of the applications prepared with Visual Basic is to manage data. Therefore, you would correctly guess that Visual Basic includes powerful data access and manipulation capabilities. The chapters in Part IV provide a detailed survey of the database development tools available in Visual Basic 6. In these chapters, you learn virtually everything you need to know to produce and use effective databases with Visual Basic.

Part V, "Integrating with Other Applications," explains the secrets and requirements of using Automation in your Visual Basic applications. Visual Basic provides the capability to share data and resources with other Windows applications. Through the wonders of Automation, Visual Basic can communicate with and control other Windows applications. For example, you can use Microsoft Word to prepare printed output from your Visual Basic programs rather than Crystal Reports. Or, you might need the number-crunching power of Excel in a financial application written with Visual Basic.

Part VI, "Developing for the Internet," discusses how to use Visual Basic to produce applications that provide live database connectivity to Internet and intranet users. The Internet is an undeniable force to reckon with these days. Visual Basic is one of the most widely used Web application development platforms, mostly because of the Web development features built into Visual Basic 6. Active Server Pages work with Microsoft's Internet Information Server and other Internet-related products to deliver real-time access to databases across the Internet.

Part VII, "Advanced Topics," discusses adding professional and highly advanced touches to your code and how to distribute your Visual Basic program to its users. I've assumed the applications you write with Visual Basic 6 will be used by people outside your immediate environment. I expect that you'll want to provide professional polish and packaging for your applications so that you'll be proud of the result of your efforts.

This book also includes several appendixes containing information that really doesn't fit anywhere else. Appendix A is a glossary of common terms you'll encounter when working with Visual Basic. Appendix B is a complete naming convention that provides guidelines you might use when applying names to the forms, modules, variables, and other components of your Visual Basic applications. The Reddick Naming Convention presented in Appendix B is one of most widely accepted conventions available for Visual Basic programs.

Wrapping Up

Visual Basic is perhaps the most exciting development platform to be working with at this time. Not only is Visual Basic powerful and easy to work with, the additional benefits from learning and using a universal programming language can't be touched by any other development environment. Never before has a development system offered programmers so much in a desktop package. Virtually any type of application can be written in Visual Basic, and it's likely that you'll go on to produce applications you never dreamed of before mastering Visual Basic.

I've done my best to provide you with a valuable learning tool and reference in this book. Because I don't feel you'd find them helpful, you won't find much hyperbole and marketing talk in these chapters. Instead, each chapter contains what you need to know to master the chapter's topic. Nothing more and nothing less than those things a developer really needs to know.

I'd love to hear from you if you have any questions or comments about this book or its contents. Feel free to drop me a line at mgroh@austin360.com or visit my Web page at http://www.praxis.net/~mgroh to find updates to this book's sample code and supplemental files and code you might find interesting.

PART I

Using Visual Basic 6

Getting Started with Visual Basic 6

Just as with most things in life, you'll learn Visual Basic fastest and most easily by building Visual Basic applications. The chapters in this book are based on several different Visual Basic 6 projects. Although the text of each chapter explains the technology associated with the chapter's projects, you won't learn much simply by reading about Visual Basic. The quickest way to learn Visual Basic is to build programs and apply what you've read in this book to the practical task of creating working applications.

One of the truly beautiful things about Visual Basic is that it supports a gentle incremental development paradigm. Most developers build applications by starting with a very general notion of how the program will work and adding features as they go. At the end of a very few hours of development with Visual Basic you'll have a surprisingly complete and sophisticated Windows program running on your computer.

This chapter takes you on a whirlwind tour of the Visual Basic 6 development environment and describes what it's like to build applications with Visual Basic. Along the way you'll learn the overall layout of the Visual Basic environment, visit each of the developer tools, and preview the VBA (Visual Basic for Applications) programming language.

> **Note:** As you work your way through this book and see different views of the Visual Basic environment, keep in mind that you might not see exactly what's shown in the figures. The exact appearance of the Visual Basic environment depends on several options that you can change at any time. These options are discussed in many different places in this book.

Experienced Visual Basic developers will probably want to skim or even bypass this chapter. However, anyone who's been working with another development system should work her way through each of the exercises in this chapter. The information in this chapter is indispensable as you move through the rest of the book. The terminology introduced in this chapter, for example, is used throughout the rest of the book without explanation. If you miss the terminology here you might not understand it later in the book when you need it to understand the technical discussions.

Visual Basic: The Fast Track to Windows Development

Before beginning you should feel a certain level of accomplishment simply from having selected Visual Basic as your next development platform. Visual Basic is enjoying unprecedented success. Over the last several years millions of applications have been written in Visual Basic. Now in its sixth major release (unlike many other applications, Visual Basic did not bypass any version numbers as it progressed toward its current release), Visual Basic continues to grow in richness and depth faster than the Windows operating system family. With few exceptions, virtually every type of application can be written in Visual Basic and probably has been.

Visual Basic is primarily a *visual* design environment. You create a Visual Basic application by designing the forms that make up the user interface, adding VBA code to the forms and the objects such as buttons and text boxes on them, and adding any required support code in additional modules.

Earlier Windows application development systems, most notably Microsoft C and C++, required extensive design and layout preparations before even a single line of code could be written. Even then, preparing a successful application required hours of painstaking adjustment and debugging to fine-tune the initial design. Many commercial Windows application projects failed simply because the developers responsible for designing and debugging these applications never quite succeeded in adding the required features to a friendly, bug-free user interface.

Your chances of success with Visual Basic are much higher simply because the Visual Basic environment makes it easy to perform the basic tasks necessary to create Windows applications. Creating a form, adding controls to the form, and writing the code behind the form (all these steps are described later in this chapter) are all managed within a friendly environment. Online help containing thousands of programming examples is available with a single keystroke. Microsoft has constructed Visual Basic from the ground up as a fast, accessible development environment.

Improving Technology for Developers

Windows is a very significant advance in technology for programmers. Think about those poor folks who grappled with the complexity of providing a commercially viable feature set in the clunky text-based DOS environment. Back then each application had to include its own set of video, keyboard, and printer drivers. Every screen had its own hard-coded navigation and selection keystrokes because no mouse was available for random screen access.

Application development once was characterized by competing interface design packages, each package claiming to provide more sophisticated and robust capabilities than its competition. Ten years ago small details such as scrolling a region of the screen or popping a child window over a portion of the main screen were considered high art.

But, no matter how much attention was lavished on a DOS screen, no matter how carefully designed the user interface was or how "intuitive" a particular navigation trick was considered, developers were limited by the miserable resolution of text-based screens. With few exceptions, DOS screens were limited to 80 characters on no more than 25 lines, much too coarse for visually appealing displays. In addition most computer screens supported at most 4 colors with a few extravagantly expensive systems supporting as many as 16 simultaneous colors.

Worse yet, many DOS programs provided virtually no user interface at all. Instead, these programs relied on complicated command-line options to control how the programs worked. Figure 1.1 shows the command-line options of a popular DOS program.

FIGURE 1.1.
Many DOS programs were driven by command-line options.

```
LHarc  version 1.13c              Copyright (c) Haruyasu Yoshizaki, 1988-89
==================================================================== 05/31/89 ===
                  <<< High-Performance File-Compression Program >>>
================================================================================
usage: LHarc [<command>] [((/|-)(<switch>[-|+|2|<option>]))...] <archive_name>
              [(<drive_name>:)|(<home_directory_name>\)] [<path_name> ...]
--------------------------------------------------------------------------------
   <command>
       a: Add files to archive             u: Update files to archive
       f: Freshen files in archive         m: Move new files into archive
       d: Delete files from archive      e,x: EXtract files from archive
       p: disPlay files in archive       l,v: View List of files in archive
       s: make a Self-extracting archive   t: Test integrity of archive
   <switch>
       r: Recursively collect files        w: assign Work directory
       x: allow eXtended file names        m: no Message for query
       p: distinguish full Path names      c: skip time-stamp Check
       a: allow any Attributes of files    v: View files by another utility
       n: display No indicator             k: Key word for AUTOLARC.BAT
       t: archive's Time-stamp option
================================================================================
 You may copy or distribute without any donation to me.  Nifty-Serve  PFF00253
 (See the User's Manual for detailed descriptions.)       ASCII-pcs    pcs02846
G:\Utils>
```

Time and time again different software companies came up with their own notion of the "perfect" user interface (UI). Users were left bewildered and frustrated by conflicting UI conventions. What worked fine in WordPerfect had no counterpart in Lotus 1-2-3. Thousands of commercial applications bit the dust simply because they were too hard to use efficiently or because their learning curves were too steep to be mastered by significant numbers of users.

Microsoft Windows changed all that. No one will ever claim that any version of Windows is perfect, but even at its very worst Windows is infinitely preferable to DOS. As a developer, you must concern yourself with only a few well-established rules of interface design, and millions of users will be able to use your application with no documentation or training. You needn't worry about what monitor or printer the user has connected to his computer. Within limits, you needn't be concerned about memory or disk limitations.

Figure 1.2 shows a typical Windows application. The toolbar and menu bar at the top of the screen and the status bar at the bottom are common Windows application features. The Eudora Light developers did not have to invent these navigation and notification aids and, instead, just used what Windows provides.

FIGURE 1.2.

Eudora Light uses Windows to its fullest.

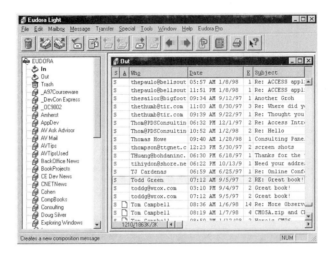

There are numerous benefits from using well-established user interface components such as those seen in Figure 1.2. Because Windows is ubiquitous, you needn't worry about having to explain how to use each part of the user interface. Menus, toolbars, scrollbars, maximize and minimize buttons, and other objects are familiar to millions of users. Although Visual Basic does not force you to use these well-established paradigms, if you use them your Visual Basic programs stand a much better chance of acceptance than if you create an entirely new and alien user interface. This basic rule is true even if you honestly feel a different approach is better than that provided by Windows.

The concept of "lowest common denominator" has virtually disappeared because the worst computer running the 32-bit versions of Windows (Windows 95, Windows 98, and Windows NT) is faster and more competent than the best desktop computer of a few years ago. Because the computers your users work with almost certainly have large amounts of memory and disk space as well as fast processors, you are free to concentrate on your program's logic rather than spend time optimizing and tweaking your applications for ultimate performance.

The best news is that Visual Basic is a "pure" Windows development tool. You'd have to try hard to create a Visual Basic application that does not comply with basic Windows design principles. The basic look and feel of the Windows 95 environment is built into all Visual Basic applications, and you can easily adopt these conventions in the programs you write. Furthermore, Windows provides drivers for thousands of different printers, video adapters, modems, and other peripherals. You needn't do a thing to enable your users to work with any Windows-compatible hardware.

Understanding the Advantages of Visual Basic

Let's take a minute to review some of the features that make Visual Basic such a robust and exciting development platform. Anyone who has been working with Visual Basic for any length of time is accustomed to these features and probably doesn't spend much time thinking about them. However, people who are new to Visual Basic should take a minute to consider why Visual Basic has become such a popular development environment. After all, there are more than three million Visual Basic developers, and it's hard to imagine that so many people would elect to use a limited and hard-to-learn programming system.

Don't worry if you are not yet familiar with the following terminology. The terminology used in this chapter and throughout this book will soon become part of your everyday vernacular. The following key points make Visual Basic an excellent development tool:

1. Visual Basic applications are *event-driven*. Event-driven means the user is in control of the application. The user generates a stream of *events* each time he or she clicks with the mouse or presses a key on the keyboard. Your Visual Basic application responds to those events through the code you've written and attached to those events.

2. Visual Basic supports the principles of *object-oriented design*. This means that you can compartmentalize different aspects of your application as *objects* and develop and test those objects independently of the rest of the application. By modifying certain properties and invoking the methods of these objects, you exert a great deal of control over the user's interaction with the Visual Basic program you've written. Although Visual Basic does not comply with all the concepts and principles behind the object-oriented development model supported by Visual C++, Delphi, and other development environments, Visual Basic includes enough of these features to more than satisfy all but the most ardent followers of object-oriented programming.

3. Microsoft has designed Visual Basic to be a *complete Windows application development system*. This means that your Visual Basic applications will look and behave like other Windows programs your users might work with. In other words, your Visual Basic applications will conform to the Windows 95 look and feel without any extra work on your part. Unlike Visual C++ and other development platforms you don't have to go to extreme measures to employ even the most sophisticated Windows features in your Visual Basic application.

4. Visual Basic is infinitely extensible through the use of *ActiveX controls, dynamically linked libraries* (DLLs), and *add-ins*. You can create these ActiveX controls, DLLs, and add-ins with Visual Basic 6 or buy them off the shelf from a large number of third-party software vendors. In fact, one of the major influences driving the rapid adoption of Visual Basic 6 is the desire of many developers to create ActiveX controls and DLLs for use in other Windows applications such as Excel, Word, or Access.

Getting Help

Visual Basic 6 includes extensive online help. Any time you need help press the F1 key and Visual Basic opens its help system to a topic related to the task you are trying to perform (see Figure 1.3).

FIGURE 1.3.

Visual Basic help is available at a single keystroke.

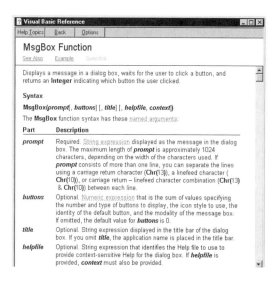

The Visual Basic online help is not intended to be tutorial. You are expected to have an idea of what it is you're looking for and the online help provides a complete reference to that topic. You'll have to find tutorial help elsewhere; this book, for example, is a good example of tutorial or "how-to" help.

The Visual Basic online help provides complete documentation of all the built-in VBA functions and subroutines, the Visual Basic objects such as forms and controls, and a great deal of information on Visual Basic concepts such as events and data access. You will not find finely detailed information such as descriptions of each of the built-in intrinsic constants (discussed in Chapter 4, "Using Visual Basic Variables").

Perhaps the biggest benefit provided by the online help facility is the hundreds of code examples (see Figure 1.4). These examples illustrate how to use most of the Visual Basic functions and subroutines. You can use the mouse to select portions of the text and code in the example window and copy that information to the Visual Basic Code window. Copying code from the online examples is a guaranteed way to use the correct syntax for the hundreds of different Visual Basic statements and commands.

FIGURE 1.4.

The code examples in the Visual Basic online help are very useful.

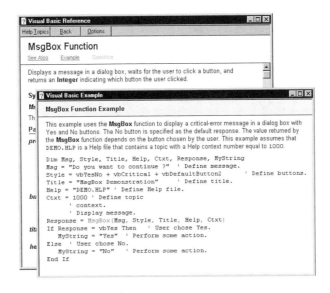

Appendix A, "Glossary," contains the descriptions of many Visual Basic terms and expressions. If you encounter an unfamiliar expression or term, check Appendix A as well as the Visual Basic online help.

Visual Basic Development Overview

Figure 1.5 shows the steps that all Visual Basic developers follow as they prepare programs destined for the user's desktop. Each of these steps is described in detail in the sections following this list:

1. Design and build the user interface.

2. Write code that responds to events.

3. Create and call other procedures as needed.

4. Test and debug.

5. Convert to runtime version.

6. Prepare distributable set of files.

These steps are not symmetrical. Some steps take longer than others do, and you will repeat several steps as the initial application design is refined and enhanced. You will spend most of your development time in the first four steps. The Visual Basic Package and Deployment Wizard helps you in the last step, which normally takes less than an hour or two. Using the Package and Deployment Wizard to package your application for distribution to end users is described in detail in Chapter 27, "Using the Package and Deployment Wizard."

FIGURE 1.5.

The prototypical Visual Basic development cycle.

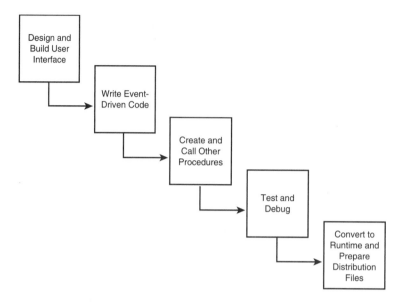

Even the most complex Visual Basic projects follow the steps described in the following sections. Most of your time with Visual Basic will be spent building the user interface and writing the code required by your application. By far the hardest part of mastering a complex development platform such as Visual Basic is learning the programming syntax required to provide the results your applications require.

Designing and Building the User Interface

The basic component of the user interface of a Visual Basic application is the *form*. A form is a window that contains several different objects. Figure 1.6 shows a form that, depending on how the form has been constructed, can be used for data entry, data display, or a combination of both.

All the objects in the form in Figure 1.6 are *controls*. The labels, text boxes, command buttons, and other controls have been placed on this form by its designer. In fact, nothing on the form is required by Visual Basic. You are free to design a form to include any controls that are required by the application's users. The form itself can look any way you want it to look. You can control the form's size and position on the screen, the color of the background, the size and position of the controls, and so on. There are virtually no limits placed on Visual Basic form design.

Almost all Visual Basic applications include several different forms, each of which performs some task required by the application. Most forms start the same way: some requirement of the application is best satisfied by a form containing certain controls. For example, the form in Figure 1.6 could be used for data entry. In which case, the text boxes would initially appear blank so the user could fill in the data to be added to the database underlying the application. Alternatively, the same form, or one very similar to it, could be used to display data already in the database and present the data to the user for modification. In fact, all these functions could be performed by the same form, depending on how the form was programmed.

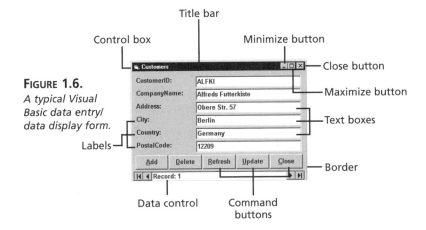

FIGURE 1.6.
A typical Visual Basic data entry/ data display form.

Building a form requires nothing more than adding a new form to the project and then dragging controls from a toolbox and dropping them on the form's design surface, as shown in Figure 1.7. Usually, you'll set several properties for each of the controls as well as for the form itself. In almost all cases you'll write code attached to the form and its controls to specify how the form actually works.

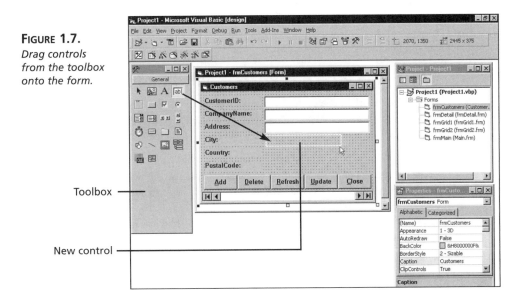

FIGURE 1.7.
Drag controls from the toolbox onto the form.

As you might expect, you must follow certain rules and requirements when using controls. For example, in most cases an Option Button control will be positioned within a Frame control, a Label control will appear to the left or above the Text Box control it's associated with, and so on.

The general rules for creating forms and using control objects are explained in detail in Chapters 2, "Understanding Visual Basic Projects," 5, "Designing the User Interface," and 6 "Putting Your Forms to Work with Controls." Because the user interface components of your programs are so important, you'll read about Visual Basic forms and controls in most of the other chapters in this book.

There is more to the user interface than just forms and controls, though. Most applications include toolbars and menus that put frequently used commands and features within easy access of the user as shown in Figure 1.8.

FIGURE 1.8.
Many forms contain a toolbar and menu.

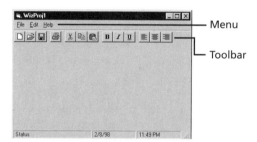

Adding and programming Visual Basic toolbars and menus are described in Chapter 7, "Mastering Menus and Toolbars." As you'll see in that chapter, menus and toolbars play important parts in most of the applications you write in Visual Basic. You can run any of several built-in commands in response to a toolbar button click or menu selection, or you can run functions that you've written for your Visual Basic applications.

Writing Code That Responds to Events

As mentioned earlier, one of the basic principles of all Windows applications is that the user is free to choose from several options rather than be confined to a predetermined sequence of interactions with the program. Visual Basic supports this principle through *event-driven programming*.

Events are generated by several different sources. Usually, you will be interested in user-initiated events that occur as the user presses keys on the keyboard or clicks an object with the mouse. There are several other sources of events such as when a form opens or closes or when Windows repaints a form because something has moved over a portion of its window.

One of the nice things about event-driven development with Visual Basic is that you needn't respond to every possible event that might occur. You write code for only meaningful events in the application you are creating. For example, even though a Command Button control supports both click and double-click events, you normally prepare code for only the click event. Unless you really mean to confuse your users, there is no need to write code attached to the double-click event.

The code you write for a form's controls exists as part of the form. This means that if you use the form in another application all the code you wrote for the form travels to the new location. You'll read more about the event procedures you add to your programs in Chapters 3, "Visual Basic Code Basics," and 4. In addition, most chapters in this book include extensive coverage of writing code for the forms in your applications.

Events happen all the time in Visual Basic applications. A small Visual Basic 6 application named Events accompanies this chapter. This application (see Figure 1.9) displays most of the events that occur as you move around the form by clicking on and tabbing into or out of the various controls.

FIGURE 1.9.
The Events project shows you a form's event sequence.

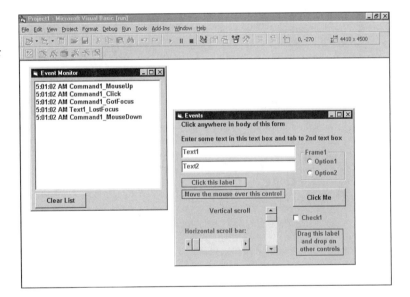

The events that occur on the form and its controls appear in reverse order in the list in the Event Monitor form. Therefore, the event at the top of the list occurred most recently.

In most cases, several events occur in response to some action on the part of the user. For example, if the focus is currently in the text box named Text2 and the user clicks the command button labeled Click Me, the following events occur in this order:

1. MouseDown (on the Click Me command button)
2. LostFocus (on the Text2 text box)

3. GotFocus (on the Click Me command button)

4. Click (on the Click Me command button)

5. MouseUp (on the Click Me command button)

You see a Click event because the mouse was used to click the Click Me command button. Notice, however, that between the time the mouse button was pressed and released, four events, seemingly unrelated to the mouse button position, fired: MouseDown, LostFocus, GotFocus, and MouseUp. Notice also that the command button got four of the events while the text box saw only one event.

Exactly which of these events you write code for depends on what you want the application to do in response to either the focus leaving the text box or the mouse click on the command button. A large part of mastering Visual Basic is knowing which of these events yields the results you want to accomplish.

> **Note:** Windows events always occur in VB programs, even if no code written is for them.

You'll read much more about events in Chapter 6. In the meantime, it's enough to know that events fire in a predictable sequence and that multiple events can occur in response to the simplest action by the user. It bears repeating that you write code for only those events that are important to your application.

Creating and Calling Other Procedures as Needed

In addition to the event-driven code behind the forms, most applications include a certain amount of code in freestanding, public modules that are part of the Visual Basic project. These modules are not connected to any of the forms in the application. By default, the code in public modules is available throughout the application and can be called from any procedure behind a form or contained in some other freestanding code module.

Chapters 3 and 4 explain what you must know about writing the Visual Basic code stored in the public and form modules in your application. If you are already familiar with C or C++, Pascal, FORTRAN, COBOL, or any other programming language, you'll be pleased to see the similarity between these languages and Visual Basic. Most of the programming concepts and rules you already know are applicable to your Visual Basic 6 programs.

In Chapters 10, "Creating Objects and Classes," and 12, "Working with Objects and Collections," you learn about class modules. A class module defines a new type of object you use in the applications you prepare. For example, you might construct a data acquisition class that retrieves data from some remote source. Alternatively, you might use a class to validate several different bits of data input by the user. Classes can simplify the task of writing Visual Basic applications. After you prepare the class module, you can easily use it in future Visual Basic applications without having to rewrite the same code repeatedly.

> **Tip:** You might be wondering when you'd want to go to the trouble of creating custom classes for your Visual Basic applications. After all, creating a class is considerably more work than building a simple code module. A general rule of thumb is to consider using a class whenever you find yourself writing code that duplicates the *functionality* you wrote into another application. If you discover a need to duplicate data access, error handling, or user interface components, you're probably better off crafting a custom class to handle the duplicated feature than simply writing the code a second time.
>
> There are so many different ways to use classes in Visual Basic applications it is difficult to provide hard and fast rules about when you should incorporate classes into your projects. As with most other things in life, use your best judgement!

Testing and Debugging

Visual Basic code tends to be complex. Even a simple project might have several thousand lines of code behind its forms and in public modules. This code might support dozens of different features, retrieve data, and perform complicated calculations. In addition, code often calls other procedures within the application, usually procedures stored in the public modules.

Problems with completed applications go far beyond obvious syntax or logical errors in the VBA code. Often, usability problems add to the difficulty.

The last step in creating a Visual Basic application is to thoroughly test and debug the user interface and code behind it. Even the most carefully designed and implemented code can contain errors and problems. If you're lucky, the errors in your code will be obvious and easily fixed. The worst bugs are those that allow the application to operate in a seemingly normal fashion but are corrupting or changing the data behind the scenes. For example, consider an inventory control application. A requirement of such an application is that it should automatically depreciate inventory on a periodic basis, perhaps on the first of the month, for tax purposes. The depreciation requirement needs precise inventory information and an accurate determination of the first day of each calendar quarter. If either of these needs is not met, the depreciation calculation may very well proceed without a glitch but will inaccurately provide the necessary tax information.

Other bugs affect the usability of the application. In many cases, aspects of the user interface you designed are not immediately obvious to your users. Perhaps it's not clear that the user is expected to click a particular button, or the user doesn't understand how to use some menu option. Often, a small design or programming change can make a world of difference to your users. Experience and good judgment provide the background necessary to create truly intuitive user interfaces.

Chapter 8, "Using the Visual Basic Debugging Tools," explains how to find and eliminate the bugs you encounter during the development cycle. Chapter 9, "Handling Runtime Errors," goes on to explain how to capture most runtime errors.

> **Warning:** Keep in mind that no debugging tool or error trapping routine can protect users from the type of bug that allows the application to appear to operate normally while it is incorrectly storing or modifying data.

> **Note:** Bugs in a program that do not cause a compiler error and are not immediately noticeable are called *logical errors*. A thorough testing plan with large amounts of good test data is the best way to prevent this type of bug.

Converting to Runtime Version

As you work with Visual Basic to produce your Windows application, you create several different files. An .FRM file contains the specification and code associated with a single form within the application, and a .BAS file contains only Visual Basic code. After you are satisfied with the design and operation of your Visual Basic application, you compile it into a distributable version. During the compilation process Visual Basic combines the information contained in the form files and code modules into a single executable file with an .EXE filename extension. The .FRM and .BAS files remain on the disk to enable you to continue making changes and improvements to the application.

Figure 1.10 provides a schematic of the compilation process. The .VBP file at the top of this diagram is the Visual Basic project file. This file, which is discussed in detail in Chapter 2 contains references to all the components of the project and is not actually compiled into the .EXE file.

The runtime .EXE is unlike most other executable Windows programs you worked with in the past. You can't run this file by itself from the Windows Explorer or by using the Run command on the Start menu. A Visual Basic executable requires a large runtime module named MSVBVM60.DLL. Usually MSVBVM60.DLL is placed into the Windows System directory as Visual Basic is installed on your computer. This file contains many of the routines and resources that are needed by your application on the end user's desktop.

FIGURE 1.10.

Compiling an application binds all the design-time elements into a single module.

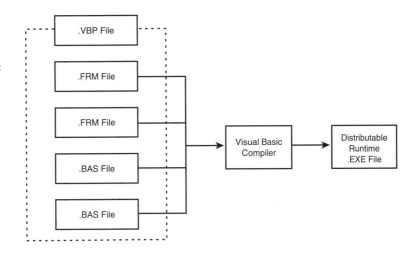

Compiling the application to an .EXE provides a small, fast file that is easily distributed to any number of users. The runtime file (MSVBVM60.DLL) and several other files must also be given to each user. Visual Basic 6 includes a Package and Deployment Wizard to help you collect the necessary files and prepare them for distribution to end users. The Package and Deployment Wizard makes sure the Visual Basic runtime (MSVBVM60.DLL) is installed into the Windows System directory on the user's computer, making it available to any Visual Basic application needing it.

Preparing a Distributable Set of Files

Preparing a Visual Basic application that will be sent out to many users is not a trivial task. The preceding section hinted at some of the challenges involved in preparing a set of files an end user can use to install the application on his desktop. Almost all Visual Basic applications require several supporting files beyond the application itself and the .EXE you built from your forms and code. These files include several DLLs (dynamically linked libraries) that provide database access and specialized functionality for the application.

No one wants to produce an application that requires hours of hands-on assistance to run properly on the user's desktop. It'd be hard to simply guess at which files must be sent to the end users, and building an installation routine that ensures the files are written to the proper locations on the user's computer is a real chore.

Fortunately, Visual Basic includes the *Package and Deployment Wizard*, which eases the process of building distributable sets of files. It produces an installation set that looks and behaves like the installation routines for any other Windows application. The Package and Deployment Wizard is smart and includes all the support DLLs and other files required by your application. The Package and Deployment Wizard is described in Chapter 27. In Chapter 27, you'll also read about some of the more common problems you'll encounter when preparing files to be sent out to your users.

> **Note:** Any time you modify a form or the code in a module the runtime .EXE must be recompiled. Therefore, after the program has been distributed to its users, changes to the application must be thought through, particularly if large numbers of users are involved.

Creating Your First Visual Basic Program

Now that you have an idea what Visual Basic development is all about, let's walk through a simple application project to build something useful. This simple demonstration illustrates most of the major aspects of developing applications with Visual Basic. Later in this chapter you'll read about several of these concepts in more detail.

This book assumes you've successfully installed Visual Basic 6 on your computer. Visual Basic is a big topic, and there aren't enough pages in this book to discuss all the available installation options. Instead, in the next section you plunge into producing an application with Visual Basic and practicing the steps that you'll repeat over and over again as you work with Visual Basic.

Keep in mind that Visual Basic supports a mind-boggling array of ways to perform most tasks. This chapter describes one way to do each of the application-building tasks but you should know that there are alternative ways to perform most of these steps.

A Simple Project

The project we'll build is shown in Figure 1.11. When the user clicks the button labeled Report Date and Time the current date is written into the text box near the top of the form and the current time is written into the text box under the date.

FIGURE 1.11.
This simple project illustrates many of the principles of Visual Basic application development.

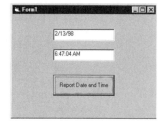

The exact appearance of this application can look any way you want it to look. You needn't put the text boxes at the top of the form or the command button near the bottom. As you develop with Visual Basic, you must continually make decisions about where to put controls and how the controls should look onscreen. In most cases, these decisions will be based on the user's requirements; however, in this simple project it's all your personal prerogatives.

At the same time, however, your designs should follow generally accepted Windows user interface guidelines. For example, most command buttons appear at the bottom or along the right side of dialog boxes. Controls are often logically grouped when they all relate to a single activity, such as setting default colors or inputting user information. The navigation sequence on most forms extends from the upper-left corner of the form down to the right corner of the form. Use familiar and successful Windows applications such as Microsoft Word, Microsoft Excel, or Quicken to get user interface ideas for your applications.

Creating the Project

You should find an entry for Visual Basic 6 on the Start Programs menu. There are several items in the Visual Basic 6 folder in addition to the Visual Basic 6 shortcut. The other utilities in this folder include the API Text Viewer, the Package and Deployment Wizard, and Crystal Reports. You'll read about these Visual Basic 6 utilities in different chapters in this book.

Figure 1.12 shows the Visual Basic 6 opening screen. The large dialog box in the middle of the screen contains three tabs below the colorful banner at the top of the dialog. For now, use the default New tab; the other tabs are discussed later in the book (mostly in Chapter 2. Also, leave the default Standard EXE icon highlighted as you click the Open button in the lower-right corner of this dialog box.

FIGURE 1.12.
Start with the default Standard EXE project type.

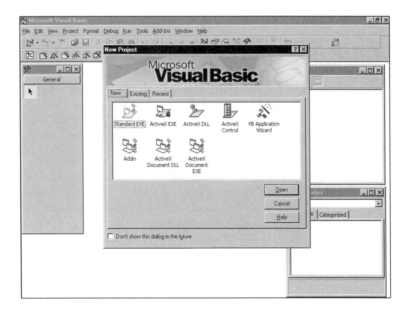

Because you've instructed Visual Basic to create a standard Windows application, the next screen you see looks similar to Figure 1.13. In this figure the Form window has been moved and resized to reveal the other Visual Basic windows under it. Visual Basic knows you need a form to serve as the user interface, so you've been provided with an empty form and all the tools necessary to populate the form with controls.

FIGURE 1.13.
Initially the Visual Basic environment is featureless.

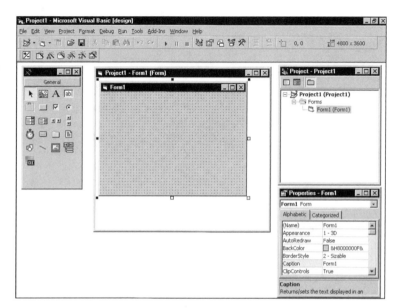

The form can be almost any size you want to make it. You can also position the form anywhere you want on the screen. These details are discussed in Chapter 5. For now, you can allow the form to open on the screen wherever it wants to.

Adding Controls to the Form

To the left of the Form window is the *toolbox*. The toolbox contains buttons or icons representing each of the types of controls you commonly add to forms. (There are many more controls you can add to forms. You'll read all about these controls in Chapter 6. Figure 1.14 shows the location of the text box and command button controls you need for this small demonstration application. Simply click one of these toolbox buttons to lock it down, move the mouse over the form, and drag the control out to its approximate size and position on the form.

You won't need much room for either the text box or the command button. The default font for Visual Basic forms and controls is 8-point MS Sans Serif, a relatively small font. You can experiment with font changes later in this chapter. The form in Design view should look similar to Figure 1.15 after you've added the text boxes and the command button. At this point neatness doesn't count. It's far more important to get the controls onto the form in more-or-less the top to bottom order you see in Figure 1.15.

FIGURE 1.14.
The Visual Basic toolbox contains many valuable controls.

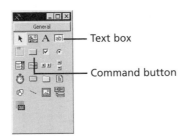

Text box

Command button

FIGURE 1.15.
This form serves as the user interface for the demonstration application.

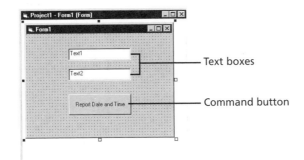

Text boxes

Command button

If you're bothered by the placement or the size of the controls on the empty form, you can move the controls to new locations by clicking (*once*, not twice!) in the center of each control and dragging it to a new location. Resize the controls by clicking the sizing handles in the corners or sides and dragging to a new size on the form.

Setting Control Properties

After you're satisfied with the size and position of each of the controls on the form, select the topmost text box by clicking it once with the mouse. If you accidentally click the text box twice, you'll open the Code window to the default event for that control.

> **Tip:** Press Shift+F7 to show the currently selected form in Design view.

Next, you must assign a name to each text box on the form and set the command button's Caption property. With the text box control selected, press the F4 key to open the Properties window (see Figure 1.16). The Properties window will be positioned to the default property for text boxes, which is the Text property. Use the mouse on the Properties window's vertical scrollbar to highlight the Name property at the top of the

Properties window. Because the Name property is at the very top of the Properties window, you could also press Ctrl+Home to move the cursor to the Name property.

FIGURE 1.16.

You should always assign a unique name to the controls on your forms.

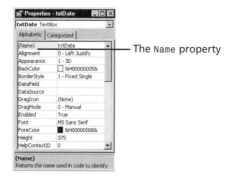

— The Name property

In either case, enter txtDate as the name of the top text box. Then click the second text box on the form, press F4 to move back to the Properties window, and set the name of the second text box to txtTime.

Set the name of the command button to cmdDateTime or something similar. While you're in the Properties window, set the Caption property of the command button to Report Date and Time. The Caption property is set to the text you want to appear on the face of the command button on the form.

> **Note:** Strictly speaking, for the purposes of this example it isn't necessary to set the name of the command button. Leaving the default command button name won't hurt anything in the example. However, providing descriptive names for the controls in your applications is a good habit to form.

In most applications you'll set more properties than just the name and caption. For example, you'll usually adjust the height, width, top, and left side of the control to precisely position it on the form. You might also want something other than the default 8-point MS Sans Serif font for the text boxes and other controls that display data.

Setting additional properties is an extension of setting the Name property. In all cases, you select the control on the form, then move to the Properties window with the mouse or by pressing the F4 key, and assign the desired values to the control's properties.

Writing Event-Driven Code

You can add code to the controls on a form at any time. After a control has been placed on the form, Visual Basic will not lose track of the control or its code. However, you should not change the name of a control after code has been written referring to the control. Visual Basic manages controls by their names, and if a control's name changes after code is written for the control Visual Basic will not understand the reference to the control.

Attaching code to a control is easy. Earlier in this chapter you saw a warning not to double-click a control because that opens the Code window, a potentially confusing situation when you're trying to set the control's properties. However, double-clicking a control is the fastest way to reach the code attached to the control.

With this in mind, double-click the command button on the form. The Code window opens, positioned to the default event procedure for the command button. Your screen should be similar to Figure 1.17. Notice how the Click event procedure for the cmdDateTime command button is positioned in the middle of the window and the text input cursor is positioned in the middle of the event procedure.

FIGURE 1.17.
The Code window is relatively empty at this point.

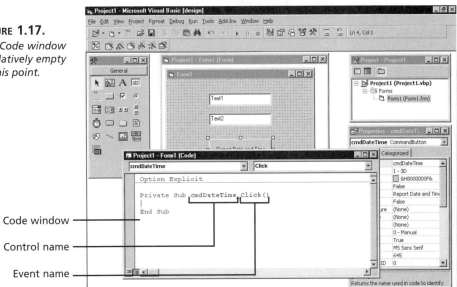

Notice the text at the top of the event procedure. In Figure 1.17 the first line of the procedure reads

```
Private Sub cmdDateTime_Click()
```

For now, ignore the Private Sub part of this line and concentrate instead on the procedure name proper, cmdDateTime_Click(). The cmdDateTime portion of the name identifies the control associated with this code, and Click() is the name of the event triggering this code. This handy naming convention, which you'll find in all the Microsoft products, makes it easy to tell which control a bit of code is attached to as well as the event that's triggering the code. This is one reason why it's so important to assign unique, descriptive names to all the controls on your forms. The default name for command buttons is something like Command1, which doesn't tell you much about how the button is used in the application.

Type the following two lines of code into the event procedure:

```
txtDate = Date()
txtTime = Time()
```

These two lines assign the current date and time, respectively, to the Text property of the text boxes named txtDate and txtTime you added to the form (the Text property is the default property for text boxes). After entering these two lines of code, the Code window should look like Figure 1.18.

FIGURE 1.18.

Two lines of deceptively simple code.

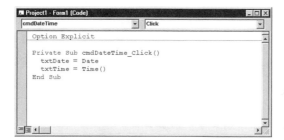

You needn't worry that Visual Basic removes the parentheses behind the Date reference. As you'll see later in this book, Date serves as both a function and as a statement. Visual Basic simply treats the Date keyword differently (by dropping the parentheses) than it treats the Time keyword.

What's "deceptively simple" about these two lines of code is that Visual Basic actually goes out to Windows, asks Windows for the current date and time, and plugs those values into the two text boxes on the form. These two programming statements are examples of how well Visual Basic integrates with the operating system. You needn't do anything fancy or special, just use the functions that provide you with the information you need in your application.

Testing and Debugging the Sample Application

Now you're ready to run the sample application. The Visual Basic toolbar contains the buttons required to run (Start), pause (Break), or stop (End) the project you're working on. Figure 1.19 shows the location of these toolbar buttons.

Very little can go wrong with this simple application. You will have problems if you neglected to name your text boxes as suggested (txtDate and txtTime) because the code behind the command button specifies these control names as the destinations for the data returned by the Date and Time function calls. However, as long as you've closely followed these instructions you shouldn't encounter any problems.

FIGURE 1.19.

You'll use these toolbar buttons a lot.

Break button

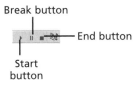

End button

Start button

Figure 1.20 shows an error dialog box you'll see when you've forgotten to properly name the text boxes on the form. The Variable Not Defined error occurs whenever Visual Basic doesn't understand some reference you've typed into the code. In this case, Visual Basic can't find anything named `txtDate` (you can see this reference highlighted in the Code window behind the error dialog box) and doesn't know where to find it.

FIGURE 1.20.

A very common error dialog box.

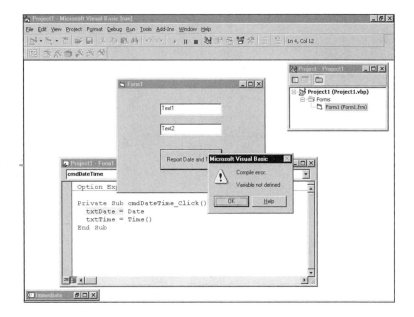

In most cases, the types of error you see illustrated in Figure 1.20 are easy to fix. Visual Basic makes it easy for you to locate the undefined reference by highlighting it in the Code window. Usually the error is due to a simple misspelling or an overlooked name change.

Converting Sample Application to Runtime

To see how easy it is to convert this application to a distributable, runtime version, drop down the File menu and select the Make Project1.exe command, as shown in Figure 1.21. This command invokes the Visual Basic compiler, which binds the various elements of your application together as a Windows-compatible .EXE file. This process was diagrammed in Figure 1.10.

FIGURE 1.21.

The Make command on the File menu creates an executable .EXE file.

The Make Project dialog box, shown in Figure 1.22, is network-aware. You can place the completed .EXE file anywhere you want on the local computer or on the network connected to the computer. You can use any Windows-compatible name for the application's executable file.

FIGURE 1.22.

Specify any location for the executable file.

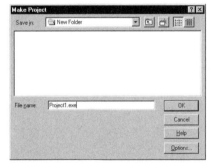

During the compilation process, Visual Basic checks the syntax of the code in the application and tests all references one last time. At the conclusion of the process, you should find an .EXE file in the location you specified in the Make Project dialog box. Use Windows Explorer to find the .EXE file and double-click the filename to run it, as shown in Figure 1.23.

That's not quite all there is to it, though. The .EXE you produce with the steps described so far in this chapter is not a full-fledged Windows application. You can't move it to just any PC and get it to run. Most Visual Basic .EXE files require large runtime files (MSVBVM60.DLL) and several other DLLs to be on the user's computer. As mentioned earlier in this chapter, you'll read about preparing distributable files for your users in Chapter 27.

FIGURE 1.23.

Run the new application from Windows Explorer.

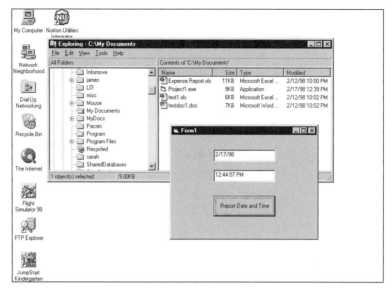

Summary

Visual Basic is a popular programming platform for a variety of Windows application development projects. More than three million developers have adopted Visual Basic as their primary programming platform. Thousands of Visual Basic add-ons are available from a large number of vendors, ensuring that Visual Basic will continue its popularity for a long time.

Development in Visual Basic is a step-wise, incremental process. From start to finish, Visual Basic applications can be broken down into smaller and smaller components that are easily tackled and completed. Large programs are built from small components that fit together in jigsaw-like fashion.

Visual Basic is a challenging environment within which to work. Such a powerful and flexible development system can't be mastered overnight. However, the benefits of learning how to program in Visual Basic are considerable.

Understanding Visual Basic Projects

Everything that you will ever do in Visual Basic is contained and controlled by a *project*. A project is a collection of files that are included with Visual Basic, created by you, or purchased from a software company to build a Windows application. In this chapter you learn how Visual Basic keeps track of what is in your projects, the types of projects you can create, and how to work with and modify the project file that Visual Basic uses.

Using Different Types of Projects

Every type of development system (for example, Microsoft Access, FoxPro, Visual C++, and so on) must provide some way for you, the developer, to maintain a list of what is being used by the programs you are creating. When you open any of these systems, such as Access, you see the objects or components that are included in the program. In Access, when you open the database file (.mdb), you see the Database tabbed dialog box (see Figure 2.1) with six tabs that contain all the different components of the database project.

FIGURE 2.1.
Microsoft Access maintains a project within the actual database file.

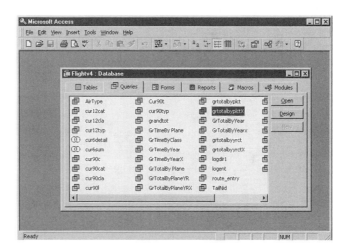

In fact, what we think of as an Access database file is actually the Access database project. Even a simple program such as Microsoft Outlook contains a way to control the different components you add to it. Figure 2.2 shows the Outlook bar and the Folder List.

FIGURE 2.2.

Outlook uses both the Outlook bar and the Folder List to maintain the different areas within the product.

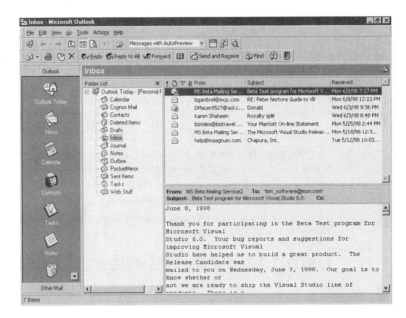

When you begin to create a new application in Visual Basic, the first thing you do is tell Visual Basic that you want to create a new project. In fact, when Visual Basic starts, it asks you which project to open or which type of project you want to create (see Figure 2.3).

FIGURE 2.3.

You must choose which project to open when Visual Basic starts.

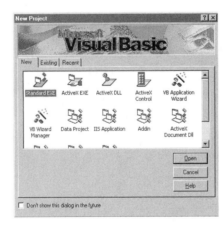

Choosing a Project

Choosing the correct project type is as important as the design of your program. If you start with the wrong project template, many options or features you are expecting to be in the project will be missing. This is annoying, and it wastes time while you add the features you need. Table 2.1 lists the project types available on the Visual Basic New Project tab.

Table 2.1. Available projects in Visual Basic.

Project Type	Description
Standard	This project contains the standard set of controls and is used to create a basic Windows application or to start a large application project.
ActiveX EXE	This project helps you create an ActiveX executable component that can be executed from other applications.
ActiveX DLL	An ActiveX DLL is used to contain controls and class code that can be used in other projects.
ActiveX Control	This enables you to create a custom ActiveX control.
Data Project	This project starts with database components already added to the project file.
IIS Application	This project is used to create an Internet application.
ActiveX Document DLL	An ActiveX Document DLL is used by Visual Basic applications that will be installed and executed from the Internet.
ActiveX Document EXE	An ActiveX Document EXE project is used to create an Internet-based Visual Basic application.
DHTML Application	This project creates a Web/HTML-based application that can be executed only in a Web browser.

In most cases, you would use the Standard project type to start a new application project. However, if you want to take a shortcut, you can use the Application Wizard on the New Project tab. This wizard creates the shell of an application, which can include the following:

- Menus
- Toolbars
- Data Access forms

- Web browser

- About box

When you choose the Standard project type, Visual Basic opens a new project file (.vbp) for you and immediately starts to add information to it. This project file is a list of the files and objects associated with the project you are working with, and it contains all the environment options that you can change. Whenever you save the project, the project file is updated to reflect the changes you have made. This provides you with a single location from which to manage your project's components. The tool that Visual Basic provides for you to manage the project and its components is the Project Explorer window (see Figure 2.4).

FIGURE 2.4.
The Project Explorer window is used to manage all the different components that you might add to a Visual Basic project.

Understanding the Different Components of a Project

A Visual Basic project can include many different types of components. Depending on the type of application you are designing, the project would consist of one or more of the file types listed in Table 2.2.

Table 2.2. Files contained in a Visual Basic project.

File Type	Description
Form (.frm)	Form files contain the textual descriptions of the form and its controls, including their property settings. These files can also have form-level declarations for constants, variables, and procedures.
Class (.cls)	Class files are similar to a form file, except they have no visible user interface. You can use a class file to create your own objects.
Standard (.bas)	These files contain public or module-level declarations of types, constants, variables, and procedures.

File Type	Description
Resource (.res)	A resource file can contain bitmaps, text strings, and other data that you can change without having to re-edit and then recompile your program code.
ActiveX documents (.doc)	These are similar to form files but are displayable only in an Internet browser.
User Controls (.ctl) and Property Pages (.pag)	These are similar to form files but are used to create custom ActiveX controls and their associated property pages.
ActiveX Controls (.ocx)	These are optional controls that you can add to the toolbox and then use on the program's forms.
ActiveX Designers (.dsr)	These files are any of the new designer components available in Visual Basic (such as Data Environment Designer and Data Report Designer).

When you start a new project, it contains only a single default form in the project. To add a file to the project, choose what you want to add by right-clicking in the Project Explorer window (see Figure 2.5) and selecting the appropriate option.

FIGURE 2.5.

Use the pop-up menu to add a component to the Visual Basic project.

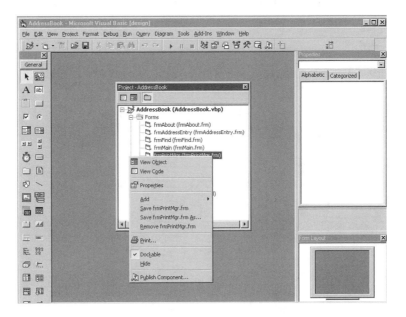

Although you add components to the project in the Project Explorer window, they are not really added to the project file until you save the project. Because you are simply including a reference to a file when you add it to your project, it can be used in any project that requires the functionality it contains. For example, you might have a form that allows the user to input a customer's name and address. This function might be needed in several different applications that you are working on. All you need to do is add the file to each project.

> **Warning:** Because the project contains only a reference to the file, any changes you make to the file will affect any project in which it is included.

The Project Explorer's pop-up menu also enables you to remove a component from the project but not delete it from the computer. If you remove a file from a project, Visual Basic updates the project file when you save it.

> **Warning:** If you delete a file from your computer, Visual Basic cannot update the project file; therefore, the next time you open the project Visual Basic will display an error message warning you that the file is missing.

Because the project file is saved as a plain text file (see Figure 2.6) you can edit it to change the references or settings in it. However, you should never make changes to it unless you know exactly what you are modifying and what the effect will be. If you make a mistake, it is possible that you will not be able to open the project again.

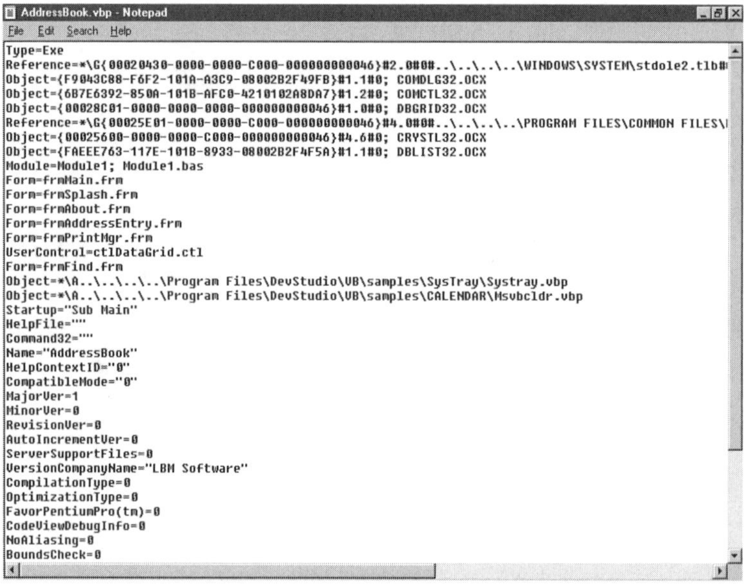

FIGURE 2.6.

View the project file's contents in Notepad.

```
AddressBook.vbp - Notepad
File  Edit  Search  Help
Type=Exe
Reference=*\G{00020430-0000-0000-C000-000000000046}#2.0#0#..\..\..\..\WINDOWS\SYSTEM\stdole2.tlb#
Object={F9043C88-F6F2-101A-A3C9-08002B2F49FB}#1.1#0; COMDLG32.OCX
Object={6B7E6392-850A-101B-AFC0-4210102A8DA7}#1.2#0; COMCTL32.OCX
Object={00028C01-0000-0000-0000-000000000046}#1.0#0; DBGRID32.OCX
Reference=*\G{00025E01-0000-0000-C000-000000000046}#4.0#0#..\..\..\..\PROGRAM FILES\COMMON FILES\I
Object={00025600-0000-0000-C000-000000000046}#4.6#0; CRYSTL32.OCX
Object={FAEEE763-117E-101B-8933-08002B2F4F5A}#1.1#0; DBLIST32.OCX
Module=Module1; Module1.bas
Form=frmMain.frm
Form=frmSplash.frm
Form=frmAbout.frm
Form=frmAddressEntry.frm
Form=frmPrintMgr.frm
UserControl=ctlDataGrid.ctl
Form=frmFind.frm
Object=*\A..\..\..\..\Program Files\DevStudio\VB\samples\SysTray\Systray.vbp
Object=*\A..\..\..\..\Program Files\DevStudio\VB\samples\CALENDAR\Msvbcldr.vbp
Startup="Sub Main"
HelpFile=""
Command32=""
Name="AddressBook"
HelpContextID="0"
CompatibleMode="0"
MajorVer=1
MinorVer=0
RevisionVer=0
AutoIncrementVer=0
ServerSupportFiles=0
VersionCompanyName="LBM Software"
CompilationType=0
OptimizationType=0
FavorPentiumPro(tm)=0
CodeViewDebugInfo=0
NoAliasing=0
BoundsCheck=0
```

Understanding the Project Explorer Window

The Project Explorer window displays all the project's components in a hierarchical list. There are three display options that you can use in the Project Explorer (see Figure 2.7).

View object

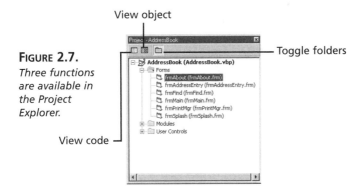

Toggle folders

FIGURE 2.7.
Three functions are available in the Project Explorer.

View code

View code and View object both display the visual interface associated with the file you selected, but View object will also display the code for the file in the Code window so you can write and edit the code associated with the selected item. The Toggle folders function toggles how the items are shown in the List window of the Project Explorer. Figure 2.8 shows the project listed in object folders, which separate the different files into types.

FIGURE 2.8.
If you toggle the folder view off, you see all the files listed alphabetically.

Note: If you are using Visual SourceSafe to control changes to a project's files, you see a check mark to the left of any filename that is checked out of SourceSafe and currently has read/write status.

Working with Multiple Projects

In most cases, you associate a project with a single application or program. However, as you start working with larger, more complex applications, you might need to have more than one project open at a time. Access to multiple projects is useful for building and testing programs involving user-created controls or other components. When more than one project is loaded, the caption of the Project Explorer window changes to Project Group and the components of all the open projects are displayed as shown in Figure 2.9.

FIGURE 2.9.

When working with multiple projects in a project group, project components are listed.

To add a second project to the current project choose File, Add Project from the Visual Basic main menu. When you save the project after adding another project, the Project Group information is also saved on your computer as a .vbg file.

Setting Project Options

Visual Basic enables you to customize each project by setting the number of properties associated with the project. To access the Project Properties dialog box, choose Project, Properties from the menu (see Figure 2.10). Any changes you make to these properties are also saved to the project file.

The Project Properties dialog box can have three to five tabbed pages, depending on the type of application project you're creating. Each page addresses unique areas of your project's information.

Using the General Page

The General page specifies the settings that your application needs to run properly. Figure 2.10 shows the default settings with which the Demo project was created. If your application will include an online help file, specify it in the Help File Name text box to set the default help file that your application will use whenever you access a help-related function or feature.

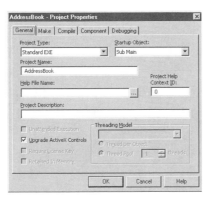

FIGURE 2.10.
The Project Properties dialog box enables you to customize your application's information and compile options.

The Startup Object combo box enables you to specify the form that you want to execute first when the application is started. You also can specify a special subprogram, Main, that executes to initialize files and settings before the first form is displayed.

Using the Make Page

On the Make page, you set the attributes for the executable file you'll create (see Figure 2.11). This page displays the name of the current project in the title so that you can choose the project to which to apply your changes. The current project is the item selected in the Project Explorer window.

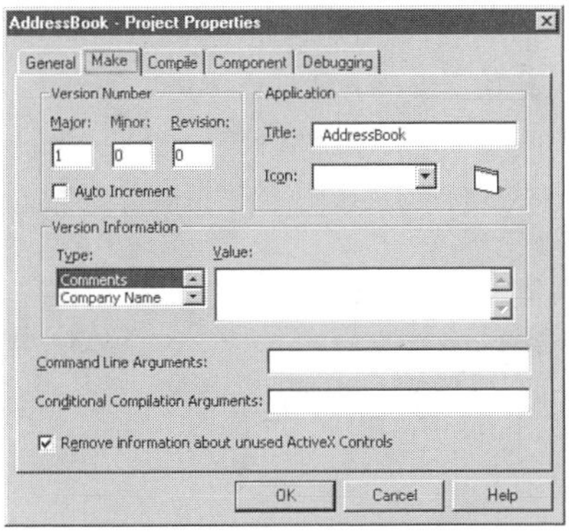

FIGURE 2.11.
The application's Make options are displayed on the Make page.

The Make page is important if you're working with a group project that contains multiple projects. When you look at the properties of an application's executable file, you see that the information available is directly related to this page. Figure 2.12 shows the Properties dialog box for a Microsoft Word executable file. (To view this dialog box, right-click a file in Windows Explorer and choose Properties from the pop-up menu.)

FIGURE 2.12.
Microsoft Word's Properties dialog box shows current information about the executable file.

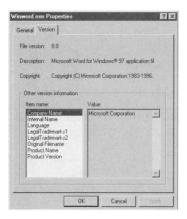

The version number and selection list at the bottom of this dialog box enable you to view the different information about the application.

The Make page is where you enter information about your application, such as the following:

- Application name
- Company name
- Description
- Copyright
- Trademark information
- Comments

The version number of an application consists of three separate values: a major release number, a minor release number, and a revision number (if needed). The Microsoft Word version number in Figure 2.12 tells you that it's version 8 of the application and there have been no minor releases.

Using the Compile Page

The Compile page (see Figure 2.13) lets you set the conditions that Visual Basic uses when computing your project. The options on this page deal with the optimization or performance of your application.

Summary

This chapter has described what a Visual Basic project is, the different types of projects that you can create, and why the project file is the most important file that you work with. The project file contains everything required by Visual Basic to create an executable program file out of the source code and form designs you created. Using the project file and the Project Explorer to display and maintain the information it contains enables you to keep track of what is included in your application's project. As you continue learning Visual Basic, you will be using the Project Explorer to add and remove forms and other components to your project.

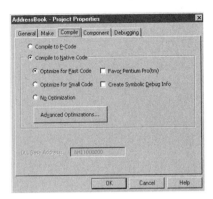

FIGURE 2.13.

The Compile page enables you to control the performance of the compilation process.

Visual Basic Code Basics

The formal name for the programming language built into Visual Basic 6 is Visual Basic for Applications (VBA), the universal language of all the major Microsoft desktop products. All the Office 97 and Office 98 applications (Word, Excel, PowerPoint, and Access) share the same language engine and programming constructs with Visual Basic 6. Visual Basic has featured VBA since Visual Basic 4.0 and most new language elements have been introduced in Visual Basic ahead of the other VBA applications.

Earlier versions of Visual Basic used proprietary syntax that was not always compatible with other Microsoft products. Beginning with Visual Basic 4.0, however, there are few differences between the programming syntax you use with Visual Basic and any of the other Microsoft desktop products. There are also many developer-oriented options in Visual Basic that influence how you interact with the Code window and the language syntax you write.

Chapter 2, "Understanding Visual Basic Projects," introduced you to the concept of a Visual Basic project and explained the roles of the different files involved in Visual Basic programs. This chapter takes you on an in-depth tour of the VBA language and offers several programming tips for writing good, solid applications. Throughout this book you'll see many examples of Visual Basic code. Some of the code examples in this chapter are shown as they appear in the Visual Basic Code window and others are presented as code listings. It's important that you are able to visualize code listings in this book as they'll appear in the Visual Basic Code window.

Understanding Visual Basic Procedures

The code in a Visual Basic application lives in containers called modules. You were introduced to modules in Chapters 1 and 2. As you learned in those chapters, modules exist behind the forms in a Visual Basic application as well as in standalone modules. The modules themselves contain many procedures, variable and constant declarations, and other directives to the Visual Basic VBA engine.

The code within the modules is composed of procedures. There are two main types of procedures in Visual Basic: *subroutines* and *functions*.

The general rules for procedures include the following:

- You must give the procedure a unique name.
- The name you assign to a procedure cannot be the same as a Visual Basic keyword or the name of a built-in Visual Basic procedure.
- A procedure can't contain other procedures within it. A procedure can, however, call another procedure and execute the code in the other procedure at any time.

The following sections cover some of the specifics regarding Visual Basic procedures. Planning and composing the procedures in your modules is the most time-consuming part of working with Visual Basic; therefore, it's important to understand how procedures fit into the overall scheme of application development.

Understanding Subroutines

Conceptually, subroutines are easy to understand. A subroutine (usually called a sub) is a set of programming statements that is executed as a unit by the VBA engine. VBA procedures can become complex, so this elementary description of subroutines is quickly overwhelmed by the actual subroutines you'll compose in the Visual Basic Code window.

Figure 3.1 shows a typical Visual Basic subroutine. Notice the Sub keyword that begins the routine, followed by the name of the subroutine. The declaration of this particular subroutine includes the Private keyword, which restricts the availability of this subroutine to the module containing the subroutine.

FIGURE 3.1.
You'll write hundreds of subroutines as you work with Visual Basic.

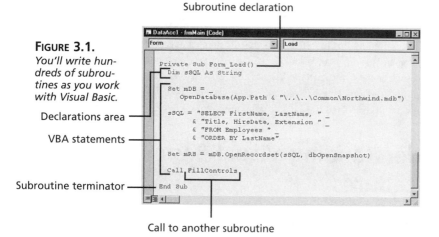

Subroutine declaration

Declarations area

VBA statements

Subroutine terminator

Call to another subroutine

```
Private Sub Form_Load()
    Dim sSQL As String

    Set mDB = _
        OpenDatabase(App.Path & "\..\..\Common\Northwind.mdb")

    sSQL = "SELECT FirstName, LastName, " _
        & "Title, HireDate, Extension " _
        & "FROM Employees " _
        & "ORDER BY LastName"

    Set mRS = mDB.OpenRecordset(sSQL, dbOpenSnapshot)

    Call FillControls
End Sub
```

The subroutine you see in Figure 3.1 contains most of the components you'll see in every Visual Basic sub or function:

- *Declaration*: All procedures must be *declared* so that Visual Basic knows where to find them. The name assigned to the procedure must be unique within the Visual Basic project. The Sub keyword identifies this procedure as a subroutine.

- *Terminator*: All procedures must be terminated with the End keyword followed by the type of procedure that is ending. In Figure 3.1, the terminator is End Sub.

- *Declarations area*: Although variables and constants can be declared within the body of the procedure, good programming conventions require variables to be declared near the top of the procedure where they'll be easy to find.

- *Statements*: A VBA procedure can contain many statements. Usually, however, you'll want to keep your Visual Basic procedures small to make debugging as painless as possible. Very large subroutines can be difficult to work with, and you'll avoid problems if you keep them small. Instead of adding too many features and operations in a single procedure, place operations in separate procedures and call those procedures when those operations are needed.

- *Call to another procedure*: This statement calls another procedure named FillControls. In Figure 3.1, the other procedure is another sub but could have been a function as well. The called procedure can be in any module (with some limitations) within the current project.

> **Note:** Use the Call keyword to invoke procedures in your application. Although normally used to run sub procedures, the Call statement also runs functions. When used to run a function, the Call statement treats the function like a sub and ignores the value returned by the function.

At the conclusion of the subroutine in Figure 3.1, program flow returns to the code or action that originally called the sub. In this particular case, this subroutine runs in response to the form's Load event. You'll read more about forms and their events in Chapter 5, "Designing the User Interface."

Understanding Functions

Functions are conceptually similar to subroutines. The main difference is that a function returns a value. This means that you can use a function name anywhere in the application as though it were the name of a variable. Visual Basic runs the function, gets the value assigned to the function (the value is assigned within the function itself, as shown in Figure 3.2), and returns the value to the code using the function name.

Parameter

FIGURE 3.2.
Functions are a common component of Visual Basic programs.

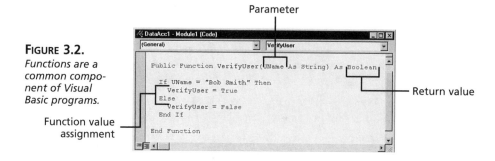

Function value assignment

Return value

The function shown in Figure 3.2 returns a Boolean value, as defined by the function declaration. The VerifyUser function accepts a string parameter named UName that is tested inside VerifyUser. If the value of the UName string is Bob Smith the value True is assigned to VerifyUser; otherwise, False is assigned.

The VerifyUser function in Figure 3.2 is laughably simple, but it illustrates how functions differ from subroutines. Keep in mind that a function is a type of procedure; therefore all the rules discussed in the section on subroutines also apply to functions.

Understanding Comments

Comments are another important part of all Visual Basic programs. A comment is a plain text message you embed in the midst of your VBA code. A comment can include any printable character but must begin with a single quote (') or the keyword Rem (shorthand for *remark*).

Figure 3.3 shows how the sub pictured in Figure 3.1 might look with a few comments added. Notice how the comments clarify how the code is being used.

FIGURE 3.3.
Comments provide inline documentation for your programs.

Comments

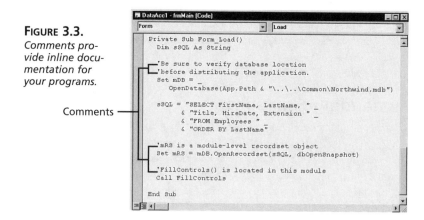

You should comment any portions of your code that might be difficult to understand. Comments are more convenient than a printed developer's guide document you might prepare to accompany your applications.

It's easy to overdo comments. It's not necessary to comment every line of code in your procedures, but it's nearly criminal to omit comments altogether. Comments do not add to the size of the completed executable nor do they slow the execution of a Visual Basic program. They do, however, reduce the amount of time you or another developer will spend deciphering the logic of a complicated procedure. A few minutes writing explanatory comments can save hours and hours of mind-bending work.

Using the Visual Basic Editor

Visual Basic includes a variety of developer-oriented features designed to make your job easier and more efficient. As you read this section, I'm sure you'll agree that the developer-oriented capabilities in Visual Basic are the type of things you've been hoping to find in a development platform.

The Visual Basic Code window (see Figure 3.4) is similar, if not identical, to the VBA editors in the other Office products. You'll compose all your VBA code with this editor, so you should become familiar with its layout and features.

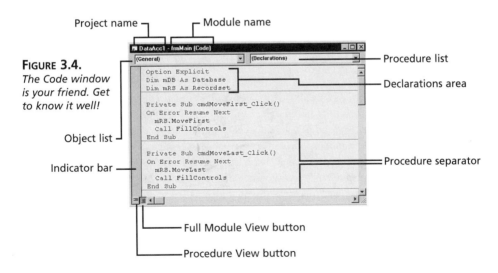

FIGURE 3.4.
The Code window is your friend. Get to know it well!

Take a close look at some of the more important parts of the Code window:

- *Project name*: As you learned in Chapter 2, all the components of a Visual Basic application are contained within a project. The module you see in Figure 3.4 is part of a project named DataAcc1. The project name always appears in the Code window's title bar.

- *Module name*: Visual Basic projects normally contain more than one component. The code in Figure 3.4 is named frmMain and is contained within a form named frmMain. From the Code window you can't tell that the code is contained within a form. The frm prefix supplies you with that information. (See Appendix B, "The Reddick VBA Naming Convention," for an example of Visual Basic naming conventions.) The module name also always appears in the Code window's title bar.

- *Object list*: Because this code lives behind a form, it has direct access to the form and all the controls on the form. The Object drop-down list contains the names of all the controls on the form, sorted alphabetically. If you are using a naming convention that places a prefix such as cmd to the names of command buttons and txt to the names of text boxes, the objects in this list will be conveniently grouped by virtue of the names you've assigned to them (see Figure 3.5). All modules include a General area where declarations and procedures that are not associated with any particular control are located. The module shown in Figure 3.5 is set to display the items in the module that are located in the General area.

FIGURE 3.5.
All the controls on the form and the form itself appear in the Object list.

Object list

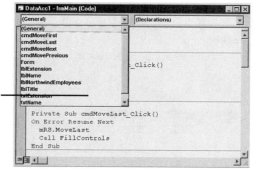

- *Procedure list*: Modules normally contain more than one procedure and several variable declarations. There are two procedures (both of which are subroutines) and two variable declarations in Figure 3.6. Because the Object list is set to the General section, the Procedure list contains the names of any procedures that are not directly related to any control on this form. These procedures are available to all the other procedures in this module (more on object scope in the next chapter). In this case, only one procedure (FillControls) is in the General section of this module. If a control had been chosen in the Object list, the Procedures list would show all the event procedures for that control.

- *Declarations area*: At the top of every module is an area reserved for declaring variables and constants used within the module (variable and constant scope are discussed in Chapter 4, "Using Visual Basic Variables." Although module-level variables can be declared anywhere in a module outside module procedures, good programming style dictates that all module-level variables and constants must be declared at the top of the module to make them easy to see.

FIGURE 3.6.

The Procedure list displays all the procedures in the area selected from the Object list.

Declarations area —

Indicator bar —

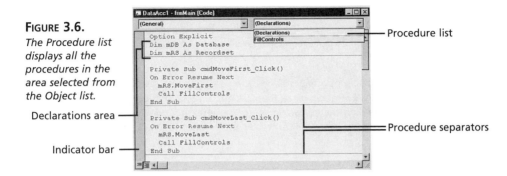

Procedure list

Procedure separators

- *Indicator bar*: The Indicator bar is a vertical gray area along the left side of the Code window. Usually the Indicator bar is featureless and gray, but during the debugging process (described in Chapter 7, "Mastering Menus and Toolbars") the Indicator bar might contain icons indicating different debugging operations. You can turn off the Indicator bar by deselecting the Margin Indicator Bar check box in the Editor Format tab of the Options dialog box (see Figure 3.13). The Indicator bar is visible by default.

- *Procedure and Full Module View buttons*: The view buttons provide a handy way to switch between Full Module view and Procedure view. In Procedure view, only one procedure is visible in the Code window at a time. Because Procedure view is so limiting, all the figures in this book feature Full Module view.

- *Procedure separator*: The procedure separator is a thin, horizontal gray line drawn between procedures in the Code window. These lines serve as an aid to help you see where procedures end or begin in the Code window. Procedure separators are visible by default. Turn off the procedure separator by deselecting the Procedure Separator setting in the Editor tab of the Options dialog box (see Figure 3.7).

FIGURE 3.7.

Several important editor settings are found in the Editor tab of the Options dialog box.

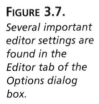
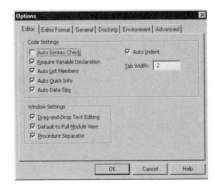

- *Procedure*: This module can contain any number of procedures. In Figure 3.7, this procedure is attached to the command button named `cmdMoveFirst` on the form and is triggered whenever a Click event occurs on that button.

> **Tip:** Visual Basic supports *drag-and-drop editing*. You can select a block of text by dragging the mouse over it; to move the block, click the highlighted area and while holding the mouse down, drag the text to a new location in the code module. This feature can be turned on and off using the Editor tab of the Options dialog box.

Opening the Code Window

There are multiple ways to open the Code window. By far the easiest is to simply double-click any control on the form in Design view. Visual Basic opens the code module attached to the form and positions the Code window on the default event for that control. Recall from Chapter 1, "Getting Started with Visual Basic 6," that each control has some type of event that is usually programmed for that control.

This behavior has the unfortunate effect of creating an empty event procedure if you choose not to use a control's default event. Because the Code window has been opened on a control's default event, Visual Basic automatically creates an event procedure template (see Figure 3.8). If you're not going to use this particular event procedure, you should delete it.

> **Note:** You are not required to remove empty procedures from your code. However, because empty procedures clutter up the Code window without adding anything to the application, removing them from your code is a good idea.

FIGURE 3.8.
Empty event procedures can clutter up a form's module.

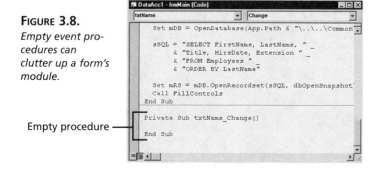

Empty procedure ──

An alternative path to the Code window is to press F7 while the form is in Design view. (You can also use the View | Code menu command.) The Code window opens on the default event of the control that has the current focus. If no control currently has the focus, meaning that the form itself must have the focus, the Code window opens on the form's Load event.

You can also right-click the name of a form in the Projects window and select View Code from the shortcut menu to open its module (see Figure 3.9). Or, you can click the View Code button at the left of the Project window's toolbar to open the module.

FIGURE 3.9.
Like everything else in Visual Basic, there are multiple ways to open a code module.

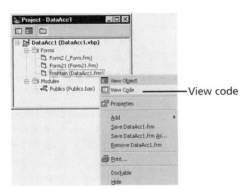

Double-clicking the name of a module in the Projects window opens that module in the Code window at the top of the module. If you double-click the name of a form in Design view, the form opens. To get to a form's module either open the form then go to its code, use the View | Code shortcut menu command, or use the Project window's View Code button.

Closing a module is like closing any other window. Click the Close button in the upper-right corner of the Code window or use Ctrl+F4 to close the window. Alt+F4 shuts down Visual Basic, so be careful when you use this keystroke combination.

Understanding Code Window Features

The Visual Basic Code window has been carefully designed to make the task of writing code for your applications as easy and painless as possible. As a result, there are several important features you'll frequently use as you work with Visual Basic.

First, Visual Basic supports a *line continuation character*. Any line of code ending in an underscore character preceded by a space is recognized as a statement that is continued on the next line, making it easy to see all of very long VBA statements. Notice the statement that starts out sSQL = in Figure 3.10. This statement actually occupies two lines of code—the one containing the sSQL = statement and the line immediately beneath it.

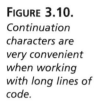

FIGURE 3.10.
Continuation characters are very convenient when working with long lines of code.

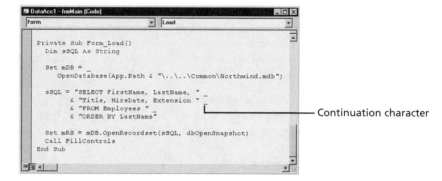

```
Private Sub Form_Load()
   Dim sSQL As String

   Set mDB = _
      OpenDatabase(App.Path & "\..\..\Common\Northwind.mdb")

   sSQL = "SELECT FirstName, LastName, " _
        & "Title, HireDate, Extension " _
        & "FROM Employees " _
        & "ORDER BY LastName"

   Set mRS = mDB.OpenRecordset(sSQL, dbOpenSnapshot)
   Call FillControls
End Sub
```

Continuation character

The line continuation in Visual Basic is quite powerful. You can split long declaration lines, such as those Windows API declares, and you can even split long strings into multiple lines. (Windows API is discussed in Chapter 25, "Mastering the Windows API.")

For example, the SQL statements you'll use to extract data from database files are often quite long and will not easily fit on a single line in the Code window. You'll find it convenient to split long SQL statements into multiple lines, joined by the continuation character. All that's needed on each subsequent line is the concatenation character (&) and as much of the string as you want to add on the line. Splitting long SQL statements makes it easy to see what's in the statement and, therefore, what fields end up in the resulting recordset. You'll learn much more about using SQL and building recordsets in Part IV, "Accessing Data."

If you use continuation characters, be sure to indent the continued lines of code so that you can recognize continued lines of code without having to keep track of the continuation characters. Figure 3.11 illustrates how omitting indention can make the code more confusing and difficult to read. The code in Figure 3.11 is the same code as in Figure 3.10 with all the leading spaces and blank lines removed. Unless you notice the continuation characters at the ends of the lines of code, you might think each of these statements stands alone and is not part of a larger statement. Omitting the blank lines bunches the code up so much that it's hard to distinguish individual statements.

Visual Basic makes it easy to indent your code. You might have noticed an option named Tab Width in the Editor tab of the Options dialog box (refer to Figure 3.7). This setting specifies how may spaces Visual Basic inserts into a VBA statement each time the Tab key is pressed. Tabs are never actually inserted into the code. Instead, spaces are inserted by the Editor in response to the Tab key. To indent a block of code, highlight the lines with the mouse and press the Tab key (see Figure 3.12). Visual Basic automatically indents all the highlighted lines.

Tip: Press Shift+Tab to outdent the highlighted lines in the Editor.

FIGURE 3.11.
Improperly indenting code and omitting whitespace makes the code hard to read.

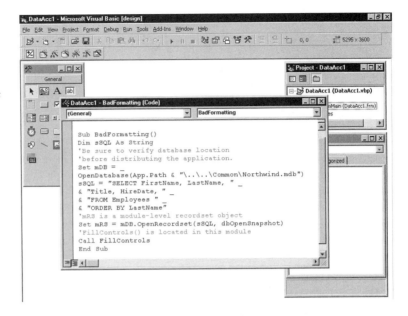

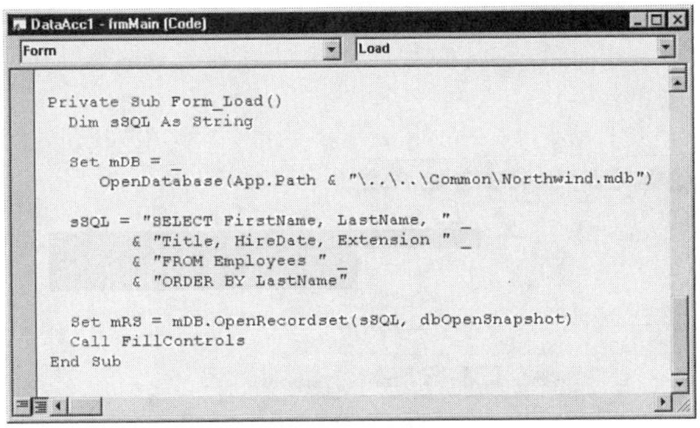

FIGURE 3.12.
Indent selected lines of code with the Tab key, outdent with Shift+Tab.

Another powerful feature of the Visual Basic VBA Code window is the color cueing used to set aside comments, keywords, and identifiers. Although it's not obvious in this book's figures, the VBA keywords like `Private`, `Sub`, `Dim`, `Set`, and `Call` are dark blue. Identifiers like `sSQL` and `mDB` are black. Comments appear dark green, and statements that contain errors are red.

You can adjust the editor font and text colors to suit your particular style. The Editor Format tab of the Options dialog box (Tools | Options) contains all the options necessary to select the font, font size, and colors for the different parts of the VBA syntax. Only one of the three drop-down lists of colors is open in Figure 3.13, but you should have an idea of the color options available to you from this figure.

FIGURE 3.13.
Visual Basic gives you many options for setting the font and font colors in the Code window.

One major improvement over earlier versions of the Microsoft family of development platforms is the global Search and Replace feature found in the VBA editor. When you open the Find or Replace dialog boxes (see Figure 3.14) notice the options in the lower-left corner. You can search for the text you specify throughout the entire project, including all standard modules, form modules, class modules, and so on. Most older development products limit you to searching through only the open code modules, which means you must continually open and close modules, restarting the search on each module in the application.

FIGURE 3.14.
You can search through the entire project for text.

Using Keyboard and Mouse Shortcuts in the Editor Window

Visual Basic 6 supports a variety of keyboard and mouse shortcuts designed to make your editing job easier. Table 3.1 lists the valid keyboard shortcuts that you can use while the Code window is open.

Table 3.1. Code window and menu shortcuts.

Shortcut	Description
F1	View Visual Basic help topic for selection
F3	Find next
F5	Start
Del	Delete
Tab	Indent selection
Home	Go to beginning of line
End	Go to end of line
Right arrow	Move to the next character
Left arrow	Move to the previous character
Down arrow	Move down one line
Up arrow	Move up one line
Page Up	Move up part of the screen
Page Down	Move down part of the screen
Ctrl+F5	Start with full compile
Ctrl+A	Select all
Ctrl+C	Copy
Ctrl+F	Find
Ctrl+H	Replace
Ctrl+I	Quick Info
Ctrl+J	List properties and methods
Ctrl+P	Print
Ctrl+V	Paste
Ctrl+X	Cut
Ctrl+Y	Delete current line
Ctrl+Z	Undo
Ctrl+Del	Delete to end of word
Ctrl+Right arrow	Move one word to the right
Ctrl+Left arrow	Move one word to the left
Ctrl+Home	Go to beginning of module
Ctrl+End	Go to end of module
Ctrl+Down arrow	Move to first line in next procedure
Ctrl+Up arrow	Move to first line in previous procedure

continues

Table 3.1. Continued.

Shortcut	Description
Ctrl+Page Up	Move to previous procedure declaration
Ctrl+Page Down	Move to next procedure declaration
Ctrl+Spacebar	Complete word
Shift+F2	View procedure definition
Shift+F3	Find previous
Shift+F10	Right-click pop-up menu
Shift+Tab	Remove indent on selection (outdent)
Shift+Right arrow	Extend selection one character to the right
Shift+Left arrow	Start selection to the left or reduce an existing selection by one character
Shift+Up arrow	Extend/reduce selection up a line
Shift+Down arrow	Extend selection down one line to current column
Ctrl+Shift+F2	Go to last position
Ctrl+Shift+J	List constants
Ctrl+Shift+I	Parameter Info

In addition, the Visual Basic Code window supports several mouse button actions. Table 3.2 lists the mouse actions.

Table 3.2. Mouse code selections.

Action	Description
Drag with left mouse down	Select code lines as they are dragged over
Double-click	Select word
Shift+Left click	Extend selection from current selection location to the current click position

Setting Bookmarks in Code

Visual Basic developers familiar with Microsoft Word have probably used bookmarks in their Word documents. A Word bookmark provides a convenient way to jump among locations in a document to make it easy to coordinate the text in different parts of the document. Visual Basic provides its own version of bookmarks that enables you to quickly jump between different locations in your VBA code.

Note: Unlike Word bookmarks, the bookmarks you insert into your VBA code are not named. Instead they simply serve as destinations for the Next Bookmark and Previous Bookmark commands.

There are several ways to toggle bookmarks in your Visual Basic code. Perhaps the easiest technique is to open the Editing toolbar. (Use the View | Toolbars menu command to open the list of Visual Basic toolbars and select Edit from the list.) The Edit toolbar (see Figure 3.15) contains several command buttons you'll use frequently while editing Visual Basic code.

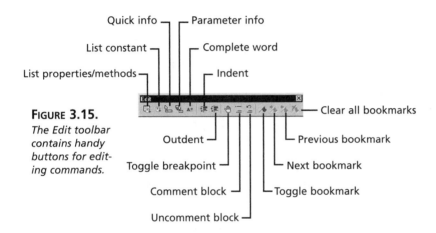

FIGURE 3.15.
The Edit toolbar contains handy buttons for editing commands.

This section deals with the four right buttons on the Edit toolbar. The other Edit toolbar buttons are mentioned later in this chapter. The purpose of the bookmark buttons is self-explanatory:

- *Toggle Bookmark*: This buttons adds a bookmark to the current line of code in the Code window. A bookmark previously set on that line will be removed.

- *Next Bookmark:* The Next Bookmark button moves the editing cursor to the next available bookmark.

- *Previous Bookmark*: As its name implies, the Previous Bookmark moves the editing cursor to the previous bookmark in the project.

- *Clear All Bookmarks*: This button removes all bookmarks in all modules in the project. Use this button whenever you've cluttered up your code with bookmarks and you want to simply throw them all away rather than remove them with the Toggle Bookmark button.

In addition to the bookmark buttons on the Edit toolbar, you can add bookmarks to your code and navigate them with the menu commands in the Edit | Bookmarks cascading menu (see Figure 3.16).

FIGURE 3.16.
Bookmarks can also be set from the Edit | Bookmarks menu.

Visual Basic remembers the sequence in which bookmarks have been added to your code and follows this sequence as you use the Next Bookmark and Previous Bookmark commands. The physical layout of the code in a module or the sequence of objects in the Project Explorer do not influence the Bookmark navigation sequence.

Bookmarks can be placed on virtually any line of code in a VBA procedure, including comments, variable declarations, procedure definitions, and so on. You can even place bookmarks on empty statements and the blank spaces between procedures. Unlike breakpoints (described in Chapter 8, "Using the Visual Basic Debugging Tools,") you aren't restricted to placing bookmarks on executable lines of code.

> **Note:** Bookmarks are not preserved when you close Visual Basic. Because bookmarks can't be saved, you are not warned or prompted to do anything with the bookmarks you've placed in your code as Visual Basic shuts down.

A bookmark set in your code appears as a blue, rounded rectangle in the margin bar of the Code window (see Figure 3.17).

FIGURE 3.17.
Bookmarks are easily seen in the Code window.

```
DataAcc1 - frmMain (Code)
Form                          Load

    Private Sub Form_Load()
        Dim sSQL As String

        'Be sure to verify database location
        'before distributing the application.
        Set mDB = _
            OpenDatabase(App.Path & "..\..\Common\Northwind.mdb")

        sSQL = "SELECT FirstName, LastName, " _
             & "Title, HireDate, Extension " _
             & "FROM Employees " _
             & "ORDER BY LastName"

        'mRS is a module-level recordset object
        Set mRS = mDB.OpenRecordset(sSQL, dbOpenSnapshot)

        'FillControls() is located in this module
        Call FillControls

    End Sub
```

> **Tip:** To jump to the last edited position in the code, which does not have to be a bookmark, use the Ctrl+Shift+F2 keystroke combination.

Using Automatic Word Completion

Visual Basic can help you by completing long keywords as you type. As soon as you've typed enough of a keyword for Visual Basic to determine which word you're typing, press Ctrl+Spacebar, and Visual Basic will complete the word. The word must be a built-in Visual Basic keyword, such as the name of an object, function, or subroutine. Automatic word completion does not recognize the names of procedures or variables you've created in your Visual Basic programs.

If you press the Ctrl+Spacebar keystroke combination and you haven't entered enough characters for Visual Basic to fill in the rest of the word, you'll see a pop-up list of words to select from. Figure 3.18 shows how the pop-up list would look after if you typed m and pressed Ctrl+Spacebar.

FIGURE 3.18.
Automatic word completion can be a useful tool as you write Visual Basic code.

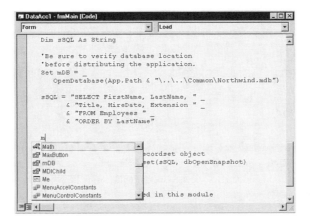

Notice that the pop-up scrolling list in Figure 3.18 starts at the top of a list of words beginning with m. If you continue typing MsgBox, the list scrolls to the correct entry on the list. As soon you've typed in enough of the word to narrow the search to the word you're typing, press the spacebar to select the word from the list and add it to the code. If you've typed enough of the word for Visual Basic to select the correct word you won't see the list at all and the word will be inserted into your code.

Using Comment Block and Uncomment Block

The Comment Block button on the Visual Basic toolbar is a handy way to comment a contiguous set of Visual Basic statements. As part of the debugging process you might need to set aside a block of code to prevent it from running. Or, you might determine that a set of statements is no longer needed in the code because of changes you've made, but you're not ready to delete the unnecessary statements. Figure 3.19 shows the location of the Comment Block and Uncomment Block toolbar buttons.

Comment block ——   —— Uncomment block

FIGURE 3.19.

The Comment Block button instantly inserts comments at the front of the selected lines of code.

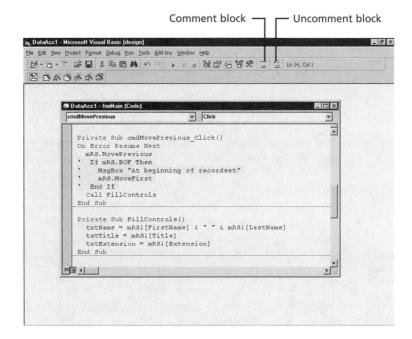

The Uncomment Block button removes the comment character from the front of the selected lines of code. If you select multiple lines of code and some of the lines do not contain comment characters, the Uncomment Block button ignores the uncommented statements.

Understanding Editor Options

Most optional settings in Visual Basic affect only developers. These features are hidden from end users and are beneficial to only the person building the application. Spend some time exploring these features so that you fully understand their benefits. You'll soon settle on option settings that suit the way you work and the kind of assistance you want as you write your VBA code. Although several of these options have been mentioned elsewhere in this chapter, a brief review of available options follows.

Understanding the Editor Tab in the Options Dialog Box

The Options dialog box contains several important settings that greatly influence how you interact with Visual Basic as you add code to your applications (refer to Figure 3.7).

- *Auto Indent*: Auto Indent causes code to be indented to the current depth in all successive lines of code. For example, if you insert four spaces or tabs in front of the current line of code, the new line of code is automatically indented four spaces when you press the Enter key to move to the next line.

- *Auto Syntax Check*: When the Auto Syntax Check option is selected, Visual Basic checks each line of code for syntax errors as you enter it in the Code window. Many experienced developers find this behavior intrusive and keep this option disabled, preferring instead to let the compiler point out syntax errors. Most of the syntax errors caught by Auto Syntax Check are obvious spelling errors, missing commas, and so on.

- *Require Variable Declaration*: If selected, this setting automatically inserts the Option Explicit directive into all VBA modules in your Visual Basic application. This means you must explicitly declare all variables you use in your program. This option is selected in Visual Basic 6 by default.

- *Auto List Members*: This timesaving option displays a list box that contains the members of an object's object hierarchy in the Code window. In Figure 3.20, the list of application objects appeared as soon as I typed the period following mDB in the VBA statement. In this case, Visual Basic knew that mDB had been declared as a Database object, so the list contains the properties and methods associated with Database objects. You select an item from the list by continuing to type it in or scrolling the list and pressing the spacebar.

FIGURE 3.20.

Auto List Members makes it easy to recall the members of an object's object hierarchy.

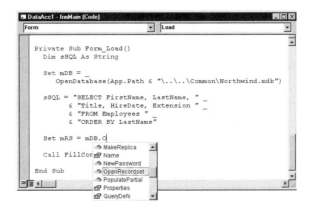

- *Auto Quick Info*: When Auto Quick Info has been selected Visual Basic displays syntax help (see Figure 3.21) when you enter the name of a procedure (function, subroutine, or method) followed by a period, space, or opening parenthesis. The procedure can be a built-in function or subroutine or one that you've written yourself in Visual Basic VBA.

- *Auto Data Tips*: Figure 3.22 shows Auto Data Tips in action. This option displays the value of variables when you hold the mouse cursor over a variable with the module in Break mode. Auto Data Tips is an alternative to setting a watch on the variable and flipping to the Debug window when Visual Basic reaches the breakpoint. (Using breakpoints and the other Visual Basic VBA debugging techniques are described in Chapter 8, "Using the Visual Basic Debugging Tools.")

FIGURE 3.21.
*Auto Quick Info
provides syntax
reminders in the
module window.*

FIGURE 3.22.
*Auto Data Tips is
a quick and easy
way to examine
the values of vari-
ables in your pro-
gram.*

Breakpoint ⎯⎯⎯⎯⎯   ⎯⎯⎯ Auto Data Tips

- *Drag-and-Drop Text Editing*: This setting toggles drag-and-drop editing.
- *Default to Full Module View*: By default, the Code window shows more than one procedure if the procedures are small enough to be seen in their entirety. Deselecting this check box forces the Code window to display one procedure at a time. (This view is called *Procedure view*). Because of the difficulty working with code in Procedure view, it is rarely chosen by most developers.
- *Procedure Separator*: The Procedure Separator selects or deselects the thin gray line that separates procedures in the Code window.
- *Tab Width*: The Tab Width option specifies how many spaces will be inserted each time the Tab key is pressed.

Because they are so handy, you'll almost certainly use one or more of the auto-help options in Visual Basic. Of the other options available to you, be sure not to overlook the ability to require variable declaration. When you get used to having Option Explicit set on every module (including public and class modules) the instances of rogue and unexplained variables (which, in reality, are simple misspellings of declared variables) disappear. With Option Explicit set in every module, your code is more self-explanatory and easier to debug and maintain.

Understanding the Editor Format Tab in the Options Dialog Box

The Editor Format tab in the Options dialog box (refer to Figure 3.13) contains settings that determine the overall appearance of the Code window. You can adjust these settings to make the Code window easier to see by selecting a larger font; show more lines of code in the window by selecting a smaller font; and make errors and other important information more visible by modifying the code colors.

- *Code Colors*: The Code window displays a variety of different types of code statements. These statements include executable commands, comments, and breakpoints, among several other programming structures. There are three color settings for each of the 10 different code structures in the Code window: Foreground, Background, and Indicator. Foreground and Background are self-explanatory. The Indicator color specifies the color to be used on the icon that appears in the window margin in certain situations, such as when a breakpoint is encountered in the program code.

- *Font and Size*: The Font and Size settings specify the font and the font size used in the Code window. Use an easy-to-read font that is small enough to display an adequate number of lines on the screen at one time.

- *Margin Indicator Bar*: The Margin Indicator Bar is the vertical, gray bar along the left side of the Code window. Normally you'll want the indicator bar to be visible so that breakpoints, the program execution point, and so on are visible. These icons are suppressed when the indicator bar is not present.

Each of these settings influences the appearance of the Code window. In most cases, the default settings are appropriate for the majority of developers, but you should feel free to customize the Code window to suit your style. The settings you change in the Options dialog box affect only your personal copy of Visual Basic and do not affect other people who might work with your code.

Controlling Program Flow

Almost all Visual Basic applications feature some way to alter the program flow at runtime. You will rarely write a program that starts at the top of a procedure and progresses through each line of code to the end. Usually, your program will have to conditionally execute portions of code depending on the value of a variable or in response to input from the user.

One common programming construct is the *loop*. A loop repetitively executes a block of code until some condition is met. Perhaps you must repeat several statements 10 times, or the statements must be repeated until an expression becomes true. In such cases, you'll use Visual Basic's looping structures.

Using Conditional Branching

A *conditional branch* executes blocks of statements depending on the value of an expression. The classic conditional branch is illustrated in Figure 3.23. In this fragment of program logic the user has requested a record deletion. A message box displays to ask the user to verify the deletion. If the user responds with Yes the record is deleted, otherwise the record deletion is ignored.

FIGURE 3.23.
Conditional branches add intelligence to your applications.

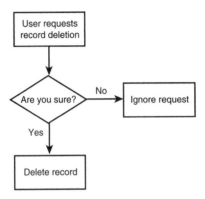

Visual Basic provides a variety of different conditional branches, which are discussed in the following sections.

Using If...Then

The most common conditional branch is some form of the If...Then branch. The simplest case of this branch is illustrated in Figure 3.24. Notice that the optional statement block is executed only when the expression is true. Regardless of the value of the expression, execution continues after the If statement with Statement 2.

FIGURE 3.24.
The If...Then branch is very common.

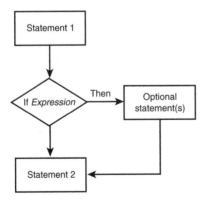

Figure 3.25 shows an example of the If loop. Notice that if the user enters anything other than Joe in the input box (a simple built-in dialog box that returns whatever the user types into its text box) the Then clause does not execute. Notice that the If statement must be terminated with an End If. Any number of statements can appear between the If and End If statements, and those statements can include calls to other procedures, nested conditionals and loops, and so on.

FIGURE 3.25.

Control execution of statements with the
If...Then *branch.*

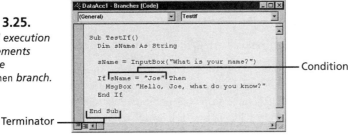

Condition

Terminator

The following code fragment shows how to nest If...End If statements. The inner If is executed only when the expression in the outer If is true. After the code verifies that the sDept variable is set to "Marketing", the input box is displayed and the value returned by InputBox is assigned to sPWD. This variable is then compared to the string "xyzzy", and if true, the customer form is displayed.

```
If sDept = "Marketing" Then
  sPWD = InputBox("Please enter the password:")
  If sPWD = "xyzzy" Then
    frmCustomer.Show
  End If
End If
```

The expression used as the conditional part of the If statement does not have to be a simple comparison as in the previous examples. The next code fragment illustrates using the built-in Len() function to determine how many characters are in the psDTS string. If the length of this string is zero, then a message box is displayed with the MsgBox statement, and Null is assigned to the object named txtDateTimeStamp.

```
If Len(psDTS) = 0 Then
  MsgBox "Assigning Null to txtDateTimeStamp"
  txtDateTimeStamp = Null
End If
```

The following is an alternative way to write an If statement:

```
If sPWD = "xyzzy" Then frmCustomer.Show
```

In this case, because the optional statement appears on the same line as the If, the End If statement isn't needed.

The only requirement of the expression used in the `If` clause is that it evaluate to either a `True` or `False` value. Therefore, all the following expressions are valid candidates for the `If` statement:

```
txtDate = #1/1/99#
iCount > 12
VerifyIdentity(sName)
```

(where `VerifyIdentity()` is a function that returns a Boolean value)

```
IsNull(txtDepartment)
```

(`IsNull()` is a built-in function that returns `True` if its argument is `Null`)

As you can see, there are multiple ways to write simple `If` statements. Because these statements are frequently nested inside other conditional statements, loops, and other constructs, it is important to indent the body of the `If` statement so that it's easy to see the statement's logic. Figure 3.26 illustrates how difficult it is to follow nested conditional statements if rigorous indenting is not followed.

FIGURE 3.26.

Poor indenting makes it difficult to understand this sub's logic.

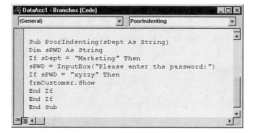

Using `If...Then...Else`

A simple `If...Then...End If` is not the only way to use this powerful branching construct. The most obvious extension to the simple `If` branch described in the last section is to add statements that execute if the expression value is `False`. You can add an `Else` clause to the basic `If` construct shown previously. Figure 3.27 illustrates the logical flow of the `If...Then...Else` statement.

From Figure 3.27 it's easy to see that certain statements execute only when the expression is `True`, and other statements execute if the statement is `False`. Examples of `If...Then...Else` abound in most Visual Basic applications. Figure 3.28 shows a typical use of `If...Then...Else`. A Boolean value, `bQuit`, is passed into this sub (more on passing parameters in the next chapter) and its value is assigned either `True` or `False`, depending on how the user responds to the `MsgBox` prompt.

FIGURE 3.27.

The `If...Then...Else` *statement is another useful conditional branching construct.*

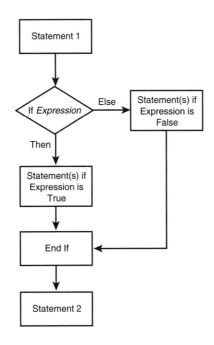

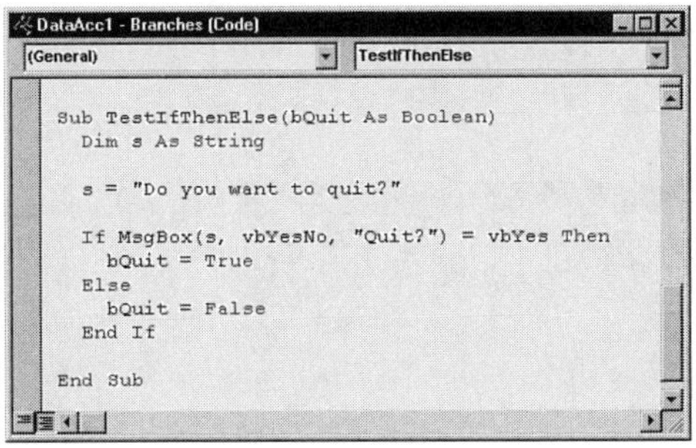

FIGURE 3.28.

The `Else` *clause provides the statements to execute if the expression is* `False`.

```
DataAcc1 - Branches (Code)
(General)                          TestIfThenElse

  Sub TestIfThenElse(bQuit As Boolean)
    Dim s As String

    s = "Do you want to quit?"

    If MsgBox(s, vbYesNo, "Quit?") = vbYes Then
       bQuit = True
    Else
       bQuit = False
    End If

  End Sub
```

In case you haven't seen the `MsgBox` function before, the statement you see in Figure 3.28 displays a simple dialog box containing Yes and No buttons. The `MsgBox` function returns the value of the button (either `vbYes` or `vbNo`). The user clicks while the dialog box is open. The `If` statement compares the selected button with the built-in `vbYes` value and performs either the `Then` or the `Else` clause, depending on whether the comparison succeeds or fails.

Using `If...Then...ElseIf...End If`

The final extension of the `If...Then...End If` branch is diagrammed in Figure 3.29. Notice how you can extend the logic supported by the `If...Then...End If` construct with additional `ElseIf` clauses. (The clause really is `ElseIf` with no space between the `Else` and the `If`.) You can string many of the `ElseIf` clauses together to accommodate complicated decision trees.

FIGURE **3.29.**

The ElseIf *clause adds complexity to the logic supported by the* If...End If *branch.*

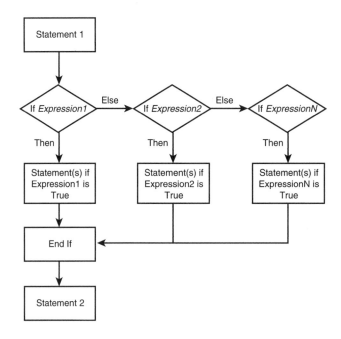

A simple example of using the ElseIf clause is shown in Figure 3.30. In this example, one of the statements specified in the ElseIf portions of the statement will be executed depending on the value of the sPet string passed into this sub procedure.

FIGURE **3.30.**

Using the ElseIf *clause quickly becomes cumbersome.*

Notice that an If expression is evaluated at each step along the way. In Figure 3.30, a single value (sPet) is examined repeatedly, but this is not necessarily always the case. For example, you could test for either a department or title before displaying a particular form (see Figure 3.31). The DeptOrTitle subroutine displays frmSecret if either the sDept or sTitle strings pass the tests conducted in this subroutine.

FIGURE 3.31.
The ElseIf *clause provides an easy way to test any of several conditions.*

It should be obvious that the code involved in using the different permutations of the If...End If branching construct quickly become cumbersome and difficult to decipher. These statements are particularly difficult to deal with when it's time to add new conditions that must be tested. The examples you've seen in this section have been extremely simple and involve very few lines of code. However, in the real world you'll often encounter instances where it's necessary to nest conditional statements, loops, calls to other procedures, and so on. In other words, don't expect such straightforward branching examples in actual practice.

Using Select Case

The Select Case branch resolves many of the issues raised by the If branch. Conceptually the Select Case is easy to understand and is diagrammed in Figure 3.32. The expression is evaluated at the top of the Select Case statement and compared with each of the candidate values in the body of the Select Case. If none of the values match the expression, the Select Case simply ends. An option Case Else can be added to the Select Case body to trap those instances where none of the candidate values match.

An example of Select Case is shown in Figure 3.33. The expression sPet is evaluated only once, then compared with "Dog", "Cat", and "Bird". If none of these values matches sPet, the Case Else clause is invoked and a message box containing None Of These is displayed.

One of the beautiful things about the Select Case statement is that you can easily extend the comparisons by simply adding new Case clauses. Unlike If...Then...ElseIf branches where you must stop and think about the impact of each additional comparison, the Select Case is simple and elegant.

The Select Case is also quite fast. The expression is evaluated only once at the top of the statement. The expression's value is cached and then compared with each of the Case values. As soon as a hit is found, Visual Basic short circuits and jumps down to the End Select. Therefore, you can optimize a Select Case by placing the most frequently matched values at the top of the comparison area.

FIGURE 3.32.

The Select Case statement elegantly solves many of the issues raised by the If...End If branching construct.

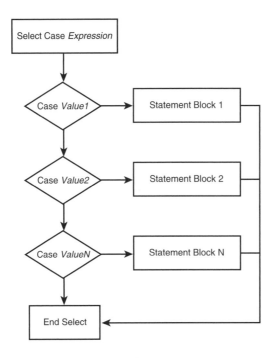

FIGURE 3.33.

Select Case statements are easy to modify by adding new values to compare.

Loops

Another frequently performed task in most databases is looping through a set of statements multiple times. For example, many login forms enable a user three or four tries to correctly enter a password. If the password is not entered accurately, the program shuts down and forces the user to start over again. Or, you might want to indefinitely loop through a process until some condition is met. For example, you might be reading data from a disk file and scanning through the data looking for certain values. Unless you know exactly how many records exist in the data file, you'll have to loop through until the end of the file is reached. Visual Basic includes looping constructs for all these types of loops.

For...Next

By far the easiest looping construct to understand is the `For...Next` loop. Figure 3.34 diagrams the logic of the `For...Next` statement.

FIGURE 3.34.

The `For...Next` *loop is very common in Visual Basic applications.*

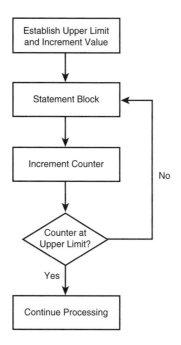

The `For...Next` is useful whenever you know how many times you must loop through the statement block. Like all the other conditional branches and looping constructs, the exact design of `For...Next` statements varies. The numbers used as the upper-limit and increment values can be hard-coded into the application or can be variables or constants established in code. The increment value is optional and defaults to `1`. The value of the counter variable is incremented after the statement block is executed.

Figure 3.35 shows a typical `For...Next` loop in action. In this function the user is given three chances to correctly enter the password. If the value entered on the input box is correct, the `ValidatePassword` function is assigned `True` and the function terminates with the `End Function` statement. If after three tries the password is not entered correctly `ValidatePassword` returns `False`.

A `For...Next` loop can be prematurely terminated if necessary. In Figure 3.35 the `For...Next` loop ends if the user enters the correct password. In this case, when the `Exit Function` statement is executed, the loop ends and processing leaves the function. Alternatively, you can use the `Exit For` statement as shown in the following subroutine:

```
Public Function ValidatePassword2() As Boolean
  Dim i As Integer
  Dim sPWD As String

  For i = 1 To 3 Step 1
    sPWD = InputBox("Enter the password")
    If sPWD = "xyzzy" Then
      Exit For
    End If
  Next i

  If i <= 3 Then
    ValidatePassword = True
  Else
    ValidatePassword = False
  End If


End Function
```

FIGURE 3.35.

The upper limit of a For...Next *loop can be hard-coded or set at runtime.*

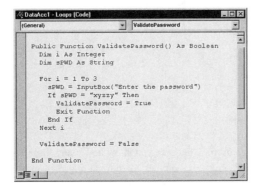

Although `ValidatePassword2` takes a few more lines of code than the previous example, the logic might be easier to understand. In `ValidatePassword2`, the `For...Next` loop prematurely ends with an `Exit For` statement if the user correctly enters the password. If the user does not enter the password correctly, the loop proceeds to its end. Because the value of `i` is incremented after the statement block, it ends up at a value of 4. That's why the `If...Then...Else` at the bottom of `ValidatePassword2` tests to see whether the value of `i` is less than or equal to 3. The value of `i` will be more than 3 if the `For...Next` loop ran all the way to its end without being interrupted by the `Exit For`.

`ValidatePassword2` also shows how you specify the increment value. The `Step 1` clause added to the `If` statement specifies that the counter (`i`) should be incremented by 1 on each pass through the loop. This example is for illustrative purposes only. Normally you wouldn't specify the step value unless you want something other than 1 because 1 is the default increment in Visual Basic `For...Next` loops.

Do...Loop

The logic of an even more flexible loop is illustrated in Figure 3.36. The first form of the Do...Loop we'll study tests the value of an expression before processing the statement block. The statement block is processed only if the expression evaluates to either True or False, depending on how the expression is constructed.

FIGURE 3.36.

The Do...Loop *offers multiple ways to loop through a block of statements.*

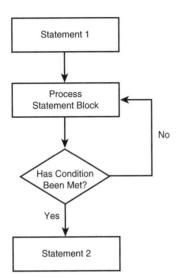

Figure 3.37 provides an example of using this form of the Do...Loop construct. Even if you're not familiar with all the Visual Basic commands you see in this example, the logic should be easy to follow. A data file named "DataFile.txt" is opened near the top of the ReadFile1() function. The code then enters the Do...Loop and a line is read from the data file. The If...End If conditional statement checks to see whether any data was actually obtained by the Line Input statement. If the length of the line read from the data file is longer than 0, then the i variable is incremented by 1. At the bottom of the loop an expression tests to see whether the end of the data file (EOF(1)) has been reached. If the expression is True, the Do...Loop ends.

When you see code similar to that at the bottom of the Do...Loop in Figure 3.36, read it as Loop until the end of the file is reached. The code in Figure 3.37 uses the Until comparison operator. The syntax diagram for the code in Figure 3.37 is as follows:

```
Do
   Statement 1
   Statement 2
   Statement n
Loop Until Expression-Is-True
```

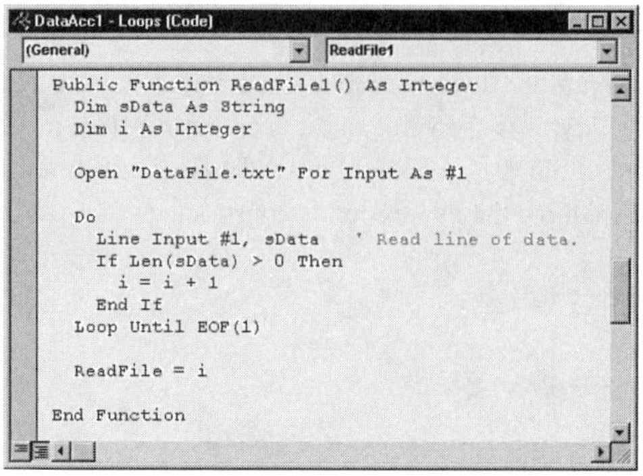

FIGURE 3.37.

This Do...Loop
*format tests the
expression at the
bottom of the
loop.*

```
DataAcc1 - Loops [Code]                                _ □ ×
(General)                    ▼    ReadFile1              ▼
   Public Function ReadFile1() As Integer
      Dim sData As String
      Dim i As Integer

      Open "DataFile.txt" For Input As #1

      Do
         Line Input #1, sData    ' Read line of data.
         If Len(sData) > 0 Then
            i = i + 1
         End If
      Loop Until EOF(1)

      ReadFile = i

   End Function
```

Depending on your programming style and the expression you choose to use, you might want to use the While keyword as an alternative comparison operator:

```
Do
   Statement 1
   Statement 2
   Statement n
Loop While Expression-Is-False
```

The following is equivalent code for the Do...Loop portion of the example shown in Figure 3.37 but using the While keyword:

```
Do
   Line Input #1, sData   ' Read line of data.
   If Len(sData) > 0 Then
      i = i + 1
   End If
Loop While Not EOF(1)
```

The Not operator negates whatever value follows it. EOF() is True when the end of the file is reached, so Loop While Not EOF() means loop while not at the end of the file.

An alternative Do...Loop logic is diagrammed in Figure 3.38. Notice that the expression is evaluated at the top of the loop and the statement block is never executed if the expression is True. The logic back in Figure 3.36 means the statement block is always processed before the expression is evaluated.

The following code listing shows how you might perform the test at the top of a Do...Loop. Notice that in this case you must read in the first line of the data file before you can test whether you've reached the end of the file. The next read is not performed until later in the loop.

```
Line Input #1, sData   ' Read line of data.
Do Until EOF(1)
   If Len(sData) > 0 Then
      i = i + 1
   End If
```

```
    Line Input #1, sData    ' Read line of data.
Loop
```

FIGURE 3.38.

You may prefer to evaluate the expression at the top of the Do...Loop *statement.*

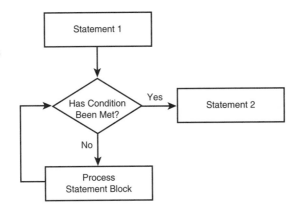

You can choose where to test the expression and how to construct the expression. Without a doubt the Do...Loop statement can be confusing. Not only can you test for positive or negative expressions, you also can test at the top or bottom of the loop. This flexibility, of course, means that the Do...Loop is one of the most common looping constructs you'll encounter in any Visual Basic application.

Using Compiler Directives

Another powerful feature in Visual Basic is the concept of *conditional compilation* directives into the VBA syntax. A conditional compilation argument instructs the VBA engine to ignore certain sections of code depending on the value of a constant you declare somewhere in the code. An example of using compiler directives is shown in Figure 3.39. In this example, two compiler constants (DEBUGGING and RETAIL) have been defined at the top of the module. Both of these constants have been set to -1, which Visual Basic evaluates as True. In the FillRecordset subroutine, you see the compiler directives at work. Because the RETAIL compiler constant is set to True, the Acme.mdb database will be opened. Because DEBUGGING is True, the Debug.Print statement later in this procedure will output the sSQL string to the Immediate window. You'll see this technique detailed in Chapter 8, "Using the Visual Basic Debugging Tools."

Visual Basic recognizes several compiler directives.

#Const: The #Const directive specifies a constant value that can be tested with the #If directive. The constant value specified by #Const is private to the module in which it appears and can be any data type (numeric, string, Boolean, and so on) recognized by Visual Basic. The syntax of #Const is

```
#Const Identifier = Value
```

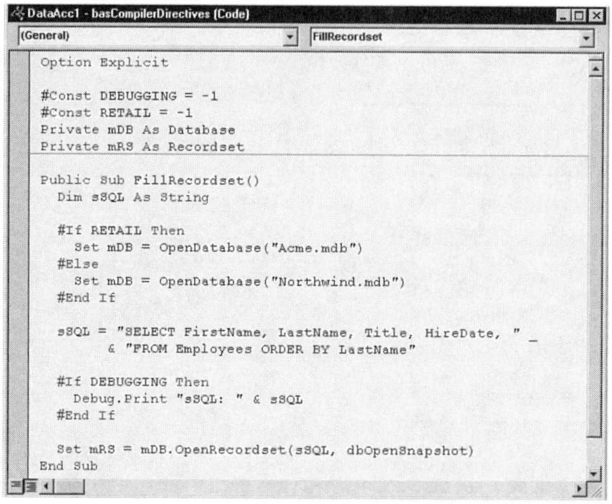

FIGURE 3.39.
Compiler directives give you a great deal of run-time control.

```
DataAcc1 - basCompilerDirectives (Code)
(General)                                    FillRecordset

    Option Explicit

    #Const DEBUGGING = -1
    #Const RETAIL = -1
    Private mDB As Database
    Private mRS As Recordset

    Public Sub FillRecordset()
      Dim sSQL As String

      #If RETAIL Then
        Set mDB = OpenDatabase("Acme.mdb")
      #Else
        Set mDB = OpenDatabase("Northwind.mdb")
      #End If

      sSQL = "SELECT FirstName, LastName, Title, HireDate, " _
          & "FROM Employees ORDER BY LastName"

      #If DEBUGGING Then
        Debug.Print "sSQL: " & sSQL
      #End If

      Set mRS = mDB.OpenRecordset(sSQL, dbOpenSnapshot)
    End Sub
```

The *Identifier* name cannot conflict with the name of a variable or constant declared elsewhere in the module and can't be the same as a Visual Basic keyword. For these reasons, you might want to adopt a naming convention, such as prefixing conditional constants with CC_, your initials, or some other text. Using a naming convention will also make the conditional constants easier to find in your code. Many developers always use full uppercase for all constants to make them easy to see in code.

#If...#Then...#Else...#End If: The #If directive evaluates an expression that returns either True or False. Place the statements you want processed when the expression is True between the #If...Then and the #Else; otherwise place them between the #Else and #End If. The syntax of these directives follows:

```
#If Expression Then
...Perform these statements
#Else
...Perform these alternate statements
#End If
```

> **Note:** The #Else portion of #If...Then is optional and can be omitted.

The constant value established with #Const is seen only by the #If compiler directive and is ignored by other VBA statements. Similarly, the #If directive can't use normal constant values established with the Const VBA keyword.

Compiler directives are a handy way to include debugging statements and optional code to an application. For example, you can use compiler directives to exclude large portions of code during development because the code is not needed as you prepare and debug certain features. You also can prepare custom versions of an application for different users. Compiler directives can turn features on and off by ignoring or including the code supporting these features as the application is compiled.

Keep in mind that the #Const directive is a module-level constant declaration. This means it won't be seen outside the module in which it appears, even if the module itself is public. This also means you can put the same compiler constant into as many modules as necessary without the name collisions you'll encounter with normal constants. In most cases the #Const directive appears in the module's Declarations section. Normally, you'll want this directive to appear where it will be easy to find and change, which means you want it in the same location from module to module. Also, if you are using compiler directives in more than one module you should probably use the same constant value in all modules to help make your code easier to understand.

If you find it necessary or helpful to use a public compiler constant, use the Conditional Compilation Arguments setting in the Make tab of the Project Properties dialog box (see Figure 3.40). Open this dialog box with the Project | Properties menu command. Enter the compiler constants just as you would in code, using a colon to separate multiple arguments. After you establish conditional compilation arguments in the Project Properties dialog box, they are applied throughout the application. This feature makes it easy to turn the effect of these arguments on and off within an application without having to make changes to the code.

Figure 3.40.

It's possible to set up public compiler constants with the Conditional Compilation Arguments setting.

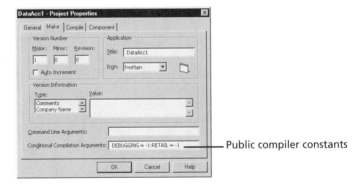

Public compiler constants

One important consideration is that the compiler directives affect the VBA code behind your application only as the code is compiled. You can't change the directive at runtime because the compiler directives are evaluated only as the code is compiled by the VBA engine. During compilation, the Visual Basic VBA compiler detects the directives and either includes or excludes the code segments as specified by the directives. After the compiled code has been prepared by the compiler, you can't change its contents.

Summary

This chapter introduces you to the powerful VBA language. Not only is VBA relatively easy to learn, you leverage your learning by applying the same syntax to a variety of other applications. For example, the entire Microsoft Office suite is VBA-compliant, and you won't have to learn new macro languages to work with Word or Excel. The principles described in this chapter provide the primary basis for carefully constructed code that is easy to debug and maintain. You'll be using the principles from this chapter throughout the rest of this book.

These procedures are essential as you move through the next several chapters. For example, Chapter 5, "Designing the User Interface," and Chapter 6. "Putting Your Forms to Work with Controls," explain how you'll use VBA code behind the forms and controls in your Visual Basic applications. The forms and controls in your applications are the essence of the user interface and define the personality and intelligence of your Visual Basic programs.

Using Visual Basic Variables

All Visual Basic applications require *variables* to hold data while the program executes. Variables are like a whiteboard where important information can be temporarily written and read later by the program. For example, when a user inputs a value on a form, a variable is used to temporarily hold the value until it can be permanently stored in a database or printed on a report. Simply put, a variable is the name you assigned to a particular bit of data in your application. In more technical terms, a variable is a named area in memory used to store values during program execution.

Variables are transient and do not persist after an application stops running. Additionally, as you'll read later in this chapter in the "Understanding Variable Scope and Lifetime" section, a variable might last a very short time as the program executes or might exist as long as the application is running.

In most cases, you assign a specific *data type* to each variable in your applications. For example, you can create a *string* variable to hold text data such as names or descriptions. A *currency* variable, on the other hand, is meant to contain values representing monetary amounts. You should not try to assign a text value to a currency variable because a run-time error might occur as a result.

The variables you use have a serious effect on your applications. You have many options when it comes to establishing and using variables in your Visual Basic programs. Inappropriately using a variable can slow an application's execution or cause data loss.

This chapter contains everything you need to know about creating and using Visual Basic variables. The information in this chapter will help you use the most efficient and effective data types in your variables while avoiding the most common problems related to Visual Basic variables.

Taking a Look at an Example

Figure 4.1 shows frmString, a form included in Variable.vbp, the Visual Basic 6 project accompanying this chapter. The frmString form demonstrates how variables are used in

Visual Basic applications. The two text boxes near the top of this form are used to capture first and last name information. When you press the Combine Names button, Visual Basic combines the first and last names and displays the results in the text box near the bottom of the form (see Figure 4.1).

FIGURE 4.1.

The frmString *form demonstrates how variables are used in Visual Basic programs.*

Listing 4.1 shows the code behind frmString. By the end of this chapter, you'll understand every line in this code, so you shouldn't worry if there's anything here that doesn't look familiar. This listing includes three string variables and the event procedure that assigns values to two of the variables and combines the variables for display in the bottom text box. The number to the left of each line of code is there simply to provide an identifier for the statement and is not part of the code.

Listing 4.1. frmString contains this code in its module.

```
1    Option Explicit
2    Dim sFirst As String
3    Dim sLast As String
4    Dim sCombined As String
5
6    Private Sub cmdCombine_Click()
7      sFirst = txtFirst.Text
8      sLast = txtLast.Text
9      sCombined = sFirst & " " & sLast
10     txtCombined.Text = sCombined
11    End Sub
```

Near the top of Listing 4.1, you see three similar statements (lines 2, 3, and 4). Each begins with the Dim keyword. These statements actually create the variables used by this form. All three of the variables (sFirst, sLast, and sCombined) are string variables that can hold text data. In case you're wondering what Option Explicit means, you'll have to wait until the "Declaring Variables" section later in this chapter.

In line 6 of Listing 4.1, you see the beginning of the Click event procedure for the command button on the middle of frmString. The Click event procedure does a lot of work.

Lines 7 and 8 take the data in the two text boxes and assign them to the sFirst and sLast string variables. Notice that the Text property of the text boxes gives access to the data in these controls. Because both sFirst and sLast were declared as string variables, there is no problem assigning them the values found in the text boxes.

Line 9 combines the sFirst and sLast string variables and assigns the combined value to sCombined. A space character (" ") is embedded between the two string variables. The ampersand you see in line 9 is called the *concatenation* operator and is used to combine string values.

Finally, the statement in line 10 stuffs the value of the sCombined variable into the Text property of the txtCombined text box at the bottom of frmString.

Although this is a very simple example of using variables, it effectively demonstrates just about everything you need to know about using Visual Basic variables.

- The Dim keyword establishes the new variable.
- You provide a meaningful name for the variable as part of the Dim statement. In Listing 4.1, the variable names are sFirst, sLast, and sCombined.
- The Dim statement includes the data type of the new variable. In Listing 4.1, all the variables are defined as the String data type.
- A variety of techniques can be used to assign a value to a variable. Listing 4.1 uses the = operator to assign values to sFirst and sLast. The data assigned to the variable should be appropriate for the variable's data type.
- The variables can be manipulated with a variety of operators. Listing 4.1 uses the concatenation operator (&) to combine sFirst and sLast as a single value.
- A control can be assigned the value of a variable.

There are several ways to perform each of the tasks you see in Listing 4.1. For example, as you'll read in the "Declaring Variables" section later in this chapter, the Dim statement is not the only way to establish a variable. In addition, the = operator is not the only way to assign a value to a variable, as you'll see in many of the chapters in this book. Also, it isn't necessary to use a variable like sCombined to hold the value being assigned to a control. The assignment to the Text property of txtCombined could have been made directly as shown in the following statement:

```
txtCombined.Text = sFirst & " " & sLast
```

Much of your use of variables in the applications you write is a matter of preference and your particular programming style. Many programmers choose to use long, verbose names for variables, whereas other developers choose more succinct identifiers. As you'll see in Chapter 28, "Professional Visual Basic Development," and Appendix B, "The Reddick VBA Naming Convention," there are good reasons to use a consistent programming style as you build your Visual Basic applications.

Understanding Visual Basic Data Types

Before you even start thinking about the variables your applications need, you must know about the different data types supported by Visual Basic. And as you've seen in other chapters in this book, Visual Basic is an incredibly flexible development platform, so you expect Visual Basic to support a variety of different data types. Table 4.1 lists the different data types supported by Visual Basic 6 as well as the memory requirement and the range of data that can be stored by each data type.

Table 4.1. Visual Basic data type specifics.

Data Type	Storage Requirement	Range
Byte	1 byte	0 to 255
Integer	2 bytes	–32,768 to 32,767
Long	4 bytes	–2,147,483,648 to 2,147,483,647
Single	4 bytes	For negative values: –3.402823E38 to –1.401298E-45
		For positive values: 1.401298E-45 to 3.402823E38
Double	8 bytes	For negative values: –1.79769313486232E308 to –4.94065645841247E-324
		For positive values: 4.94065645841247E-324 to 1.79769313486232E308
Currency	8 bytes	–922,337,203,685,477.5808 to 922,337,203,685,477.5807
Boolean	2 bytes	True or False
Date	8 bytes	January 1, 100 to December 31, 9999
Object	4 bytes	Reference to any type of object
String	Varies	0 to 2 billion (see section on string data type)
Variant	Varies	Same range as any numeric or string data type

Think of a variable as a little bucket in memory. The shape and size of the bucket determines the kind of data you can store in it and how much of that type of data will fit. Table 4.1 shows the different data buckets you can create and how big they can be. Obviously, based on the information in Table 4.1, there are very few limits on the data you can manipulate in your Visual Basic programs.

The next several sections describe each of the different Visual Basic data types and give you an idea of when you'll use each of these data types. In most cases, small code listings give you an idea about how you might use each of these data types in your applications. Don't worry too much about the Visual Basic syntax you see in these listings. All the Visual Basic statements you see in these listings will be explained by the end of this chapter.

Byte

A byte variable occupies only 8 bits (1 byte) of memory. Byte variables can contain unsigned whole number values from 0 through 255. Negative numbers and numbers larger than 255 are not allowed. An attempt to assign a negative value or a value larger than 255 to a byte variable results in a runtime overflow error.

Figure 4.2 shows frmByteTest, a form included in the Variable.vbp project. This form demonstrates the error that occurs when a value larger than 255 is assigned to a byte data type variable. The variable named bByte starts at 250 and is incremented by 1 each time the Go! button is clicked. The error you see in Figure 4.2 occurs when you try to force bByte past 255.

FIGURE 4.2.

The frmByteTest form shows how easy it is to overflow byte variables.

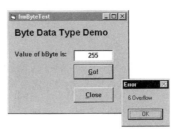

The code behind frmByteTest is shown in Listing 4.2. Again, the line numbers are provided as a guide to the statements in the listing and are not part of the actual code behind frmByteTest.

Listing 4.2. This code quickly drives the bByte variable beyond 255.

```
1    Dim bByte As Byte
2
3    Private Sub Form_Load()
4      bByte = 250
5      txtResult.Text = bByte
6    End Sub
7
8    Private Sub cmdGo_Click()
9    On Error GoTo Err_cmdGo_Click
10     bByte = bByte + 1
```

continues

Listing 4.2. Continued.

```
11     txtResult.Text = bByte
12   Exit_cmdGo_Click:
13     Exit Sub
14   Err_cmdGo_Click:
15     MsgBox Err.Number & " " _
16         & Err.Description, , "Error"
17   End Sub
```

In lines 4 and 5 of Listing 4.2, bByte is assigned its initial value and that value is written into the text box on frmByteTest. The cmdGo_Click event procedure increments bByte in line 10 each time the Go! button is clicked and the new value is assigned to txtResult in line 11. All the other code in the cmdGo_Click event procedure traps the inevitable over-flow error that occurs when a value higher than 255 is assigned to bByte in line 10. (You'll read all about error trapping in Chapter 9, "Handling Runtime Errors.") The message box you saw in Figure 4.2 displaying the error number and error message is opened in lines 15 and 16 in Listing 4.2.

Because byte variables require a single byte of memory, they are very fast for counting and holding small numbers. You might use a Byte data type variable to hold the number of cars owned by a customer or the number of items in inventory if you are absolutely sure the number of items will never be more than 255.

Integer

The integer data type is similar to byte, except that it's larger and can store negative numbers. An integer occupies 16 bits (2 bytes) of memory and can hold whole numbers between –32,768 to 32,767. This makes integer variables useful for counting reasonably large numeric values, performing simple addition and subtraction, and for counting things. Because integer variables occupy only two bytes of memory, they are quite fast when used in calculations and loops. Because they store only whole numbers, integer variables are not appropriate for calculations involving fractional portions of numbers.

Figure 4.3 shows frmIntTest from the Variable.vbp project on this book's companion CD-ROM.

FIGURE 4.3.

The frmIntTest form demonstrates that fairly large numbers are required to overflow integers.

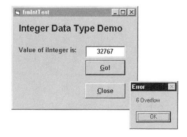

Long

Long integers behave exactly as integer values, except that long integers can be assigned much larger and much smaller values than integers. Because long integers are 32 bits in size, they can hold positive whole numbers as large as 2,147,483,647 and negative whole numbers as large as –2,147,483,648 in the negative direction. However, long integers occupy twice as much memory as integers, and they are considerably slower because the computer must move more data into and out of memory locations. They should not be used for simple counting tasks. Instead, reserve long integers for counting large values or for those situations in which the sum or difference between two numbers in a calculation might result in a large value.

The Variable.vbp sample project accompanying this chapter includes frmLongTest, which demonstrates the error condition triggered when a number larger than 2,147,483,647 is assigned to a long integer variable.

Single

The single data type contains *floating-point numbers*. Use the single data type for variables that must store fractional numeric values, such as those returned by calculations involving division or percentages. Visual Basic *floats* the decimal point to provide the highest possible precision permitted by the 32 bits of storage occupied by the variable. This means that relatively small numbers, such as the square root of 2, can be displayed and stored with fairly good precision, and extremely large numbers, such as 7.000001 raised to the 40th power, might not be as precise as necessary for critical calculations. Therefore, the single data type might not be appropriate for very precise financial and scientific calculations and variables.

Double

The double data type solves most of the precision problems encountered with the single data type. A double variable occupies 8 bytes (64 bits) of memory and can hold extremely large and small floating-point numbers. (Refer to Table 4.1 to see the range of values accommodated by the double data type.) The double data type is ideal for calculations requiring extreme precision, such as programming the trajectories of satellites billions of miles from earth or measuring the tolerance specifications of computer chips. Because the double data type is so large, calculations involving this type of variable are quite slow.

Currency

The currency data type is reserved for storing numeric monetary values such as bank account balances, prices, and payroll information. The currency data type is stored internally in a rather odd fashion. All currency values are stored as very large integer values that contain no decimal points. When the value is needed, Visual Basic divides the integer value by 10,000 to yield a number with four digits to the right of the decimal point.

You are therefore guaranteed extreme accuracy to the left of the decimal point and four digits of precision to the right of the decimal point in all calculations involving currency data types.

In most cases, these characteristics of currency variables are adequate for monetary calculations such as payroll and inventory control. However, the four digits of decimal precision is probably not appropriate for calculating daily interest payments on large loans, effective yield of long-term bonds, and so on. In such cases, the calculations require more precision in the fractional part of the number. The difference between a billion dollars earning 0.0301 percent per day and a billion dollars earning 0.03014 percent per day is a lot of money ($40,000 a day)! Therefore, you should use the double data type when you perform financial calculations that require precision beyond the fourth decimal point.

Boolean

Visual Basic supports true Boolean data types. Boolean variables accept only True or False values. Booleans are stored internally as integer numbers. True is stored as –1, and False is stored as 0. Although you could use an integer data type variable to represent True and False, code written with Booleans is easier to understand. Functions, for example, can return Boolean True or False values, instead of integers that must be interpreted by the calling routine. Because the default values of all numeric data types is zero, the default value for a Boolean variable is False (zero).

Use the Visual Basic True and False keywords to assign values to Boolean variables. Alternatively, assign a Boolean to an expression that evaluates to True or False. A zero value is always interpreted as False, whereas any nonzero value is considered True. By convention, –1 is used to indicate True values in Visual Basic VBA code.

Date

Visual Basic includes a date data type. A date variable contains only date and time data. There is no ambiguity about the value stored in a date variable, and Visual Basic always correctly interprets the date.

A date variable occupies 8 bytes of storage and is stored internally as a floating-point number. Dates store all date and time values from January 1, 100 through December 31, 9999 and times from 00:00:00 (midnight) to 23:59:59 (one second before midnight) in one-second increments. The date data type, therefore, does not store fractional parts of seconds or dates in the extreme future or past.

By default date variables are displayed in the short date format determined by the international settings on your computer (see the Regional Settings applet in the Control Panel). The hour portion is displayed in 12- or 24-hour time as specified by your computer's Control Panel settings.

When converting numeric variables to dates, the portion of the number to the left of the decimal point becomes the date, and the decimal portion become the time. A numeric value with a zero to the right of the decimal point is considered to occur at midnight, and .5 is noon. Negative numbers represent dates before Dec. 30, 1899.

The Year 2000 and Visual Basic

Much has been written in the last year or so concerning the impending change in date data as the century rolls over to the year 2000. The problem comes from the fact that most applications, when given a date in *short date* format (such as 11/19/98) assume the century portion of the year is the same as the century portion of the system time. Therefore, in the year 1999, a date like 11/19/98 is assumed by most applications to be November 19, 1998. In the year 2001, a date like 11/19/98 is interpreted to be November 19, 2098. Obviously, these long-held assumptions are inappropriate when dealing with dates in the future or the past.

The obvious way to rectify this situation is to force users to consistently input dates with all four digits of the year. Therefore, 11/19/98 would have to be input as 11/19/1998 (or 11/19/2098, as the case may be). Providing all four year digits removes the ambiguity surrounding the date and provides the application with enough information that no assumptions have to be made about the date.

The problem with this solution is that most users have grown accustomed to inputting only two digits of the year in most applications. A certain amount of retraining will be required to get users to consistently enter all four digits of the year portion of date data. Additionally, many forms and reports do not allow enough room to display all four digits of the year, which would mean redesigning those forms and reports to accommodate the extra two digits.

How Visual Basic Handles Year 2000 Issues

Visual Basic simplifies handling year 2000 issues. Visual Basic assumes any date entered between 1/1/00 and 12/31/29 actually falls between January 1, 2000 and December 31, 2029. Date data between 1/1/30 and 12/31/99 is assumed to fall between January 1, 1930 and December 31, 1999.

The rationale for this policy is that most dates, like 11/19/39, are birth dates or *historic* data such as order dates, purchase dates, and so on. Such dates are likely to fall between the beginning of 1930 and the end of 1999. Any date, such as 11/19/08, is presumably a reference to a *future* date and therefore falls somewhere near the beginning of the 21st century.

The only time users must enter all four digits of the year is when the date falls outside the range from January 1, 1930 and December 31, 2029. If, for example, the user really means to enter the date September 30, 1916, they must enter it as 9/30/1916 or Visual Basic will interpret it as September 30, 2016.

String

Almost every application must manage text data. It's a rare application that handles only numeric values. Names, addresses, descriptions, serial numbers, ZIP codes, and thousands of other bits of information fall into the text data category. To handle this very broad category of data, Visual Basic provides the string data type.

A string variable holds data made up of letters, numbers, and the symbols you see on a computer keyboard. In addition, a string variable can also contain unprintable characters such as Ctrl+G.

There is a temptation to use a numeric data type variable such as a long integer to hold values that look like numbers but really aren't. Zip codes, phone numbers, employee IDs, and Social Security numbers are examples of data that look like numbers but are actually text. Although these values contain only numeric digits (neglecting for the moment the dashes used to separate groups of digits) they are not numbers. Because Visual Basic will not store leading zeros, a ZIP code like 02173 is stored and used internally by Visual Basic as 2173. ZIP codes, phone numbers, and Social Security numbers are actually string data. In fact, unless you're planning to perform mathematical operations on the data, in most cases you'll find the string data type works best.

Visual Basic provides two forms of string variables.

Fixed-Length Strings

A fixed-length string contains at most approximately 65,000 characters, whereas a variable-length string can be as long as 2 billion characters. The declarations for fixed and variable-length strings are slightly different:

```
Dim sFixed As String * 10   ' A 10-character fixed width string
Dim sVariable As String     ' A variable length string
```

Fixed-Width Strings

Fixed-width strings are padded with spaces to fit the width defined for the string. Therefore, if the word "Windstar" is assigned to the sFixed variable declared in the example above, the data actually stored and used by Visual Basic is "Windstar ".

This means that fixed-width string variables might contain unwanted spaces, possibly interfering with formatting and data storage. You should use the various trim functions to remove unwanted spaces before using fixed-width variables in critical situations. The trim functions are Ltrim, which removes leading spaces, Rtrim, which removes trailing spaces, and Trim, which removes both leading and trailing spaces.

You'll see many examples of using string variables in this book and other publications you read. Strings are probably the most common type of data managed by Visual Basic applications.

Object

Visual Basic can do much more than work with numbers and letters. Visual Basic can work with things that do not fit the usual definition of *data*. You've already seen how Visual Basic can manipulate complex objects such as forms and controls. Later in this book, you'll learn how to use Visual Basic to create and work with sophisticated data structures, special-purpose controls and hardware devices, such as the printer connected to your computer.

All these things fall into the broad category of *objects*. Visual Basic provides everything you need to work with built-in objects such as the `Printer` object, as well as objects you create yourself out of Visual Basic programming statements.

There will be occasions when you'll want to refer to a form or a control on a form in code, or establish a variable that represents a complex object with several different properties rather than a single value. In such cases, the object data type might be suitable.

Using the Object Variable

Listing 4.3 demonstrates one way to use an object variable. This code is included in `frmObject` in the `Variable.vbp` project on this book's disk.

Listing 4.3. Object variables can provide a lot of flexibility in your Visual Basic projects.

```
Private Sub Form_Load()
  frmBuddy.Show
  Call UpdateCaptions(Me, txtCaption1)
  Call UpdateCaptions(frmBuddy, txtCaption2)
  bChanged = False
End Sub

Public Sub UpdateCaptions(frm As Object, txt As Object)
  txt.Text = frm.Caption
End Sub
```

Notice how the `UpdateCaptions` sub in Listing 4.3 references the `Object` variable type in its argument list. There is no need to hard-code form and text box names into this sub, nor is there a need to hard-code the type of object passed to `UpdateCaptions`. Visual Basic figures out the references to these objects from the names passed to `UpdateCaptions`. After Visual Basic has a handle on which form or text box has been passed to the `UpdateCaptions` subroutine, the code adjusts the object's properties.

In Listing 4.4, the generic object variable declarations have been replaced with references to `Form` and `TextBox` object variable types. Both of these variable types are objects built into Visual Basic 6.

Listing 4.4. Specific object type references run faster than the generic
object type.

```
Private Sub Form_Load()
  frmBuddy.Show
  Call UpdateCaptions(Me, txtCaption1)
  Call UpdateCaptions(frmBuddy, txtCaption2)
  bChanged = False
End Sub

Public Sub UpdateCaptions(frm As Form, txt As TextBox)
  txt.Text = frm.Caption
End Sub
```

The code in Listing 4.4 is identical to Listing 4.3, except that it runs a bit faster because
Visual Basic does not have to spend any time figuring out the object that has been passed
to the UpdateCaptions sub procedure.

Understanding Object-Oriented and Object-Based Languages

Although Visual Basic is not considered an object-oriented programming language,
Visual Basic is very much an *object-based* programming language. Because of the
importance of objects to Visual Basic 6, you'll see many examples of the use of objects
in this book. In the meantime, it's important to know there are two main sources of the
objects you work with in Visual Basic:

- Built-in object types such as Form, TextBox, and Recordset as well as the generic
  object data type. Listing 4.3 uses the object data type, whereas Listing 4.4 uses
  specific built-in objects.

- Objects you create yourself through the use of *classes*. Creating custom classes is
  discussed in Chapter 12, "Working with Objects and Collections."

As you'll see in the following chapters, objects are a natural and logical way to manage
forms and other components of your Visual Basic applications. The built-in objects like
Form, Control, and TextBox are a great way to write reusable code. You needn't hard-
code every reference in your procedures.

Variant

The default Visual Basic data type is the variant, a very special type of variable. The
variant is a true chameleon and can accept any value. Unlike the other Visual Basic data
types, a variant is perfectly happy storing a date one moment and a currency value the
next. Visual Basic intelligently adjusts the internal memory storage required to accommodate the value assigned to the variant variable.

Variants are discussed in detail in the section titled "Understanding the Variant Data
Type" later in this chapter. In the meantime, you should understand that the variant data

type requires more storage space and consumes more CPU cycles at runtime than other data types.

Declaring Variables

There are two principle ways to add variables to your applications. The first method—called *implicit declaration*—is to let Visual Basic automatically create the variables for you. As with most things that are not carefully controlled, you'll find that letting Visual Basic prepare your variables for you is not necessarily a good idea. It does not lead to the best performance or efficiency in your programs. See the section titled "Comparing Implicit and Explicit Variable Performance" later in this chapter for a comparison of implicit declaration with the alternatives.

Implicit declaration means that Visual Basic automatically creates a variant for each identifier it recognizes as a variable in an application. In Listing 4.5, there are two implicitly declared variables (FirstName and LastName). This code is behind the form named frmImplicit in the Variable.vbp sample application.

Listing 4.5. Implicit variables work just fine.

```
Private Sub cmdCombine_Click()
  FirstName = txtFirstName.Text
  LastName = txtLastName.Text
  txtFullName = FirstName & " " & LastName
End Sub
```

The second approach to declaring variables is to *explicitly* declare them with one of the following keywords: Dim, Static, Private, and Public. The choice of keyword has a profound effect on the variable's scope within the application and determines where the variable can be used in the program. Variable scope is discussed in the "Understanding Variable Scope and Lifetime" section later in this chapter.

The syntax for explicitly declaring a variable is quite simple:

```
Dim VariableName As DataType
Static VariableName As DataType
Private VariableName As DataType
Public VariableName As DataType
```

In each case, the name of the variable and its data type are provided as part of the declaration. Visual Basic reserves the amount of memory required to hold the variable as soon as the declaration statement is executed. After a variable is declared, it is not possible to change its data type, although it is quite easy to convert the value of a variable and assign the converted value to another variable.

Listing 4.6 shows the cmdCombine_Click event procedure in Listing 4.4 rewritten to use explicitly declared variables.

Listing 4.6. Explicit variable declarations are unambiguous.

```
Private Sub cmdCombine_Click()
  Dim FirstName As String
  Dim LastName As String
  FirstName = txtFirstName.Text
  LastName = txtLastName.Text
  txtFullName = FirstName & " " & LastName
End Sub
```

So, if there's often very little difference between using implicit and explicit variables, why bother declaring variables at all? Listing 4.7 demonstrates the importance of using explicitly declared variables in your applications.

Listing 4.7. Implicit variable declarations lead to bugs in your code.

```
Private Sub Form_Load()
  Department = "Manufacturing"
  Supervisor = "Joe Jones"
  Title = "Senior Engineer"

  'Dozens of lines of code go here

  txtDepartment = Department
  txtSuperviser = Supervisor
  txtTitle = Title
End Sub
```

In this sample code, the txtSupervisor text box on frmImplicit is always empty and is never assigned a value. The second-to-last line of this procedure assigns the value of Supervisor to the nonexistent identifier, txtSuperviser. Because the recipient of the assignment appears to be a variable, Visual Basic simply creates a new variant named txtSuperviser and assigns the value of Supervisor to it. Misspellings such as this are very common and easy to overlook in long or complex procedures.

Comparing Implicit and Explicit Variable Performance

The default data type for Visual Basic variables is the variant. This means that, unless you specify otherwise, every variable in your application will be a variant. As you read earlier in this chapter, the variant data type is not very efficient. Its data storage requirements are greater than the equivalent simple data type (a string, for example). The computer spends more time keeping track of the data type contained in a variant than for other data types.

Listing 4.8 shows how you might test for the speed difference when using implicitly declared variant variables and explicitly declared variables.

Listing 4.8. The explicit declarations in `cmdTestDecimal_Click` include a decimal data type variable.

```
Private Sub cmdGo_Click()
  Dim i As Integer
  Dim j As Integer
  Dim sExplicit As Single

  txtImplicitStart = timeGetTime()
  For o = 1 To 10000
    For p = 1 To 1000
      q = i / 0.33333
    Next p
  Next o
  txtImplicitEnd = timeGetTime()
  txtImplicitElapsed = txtImplicitEnd - txtImplicitStart

  DoEvents

  txtExplicitStart = timeGetTime()
  For i = 1 To 10000
    For j = 1 To 1000
      sExplicit = i / 0.33333
    Next j
  Next i
  txtExplicitEnd = timeGetTime()
  txtExplicitElapsed = txtExplicitEnd - txtExplicitStart
End Sub
```

In this small test, the loop using implicitly declared variables required approximately 18.6 seconds to run, whereas the loop with the explicitly declared variables required only 15.5 seconds. This is an approximately 17 percent performance enhancement just by using explicitly declared variables.

Providing Names for Your Variables

Visual Basic provides extremely liberal rules for naming variables. Briefly, all variable names must conform to the following requirements:

- The name must begin with a letter of the alphabet.
- The name must consist only of letters, digits, and the underscore character. (No punctuation marks are allowed.)

- The name can be as long as 255 characters.

- Variable names can't be duplicated within the same scope. This means, for example, that you can't have two variables of the same name within a procedure. You can, however, have two variables with the same name in two different procedures.

Because Visual Basic's variable naming rules are so liberal, you should strive to provide descriptive, meaningful names to the variables in your application. There is no reason to settle for cryptic, hard-to-understand names such as LN when strLastName says so much more. You'll avoid many simple errors by providing descriptive names to the variables in your application. For example, it is hard to misunderstand what kind of data is contained in a variable named strLastName, especially after you recognize str as the prefix applied to all string variables in the application. Naming conventions are discussed later in this chapter in the section titled "Using a Naming Convention."

Forcing Explicit Declaration

Visual Basic provides a simple compiler directive that forces you to always declare the variables in your applications. You read about several other compiler directives in Chapter 3, "Visual Basic Code Basics." When the Option Explicit statement is inserted at the top of a module, it instructs Visual Basic to require explicit declaration of all variables in the module. If, for example, you are working with an application that contains several implicitly declared variables, inserting Option Explicit at the top of each module results in a check of all variable declarations the next time the application is compiled.

Because explicit declaration is such a good idea, it might not come as a surprise that Visual Basic provides a way to automatically ensure that every module in your applications uses explicit declaration. The Editor tab of the Options dialog box (see Figure 4.4) includes a Require Variable Declaration check box. This option automatically inserts the Option Explicit directive at the top of very module created from this point in time.

FIGURE 4.4.

Requiring a variable declaration is a good idea in most Visual Basic applications.

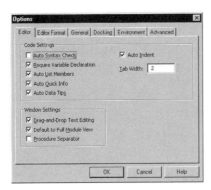

Note: The Require Variable Declaration option does not affect modules already written. This option applies only to modules created after this option is selected. Therefore, you must insert the `Option Explicit` directive in existing modules.

Using a Naming Convention

Like most programming languages, applications written in Visual Basic tend to be long and complex, often occupying several thousand lines of code. Even simple Visual Basic programs might require hundreds of different variables. Visual Basic forms often have dozens of different controls on them, including text boxes, command buttons, option groups, and other controls. Keeping track of the variables, procedures, forms, and controls in even a moderately complicated Visual Basic application is a daunting task.

One way to ease the burden of managing the code and objects in an application is to use naming conventions. A naming convention applies a standardized method of supplying names to the objects and variables in an application. Appendix B describes the most popular naming convention used by Visual Basic developers.

The Reddick naming convention was authored by Greg Reddick, a well-known and successful Visual Basic developer and author. Reddick uses a three- or four-character prefix (a tag) attached to the base name of the objects and variables in a Visual Basic application. For example, a text box that contains a person's last name might be named `txtLastName` while a command button that closes a form would be named `cmdClose`.

The names for variables follow a similar pattern. The string variable holding a customer name might be named `strCustomer` and a Boolean variable indicating whether the customer is currently active would be either `boolActive` or `fActive` (the `f` indicates a flag value).

Using a naming convention is not difficult. The code in this book uses one- and three-character prefixes exclusively. In most cases, when the use of the variable is obvious a one-character prefix is used (for example, `sLastName`) to keep code examples short and simple. In longer procedures, three-character prefixes are used on most variables. All controls on the Visual Basic forms in the projects on this book's disk use three-character prefixes.

The Reddick naming convention even helps you select the most logical name to apply to the variables and objects in your applications. In virtually every case, you assign a name to a variable or object based on how that item is used in the application. In other words, the Reddick convention encourages names based on the functionality provided by the variables and objects in your applications. After all, you should not be adding variables and objects to an application that do not have specific jobs to perform.

Understanding Variable Scope and Lifetime

A variable is more than just a simple data repository. Every variable is a dynamic part of the application and can be used at different times during the program's execution. The declaration of a variable establishes more than just the name and data type of the variable. Depending on the keyword used to declare the variable and the placement of the variable's declaration in the program's code, the variable might be visible to large portions of the application's code. Alternatively, a different placement might severely limit where the variable can be referenced in the procedures within the application.

Examining Scope

The visibility of a variable or procedure is called its *scope*. A variable that can be seen and used by any procedure in the application is said to have *public* scope. Another variable, one that is usable by a single procedure, is said to have scope that is *private* to that procedure.

There are many analogies for public and private scope. For example, a company is likely to have a public phone number (the main switchboard number) that is listed in the phone book. In addition to the main switchboard number, each office or room within the company might have its own private extension number within the company. A large office building has a public street address that is known by anyone passing by the building. Each office or suite within the building has a number that is private within that building.

Variables declared within a procedure are *local* to that procedure and cannot be used or referenced outside that procedure. Most of the listings in this chapter have included several variables declared within the procedures in the listings. In each case, the Dim keyword was used to define the variable. Dim is shorthand for *dimension* and is a rather archaic expression that instructs Visual Basic to allocate enough memory to contain the variable that follows the Dim keyword. Therefore, Dim i As Integer allocates less memory (2 bytes) than Dim s As Double (8 bytes). There is no way to make a variable declared within a procedure visible outside of that procedure.

The Public keyword is used to make a variable visible throughout an application. Public can be used only at the module level and cannot be used within a procedure. Usually, the Public keyword is used only in standard (standalone) modules that are not part of a form. Figure 4.5 illustrates variables declared with three very different scopes.

Every variable declared in the general section of the standard module is public throughout the application unless the Private keyword is used. Private restricts the visibility of a variable to the module in which the variable is declared. In Figure 4.5 the X1 integer declared with Public scope at the top of the module will be seen everywhere in the application, while the Private Y1 integer declared in the next statement is accessible only within the module.

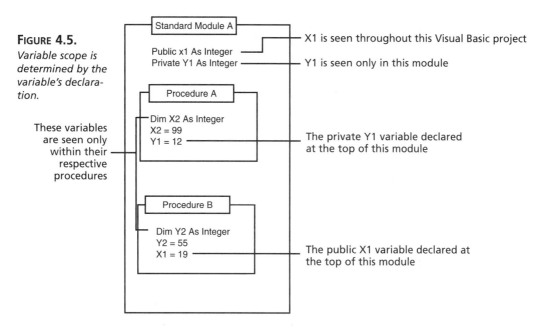

FIGURE 4.5.

Variable scope is determined by the variable's declaration.

These variables are seen only within their respective procedures

A bit farther down in Figure 4.5, you see two procedures (A and B). Each procedure declares a variable that is usable only from within the procedure. In Procedure A, you see a variable named X2 declared as an integer and assigned the value 99. Just below this assignment is a reference to the Y1 variable defined at the top of the module. This variable is accessible only from within the module. Procedure B defines an integer variable named Y2 and assigns it a value of 55. The X1 variable, assigned the 19 value, is the public variable declared at the top of the module.

Determining a Variable's Lifetime

Variables are not necessarily permanent citizens of an application. Just as their visibility is determined by the location of their declaration, their lifetime is determined by their declaration as well. A variable's lifetime determines when it is accessible to the application.

By default, procedure-level variables exist only while the procedure is executing. As soon as the procedure ends, the variable is removed from memory and is no longer accessible. For example, the X2 and Y2 variables in Figure 4.5 expire as soon as their respective procedures end. As already discussed, the scope of procedure-level variables is limited to the procedure and cannot be expanded beyond the procedure's boundaries.

A variable declared in the declarations section of a form's module exists as long as the form is open. All the procedures within the form's module can use the module-level variables as often as they need. When the form is closed and removed from memory, all its variables are removed as well.

The greatest variable lifetime is experienced by the variables declared in public (standard) modules. These variables are available as soon as the Visual Basic application starts up and they persist until the program is shut down and removed from memory. Therefore, any public variables retain their values throughout the application and are accessible to any procedures within the program. Private variables, declared at the top of standard modules, endure throughout the application, but following the rules of variable scope, are accessible only from within the module.

There is one major exception to the general rule that procedure-level variables persist only as long as the procedure is running. The Static keyword makes a variable persist between calls to the procedure. After a value has been assigned to a static variable, that variable retains that value until it is changed in another call to the procedure. Figure 4.6 shows frmStatic, part of Variable.vbp. This form demonstrates how to declare and use static variables.

FIGURE 4.6.

Static variables are not re-created each time the procedure is called.

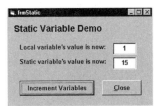

The frmStatic form includes the code shown in Listing 4.9. Notice how the variables declared in the StaticTest1 sub are incremented each time the procedure is called by cmdIncrement_Click. As shown in Figure 4.6, however, only iStatic, the static variable, actually increments each time StaticTest1 is called. The iLocal variable is created from scratch each time StaticTest1 is called, and each time it is created its initial value is zero (0). Therefore, its text box on frmStatic shows only 1.

Listing 4.9. Static variables retain their values between calls to their procedures.

```
Private Sub cmdIncrement_Click()
  Call StaticTest1
End Sub

Private Sub StaticTest1()
   Static iStatic As Integer
   Dim iLocal As Integer

   iStatic = iStatic + 1
   iLocal = iLocal + 1

   txtStatic = iStatic
   txtLocal = iLocal
End Sub
```

An alternative to using static variables is to declare a *global* or *module-level* variable and use it each time a particular procedure is called. The problem with this approach is that a global or module-level variable is accessible to other procedures that are also able to modify its value.

You can experience undesirable side effect bugs by unwittingly changing the value of a widely scoped variable without realizing what has happened. For example, consider an application that uses a global variable that contains the current exchange rate. Consider the consequences of a small bug that alters the value of the exchange rate global variable at an unexpected time. From this point on, every calculation in every procedure relying on the exchange rate variable will be in error. Because of their procedure-limited scope, static variables are one way to avoid side effect bugs.

Incidentally, making a procedure static makes all variables in the procedure static as well. In Listing 4.10 both variables in the `StaticTest2` sub are static, in spite of their local declarations within the procedure. The `Static` keyword used in the procedure's heading makes them both static.

Listing 4.10. All the variables in `StaticTest2` are static because of the declaration used to set up this procedure.

```
Private Static Sub StaticTest2()
    Dim iStatic As Integer
    Dim iLocal As Integer

    iStatic = iStatic + 1
    iLocal = iLocal + 1

    txtStatic = iStatic
    txtLocal = iLocal
End Sub
```

Converting Between Data Types

Visual Basic provides several ways to convert values between different data types. The easiest way is to use a variable in a new context. In many cases, Visual Basic automatically converts between the data types in the expression. Listing 4.11 shows how Visual Basic's automatic conversion works.

Listing 4.11. Strings are easily coerced into numeric values such as doubles.

```
Public Sub Conversion1()
    Dim sStr As String
    Dim dDbl As Double

    sStr = "12345.67890"
```

continues

Listing 4.11. Continued.

```
  dDbl = sString

  MsgBox "Value of dDbl: " & dDbl & vbCrLf _
      & "TypeName(dDbl): " & TypeName(dDbl)
End Sub
```

The message box reports the value of dDbl as 12345.6789 and its data type as double. No error occurs as the string value contained in sStr is assigned to dDbl. This process of automatic conversion is called *coercion* because Visual Basic coerces the string value to a numeric value.

Coercion is not necessarily the best way to perform data conversion. If sStr in Listing 4.11 contains any non-numeric characters (for example, punctuation other than a period or a letter of the alphabet) a runtime error occurs. Visual Basic is able to coerce variable values that are perfect fits for the destination variables.

Also, Visual Basic rounds rather than truncates values as it coerces fractional values to integers. Listing 4.12 shows the Conversion2 procedure from basConversion in Variable.vbp. In this case, the value of iInt at the end of the procedure is rounded to 12346 as the decimal fraction is coerced into an integer.

Listing 4.12. Integers are rounded during coercion.

```
Public Sub Conversion2()
  Dim sStr As String
  Dim iInt As Integer

  sStr = "12345.67890"
  iInt = sStr

  MsgBox "Value of iInt: " & iInt _
      & vbCrLf & vbCrLf _
      & "TypeName(iInt): " & TypeName(iInt)
End Sub
```

Although VB automatically converts (coerces) values to fit particular data types during assignment (for example, a floating-point number to a string), doing so is not considered a good programming practice. It's entirely too easy to encounter a runtime error during the conversion or to lose data in the process. Additionally, the outcome of some conversions might be unexpected. For example, it's easy to end up with a single value instead of a double. In many critical applications, the difference in resulting data types is important.

Instead of allowing Visual Basic to coerce values into new data types, use the built-in conversion functions provided by the VBA language. Table 4.2 shows the values returned by several of the VBA conversion functions when passed the string 12345.67890.

Table 4.2. Results of VBA's conversion functions.

Function	Result	Resulting Data Type
CByte	Overflow	Byte cannot contain a value this large
CCur	12345.6789	Currency
CDate	10/18/33 4:17:37 PM	Date/Time
CDbl	12345.6789	Double
CDec	12345.6789	Decimal
CInt	12346	Integer
CLng	12346	Long
CSng	12345.68	Single
CStr	"12345.67890"	String
CVar	"12345.6789"	String

The data being converted by the VBA conversion functions must be appropriate for the destination variable. For example, if the CInt function is used to assign a value to an integer and the value is too large to fit, a trappable runtime error occurs. You'll learn about trapping and handling runtime errors in Chapter 9.

Working with Arrays

Visual Basic arrays give you a way to work with a group of variables as a single object. An *array* is a series of variables of the same type (integer, string, and so on). When working with arrays you use an index number to tell the elements of the array apart.

Think of an array as a string of boxcars, each containing the same type of data. Each boxcar has a number, and you use that number to retrieve the value stored in a boxcar. There is nothing about the boxcars to distinguish them from one another except their index numbers.

Declaring Arrays

Arrays must be declared just like any other variable. Visual Basic recognizes both *fixed-size* arrays, in which the number of elements in the array does not vary during execution, and *variable-size* arrays, in which the number of elements in the array can change during execution. The syntax of a fixed-size array declaration is as follows:

```
Dim ArrayName([LowerBound To [UpperBound]]) [As DataType]
```

In this declaration, *ArrayName* is the name of the array and *UpperBound* and *LowerBound* indicate the lowest and highest index values, respectively, of the array. The upper and lower bounds are long integers, so Visual Basic arrays can be quite large.

The name of the array is any valid Visual Basic name. The *UpperBound* and *LowerBound* designations are optional and the *UpperBound* value can be supplied without an accompanying *LowerBound* value. If no *LowerBound* value is provided, Visual Basic automatically assigns 0 as the lower bound of the array.

The *DataType* of an array is any valid Visual Basic data type, including simple numeric and string data types as well as user-defined data types. (User-defined data types are described later in this chapter.) If the data type portion of the declaration is omitted, an array of variants is created.

Array Limitations

The only data limitation of arrays is that all the elements of the array must be of the same data type. If this limitation is a problem to you, a collection might be a better solution than an array. (See Chapter 12.) Of course, when working with an array of variants, each element of the array can hold a different data type value. However, the extra memory and processing requirements of using variants in an array limit this approach.

Declaring a variable-size array requires syntax similar to fixed-length arrays:

```
Dim ArrayName() [As DataType]
```

In this case, the *UpperBound* and *LowerBound* are purposely omitted. Visual Basic recognizes this declaration as a variable-size array and expects you to eventually establish the array size with the Redim statement:

```
Redim ArrayName([LowerBound To [UpperBound]])
```

As soon as the Redim statement is applied, Visual Basic allocates as much memory as required to contain the array. You can redim an array multiple times, dynamically altering the amount of memory occupied by the array.

The bounds of an array can be determined with the UBound (upper bound) and LBound (lower bound) functions. The syntax of these functions are as follows:

```
UBound(ArrayName)
LBound(ArrayName)
```

Because the bound values of arrays are long integers, both of these functions return long values.

Listing 4.13 shows how you might use fixed and dynamic arrays in an application. Notice how the dynamic arrays are set to specific sizes by the Redim statement before they are used. Notice also that, because the Redim statements do not include the *LowerBound* specifier, each of the dynamic arrays begins at index 0.

Listing 4.13. The `ArrayDemo` sub (included in `basArrays`) exercises.

```
Sub ArrayDemo()
  Dim aintInt1(1 To 10)  'Fixed array of integers
  Dim astrStr1(1 To 10)  'Fixed array of strings

  Dim aintInt2()  'Dynamic array of integers
  Dim astrStr2()  'Dynamic array of strings

  Dim i As Integer

  ReDim aintInt2(5) 'Now a fixed array of integers
  ReDim astrStr2(5) 'Now a fixed array of strings

  For i = 1 To 10
    aintInt1(i) = i * 100
    astrStr1(i) = Format(i * 100, "0000")
    MsgBox i & " " & aintInt1(i) & " " & astrStr1(i)
  Next i

  For i = 0 To 5
    aintInt2(i) = i * 100
    astrStr2(i) = Format(i * 100, "0000")
    MsgBox i & " " & aintInt2(i) & " " & astrStr2(i)
  Next i

End Sub
```

The `Redim` statement discards the contents of an array if data is already present. Use the `Preserve` keyword when it is important to retain the contents of an array as it is redimensioned:

```
ReDim Preserve astrInt2(1 to 15)
ReDim Preserve astrStr2(1 to 15)
```

The `Preserve` statement instructs Visual Basic to create a new array with the bounds specified in the `Redim` statement and then copy the contents of the original array into the new array.

Understanding the Variant Data Type

Variants are very useful in situations in which the data coming into an application is unknown. For example, Visual Basic applications frequently work with data stored in text files. As the data is read from a text file, certain fields might be missing or contain inappropriate values. Assigning a missing value to a string or numeric data type often generates a runtime error that must be trapped and handled by the application. If the attempt to assign the missing value is not trapped, a runtime error occurs, possibly crashing the application.

The missing value referenced in the preceding paragraph is called a *null value*. *Null* is a special term applied to a value that is not known or is unavailable. For example, the middle initial of a person who does not have a middle name is NULL. A Null value is not the same as an empty string (which is " ") or zero. (Zero appears on the imaginary number line we all learned about in algebra class.) You'll see many instances in this book where the VBA code is written in such a way as to handle null values. In fact, Chapter 15, "Reading and Writing Text Files," explains how to read data from text files and handle the errors that occur when null values are not handled appropriately.

Variant Storage Requirements

Variants have large storage requirements. A variant requires all the memory as needed by the data type stored in the variant, plus another 16 bytes or so as overhead. Additionally, because Visual Basic is able to dynamically adjust the memory occupied by a variant, more CPU cycles are consumed managing variants than simple data types. For these reasons, calculations and data manipulations involving variants tend to be slower than the same operations on simple data types.

Figure 4.7 shows frmVariant, one of the forms in the Variable.vbp application on this book's CD-ROM. frmVariant uses the code in Listing 4.14 to assign different values to a variant.

FIGURE 4.7.

The frmVariant *form demonstrates the versatility of the variant data type.*

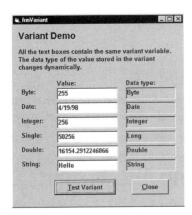

Listing 4.14. The cmdTestVariant_Click event procedure shows how easily the variant data type is converted.

```
Private Sub cmdTestVariant_Click()
    Dim b As Byte
    Dim v As Variant
```

```
    v = Date
    txtDate = v
    lblDate = TypeName(v)

    b = 255
    v = b
    txtByte = v
    lblByte = TypeName(v)

    v = v + 1
    txtInteger = v
    lblInteger = TypeName(v)

    v = v + 50000
    txtSingle = v
    lblSingle = TypeName(v)

    v = v / 3.111
    txtDouble = v
    lblDouble = TypeName(v)

    v = "Hello"
    txtString = v
    lblString = TypeName(v)
End Sub
```

Variants are automatically promoted to the numeric data type required to contain the value of a mathematical operation. For example, adding 1 to a variant containing a value of 255 promotes the variant from a byte to an integer data type.

Because variants are slower than other data types, you should reserve variants for those situations requiring the special features of variants. Any time you'll be taking data out of a disk file, database table, or directly out of a control on a form, you should probably use a variant to receive the value. Otherwise, you risk running into the dreaded runtime null error.

Table 4.3 shows the different storage requirements of variant variables. Notice how the storage requirement depends on which kind of data is stored in the variant.

Table 4.3. Variant data storage requirements.

Data Type	Storage Requirement	Range
Numeric	16 bytes	Any numeric value up to the range of a double
String	22 bytes + string length	Same range as for variable-length string

continues

Table 4.3. Continued.

Data Type	Storage Requirement	Range
Decimal (no decimal point)	14 bytes	+/–79,228,162,514, 264,337,593,543,950,335
Decimal (with decimal point)	14 bytes	+/–7.9228162514264 337593543950335 (see section on decimal data type)

The last item in Table 4.3 is a special, seldom-used data type that only a variant variable can assume. The decimal data type is stored internally as a 96-bit (12-byte) unsigned integer. The value stored in a decimal variable is automatically scaled by a power of 10 to yield the highest precision possible.

A decimal data type variable displays as many as 28 digits to the right or left of the decimal point. The largest possible number that can be stored in the 96 bits occupied by a decimal is +/–79,228,162,514,264,337,593,543,950,335. The smallest number that can be stored in a decimal is 0.0000000000000000000000000001.

In those rare occasions where a decimal data type variable is necessary, use the CDec function to convert a variant to a decimal. Listing 4.15 is found behind the form named frmDecimal in Variable.vbp. This routine exercises a decimal variable and forces it to overflow after several thousand iterations of its For...Next loop.

Listing 4.15. The cmdTestDecimal_Click event exercises a decimal data type variable.

```
Private Sub cmdTestDecimal_Click()
  Dim v As Variant
  Dim i As Integer
On Error GoTo Err_Decimal
  v = 1
  v = CDec(v)      'Convert the variant to decimal
  v = 1000000
  For i = 1 To 10000
    v = v * (9.999999 / 0.11111111)
    txtDecimal = Format(v, "#########.#########")
    lblCount.Caption = i
    DoEvents
  Next i
Exit_Decimal:
  Exit Sub
Err_Decimal:
  Resume Exit_Decimal
End Sub
```

Special Values of Variant Variables

In addition to its other features, variants include several values that other variables never assume:

- Null: Null has already been discussed. Null means that the actual value of something is unknown or has not been provided.

- Empty: A variant that has never been assigned a value contains the special Empty value. As soon as the variant is assigned any value (even Null) the Empty value vanishes and does not return.

- Error: A variant can be assigned a user-defined error value with the CVErr function. For example, the function in Listing 4.16 returns either a formatted date string or a user-defined error number (9999) if the function's argument cannot be expressed as a date.

Listing 4.16. GetFormattedDate shows how to add user-defined error numbers to an application.

```
Function GetFormattedDate(dtmDate As String) _
    As Variant
  If IsDate(dtmDate) Then
    ' Return result
    GetFormattedDate = Number * 2
  Else
    ' Return a user-defined error
    GetFormattedDate = CVErr(9999)
  End If
End Function
```

- Nothing: If the variant contains an object of some sort or other, setting the variant to Nothing releases the memory occupied by the object. Objects are discussed in detail in Chapter 10, "Creating Objects and Classes."

The IsNull function returns True when the value of a variant is Null:

```
If IsNull(VariantVariable) Then...
```

It is always a good idea to test whether a variant is Null before assigning its value to another variable or using the variant in an expression.

Similarly, test whether a variant has ever been assigned a value with the IsEmpty function:

```
If IsEmpty(VariantVariable) Then...
```

The variant data type's capability to assume new identities is unequaled by any other data type. Although variants have a few limitations (mostly speed and storage

requirements) the flexibility they give your programs make them a valuable addition to
most Visual Basic applications.

The VarType function returns a value indicating what type of data is stored in the variant.
The VType function in Listing 4.17 returns a string indicating what type of data is stored
in the variant v passed into the function as an argument. VType is included in
basVariants in the Variable.vbp project.

Listing 4.17. Use the VarType function to determine what kind of data is
stored in a variant.

```
Function VType(v As Variant) As String
  Select Case VarType(v)
    Case vbEmpty:     VType = "Empty"
    Case vbNull:      VType = "Null"
    Case vbInteger:   VType = "Integer"
    Case vbLong:      VType = "Long"
    Case vbSingle:    VType = "Single"
    Case vbDouble:    VType = "Double"
    Case vbCurrency:  VType = "Currency"
    Case vbDate:      VType = "Date"
    Case vbString:    VType = "String"
    Case vbObject:    VType = "Object"
    Case vbError:     VType = "Error"
    Case vbBoolean:   VType = "Boolean"
    Case vbVariant:   VType = "Variant"
    Case vbDecimal:   VType = "Decimal"
    Case vbByte:      VType = "Byte"
    Case vbArray:     VType = "Array"
    Case Else:        VType = "Unknown"
  End Select
End Function
```

The VarType function returns an integer matching one of the intrinsic constants
(vbEmpty, vbNull, vbInteger, and so on) you see in Listing 4.17. Visual Basic does a
good job of guessing the data type contained in a variant, and you can rely on the value
returned by VarType to determine whether your program has received the type of data
expected.

Passing Variables to Procedures

Variables are used in many ways other than demonstrated in the code listings you've seen
so far in this chapter. One of the basic principles of application development with Visual
Basic is to *compartmentalize* functionality whenever possible. In many cases, this means
treating procedures as black boxes that perform certain tasks as the application runs.
You've already seen examples of black box procedures. Listings 4.16 and 4.17 both follow the pattern outlined in Figure 4.8.

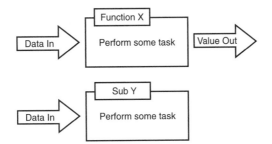

FIGURE 4.8.
Compartmental-ization means treating proce-dures as black boxes that perform tasks.

Figure 4.8 illustrates how a function accepts optional data as input and returns some value that can be used by whatever object in the application that called the function. Subs are different in that they accept data as input but do not return a value.

By default, the values passed into procedures as input can be modified by the procedure. This means that the calling routine must be careful not to send data to a procedure that will be damaged if its value is changed by the called routine. Allowing a procedure to modify a value in its argument list means that the argument is passed *by reference*, allowing the procedure access to the argument's location in memory. Passing arguments by reference is the default behavior in Visual Basic 6.

If it is important that a called routine not change the value of arguments passed to it, the procedure must receive the arguments *by value*, which means that Visual Basic prepares a copy of the argument before invoking the procedure's code. The ByVal keyword in the procedure's argument list specifies that the procedure receives an argument by value.

Listing 4.18 illustrates how ByVal influences how arguments are passed to procedures. The i variable is not modified by Proc2, but the value of i can be used inside Proc2.

Listing 4.18. ByVal instructs Visual Basic to pass a copy of a variable to a procedure in the procedure's argument list.

```
Sub TestArgs()
  Dim i As Integer

  i = 23
  MsgBox "Before Proc1 - i: " & i

  Call Proc1(i)
  'Value of i is now 99
  MsgBox "After Proc1 - i: " & i

  Call Proc2(i)
  'Value of i is still 99
  MsgBox "After Proc2 - i: " & i
```

continues

Listing 4.18. Continued.

```
End Sub

Sub Proc1(iInt As Integer)
  'iInt is received "by reference"
  iInt = 99
  MsgBox "In Proc1 - iInt: " & iInt
End Sub

Sub Proc2(ByVal iInt As Integer)
  'iInt is received "by value"
  iInt = 999
  MsgBox "In Proc2 - iInt: " & iInt
End Sub
```

Notice that both Proc1 and Proc2 specify the data types of their arguments. As with many other things in Visual Basic, you are not required to specify an argument's data type. If the data type is not specified, Visual Basic assumes the argument is a variant data type.

Optional Arguments

Visual Basic enables you to prepare procedures that accept optional arguments. The Optional keyword tells Visual Basic that an argument might not be provided at runtime. You can also provide a default value you want the procedure to use in the event the argument has been omitted. Listing 4.19 (part of basOptional in Variable.vbp) illustrates the Optional keyword and how default values are provided for optional arguments.

Listing 4.19. Optional arguments add flexibility to procedures.

```
Sub TestOptional()
  Call ProcOptional(99, 12)
  Call ProcOptional(88)
End Sub


Sub ProcOptional( _
    iIntX As Integer, _
    Optional iIntY As Integer = 9999)

  MsgBox "ProcOptional has these values: " & vbCrLf _
    & "iIntX: " & iIntX & vbCrLf _
    & "iIntY: " & iIntY
End Sub
```

In the first call to ProcOptional1, both arguments are provided so the message box opened in ProcOptional1 displays both values (99 and 12). The second call to ProcOptional1 omits the second argument. In this case, the message box displayed by ProcOptional1 displays 88 and 9999 (the default value for the second argument to ProcOptional1).

Visual Basic provides a special function to test whether an optional argument has been provided. The IsMissing function works only with variant type arguments and enables you to run alternative code if the optional argument is not provided. In Listing 4.20 notice that iVarY is passed into ProcOptional2 as a variant.

Listing 4.20. The IsMissing function identifies variant arguments that are not provided to the procedure.

```
Sub ProcOptional2(iIntX As Integer, _
    Optional iVarY)

  If IsMissing(iIntY) Then
    MsgBox "ProcOptional2 has this value: " & vbCrLf _
      & "iIntX: " & iIntX
  Else
    MsgBox "ProcOptional2 has these values: " & vbCrLf _
      & "iIntX: " & iIntX & vbCrLf _
      & "iIntY: " & iIntY
  End If


End Sub
```

When the second argument to ProcOptional2 is omitted, the Else clause of the If...End If statement executes, displaying the single value that was passed into ProcOptional2. Keep in mind that IsMissing works only for variant type arguments.

It is a good practice to provide default values for optional arguments, as shown in Listing 4.19. However, in situations in which you cannot determine beforehand which type of data will be passed into a procedure, using a variant type argument coupled with the IsMissing function enables you to intelligently handle missing arguments.

The primary restriction of optional arguments is that the optional arguments must come at the end of the argument list. After the Optional keyword appears in the argument list, all arguments following the Optional keyword must also be optional.

Using Named Arguments

One of the exciting features of Visual Basic VBA is the ability to use *named parameters*. How many times have you found yourself counting commas and writing code like this if you wanted to open up the form as a dialog box?

```
DoCmd.OpenForm "frmOrders", , , , , acDialog
```

With named parameters, you can now use the following code instead:

```
DoCmd.OpenForm "frmOrders", WindowMode:=acDialog
```

Using the named parameter means that Visual Basic doesn't have to evaluate each parameter in the parameter list. Even if the parameter is empty and is indicated only by the comma, the evaluation takes a little bit of time.

Using named arguments is not only easier than having to remember how many commas to place, but it allows your code to be self-documenting as well. Named arguments work just as well with user-defined functions and subs as with the built-in Visual Basic procedures.

Using Constants

Many applications require data that is used as if it were variable in nature but is actually unchanged during the program's execution. A *constant* is defined in the application and is assigned a value during its declaration. Then, as the program executes the constant's value can be used anywhere a variable could be used, but its value cannot be changed by the program's code.

The syntax of a constant's declaration is as follows:

```
[Public¦Private] Const ConstName [As DataType] = Value
```

The same naming conventions apply to constants as to variables. The constant's name must begin with a letter of the alphabet and can't contain any punctuation other than the underscore character. Constant names must be 255 characters or less in length.

The same scoping rules apply to constants and variables. Constants defined in standard modules are public throughout the application by default. Constants defined within form modules are private to the form in which their declarations appear by default. Use the Public and Private keywords to emphasize and clarify the scope of the constant.

If the data type is not provided in a constant's declaration, Visual Basic assumes the data type from the data used to initialize the constant's value. Any data type except objects and user-defined types can be used to initialize constants. Constants can even be defined in terms of other constants:

```
Const conVersion = "5.1"
Const conVerDate = "13-Nov-99 " & conVersion
```

You cannot, however, use functions in a constant's declaration. The following constant declaration generates a compile-time error:

```
Const conVerDate = Date()
```

Because you can define a constant in terms of other constants, it is possible to set up a *circular reference*. A circular reference occurs when a constant includes itself in its definition. Visual Basic warns you of the presence of circular constant references by generating a compile-time error. You cannot run the code until the circular reference has been removed.

User-Defined Data Types

So far in this chapter, you've read about fairly simple data types. With the exception of arrays, each variable has been declared as a solitary instance of a particular simple data type. However, the data most applications manage is somewhat more complex than that. For example, consider the information managed by an inventory control system. This application must handle the item's part number, its description and price, location in the warehouse, and the wholesale vendor providing the part for resale.

Handling this complex kind of data requires different discrete variables. It'd be nice to be able to combine the individual pieces of each inventory item together as a single unit. The Visual Basic Type statement, which enables you to define a data structure, is ideally suited for this type of work. The syntax of the Type statement is shown in Listing 4.21.

Listing 4.21. The Type statement enables you to define complex data structures.

```
[Private ¦ Public] Type TypeName
   ElementName As DataType
   [ElementName As DataType]
   ...
End Type

[Public¦Private¦Dim] VarName As TypeName
```

The Type statement itself defines the data structure's template, whereas the variable declaration below the Type statement sets up a variable from the Type's data structure. Often, an array of the data structure will be established to handle several different items (see Listing 4.22).

Listing 4.22. How to define the inventory control data structure and declare an array of 1000 inventory items.

```
Public Type InvItemType
   strPartNumber As String
   strDescription As String
   curPrice As Currency
   strLocation As String
   strVendorID As Long
End Type

Public InvItems(1 To 1000) As InvItemType
```

Referencing one of the elements of the data structure is straightforward. The following statement sets the price of the 109th element of the `InvItems` array:

```
InvItems(109).Price = $12.09
```

A type structure can contain as many different elements as necessary to define the object. Any elements that are not data typed will be treated as variants. As indicated in Listing 4.22, you can easily establish arrays of type structures to manage several similar complex objects.

A more sophisticated approach to creating user-defined data structures is to create a class module that defines the object. Chapter 10 describes this approach to handling complex data.

Summary

Visual Basic is an exceedingly flexible application development system. This flexibility requires Visual Basic to handle a wide variety of data types, including numeric, string, and object data. Fortunately, Visual Basic provides a wealth of different data types that enable you to tailor the data management features of your applications to suit the user's needs.

Visual Basic variables is a big topic, requiring an entire chapter in this book just to work through some of the details of setting up and handling variables in Visual Basic applications. This chapter has established the variable usage guidelines you'll see applied throughout the other chapters of this book.

Now that you have a firm basis in programming with Visual Basic, it is time to move on to the more visible parts of the applications you'll create. The next several chapters document how you'll build user interfaces in Visual Basic. Chapter 5, "Designing the User Interface," discusses how you'll build the forms that serve as the main component of the user interface. Chapter 6, "Putting Your Forms to Work with Controls," explains how controls add utility and intelligence to your applications, reducing support and training requirements. Finally, Chapter 7, "Mastering Menus and Toolbars," shows you how to top off the user interface with components that provide instant access to the application's features.

Designing the User Interface

In this chapter, you begin to create the graphical user interface (GUI) for your program. That is a fancy way to refer to the text boxes, labels, command buttons, and other controls that make up the visible, interactive part of your project.

This chapter shows you how to create and customize the basic building block of the Windows GUI, called the *form*. First, you take a look at forms and learn their design-mode properties and then move on to their runtime properties, methods, and events.

Chapter 6, "Putting Your Forms to Work with Controls," discusses how to populate your forms with controls such as text boxes and command buttons. Chapter 7, "Mastering Menus and Toolbars," completes this overview of the user interface with a look at the menus and toolbars that make it easy for users to work with the application.

This chapter is accompanied by a large number of projects on this book's CD-ROM. All the forms you see in this chapter's figures and sample code listings are taken from the projects accompanying this chapter.

Understanding the Visual Basic Form

Think of a form as the structural plan for an application window—a window under construction. You create a form inside the Visual Basic Form Editor window or Form Designer window. When you run your program, the form you've created becomes an independent window in the working application.

Figure 5.1 shows a typical Visual Basic form with some of its components labeled. Become familiar with Visual Basic forms and their anatomy because you'll spend a lot of time creating these important parts of most every Visual Basic application.

The relationship between a form and an application window can be confusing at first. The same object is sometimes called a form and other times a window. There is a logic to this. The object is called a *form* when describing its appearance and behavior in the Visual Basic design-mode environment. A form is often called a *window* when referring to its runtime behavior and appearance.

Control box   Title bar   Minimize button

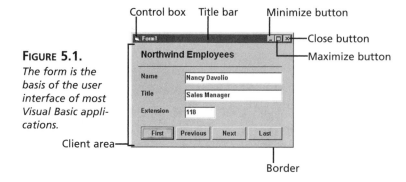

FIGURE 5.1.
The form is the basis of the user interface of most Visual Basic applications.

Client area

Border

Getting the Look and Feel of Windows

The Windows operating system has its own GUI standard that is different from other operating systems such as UNIX. Visual Basic creates programs that are compatible with the Windows GUI standard. In fact, Visual Basic applications utilize the same GUI components that the Windows operating system uses. Those components include windows, buttons, check boxes, text boxes, and the other standard Windows controls. Figure 5.2 shows the Word 97 Options dialog box, which contains many common Windows user interface elements.

Tabs

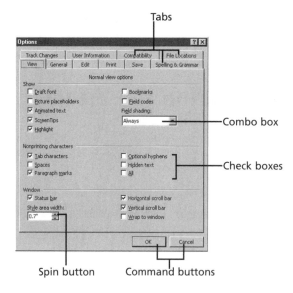

FIGURE 5.2.
The Word Options dialog box features many Windows GUI elements.

Combo box

Check boxes

Spin button   Command buttons

Because Visual Basic programs are written for use under the Windows operating system, it makes sense that programs written with Visual Basic should be consistent with Windows conventions and standards. There are important benefits gained by consistency:

- Visual Basic program will not clash visually with its Windows environment.
- Visual Basic programs leverage the maximum benefits of compatibility with other programs, utilities, and operating system resources.
- A consistent GUI minimizes training time for new users of your application.

Keeping your Visual Basic applications consistent with the Windows operating system, and within itself, means your program is immediately intuitive and familiar to your users.

Following Windows conventions does not mean abandoning your own creativity. Visual Basic offers unlimited flexibility so you can create a unique look and feel for your applications while remaining within the bounds of Windows programming conventions. The next few chapters show you how to design compatible and consistent user interfaces and introduce you to ways you can add your own personal style and flair to your creations.

Creating Your First Form

Because the vast majority of Visual Basic programs have at least one window, Visual Basic automatically creates the first form for you when you create a new project.

To try this, run Visual Basic and select the File, New Project menu item. The New Project dialog box appears (see Figure 5.3) enabling you to select the type of project you intend to create. Later in this book, you learn how to create some of the more specialized application types (such as ActiveX Control) offered in this dialog box. For now, make sure the Standard EXE icon is selected and click OK. Most applications you create are Standard EXE type projects.

FIGURE 5.3.
All Visual Basic projects start with this dialog box.

The Visual Basic Form Designer window appears (see Figure 5.4). Inside the Form Designer window is a blank form with its caption set to Form1. This is the first form of your application.

FIGURE 5.4.
Visual Basic creates the startup form for you.

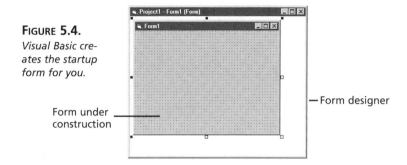

—Form designer

Form under
construction

The new form is also the project's startup form. This means that this form is the window that is automatically displayed when your program starts up. Any additional forms you create must be displayed by program commands.

Select the Run, Start menu item to run your new application so that you can see the form as a window. You can also start your program by pressing the F5 key to run the project. If you are shown a dialog box prompting to save your project, you can do so or you can click the Cancel button to indicate that you don't want to save the project at this time. You then see your form displayed as an application window (see Figure 5.5). Although you have not written a single line of code, you can do a lot with your new application window; you can move, resize, minimize, restore, and close it.

FIGURE 5.5.
This application window doesn't do much but was easy to create!

You have now created a Visual Basic program that displays a blank application window. Not many years ago, this simple, do-nothing application would have required a formidable programming effort! It's important to understand that the form shown in Figure 5.5 is a real Windows application. The form can be minimized, maximized, and moved about on the screen. It has an icon associated with it (notice the icon in the leftmost position on the title bar), and a control menu under the control box next to the program icon. Visual Basic is unique in its capability to get Windows-compatible applications running in a very short time with so little effort.

The form you see in Figure 5.5, Form1, is part of the First1.vbp project found on the CD-ROM accompanying this book.

Adding New Forms

Most applications require more than the one form that Visual Basic adds automatically to new projects. To add new forms to your project, click Project, Add Form. Visual Basic opens a dialog box offering you a list of typical form types to choose from (see Figure 5.6).

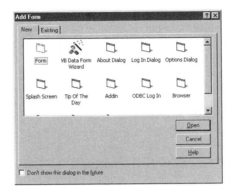

Visual Basic offers you the option of starting with a blank form or with a form that has already been preconfigured for specialized purposes, such as an About Box form or a Login form.

Later, you can select one of the preconfigured form types if it fits your needs. For now, select the blank form labeled Form. Visual Basic creates a new blank form and adds it to your project.

> **Tip:** Don't feel you need to add all your planned forms at one time. Add each one when you are ready to work on it.

Understanding Form Properties

Your new form has several property settings that determine its appearance and behavior. Because you have not changed any property settings up to this point, your new form looks and behaves according to its default property settings.

These property settings can be viewed and modified in the Properties window (see Figure 5.7). If you do not see the Properties window, select View, Properties Window from the menu or press F4. The Visual Basic Properties window appears. The Properties window displays the property names and values for the form or control selected in the Form Designer window.

FIGURE 5.7.

The Properties window contains most of the property settings for the object selected in the Form Designer window.

To change the style or behavior of your new form, you need only change the related properties in the Properties window. We will go through some of the most common form properties to learn what they do. Remember that when you are writing a Visual Basic application, you can get context-sensitive help on any property by positioning the cursor in the Property Name box in the Properties window and pressing F1.

There are several ways to change property values:

- Type the property setting into the Property text box in the Properties window.
- Select a property from a drop-down list in the Property box.
- Click a Build button in the Property box to open a palette or other selection device.
- Double-click the property to cycle through the acceptable values for the property.

Not all properties support all these selection techniques. The BackColor property, for example, contains a drop-down button that opens a color selection palette (see Figure 5.8). The Alignment property uses a drop-down list of acceptable values. The double-click method works only on properties that have drop-down lists for selection.

The Properties window shows you the relevant properties for the object selected in the Form Designer window. You'll become familiar with the properties that are relevant for common controls. For example, a text box control has both ForeColor and BackColor properties, whereas a command button has neither of these properties but has a DownPicture property not shared with text boxes.

Setting properties at design time modifies the initial characteristics for the form. Many properties can be changed at runtime as needed by setting the properties from within your code. Later in this chapter, you'll see many examples of using VBA code to modify properties at runtime.

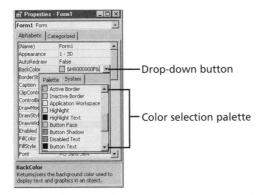

FIGURE 5.8.
Many properties include selection palettes or dialog boxes to help you set values.

Drop-down button

Color selection palette

Form Appearance Properties

All Visual Basic forms include several properties that influence the appearance of the form. You'll often use these properties to call attention to a form or to draw distinctions between the forms in your applications.

BorderStyle

The BorderStyle property is one of the most important form properties. BorderStyle determines the kind of window your form becomes at runtime. Visual Basic provides several preconfigured styles for the BorderStyle property.

The most flexible style is the Sizable border style. Sizable forms (see Figure 5.9) can be resized by the user at runtime to make the form larger or smaller. Sizable forms can have a control menu box, a minimize button, a maximize button, and a close button in the title bar. Sizable forms always have "stretchable" borders.

Control box   Minimize button

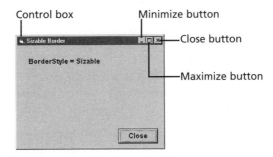

Close button

Maximize button

FIGURE 5.9.
Sizable borders are common in Visual Basic applications.

Equally common is the Fixed Single border style. This style (see Figure 5.10) can include a control menu button, a minimize button, and a maximize button. It cannot be resized. Use this style if you want to enable the user to minimize or maximize the window but not to freely resize it.

FIGURE 5.10.
The Fixed Single border style is useful when you don't want users dragging the margins of a form to a new size.

The Fixed Single border style and Sizable border look similar. Therefore, you should use whichever of these styles is best suited for the application you are developing. If it's important that the user not resize the form's borders (perhaps to prevent the form from obscuring other important information on the screen) use the Fixed Single border style. Otherwise, you might want to use the Sizable border, which is the default for all Visual Basic applications.

Another common border style is the Fixed Dialog. A fixed dialog form (see Figure 5.11) can include a control-menu button but is not sizable and cannot have a minimize or maximize button. Fixed Dialog style forms are routinely used for most pop-up displays or data entry windows.

FIGURE 5.11.
The Fixed Dialog border is often used on pop-up dialog boxes. Notice the absence of minimize and maximize buttons.

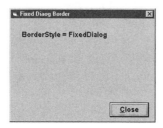

In Figure 5.11 notice that the minimize and maximize buttons are not displayed in the form's title bar. These buttons are missing although the MinButton and MaxButton properties are both True. These buttons have been removed because the Fixed Dialog border is intended to be used on forms such as dialog boxes in Visual Basic applications and other situations in which the form will not be maximized or minimized by the user.

Somewhat less common is the Fixed ToolWindow BorderStyle property setting. This setting (see Figure 5.12) creates a form with a title bar half the size of a normal title bar, and no control box, minimize, or maximize buttons. The caption in the title bar of a Fixed Toolwindow form uses a smaller font than a normal form. A form with its BorderStyle set to Fixed ToolWindow is intended for use as a toolbox type of window. Toolboxes typically display several settings or tools that are used in an application. A tool window does not appear in the Windows taskbar.

Figure 5.12.
The Fixed ToolWindow setting creates a unique form for selection purposes.

There is a corresponding Sizable ToolWindow setting for the BorderStyle property. In this case the border of the tool window can be stretched into new positions on the screen.

Unlike many other form properties, the BorderStyle property is read-only at runtime. You can alter this property only at design time and cannot change its value while the application runs.

Name

The Name property is the name by which your code references this form. The Name property of the first form defaults to Form1. Additional forms are automatically named Form2, Form3, and so on. You should provide meaningful names for your forms using the frm prefix as a convention. For example, frmMain is the recommended name for the startup form because it is the main form in the project. Naming this important form frmMain lets everyone know which form is the startup form. Additional forms can be given names like frmReport or frmInput.

The name of a form is assigned at design time and cannot be changed at runtime.

Caption

The Caption property designates the text appearing in the form's title bar. The caption should be short and clear to identify the window to the user. The caption, as with many other form properties, can be changed at runtime.

Icon

The icon displayed in the form's title bar is set with the Icon property. To assign an icon, select the Icon property in the Properties window. A browser button with three dots (often called an ellipsis) appears in the Property box. When you click the browser button, a file selection window lets you choose an icon file for your window icon (see Figure 5.13). This icon data is stored as part of the project, so the original icon file is no longer needed.

FIGURE 5.13.
A Browser button makes it easy to locate and select an icon for the form.

Icon selection dialog box

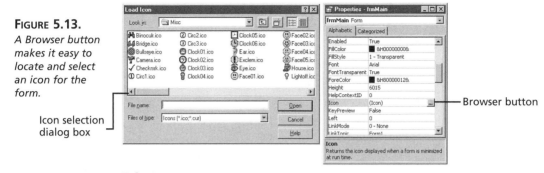

Browser button

Picture

A form can display a picture in its *client area*, the working area of the window. The picture file, which can be virtually any Windows-compatible image file such as .BMP, .PCX, or .WMF, is designated by the form's Picture property. The picture file can be selected the same way as an icon.

The frmPicture form, part of FormProp.vbp on this book's CD-ROM, is shown in Figure 5.14. This form contains several command buttons that load different images into the form's Picture property.

FIGURE 5.14.
The frmPicture *form, part of* FormProp.vbp, *demonstrates how to change the* Picture *property of a form at run-time.*

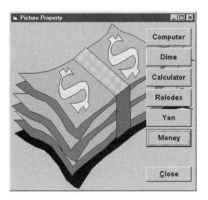

Each command button on frmPicture uses the LoadPicture function to load a picture into the form's Picture property. The code behind the Computer command button on frmPicture is shown in Listing 5.1.

Listing 5.1. Very little code is required to change the picture displayed on a Visual Basic form.

```
Private Sub cmdComputer_Click()
  Me.Picture = LoadPicture(App.Path & "\Computer.wmf")
End Sub
```

Notice the code behind frmPicture requires that the bitmaps displayed in the form's Picture property reside in the same directory as the application itself. The Path property of the App object returns the location of the program's .EXE file.

The Picture property is seldom used because Image or Picture Box controls are more flexible and powerful to use. One situation in which the form's Picture property is frequently used is when a form is used as an application's splash screen.

BackColor

The BackColor property designates the color of the client area of the form. The Properties window displays a color selector that lets you choose from a list of Windows system colors or a palette of standard colors (see Figure 5.15).

FIGURE 5.15.
Visual Basic provides the Define Color dialog box for specifying custom colors.

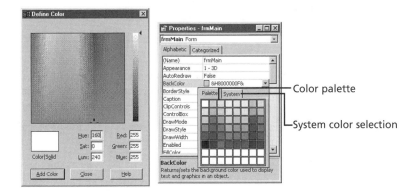

When using the palette portion of the color selector, you can select a custom color by right-clicking the palette's lower area of the color palette to bring up the Define Color dialog box, shown in Figure 5.15. If you know the hexadecimal value for the desired color, you can enter it directly as the BackColor property.

> **Tip:** Normally you get the best results by leaving all colors set to their default Windows system colors. By using standard Windows system colors, your program color scheme changes to match whatever Windows color scheme the user selects. If you set your own colors, you have more control over the appearance of your product, but users have none. Many users might hate your choices and think that their own combinations (no matter how garish) are far better. If they do change their Windows scheme, your color scheme might look awful against the user's custom color choices and give the impression that you are not fully Windows-aware. The best choice is usually to allow your program to remain color-consistent with the user's desktop by using system colors.

Font Properties

Visual Basic provides several font properties applicable to forms. A form's font properties determine the default font applied to all controls added to the form as well as the font used for drawing operations on the form.

The font properties applicable to forms include the following:

- `FontName` —The name of the font used on the form. The font must be available on the computer. A runtime error occurs if an invalid font is specified. The `FontName` property is a string data type.

- `FontBold`—The `FontBold` property displays the fonts in bold typeface by default. Valid values for `FontBold` are `True` and `False`.

- `FontItalic`—Similar to `FontBold`, the `FontItalic` property sets the default font display to italics. `FontItalic` is a Boolean data type like `FontBold`.

- `FontSize`—The `FontSize` property is an integer specifying the size of the form's default font in points.

- `FontStrikeThru`—The `FontStrikeThru` property displays the form's fonts with a strikethrough. This is another Boolean (`True` or `False`) property.

- `FontUnderline`—`FontUnderline`, like several other properties, affects the typeface applied to the form's fonts. In this case, characters are displayed with an underscore under them. This is another Boolean property.

The `frmFonts` form in the `FormProp.vbp` project is shown in Figure 5.16. This form demonstrates how to set a form's font properties at runtime. The check boxes on this form set the `FontBold`, `FontItalic`, and other font properties for `frmFonts`. The Print On This Form button uses the `Print` statement to print directly onto the face of the form while the Clear Form button invokes the form's `Cls` method (discussed later in this chapter) to clear the form.

FIGURE 5.16.

A form's font properties provide a lot of text-display flexibility.

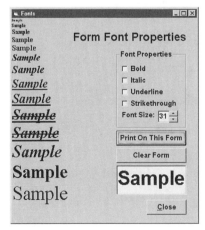

Form Control Properties

By default, Visual Basic displays several buttons in a form's title bar. These buttons enable the user to maximize the form so that it occupies all the available space on the computer screen or shrink it down to an icon on the Windows 95 taskbar. In many applications, you'll want to inhibit these actions by the user, so you might need to explicitly remove these buttons from the title bar.

Many properties discussed in this section are exercised in the FormProp.vbp project on the CD-ROM accompanying this book.

ControlBox

The ControlBox property is a True/False value that determines whether the standard Windows control menu is visible in the leftmost position on the form's title bar. When ControlBox is set to True (its default value) the minimize, maximize, and close buttons appear in the title bar as well. The minimize and maximize buttons can be hidden by adjusting their respective properties.

Figure 5.17 shows the control menu hidden under the control box button. This menu contains certain commands (such as Maximize and Minimize) that you might not want available to your users. You hide this menu by removing the control box from the form's title bar.

Control box

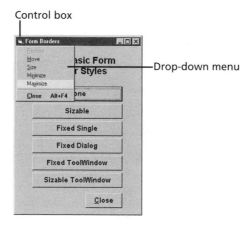

FIGURE 5.17.

The control box hides the control menu containing some important and potentially dangerous commands.

Drop-down menu

If the ControlBox property is set to False to remove the control box from the title bar (suppressing the close button at the same time), you should provide some way for the user to close the form. You can, for example, add Cancel and OK buttons on a form to give the user a way to dismiss it.

MinButton and MaxButton

For forms with a Sizable or Fixed Single border style, the MinButton and MaxButton properties (both are Boolean values) enable or disable the minimize and maximize buttons in the title bar.

> **Note:** Changing the BorderStyle property might cause a change in the MinButton and MaxButton properties.

Form Size and Positioning Properties

Visual Basic also provides the properties required to precisely position a form in a specific location on the screen. These properties are provided to enable you to perform such actions as opening two forms side-by-side on the screen, popping up a dialog box in a predictable location, and altering a form's horizontal and vertical dimensions at runtime.

StartupPosition

The StartupPosition property specifies how you want the form to be initially positioned on the screen as it opens. The StartupPosition property has just a few acceptable settings:

- The Manual setting opens the form at whatever position is determined by the form's Top and Left property settings.
- CenterOwner centers the form over the form that opened it.
- CenterScreen positions the form in the center of the computer's screen, regardless of the video resolution (640×480, 800×600, and so on) of the computer's monitor.
- Windows Default (the default setting) initially positions the form near the upper-left corner of the screen. Each subsequent time the form is displayed it is positioned somewhat arbitrarily to the right and left of the initial position.

CenterScreen is the most common and the most reliable setting. Both CenterOwner and CenterScreen override the Top and Left property settings (described in the following section) that otherwise determine where the form appears on the screen. The Manual setting requires the programmer to set the form's position through the form's property settings at design time or in code at runtime.

Left, Top, Height, and Width

In Design mode, these properties set the starting position and size of the window. They can also be set at runtime to change the location and size of the window. Note that you can also change the Height and Width property settings by resizing the form in the Form Design window with the mouse.

Visual Basic provides a handy tool that helps you position a form on the screen. Select View, Form Layout from the Visual Basic menu at design time. When a form is open in the Form Design window, a small facsimile of the form appears in the Form Layout window (see Figure 5.18). You set the form's Left and Top properties by moving the facsimile around in the Form Layout window with the mouse. The form's StartupPosition is also set to Manual as you move the facsimile in the Form Layout window.

FIGURE 5.18.

The Form Layout window is a handy tool for positioning a form on the screen.

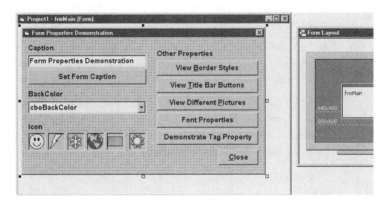

Movable

The Movable property is seldom used in most Visual Basic applications. The default value for the Movable property is True. By setting this property to False, you prevent the user from being able to move the window (by dragging the title bar with the mouse) at runtime.

There are few situations in which you would want to immobilize a form on the screen. One situation in which an immovable form is useful is when displaying a pop-up form next to another form. Perhaps you want to make sure the user is able to see important data on the form under the pop-up form. You might consider immobilizing the form under the pop-up form as well as the pop-up form itself to ensure that both forms are visible at the same time.

> **Tip:** You can easily toggle True/False (Boolean) properties by double-clicking the property name in the Properties window.

WindowState

The WindowState property sets the initial state of the form. The form in your application can start out in its default size and position on the screen, minimized, or maximized. If

you set the MinButton, MaxButton, and ControlBox properties to False, you can prevent
the user from changing the state of the application after it has been opened.

ShowInTaskbar

The ShowInTaskbar property determines whether the form appears in the Windows 95
taskbar. Your startup form, if it is also the primary form in your application, should have
this property set to True so that the program appears in the taskbar. It should normally be
set to False for secondary forms so as not to clutter up the Windows taskbar.

If, for some reason, your application is meant to appear unobtrusively on the user's
Windows 95 desktop, set the ShowInTaskbar property to False. When ShowInTaskbar is
set to False the user is not able to Alt+Tab to the application in the Windows task list.

Note that changing the BorderStyle property might cause an automatic change in the
ShowInTaskbar property to reflect the conventions described earlier in this chapter. For
example, the Fixed ToolWindow setting for the BorderStyle property prevents a form
from showing in the Windows taskbar.

The ShowInTaskbar property is read-only at runtime and cannot be changed with VBA
code.

More Form Properties

As you can see in the Properties window, there are many more form properties. In later
sections of this chapter and in other chapters you learn many more of these properties.
Many other properties are seldom used in Visual Basic 6 applications and several properties are maintained simply for backward compatibility with earlier versions of Visual
Basic.

Other Form Properties

Visual Basic forms include several miscellaneous properties in addition to the properties
you've already studied. These properties affect how your code interacts with a form to a
certain extent. Most often, the default values for these properties work fine, but you
sometimes might have to make adjustments.

Tag

The Tag property is a text string that tags the form. This string has no purpose other than
whatever you want to do with it. You can use the Tag property to store any string information you need to associate with the form.

In many cases, you'll use the Tag property as a place to document something about a
form. Alternatively, you might use the Tag property to hold some flag value that tells
your code how to handle the form. Listing 5.2 shows how to use the Tag property to display a version number on the form. The Tag property in this case is updated each time

you make a change to the form. The user displays the form's modification date in a label near the bottom of the form by double-clicking anywhere on the body of the form.

Listing 5.2. The `Tag` property of this form stores the date of the form's most recent modification.

```
Private Sub Form_DblClick()
  lblVersion.Caption = "Version: " & Me.Tag
End Sub
```

The form itself (`frmTag` in the `FormProp.vbp` project) is shown in Figure 5.19. A double-click on the body of this form displays the form's `Tag` property in the label near the bottom of the form.

FIGURE 5.19.

The `frmTag` *form shows one use of the* `Tag` *property.*

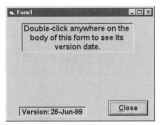

ScaleMode, ScaleTop, ScaleLeft, ScaleWidth, ScaleHeight

Visual Basic provides form drawing methods discussed later in this chapter. These enable you to draw graphics directly on the form's client area. The form's client area becomes a drawing canvas or sketchpad in the process.

The `ScaleMode` property determines the units used to measure the canvas area. The `ScaleMode` settings include Twip, Pixel, Character, Inch, Centimeter, and Millimeter. The dimensions of the client area are the physical dimensions of the client area measured in these units. For example, as the user stretches the form wider, the `ScaleWidth` increases.

> **Note:** The twip unit of measurement requires a bit of explanation. A twip is 1/20th of a printer's point. There are 72 printer's points per inch on a printed page. Therefore, each twip is only 1/1440th of an inch, an exceedingly small unit of measurement.

To keep the canvas dimensions fixed, no matter how the user sizes the window, set the `ScaleMode` property to User. With this property setting, the `ScaleWidth` and `ScaleHeight` are set to arbitrary values (such as 1000 and 1000, respectively) that define the interior dimensions of the form. Visual Basic then maintains the 1000×1000 user-defined units regardless of the actual physical dimensions of the form on the screen. Setting a control's Left property to 100 always positions the left margin of the control at 1/10 of the total width of the form, no matter how wide the form is on the screen.

The ScaleWidth and ScaleHeight properties affect only the interior of the form, exclusive of the form's border area and title bar.

Referencing Form Properties

Up until this point in the discussion of form properties, you have learned about setting the initial properties of a form in Design mode, using the Properties window. Now you move on to setting or retrieving window properties using Visual Basic code at runtime.

Properties are linked to a particular form object. Use this general syntax to set a form's property:

```
FormName.PropertyName = Value
```

Retrieving a form's property is the opposite operation:

```
Value = FormName.PropertyName
```

You can always reference properties this way from any form or code module in the project.

Referencing a form's properties from within that form's code module uses a shorthand notation:

```
Me.Property
```

The Me keyword refers to the current form and is properly used only with a form's module. An error is generated if you attempt to reference the Me object within a standard or public code module. Alternatively, some properties assume the Me object as the default without specifying it at all. In those cases, you can just say

```
Property = Value
```

One example of this is the Caption property. If you do not specify an object, the current form object is assumed. Therefore you can set the Caption of the current form (from within that form's code module) by saying

```
Caption = "Form Caption"
```

Omitting the reference to the form, however, is considered bad programming style by many developers. Including the Me reference removes any ambiguity from the code and is much easier to understand.

> **Note:** The preceding comments are true for form methods as well as form properties.

Setting Properties in Code

If you want to change form properties at runtime, as in the `FormProp.vbp` sample application, you must set the properties in your code. It is easy to do this in Visual Basic. Here is the event procedure from `frmMain` in the `FormProp.vbp` project that changes the title bar caption:

```
Private Sub cmdCaption_Click()
frmMain.Caption = txtCaption.Text
End Sub
```

In this event procedure, the `Caption` property of `frmMain` is set to the value of the `Text` property of a text box on the form.

All other properties are set in the same way. For example, the following routines set the size and position of the form on the screen at runtime:

```
Private Sub cmdMove_Click()
  frmMain.Left = 1000
  frmMain.Top = 2000
End Sub

Private Sub cmdResize_Click()
  frmMain.Width = 5000
  frmMain.Width = 6000
End Sub
```

> **Note:** Not all properties can be set at runtime. Some properties, such as the `ShowInTaskbar` property, are read-only at runtime. That means that if you try to assign new values to these properties, a runtime error occurs. In particular, many of the form configuration properties are read-only at runtime. If you are not sure, check the property's online help topic. It should tell you whether the property is read-only at runtime.

Positioning the Form with Methods

In addition to properties, forms, like other objects, have several *methods*. A method is an action performed on the object.

You've already read about the `Top`, `Left`, `Width`, and `Height` properties. These properties, which can be set at runtime as well as design time, specify the precise size and location of the form on the screen. In addition, Visual Basic forms support several methods specifically designed to manipulate the form's size and position at runtime. Generally speaking, these methods are faster to use than setting the equivalent properties.

Move

You can use the Move method instead of individually setting the Left, Top, Width, and Height properties as shown earlier in this chapter. The Move method includes parameters that parallel the function of the Left, Top, Width, and Height properties. As an example, frmMain in the Forms.vbp project includes the following event procedure:

```
Private Sub cmdMoveResize_Click()
  frmMain.Move 1000, 2000, 5000, 6000
End Sub
```

The syntax diagram of the Move method is

```
FormName.Move Left, [Top], [Width], [Height]
```

where Left, Top, Width, and Height are the dimensions you want to apply to the corresponding form properties. Notice that only the Left parameter is required.

The Move method executes much faster and uses less code space than setting the four properties (Left, Top, Width, and Height) separately.

ZOrder

Windows can overlap onscreen, giving them relative positions in the third dimension, or along the z-axis perpendicular to the screen. The ZOrder method enables you to move a form to the front or the back position along this dimension.

By calling the ZOrder method and passing it a value of 0, the form is moved to the top of the screen. By passing the method a value of 1, the form is moved behind all other forms. The ZOrder method is very useful to ensure that the desired form is on top of the other windows open onscreen.

Using Form Drawing Methods

Visual Basic provides several methods that support drawing graphical objects and text directly on the surface of the form. Earlier in this chapter you learned about the properties (ScaleMode, ScaleWidth, ScaleHeight, and so on) that specify the interior dimensions of the form. The methods described in this section draw the graphics primitives you can use to graph numeric data directly on Visual Basic forms.

Several of these methods use the paradigm of a drawing pen that is positioned at some X and Y position of the form. The origin of the form's axes (point 0,0) is at the upper-left corner of the form. The X values increase as you move to the right across the form, whereas the Y values increase as you move down the form. The position of the drawing pen is indicated by the form's CurrentX and CurrentY properties.

The drawing methods discussed in this section are demonstrated in frmDrawing, part of the FrmMeths.vbp project on this book's CD-ROM.

Circle

The syntax of the `Circle` method is

```
FormName.Circle [Step], (X,Y), Radius, [Color]
```

The optional `Step` parameter indicates the center of the circle relative to the form's `CurrentX` and `CurrentY` properties.

The `Click` event procedure for the `Circle` button on `frmDrawing` is shown in Listing 5.3. This code shifts the circle's center and radius on each loop through the `For..Next`. The circle in this example is always red.

Listing 5.3. The `Circle` method draws a circle at the location and radius specified in the method's parameters.

```
Private Sub cmdCircle_Click()
  For i = 100 To 10000 Step 100
    Me.Circle (i, i), i, RGB(255, 0, 0)
  Next i
End Sub
```

The effect of the `Circle` method is shown in Figure 5.20.

FIGURE 5.20.
The `frmDrawing`
form includes this
`Circle` *method*
demonstration.

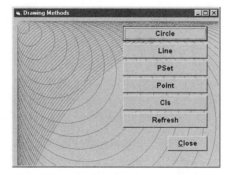

Line

The `Line` method draws a line from a point defined by an X and Y coordinate to another point defined by a different X, Y coordinate. The syntax of the `Line` method is as follows:

```
FormName.Line (x1, 1) - (x2, y2), [color]
```

The `Click` event procedure behind the Line button on `frmDrawing` is shown in Listing 5.4. This procedure draws two sets of straight lines on the form.

Listing 5.4. The Line method draws straight lines on Visual Basic forms.

```
Private Sub cmdLine_Click()
  Dim i As Integer
  ScaleMode = 3 ' Set ScaleMode to pixels.
  For i = 10 To 250 Step 3
    Me.Line (10, i)-(250, i), RGB(0, 0, 255)
    Me.Line (i, 10)-(i, 250), RGB(255, 0, 255)
    DoEvents
  Next I
End Sub
```

The cmdLine_Click behind frmDrawing produces the results you see in Figure 5.21. The line color is set to blue by the RGB function call you see in Listing 5.4.

FIGURE 5.21.

The frmDrawing *form demon-strates how to draw straight lines with the* Line *method.*

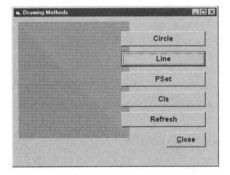

PSet

The PSet method is easy to understand. Given an X and Y position it draws a single point on the screen in a particular color. The syntax of the PSet method is as follows:

```
FormName.PSet (X, Y), [Color]
```

The Color parameter is optional, but you must provide the X and Y parameters.

The frmDrawing form in the FrmMeths.vbp project includes a demonstration of the PSet method. The Click event procedure of cmdPSet paints a colorful square on frmDrawing (see Listing 5.5).

Listing 5.5. The code behind cmdPSet paints a colorful square on frmDrawing.

```
Private Sub cmdPSet_Click()
  Dim i As Integer
  Dim j As Integer
  Dim Red As Integer
  Dim Green As Integer
  Dim Blue As Integer
  ScaleMode = 3 ' Set ScaleMode to pixels.
```

```
    For i = 1 To 200
        For j = 1 To 200
        Red = CInt(Rnd * 255)
        Green = CInt(Rnd * 225)
        Blue = CInt(Rnd * 255)
        Me.PSet (i, j), RGB(Red, Green, Blue)
      Next j
    Next i
End Sub
```

Point

The `Point` method is the opposite of `PSet`. Rather than setting a point on the screen to a particular color, `Point` returns the color of the screen at the location specified by its X and Y parameters.

The syntax of `Point` is as follows:

```
LongIntegerVariable = FormName.Point(X, Y)
```

`Point` returns a long integer value.

Cls

The `Cls` method clears the form of any drawing objects or text. Use the `Cls` method to erase a drawing from the form. The `Cls` method requires no parameters:

```
FormName.Cls
```

Refresh

The `Refresh` method is used frequently. `Refresh` forces a window to repaint itself. Often, you must ensure that drawing changes to the window are drawn immediately. The `Refresh` method instructs Windows to repaint the window, refreshing its display in the process. Without an explicit refresh call, changes to a window might sometimes be delayed while other code is executed.

The syntax of the `Refresh` method is simple:

```
FormName.Refresh
```

TextWidth, TextHeight

`TextWidth` and `TextHeight` return the width and height of a text string passed as its argument. These methods return a value in current form scale units. These are commonly used to position text on a form without colliding with other graphic elements on the form.

The syntax of these methods is

```
LongIntegerVariable = FormName.TextWidth(String)
LongIntegerVariable = FormName.TextWidth(String)
```

SetFocus

SetFocus is an important method that makes the object form the *active form* in the application. The active form is whichever form is currently receiving user interaction.

The code shown in Listing 5.6, found behind frmMain in the FrmMeths.vbp project, shows how to open several forms and set the focus on any of the forms that are open. frmMain contains a command button (Set Focus Experiment) and a set of option buttons. After the three forms are opened with the command button, one of the three forms receives the focus when an option button is clicked with the mouse.

Listing 5.6. This code demonstrates how to use the SetFocus method to put the focus on a particular form.

```
Private Sub cmdSetFocusExp_Click()
  Frame1.Enabled = True
  frmForm1.Show
  frmForm2.Show
  frmForm3.Show
  frmMain.SetFocus
End Sub

Private Sub optForm_Click(Index As Integer)
  Select Case Index
    Case 0: frmForm1.SetFocus
    Case 1: frmForm2.SetFocus
    Case 2: frmForm3.SetFocus
  End Select
End Sub
```

Each of the three forms includes the following code in its GotFocus event. This short procedure unhides a label containing the message This Form Just Got the Focus to indicate which of the three forms received the focus.

Showing and Hiding Forms

The OpenMode.vbp project demonstrates how to display forms in Visual Basic applications. Use the Show method to open a form and make it visible on the screen. The Show method has two optional parameters. The syntax for the Show method is as follows:

```
FormName.[ShowStyle], [OwnerForm]
```

The style parameter is the most important one. It determines whether the form is displayed as a *modal* or *modeless* form. The OpenMode.vbp sample project opens forms in both the modal and modeless modes. When you click the button for the modal type form, the following code is executed:

```
frmModal.Show vbModal
```

A modal form prevents user interaction with any window in the application besides the one that is shown. No code is executed in the calling routine after the Show statement until the user releases the form. Modal forms are frequently used when the user must respond to a dialog window before the application can proceed. The Visual Basic system constant vbModal (which has a value of 1) is used as the style option to specify this behavior.

Omitting the ShowStyle parameter causes the form to open in modeless mode. There is no restriction on the user while a modeless form is open. The user is free to navigate to any other form in the application, use any menu or toolbar, or use any part of the application normally.

A modeless form can remain on the screen while other windows in the application are used. The user can switch back and forth between modeless forms. When the Show method is called with the vbModeless system constant used as the style option, the form is displayed modeless. Note also that vbModeless is the default style for this method. Therefore, you only need to include a style parameter if you want to display modal forms.

The Show method makes the form visible to the user. What if you want to make the form invisible to the user? To do this, use the Hide method.

```
FrmDialog.Hide
```

This method makes the form invisible by setting the form's Visible property to False. The hidden form and its controls cannot receive events, so you needn't worry about a user accidentally clicking a button or changing text or other data on a hidden form. You can still access any form properties with code, but the user does not see the form.

The Show method's OwnerForm parameter specifies the window that owns the new window to be shown. This parameter isn't normally specified because the current form is the default and this is normally desired. As one example of the effect of this optional parameter, if the StartupPosition property is set to CenterOwner, then the new form is centered on the current form or the alternative form specified by the OwnerForm parameter.

Loading Forms

Sometimes you might want to assign properties to a form, but delay showing it to the user. In this case, you want to load the form into memory but not show it on the screen. In fact, when you call the Show method on a form that has not been loaded as in the previous examples, the Show method loads the form automatically. Forms also are loaded automatically if you reference a property of that form.

For example, take the case where the first line in your program is as follows:

```
frmCustomer.Caption = "New Form"
```

In this example, you are referencing a form, frmCustomer, which has not been loaded or shown. This statement automatically loads the form and sets the Caption property.

Loading forms, especially complex forms, takes time to execute. Suppose you want to load a form at the start of your program so that the user experiences that delay at startup, not when he clicks the button to bring up the form. You can't use the Show method in this case because you don't want to display the form until the user asks for it. You could load it by setting the property on the form, but let's further suppose that you don't have any need to do that.

In this case, you can load the form by executing the following statement:

```
Load frmCustomer
```

This Visual Basic statement explicitly loads frmCustomer but doesn't show it. Later, when the user asks for the form, use the Show method to display the form and it appears more quickly because the form has already been loaded into memory.

Other uses of the Load statement are discussed later.

Unloading Forms

Loading forms might take some noticeable time to execute because Windows resources must be allocated for the form and the objects on it. This is normally quite fast, but it is efficient to keep your forms as lean as possible.

Because memory resources have been allocated to the form, these should be returned to the operating system when the form is no longer needed. When the user exits a form that is no longer needed, the code should execute the Unload statement as in the following example:

```
Unload frmCustomer
```

This statement unloads the frmCustomer form object along with all the control objects and the code modules it contains. This might not be enough, however, to free all resources allocated by the form. To ensure that all resources are completely freed, the program should also execute the following statement:

```
Set frmCustomer = Nothing
```

This statement releases any remaining memory that might still be reserved by the form object or its code module.

Consider the following hypothetical series of statements:

```
frmDialog.Tag = "No Response"
```

This statement loads the form but does not show it. It then sets the form's Tag property to the string "No Response":

```
Load frmDialog
```

This statement does nothing because frmDialog was loaded in the previous statement, but it doesn't hurt anything:

```
frmDialog.Show vbModal
```

This statement displays the dialog form.

When the user clicks the OK button on frmDialog, the following statement is executed within frmDialog:

```
Me.Tag = "OK"
Me.Hide
```

The Hide method causes frmDialog to become invisible. We don't unload the form yet because we want the calling program to be able to read the Tag property.

Back in the calling routine, the next statements after the Show statement are now executed:

```
If frmDialog.Tag = "OK" then ProcessDialog
Unload frmDialog
Set frmDialog = Nothing
```

These statements check to see whether the Tag property was set to "OK". If so, it executes some processing code. If you intended to show the form again, you would be finished. However, in this case, the form consumes a large amount of resources and you are not sure you need it again. It is best to immediately free up the form's resources. Therefore, execute the Unload statement and set the form object to Nothing to free up all memory used by it.

The decision when to unload a form is based on many factors. How likely is the user to need the form again? How long does it take to load? How many resources does the form and its code module reserve? Do you need to access information from the form after the user is finished with it? Do you want to redisplay the form with the same settings it had when it was hidden previously? Based on all these issues, the programmer must decide whether to unload a form immediately, after additional processing, or when the application terminates. Whenever it is done, all forms must be unloaded properly.

Understanding Form Events

Visual Basic is an *event-driven* language. This means that when the user interacts with the GUI, events are fired to trigger responses in the program code. The most practical definition of an event is that it is an action recognized by a program. In most cases, the user performs the action that triggers the event.

You can see two drop-down lists at the top of the form's Code window (see Figure 5.22). The left drop-down list is a list of all the objects (such as controls) contained by the form, including the form itself. Choose the object name from that list. The right drop-down list is a list of all event procedures for the object selected in the left drop-down list. You can select an event to view its code.

FIGURE 5.22.

The Code window makes it easy to write code for an object's events.

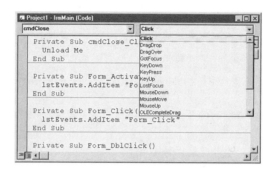

Form Maintenance Events

Several events are associated with a form's appearance on the screen. In addition, after a form is open, certain events fire every time the user moves to that form from another location in the application.

Initialize

This is the first event triggered when a form is loaded. This event is normally used to initialize variables, which the form uses. Initialize is followed by the Load event in which these variables can be used to configure the form.

Load

When a form is loaded into memory, either using the Load statement or as a result of a Show statement or by referencing a form property, the Load event is triggered. This happens one time for each form. The Load event includes code that is executed with this event occurs.

> **Note:** If you unload a form and reload it, the Load event fires again. If you have time-consuming code in your Load event, you might want to use the Hide method so that you can show the form again without triggering another Load event.

Activate, Deactivate

The `Activate` event occurs whenever the form becomes the *active* window, meaning the window that is receiving user events. It becomes the active window when the user clicks the mouse on it or when its `Show` or `SetFocus` method is called. Normally, you put code that you must execute every time the user displays the window in the `Activate` event. You might use the `Activate` event to reveal a hidden dialog box or object used by the form.

The `Deactivate` event is triggered by the opposite conditions; that is, a different window becomes the active window.

QueryUnload, Unload

When the user closes the form, or when the form `Unload` method is invoked, the `QueryUnload` event is fired, followed by the `Unload` event. The `QueryUnload` event allows the option of canceling the unload. This is done by setting the `Cancel` parameter of the `QueryUnload` event to `True`.

The `Unload` event is where all cleanup of objects and variables should occur. Any remaining object variables should be set to `Nothing` in this routine.

Terminate

This is the final event triggered for a form. It occurs when the form is set to `Nothing`. The `Terminate` event indicates that Visual Basic has removed the form and its module from memory.

Form Operation Events

While the form is on the screen, certain events occur as the form becomes the center of attention or as the dimensions of the form are changed by the user or through code.

GotFocus, LostFocus

The `GotFocus` event occurs when a form gains focus. The `LostFocus` event occurs when the form loses focus. If the form has any controls on it, the `GotFocus` event might never fire. Instead, the focus might move to a control on the form, effectively disabling the form's `GotFocus` event.

> **Note:** The `Activate` event occurs before the `GotFocus` event, and the `LostFocus` event occurs before the `Deactivate` event.

Paint

The Paint event fires when the form's AutoRedraw property is set to False. Some detailed explanation is required to explain this.

When another window is moved onto or off of your window, the client area of your window must be redrawn. There are two ways this can occur. If the AutoRedraw property is True, Windows stores an image of the form's client area and uses the stored image to automatically redraw the form. If AutoRedraw is False, Windows does not redraw your client area, but instead fires a Paint event. In the latter case, all code to regenerate your client area must be in the form's Paint event procedure.

> **Note:** AutoRedraw requires that memory be allocated for the image, consuming resources. To conserve resources, it might be beneficial to repaint the image every time from scratch, provided it does not take too long.

Resize

The Resize event fires when the user resizes the form or changes the window state with the minimize, maximize, or restore buttons. It is also fired the first time the form is displayed.

> **Note:** For a nonsizable dialog box, no code is necessary in this event. For sizable forms, however, there must be code in the Resize event to redraw or recalculate the layout of the window to utilize the resized client area.

Form Mouse Events

Visual Basic provides several mouse-specific events. These events are fired when the user moves the mouse or presses a mouse button. The mouse events are shared with other Visual Basic components such as command buttons and text boxes.

Be aware that more than one of these events might fire as a result of a single user operation. For example, when the user presses a mouse button, the Click, MouseDown, and MouseUp events all fire. It is up to you to determine which of the events to utilize. You must also sometimes be aware of the order of multiple events.

The CD-ROM accompanying this book contains Events.vbp, a project demonstrating many of the events discussed in this section.

Click, DblClick

The Click event indicates that the user has pressed and released the mouse button, whereas the DblClick event indicates two mouse clicks in rapid succession. The DblClick event is like the Click event in every way.

The Click event is one of the most frequently programmed events in Visual Basic applications. In fact, the Click event is the default event for several types of controls, including command buttons, list boxes, and labels. You might use a form's Click event to pop up help, begin an operation, or provide some other helpful response to the user.

Several controls (such as the Label and ListBox controls) support both the Click and DblClick events. In these cases, you should not write code for both these events. Visual Basic ignores the second click of a double-click action by the user when code exists in the Click event procedure.

The Click and DblClick event procedure has no arguments. The click occurs, the code you added to the Click event procedure runs, and that's the end of it. As you'll read in the following sections, several other mouse events have certain arguments associated with them. You use these arguments to obtain more information about where the event has occurred on a form.

MouseDown, MouseUp

As the names imply, a MouseDown event indicates the user has pressed a button on the mouse, whereas the MouseUp event indicates the user has released the mouse. Both the MouseDown and MouseUp events fire in addition to the Click event whenever there is a mouse click on a form. The sequence of these events is as follows:

1. MouseDown
2. MouseUp
3. Click

Because the Click event has no arguments, it is not easy to determine where the mouse was clicked on a form. Instead, use the MouseUp event, which provides several arguments telling you which mouse button (right, left, or middle) was pressed and the exact position on the form that was clicked. The syntax of the MouseUp event procedure is as follows:

```
Private Sub Form_MouseUp(Button As Integer, _
    Shift As Integer, X As Single, Y As Single)
```

The Button parameter tells you which of the mouse buttons was actually pressed; the Shift parameter tells you which key was pressed as the button was clicked. The X and Y parameters return the exact position of the mouse pointer's hot spot at the instant the mouse was clicked. The syntax of the MouseDown event is the same as MouseUp.

Visual Basic provides several constants representing the mouse buttons and shift values. Tables 5.1 and 5.2 show these values.

Table 5.1. Visual Basic mouse button constants.

Constant	Value	Description
vbLeftButton	1	Left button is pressed
vbRightButton	2	Right button is pressed
vbMiddleButton	4	Middle button is pressed

Table 5.2. Visual Basic shift key constants.

Constant	Value	Description
vbShiftMask	1	Shift key is pressed.
vbCtrlMask	2	Ctrl key is pressed.
vbAltMask	4	Alt key is pressed.

The use of built-in Visual Basic constants to identify mouse buttons and states greatly improves the readability of mouse event handling code (see Listing 5.7). Similarly, Visual Basic constants should be used not only for mouse handling, but also for any operations for which they have been defined.

Listing 5.7. The MouseUp event procedure behind frmMain in the Events.vbp project on this book's CD-ROM.

```
Private Sub Form_MouseUp(Button As Integer, _
  Shift As Integer, X As Single, Y As Single)
  Dim s As String

  Select Case Button
    Case vbLeftButton:   s = "Left button,"
    Case vbRightButton:  s = "Right button,"
    Case vbMiddleButton: s = "Middle button,"
  End Select

  Select Case Shift
    Case vbShiftMask: s = " Shift key"
    Case vbCtrlMask:  s = " Ctrl key"
    Case vbAltMask:   s = " Alt key"
  End Select

  lstEvents.AddItem "Form_MouseUp "
  lstEvents.AddItem "         " & s
  lstEvents.AddItem "         " & "X: " & X
  lstEvents.AddItem "         " & "Y: " & Y

End Sub
```

MouseMove

The MouseMove event is similar to MouseUp and MouseDown. The MouseMove event fires every time the computer detects that the mouse has been moved. In the case of a typical 300 dot per inch mouse, this means the MouseMove event fires 300 times as the mouse is moved one inch on the desktop.

The syntax of the MouseMove event procedure is identical to MouseUp and MouseDown:

```
Private Sub Form_MouseMove(Button As Integer, _
    Shift As Integer, X As Single, Y As Single)
```

Because of the frequency of the MouseMove event (it fires several thousand times in most cases as the mouse is moved across the form) it is rarely programmed on most forms.

Form Keyboard Events

Visual Basic forms support several keyboard events. Use these events to determine when a key has been pressed and which key was pressed by the user. You can also determine whether the Shift key was held down as the key was pressed.

An interesting aspect of the keyboard events is that you must set the form's KeyPreview property to True in order for the form to see all keyboard events. With KeyPreview set to True, the form receives keyboard events ahead of the controls on the form. For example, assume the focus is in a text box named txtLastName on a form. With the form's KeyPreview set to True, the form's keyboard events fire ahead of the text box's equivalent events. If the form ignores the keystroke, the keyboard events attached to txtLastName fire, allowing the text box to respond to the keystroke.

KeyDown, KeyUp

The KeyDown and KeyUp events are triggered when any key on the keyboard is pressed, including special-purpose keys such as Alt, Tab, and the function keys F1 through F12. The syntax of KeyDown is as follows:

```
Private Sub Form_KeyDown(KeyCode As Integer, _
    Shift As Integer)
```

The KeyCode parameter is any of a number of different values, depending on which key on the keyboard was pressed. Visual Basic provides several different constants (such as vbKeyF1, vbKeyAlt, and vbKeyShift) that indicate which key on the keyboard was pressed. The Shift parameter is identical to the Shift parameter you saw in the discussion of the MouseDown and MouseUp events. Use the same constant values (vbShiftMask, vbCtrlMask, and vbAltMask) to determine whether the Shift, Ctrl, or Alt key (respectively) was held down as they key was pressed.

An interesting effect of the way the KeyDown and KeyUp events work is that the KeyCode parameter reports which physical key was pressed, not the ASCII value of the character or letter on the key. For example, the same key code (its value is 16) is returned whether an "a" or "A" was typed. Use the KeyPress event when it's important to know which ASCII character on the keyboard was pressed.

Your forms might need to ignore certain keystrokes such as Esc, PgDn, or PrtSc. The KeyDown event provides the perfect way to absorb these keystrokes without affecting the program (see Listing 5.8).

Listing 5.8. It's easy to use the KeyDown event to ignore certain keystrokes.

```
Private Sub Form_KeyDown(KeyCode As Integer, Shift As Integer)
  Select Case KeyCode
    Case vbKeyEscape, vbKeyPageDown, vbKeyPrint
        KeyCode = 0
        Exit Sub
  End Select
End Sub
```

In Listing 5.8, the KeyCode is set to 0 (zero) if it matches any of the following values: vbKeyEscape (Esc key), vbKeyPageDown (PgDn key), or vbKeyPrint (PrtSc). In effect, the KeyDown event procedure you see in Listing 5.8 forces the form to ignore the keystroke in any of these three cases.

KeyPress

The KeyPress event is very similar to KeyDown or KeyUp. In this case, KeyPress reports which ASCII key (A through Z, 0 through 9, and punctuation) was pressed. The KeyPress event fires only when a printable key is pressed. The syntax of the KeyPress event procedure is as follows:

```
Private Sub Form_KeyPress(KeyAscii As Integer)
```

The KeyAscii parameter returns the ASCII value of the key pressed on the keyboard. In the case of KeyPress, a lowercase a (KeyAscii = 97) is a very different value than an uppercase A (KeyAscii = 65).

KeyPress is valuable when you want code to respond to keystrokes on printable characters, such as letters of the alphabet, numeric digits, and punctuation. KeyPress does not fire in response to function keys or special-purpose keys such as Esc and PgDn.

Making the Most of Built-In Dialog Boxes

Visual Basic offers easy access to two types of built-in forms that can be used in many situations. The first of these dialog boxes is the message box, and the second is the input box. These dialog boxes can save you a lot of work by relieving you of the chore of creating your own dialog box forms.

The Message Box

Unless you are brand-spanking new to Windows, you have already seen the message box dozens if not hundreds of times. The message box, in all its different formats, is certainly the most commonly used Windows form. Because the user is likely to be familiar with message boxes, it makes sense to use them in your application.

The message box is the familiar dialog box that appears to ask short Yes/No and Cancel/Retry questions. Figure 5.23 shows a typical message box displaying an informational message.

FIGURE 5.23.

A message box is a common feature of most Windows applications.

The message box in Figure 5.23 can be called with this simple line of code:

```
MsgBox "This is an example of a message box."
```

Many developers, however, prefer a more formal syntax when using the MsgBox function:

```
Call MsgBox("This is an example of a message box")
```

This alternative syntax emphasizes the fact that MsgBox is a Visual Basic function. Using the Call keyword instructs Visual Basic to ignore the return value of the MsgBox function.

A message box is a modal form. The program halts at the MsgBox statement until the user dismisses the message box by clicking one of the buttons in the dialog box. In most cases, you want to make sure the user has read the message displayed in the message box before continuing program execution.

Although the simplest message box contains just an OK button, there are many ways to extend the functionality of the MsgBox call. Here is the full syntax of the MsgBox statement:

```
nRet = MsgBox(Prompt[, Buttons] [, Title] [, Helpfile, HelpContextID])
```

The following is the description of the statement:

- Prompt is the message to appear on the message box.
- Buttons specifies which buttons and icons appear on the box. The various button constants are found in the Visual Basic help documentation. The default button is the OK button.

- `Title` enables you to change the default message box caption.
- `Helpfile` and `HelpContextID` enable you to specify the help file and the help context number for the message box.

The `Buttons` parameter has a profound effect on the appearance of the message box. You control the number and type of buttons on the message box by specifying any of several built-in Visual Basic constants. In addition, you might add another constant that displays an icon in the message box. Table 5.3 lists the button constants commonly used with the Visual Basic `MsgBox` statement. Following Table 5.3 are a few examples that show how to use the message box button constants.

Table 5.3. Visual Basic constants for message box buttons and icons.

Constant	Value	Description
vbOKOnly	0	Displays only the OK button.
vbOKCancel	1	Displays both the OK and Cancel buttons.
vbAbortRetryIgnore	2	Displays the Abort, Retry, and Ignore buttons.
vbYesNoCancel	3	Displays Yes, No, and Cancel buttons.
vbYesNo	4	Displays Yes and No buttons.
vbRetryCancel	5	Displays Retry and Cancel buttons.
vbCritical	16	Displays Critical Message icon.
vbQuestion	32	Displays Warning Query icon.
vbExclamation	48	Displays Warning Message icon.
vbInformation	64	Displays Information Message icon.
vbDefaultButton1	0	The first button is the default.
vbDefaultButton2	256	The second button is the default.
vbDefaultButton3	512	The third button is the default.
vbDefaultButton4	768	The fourth button is the default.
vbApplicationModal	0	Makes the message box application modal. The user must respond to the message box before continuing work. (Default)
vbSystemModal	4096	Makes the message box system modal. All Windows applications are suspended until the user responds to the message box.
vbMsgBoxHelpButton	16384	Adds a Help button to the message box.

Constant	Value	Description
VbMsgBoxSetForeground	65536	Makes the message box window as the foreground window
vbMsgBoxRight	524288	Right-aligns the text in the message box.

As indicated by the variety of button constants in Table 5.3 the message box is very versatile. You can combine the button and icon constants to obtain precise results. For example, the following statement produces the message box shown in Figure 5.24:

```
intRetValue = MsgBox("Are you sure", _
    vbYesNo + vbQuestion, "Response Required")
```

FIGURE 5.24.

The MsgBox *function returns a value indicating which button the user clicks.*

vbYesNo instructs Visual Basic to include Yes and No buttons on the message box. Notice how the vbQuestion value is added to vbYesNo. vbQuestion adds the question mark icon to the message box to indicate the type of message displayed by the message box.

A somewhat more complex example is displayed in Listing 5.9. In this case, the user must select either the Yes, No, or Cancel buttons. The Select..End Select construct following the MsgBox statement executes whichever statement block is appropriate for the user's response.

Listing 5.9. Very little code is required to change the picture displayed on a Visual Basic form.

```
Private Sub cmdComplex_Click()
    Dim intRetValue As Integer
    intRetValue = MsgBox("About to delete this record" _
        & vbCrLf & "Once the deletion has occurred you " _
        & "will not be able to recover this data." _
        & vbCrLf & "Are you sure you want to continue?", _
        vbYesNoCancel + vbCritical, "Confirmation Required")
    Select Case intRetValue
        Case vbYes
            lblMessage2.Caption = "Perform deletion"
        Case vbNo
            lblMessage2.Caption = "Abort deletion"
        Case vbCancel
            lblMessage2.Caption = "Operation canceled"
    End Select
End Sub
```

Using the MsgBox function is much easier than constructing your own dialog boxes and interpreting the user's responses to the dialog box. Because Visual Basic provides such a rich selection of button and icon styles you will almost certainly find a combination that suits most of your simple interactions with your users.

Using the InputBox Function

The message box enables you to alert the user of important information and to return one of several buttons that the user clicks in response. It cannot return text or numeric input from the user.

The Visual Basic input box is designed to serve that purpose. An input box is a modal, pop-up dialog box that contains a prompt and a text entry box. The input box returns whatever text the user types into the text box in response to the prompt. A sample of a typical input box is shown in Figure 5.25.

FIGURE 5.25.

The InputBox *function provides a simple but useful dialog box for your applications.*

You display an input box with just one line of code as follows:

```
strInitials = InputBox("New High Score! Please enter your initials.")
```

Like the message box, the input box is also a modal form. The program halts at the InputBox statement until the user dismisses the input box. In this example, processing halts until the user enters her initials in the input box's text box or cancels.

Here is the full syntax of the InputBox function:

```
strRet = InputBox(Prompt[, Title] [, Default] [, XPos] _
    [, YPos] [, HelpFile, HelpContextID])
```

strRet is the variable that contains the string returned by the input box. The InputBox function is quite complex and includes these parameters:

- Prompt is the message to appear on the input box.
- Title is the caption that appears in the input box's title bar.
- Default is the value returned by the input box when the user dismisses the input box without entering a response in its text box.
- XPos and YPos specify the position of the upper-left corner of the input box.
- HelpFile and HelpContextID specify the custom help file and the help context ID for the message box.

Understanding MDI Applications

When you went to the Project Menu to add a new form, you might have noticed another menu item called Add MDI Form. Selecting this menu item creates a special type of form called an MDI *parent form*. MDI stands for Multiple-Document Interface. An MDI parent form becomes a special window that can serve as the container for other forms in the application (see Figure 5.26). In an MDI application, child forms appear within the client area of the MDI parent.

FIGURE 5.26.
MDI applications are a convenient way to control the user interface.

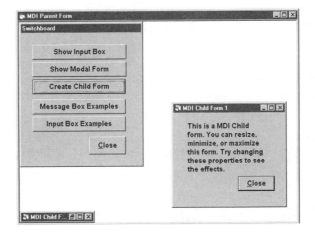

One big advantage of the MDI architecture is that it keeps child forms together within the client area of the parent. The user can move the parent and retain the positions of all child forms within it. If the user minimizes the MDI parent form, all child forms remain inside the minimized parent.

You can have forms in an MDI application that are not forms. Most applications, for example, include an About box that displays the version and copyright information about the application. There is no reason to make an About box a child of the parent form.

Microsoft Word is a good example of an MDI application. The Word MDI Parent includes the main menu bar and toolbar. Each document appears in a separate child window that cannot move outside the client area of the parent. Visual Basic 6 is another great example of an MDI application. The form design windows, the Properties window, the Project window, and the others are all child windows of the Visual Basic environment.

You do not need to have an MDI parent form in your project. By default, Visual Basic applications are not MDI. If you don't have an MDI parent form in your application, it is a single-document interface (SDI) application.

Notepad is an example of an SDI application. It has one main window, and that window does not contain any child windows. You cannot open multiple text files in Notepad at a time. There are other windows in Notepad such as the Search window, but these are not MDI children. They are independent windows that can be moved anywhere on the screen.

This comparison is not to imply that that MDI applications are inherently more complex or sophisticated than SDI applications. The choice between MDI and SDI is not based on complexity, but on which design delivers the best architecture for the application.

Creating an MDI Parent Form

If you decide that your application should be based on an MDI architecture, you must add the MDI parent form to your project. To create an MDI parent, select Project, Add MDI Form. Visual Basic creates what looks like a standard, sizable form. It is much more however, because this form can serve as a container for MDI child forms.

> **Note:** You can have only one MDI parent form in a project. To confirm this fact, add an MDI parent form to your project then look at the Project menu. The Add MDI Parent item is disabled.

Turning Forms Into MDI Child Forms

You can make any standard form an MDI child form simply by setting the form's MDIChild property to True. When the MDIChild property is True, the form can be displayed only within the client area of the MDI parent form. It is subject to other restrictions, but gains substantial benefits too.

Behavior of MDI Child Forms

Several behaviors are peculiar to MDI child forms. These behaviors should not cause you any problems and are actually desirable in MDI environments:

- When an MDI child window is maximized at runtime, its caption is merged with that of the MDI parent.
- MDI child forms cannot be modal, that is, they cannot block the user from selecting other MDI child windows.
- The StartupPosition property is automatically set to Manual. The MDI child's startup position is determined by the operating system unless you set the position with runtime code.
- When you minimize a child form, it shrinks to an icon within the MDI parent's client area.

- Multiple MDI child forms can be arranged in the MDI parent's client area using the Arrange method of the parent form.

- If a child window has a menu, its menu replaces the parent's menu when the child form has the focus.

Making the MDI Parent the Startup Form

In an MDI application, you usually want your MDI parent form to be the startup form. To do this, go to the Project Menu and find the <ProjectName>, Properties item where <ProjectName> is the name of your project. Select this menu item, and the Project Properties dialog box appears.

On the first tab is a Startup Object drop-down selector. Choose the name of your MDI parent form as your startup form object. Now when you run your application, the MDI parent form appears automatically.

> **Note:** When the MDI parent is the startup form, no child forms are automatically displayed in it. Child forms can be shown by using commands in your code as described in the following section. If an MDI child form is the startup form, however, the MDI parent is displayed automatically when the program runs. The child startup form is shown automatically inside the parent.

Creating Multiple Instances of Forms

In Visual Basic 6, there can be many instances of the Form Design window or the Code window. In Microsoft Word, there is an instance of the Edit window for each open document. These application windows are all copies of the same form.

Creating multiple instances of a Visual Basic form is not difficult. A Visual Basic form is an object. You'll read much more about objects in Chapter 10, "Creating Objects and Classes." You can declare new instances of the form object, or any object, as follows:

```
Dim frmCopy1 As New frmMaster
Dim frmCopy2 As New frmMaster
```

In this code, two new instances of the frmMaster object are created, named frmCopy1 and frmCopy2. You can show either or both of these new forms using the Show method just as you would show the master copy:

```
frmCopy1.Show
```

The switchboard form in the FrmTypes.vbp project includes the code shown in Listing 5.10 behind the Create Child Form command button.

Listing 5.10. Multiple instances of forms are easily created in Visual Basic 6.

```
Private Sub cmdCreateChild_Click(Index As Integer)
  Static intCount As Integer
  Dim frmChildForm As New frmChild
  intCount = intCount + 1
  'Create a new instance of frmChild
  With frmChildForm
    .Caption = "MDI Child Form " & intCount
    .Show
  End With
End Sub
```

The logic behind Listing 5.10 is a bit too complex to discuss at this point in this book. Please visit Chapter 10 for a complete explanation of objects, object types, and creating objects with Visual Basic 6.

Wrapping Up Forms

At this point, you can only gain more familiarity with forms by working with them. I strongly recommend that you take some time to experiment with the sample projects once more, this time in more depth. Only by playing around with Visual Basic can you hope to become comfortable with this powerful development system. Here are some suggested areas to explore forms on your own:

1. Display the frmMain form window.

2. View the properties for frmMain in the Properties window.

3. Select each form property and experiment by changing its value. For each property, notice whether new values are entered as text, selected with a file selector, or selected from a drop-down list.

4. As you change property values, notice whether the changes affect the form's appearance or behavior.

5. Press F1 to view the help information for each property. Pay special attention to whether the properties are read-only at runtime and the meaning of alternative property values.

6. Now run the program. Notice that in the Debug window diagnostic statements appear. The Debug.Print statements are located in different form events to show you the sequence of the form's events.

7. Experiment with modifying the code to display a message box and an input box.

8. Continue to play with properties, running the program to see the effects. Try modifying the code to see the effect.

9. Create some forms of your own.

After you are all played out, you can switch back to right-brain learning and continue with Chapter 6, "Putting Your Forms to Work with Controls."

Summary

In this chapter you learned how to create, configure, and display the Visual Basic forms that become the application windows in your programs. Visual Basic forms, the basis of the user interface in most Visual Basic applications, are complex and interesting objects. Forms include many different properties and methods that determine their appearance and behavior at runtime. In addition, Visual Basic forms can be programmed to add to their utility and usefulness to the users of your application.

Of course, forms aren't much good in themselves. Their main purpose is to contain other user interface objects called *controls*, the objects that interact with the application's users. In Chapter 6 you learn how to populate your windows with controls and program these controls to add utility, intelligence, and personality to your applications.

Putting Your Forms to Work with Controls

In the last chapter, you learned how to create forms, the basic building blocks of the Windows graphical user interface. Now you learn how to add functionality to your forms by adding controls. In fact, the main purpose of a Visual Basic form is to serve as a container for controls. The controls in Visual Basic programs include text boxes, command buttons, list boxes, and combo boxes.

Visual Basic 6.0 provides a variety of controls. Each is designed to perform a unique and frequently used function. Think of a control as an intelligent little subroutine, except that this subroutine usually includes a graphical user interface. The benefits of controls, like subroutines, include easy reuse and insulating the programmer from the details of the control implementation.

You will often hear controls referred to as *components*. Actually a control is a particular type of component. DLLs (dynamically linked libraries) are another type of program component, but they are not controls. You'll read more about DLLs in Chapter 25, "Mastering the Windows API." A control meets certain design specifications so that it can be accessed in standard fashion from within Visual Basic.

Getting to Know the Toolbox

Controls are kept in the Visual Basic toolbox. You can go to the toolbox to get a control whenever you need one. If the toolbox window is not visible you can display it by selecting View, Toolbox. The Toolbox window shows all the available control components as icons (see Figure 6.1). When you hold the mouse pointer over a control icon on the toolbox, a ToolTip appears to show the name of the associated control.

FIGURE 6.1.

ToolTips help you identify the controls on the Visual Basic toolbox.

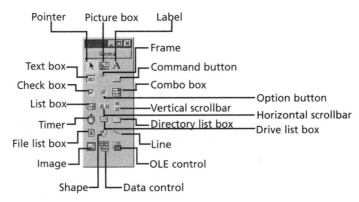

The arrow icon in the upper-left corner of the toolbox (its ToolTip says Pointer) is not actually a control. This icon enables you to select the normal mouse pointer cursor. When you are not in the process of adding a control to a form, the pointer icon should be selected. In this mode, the mouse can be used to select, move, or resize objects or to perform other normal windows operations. In fact, if you select a control icon and add it, the cursor automatically reverts to the normal mouse pointer.

Getting to Know the Visual Basic Tools

Visual Basic provides certain basic controls that always appear in the toolbox (see Table 6.1). These are called the *standard* controls. Each of these controls is labeled in Figure 6.1.

Table 6.1. Standard Visual Basic controls and their functions.

Control	Function
Label	Display text
Text Box	Display or edit text
Frame	Border or container
Command Button	Button to trigger code
Check Box	Check box selection
Option Button	Option button selection
List Box	Display a list of values
Combo Box	Display a drop-down list of values
Horizontal Scrollbar	Scroll horizontally
Vertical Scrollbar	Scroll vertically

Control	Function
Timer	Trigger timed events
Drive List Box	Select a drive
Directory List Box	Select a directory
File List Box	Select a file
Line	Draw lines
Shape	Draw shapes
Image Box	Display images
Picture Box	Display images
Data Control	Provides database connection
OLE Control	OLE Container

The standard controls listed in the table are just the beginning. In addition, Visual Basic enables you to use custom controls such as Grid Boxes and Tab controls. Visual Basic includes many custom controls, and others are available from third-party vendors. The latter are referred to as *third-party controls*.

You can even create your own custom controls using Visual Basic 6.0. You learn how to do this in later chapters.

Customizing the Toolbox

Custom controls, whether supplied with Visual Basic, purchased from third-party control vendors, or homemade, can be added to or removed from the toolbox. You can't remove the standard controls listed in Table 6.1 from the toolbox.

Your toolbox will have less clutter if you configure your toolbox with only the added controls that you care about. Adding or removing custom controls from your toolbox is easy. To do so, select Project, Components from the Visual Basic menu. You see the Components dialog box, which displays all controls installed on your system under the Controls tab (see Figure 6.2). The checked components appear in your toolbox.

To remove a component from the toolbox, uncheck it in the list in the Components dialog box. To add a component to the toolbox, check it. When you apply the changes, the toolbox will be automatically updated. Of course, if you remove a component and then decide later that you need it, you can always return to the Components dialog box and restore it to your toolbox.

Before you can remove a component, you must first delete all instances of the control from the project. Visual Basic does not enable you to remove a component that is currently used in your project.

FIGURE 6.2.

Add controls to the toolbox with the Components dialog box.

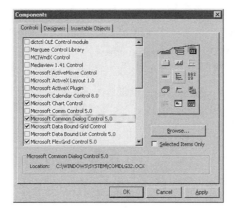

Adding Controls to Forms

Controls included in the toolbox can be added to your forms to create your user interface. To try out this process, start a new project and be sure that the initial blank form is displayed. If you are not sure how to do this, review Chapter 5, "Designing the User Interface."

Now be sure that the Toolbox window is displayed, if necessary, by selecting the View, Toolbox menu item. Look at the icons on the Toolbox window and find the black "A" icon (the Label control). The ToolTip for this control says Label.

Click the Label Control icon. The selected toolbox icon appears pressed down. Now move your mouse pointer over your blank form. The mouse pointer appears as a crosshair. Hold the left mouse button down and drag the mouse pointer to create the outline of the new control. After making the outline box, release the mouse button and the Label control appears on your form, displaying its default name.

The other controls are created in the same manner. You click the control's icon and drag an outline for it on the form. Each control appears on the form with its own distinctive user interface. Each control is added to the form with its properties set to the default values.

You can put as many controls of the same type on a form as you want. Most forms, for example, have many label objects on them.

Using the Alignment Grid

When you place controls on a form, the alignment grid makes it easy to align control positions. By default, controls automatically snap to the closest grid positions when you place or move the controls on the form.

The horizontal and vertical spacing of the grid can be adjusted to suit your preferences. To set the grid resolution in Visual Basic 6.0, select Tools, Options to display the Options dialog box. On the General tab is a frame named Form Grid Settings (see Figure 6.3). In this frame you find options to set the granularity of the grid spacing as well as an option to turn grid alignment on or off.

FIGURE 6.3.

Set the grid's granularity in the Options dialog box.

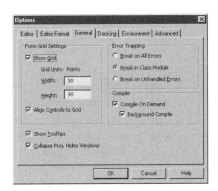

If you cannot move a control exactly where you want it on a form, you can either turn off grid alignment completely or just reduce the grid spacing to allow finer placement. The numbers in the Width and Height text boxes on the Options dialog box specify how many measurement units are in each grid point. Larger numbers mean a coarser grid; smaller numbers mean a finer grid.

If you turn off automatic alignment, you can still set the Left and Top properties directly to ensure that controls are aligned, but this is a tedious process when a lot of controls are involved. One way or another, however, you must make sure your controls are aligned so as not to appear misaligned to the eye.

Multiselecting Controls

You can select as many controls as you want by clicking on them with the Shift key held down. Alternatively, drag a rubber band box around the controls you want to select. All the selected controls appear with sizing handles in each corner and along each side (see Figure 6.4).

Form Layout Functions

In addition to aligning to a grid, there are other cases in which you might want help to position controls on a form. For example, you might want to set the same width for a series of option buttons. You could set the widths individually or you could multiselect all of them and set the Width property once.

FIGURE 6.4.
All the selected controls display sizing handles in their corners and along their edges.

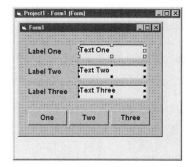

There is a third alternative. You could multiselect the option buttons and select the Format, Make Same Size|Width menu option. Many additional form layout functions in the Format menu can be used to center controls on a form, to align controls, to set the spacing between controls, or to perform other layout functions. The selected item with the bright yellow sizing handles is used as the anchor for sizing and alignment operations. In Figure 6.4, the text box containing Text One serves as the anchor for sizing and alignment operations affecting the three selected text boxes.

Control Properties

The label object you just created simply places a text block on your form. Although it might not seem to do much, it will probably be your most frequently used control. And despite its simplicity, the Label control has several properties that make it flexible and powerful.

To view the default properties of your new label object, select the label and press F4. The Properties window displays the property settings for the selected Label control.

When multiple controls are selected, you can still use the Properties window. In this case, only those properties common to all the selected controls will be displayed. This is a powerful way to modify properties of many controls at one time.

Many control properties might be familiar to you from the discussion of form properties in Chapter 5. In fact, most controls have many of the same properties in common. One reason for this is that certain properties (such as the Name property) are found in almost every Visual Basic control. Another reason is that adherence to standard conventions makes the control more familiar and easier to learn for the programmer using it.

Typical, but not required, control properties include Left, Top, Width, Height, Font, BackColor, Enabled, Visible, Tag, Index, TabStop, TabIndex, and ToolTipText. In addition, each control has several unique properties that are needed to support its unique functionality.

We will not attempt to cover every property setting for every control in this book. You can easily get help on any control property just as you did for form properties. Even highly experienced Visual Basic programmers refer to the help file routinely.

Note that well-written third-party controls provide the same context-sensitive help on properties and methods that you have available for the controls shipped with Visual Basic. If context-sensitive help is not available, you must resort to reading the printed documentation from the control vendor or trial-and-error to learn the control's properties and acceptable settings. This does not necessarily mean the control is substandard, but just that the developers did not fully utilize the help system.

At this point, you must learn the standard Visual Basic controls. Instead of merely repeating the help listing, you learn common programming tasks and the controls you will probably need to use to accomplish that task. You will also learn the properties, methods, and events used most frequently.

Displaying Simple Text

For displaying simple text on a form, such as captions, labels, and informational messages, the Label control is your workhorse. You must set the Caption property to the text you want to display. You can then position and size the label on the form using the mouse.

There are many properties you can use to customize the appearance of the text. One important one is the WordWrap property. When the WordWrap property is True, the caption wraps onto multiple lines if the label's width is not large enough to accommodate all the caption text. If WordWrap is False, text will be cut off at the left or right margin (depending on the Alignment property setting) of the label if the caption does not fit into the width of the label area.

Note that you can force new lines by putting line terminators in your caption string. For example, the following line of code displays two lines in Label1 regardless of the width of the control or what the WordWrap setting is. Be sure the height of the label is big enough to see both lines.

```
Label1.Caption = "Line 1" & vbCrLf & "Line 2"
```

The ForeColor property specifies the color of the text.

The Alignment property specifies whether the caption is left-justified, right-justified, or centered in the Label control. For example, to center a caption over an area, you can place a Label control above the area, stretch it to the same length as the area, and set the Alignment property to Centered.

Another important property is the BackStyle property. This can be set to either Transparent or Opaque. Although the default setting is Opaque, you might get preferable behavior by routinely changing BackStyle to Transparent. If Opaque, the text is drawn on a background color specified by the control's BackColor property. If the user changes his Windows color scheme, the control's BackColor setting can result in an oddly colored label region. By setting BackColor to transparent, the background is always the color of the form's client area.

The Font property specifies the font characteristics. Unless you have special needs, leave this at the default font settings to ensure that your program looks Windows-compliant at all resolutions.

Displaying a Button

Like the Label control, the command button is another simple but frequently used component. Most programs have at least a couple of buttons on them. You can place a new command button on a form like any other control and can move it and size it to fit attractively on the form.

Again, for visual consistency, it is recommended that you set the Height and Width properties to make sure that each button is the same size as all other buttons in your project.

Other than the name, the caption is really the only property you must set on a command button. The caption should identify the button to the user and describe its function. Try to use consistent captions on command buttons supporting the same operation throughout your program. If these captions are consistent with other Windows applications, all the better. For example, most programs use Cancel and OK buttons. These might not be the most descriptive captions for a particular situation, but the goal of consistency takes precedence.

> **Tip:** An ampersand (&) in the Name property indicates that the character following it is a keyboard equivalent for that button. For example, the Name property &Cancel will appear as Cancel on the button. The user will be able to press Alt+C to invoke that button.

Two additional command button properties (Default and Cancel) are worth mentioning. If a button's Default property is set to True, that button is invoked when the user presses the Enter key, even if the button is not selected. Similarly, if a button's Cancel property is set to True, the button is invoked when the user presses the Esc key. There can be only one Default and only one Cancel button on a form (see Figure 6.5). When either of these properties are set to True, the property is set to False on all other controls on that form automatically.

Responding to command button events is very simple. Just put the appropriate code into the command button's Click event procedure.

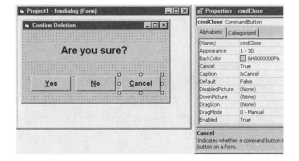

FIGURE 6.5.

Only one button on a form can have its Cancel *property set to* True.

Displaying a List

The list box enables you to display a scrollable list of text data. You can select lines of text, but not edit them. Figure 6.6 shows a typical list box containing the names of some cities in the United States.

FIGURE 6.6.

A list box is a handy way to present the user with a number of alternative values.

After positioning and sizing a list box control on your form, there is not much else to do in Design mode. There is just one property you might want to specify at design time. That is the MultiSelect property. This property cannot be modified at runtime so you must decide upon this setting in Design mode.

There are three possible MultiSelect settings. They specify how the user will be able to select lines. When MultiSelect is set to None, the user cannot multiselect values on the list, which means he can select only a single item in the list box. When MultiSelect is set to Simple, the user can select multiple items in the list by clicking on each line to toggle the selection status. The third MultiSelect setting is Extended in which the user gains additional functionality to select blocks of lines using the mouse and keyboard controls. When MultiSelect is set to Extended, the user can use the Ctrl key in conjunction with the mouse to select and deselect multiple items and use the Shift key to select blocks of items in the list.

The `Sampler.vbp` project on the CD-ROM accompanying this book includes `frmSampler`, shown in Figure 6.7. This form includes examples of all three settings of the list box `MultiSelect` property.

FIGURE 6.7.

The `MultiSelect` *property gives the user a lot of flexibility when working with list box controls.*

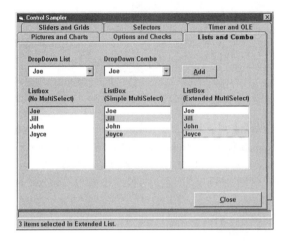

After you have added the list box and chosen the `MultiSelect` mode, the rest of the work usually takes place in code. At runtime you can add lines to the list box by appending members to the list box's list collection. Each item added to the list box can have a number (a long integer) associated with it.

Listing 6.1 contains some sample code to add two names to a list box.

Listing 6.1. Add items to the list box with the `AddItem` method.

```
With lstNames 'List Box control
   .Clear   'Remove any previous lines
   .AddItem "Jim"
   .ItemData(.NewIndex) = 1000
   .AddItem "Sally"
   .ItemData(.NewIndex) = 1001
End With
```

Notice the lines referring to the `ItemData` property. This is a very useful property that enables you to attach a number to every line. This number can be used to identify the line. In the listing, Jim is identified by an `ItemData` number of `1000` and Sally is identified by an `ItemData` number of `1001`. `NewIndex` is a method of the list box control that returns the index (or pointer) to the item most recently added to the list box. In Listing 6.1 the number `1000` is added to the `Jim` item, and `1001` is added to the `Sally` item.

When the user double-clicks a line, the list box's DblClick event fires. In the DblClick event, you can display the line that the user double-clicked by using the code in Listing 6.2.

Listing 6.2. Retrieving values from the list box.

```
'The selected line:
nLineClicked = lstNames.ListIndex

If nLineClicked = -1 Then
  Exit Sub 'Did not click on a valid line
End If

'Jim or Sally:
sName = lstNames.List(lstNames.ListIndex)
'1000 or 1001
lNumber = lstNames.ItemData(lstNames.ListIndex)
```

This technique works for list boxes in which the MultiSelect property is set to None. For multiselect boxes, you can determine what lines are selected using the code in Listing 6.3.

Listing 6.3. Use the Selected property to determine which items in a multi-select list box are selected.

```
With lstNames
  For i = 0 to .ListCount - 1
    If .Selected(i) then
      Debug.Print .List(i), .ItemData(i)
    End If
  Next
End With
```

Displaying a Drop-Down Selection List

In some situations, you must display a simple selection list but can't afford much space on the form. In this case, a drop-down selector might be the best control choice. The only limitation is that users cannot see more than the current choice unless they drop down the selection list.

To create a drop-down type selector, put a combo box control on your form. Set the combo box's Style property to Dropdown List. Populate the list the same way as the list box described previously, by using the AddItem method.

Use the ListIndex property to find the index of the currently selected item, or use the Text property to get the text value of the selected item.

It is also possible to edit the currently selected item. To do this, set the `Style` property to DropDown Combo. The users will be able to edit the selected item. This lets the user add new items to the list or edit existing items, but does requires some code to capture control events and update the list. The `frmSampler` form in the `Sampler.vbp` project includes examples of both kinds of combo boxes.

Displaying a Check Box

A check box is a nice control to use when the user must check off one or more options. The options are not mutually exclusive and any combination of check boxes can be selected. For example, you can use check boxes to enable users to select any number of foods they like from a short list.

To put a check box on a form, select and place the check box control. Set the `Caption` property to display the description of the option and size the control as necessary to display the entire caption.

Normally, you won't want to respond every time the user checks or unchecks the check box. Instead you will probably want to retrieve its value when the user clicks a command button or performs some other action. To determine whether a check box is currently checked or unchecked, read its `Value` property. The value of an unchecked check box is 0, while the value of a checked box is 1.

Figure 6.8 shows how check box controls might be used to select favorite animals. The options are not mutually exclusive. Any combination of dogs, cats, birds, and fish can be selected by checking the corresponding check boxes.

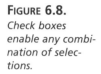

FIGURE 6.8.

Check boxes enable any combination of selections.

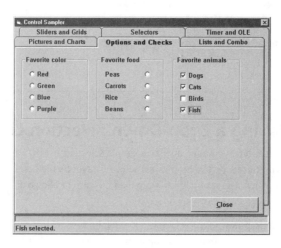

There are two possible settings for the check box `Style` property. Standard is the normal check box style in which you have an x-box and a caption. You can also select the Graphical style setting, which displays the control as a button that the user can toggle between up (unchecked) and down (checked) states. Figure 6.9 shows the difference between the two `Style` property settings.

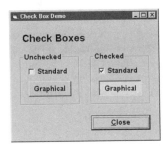

FIGURE 6.9.

Check boxes can be displayed in either of two styles.

Providing Mutually Exclusive Options

In the previous check box example, a Check Box control was used to enable users to select any number of favorite animals from a number of alternative values. What if the goal was to ask them to select only one item? It is possible to program check boxes to enable only one item in a group to be selected, but to do so requires a lot of code and gives the user no visual clue that only one option can be checked.

Instead, the Option Button control is used to select only one item from a group of options. An option button operates just like a Check Box control, but only one option button in a group of option buttons can be selected at a time. When the user selects an option button, all other option buttons in the same group are deselected.

It is possible to have more than one group of option buttons on one form. The easiest way to create a group of related option buttons on a form is to place them in a Frame control. Figure 6.10 shows two groups of option buttons enclosed within Frame controls. Only one option button within each group can be selected at a time.

FIGURE 6.10.

Option buttons provide mutually exclusive selection.

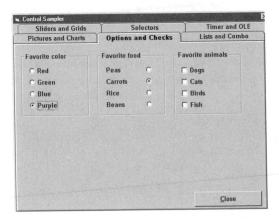

> **Tip:** In Figure 6.10 you might have noticed that the labels in the Favorite Color group appear to the right of the option buttons while the labels in the Favorite Food group appear to the left of the option buttons. The text arrangement is determined by the `Alignment` property applied to the option button. With `Alignment` set to Left Justify the labels appear to the right of the option button, whereas Right Justify causes the label to appear to the left of the option button.

Using the Frame Control

A *frame* is a box with a caption on it. The Frame control can act as a container for other controls within it. There are many reasons why you will want to use frames on your forms. First, a frame groups controls into distinct areas to enhance clarity for the user. Second, a frame enables you to move a group of controls as a group by moving the frame. Third, a frame enables you to hide a group of controls at runtime just by making the frame invisible. Finally, a frame enables you to group option buttons. Without frames to establish option groups, you could have only one selected option on a form.

You can place a frame control on your form like any other control, and can set its `Caption` property to identify its contents to the user. After you put a frame on your form, you can place new controls within it.

If a control already exists elsewhere on your form and you want to place it in a frame, you must cut and paste it into the frame.

Entering Text

Another extremely common operation is inputting text or numeric information from the user. This is typically done using the Text Box control. A text box displays a text or numeric string, and enables the user to modify it.

The text string is set and retrieved using the text box's `Text` property. Another important property to consider using is the `MaxLength` property. `MaxLength` sets the maximum number of characters that can be entered into the text box and is very useful in ensuring that a string cannot be entered that is too long.

Another set of important text box properties is `SelStart` and `SelLength`. These properties determine which portion of the string is currently selected. For example, the following code selects the entire string in a text box so that it can be easily replaced when the user starts typing:

```
txtInput.SelStart = 0
txtInput.SelLength = Len(txtInput.Text)
```

Drawing Shapes and Displaying Pictures

Sometimes you might need to draw your own line art pictures using Line, Pset, and Circle methods. These methods can be used directly on a form object's surface as described in Chapter 5.

These methods are also available on the Picture Box control. Using the Picture Box control as your drawing canvas provides greater flexibility than drawing directly in the form client area.

For example, the picture box can be hidden by setting its Visible property to False, temporarily hiding the drawing. Multiple Picture Box controls can be placed on the same form, each displaying a different drawing.

In addition, like the Form object, the picture box has a Picture property that specifies a bitmap image to display within the picture box. Using a picture box with the drawing methods and Picture property, you can meet almost any imaging requirements.

The Picture Box control features a full set of properties and methods for drawing on its surface and controlling its internal scale characteristics, positioning the control on the form, and changing its image.

Although the picture box is the most powerful standard graphics control, you might want to consider using the Image control if all you need to do is display a bitmap image. The Image control does not provide as much functionality as does the Picture Box, but it also uses fewer resources. The Image control, for example, does not feature any of the drawing methods of the Picture Box control (see Figure 6.11).

FIGURE 6.11.

The frmSampler *form in* Sampler.vbp *includes two Picture Box controls.*

Picture Box controls

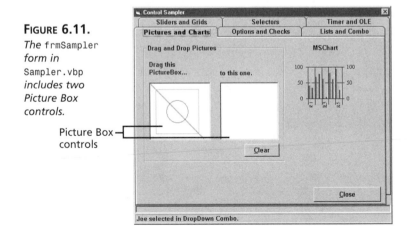

Selecting Files, Colors, Fonts, Printers, and Help

There are several common selection tasks that most programs rely upon. Visual Basic provides many of these selection dialog boxes in its Common Dialog control. This control includes several general-purpose selection dialog boxes, such as a file selector, a color selector, a font selector, and a printer selector. It also enables your Visual Basic program to display Help files.

The Common Dialog control has no user interface until invoked. The Common Dialog control can display several different dialog boxes, depending on which of the methods listed in Table 6.2 is invoked.

Table 6.2. Common Dialog control methods.

Method	Function
ShowColor	Color Selector
ShowFont	Font Selector
ShowHelp	Display Help
ShowPrinter	Printer Selector
ShowOpen	Open File Selector
ShowSave	Save File Selector

Each method is initialized with different common dialog properties. The user's selections are returned through different property values. You can learn these in the Visual Basic Help file. The Help file also shows examples of using the Common Dialog with the different methods.

For file selection, Visual Basic also offers some additional controls to enable you to create your own customized file or folder selectors. The Common Dialog control is not well suited to folder selection, for example, because it lacks a property indicating which folder has been selected. In this case, you are better advised to use the DirListBox control, which is specifically designed to return a string indicating which folder has been selected.

There are three controls you can use to construct custom file selectors. The first is the DriveListBox control. This enables you to select a drive. The second is the DirListBox control, which enables you to select folders. The third is the FileListBox control, which displays a selectable list of files.

These three controls are designed to coordinate together. For example, if the user selects a new drive, the DirListBox can be updated with some simple code. I will not go into further implementation details here because the Common Dialog will probably meet all your initial file selection needs. Figure 6.12 shows the Common Dialogs tab of the frmSampler in Sampler.vbp. The controls at the left side of this form contain examples of the DriveListBox, DirListBox, and the FileListBox controls.

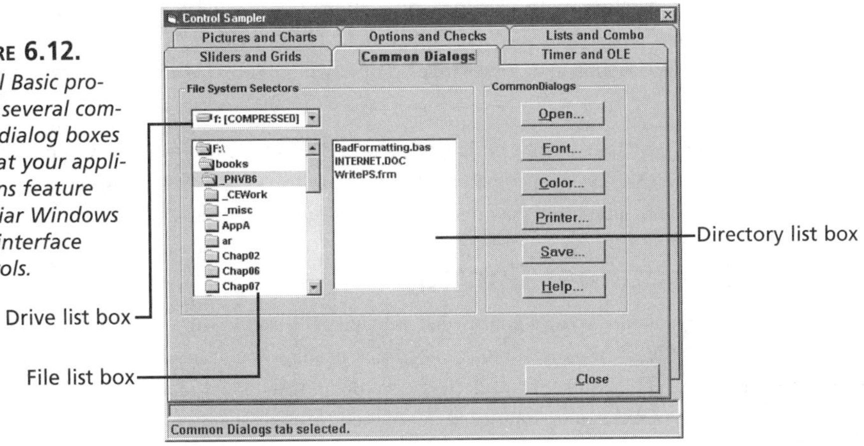

FIGURE 6.12.
Visual Basic provides several common dialog boxes so that your applications feature familiar Windows user-interface controls.

The buttons along the right side of the Common Dialogs tab of frmSampler invoke the different methods of the Common Dialog control. You cannot actually see the Common Dialog control on this form because it is invisible until one of its methods has been invoked. Figure 6.13 shows the Open dialog box produced when the Common Dialog's ShowOpen method is invoked.

FIGURE 6.13.
The Open dialog box is just one of the dialog boxes displayed by the Common Dialog control.

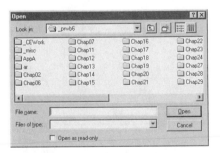

Generating Timed Events

Visual Basic has a Timer function that returns the number of seconds elapsed since midnight. Visual Basic also provides a Timer control. The Timer control is different from the Timer function in that the control generates a Timer event when a specified number of milliseconds has elapsed.

The Timer control has no user interface and does not appear visible to the user. It has just a few essential properties and one event. To use the Timer control, set the Interval property to the number of milliseconds between Timer events. Put any code you want to execute each time the Timer event is fired in the Timer event procedure of the Timer control. Set the Enabled property to True to start the timer. (Setting the Interval property to any positive value other than 0 also starts the timer.) The timer fires Timer events every Interval milliseconds until the Enabled property is set to False or the Interval property is set to 0.

Remember that Timer events are independent and occur automatically. If you need to halt the firing of Timer events, set the Enabled property to False or set its Interval property to 0. You can include more than one Timer control on a form.

OLE Container Control

The OLE Container control is provided with Visual Basic to support object linking and embedding (OLE), a powerful technology that enables you to insert objects into your Visual Basic applications. Objects like Word documents, Paint images, and Excel spreadsheets can be linked to or embedded in your application (see Figure 6.14).

FIGURE 6.14.

The frmSampler *form includes an OLE control containing a Word document. Double-click the document's image to invoke Microsoft Word and edit the document.*

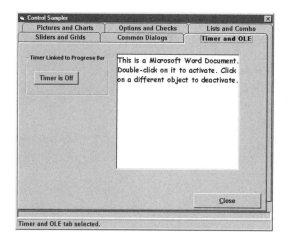

Although I can't go into detail about this powerful technology here, I can give you a flavor of what all this terminology means to you. Create a new project and select the OLE control. Place it on your form, making it large so that it covers most of the client area. As soon as you release the mouse, a dialog box appears asking you to select an insertable object. Choose Paintbrush Picture. Now press F5 to run your program. Right-click the OLE control to get the pop-up menu and select Edit. A Paintbrush menu bar appears on the surface of your Visual Basic application and you will be able to create the image using the Paintbrush drawing tools. After you play around a bit, close the application.

In this small example, you inserted a Paintbrush object into your application and ran it as a part of your program. This is just one very modest example of what can be accomplished using the OLE Container control. You are encouraged to explore the capabilities of this control and its applicability to your needs. It might open up fertile new windows of opportunity.

Grid and Spreadsheet Controls

Eventually, almost every programmer needs to use a data grid for one project or another. A grid enables users to view and edit data in a scrollable table form. This is often the only practical way to display multiple sets of data.

Today, there are a large number of grid and spreadsheet controls to choose from. Years ago, there was a real difference between grid and spreadsheet controls. The grids were better at displaying data, and the spreadsheet controls were better at editing and calculating data. In recent years, however, the two have expanded to overlap so completely that any distinction is almost moot.

Visual Basic includes two grid controls: the Data Bound Grid (DBGrid) and the FlexGrid (MSFlexGrid). The Data Bound Grid is better at displaying data retrieved directly from a database. The FlexGrid is better at displaying data in *Unbound* mode, that is data supplied by the program. FlexGrid does offer some binding capability, but bound data must be read-only.

FlexGrid makes it easy to access data from individual cells with its TextMatrix property. Listing 6.4 is an example of how to set up and populate a FlexGrid display and retrieve the contents of a cell.

Listing 6.4. This code sets up and fills a FlexGrid control on frmSampler.

```
Dim i As Integer
With grdMembers 'FlexGrid control
   'Clear grid
   .Clear
   'Set up rows and columns
   .Rows = 3: .Cols = 3
   'Label rows and columns
   .TextMatrix(0, 1) = "First Name"
   .TextMatrix(0, 2) = "Last Name"
   .TextMatrix(1, 0) = "Member 1"
   .TextMatrix(2, 0) = "Member 2"
   'Add data
   .TextMatrix(1, 1) = "Sam"
   .TextMatrix(1, 2) = "Jones"
   .TextMatrix(2, 1) = "Jenny"
```

continues

Listing 6.4. Continued.

```
.TextMatrix(2, 2) = "Smith"
'Print members to debug window
For i = 1 To .Rows - 1
  Debug.Print .TextMatrix(i, 1) & " " & .TextMatrix(i, 2)
Next
End With
```

The completed grid is shown in Figure 6.15.

FIGURE 6.15.
The FlexGrid control displays either numeric or text data.

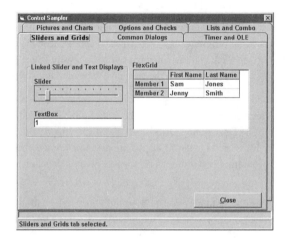

Creating Tabbed Displays

Sometimes you simply have too much information to fit on one form. Other times you would prefer that the user not be exposed to all information at one time. In these cases, a Tab control might be the way to go. A Tab control enables you to display different information on different pages of the Tab control. The Tab control can save you from having to display multiple forms at runtime.

Visual Basic provides two Tab controls: TabStrip and SSTab. To add the TabStrip to the toolbox, select the Microsoft Windows Common Controls from the component list. To get an SSTab control, select Microsoft Tabbed Dialog Control.

Apart from some minor differences, the biggest difference between the two is that SSTab is a container, whereas TabStrip is not. This means that you can place controls on each tab of the SSTab control. When you change tabs, only the controls placed on that tab appear.

The TabStrip merely triggers an event when a new tab is chosen. It is up to the program to modify the display as necessary. The TabStrip is the lower overhead option in cases where the display can be easily modified for each tab. For example, take the case where the same grid is displayed on every tab, but with different data. In this situation, the TabStrip makes more sense because the grid control can be easily modified. Also, a separate copy of the grid on each tab would just consume resources unnecessarily.

Figure 6.16 illustrates the two different types of tab controls in Visual Basic 6.0. Notice that the SSTab control at the top of frmTabs is able to contain other controls (such as this label) within it whereas the TabStrip is a much simpler control. The TabStrip is not able to host controls on its surface, but does have a complete set of properties and events.

FIGURE 6.16.
Visual Basic provides two different styles of tab controls.

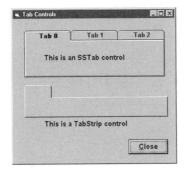

Other Controls

Many other controls can make your programming task easier. Some of the other frequently used controls that you should know about include the following:

- *Status Bar* is used to display the partitioned status bar you see at the bottom of many popular applications.
- *Progress Bar* is used to provide a graphical progress indicator during long operations.
- *TreeView* is used to create outline type lists and Explorer-type interfaces.
- *Chart* is used to create pie, bar, line, and many other types of charts.
- *Multimedia* is used to play WAV audio or AVI movie files.
- *RichTextBox* provides the display and editing of text in Rich Text Format (RTF). RTF format enables tabs, colors, styles, and other settings in the text to create complex text layouts.
- *Slider* offers a graphical slider control that enables users to easily select values on a linear scale.

Naming Controls

Just as in naming variables, it is important to follow standard conventions when naming controls. Table 6.3 contains a list of suggested name prefixes for the standard Visual Basic controls. For example, rather than use the default name Command1 for a command button, it would be better to name it something like cmdCancel, using the standard prefix and a short, clear description of the control's function.

Table 6.3. Standard Visual Basic controls and their name prefixes.

Control	Name Prefix
Label	lbl
Text Box	txt
Frame	fra
Command Button	cmd
Check Box	chk
Option Button	opt
List Box	lst
Combo Box	cbo
Horizontal Scrollbar	hsb
Vertical Scrollbar	vsb
Timer	tmr
Drive List Box	dir
Directory List Box	drv
File List Box	fil
Line	lin
Shape	shp
Image Box	img
Picture Box	pic
Data control	dat
OLE control	ole

Providing consistent names for controls is one important practice to ensure that your code is clear and maintainable.

Copying Controls

You can cut, copy, and paste controls just like text in an editor. To copy a control, select the control then Edit, Copy or Ctrl+C. To paste the copied control, select Edit, Paste or Ctrl+V. The copied control is then pasted onto the current form. Be sure to read the next section on control arrays because Visual Basic interprets the paste operation as an attempt to create a control array on the form.

Copying controls helps you avoid errors and saves you time setting the design-time properties of controls. Imagine that you spend a lot of time setting the initial properties of a control. Now you need three more duplicates of the control with the same settings. It would take a lot of time to set up each one from scratch, and would be prone to error. When you copy a control, all current property settings are copied with it. Unfortunately, the code you've written in the control's event procedures does not copy as well.

To move a control from one form to another or to move it into or out of a frame, use Edit, Cut or Ctrl+X to cut the control and then paste it back into the new location.

When you multiselect controls, the Cut, Copy, and Paste functions affect all the selected controls. This is a quick shortcut to move many controls from one container to another.

Control Arrays

When you add a second control of the same type to a form, Visual Basic presents you with a message asking if you want to create a control array (see Figure 6.17). A control array is an array of controls, in the same way that an integer array is an array of integers.

FIGURE 6.17.
Copying and pasting a control provides you with a way to create a control array.

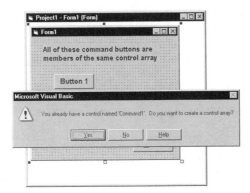

There are many benefits to using control arrays instead of several individual controls. First, control arrays use fewer resources than individual controls. Second, control arrays share common events. For example, if you have an array of command buttons, the same Click event procedure is called no matter which button is pressed.

If you start with a text box named Text1 and elect to create a control array, Visual Basic assigns Text1 an index number of 0 and creates a new member of the Text1 array, with an index number of 1. If you make additional copies of Text1 or Text2, their index properties are set to 3, 4, and so on.

Control arrays are referenced by name and index. For example, the two members of the text box array mentioned previously would be referenced by Text1(0) and Text1(1).

Listing 6.5 shows how to handle a Click event for control arrays.

Listing 6.5. Control arrays simplify managing code for multiple controls.

```
Private Sub cmdButtonArray_Click(Index As Integer)
  Select Case Index
    Case 0: txtIndex.Text = 1
    Case 1: txtIndex.Text = 2
    Case 2: txtIndex.Text = 3
    Case 3: txtIndex.Text = 4
    Case 4: txtIndex.Text = 5
    Case 5: txtIndex.Text = 6
  End Select
End Sub
```

Notice in this code fragment that the Index property of the control array member that received the event is passed as an argument to the event. However, instead of using index numbers directly in the Select statement, it is more maintainable to assign these to constants. That way, if for any reason control indexes change, you only need to change the constant declarations to fix all the code referencing those indexes. Listing 6.6 is an improvement over the Listing 6.5 code sample.

Listing 6.6. Code can be easier to maintain by using constants in place of hard-coded values.

```
CONST CHOICE_BUTTON_1 = 0
CONST CHOICE_BUTTON_2 = 1
CONST CHOICE_BUTTON_3 = 2
CONST CHOICE_BUTTON_4 = 3
CONST CHOICE_BUTTON_5 = 4
CONST CHOICE_BUTTON_6 = 5
```

```
Private Sub cmdButtonArray_Click(Index As Integer)
  Select Case Index
    Case CHOICE_BUTTON_1: txtIndex.Text = 1
    Case CHOICE_BUTTON_2: txtIndex.Text = 2
    Case CHOICE_BUTTON_3: txtIndex.Text = 3
    Case CHOICE_BUTTON_4: txtIndex.Text = 4
    Case CHOICE_BUTTON_5: txtIndex.Text = 5
    Case CHOICE_BUTTON_6: txtIndex.Text = 6
  End Select
End Sub
```

Referencing Controls

Controls and their properties and methods can be referenced using the same techniques described for forms in the previous chapter. Complete the following steps:

1. Within the same form, you can reference a control by name; for example, txtInput.Text or lstChoices.Clear.

2. Controls can be referenced from outside their form, but you must specify the form; for example, frmMain.txtInput.Text or frmInput.lstChoices.Clear.

3. You can use a With block to avoid repeating the object "path" of the control.

A note of caution: With blocks can greatly enhance the readability of the code (see Listing 6.7), but it is best not to use them to avoid making just a couple of references. They can have a net complicating effect due to additional nesting. Also, always be sure to exit a With block with an End With statement. If you jump out of a With block, you might generate errors that are difficult to debug.

Listing 6.7. A With block simplifies references to the properties and methods of a control.

```
With frmInput.lstChoices
  .Clear
  .AddItem "Line 1"
End With
```

Passing a Control as an Argument

It is possible to pass a control to a subroutine. For example, the code in Listing 6.8 passes a text box to a subroutine to set the Caption property.

Listing 6.8. Passing a control to another routine requires careful declaration of the procedure arguments.

```
Sub CallingRoutine()
  SetCaption txtName 'passes the TextBox control
End Sub

Sub SetCaption(txtBox as TextBox)
  txtBox.Text = "My Name"
End Sub
```

If txtName were a control array, you could pass the first member by using SetCaption txtName(0) as the subroutine call.

Determining the Type of Control

Notice in the previous example that the argument txtBox is declared as a TextBox type. This could be more general by declaring it an Object type. In Listing 6.9, any control can be passed to the same routine.

Listing 6.9. Sometimes a generic reference to a control is best.

```
Sub CallingRoutine()
  'passes the TextBox control:
  SetCaption txtName

  'passes the ComboBox control
  SetCaption cboName
End Sub

Sub SetCaption(ctrl as Object)
  ctrl.Text = "My Name"
End Sub
```

In the previous example, either a text box or a combo box can be safely passed to the SetCaption procedure.

If the SetCaption subroutine were made generally available, it would be wise to add protections. What if some programmer, misinterpreting the name, passed a Label control to it? Because the Label control does not have a Text property, an error would result.

To protect the routine and make it more versatile, it could check for the type of the passed object using the TypeOf operator as in Listing 6.10.

Listing 6.10. It's not difficult to check the type of control passed to a procedure.

```
Sub SetCaption(ctrl as Object)
  if TypeOf ctrl Is MsgBox _
  or TypeOf ctrl Is ComboBox Then
    ctrl.Text = "My Name"
  ElseIf TypeOf ctrl is Label Then
    ctrl.Label = "My Name"
  End If
End Sub
```

Using the Controls Collection

The controls on a form are actually members of the Controls collection for that form. Listing 6.11 displays the name of every control on frmMain in the Debug window.

Listing 6.11. The Controls collection provides a fast way to reference all the controls on a form.

```
Dim i As Integer
For i = 0 To frmMain.Controls.Count - 1
  Debug.Print frmMain.Controls(i).Name
Next
```

Other control properties can be accessed in the same way as the Name property in the previous example.

Control Focus

In the last chapter you learned that only one window on the screen can be the active window. Likewise, only one control can be active on a form. The active control is said to have *focus*. The control with focus is the one that receives user events.

Sometimes it is necessary to set the focus to a particular control at runtime. To do this, you can call the SetFocus method for a control.

For example, after an error you might want to set focus on the control that caused the error so that the user can make a correction. Listing 6.12 displays an error message and sets focus on the control that the user must correct.

Listing 6.12. Use the SetFocus method to move the focus to a specific control.

```
Sub DisplayError(sMsg as string, ctrl as Object)
  On Error Resume Next
  ctrl.SetFocus
  On Error Goto 0
  MsgBox sMsg, vbCritical, "Error"
End Sub
```

Notice that in this sample routine the SetFocus method is within an On Error block. It is highly recommended that you always protect the SetFocus method this way because a control can be unable to receive focus under certain circumstances due to a variety of situations that are unpredictable and difficult to reproduce. Handling errors in VBA code is documented in Chapter 9, "Handling Runtime Errors."

Setting Tab Order

When the user presses the Tab key, it is the normal Windows convention that the focus move to the next logical control on a form. This is to enable keyboard-only operation. The order that the focus moves across the controls is dictated by two general control properties called TabStop and TabIndex.

If TabStop is set to False for a control, it is skipped during tabbing. The order in which the controls are tabbed is governed by TabIndex. The Tab key moves to the control with the next TabIndex. The Shift+Tab key moves focus to the control with the previous TabIndex.

Generally, setting the TabIndex is the last thing you should do to complete your form. After no further changes are likely to take place that could affect the tab order, select each control in a logical order and increment the TabIndex. The tab order should correspond to the intuitive or typical order that the user would want to follow to attend to the controls on the form.

Binding Controls

Many controls have the capability to *bind* to a database. This means that they can be directly tied to particular data in the database. They can automatically display and update the data to which they are bound.

Generally, it is the Data control that actually binds directly to the database. Other data-aware controls can bind through the Data control.

Data-aware controls include most standard Visual Basic controls. For a control to bind to the Data control, it must have a DataSource property. The DataSource specifies the Data control that is the source of the data. Data-aware controls must also have a DataField property specifying the particular database field to bind.

The Data control has a DatabaseName property that enables you to specify the database and a RecordSource property to specify the records and fields to access. The fields specified are available to data-aware controls through their DataField property. The RecordSource is a SQL selection statement.

The Data control has methods that enable the program to move through its recordset. As the recordset cursor changes, the bound controls are automatically updated.

The use of the Data control and data-aware controls can make it very easy to access information in the database. However these techniques are somewhat limited and should not be considered to be a complete alternative to more complete database programming techniques.

You'll read more about the Data control and using data-aware controls in Chapter 16, "Mastering the Visual Basic Data Control."

Dragging and Dropping

Another common functionality that many controls share is *drag-and-drop* operation. This enables the user to drag one control onto another to perform an action or establish a relationship.

Drag-and-drop operation seems like a really sophisticated interface to the user, but in reality is not difficult to implement using Visual Basic. There are two properties of controls that support drag-and-drop operation. The DragMode property specifies whether the user can initiate a drag-and-drop operation. If DragMode is set to Automatic, the user can initiate drag-and-drop. If it is set to Manual, drag-and-drop operations can be initiated only by the program. The second property is the DragIcon, which specifies the mouse icon displayed while dragging.

After a drag-and-drop action is initiated, two events control the program's response: DragOver and DragDrop. The DragOver event is fired by a control when another control is dragged over it. The program can respond with some graphical feedback to let the user know whether it is valid to drop on this control. The DragDrop event is fired when the user releases the mouse button to drop an object on the control. This is the event that should process the final drag-and-drop actions.

Implementing drag-and-drop can be a lot of fun and greatly enhance the user interface, especially when it is intuitive and entertaining. If not obvious, however, drag-and-drop can be a hidden and confusing approach. It is wise to provide an explicit interface strategy and offer drag-and-drop as an alternative method for more experienced users.

Handling Keyboard Events

Although Windows is primarily a mouse-based interface, you should never underestimate the importance of designing programs that make effective use of the keyboard. Many programs rely heavily upon the keyboard for text and numeric entry. In those programs, it can be very awkward and inefficient for the user to be forced to shift to the mouse frequently. Further, many handicapped users rely upon the keyboard heavily.

Earlier you learned about the `Default` and `Cancel` properties of command buttons, which offer keyboard shortcuts for the user. You also learned that the ampersand (&) character can be used in the `Caption` property of some controls to provide keyboard equivalents. Additionally, Visual Basic programs reserve certain keys such as the Tab key for control focus and the F1 key for help.

Beyond these, you can include any custom keyboard handling that makes the program operation more efficient. Note however, that some designers simply create keyboard shortcuts for every program operation as a matter of policy. This can backfire, causing an overly complicated program design in which few keyboard commands are used because there are far too many to learn. As in all things, at some point more is no longer better. Analyze user operation and include keyboard shortcuts intelligently.

You also saw earlier that whichever control has focus receives keyboard events. Three events are fired in the active control when a key is pressed: `KeyDown`, `KeyUp`, and `KeyPress`. `KeyDown` and `KeyPress` are fired when a key is pressed. `KeyUp` is fired when the key is released. Chapter 5, "Designing the User Interface," described the `KeyDown`, `KeyUp`, and `KeyPress` events in detail.

You can use any or all of these events. The `KeyDown` event is most commonly used to provide a quick program response. However, there are times when it is desirable to wait until the `KeyUp` event. For example, because the `KeyDown` and `KeyPress` events autorepeat if the user holds down a key, it is preferable to use the `KeyUp` event to avoid repeated event processing.

Why have both the `KeyPress` and the `KeyDown` events? These receive slightly different information. The `KeyPress` receives only the ANSI code for the simple character selection. `KeyDown` and `KeyUp` receive an extended key code, which includes function keys and other named keys, as well as the state of the Shift, Alt, and Ctrl keys.

Note that some keys are trapped prior to reaching a control. For example, the Tab key is normally processed for control navigation and does not trigger control events. The Esc and Enter keys are trapped and handled by command button controls.

Visual Basic has key code constants defined for all keys. Be sure to use these in your code rather than ANSI numbers. These can be found in the Visual Basic help documentation.

Sometimes it is necessary to handle keystrokes for the entire form, no matter which control has focus. It would be very undesirable to try to put the same code in the keyboard events for every control on the form. Even if you did, what if the form itself has focus?

To solve this common situation, forms have a property called KeyPreview. If the KeyPreview property of the form is True, all keyboard operations first trigger form events, and then control events. Therefore, by placing keyboard-handling code at the form level, the code can be executed no matter which control has focus. Of course, some keys still can be handled at the form level, and others are handled at the control level.

Handling Mouse Events

There are three mouse events called MouseDown, MouseUp, and MouseMove. MouseDown and MouseUp are analogous to the KeyDown and KeyUp events described previously. They are fired when a mouse button is pressed. The mouse button (left, middle, and right) that was pressed is passed as a parameter.

The MouseMove event is triggered when the mouse is moved over a control. The event parameters include the x and y location of the mouse. Chapter 5 explains the mouse events in more detail.

Summary

Now you have a good foundation to use controls effectively in building applications. A tremendous number of controls are available to you, and I was only able to touch on some of the most common ones. Even among those, I could describe only a small number of their properties, methods, and events. Nevertheless, there is such a high degree of consistency in control designs that you should be able to easily translate and extend the concepts presented in this chapter to fully utilize any of them.

Remember however, not to get caught up in the novelty of using a large number of controls and property variations. The best applications have the smallest number of controls possible, presented in the most consistent and familiar fashion.

The next chapter expands the discussion of user-interface design to include menu bars and toolbars. These have become almost indispensable components of modern program design.

Mastering Menus and Toolbars

In Chapter 5, "Designing the User Interface," you learned about forms. In Chapter 6, "Putting Your Forms to Work with Controls," you added controls to your forms. In this chapter, you add two more important program components: menus and toolbars.

It is with good reason that menus and toolbars appear on almost every Windows program. Menus can contain a large number of logically organized user options yet they take up only a small amount of screen space. Toolbars supplement menus by providing quick, graphical shortcuts to frequently used options. Both can be easily modified at runtime to provide situation-dependent configurations.

The menu and the toolbar enable the user to access the functionality available in your program. Providing standard buttons for every possible program option would not only be an inefficient use of space but would also appear cluttered and confusing to the user.

This chapter shows you how to design and implement effective menus and then moves on to enhancing the user interface with attractive and functional toolbars.

Understanding Menus

A *menu system* consists of a menu bar that displays a row of menu titles. When the user clicks a menu title, its menu, which includes a list of menu items, is displayed. When a menu item is clicked, a menu Click event is triggered to allow a program response to the menu selection.

You have full control over what appears in the menu system. Although the title and menu item captions are completely configurable, the width of menus are automatically adjusted to fit the captions.

Each menu item can have its own submenu, which appears when the mouse is moved horizontally to the next child menu. There can be up to four child menus. That means that there can be up to five menus displayed horizontally (the main menu and up to four sub-menus).

Items that have child menus are identified by a graphical arrow on the right side of the item. Menu titles and items can be disabled to make them unavailable, or made invisible to hide them from the user. Menu items can have check marks to provide toggle-type settings, keyboard equivalents for keyboard navigation of the menu, and shortcut keys for hot-key operation. A menu can also contain separator lines to logically group menu items.

A menu system is tied to a form and cannot exist independently of it. When a form is deleted, any menu system on it is deleted as well. Although each form can have its own menu, only the main form has a menu in most programs. Because a menu system is not a selectable object as are other controls, there is no simple way to copy a menu from one form to another. You cannot select, cut, and paste menus. They can only be created and modified using the Menu Editor.

Using the Menu Editor

Menus are so tightly integrated into the Visual Basic application that very little programming is required to create and program them. Visual Basic provides a tool called the Menu Editor to make it easy to create and modify menus.

To use the Menu Editor, first create a new project. Select the starting form and click Tools, Menu Editor to create a menu for that form. The Menu Editor dialog box appears.

There are three logical sections in the Menu Editor dialog box (see Figure 7.1). It is easiest to describe them from the bottom up. At the bottom of the dialog box is the menu item list. It summarizes how a menu will appear on the form. This list box shows all current menu entries in an outline-type display. Each line is a single menu entry. Entries positioned all the way to the left are menu titles, and entries that are tabbed in are child items under the menu entry above it.

FIGURE 7.1.

You build menus with the Visual Basic Menu Editor.

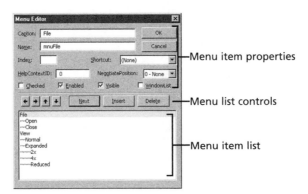

The menu list shown in Figure 7.1 will have two menu titles in the menu bar, File and View. The File menu will have two menu items, Open and Close. The View menu will have two menu items, Normal and Expanded. The Expanded menu item will have a sub-menu with three items, 2x, 4x, and Reduced.

Above the menu list in the middle of the dialog box are the menu list controls. These buttons modify each line in the menu list. Table 7.1 contains a description of their functions.

Table 7.1. Menu list controls and their functions.

Button	Action on Selected Item
Left Arrow	Tab item left
Right Arrow	Tab item right
Up Arrow	Move item up in list
Down Arrow	Move item down in list
Next	Select next item
Insert	Add new row before item
Delete	Delete item

At the top of the dialog box is a group of controls that set the various properties for the selected menu item (see Table 7.2).

Table 7.2. Menu item property controls and their functions.

Control	Action on Selected Item
Caption	Set the item text
Name	Set the name of the item
Index	Set the control array index
Shortcut	Assign a shortcut key
HelpContextID	Assign a help context ID
NegotiatePosition	Should be None for standard executables
Checked	Sets the initial `Checked` property
Enabled	Sets the initial `Enabled` property
Visible	Sets the initial `Visible` property
WindowList	Used for MDI parents to create a list of child windows in the menu

Menu Arrays

Just as controls can be added to a control array, menu items can be added to a menu array. The primary advantage of this is to allow many items to be handled in one event routine. Menu arrays can greatly reduce the number of event procedures in the code and simplify the application.

To create menu arrays, simply give a contiguous set of menu items the same name and unique index numbers. The index numbers do not have to be consecutive, but they must be in ascending order. It is wise to increment your indexes by 10 to leave room for additions without forcing code modifications to correct the references.

Listing 7.1 is a sample of code to demonstrate how to handle the event processing of a menu array.

Listing 7.1. Handling the event processing of a menu array.

```
Private Sub mnuEditItem_Click(Index As Integer)

   'Handle Edit menu event
   'The Index constants are defined in the module declarations
   Select Case Index

     Case EDIT_COPY
        lblStatus.Caption = "Edit¦Copy Selected"

     Case EDIT_CUT
        lblStatus.Caption = "Edit¦Cut Selected"

     Case EDIT_PASTE
        lblStatus.Caption = "Edit¦Paste Selected"

     Case EDIT_DELETE
        lblStatus.Caption = "Edit¦Delete Selected"

     Case EDIT_UNDO
        lblStatus.Caption = "Edit¦Undo Selected"

   End Select

End Sub
```

Applying Menu Conventions

As with any caption or label, menu titles and item captions should be as short as possible to convey their meaning. Normally menu captions should be in *title case* (meaning that all words other than articles are initial capitalized).

Because there are no separators in the menu bar, menu titles longer than one word can be confusing. Menu items should be limited to three words or less. Grouping, through the use of menu separator bars, can be helpful to provide context clues for the items.

Menus can extend below the bottom or past the right edge of their form. If menus extend off the screen, they will wrap to stay on screen. This is one reason why it is not good technique to make menu lists too long or to add many submenus. Another reason to keep menu lists short is that long lists are difficult for the user to scan. Try to achieve a good balance between the number of menu titles and menu lengths to organize all options most conveniently for the user.

Submenus help to keep main menu lists short by moving option sets into child menus. However, submenus should be used frugally. Submenus require more mouse movement to navigate and can be frustrating for the user if overused. Novice mouse handlers might have difficulty selecting nested submenu items. Although Visual Basic allows four submenus, that many should rarely be used. Typically, more than two submenus is undesirable.

Users expect to find certain menus and menu items in standard places in the menu bar. By convention, a File menu is always the first menu on the left. Even if you don't actually require a File menu, it is still not a bad idea to add one with at least a Quit option to make the menu system feel familiar to the user. The Quit option should always appear at the bottom of the File menu, isolated with a separator bar.

The last two menus are generally the Window menu, if needed, and the Help menu. A Help option should appear first in the Help menu, and an About item should appear last.

Between those ends of the menu bar, you can place any program-specific options. In designing your menu, consider both the logical placement of your items and the typical naming and placement of analogous items in other programs.

Using Ellipses

An alternative to submenus is to display a dialog box that enables the user to select a submenu option. By Windows convention, any menu item that displays an intermediate dialog box before executing its function is identified by adding an ellipsis (three dots) after the menu caption. This alerts the user that clicking the menu item does not cause an immediate action until further information or confirmation is received. It enables the user to explore the option without worry of triggering some irreversible action.

For example, consider a menu item that says Delete. If users are not sure exactly what this means, they might be afraid to try it. However, if the menu item says Delete..., users will feel confident that they can click it to obtain further information before proceeding or canceling.

Allowing Keyboard Navigation

Another convention is that all menu titles and items should have keyboard navigation controls. This means that the user can select menu items using the keyboard only, through the use of Alt+key combinations. This is accomplished in menus just as with controls like the command button, by means of the ampersand character in the Caption property.

Each menu title or menu item should have an ampersand (&) in the caption string. For example, the menu title &File displays File in the menu bar. The menu item Save &As displays Save As in the menu.

The typical method for deciding which letter to use as the keyboard equivalent is to use the first letter. If the first letter has already been used, use the next letter that has not been used. Of course, this should be violated if other keyboard equivalents are more natural or easier to remember.

Letters assigned to keyboard equivalents cannot be assigned to two titles in the menu bar or two items in a menu. The same letter can be assigned in different menus.

Using Shortcut Keys

Another Windows convention is to provide a shortcut key for frequently used menu items. A shortcut key is different than a navigation key. A shortcut key is typically a function key or a Ctrl+key combination that immediately executes a menu option without displaying the menu.

Shortcut keys are assigned using the Shortcut property of each menu item. They are automatically right-justified on each menu item line (see Table 7.3).

Don't overuse shortcut keys—use them strategically for critical operations such as a Save command. Also, try to assign the same shortcuts that other programs use to make your program feel more familiar to users.

Table 7.3. Typical shortcut key assignments.

Shortcut	Menu Operation
Ctrl+A	Select All
Ctrl+C	Copy
Ctrl+F	Find...
Ctrl+G	Goto...
Ctrl+H	Replace...
Ctrl+N	New...
Ctrl+O	Open...
Ctrl+P	Print...

Shortcut	Menu Operation
Ctrl+Q	Exit
Ctrl+S	Save...
Ctrl+V	Paste
Ctrl+X	Cut
Ctrl+Z	Undo
F1	Help

Using Pop-Up Menus

A pop-up menu is a menu that appears at the mouse location when you press the right mouse button. Although pop-up menus are not normally visible in the main menu, they are a part of the menu system.

To create a pop-up menu in the Menu Editor, first create the menu as you would a normal visible menu. Select the title item of the menu that will become a pop-up menu. Set its Visible property to False. The menu will not appear in the menu bar.

To display the invisible menu at runtime, use code similar to Listing 7.2.

Listing 7.2. Displaying the invisible menu at runtime.

```
Private Sub Form_MouseDown(Button As Integer, Shift As Integer, X As Single,
➥Y As Single)

   If Button = 2 Then 'Right mouse button
     'Display popup menu
     PopupMenu mnuPopup 'mnuPopup is the name of the menu to display
   End If

End Sub
```

That is all there is to it. You handle Click events for the pop-up menu items just as you would for any other menu item.

Configuring Menus at Runtime

You can modify your menus extensively at runtime. You will often change the Checked property, usually in two situations: to indicate whether a particular menu item is toggled on or off and to indicate which item in a group is currently selected.

Another commonly modified property is the Enabled property. You can enable or disable menus and menu items if their function is not allowed in a particular circumstance. The Visible property can also be changed to show or hide menu items as required.

Menu item captions can also be modified at runtime to provide situation-dependent options. You can even create or delete menu array members to create completely custom menus at runtime.

Don't automatically apply all that flexibility. Some users are perfectly comfortable with dynamically changing menus; however, others might be confused by menus that change in different situations. If a menu item is missing or disabled, they might be bewildered about how to enable it. Therefore, always know your target audience well before deciding upon how extensively to modify menus. The best approach is to use dull, static menus that all users can understand and remember easily.

Understanding Toolbars

Menus are great, but users want even faster access to frequently used program functions. Toolbars are most commonly used to provide this interface (see Figure 7.2). A toolbar is a set of buttons, each identified by a unique icon. Buttons on a toolbar can be simple buttons, toggle-type buttons, or group option type buttons. These varieties offer great flexibility and provide more visible status information than do check marks on a menu.

FIGURE 7.2.
Toolbars are a handy navigation device for users.

A toolbar can be used without a menu bar. This might be appropriate if few menu options are required and those options are used frequently. Normally, however, a toolbar is a supplement to a menu bar, offering mouse shortcuts to frequently used menu items. It is good practice to provide a menu item for every corresponding toolbar button.

In order to save screen space, many programs provide a Preferences or View Toolbar menu option to hide the toolbar. If all toolbar buttons have duplicate items in the menu system, then this is not a problem. When the toolbar is hidden, the user can still get to all toolbar functions using the menu system.

Finding the Perfect Icons

Whereas menus communicate options through short text descriptions, toolbars communicate their functions by means of graphic images. Some functions can be communicated with equal effectiveness using either a text description or an icon. Other functions are difficult to represent in one form or the other.

Finding the right icons can be the biggest challenge to creating a toolbar. Some common functions like New, Open, or Save have fairly standard icons that are readily available and quickly recognized. More specialized functions might require custom icons that can be hard to find or design.

Even some commercial icon libraries on CD-ROM include low-quality icons that detract from the professional appearance of your product. Further, it is hard to find a set of icons to meet your needs and look like a coordinated family when displayed together. You might find nice icons, but their styles appear like a hodgepodge when side-by-side on a toolbar.

An application with poor quality, nonintuitive, or inconsistent icons looks shabby. If the impact of the icons on the product is negative, or if the icons are not intuitive, consider not using a toolbar at all. Often an icon that you find intuitive is completely incomprehensible to users. Always test the icons with beta testers. If they have trouble understanding or remembering the meaning of an icon, it should be improved or removed.

There is good news about icons, however. If you need only standard icons, Visual Basic includes many of them in the Toolbar Builder Wizard.

Adding Toolbars to Your Application

Assuming you can find or create a high-quality set of icons that look compatible together, the process of creating a toolbar is relatively simple.

If you do not already have the Toolbar Control icon in your toolbox, you can add it by selecting the Microsoft Windows Common Controls component from the Visual Basic component list. Select the Toolbar Control icon and place a new toolbar on your form. A wizard called the Toolbar Builder appears.

The Toolbar Builder helps you create your new toolbar with ease. Simply find the toolbar icons you want to include in the source list on the left and click the Move button to move them to the toolbar list on the right side. You can change the order of the icons in the toolbar list using the Move Up and Move Down buttons. You can add separators by adding separator bars.

Following is a list of standard icons that are available within the Toolbar Builder:

Align Left	Align Right
Arc	Back
Bold	Button
Camera	Center
Copy	Cut
Delete	Disconnect Net Drive
Double Underline	Drawing
Ellipse	Find
Forward	Freeform
Help	Help What's This
Italic	Justify
Line	Line Style
Macro	Map Network Drive
New	Open
Paste	Print
Properties	Rectangle
Redo	Save
Small Caps	Sort Ascending
Sort Descending	Spell Check
Strikethrough	Sum
Tab Center	Tab Decimal
Tab Left	Tab Right
Underline	Undo
Up One Level	View Details
View Large Icons	View List
View Small Icons	Word Underline

To add an icon that is not in the list, click the bottom button. Its ToolTip text says Load External Bitmap or Icon. This button displays a file selector enabling you to select the image file for your icon. The new icon is added to the toolbar list and displayed in the preview.

The text to the right of each icon is the ToolTip. This ToolTip will be assigned to that toolbar button. To change the ToolTip for an icon, click the ToolTip in the toolbar list and it becomes editable.

A toolbar preview is displayed on the top of the Toolbar Builder while you work. The preview toolbar displays your ToolTip text when you hold the mouse over a button. When you are satisfied with the icons, their order, the grouping arrangement, and the ToolTips, click Finish.

The Toolbar Builder Wizard adds the working toolbar to your project, which includes two controls. The first is the Toolbar control. The second is an ImageList control. The ImageList control is required to store the icons selected for use by the toolbar. Therefore, the Toolbar control requires that the ImageList be present. The `ImageList` property of the Toolbar control identifies the ImageList control it uses. The `ImageList` property can be set only in the Properties dialog box of the Toolbar control.

Toolbar and ImageList properties can be modified in their Properties windows or in their Properties dialog boxes. The properties can be displayed by right-clicking the control and choosing Properties from the pop-up menu. They can also be displayed by clicking the `Custom` property in their Property windows.

Customizing the Toolbar

After you create your toolbar using the Toolbar Builder Wizard, you can customize it by setting properties of the Toolbar and ImageList controls.

There are several general toolbar properties that you will use frequently. By setting the toolbar `BorderStyle` property, you can elect to outline your toolbar with a border. By setting the `ShowTips` property to `False`, you can suppress ToolTips. In many programs this is a Preferences setting. The `AllowCustomize` property determines whether the user can double-click the toolbar at runtime to customize it.

The customization of specific button properties requires a bit more work. The following sections list some typical toolbar button modifications and how to use them.

Removing a Button

To remove a button, complete the following steps:

1. Bring up the properties for the toolbar.
2. Go to the Buttons tab and select the Index for the button you want to delete.
3. Click Remove Button.

Changing a ToolTip

To change the ToolTip for a button, complete the following steps:

1. Bring up the properties for the toolbar.
2. Go to the Buttons tab and select the Index for the button you want to change.
3. Edit the `ToolTipText` property and click the Apply button.

Many programs do not include ellipses in toolbar ToolTips even if the corresponding menu item does have an ellipsis. Although ellipses are not expected, it can't hurt to include them for the same reasons they are included in menu items.

Changing an Icon

To change the icon for a button, you must add that icon to the ImageList control. Before you can do that, however, you must first unbind the Toolbar control from the ImageList control. ImageLists that are bound to another control cannot be modified.

To unbind the ImageList control, complete the following steps:

1. Bring up the properties for the toolbar (see Figure 7.3).
2. Select None from the ImageList Property combo box. Now you can edit the ImageList.
3. Go to the ImageList Property Pages dialog box and select the Images tab.
4. Click Insert Picture and select the image file to add.
5. Give the new icon a name in the Key property text box. While you are there, mark down the key names of all the icons. You will need them!

FIGURE 7.3.

The ImageList control serves as an image storage area.

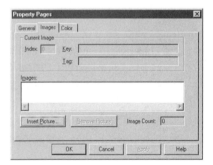

6. Apply the changes and close the properties for the ImageList control.

Now look at your toolbar. All the images are gone! When you unbound the ImageList control, you lost all your image references and must reassign them all. To do this, go back to the toolbar properties and reselect the ImageList control name in the ImageList Property combo box. Then enter the correct icon key in the Image Property combo box for each button. Of course, you enter the new key for the icon you want to change (see Figure 7.4).

In many Visual Basic tasks, such as creating menus, you can start small and add more options as you need them. For toolboxes, it is much more efficient to plan all your buttons before you start and create them all using the Toolbox Builder Wizard.

FIGURE 7.4.
Set toolbar properties in the Property Pages dialog box.

Adding a Button

If you do not already have an icon for the new button in the ImageList, you must add it as described in the previous section. After you have reassigned the ImageList property of the toolbox, complete the following steps:

1. Go to the button before the position where you plan to add a button and click Insert Button.
2. Enter the Key, ToolTipText, and Image properties for the new button.
3. Reassign the Image properties for the remaining buttons.

Moving a Button

To move a button, complete the following steps:

1. Move to the button before the new button position.
2. Click Insert Button and assign the properties to match the current button.
3. After copying all properties, move to the current button and delete it.

Creating Toggle-Style Buttons

The default button style property setting is tbrDefault, which creates a normal button. By changing the style property to tbrCheck, the button will toggle between up and down states.

If you want to change the icon of a check style button at runtime depending on the toggle state, you should first load both icons in the ImageList. Then you can change the Image property at runtime based on the Value property of the button.

A big advantage of toolbars is that the user can easily see the state of selected items without having to navigate the menu system to see whether a particular item is checked. Toolbar buttons are always visible, and their state is usually apparent from the button up/down position and icon.

Creating Option-Style Buttons

In addition to toggle-style buttons, it is also possible to create option-style buttons in which only one button in a button group can be pressed at one time. To create option-style buttons, set their Style property to tbrButtonGroup. A toolbar can have many button groups, divided by separator buttons.

Adding Captions to Buttons

The toolbar supports text captions as well as icons on each button. To add a caption, simply enter the Caption property for each button. Note that the caption might not display properly if the ButtonHeight property is not large enough to display it. The ButtonWidth of all buttons automatically adjusts to fit the widest caption; therefore it is practical to use anything but very short captions.

Configuring the Toolbar at Runtime

One of the powerful features of a toolbar is its capability to be configured at runtime. Depending on the program state, certain toolbar buttons can be disabled or modified. Buttons can even be added or removed by the program or by the user at runtime.

Button properties such as Enabled, Visible, ToolTipText, Image, and Caption can be accessed through the Buttons collection of the Toolbar control. The Buttons collection is a collection of button objects. Either the Key or Index property is used to identify a button object in the collection. Listing 7.3 is a code sample showing how to reference button properties and also how to change images on a button.

Listing 7.3. Referencing button properties and changing images on a button.

```
'Disable the Save button
tbrToolbar.Buttons("SaveButton").Enabled = False

'Show the disabled version of the Save icon
'SaveDisabledImage is an ImageList key. The index number could also be used.
tbrToolbar.Buttons(1).Image = "SaveDisabledImage" '1 is the SaveButton Index
```

Handling Toolbar Events

The only toolbar event of real interest is the ButtonClick event, which is fired whenever a button is clicked. The Button object of the button that was clicked is passed to the event. The most typical way to handle toolbar events is illustrated in the code fragment as follows:

```
Private Sub tbrMain_ButtonClick(ByVal Button As ComctlLib.Button)

    'Send toolbar events to the appropriate menu item
    Select Case Button.Key

        Case "New"
            mnuFileItem_Click FILE_NEW

        Case "Open"
            mnuFileItem_Click FILE_OPEN

        Case "Save"
            mnuFileItem_Click FILE_SAVE

        Case "Print"
            mnuFileItem_Click FILE_PRINT

    End Select

End Sub
```

Running the Menu and Toolbar Demo Program

Run the Menu and Toolbar Demo program to experiment with a simple program that includes both components (see Figure 7.5). The menu and toolbar samples demonstrate all their standard features, including a pop-up menu. By examining the code, you will quickly see how to coordinate a menu bar with a toolbar and how to handle their events.

FIGURE 7.5.
MenuTbar.vbp *is included on this book's CD-ROM.*

Summary

In previous chapters you learned to create forms and to put them to work using controls. In this chapter, you learned to make that functionality accessible through menus and toolbars. Building on this foundation you can develop sophisticated, full-featured Visual Basic applications.

However, this is only the beginning. Visual Basic has much more to offer. In Chapter 8, "Using the Visual Basic Debugging Tools," you learn how to perform design-time debugging on the VBA code you write in your applications. Chapter 9, "Handling Runtime Errors," explains how to effectively trap and handle the errors that can cause problems for your users.

Using the Visual Basic Debugging Tools

Even the best Visual Basic developers make mistakes. Visual Basic applications tend to get pretty complicated by the time all the various forms, controls, modules, and other components have been added. Because of its modular nature, most Visual Basic applications include diverse pieces that must be hooked together to produce the finished product. All it takes is a misspelling, incorrect reference, or out-of-place comma to cause a runtime or compile-time error.

Sooner or later, something goes wrong as you develop an application, and often the thing that's wrong is not immediately obvious. Simple misspellings are usually easy to identify and correct, but more subtle errors can take hours to debug. A worse situation is when you know there's a problem (perhaps the data is being unexpectedly modified by the application), but you can't find out where the data corruption is occurring. The worst situation is where a data-changing bug exists in the program but its effect is either so subtle or infrequent that you aren't even aware there's a problem. Such bugs can exist for years before their existence is discovered.

This chapter examines the different types of errors you're likely to encounter when using Visual Basic and the steps required to detect and eradicate these bugs. As you'll soon see, Visual Basic provides a powerful set of debugging tools that are adequate to detect and remove virtually any coding or logical error in your Visual Basic code.

This chapter doesn't cover bugs that are caused by poor application design such as incorrect data entry or improper action on the part of the user, data-entry errors caused by misunderstood user-interface conventions, and so on. If, after you release a new version of an application you hear of problems with the data or performance of the application, the user interface might be at fault. Sometimes a simple change—perhaps as small as replacing a text box with a combo box containing the acceptable values for a particular field—is all that's necessary to avoid a seemingly insurmountable problem.

What this chapter does help you with, however, are the bugs that inevitably creep into VBA code. Bugs are to be expected and, to a certain extent, are unavoidable in programming projects. The larger and more complex your applications become, the more bugs you can expect to encounter. This chapter assumes you're familiar with writing code behind Visual Basic forms and in standard modules. You should also understand program flow concepts, variable usage, and how subroutines and functions call each other in Visual Basic programs.

Finding Errors

Most VBA errors fall into either of two broad categories: syntax and logical. *Syntax* errors are mistakes in the VBA language you've written. Syntax errors include spelling mistakes, missing or duplicated commas or parentheses, and misplaced spaces in identifiers. Most syntax errors are easy to detect and repair. In fact, most syntax errors are immediately detected by Visual Basic as the statement is composed. When this happens the lines of code affected by the syntax error are changed to red in the Code window to indicate that an error exists.

> **Tip:** The Auto Syntax Check option of the Code Editor prevents many spelling errors, as well as syntax errors.

Logical errors, on the other hand, can be difficult to detect and remove. A logical error means that the program is not performing as expected. Some logical errors are easy to detect, such as a program crash whenever a particular text box is left empty. In this case, the empty text box might be causing a crash when its null value is used in a calculation or expression requiring non-null operands.

You'll spend what might appear to be an inordinate amount of time finding and repairing bugs in the code you write. This does not mean that your Visual Basic programming skills are lacking. Instead, it might mean that your applications are getting complex enough to tempt fate and bring out unexpected bugs. The only solution to many common problems in Visual Basic programs is careful attention to coding techniques and rigorous adherence to programming standards and conventions, which are designed to help you avoid trouble later. Throughout this book, you've been exposed to consistent naming conventions, careful use of indenting, and appropriate application of VBA looping constructs.

Identifying Syntax Errors

You'll frequently encounter syntax errors as you work with Visual Basic. Every time you misspell a keyword or omit a required comma or parenthesis, you generate a syntax error. Syntax errors have other, less obvious, causes as well. For example, misuse of a procedure call or variable name can also generate syntax errors.

In most cases, syntax errors are easily trapped by Visual Basic. In fact, by default Visual Basic informs you every time a syntax error exists in a line of VBA code. Figure 8.1 shows the Editor tab of the Options dialog box, which you open with the Tools I Options menu command. Notice the Auto Syntax Check option in the upper-left corner of this dialog box.

FIGURE 8.1.

The Editor tab of the Options dialog box contains several important VBA code settings.

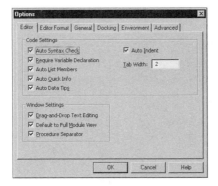

Auto Syntax Check, which is selected by default, instructs Visual Basic to test the syntax of a line of VBA code as you move off the statement. For example, Figure 8.2 shows a small Visual Basic procedure with a rather obvious syntax error.

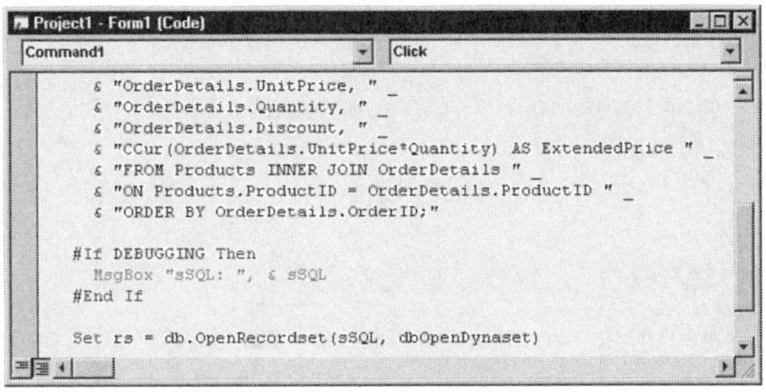

FIGURE 8.2.

Most Visual Basic syntax errors are easy to see.

The MsgBox statement near the bottom of this procedure contains a stray comma. This MsgBox statement is meant to display the value of the sSQL string when the DEBUGGING compiler directive is True. Normally, a comma is used to separate arguments to the MsgBox statement. Because a comma appears in this statement, Visual Basic thinks a second (optional) argument is being set up. (The second argument is a numeric value that specifies the icon to use in the message box.) As you can see, the second argument is actually the right operand of the concatenation operation, and the comma doesn't belong here. If the figures in this book were reproduced in color, you could see that the MsgBox statement appears in red to make it easy to see.

If you prefer some color other than red for syntax errors—in fact, if you prefer any other color for any of the VBA statements in your Visual Basic project—the Editor Format tab of the Options dialog box (see Figure 8.3) lets you specify a new font and custom color scheme for the Code Editor. You select the foreground, background, and indicator colors for the VBA statements in the Editor window from the drop-down lists in the lower-left corner of the Editor Format tab.

FIGURE 8.3.
Set the colors in the Code window the way you want them.

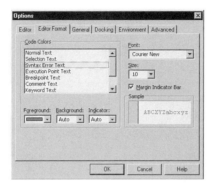

Fixing syntax errors involves nothing more than correcting the spelling or composition error in your code. If a simple spelling error is not the cause of a syntax error, more often than not it'll be a stray or missing character somewhere on the offending line of code.

> **Tip:** Strict adherence to even the simplest naming convention (that is, assigning meaningful names to objects, variables, and procedures) will help you avoid making silly syntax errors and bugs.

Identifying Logical Errors

In contrast to simple syntax errors, logical errors can be difficult to detect and remove. Logical errors occur when there's a mistake in the program flow, misuse of the data or variables in an application, or an error in the code that causes an unexpected behavior in the application.

As an example, consider a typical data entry form where the user is expected to provide both the first and last names of the customer. Because the order entry form contains text boxes for the information, the user will understand he is required to provide both of these bits of information, right? The reality is that, in many cases, the user assumes the data in a text box is optional and not required by the application. If the code behind the data entry form assumes there is valid data in both text boxes, you are likely to encounter a *null error* if a variable is assigned the value of a text box that is empty. In all VBA applications, a runtime error is generated when a null value (meaning a nonexistent value) is assigned to a variable that is not a Variant.

Therefore, the only way to protect yourself against such a logical error is to consistently test for null values in the text boxes and other controls on your forms. If a required text box or control is left empty, notify the user by displaying a message or dialog box that provides the user with information regarding the type of data required by that control.

Chapter 9, "Handling Runtime Errors," provides solutions for the type of error described in the preceding paragraph. It deals with the problems you encounter as you develop a Visual Basic application and helps you resolve issues reported by users after an application has been distributed. The logical problems captured and removed by the Visual Basic debugging tools include calculation errors, incorrect branching or evaluation of expressions, and so on. As you'll soon see, Visual Basic provides several tools for eradicating most logical errors in your applications.

Dealing with Runtime Errors

Runtime errors are frequently caused by hardware failures of one type or another. For example, a hard disk might fail, causing an application to stop working. Such an error, of course, is easily detected and resolved by the user and there is nothing you can do in code to avoid such a catastrophic problem.

Other hardware problems might be more subtle and difficult to deal with. For example, noise on the network, or an unavailable printer, might cause an application to either hang up and appear to stop working, crash unexpectedly, or confound the user with erratic behavior.

Memory errors are tricky to deal with, particularly under Windows 95, Windows 98, and Windows NT. These advanced operating systems utilize disk space as *virtual memory*, and simply running out of disk space causes an application to report a memory error. Often, the apparent memory error causes the application to slow down or behave erratically as its memory requirements change at runtime. The larger the installed user base and the more varied the hardware users are working with, the more likely it is your applications will encounter hardware-related, runtime problems.

Detecting and avoiding hardware-related runtime errors is difficult. For example, there is no easy way for your application to determine when disk space is running low. There are several Windows application programming interface (API) calls that report on the current status of the computer's hardware and accessories. Chapter 25, "Mastering the Windows API," describes how to exploit the hundreds of functions and subroutines written into the Windows API to determine the amount of free disk space, free memory, and other resources available on the user's computer.

You can then use that information in your application to notify the user when disk space appears to be running low, operations are taking longer than expected, and so on. You might be able to avoid some of the most common and grievous hardware problems through these API calls. Other than anticipating and planning for these failures, there is not much you can do about the status of the hardware on the user's desktop.

Avoiding Errors

It goes without saying that your personal coding style and habits have more to do with your ability to avoid bugs than any other factor. A sloppy programmer who pays little attention to naming conventions, indenting, or program organization is more likely to encounter difficult, sneaky bugs that cause crashes, lock up an application, or damage the data the application's users rely on. A careful, fastidious programmer, on the other hand, is likely to avoid most of the bothersome errors that can tie up a developer's time.

One of the simplest suggestions for any VBA programmer is to include only one variable declaration in a single line of code. Many programmers seem compelled to conserve the number of lines of code in their applications, even when procedures are complicated and require dozens of variables. Rather than stacking up variable declarations as you see in Figure 8.4, try spreading out the variable declarations as shown in Figure 8.5. Although grouping variable declarations as a large block of text occupies fewer lines of code, locating an individual variable to determine its data type is very difficult. There's no rhyme or reason to the order of the variable declarations at the top of the procedure shown in Figure 8.4, further complicating the process of understanding how the variables are used in this procedure.

FIGURE 8.4.

Multiple variable declarations in a single statement can be hard to work with.

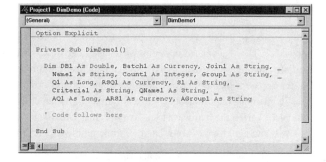

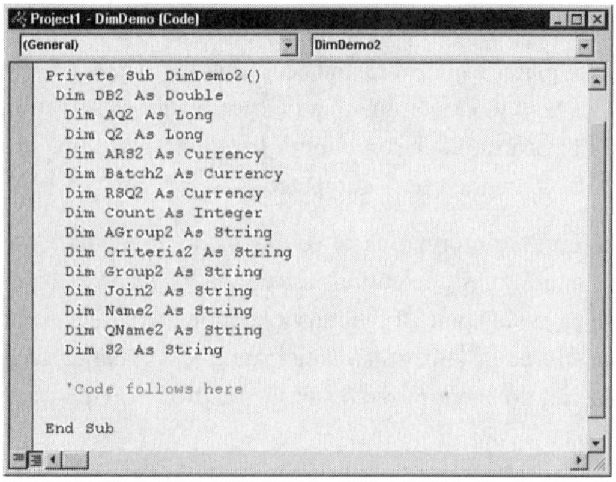

FIGURE 8.5.

A few minutes spent carefully formatting variable declarations yields handsome rewards.

Another, less obvious improvement in the declarations list from Figure 8.4 to Figure 8.5 is that the variables are grouped by data type. In fact, the variable names appear in alphabetical order within each data type group. This arrangement makes it easy to see all the string variables at a glance. Although alphabetically sorting each group of variables might be carrying things a bit far, there's no denying that it's easy to find the string variable named Join2.

> **Note:** Using a separate line for each variable declaration takes no more time to compile and run than placing all variable declarations on a single line. The only difference is to you, the developer. Anything you can do to make your code easier to understand and work with reduces the chance of future bugs.

Using the Module Options

The General tab in the Options dialog box (shown in Figure 8.6) contains several important settings options that affect the way errors are trapped in your VBA code. These options are summarized here:

- **Break On All Errors:** Break On All Errors causes Visual Basic to behave as if On Error GoTo 0 (explained in Chapter 9) is always set, regardless of any error trapping you might set up in code. This means that Visual Basic stops at each error so you can debug the statement generating the error. Although this option will make more sense after you've read Chapter 9, usually you'll want to see errors as they occur during the development process. This way you'll be sure to see every error that occurs rather than having them trapped and (perhaps ineffectively) handled by an incomplete error-handling routine.

FIGURE 8.6.

The General tab of the Options dialog box contains additional useful settings.

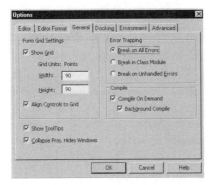

> **Warning:** Be sure to turn off the Break On All Errors option before distributing the application to its end users.

- **Break in Class Module:** Class modules (explained in Chapter 10, "Creating Objects and Classes") are often developed independently of the rest of the application. In these cases you want errors to occur in the class module's project, not the project using the class module. Use this option to ensure errors are seen where they actually occur.

- **Break on Unhandled Errors:** This option causes program execution to stop only on errors that are not being handled by VBA code. Normally you want this setting so you'll see only those errors requiring more work.

- **Compile on Demand:** The Compile on Demand option instructs Visual Basic to compile modules only when their functions are required somewhere else in the database. When this option is unchecked, all modules are compiled any time any function is called. Deselecting this option ensures that you see all errors detected by the compiler each time you make changes to the modules in your application. However, it takes more time because of the extra compilation that occurs each time you run the code. If you leave this option selected, the Visual Basic compiler will not recompile all the code in the application, which means that some errors might slip through but the compilation process will go much more quickly.

- **Background Compile:** Compiling a Visual Basic application can take a long time. Rather than sit and wait for compilation to complete, the Background Compile option instructs Visual Basic to perform as much of a program's compilation in the background as possible. This way you'll be able to use compiled portions of the application while Visual Basic is compiling other parts of the project.

Traditional Debugging Techniques

Two widely used debugging techniques have been available since Visual Basic 1.0. The first is to insert MsgBox statements to display the value of variables, procedure names, and so on. The second common technique is to insert Debug.Print statements to output messages to the Immediate window. The following sections discuss these methods.

Using MsgBox

Figure 8.7 shows an example of a MsgBox statement and the message box produced by the statement. The message box in the lower-right corner of this figure appeared in response to the MsgBox statement in the Code window. Program execution halts while this message box is on the screen and resumes only when the message box has been dismissed.

The advantages of using the MsgBox statement are obvious. MsgBox is easy to use and can be used to output virtually any type of data. Simply concatenate a message with the data you'd like to display. The message box itself appears on the user interface, and you don't have to have the Immediate window open or flip to the Immediate window to view the message box. Also, the MsgBox statement is simple and easy to use and occupies only a single line of code.

FIGURE 8.7.

Using the MsgBox *statement is a crude but effective debugging tool.*

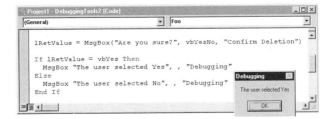

Figure 8.7 illustrates one of the most common sources of confusion in Visual Basic. MsgBox is a function as well as a statement. When MsgBox is followed by an opening parenthesis (as at the top of Figure 8.7), Visual Basic assumes you mean to use MsgBox as a function. Therefore, you must provide a variable (in this case lRetValue) to capture the return value of the MsgBox function. Later in this code fragment you see MsgBox being used as a simple VBA statement. In this case, MsgBox simply displays the information provided as arguments to the MsgBox statement, and the parentheses are not needed.

> **Warning:** Don't forget to remove all MsgBox statements from your code before shipping to end users. Any MsgBox statements remaining in the code after the debugging process will appear in front of the end user, which can cause confusion and other problems.

There are also problems associated with MsgBox statements. Message boxes are modal, which means you can't flip to the Code Editor window or debug windows to examine the value of variables or view the code underlying the application. Using the MsgBox statement is an all-or-nothing proposition (with the one exception described in the following paragraph).

A refinement of the MsgBox technique is to use the Visual Basic compiler directives to suppress the MsgBox statements unless a compiler constant has been set in the code or Visual Basic environment. Chapter 3, "Visual Basic Code Basics," discusses using compiler directives in depth; so a simple example here should suffice. Examine the ConfirmDeletion() function shown in Figure 8.8. Notice the #Const compiler directive above the MsgBox statement and the #If and #End If directives surrounding the If...Then...Else statement.

The #Const directive establishes a constant value that is seen only by the compiler. In this case, a reference to the DEBUGGING compiler constant anywhere in the application other than from within a compiler directive causes a compile-time error. The #If, #Else, and #End If directives establish a normal If...Then...Else construct that tests the value of a compiler constant. In Figure 8.8, because the DEBUGGING compiler constant has been set to -1 (true), the code within the #If and #End If directives executes each time the ConfirmDeletion() function runs. Later, the #Const statement at the top of the module can be removed or the value of DEBUGGING changed to 0 (false), which will cause Visual Basic to ignore this bit of code at all times.

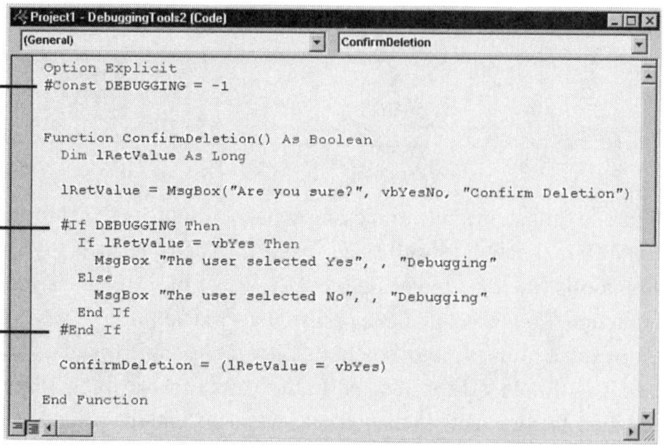

FIGURE 8.8.
Compiler direc-tives are seen only by the VBA com-piler and do not affect other code in the application.

Compiler directives —

```
Project1 - DebuggingTools2 (Code)                                _ □ ×
(General)                              ▼   ConfirmDeletion          ▼
    Option Explicit
    #Const DEBUGGING = -1


    Function ConfirmDeletion() As Boolean
        Dim lRetValue As Long

        lRetValue = MsgBox("Are you sure?", vbYesNo, "Confirm Deletion")

    #If DEBUGGING Then
        If lRetValue = vbYes Then
            MsgBox "The user selected Yes", , "Debugging"
        Else
            MsgBox "The user selected No", , "Debugging"
        End If
    #End If

        ConfirmDeletion = (lRetValue = vbYes)

    End Function
```

> **Note:** You can't use built-in values such as True and False in the #Const declara-tion. You must use the internal representation of these values (–1 and 0, respec-tively) in the #Const syntax.

The #Const directive in Figure 8.8 can appear anywhere in the module as long as it is placed above the #If directive. The logical place for the #Const is in the module's decla-ration section because #Const values are seen throughout the module. You might also want to place your #Const declarations (along with any other application constants, pub-lic variables, and public procedures) in a standard module named Publics.

The name you choose for your compiler constants is up to you. In Figure 8.8, DEBUGGING was chosen because the use of this compiler constant in the application is strictly for debugging purposes. Use whatever compiler constant names you want, and use as many compiler constants as your application needs.

Alternatively, use the Conditional Compilation Arguments option near the bottom of the Make tab of the Project Properties dialog box to specify the constant value (see Figure 8.9). (You open this dialog box from the Project menu.) A conditional compilation con-stant entered in the Project Properties dialog box is available throughout the entire appli-cation, making it easy for you to consistently activate or deactivate the MsgBox state-ments.

> **Note:** Multiple conditional compilation arguments must be separated by semi-colons in the Conditional Compilation Arguments text box.

FIGURE 8.9.
*Setting
Conditional
Compilation
Arguments
applies compiler
constants globally
throughout the
application.*

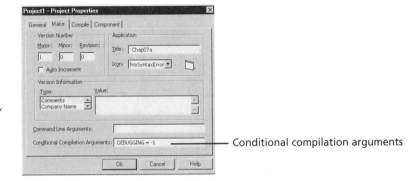

— Conditional compilation arguments

The conditional compilation arguments are preserved with other information associated with your project and will be compiled into the final runtime EXE unless you remove or change the setting. If you use this powerful feature, be sure to remove any debugging or development-only settings or your users will encounter whatever statements you've sequestered with the #If...#End If directive.

Using Debug.Print

Another common debugging statement is Debug.Print, which is used to output messages to the Immediate window. Print is actually a method (the only method, in fact) of the Debug object. Figure 8.10 shows how the sSQL variable appears in the Immediate window. In this figure, the Debug.Print statement is enclosed within the #If and #End If compiler directives.

FIGURE 8.10.
*Using Debug.Print
to output infor-
mation to the
Immediate win-
dow is a common
debugging tech-
nique.*

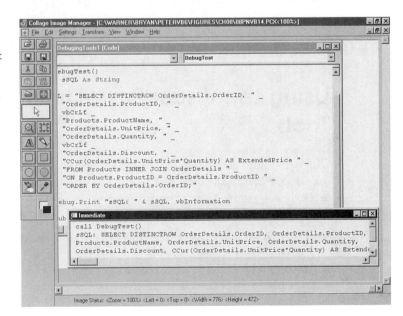

Unlike the MsgBox statement, you don't have to do anything special to suppress its output from the user interface. The output of Debug.Print goes to the Immediate window only, and because end users never see the Immediate window, you needn't worry about a user encountering debug messages. Therefore, the compiler directives surrounding the Debug.Print statement in Figure 8.10 are not strictly needed, but they might help someone understand that this statement is included for debugging purposes only.

> **Tip:** Unfortunately, there's no easy way to save or print the contents of the Immediate window. You can, however, easily copy the contents of the Immediate window to the Windows Clipboard. Whenever the Immediate window has the focus, Ctrl+A highlights all the contents of the Immediate window. Ctrl+C then copies all the selected text to the Windows Clipboard. From there it is a relatively simple process to paste the Clipboard contents (with the Ctrl+V keystroke combination) into Notepad or another editor for printing or to save it as a text file.

The problems with Debug.Print are obvious from Figure 8.10. Long strings do not wrap in the Immediate window unless you concatenate the vbCrLf (carriage return/line feed) intrinsic constant. Also, the Immediate window must be brought to the top in order for you to view its output. But these limitations are relatively harmless, and it's likely you'll frequently use Debug.Print in your applications.

> **Note:** There have been some reports that excessive numbers of Debug.Print statements can slow an application. Although the Immediate window is not visible, Visual Basic executes the Debug.Print statements it finds in its code. You might consider surrounding each Debug.Print statement with compiler directives and execute them only when debugging.

Using the Visual Basic Debugging Tools

Debugging an application, of course, presumes that you've encountered a problem with your code. Perhaps the code has failed to run as expected or crashes as it executes certain commands. Frequently, an application performs well under certain conditions but fails miserably under others. Your challenge during the debugging process is to determine why the program's execution fails under some conditions but not others.

Visual Basic 6 provides several powerful debugging tools. You use these tools when you encounter a problem that requires more than correcting a simple syntax error. The Visual Basic debugging tools enable you to pause a program's execution, examine the values of variables used by the program, and redirect the flow of execution to another point in the halted procedure. You can even play what-if games with variable values and change code on-the-fly to see what happens when you make minor changes to a program's logic.

Basically, debugging a Visual Basic application involves the following tasks, which are not necessarily performed in this order:

- **Execute procedures:** Any of the *public* procedures in your Visual Basic programs can be run during the development process. It isn't necessary to actually run the entire application to test a single public subroutine or function.

- **Suspending execution:** A *breakpoint* suspends program execution at a specific point in the application, enabling you to work with the code and variables while the program is suspended.

- **Single-stepping through code:** While in Break mode you can step through your VBA code one statement at a time. As you single-step through the code, you can modify the code, watch the value of variables change, or manually set the value of variables to see what effect these changes have on the program's execution.

- **Examine variables:** You set *watches* or *watch points* on important variables to automatically audit the status of these variables as the code runs. There are several other ways to examine the values of variables, all of which are explained in this chapter.

- **Redirect program flow:** Visual Basic also offers a rather unique option in that you can specify which line of code the execution point should jump to.

All these debugging techniques are described in the following sections.

Using the Debug Toolbar

Most of the Visual Basic debugging tools are conveniently located on the Debug toolbar. This toolbar is not displayed by default and must be explicitly opened by right-clicking an existing toolbar and selecting Debug from the toolbar drop-down list. Alternatively, choose the Toolbars command from the View menu and select Debug from the toolbar drop-down list that appears. Both of these techniques are shown in Figure 8.11.

All the command buttons on the Debug toolbar are also available as menu commands, but keeping the Debug toolbar open on the desktop provides you with quick access to those commands. Figure 8.12 shows the Debug toolbar.

Like other Windows toolbars, the Debug toolbar is context-sensitive. Often, one or more of the buttons on this toolbar will be grayed out because nothing in the Visual Basic environment is applicable to the grayed-out buttons. The purpose of each of the Debug toolbar buttons is described in the following sections.

Figure 8.11.
Like so many other things in Visual Basic, there is more than one way to open the Debug toolbar.

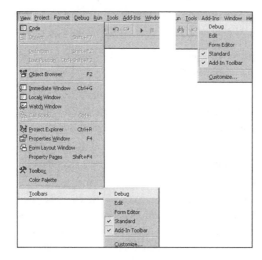

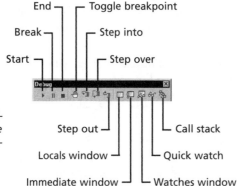

Figure 8.12.
The Debug toolbar contains the essential debugging tools.

Suspending Execution with Breakpoints

You suspend execution by setting a *breakpoint* in the code. When Visual Basic encounters a breakpoint, execution immediately stops, allowing you to switch to any of the debugging windows (Immediate, Locals, or Watches) to set or examine the value of variables. While in Break mode, you can also use the other debugging tools such as stepping into code, using the Auto Data Tips, or setting watches on variables. Finally, Visual Basic enables you to modify the code in your procedures while you are in Break mode. You can redirect the program's flow to execute the new or modified lines of code to see what effect the changes have on the program's execution.

Setting a breakpoint is easy. As with most tasks in Visual Basic, there is more than one way to set a breakpoint. Open the Code window and click the gray bar (called the Margin Indicator bar or simply the margin) next to the statement on which you want execution to stop (see Figure 8.13). Alternatively, position the cursor on the line and click the Breakpoint toolbar button. The breakpoint itself appears as a large brown dot in the gray bar along the left edge of the Code window and as a brown highlight behind the code while the code itself is displayed in bold typeface. All these colors and font characteristics can be changed in the Editor Format tab of the Options dialog box.

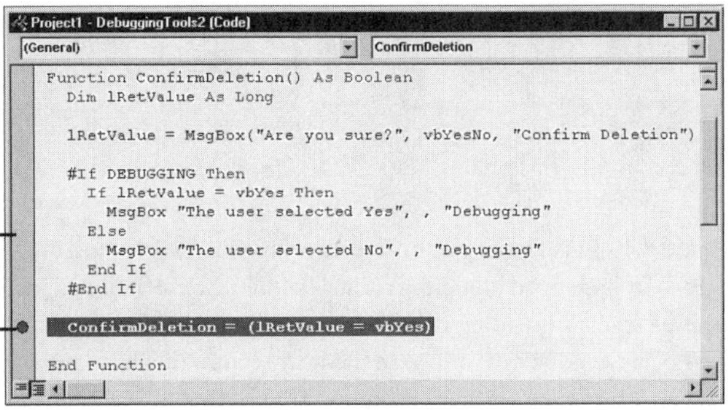

FIGURE 8.13.
Breakpoints are an indispensable debugging tool.

Margin Indicator bar

Breakpoint

To remove a breakpoint simply click the large breakpoint dot in the Margin Indicator bar. Breakpoints are also automatically removed when you close the module and leave Visual Basic. Breakpoints are not preserved as Visual Basic shuts down, but they persist from invocation to invocation of the code until you remove them. You can place as many breakpoints in your code as you want, but setting too many breakpoints can impede your development efforts. Remove all breakpoints by selecting the Clear All Breakpoints command from the Debug menu or by pressing Ctrl+Shift+F9.

Note: You can't put a breakpoint on just any line of code in your application. The line must be an executable statement. For example, you can't set breakpoints on variable declarations (Dim, Private, Public, and so on) or comments.

When execution reaches the breakpoint, Visual Basic halts execution and opens the module at the breakpoint (see Figure 8.14). The line of highlighted code has not yet run, so think of the breakpoint as occurring at the front of the line containing the breakpoint. You can now use the Immediate window to examine the values of variables and perform other operations. Neither the Code window nor the Immediate window are modal, so you still have full access to the development environment.

While in Break mode, execution is suspended but not halted. The line of code that is about to execute is indicated by a yellow arrow in the Code window margin. Later, as you step through the code, the execution point will sequentially move to the VBA statements just before they are executed by the VBA engine.

FIGURE 8.14.

The execution point is indicated by the arrow in the Editor window's left margin.

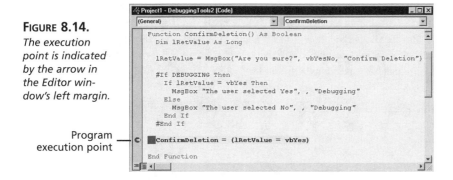

Program execution point

Figure 8.15 illustrates three different techniques for viewing the values of variables while execution is stopped at a breakpoint. The first two techniques you've already seen. The mouse cursor is hovering over the name of the lRetValue variable in the Code window; the Locals window (described in the next section) contains the names and values of all the variables in the current procedure. If you want to see the value of a variable in a slightly different format, use the Debug Print command to display the variable's value in the Immediate window.

FIGURE 8.15.

Visual Basic provides several ways to read a variable's value while in Break mode.

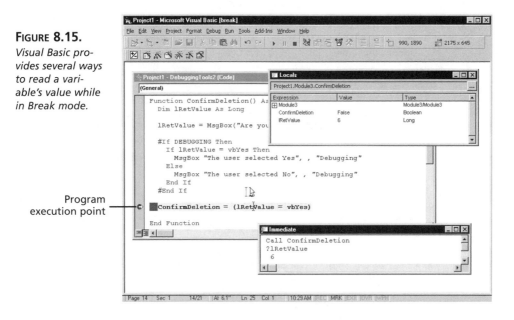

Program execution point

An alternative to setting breakpoints is to use Stop statements. The Stop statement, a VBA command like MsgBox or Debug.Print, halts execution but is more permanent than breakpoints. Otherwise, a Stop behaves exactly like a breakpoint, halting execution on the Stop statement, enabling you to use the other Visual Basic debugging tools.

A Stop statement, like any other VBA statement, persists from session to session until explicitly removed. You can, however, surround the Stop statement with conditional compilation expressions. Figure 8.16 illustrates using the Stop statement.

FIGURE 8.16.
A Stop *statement behaves like a permanent breakpoint.*

Program execution point

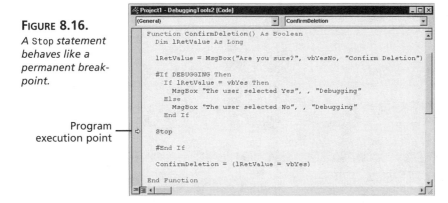

```
Function ConfirmDeletion() As Boolean
    Dim lRetValue As Long

    lRetValue = MsgBox("Are you sure?", vbYesNo, "Confirm Deletion")

    #If DEBUGGING Then
        If lRetValue = vbYes Then
            MsgBox "The user selected Yes", , "Debugging"
        Else
            MsgBox "The user selected No", , "Debugging"
        End If

        Stop

    #End If

    ConfirmDeletion = (lRetValue = vbYes)

End Function
```

In Figure 8.16 the Stop statement is enclosed by the #If and #End If compiler directives. In this situation, it's safe to leave the Stop in place and deliver the application to its end users without removing the Stop as long as the value of the DEBUGGING compiler constant is changed to false.

Stepping Through Code

After you reach a breakpoint you can control the execution of the application. You can step through code one statement at a time, continue execution to a specific point in the procedure, or step over the procedure and continue execution on the other side of the procedure. You can also resume normal execution and allow the application to progress in a normal fashion.

In Figure 8.17, a breakpoint has been inserted near the top of the ConfirmDeletion() function. When execution reaches this point a break occurs, allowing you to take control of program execution.

In Figure 8.18, the break has occurred and I've clicked the Step Into button on the Debug toolbar. Alternatively, I could have pressed the F8 button or selected the Step Into command in the Visual Basic Debug menu. The Step Into button executes the next statement in the program's flow of execution, which in this case is the MsgBox command, which displays the message box you see in the lower-right corner of Figure 8.18.

Notice the execution pointer (the yellow arrow) in the Margin Indicator bar to the left of the stopped statement. The line the arrow is pointing to is about to run, so any variables that will be assigned by that line still have their most recent values and any procedures called by that line have not yet been run.

FIGURE 8.17.

The breakpoint suspends the program before this line of code executes.

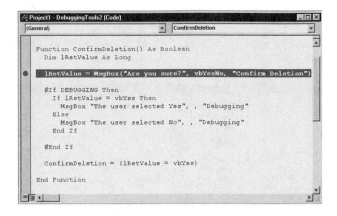

FIGURE 8.18.

Step Into executes one line of code at a time.

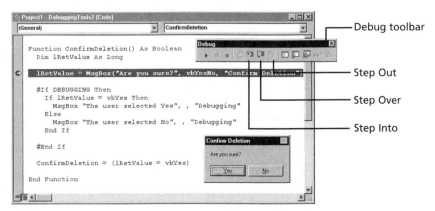

Consecutively clicking the Step Into button walks you through the code one statement at a time. If a statement includes a call to another procedure, you will be taken to that procedure and walked through it one step at a time. If the new procedure is located in a different code module, Visual Basic opens that code module and places the execution point at the appropriate spot. If you want, you can use the Step Over button to step through the called routine rather than be taken to it. If you previously debugged the called routine and are sure it contains no errors, there is no reason to walk through its code. The code in the called routine is actually executed when you click the Step Over button; this changes any variables involved in that other procedure.

When you're satisfied, you needn't continue walking through the code; click the Step Out button to complete the procedure or use the Continue button (or press F5) to resume normal execution. The Step Out button is handy if you've stepped into a called routine and are sure there's nothing interesting going on in it. In this case, Step Out instructs Visual Basic to complete the called procedure and return you to the original function or subroutine. Pressing the Continue button, on the other hand, is a signal to Visual Basic that you're finished with Break mode and want to return to normal operation.

Controlling Program Flow

Visual Basic provides two different ways to control the program's execution point while the code is suspended in Break mode. Perhaps you've made a change to a procedure's code and you want to backtrack to see what effect the changes will have on the procedure's execution. Or, you might simply want the code to complete a loop without stopping on a breakpoint you have set within the loop each time the breakpoint is reached. Before reading the following discussion, keep in mind that all these redirection features operate only while the code is in Break mode. Also, all these operations work only within the current function or subroutine. You can't use the Run to Cursor command to redirect execution out of the current procedure.

The Run to Cursor feature instructs Visual Basic to execute all statements from the current breakpoint down to where the mouse cursor is positioned in the code. To set this feature, right-click the line you want to run to and select Run to Cursor from the shortcut menu that appears (see Figure 8.19). As soon as you've specified the Run to Cursor target, the code automatically executes down to that point. Any procedure calls, variable assignments, and other operations occur as execution proceeds to the Run to Cursor target. Execution then breaks on the Run to Cursor target statement.

FIGURE 8.19.
Run to Cursor is handy for executing blocks of code.

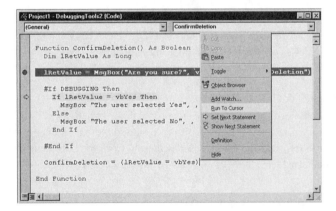

Run to Cursor is particularly useful for executing blocks of complicated code when you're not interested in viewing each line in sequence. Perhaps you're more interested in whether the block of code manipulates variables the way you expect it to. You can easily run to a point past the complicated code and examine the variables after the block has executed.

Another way to redirect program flow is with the Set Next Statement command, seen also in the shortcut menu in Figure 8.19. Conceptually, Set Next Statement works like Run to Cursor with a major difference. With Set Next Statement program execution jumps to the Set Next Statement target without executing the lines of code between the current execution point and the Set Next Statement target. Therefore, Set Next Statement is useful for restarting procedures after making changes to the code.

If you're in the middle of a complicated bit of code and you're not quite sure which line of code will execute next (perhaps because of the complexity of the logic), use the Show Next Statement command on the shortcut menu you see in Figure 8.19. In most cases, Show Next Statement is less useful than either Run to Cursor or Set Next Statement, but it's a nice debugging tool to have.

Getting to Know the Debugging Windows

This section covers some of your most valuable debugging aids. Visual Basic offers several design-time windows that you can open to view different aspects of your program. These windows include the following:

- **Immediate window:** Permits "immediate" execution of Visual Basic commands and application procedures.
- **Locals window:** Displays the values of variables currently in scope.
- **Watches window:** Displays the values of program variables whose values are being watched.

Access 97 developers will recognize each of these debug window types. A major difference between the Access 97 and Visual Basic 6 debug windows is that all three of these windows are combined as a single unit in Access 97, whereas Visual Basic maintains a separate window for each debugging purpose.

Using the Immediate Window

The Immediate window supports several different debugging tasks. You use the Immediate window to test VBA procedures, display the values of program variables, and as the target of the Debug.Print statement. Open the Immediate window by selecting its command from the View menu or by pressing Ctrl+G. The Visual Basic Immediate window can be opened at any time.

The Visual Basic Immediate window is shown in Figure 8.20. The Immediate window contains as many as 100 lines of text and can be scrolled horizontally and vertically to show data that extends beyond the margins of the window. You must manually select and delete text in the Immediate window to clear its contents.

FIGURE 8.20.

The Immediate window is an important debugging tool.

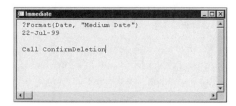

It's easy to run a built-in Visual Basic command or a procedure (function or subroutine) you've written from the Immediate window. If the command or procedure is a function, precede the command with a question mark as shown at the top of Figure 8.20. The question mark is shorthand for "print the value of..." and is equivalent to using the Debug.Print statement in code. Figure 8.20 displays the value returned by formatting the current date in the Medium Date format.

If the Visual Basic command or procedure is a subroutine, you can either use the Call keyword as in Figure 8.20 or simply type the name of the subroutine in the Immediate window. In either case, if the command or procedure requires arguments you must provide the arguments in the Immediate window just as when you run the command from within the program.

A second use of the Immediate window is to display or set the value of variables within the application. Earlier in this chapter you saw an example of a function that uses a procedure-level variable named lRetValue. You could use the breakpoint feature described later in this chapter to temporarily halt execution of the function, assign a new value to the lRetValue variable, and continue execution to see the effect of the different values of the lRetValue variable. See Figure 8.21 to see how this technique works.

FIGURE 8.21.
Use the Immediate window in Break mode to run code or display variable values.

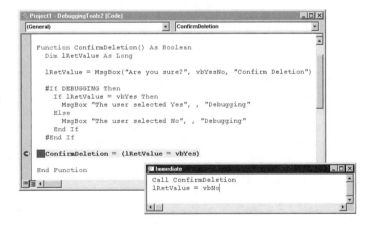

In Figure 8.21, a breakpoint has been used to halt execution on the highlighted line of code. The user has used the Immediate window to assign a new value to the lRetValue variable by typing the variable assignment into the Immediate window. When the user clicks the Continue button on the Debug toolbar, execution proceeds from the breakpoint in the code to the next executable statement.

Using the Locals Window

You might have noticed the items in the Locals window in Figure 8.15. The Locals window shows the value for any variables, functions, and identifiers that are currently in scope. For example, in Figure 8.15 the ConfirmDeletion() function is running but not complete, so it's in scope and its value is currently `False` (the default for any Boolean variable or function). The value of `lRetVal`, a long variable, is 6 (`vbYes`) because the user has clicked the Yes button in the message box near the top of the `ConfirmDeletion()` function.

Any line in the Locals window that begins with a plus sign can unfold to reveal more information. For example, in Figure 8.22 the `DebuggingTools` module contains three module-scope variables: `db`, `rs`, and `sSQL`. At this time these variables have not yet been assigned values, so they are set to their respective defaults. Later at another breakpoint, these variables can be set to other values.

FIGURE 8.22.

Use the Locals window to monitor the values of variables and functions.

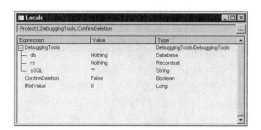

Using Watches

So far, most of the debugging tools you've looked at have been static. That is, they're useful only when the code is halted at a breakpoint or before the code has been started. A *watch* is a dynamic view of an expression. The expression can be as simple as a variable name or as complex as a lengthy calculated value. You don't have to set breakpoints in your code to use watches. After a watch has been set on a variable or expression you can examine its status in the Watches window at your leisure. You can also set a *conditional watch* that will force a break when a certain condition has been met. Watches are similar to the operations you can perform in the Immediate window but are much more convenient.

You set variable watches by positioning the cursor within a variable name in the code and then selecting the Quick Watch command in the Debug menu, clicking the Quick Watch button in the Debug toolbar, or pressing Shift+F9. The dialog shown in Figure 8.23 opens in response to any of these actions.

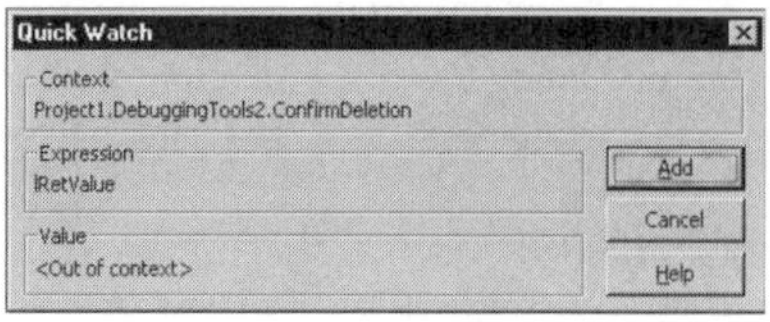

FIGURE 8.23.

A quick watch provides a dynamic look at a variable.

After you verify the watch by clicking the Add button, Visual Basic adds the variable to the Watches window (see Figure 8.24). The value of the watched variable is updated as the code executes until either you close Visual Basic or remove the watched variable from the Watches window.

FIGURE 8.24.

The value of a watched variable is dynamically updated in the Watches window as the code runs.

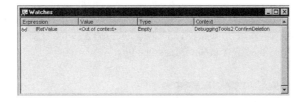

The value of a watched variable changes dynamically as the code runs. (You must be at some kind of breakpoint or stopping point in the code, of course, to actually see the values.) The advantage of using the Watches window is that the variables displayed do not have to be from the local procedure. In fact, the variables in the watch can be from any part of the application and do not necessarily have to be in scope.

Removing a watch is easy. Right-click the watched variable in the Watches window and select Delete Watch from the shortcut menu that appears (see Figure 8.25).

FIGURE 8.25.

This shortcut menu contains the commands necessary to manage watched variables.

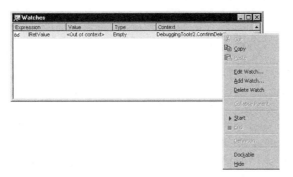

All the watched variables are evaluated each time a Visual Basic statement executes. Obviously, a lot of watches will slow execution considerably. Also, even though Visual Basic doesn't limit the number of watches you've placed in your program, having too many watches is probably counterproductive because you'll end up with a lot of different values to track.

Variables are not the only values you can track with watches. You can also establish watches on expressions like the following:

```
lRetValue = vbYes
```

This expression returns True only when the lRetValue is set to vbYes. The watch you set on this expression can conditionally force a break whenever the expression (or variable) changes or whenever the expression evaluates to True.

Use the Add Watch command in the Debug menu. The Add Watch dialog box appears, enabling you to set the details of the type of watch you'd like to establish. Figure 8.26 shows how to set a conditional watch that breaks execution whenever the lRetValue variable equals vbYes. This watch would be useful to break the code when the user clicks the Yes button in the Are You Sure? message box.

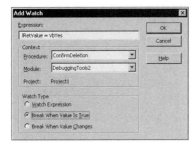

The Add Watch dialog box includes some important options. In addition to the name of a variable or expression, there are options for specifying the module and procedure within the module to watch. (These names appear in the drop-down lists in the center of the Add Watch dialog box.)

At the bottom of the Add Watch dialog box are the following options:

- **Watch Expression:** The variable's value dynamically changes in the Watches window. You must use an explicit breakpoint or Stop statement in order to observe the value of the watched variable. Otherwise, Visual Basic is unable to keep the watch updated as the code runs.

- **Break When Value Is True:** This option generates a break whenever the value of the watched variable or expression becomes True. An example was described a few paragraphs ago. If you set the expression to lRetValue = vbYes the code shifts into Break mode whenever the value of the lRetValue variable is 6. Keep in mind that you can negate any expression with the Not operator.

- **Break When Value Changes:** This directive causes Visual Basic to halt execution whenever the value of the variable or expression changes. This setting can generate a *lot* of breakpoints.

Use watches wisely. You don't want to be breaking into program execution too frequently or you'll never get through the code. On the other hand, you don't want to overlook some important change in the value of a variable because you didn't set a watch appropriately.

A conditional watch looks a bit different in the Watches window than a simple watch. Figure 8.27 shows how a conditional watch (the lower one) looks compared to a simple watch (the upper one).

FIGURE 8.27.
It's easy to tell conditional watches from simple watches in your code.

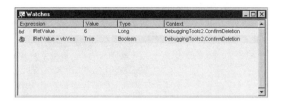

The Watches window displays the watched expression, its current value, the type of data returned by the watch (usually Boolean), and the context of the watched expression. The context is the procedure or module you specified for the watched expression. You can set different watches on the same variable as long as you've specified different contexts for each watch.

Note: Watches are not preserved after you leave Visual Basic.

Using the Call Stack

The last debugging tool we'll examine in this chapter is the *call stack*. It can be difficult to tell how the code has gotten to a certain procedure in a complex application. You might encounter a problem that appears only when the code has taken a certain path through the code. One procedure calls another and that one calls yet another in turn. Because of the myriad ways you can design the flow through your programs and because program logic can actually dynamically change a program's flow, it's important to understand how the execution point has ended up in a particular subroutine or function.

The call stack is a list showing the sequence in which procedures in the application have been called. The call stack is useful only with the application in Break mode, so place a breakpoint in a procedure then run the application. When the program reaches the breakpoint, click the Call Stack button on the Debug toolbar or select the Call Stack command in the View menu (Ctrl+L opens the Call Stack as well). Figure 8.28 shows a rather trivial example of the Visual Basic call stack in action.

In Figure 8.28 the A subroutine was the first procedure to run and appears at the bottom of the call list. The A subroutine called B, which in turn called C, and so on. The breakpoint was actually placed in subroutine D. The Call Stack window is modal, so you are not able to modify code or examine variables while this dialog box is open. You can't even single step through the code with the F8 button or Step Into button on the Debug toolbar.

FIGURE 8.28.

The call stack provides a peek at a program's execution path.

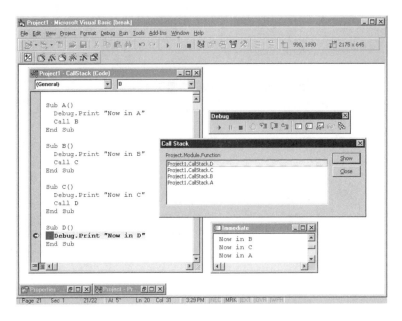

One thing you can do with the Call Stack dialog box, however, is instantly show the code in any of the procedures in the call list. Figure 8.29 shows how the code window looks when Project1.CallStack.B is selected in the call list and the Show button is clicked.

FIGURE 8.29.

The Show button takes you to the procedure you've selected in the Call Stack dialog box.

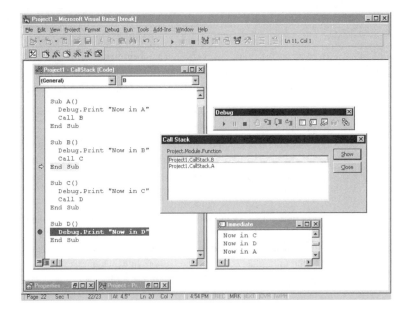

It's important to note that the execution point does not actually change to the selected procedure. Instead, the green arrow in the Code Window Indicator bar tells you that you are simply viewing the code in this procedure and that the execution point is actually somewhere else in the program. The execution point is visible in Figure 8.29, but that is not necessarily the case. The call stack will take you anywhere you specify in the current project. This means you might be taken to another module and might lose track of the execution point.

While you're in the other procedure, however, you can make code changes, examine the values of variables, and perform any other debugging operation. When you click the Step Into button or command, however, you'll be returned to the statement that contains the breakpoint, and execution will proceed from there.

Figure 8.30 shows the effect of pressing the F8 key a few times while the code is in Break mode in the D subroutine. The code steps out of D, back through C, and is now in B. The call stack shows that you're now in B and that you got there from A. The call list does not show the history of how you got here. Instead, it shows the list of procedures that have been called but have not completed execution.

FIGURE 8.30.
The call list dynamically changes as you single-step through code.

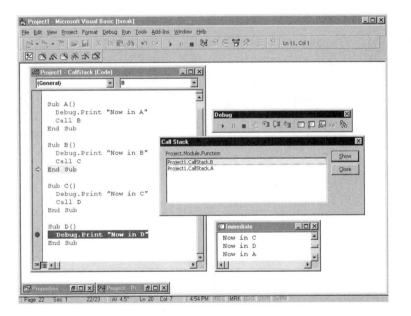

Summary

This chapter has taken a quick look at the important topic of debugging Visual Basic VBA code. The techniques you apply and the tools you use to debug your code are highly individual choices. Not all developers feel comfortable using the Immediate window to watch variables, and not every developer wants to use watches in their code. At the same time it's nice to know these powerful tools are available for your use when you're ready.

A key objective in any Visual Basic project is to avoid errors in the first place. Well-written, carefully organized, and highly disciplined code will not only generate fewer errors, it'll be easier to debug when a problem exists.

Chapter 9, "Handling Runtime Errors," discusses how to handle the problems that inevitably occur as the user works with your applications. Try as you might, there is no way you can code around every possible runtime problem. Because of network noise, missing files, or a change in the user's desktop configuration, even the best-written application will encounter problems at runtime now and then.

Handling Runtime Errors

Several situations can cause great frustration for the users of your applications:

- A program that has been operating without a hint of trouble suddenly crashes and displays a dialog box that contains a contradictory or confusing error message.

- Sometimes a program behaves inconsistently. In one situation, the program operates in a predictable fashion, reliably churning out reports and displaying the results of calculations. Under other conditions the same program, operating on seemingly identical data, behaves erratically, stopping execution or perhaps displaying the data in unexpected ways.

- A program also might appear to be functioning properly but in fact corrupts data. This program silently makes changes to the data or reports erroneous values without indicating that an error exists. An example is a program that calculates currency exchange rates. The user of this program might believe the program is correctly calculating the correct monetary exchange values whereas the program is actually reporting incorrect results. The worst situation occurs when the values returned by the program appear to be correct, but are wrong.

The Visual Basic error-handling techniques described in this chapter will protect your users from the first two types of runtime errors. After reading this chapter, you will be able to add code to your applications to prevent unexpected crashes or inconsistent behavior. You'll learn how to bulletproof your Visual Basic code so that no error can crash the applications containing the code. You'll see how to intercept the confusing and sometimes misleading error messages Visual Basic displays in response to unmanaged errors in code.

Unfortunately, little can be done to correct a poorly programmed application. If the calculations are being performed incorrectly, there is nothing that the VBA engine can do to correct the error. Your only defense against deadly *logical errors* (the types of errors commonly encountered in most computer programs were discussed in Chapter 8, "Using the Visual Basic Debugging Tools") is carefully applied error trapping and error handling code added to each procedure in your applications.

> **Note:** This chapter includes some code that is used when working with databases in Visual Basic. This code, part of the Data Access Objects (DAO) syntax common to Visual Basic applications, is explained in Chapter 18, "Mastering Jet DAO." Although you haven't yet studied working with databases in Visual Basic, the database code is included in this chapter to demonstrate real-world uses of error handling.

Recognizing Runtime Errors

Access, Visual Basic, and the other VBA applications such as Word and Excel handle most runtime errors for you. When a program like Word cannot open a particular document file the user sees an error message indicating that a problem exists. Similarly, the Visual Basic programs you prepare will display error messages and respond to runtime errors without any effort on your part. If you are happy with the default error messages and application behavior that occurs in response to runtime errors, you needn't change a thing in your Visual Basic code.

Unfortunately, the built-in error handling in applications is not helpful for most end users. Figure 9.1 shows a typical runtime error message produced by Visual Basic 6.0. Notice how unhelpful the message is. Most users have no idea how to respond to the error message you see in Figure 9.1. This error message (No Current Record) is fairly technical and is not intended for end users.

Figure 9.1.

Built-in error messages usually are not helpful.

Unless training has been provided explaining how to respond to this error it is unlikely the user will simply guess at the correct action to take in response. The default response to the message box in Figure 9.1 is to shut down the application. After the user has innocently stepped off the end of the set of data under the form there is no way to prevent the form from shutting down. (You'll learn how to create data-driven forms in Part IV of this book, "Accessing Data.") The correct way to handle this error is to detect the end of the data under the form, and put the record pointer back on the last record under the form. It is a fatal error to leave the record pointer pointing at a nonexistent record.

The following sections describe the Visual Basic code that you must add to your Visual Basic programs to effectively trap and handle runtime errors. Because the same pattern of Visual Basic statements is required for trapping and handling any runtime error, you'll find yourself writing this code repeatedly in your applications. Fortunately, as with most other things, Visual Basic is flexible and provides a variety of solutions to most runtime error situations. You'll discover that intercepting runtime errors and providing the user with several different responses to the error is not that difficult. You needn't worry about your Visual Basic forms shutting down every time an error occurs.

Trapping Errors in Visual Basic Applications

Visual Basic provides extensive runtime error handling capabilities. You can add code to the applications you create to detect when an error occurs. Other code directs the program to handle anticipated errors in a predictable fashion. Still other code can catch unanticipated errors, defusing them and preventing the loss of data, and reducing support costs.

Almost all error-handling routines in Visual Basic programs follow these three steps:

1. Trap the error and redirect program flow to the error handler.

2. Handle the error (for example, ignore it, perform corrective actions, and so on).

3. Direct the program flow out of the error handler back to the main body of the procedure.

It is important to note that all Visual Basic error handling is done locally. That is, each procedure contains its own error-handling code. Although a procedure's error handler can call other functions and subroutines, the error handler exists entirely within the procedure causing the error. In fact, as discussed later in this chapter, after you start implementing error handling, it's important to include error-handling code in almost every procedure in your program. An error that occurs in a procedure without error handling is passed back to the routine from which it was called; this causes confusion about which procedure actually failed.

Trapping the Error

The VBA engine is constantly looking for problems and immediately notifies you when something unexpected happens. The default error message is generally technical in nature. Figure 9.1 showed an example of how Visual Basic normally handles most errors. The error message box in this example did not provide the user with any alternative other than to shut down the form.

A single line of code is all that's necessary to intercept the error and redirect program flow to code that provides a more user-friendly approach to error resolution. After the error has been managed by the code, the program flow is redirected to another location within the procedure.

The code in Listing 9.1 shows how error handling is implemented in Visual Basic procedures. The `On Error` statement near the top of this routine sets the error trap for this subroutine. Code near the bottom of the routine implements the error-handling mechanism for this subroutine. The line numbers to the left of each statement are not part of the subroutine. They have been placed there to make the code in Listing 9.1 easier to reference in the paragraphs that follow. Listing 9.1 is included in the form named `frmDefault` in the `Errors.vbp` project.

Listing 9.1. A typical Visual Basic procedure implementing error handling.

```
 1  Private Sub cmdNext_Click()
 2  On Error GoTo Err_cmdNext_Click
 3     rs.MoveNext
 4     Call FillLabels
 5  Exit_cmdNext_Click:
 6     Exit Sub
 7  Err_cmdNext_Click:
 8     MsgBox Err.Description
 9     Resume Exit_cmdNext_Click
10  End Sub
```

The error-handling code in Listing 9.1 is the very least you can include in your procedures to effectively handle runtime errors. The error-handling statements you see in Listing 9.1 are the template you'll consistently use in all your Visual Basic programs.

Let's take a moment to examine the syntax diagram of the On Error statement in Listing 9.1 (line 2):

```
On Error GoTo Err_cmdNext_Click
```

The On Error clause informs Visual Basic that you want to override the built-in Visual Basic error-handling system. The GoTo Err_cmdNext_Click statement is an unconditional branch to a label somewhere within the procedure. In Listing 9.1 the name of the label is Err_cmdNext_Click, but it could be named anything you want. This label appears near the end of the procedure and marks the beginning of the error handler for this subroutine. The error handler itself contains only two lines of code and is discussed in the next section, "Handling the Error."

The On Error statement is a switch that disables the default Visual Basic error handling. This statement switches the VBA engine away from its built-in error handling and redirects error handling to your code. After you set the error trap with the On Error statement, you suppress the appearance of the default error dialog boxes.

There are several other forms of the On Error statement. The general syntax of On Error is as follows:

```
On Error [Perform Some Action]
```

Depending on what you want you want the code to do, you can use either of the following statements as the error trap in your procedures:

```
On Error Resume
On Error Resume Next
```

These two forms of the Resume statement control the program's execution in different ways. You'll read more about the Resume statement in the section titled "Redirecting the Program Flow," later in this chapter.

Handling the Error

After an error occurs, the VBA engine's normal operation is suspended. Normal execution is directed to the error handler, and further error trapping within the error handler is inactive. If an error occurs in your error handler, Visual Basic responds with its default behavior.

In Listing 9.1 the error handler consists of only two lines of code (lines 8 and 9):

```
MsgBox Err.Description
Resume Exit_cmdNext_Click
```

The first of these lines displays the description of the error in a simple message box. As explained earlier in this chapter, in most cases the default error description is not very helpful to the users of the application. Later in this chapter, in the section titled "Using the Err Object," you'll see how you can display your own error message in response to problems managed by your error handlers.

Redirecting the Program Flow

The second line of the error handler (line 10) redirects program flow to another label in the procedure. (The redirection label appears on line 5.) In this particular case, the line following the redirection label (line 6) is Exit Sub, which ends the subroutine. In most cases, the statements following the redirection label do more than simply end the procedure. As you'll read in the section titled "Using the Resume Statement," you'll usually put code under the redirection label that releases the variables, closes files, and performs other cleanup operations.

Using the Err Object

As soon as an error occurs in Visual Basic code, the special built-in Err object becomes active. The Err object includes properties that report the number of the error, the error's description, as well as other useful information.

Using the Err.Description Property

The Err.Description property returns the default description of the error that has occurred. For example, in line 8 of Listing 9.1 you see the following line of code:

```
MsgBox Err.Description
```

This Description property's value is the same text that appears in the dialog box in Figure 9.1. Whether or not you choose to use this description is entirely up to you. You can easily display a more helpful message using the technique demonstrated in Listing 9.2, in the following section.

Using the `Err.Number` Property

The most important property of the `Err` object is the number associated with the error that occurred. Listing 9.2 shows how you might use the `Err.Number` property to determine which error has triggered the error handler. Listing 9.2 appears in the module named `basGeneric` in the `Errors.vbp` project.

Listing 9.2. Using `Err.Number` to determine which error has occurred.

```
Sub GenericHandler()
On Error GoTo Err_GenericHandler
  'Other Visual Basic statements here
Exit_GenericHandler:
  'Shut down statements here
  Exit Sub
Err_GenericHandler:
  Select Case Err.Number
    Case X
      'Handle X case
    Case Y
      'Handle Y case
    Case Z
      'Handle Z case
    Case Else 'Unanticipated error
      MsgBox Err.Number & " " & Err.Description
      Resume Exit_GenericHandler
  End Select
End Sub
```

The `Select Case` statement in the error handler in `GenericHandler` uses the `Err.Number` property to execute any of a number of responses to the error. The beauty of `Select Case` is that the error-handling code can be extended as far as necessary. There is no practical limit to the number of `Case` statements that can be contained within the `Select Case` construct, and multiple `Err.Number` values can be handled by the same `Case`.

Obviously, the `Select Case` construct is not the only way to handle multiple error conditions. You could, for example, use nested `If..Then..Else` statements. However, you'll find that the `If` statement is not easily extensible, and the logical flow through nested `If..Then..Else` statements can be difficult to follow.

Displaying More Helpful Information

The `Err.Number` property makes it easy to replace the default error messages with more helpful text. Listing 9.3 shows how the `cmdNext_Click` event procedure you saw earlier in this chapter can be rewritten to display more helpful information to the user.

Listing 9.3. Your users will appreciate helpful error messages.

```
1   Private Sub cmdNext_Click()
2   On Error GoTo Err_cmdNext_Click
3     rs.MoveNext
4     Call FillLabels
5   Exit_cmdNext_Click:
6     Exit Sub
7   Err_cmdNext_Click:
8     Select Case Err.Number
9       Case 3021
10        MsgBox "No more records in that direction"
11      Case Else
12        MsgBox "Error: " & Err.Number _
13          & vbCrLf & Err.Description, _
14          vbOKOnly, "Error Condition"
15    End Select
16    Resume Exit_cmdNext_Click
17  End Sub
```

In Listing 9.3, the most common error is number 3021, the No current record error that occurs as the user tries to move beyond the set of records behind the products form. The first Case clause in Listing 9.3 (see line 9) provides the statement necessary to display a helpful message to the user. Figure 9.2 shows the results of the changes you see in Listing 9.3. Surely the message No more records in that direction is easier to understand than No current record.

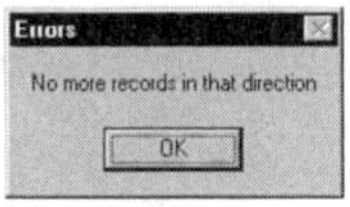

FIGURE 9.2.

It's easy to display helpful information in place of the default error message.

Because the Select Case statement is so extensible, it is easy to add handling for as many anticipated errors as necessary. Additionally, the Case Else clause catches everything that is not explicitly handled by the Case clause. Listing 9.4 exhibits a more generic approach to providing helpful error messages. In this case, instead of including all the error messages in every procedure, a public subroutine displays any number of different messages.

Listing 9.4. A more generic approach to handling errors.

```
Private Sub cmdNext_Click()
  On Error GoTo Err_cmdNext_Click
  rs.MoveNext
  Call FillLabels
Exit_cmdNext_Click:
```

continues

Listing 9.4. Continued.

```
  Exit Sub
Err_cmdNext_Click:
  Call PublicMessenger1
  Resume Exit_cmdNext_Click
End Sub

Public Sub PublicMessenger1
  Select Case Err.Number
    Case 11 'Divide by zero
      MsgBox "Can't divide by zero!"
    Case 53 'File not found
       MsgBox "Can't locate the data file"
    Case 71 'Disk not ready
      MsgBox "Make sure a disk is in the drive"
    Case 3021 'No current record
      MsgBox "No more records in that direction"
    Case 3026 'Not enough space on disk.
      MsgBox "Not enough free disk space to save file"
    Case Else
      MsgBox "Error: " & Err.Number _
        & vbCrLf & Err.Description, _
        vbOKOnly, "Unexpected Error"
  End Select
End Sub
```

The `PublicMessenger1` sub is called by any routine needing its services. `PublicMessenger1` uses the `Err.Number` property to select the appropriate message. If the error number does not match any of the anticipated errors, a default message is opened, displaying the `Err.Number` and `Err.Description`.

Notice that `PublicMessenger1` uses `Err.Number` although the error did not occur in the `PublicMessenger1` routine. The `Err` object is available everywhere in the Visual Basic project and can be referenced by routines such as `PublicMessenger1` called from error handlers throughout the project.

Knowing Which Errors to Trap

Several hundred trappable errors can occur in Visual Basic applications. Only a minor portion of these hundreds of errors is likely to occur in your applications. The question is, then, which of the remaining 50 or 100 relevant errors should you trap in your applications?

Most developers begin simply and write an error handler that catches one or two of the most obvious errors. In the case of the navigation buttons on a Visual Basic form, you should trap error number 3021. Such an error is readily anticipated and is the result of normal navigation through a form's recordset.

However, the situation in which the recordset itself cannot be created might not be as obvious. An application might fail to retrieve data from a database for many reasons. Perhaps the database table can't be found because it has been deleted, or there could be an error in the statement used to retrieve the data and no database records are returned. During development, you might never see an error caused by missing data because your test data is always available.

Experience will tell you which errors are expected as you write your Visual Basic procedures. However, you should always prepare for the unexpected. The `Case Else` clause, in Listings 9.3 and 9.4, catches every error that is not explicitly handled by the `Case` clauses. You could easily add code to the `Case Else` to log the unhandled errors in a database table or add them to a text file on disk. Later, review the contents of the error log table or file to see what additional error handling must be added.

Using the Resume Statement

You shouldn't allow processing to simply fall out of the error handlers in your procedure. You've probably noticed that the error handler customarily appears near the very bottom of the procedure. It's tempting to just let the `End Sub` statement after the error handler terminate the procedure after the error has been managed. There are several problems with this approach:

- The Visual Basic error mechanism is left in an indeterminate state. Recall that as soon as the error occurs, Visual Basic enters a special "error" mode. This mode persists until the VBA engine encounters a `Resume` statement (more on `Resume` later). Although the end of the procedure resets VBA's error mode, you should not count on this happening, particularly in deeply nested procedure calls.

- The `Err` object is reset by the `Resume` statement. The VBA engine resets `Err.Number` to 0 and `Err.Description` to `""`. Unless `Resume` is executed before processing recommences any code dependent on the value of `Err.Number` may run incorrectly.

- Visual Basic procedures often open sets of data, establish object variables, and perform other tasks that might be left incomplete unless shut down in a predictable fashion. For example, assume a procedure has opened a disk file and an error occurs. Unless the disk file is explicitly closed, you run the risk of damaging the disk's file structure. Using the `Resume` statement to redirect flow to the procedure's shut-down code provides a single point at which to close resources that are no longer needed.

Every Visual Basic error handler should include some form of the `Resume` statement. This special Visual Basic command instructs the VBA engine to resume normal execution. Depending on how you write the `Resume` statement, you can redirect program execution to any of a number of different points within the procedure.

> **Note:** The GoTo statement will not work in place of Resume. GoTo is an uncondi-
> tional branch to another location within the current procedure and does not
> reset the VBA engine error status.

Resume Label

The simplest form of Resume follows this syntax:

```
Resume Label
```

Label must be a label appearing within the current procedure. You cannot resume execution at a point outside the currently executing procedure. If you must use code in another
procedure as part of the error handler, simply call it at some point above the Resume
statement.

The Resume statements in Listings 9.2 and 9.3 redirect program flow to labels immediately preceding the Exit statement. Put the statements required to release the procedure's
variables, close open recordsets and files, and perform other shutdown tasks here.

Resume Next

The Resume Next statement instructs the VBA engine to resume processing at the first
executable statement following the statement that caused the error. The assumption with
Resume Next is that either the error handler corrected the error condition or the error was
relatively minor in nature and that it's appropriate for processing to proceed.

Listing 9.5 shows how to use On Error Resume Next. This simple error logging routine
tries to create a recordset object by selecting all fields from a table named tblErrorLog.
The call to the OpenRecordset method fails if tblErrorLog is unavailable. If
tblErrorLog cannot be opened, an error occurs. However, because of the Resume Next
directive, processing simply falls through to the If statement immediately following the
OpenRecordset. The code to create tblErrorLog is missing from this routine, but the
logic should be clear.

Listing 9.5. Resume Next lets you handle simple error conditions.

```
Sub LogError(iNumber As Integer, sDesc As String)
  Dim db As Database
  Dim rs As Recordset

On Error Resume Next

  Set ws = DBEngine.Workspaces(0)
  Set db = _
    ws.OpenDatabase(App.Path & "\Products.mdb")
  Set rs = db.OpenRecordset("SELECT * FROM tblErrorLog")
  If Err.Number <> 0 Then
```

```
        'Put code here to create tblErrorLog
    End If

    rs.AddNew
    rs![TimeStamp] = Now()
    rs![Number] = iNumber
    rs![Description] = sDesc
    rs.Update
    rs.Close
End Sub
```

The `LogError` sub in Listing 9.5 does not capture the situation that occurs if `tblErrorLog` cannot be created. In fact, if errors occur as the code tries to assign values to the fields in `tblLogError`, processing falls through to succeeding statements until a successful statement is executed. In most cases, this means execution will end up in an unpredictable location. It also means subsequent errors are not properly trapped. Later, in the section titled "Using `On Error GoTo 0`," you'll see how to reset the error handler to disable this undesirable side effect of `Resume Next`.

Resume

The simplest way to leave an error handler is with the `Resume` statement. `Resume` by itself simply redirects program flow back to the statement that generated the error. `Resume` assumes that the error handler repairs the error condition. If the error condition is not corrected, every time the line causing the error is executed the error reoccurs, triggering the `Resume` statement, causing the cycle to repeat itself an infinite number of times.

Listing 9.6 shows how the `Resume` statement fits into a robust error handler.

Listing 9.6. Judicious use of `Resume` simplifies your code.

```
Public Sub ResumeDemo()
On Error GoTo Err_ResumeDemo
    'Statement causing error occurs here:
    Kill "C:\Temp.txt"
Exit_ResumeDemo:
    Exit Sub
Err_ResumeDemo:
    If MsgBox("Error! Try again?", vbYesNo) = vbYes Then
        Resume
    Else
        Resume Exit_ResumeDemo
    End If
End Sub
```

If the `Temp.txt` file cannot be found, processing jumps down to the error handler. A message box pops up with Yes and No buttons on it asking the user whether to try again to delete the file. If the user selects the Yes button (vbYes) processing returns to the Kill statement. The cycle repeats itself until the Temp.txt file becomes available and is deleted or until the user presses the No button on the message box.

Using On Error GoTo 0

Listing 9.7 shows an example of using GoTo 0. The Resume Next statement in this sub simply ignores the Item Not Found In This Collection error that occurs if tblTemp does not exist when the Delete method is run against it. After processing has bypassed the Delete method, the On Error GoTo 0 statement disables further error traps. This means any errors that occur after this statement will be handled by the default VBA error mechanism.

Listing 9.7. Using On Error GoTo 0 to disable error handling.

```
Sub DeleteTable()
  Dim ws As Workspace
  Dim db As Database

  Set ws = DBEngine.Workspaces(0)
  Set db = _
    ws.OpenDatabase(App.Path & "\Products.mdb")

  On Error Resume Next
  db.TableDefs.Delete "tblTemp"
  On Error GoTo 0

  'More code here

End Sub
```

Although in most cases it is not desirable to let Visual Basic handle its own errors, one situation in which you might choose to use On Error GoTo 0 is during the development process. Assume you're working on a complex procedure that has several different failure modes. You're never really sure you're trapping for all possible errors, so you might want to temporarily disable error traps so that you'll be sure to see all errors that occur past the error trap you've prepared. Listing 9.7 shows how this is done.

Handling Errors Locally

Earlier in this chapter, you read that Visual Basic procedures should always handle errors locally. This means that most every Visual Basic procedure should contain the On Error statement as well as some kind of error-handling code. Because error conditions are global throughout the application, it's easy for a procedure to trap an error generated by another procedure. (Recall in the section "Using the `Err` Object," that procedures can read the `Err.Number` and `Err.Description` properties that are triggered by other procedures in the project.) Figure 9.3 illustrates this concept.

FIGURE 9.3.
Untrapped errors are passed up the Visual Basic call stack.

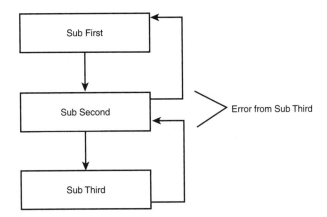

Chapter 8, "Using the Visual Basic Debugging Tools," discussed the Visual Basic call stack. The call stack in a Visual Basic application is the sequence of procedures that have been called by other procedures. In Figure 9.3, `Sub Second` is called by `Sub First`. `Sub Second` calls `Sub Third`. An error has occurred in `Sub Third`. Because `Sub Third` does not contain an error trap and error-handling code, the error condition is passed back up to `Sub Second`. Again, because `Sub Second` does not contain an error handler the error condition is passed up the call stack to `Sub First`. Finally, the error is trapped by `Sub First` and reported by the error handler in `Sub First`. Listing 9.8 contains the code demonstrating this phenomenon. Listing 9.8 is included in `basCallStack` in `Error.vbp`.

Listing 9.8. It is important to trap errors in each procedure in a call stack.

```
Sub First()
On Error GoTo Err_First
  Call Second
Exit_First:
  Exit Sub
Err_First:
  MsgBox Err.Number & " " _
    & Err.Description
  Resume Exit_First
End Sub

Sub Second()
  Call Third
End Sub
```

continues

Listing 9.8. Continued.

```
Sub Third()
  Dim i As Single
  i = 1 / 0
End Sub
```

In a real-world situation, Sub Third might be a routine that retrieves data from the computer's hard disk. Sub Second could be a formatter or display routine that plugs the data onto a Visual Basic form. Sub First is the routine supporting the navigation buttons on the form. Assume a null error occurs in the data retrieval routine. (A null error happens if you try to assign a null value to a variable.) If the error is not handled in the data retrieval routine, it'll be passed back up the call stack until some error handler is able to trap it. In this particular case, the navigation button code might report Invalid Use of Null. Because the navigation buttons have nothing to do with data assignments, you might be confused or mislead by the error message.

In the worst case, you might spend hours debugging code that isn't broken. Visual Basic routines can become lengthy and complicated. Procedures frequently call other procedures that in turn call other procedures. A routine that works well when called from one procedure might fail when called by another. It is important to trap errors as close to the error incident as possible. Try to make the error reporting as specific as possible and include information (such as the procedure name) that makes it easy for you to pinpoint the error incident. Finally, as suggested by the next section of this chapter, it is always a good idea to produce a permanent record of the error event.

Logging Errors

Earlier in this chapter, you read that one technique to determine which errors should be trapped by your application involves setting up simple error trapping, then collecting error information as it occurs. This technique requires an easy and foolproof way to record errors as they occur. Later, you can review the error log to see which errors are not yet handled by the procedures in the application.

One such error logging routine appears in Listing 9.9. The Logger subroutine uses a text file to record the date and time of the error incident as well as the name of the procedure triggering the error and the other error information you've seen earlier in this chapter.

Listing 9.9. A simple error logging routine for your Visual Basic applications.

```
Public Sub Logger(sProcName As String)
  Dim sFName As String

  sFName = App.Path & "\ErrorLog.txt"
```

```
    Open sFName For Append As #1
    Write #1, Now(), sProcName, Err.Number, Err.Description
    Close #1
End Sub
```

Using Logger is easy and requires a single additional line of code in each procedure. The only argument passed into Logger is the name of the procedure making the call. Listing 9.10 shows how Logger is used to trap the record navigation problem described earlier in this chapter (see the cmdNext_Click procedure in Listing 9.4).

Listing 9.10. A more generic approach to handling errors.

```
Private Sub cmdNext_Click()
  On Error GoTo Err_cmdNext_Click
  rs.MoveNext
  Call FillLabels
Exit_cmdNext_Click:
  Exit Sub
Err_cmdNext_Click:
  Call PublicMessenger1
  Call Logger("cmdNext_Click")
  Resume Exit_cmdNext_Click
End Sub
```

The only difference between Listing 9.10 and the cmdNext_Click procedure in Listing 9.4 is the addition of the call to Logger. Listing 9.4 simply calls PublicMessenger without logging the error. Notice in Listing 9.10 that the error must still be handled and the user must be notified of the error through the PublicMessenger procedure. All Logger does is record the error in the ErrorLog.txt file for examination at a later time.

Listing 9.5 shows how to log errors to a database file. Although creating and maintaining a database table is considerably more work you'll find a database table provides more information than a simple text file. In a large application where dozens or even hundreds of error incidents are logged each day you could search and sort the database log table using standard database techniques. It's also easy to count incidents and perform other statistical calculations on the data in a database table. Chapter 18 explains how to create and use database tables with Visual Basic.

Summary

This chapter has explored several techniques to debug the Visual Basic code in your applications and to handle runtime errors. Visual Basic provides several statements and different constructs that enable you to build virtually bulletproof applications. Trapping and handling runtimes does not require extensive changes to the basic code in an application.

You are rewarded for time spent mastering the Visual Basic debugging tools by reduced and more effective development time. Your users will appreciate your efforts to trap and handle runtime errors to prevent data loss and downtime on their desktops.

PART II

Object-Oriented Programming

Creating Objects and Classes

Visual Basic provides a comfortable, gradual transition from procedural to event-driven programming. Although an event is required to invoke a response from the Visual Basic application, after processing has entered the event's subroutine the code is processed by the VBA engine in a procedural fashion. Events help keep Visual Basic code modularized; the code attached to an event is invoked only when the event is triggered. In other words, the event procedure is a modular component attached to the event.

Surely, you've noticed how Visual Basic is *object based*. Almost everything in a Visual Basic application is some kind of object. All the forms, controls, and other visible parts of your programs are objects. In addition to these familiar objects, there are *hidden objects* lurking within the computer memory occupied by your program. These objects are another way that Visual Basic is modular in nature. Each built-in object, such as a form or control, is a modular component that performs some task within the application.

Visual Basic is often criticized for not being truly object-oriented in the sense that programming languages such as Visual C++ are. With the emphasis on modularization and code reuse, so say the critics, Visual Basic does not provide the tools required to write strong, object-oriented applications that exhibit all the desirable benefits of object-oriented programming.

Rather than getting into a long and senseless defense of Visual Basic's implementation of object-oriented principles, let us instead examine what it means to work with objects and examine how Visual Basic approaches object-oriented programming.

This chapter concerns itself with the important topic of objects. Here you will learn what objects are and how to use them in your programs. You'll also learn how to build your own objects using VBA code. This chapter emphasizes the technology of creating and using custom objects in your Visual Basic applications. In this chapter, you learn the general technology and techniques for using the built-in Visual Basic 6.0 objects and creating new objects. Chapter 11, "Advanced Class Concepts," continues the discussion of class modules and object-oriented programming by enhancing the class module built in this chapter. Finally, Chapter 12, "Working with Objects and Collections," discusses how to use aggregates of objects called collections.

Understanding the Benefits of Object-Oriented Development

Why even bother with objects? Why not just accept the fact that Visual Basic comes with a fixed set of items that can be added to an application? Following this line of reasoning, a form is just a rectangle on the screen and you work with it by setting its properties and programming it with Visual Basic code. Why complicate things by introducing the complexity of building and maintaining custom objects when the old procedural programming techniques have worked so well?

You've already seen how Visual Basic's object-based programming is a benefit to Windows developers. The built-in Visual Basic objects like forms and controls provide properties that are easily manipulated at design time and as the application runs on the user's computer. Traditional Windows development systems such as Visual C++ require extensive programming to modify even simple properties such as a form's caption or back color.

The greatest advantage of using objects is *encapsulation*, which is the capability to wrap all aspects of functionality and user interface into a single entity. A Visual Basic object enables you abstract complex activities and tasks as a simple, compact object you can use in any Visual Basic or VBA project. An encapsulated object can be much easier to maintain than a traditional module or VBA procedure. Because an object contains all its functionality and appearance as a single entity, there is a single thing to modify or maintain as improvements are made to the program.

Most applications include extensive data validation routines. Depending on the type of data being entered by the user, data validation ranges from a single VBA statement to extensive modules containing dozens or hundreds of lines of code. By using Visual Basic's object-oriented programming features, it's possible to wrap all data validation routines into a single object that can be used by setting its properties and invoking its methods.

Custom objects, therefore, provide a simplified interface to complex operations. When properly designed and implemented, custom objects can be used in virtually any compatible VBA programming system, exposing the same properties and methods you work with when incorporating the objects in your Visual Basic projects.

Understanding the Component Object Model (COM)

All these features and benefits of using objects are wrapped up in what Microsoft calls the Component Object Model (COM). The main objective of the COM philosophy is reusability: Create an object once and use it in many applications. Following the COM principles, applications are constructed from several object components that are bound together with a programming language like Visual Basic.

On the surface, COM is a great idea whose time has come. An accessible and powerful development system such as Visual Basic provides all the tools necessary to construct nonobject-oriented programs and also to create objects from scratch (or from existing code) and bind them together in a COM-type application.

The reality, however, is that most Visual Basic applications are still stick-built, one line of code at a time. In this regard there has been little improvement from the bad old days of the COBOL and C programming languages. On the other hand, more and more Visual Basic developers are creating powerful and useful objects and other components that are easily dropped into new and existing Visual Basic projects. In many cases, these components (class modules, OLE servers, and ActiveX controls, to name three) replace hundreds or thousands of lines of stick-built code.

At the very least, constructing objects in Visual Basic provides you with a single point of maintenance and improvement. Consider the custom data validation object suggested earlier in this chapter. In many businesses, this object would be used in dozens of different applications. Theoretically, at least, those dozens of applications would be easily updated by improving and enhancing the single copy of the object on the network. The next time any one of the applications was used, the newly enhanced control would be in place, ready to use. Because an object can be used in multiple settings, you have the perfect example of *code reuse*. Construct the object one time and use it repeatedly in different programs.

Getting Started with Objects

Our world is filled with objects. The chair you sit on, the car you drive, and the television you watch are all examples of objects. Some objects, like a coffee cup, are relatively simple, while other objects such as a 757 jet airliner are more complex.

In addition to physical objects, our world is filled with objects that can't be felt or touched. Light, sound, and radio waves are all examples of objects that can be produced, measured, and used by people but aren't experienced as physical entities. An object's visible characteristics have little to do with its value to people. An invisible radio wave carrying an important message can be as valuable as the jet airliner whisking you away to a vacation destination.

You'll find any number of visible and invisible objects in most Visual Basic projects. As with the objects that make up our environment, the invisible objects in a Visual Basic project can be as valuable as the forms, menus, and toolbars the user sees.

A Visual Basic object is a programmable entity of one sort or another. So far in this book, the expression *object* has referred to just about every aspect of Visual Basic programs. Back in Chapter 9, "Handling Runtime Errors," you learned about the special Err object that helps you determine which of the several hundred runtime errors possible in a Visual Basic application has been triggered. The `Err` object is an example of an invisible, but valuable, object built into Visual Basic 6.0.

Examining Objects

Although there is an endless variety of objects, all objects share several common features. You read earlier that an object is a programmable entity. This means that most objects contain many properties that can be read or set at runtime. In addition, most objects include methods that can be run to perform tasks.

> **Note:** Recall from discussions in earlier chapters that a property is an attribute that describes an object and a method is an action that can be performed by an object.

The fact that most objects are programmable means that objects can be written to adapt to changing environments and user requirements. Object programmability is usually implemented by changing the object's properties and running its methods. However, a custom object can be engineered in such a way that the object automatically adapts to differing conditions by running different internal routines.

Most object types can be created multiple times within an application. This means that a single Visual Basic program can host more than one instance of the object. Each object can operate independently of the others (possibly even cooperating with the other objects) and maintain its own set of properties and other data.

Using Objects in Applications

You've already seen many examples of objects in this book. Every time you've seen code setting a label's `Caption` property to a value or returning the contents of a text box's `Text` property, you've seen component objects at work. Although it's true that a Label or Text Box control is a very simple type of object, the principles of using these simple objects are the same as using more complex and more intelligent objects you create yourself.

One popular expression describes an object as a *provider* of services or functionality. The program using the object can be considered a *consumer* of the object's services. In most cases, the interface (that is, the properties and methods) to the object's services is the same regardless of where the object is used. It's possible that some programs will ignore an object's certain properties and methods whereas other programs will make full use of all an object's features.

The following series of statements is typical of how objects are used in Visual Basic applications:

```
Dim obj As ObjectClass
```

```
Set obj = New ObjectClass
obj.Property = SomeValue
obj.Method
```

In this code fragment, the name of the object is `obj` and its object class (described in the next section) is `ObjectClass`. The object is declared in the `Dim` statement and is *instantiated* (created) by the `New` keyword. The last two statements assign a value to a property of the object and run a method of the object.

Understanding Classes

Objects don't just happen. There must be a template for Visual Basic to use when creating an object. An object's class defines the object and serves as the template or blueprint for all the objects created from that class.

A Visual Basic class is a special type of code module. Visual Basic recognizes the module as an object's definition and lets you create new instances of the object from the code in the module. Any of the object's special features, including properties, methods, and events, are handled by the code in the class module.

An object is an instance of an object class. As an example, the Mercury Marquis is a particular class of automobile. The Mercury Marquis owned by your Aunt Millie is a particular instance of the Mercury Marquis class of automobile. Although Aunt Millie's car looks much like every other Mercury Marquis, certain attributes of her car set it apart from all the other Mercury Marquis's on the road.

Carrying the car analogy a bit further, consider the properties and methods of the automobile object class. A car has a color property that defines the color of the paint applied to the exterior of the car. It is likely that the color of any car matches the color applied to several other cars produced by the car's manufacturer. A car also has a vehicle identification number (VIN) that is not shared with any other car anywhere on earth.

An object's property values, therefore, are a combination of values shared with other objects of the same class and values that are unique to the particular instance of the class.

If you were to construct a car class module in Visual Basic, you'd include properties such as `Color` (a string), `VIN` (a string), `NumberOfDoors` (an integer), `TypeOfRadio` (probably a string), and `Convertible` (a Boolean value). Depending on how the car object is to be used in the application, you might add additional properties to contain the license number, the owner information, mileage, and other data relevant to the application.

The point is that, because you are constructing the class in VBA code, you can add any properties necessary to support the application you are constructing. When you build Visual Basic classes, you have access to all the power and utility available through the Visual Basic data types and features.

Within a class module, properties are handled by variables internally managed by the module's code. As you'll see later in this chapter, the mechanism for implementing properties is part of the special qualities of class modules. Certain rules and coding conventions must be followed to successfully implement properties in Visual Basic class modules.

In addition to properties, most objects support several methods, the actions performed by the class to implement tasks associated with the class. An automobile has several rather obvious methods: go, stop, turn, and park, among others. The classes you construct in Visual Basic will implement whatever functionality you want the objects created from the class to support.

The methods of the custom objects you create with Visual Basic exist as public procedures (functions and subroutines) within the class module. As with properties, you have the full power and flexibility of Visual Basic at your disposal as you write the methods of your custom classes.

Creating a Simple Class

Usually, the classes in your applications will model some real-world object. Examples are customers, patients, inventory items, and employees. Your knowledge and understanding of the physical object will be translated directly into VBA code and will become the properties and methods of the Visual Basic objects created from the class module's code.

This chapter's project (Objects.vbp) implements a car class similar to the one described in the preceding sections. The car class module (clsCar1) in Objects.vbp includes the properties and methods listed in Tables 10.1 and 10.2, respectively.

Table 10.1. Properties of the car class.

Name	Data Type	Purpose
Make	String	The car's manufacturer
Color	String	The car's exterior color
Model	String	The model of the car
Year	String	The year the car was built
Speed	Integer	How fast the car is moving
Clean	Boolean	Whether the car has been cleaned recently

Table 10.2. Methods of the car class.

Name	Purpose
Accelerate	Make the car go faster
Decelerate	Slow the car down
Stop	Halt the car
Wash	Wash the car (makes the car clean)

The car class object in Objects.vbp is not meant to completely model a real vehicle. There are many other properties and methods that could be added to this class to more effectively model a real automobile, but this simple class does show how you approach modeling a physical object in Visual Basic.

The car created from the class might be described as follows:

> The car has been produced during a certain model year (indicated by the Year property) by a certain car manufacturer (the car's Make) and is painted a certain color (the Color property). Driving the car makes it dirty (indicated when the Clean property is False). From time to time the car should be washed (with its Wash method, which sets the Clean). Accelerating the car (by invoking its Accelerate method) increases its velocity (the Speed property) while decelerating the car (through its Decelerate method) decreases its speed. The car can also be stopped (with its Stop method) to bring the car's speed to zero.

Each of these behaviors and actions (accelerate, decelerate, wash) is supported through a corresponding method (Accelerate, Decelerate, and Wash, respectively). It is not required that the method's name matches the action provided by the method, but it makes sense to add this symmetry to your object classes.

Beginning the Class Module

We've already completed the first step of building the car class module. Tables 10.1 and 10.2 list the properties and methods to be implemented in the class module. Select Project, Add Class Module to open the new class module in the Code window and provide a name for the module in the Visual Basic Property window (see Figure 10.1).

The name of the module is the name given to the class and is how Visual Basic identifies the objects created from the class. The name you provide for the class modules is similar to the names you've given other objects in your projects. Appendix B, "The Reddick VBA Naming Convention," contains a complete description of a valuable naming convention you might consider using when creating objects in your applications.

The name you assign to your class module should be descriptive but not excessively long. Furthermore, the name should be meaningful to you, the developer. Your users never see the name of the class, so use a name that means something to you.

FIGURE 10.1.

The name you provide for the class module is used for the object type supported by the module.

Class module icon

Class module name

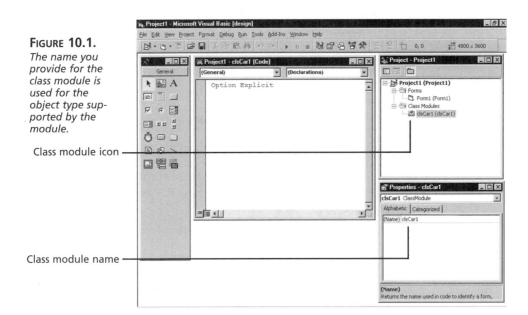

The class module itself is seen in the Code Editor window in Figure 10.1. Notice that the Property window identifies the module as a `ClassModule` type of object. The module itself looks like any other module in the Editor window. Visual Basic treats the class module as a special type of module, as you'll see in several places later in this chapter.

Adding Properties to the Class

Most objects include properties that describe the object. The car class includes five properties that define the car object created from the class: `Make`, `Color`, `Year`, `Speed`, and `Clean`. Each of these properties tells you something about the object created from the car class of objects.

The easiest way to establish the properties of a class, and the technique we'll use in our first class example, is to simply declare each of the properties as a public variable within the `clsCar1` class module (see Listing 10.1). Locating a public variable within a class module makes the variable into a property of the class while its public scope makes it accessible to other routines within the project. Later in this chapter, in the section named "Using Property Procedures," you'll see an alternative way to create properties for your class modules.

Listing 10.1. The `clsCar1` class properties are implemented as public variables within the class module.

```
Public Make As String
Public Year As String
Public Color As String
```

```
Public Speed As Integer
Public Clean As Boolean
```

Each public variable within a class module is treated as a property of the objects created from the class. Because the public variables are declared within a class module, Visual Basic uses the variables as properties of the class's objects without further work on your part. Figure 10.2 shows how Visual Basic's Intellisense displays the properties in the AutoList Members drop-down list in a module using an object created from the class.

FIGURE 10.2.
Visual Basic's Intellisense shows you the properties and methods you've created for the new object class.

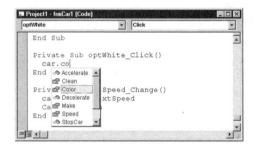

The Intellisense list in Figure 10.2 shows the properties and methods that have been created for the clsCar1 object class. The names you provide for an object's properties and methods should be descriptive and easy to recognize. Because the class's properties are actually variables within the class module, the names you assign to these items must conform to Visual Basic's variable naming requirements. That is, property names should be 64 or fewer characters and contain only alphanumeric characters and the underscore character. Property names must begin with an alphabetic character and should never begin with the underscore character or a number.

Creating Methods for the Class

The clsCar1 class includes several methods. These methods, like all object methods, provide the actions supported by the objects created from the class. Each method of an object's class is nothing more than a public procedure in the object's class module.

Listing 10.2 shows the procedure implementing the car object's Wash method. Because all procedures in a class module are public by default, the Public keyword is optional and is added to the Wash method to clarify the status of the procedure.

Listing 10.2. The procedure supporting the Wash method of the car class.

```
Public Sub Wash()
  Clean = True
End Sub
```

Notice that there is nothing special about the Wash method's procedure. There is no special declaration for this procedure, nor is there reference to its status as a method of the class. Methods are an example of how Visual Basic treats class modules differently than simple code modules. As long as the procedure (sub or function) is declared with the Public keyword, Visual Basic treats it as a method of the objects created from the class module.

Because it is a subroutine, the Wash method does not return a value, although it could have been declared as a function, if necessary. As a function, it could return any valid Visual Basic data type. The Wash procedure also does not require any arguments, although arguments could be provided if the method supported by the procedure required them.

The Wash procedure operates as any other subroutine in a Visual Basic application. In this case, the Wash procedure sets the Clean public variable to True. Later, when the value of the Clean variable is retrieved as a property of the class's object, the Clean value is returned to the class's consumer.

A class's methods can be simple, as in the case of Clean, or a bit more complex as the Accelerate method, shown in Listing 10.3. Accelerate uses an If..End If conditional to check whether the car's speed exceeds its maximum permitted value. If the increase in the Speed variable means the car is traveling more than 150 miles an hour, Accelerate sets Speed to 150. In this way, Accelerate enforces a fixed top speed for the car object.

Listing 10.3. The Accelerate method makes sure the car does not exceed the maximum speed.

```
Public Sub Accelerate()
  Speed = Speed + 10
  If Speed > 150 Then
    Speed = 150
  End If
End Sub
```

Obviously, much more could be added to the car class. The section titled "Enhancing the Simple Class," in Chapter 11 shows a few changes that can be made to clsCar1 to make it more effective as a model of a car's behavior.

Eventually, with enough work and attention to detail, the car class could be refined to the point where it virtually duplicates a real automobile. Other classes could model other physical objects such as airplanes, manufacturing equipment, and lawnmowers. In fact, most video games utilize just this kind of object-oriented programming technique to model spaceships, karate fighters, and army tanks. The objects created from Visual Basic class modules in your computer's memory needn't have ever existed in reality. The computer's virtual reality is real enough for an object made of electronic pulses inside your computer's memory.

Using the Class Module

After the class module has been assembled, new objects can be created from the class in any VBA module. Figure 10.3 shows frmCar1, a form included in Objects.vbp, the project accompanying this chapter. The controls along the left side of this form display the object's properties, whereas the buttons to the right side of this form invoke the object's methods.

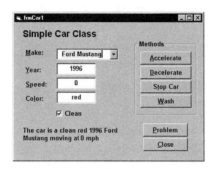

The code behind frmCar1 is quite simple. After all, simplicity is one of the basic concepts behind using objects. If using objects in an application were as difficult as using the equivalent traditional procedures, there'd be no reason to resort to object-oriented programming in the first place.

Creating a new car object requires the use of the New keyword. The following statement creates a new instance of a car object at the same time the object is declared:

```
Private Car As New clsCar1
```

Alternatively, the car object can be declared and then instantiated as separate statements. For example, the following statement, placed in the form module's Declarations section, establishes the initial clsCar1 object:

```
Private Car As clsCar1
```

Later, perhaps in the form's Load event procedure, the car object is actually instantiated:

```
Set Car = New Car
```

In either case, the new car instance is created at the instant the New keyword is executed. The code behind frmCar1 actually declares the car object as mCar to emphasize its module-level scope:

```
Private mCar As New clsCar1
```

In frmCar1 the car object is instantiated as soon as the form is loaded into memory. Therefore, the car object is available as the form's Load event runs and its initial properties are set at that time.

After the car is created, its properties and methods can be referenced. References to the car object's properties are similar to property references anywhere else in VBA. The following statement retrieves the current value of the car's Speed property and assigns it to the text box named txtSpeed on frmCar1:

```
txtSpeed.Text = car.Speed
```

The frmCar1 form makes several property assignments from the form's Load event procedure. Listing 10.4 shows the entire Form_Load sub from frmCar1.

Listing 10.4. The Form_Load event procedure from frmCar1.

```
Private Sub Form_Load()
  With mCar
    .Make = "Ford Mustang"
    .Color = "red"
    .Year = "1996"
    .Speed = 0
    .Clean = True
  End With
  Call FillForm
End Sub
```

Similarly, you increase the car's speed by invoking the car's Accelerate method. The four buttons on frmCar1 that invoke the Accelerate, Decelerate, StopCar, and Wash methods of the car object are members of a control array named cmdMethods. Clicking any of these buttons triggers a Click event on the cmdMethods control array. Which button is clicked is indicated by the Index parameter of the cmdMethods_Click event procedure, as shown in Listing 10.5.

Listing 10.5. The cmdMethods control array runs each of the car object's methods.

```
Private Sub cmdMethods_Click(Index As Integer)
  Select Case Index
    Case 1: car.Accelerate
    Case 2: car.Decelerate
    Case 3: car.StopCar
    Case 4: car.Wash
  End Select
  Call FillForm
End Sub
```

As the car's speed is increased with the Accelerate method, the new speed is plugged into txtSpeed on the form. In a similar fashion, the Decelerate button calls the car's

Decelerate method to decrease the car's Speed property. The Decelerate method (see Listing 10.6) makes sure the car's speed never drops below zero.

Listing 10.6. The cmdMethods control array runs each of the car object's methods.

```
Public Sub Decelerate()
  Speed = Speed - 10
  If Speed < 0 Then
    Speed = 0
  End If
End Sub
```

In Chapter 11 we'll revisit the car class in the section "Enhancing the Simple Class" and make a few changes that enhance the car object's capabilities, resulting in a more interesting example to work with.

Using Property Procedures

The car class module works pretty well. It performs several essential tasks required of any car object. The class module itself is simple enough that new properties and methods can be added at any time without complicating the car object's features. The new properties and methods can be referenced from the car form as enhancements to the application's capabilities.

However, one major problem exists in the clsCar1 module. You might have noticed the button labeled Problem in the lower-right corner of the form, just above the Close button. Clicking the Problem button assigns the values you see in Table 10.3 to the car's properties.

Table 10.3. Invalid property assignments.

Property	New Value
Make	Fiat 850
Color	Orange
Year	1971
Speed	900
Clean	False

The Click event procedure for the Problem button is shown in Listing 10.7. This code is identical to other code you've seen in this chapter for assigning values to the car object's properties. The only difference is that in Listing 10.7 inappropriate values are being assigned to the car object.

Listing 10.7. The Problem button's `Click` event procedure assigns the new values to the car object's properties.

```
Private Sub cmdProblem_Click()
  With mCar
    .Make = "Fiat 850"
    .Color = "orange"
    .Year = "1971"
    .Speed = 900
    .Clean = False
  End With
  Call FillForm
End Sub
```

The Problem button is provided on `frmCar1` to demonstrate the kind of mischief that can occur when a property is assigned an undesirable value. Because there is no way to manually add bad values to the car object's properties, it is necessary to assign these values through code. Clicking the Problem button creates a dirty orange 1971 Fiat 850 going 900 miles an hour, a very unlikely combination of property values. Although nothing in our application breaks because of the erroneous values, in many class modules inappropriate property assignments can cause runtime errors. For example, consider an inventory control system that does not prevent negative value assignment to quantity or cost properties, or a medical test results program that accepts values that are impossible to observe in a patient (such as a body temperature of 400 degrees).

You needn't use the Problem button to assign bad values to the object's properties. The same effect can be obtained by typing unusual vales into the text boxes on `frmCar1`. Each text box on `frmCar1` updates its corresponding property values using code similar to Listing 10.8. In this case, the text box's `Change` event is used to write the value of the text box into the object's property.

Listing 10.8. The `frmCar1` form uses code like this to assign values to the car object's properties.

```
Private Sub cboMake_Change()
  mCar.Make = cboMake
  Call FillForm
End Sub
```

The `Change` event procedure is needed so that the person using the form can make changes to the car's properties. In fact, because the `Change` event is used here, the description of the car in the label near the bottom of the form changes dynamically as the user types new information into the text boxes on the form.

The problem here is that the class module has no control over what values are assigned to its properties. Therefore, extreme values such as 900 (or –900) can be assigned to the

Speed property without generating an error. Although the Accelerate and Decelerate methods check for and correct extreme Speed values, there is no way for the clsCar1 class module to prevent the assignment in the first place.

When using public variables as properties of a class, the *consumer* of the class's features must make sure that invalid values are not assigned to the object's properties. This requirement violates the concept of encapsulation—that is, all the object's intelligence and functionality is wrapped up within the object. The consumer should not be required to validate property values.

Visual Basic provides a way to control property assignment. The special *property procedures* you can add to class modules provide you with a way to validate property values before the assignment is made and stored within the class. Furthermore, you can use property procedures to make certain properties read-only and to provide a default value when the candidate value for a property is inappropriate. You can also use property procedures to restrict property values to a limited selection of values if you want.

Understanding Property Procedure Types

A property procedure is a procedure within the class module that includes the code necessary to perform whatever actions (such as validation, bounds checking, and so on) are necessary when setting, changing, or retrieving a property's value. Property procedures are the primary way a class module protects the properties managed by the class module.

The Visual Basic 6.0 property procedures include the following:

- Property Get retrieves the value of a property and makes it available within the class's consumer.
- Property Let sets the value of a property.
- Property Set sets the value of an object type of property.

The general syntax of a property procedure is simple. For example, the following syntax shows how a Property Let works:

```
Property Let PropertyName(PropertyValue)
  'Validate PropertyValue here
  PrivateVariable = PropertyValue
End Property
```

Property procedures do more than validate the value passed into the class module as the property's new value. Previously, you saw properties stored within the class module as public variables. When using property procedures, in most cases the property is stored as a private variable within the class module. For example, the declarations in Listing 10.9 appear in clsCar2, a class module in the Objects.vbp project.

Listing 10.9. The internal storage variables in `clsCar2`.

```
Private mstrMake As String
Private mstrYear As String
Private mintSpeed As Integer
Private mstrColor As String
Private mboolClean As Boolean
```

Notice that all the variables in Listing 10.9 are private to the class module. This means that these variables are not accessible outside the class module. The only way to modify or retrieve the values of these variables is through the property procedures introduced earlier in this section.

The `Property Let` for the `Color` property is shown in Listing 10.10. Notice that all it does is take the incoming color passed as the `strColor` argument and assign it to the private `mstrColor` variable.

Listing 10.10. A `Property Let` for the `Color` property.

```
Property Let Color(strColor)
   mstrColor = strColor
End Property
```

The `Property Get` procedure for the `Color` property (see Listing 10.11) is similar to the corresponding `Property Let`. In this case, the `Property Get` returns the value of the private `mstrColor` variable. Because `mstrColor` is private to the class module, the only way for a procedure outside the class module to obtain the value of `mstrColor` is through the `Property Get` procedure.

Listing 10.11. This `Property Get` returns the value of the private `mstrColor` variable.

```
Property Get Color() As String
   Color = mstrColor
End Property
```

`Property Let` (assigning a property value) and `Property Get` (retrieving the value of a property) normally appear in pairs in a class module. Either can be omitted to endow the property with special characteristics. For example, a `Property Get` without a matching `Property Let` means the property can be retrieved but not set or changed to a different value. In other words, such a property is read-only. (Read-only properties are discussed in the section titled "Creating a Read-Only Property" in Chapter 11.) In this case, the property's private value is either set as the class module is initialized or through a constant within the module.

The arguments of a `Property Let` and its matching `Property Get` must match. Listing 10.12 shows the property procedures for the `Make` property of a class module similar to `clsCar1`.

Listing 10.12. Property procedure arguments must match.

```
Property Let Make(strMake As String)
  mstrMake = strMake
End Property

Property Get Make() As String
  Make = mstrMake
End Property
```

Notice that the incoming value of the `Property Let Make` procedure is a string as is the value returned by the `Property Get Make` procedure. It would be an error to set a property as a string value, for example, and retrieve it as a floating-point value.

Bulletproofing Property Procedures

In many cases, assigning an invalid value to a property results in a runtime error or other bug. If you're lucky, the invalid value will cause the application to halt and display an error dialog box to the user. Such a message is preferable to having the application continue operating as if nothing is wrong when in fact the class module is working with invalid data. The best situation is when the class module itself validates property values as they are assigned, rather than waiting until the properties are used in the application.

For example, consider a banking application that calculates exchange rates for foreign currency deposited in the bank's vault. A class module is the ideal vehicle for handling foreign currency exchange calculations. Keeping these calculations within a class module isolates these complicated routines from the rest of the application and makes it easy to maintain the calculations as currency values fluctuate.

Ideally, the class module would not accept invalid exchange ratios or would check the exchange ratios input by the user at runtime. Perhaps the class module could check online sources such as the *Wall Street Journal* or other financial publications to verify that the data input by the user is correct.

In simpler class modules, property errors might occur if a string is passed when a numeric value is required or when a property value is less than zero. The following methods will help bulletproof properties and help you avoid runtime errors:

- Set default property values if inappropriate data type is passed. Use conversion routines.
- Use private procedures within the class module to validate data types. These data validation routines can be class module-specific.

- Use error trapping everywhere in the class module, especially on the class's properties and methods. The property procedures and methods (the public procedures within the class) are where most unexpected behaviors occur.

Keep in mind that a basic principle of using object-oriented programming is encapsulating functionality. Whenever possible anything that affects how the class operates should be included within the class module. Keeping the property validation, method error handling, and other features within the class module makes the class more portable and reusable.

Summary

This chapter has taken on the important topic of creating and using object classes. Visual Basic's object-oriented features are a powerful way to encapsulate functionality, enabling you to design modular applications that are easy to create and maintain. Breaking complex features into discrete objects is a powerful way to incrementally build applications from a series of components, each of which performs a single job within the application.

Chapter 11 continues the discussion of objects and classes. In it you learn how best to take advantage of the classes you build for your applications. You'll see how to define default properties and methods and how to add read-only and write-only properties to Visual Basic classes.

Advanced Class Concepts

Chapter 10 introduced you to the basics of object-oriented programming with Visual Basic 6. You learned how to create object classes, add properties and methods to the class, and how to create objects from the class modules you've created. This chapter extends the discussion begun in Chapter 10 by enhancing the class modules you created in that chapter, adding new functionality, and making the class modules more robust and trouble-free.

Many important object-oriented topics were mentioned in passing in Chapter 10. It is now time to drill into those topics in more detail, filling in your expanding knowledge and understanding of object-oriented programming in Visual Basic 6.

Understanding Initialize and Terminate

So far, we've been treating the class module as though it were no different than a standard code module. The fact is, however, that as soon as you tell Visual Basic that you intend to use the module to define a new class of objects, Visual Basic adds a few special features to the module.

Among these features are the `Class_Initialize` and `Class_Terminate` event procedures. These two procedures, which are analogous to the `Initialize` and `Terminate` events behind all Visual Basic forms, are the perfect place to put operations that must be performed as the class's objects are created and destroyed. Listing 11.1 shows a generic class module that contains code in the `Class_Initialize` and `Class_Terminate` event procedures.

Listing 11.1. An entire generic class module.

```
Private mstrName As String
Private mstrColor As String

Property Get Name() As String
  MsgBox "Reading the Name property"
  Name = mstrName
End Property

Property Get Color() As String
  MsgBox "Reading the Color property"
  Color = mstrColor
End Property

Private Sub Class_Initialize()
  'Perform initialization operations here.
  MsgBox "Now in Class_Initialize"
  mstrName = "Bobby"
  mstrColor = "Red"
End Sub

Private Sub Class_Terminate()
  'Perform clean up operations here.
  MsgBox "Now in Class_Terminate"
End Sub
```

Looking at `Class_Initialize`

The `Class_Initialize` event fires as soon as an object created from the class is referenced. Examples of `Class_Initialize` operations include the following:

- Setting class properties to default values.
- Logging onto a data source such as a SQL database back end.
- Displaying a login dialog box.
- Performing environment checks such as verifying free disk space, retrieving the computer's video system parameters (screen resolution, color depth, and so on).
- Setting temporary variables to their initial values.

The `Class_Terminate` event is the opposite of `Class_Initialize`. `Class_Terminate` fires the moment an object variable created by the class goes out of scope or is set to `Nothing`. Setting an object variable to the special `Nothing` value removes all traces of the object from memory. Here are a few examples of the operations you might perform in a `Class_Terminate` event procedure:

- Logging off of a remote database server
- Closing open files

- Releasing local variables used within the class module
- Informing the user that the resources provided by the class module's object are no longer available

Using Class_Terminate

Use Class_Terminate to perform any cleanup that might otherwise lead to errors or other problems. All disk files that are opened in a Visual Basic application, for example, must be explicitly closed. Otherwise, you might encounter lost chain errors on the computer's hard disk that must be corrected with Windows Scandisk or another disk utility.

The Objects.vbp project on this book's disk includes frmGeneric, shown in Figure 11.1. This form includes the code you see in Listing 11.2, which simply creates an object named objGeneric, reads the properties set in the object's Class_Initialize event procedure, and then destroys the object by setting it to Nothing.

FIGURE 11.1.

The frmGeneric *form contains the code shown in Listing 11.2.*

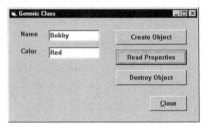

Listing 11.2. The code behind frmGeneric.

```
Dim objGeneric As clsGeneric

Private Sub cmdCreateObject_Click()
  Set objGeneric = New clsGeneric
End Sub

Private Sub cmdReadProperties_Click()
  txtName = objGeneric.Name
  txtColor = objGeneric.Color
End Sub

Private Sub cmdDestroyObject_Click()
  Set objGeneric = Nothing
End Sub
```

Looking at the code behind frmGeneric, you see how the simple object defined by clsGeneric works. The object itself (objGeneric) is a module-level variable declared at the top of the form's module. The objGeneric object is actually created when the object is instantiated in the cmdCreateObject_Click event procedure. At that moment, the

`Class_Initialize` event procedure in the class module runs and you see the message box opened in this event procedure pop up on the screen (see Figure 11.2).

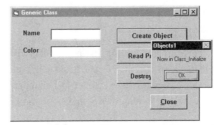

Figure 11.2.
This message box tells you the `Class_Initialize` *event is running.*

At the same time, the object's two properties (`Name` and `Color`) are initialized to `"Bobby"` and `"Red"`, respectively.

Clicking the Read Properties button assigns the `Name` and `Color` properties from `objGeneric` to `txtName` and `txtColor` on `frmGeneric`.

Later, when you click the Destroy Object button, the message box you see in Figure 11.3 appears, telling you that the `Class_Terminate` event procedure is running. The `objGeneric` object is destroyed by the following statement in the code behind `frmGeneric`:

```
Set objGeneric = Nothing
```

The `Nothing` keyword notifies Visual Basic that you are finished with the object and you want to release the memory occupied by the object and its class module. As soon as the `Nothing` statement is executed, you can no longer reference the object or its properties. Visual Basic automatically runs the `Class_Terminate` event as the object is destroyed.

Testing for Existing Class Objects

The code you've seen in this section leads to a potential problem. Notice that the `cmd_CreateObject` button simply creates a new object without regard to prior settings. What happens if `objGeneric` already exists when the `Set objGeneric = New clsGeneric` statement is executed? It turns out that an error is not generated in response to this situation, but the existing object is destroyed at the same time the new object is created. That means that all the properties and other work done by the previous instance of the object are lost as the object is destroyed.

It is easy to test whether an instance of the object currently exists in the application. Listing 11.3 shows how you can use the `Nothing` value to determine whether `objGeneric` is set to an actual value. We really don't care what the value is as long as it's not `Nothing`. Then, depending on whether the user clicked the Yes or No button in the message box, either a new object is created or nothing is done and the existing object remains in memory.

Listing 11.3. Checking to see whether an object already exists.

```
If objGeneric Is Nothing Then
  Set objGeneric = New clsGeneric
Else
  If MsgBox("objGeneric exists. Kill it?", _
      vbYesNo) = vbYes Then
    Set objGeneric = Nothing
    Set objGeneric = New clsGeneric
  Else
    'Do nothing
  End If
End If
```

Creating Special Types of Properties

Not all properties are created equally. So far the class properties we've looked at have been fully accessible as the program executes. You are able to read and write these properties at any time. This section discusses several other types of properties and methods, specifically, properties are read-only or write-only. For example, it doesn't make sense to try to set the model year of a car object. The year a car was built is a fixed value and there's no need to make it a property that can be changed by the application.

Creating a Read-Only Property

In Chapter 10, you saw how you make a property available for reading by writing a Property Get procedure. A Property Let procedure performs the opposite action—that is, a Property Let assigns a new value to a property. By simply omitting the Property Let, you make a property read-only because there is no way for the class's consumer to set the value of the property without a Property Let.

You've seen several examples of read-only properties in several listings in this chapter. In Listing 11.4, both the Name and Color properties in clsGeneric are read-only. Without a Property Let procedure neither of these properties can be changed at runtime.

Listing 11.4. Omitting the Property Let makes a property read-only.

```
Private mstrColor As String
Private Const pconSize = "Large"

Property Get Color() As String
  Color = mstrColor
End Property
```

continues

Listing 11.4. Continued.

```
Property Get Size() As String
  Size = mconSize
End Property

Private Sub Class_Initialize()
  mstrColor = "Red"
End Sub
```

In most cases, the read-only property's value is set by the class module's during the `Class_Initialize` procedure (as in Listing 11.1), or is stored as a private scope constant within the class module. Listing 11.4 shows these two ways to establish a read-only property. Notice that the `Property Get` for the `Size` property simply returns the value of the `mconSize` constant. Because `mconSize` is private to the class module, there is no other way for another routine in this application to access this value.

The advantage of using a private constant to specify the value of a read-only property is that, like all constants, there is only one place in the module you need to look for the property's value. Keeping the constant declarations near the top of the module greatly simplifies maintenance on the read-only properties in the class module.

You might need to use a private variable to store a read-only property value because the module doesn't know in advance what the value of the property will be. An example is the number of customer records to be printed by the class or the name of a data file to be opened. In such cases, the `Class_Initialize` event procedure determines the value of the property and sets it. The `Property Get` then returns the property value as needed.

Setting Up Write-Only Properties

In a fashion completely analogous to read-only properties, a write-only property is created by providing the `Property Let` procedure without a parallel `Property Get`. You might think it's strange that you'd have a `Property Let` to set a value without being able to read it back out of the class module.

Consider for a moment a data acquisition class. This class module will need the name of the database file, the user's name, and his password. Normally, these properties are provided on a write-only basis. After the database name, the username, and password are provided, the class module has everything it needs to open the data source and begin reading data. Normally there'd be no need to go back and read the values of these properties after they've been set. In fact, making these properties available for reading might actually violate data security in the application.

Setting Up a Default Property or Method

Many classes have some property that is designated as the class's default. In most cases, the default property of an object is the property that is most often modified at runtime.

The default property of a text box object, for example, is its Text property while the default property of a label object is its Caption, and so on.

A class can have a default method instead of a default property. (You cannot create a class that has both a default property and a default method, however.) A default method, obviously, is the most-frequently used public procedure within the class.

Using a default property or method simplifies the code required to reference the objects created from the class. The following two statements perform exactly the same task, changing the Text property of a text box control named txtLastName:

```
txtLastName.Text = "Jones"
txtLastName = "Jones"
```

The second statement assumes the default Name property is to be changed by the assignment.

Your classes can support default properties and methods the same way. You simply change the attributes of a procedure within the class module to specify it as the class's default. After a default procedure has been designated, you can omit the corresponding property or method's name when invoking its procedure.

To specify a property or method procedure as the class's default, first open the module in the editor window. Next open the Tools, Procedure Attributes dialog box (see Figure 11.3) and select the procedure's name from the drop-down list at the top of the dialog box. Then open the Procedure ID drop-down list and select (Default) from the entries on this list.

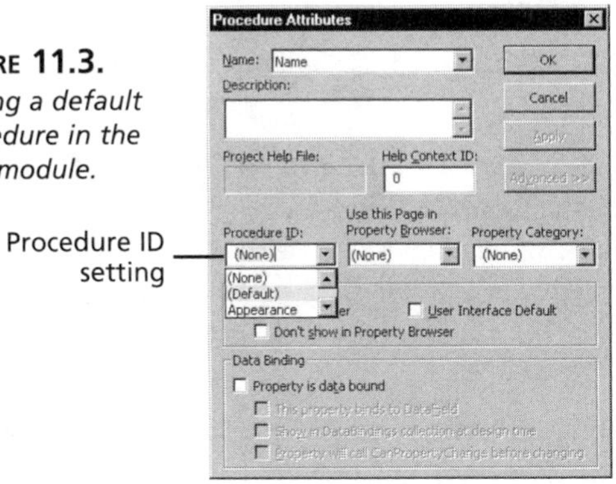

FIGURE 11.3.

Setting a default procedure in the class module.

Procedure ID setting

Figure 11.3 shows how to set the Name property of clsGeneric as the default for the class. Making this change simplifies references to the object's Name property:

```
Dim objGeneric As clsGeneric
Set objGeneric = New clsGeneric
objGeneric = "Bobby"
txtName = objGeneric
```

You may choose not to use defaults in your classes. Because references to the default property or method are simplified there is a chance you or another developer might misinterpret a statement that makes an assignment to the default property or invokes the default method of a class.

Enhancing the Simple Class

The clsCar1 class built in Chapter 10 features several properties and methods that support obvious behaviors of most automobiles. In many ways, however, the car objects created from this class do not reflect the behavior of a real car. For example, most cars experience mechanical failure if the engine's maximum speed is maintained for very long. Additionally, cars tend to get dirty and must be washed from time to time.

Most importantly, though, is that the consumer of the clsCar1 class must be careful of some of the car's properties. For example, the only way the car gets dirty is if the consumer (frmCars1) sets the Clean property to False. Similarly, the make, year, and color must be specified on frmCar1 and can be virtually any value. Additionally, as you learned in the section titled "Using Property Procedures" in Chapter 10, the car's speed can be assigned to any integer value without generating an error. It'd be nice to add property procedures to the car class to restrict property values and more closely model the behavior of a real car.

> **Note:** frmCars1 is included in the AdvObjs.vbp project accompanying this chapter. Although this form is not used in this chapter, it and its class module (clsCar1) are included so that you can easily compare the code discussed in Chapter 10 with the advanced discussions in this chapter.

Looking at the Class_Initialize Procedure

The clsCar2 class module includes a private constant and several private variables that are used by the module's procedures. Listing 11.5 shows the constant and variable declarations and the Class_Initialize procedure used to set several variables to their initial values.

Listing 11.5. clsCar2 includes a private constant and several private variables.

```
Private Const pintMaxSpeed = 150

Private mstrMake As String
Private mstrYear As String
Private mstrColor As String
Private mintSpeed As Integer
Private mboolClean As Boolean
```

```
Private mboolEngineOK As Boolean

Private Sub Class_Initialize()
  mboolClean = True
  mboolEngineOK = True
End Sub
```

You'll see how clsCar2 uses the mboolEngineOK Boolean variable later in this chapter in the section titled "Enhancing the Accelerate Method." In the meantime, notice that this variable is initialized to a True value. The mboolClean Boolean is also set to True by the Class_Initialize event procedure.

Adding Simple Property Procedures

The first and easiest enhancement is to add several simple property procedures for each property in clsCar1. The enhanced class module (clsCar2) includes the property procedures shown in Listing 11.6. Not all the class module's property procedures are shown here. Several are discussed in the next section of this chapter.

Listing 11.6. The first enhancements involve adding simple property procedures to the car class.

```
Property Let Make(strMake As String)
  mstrMake = strMake
End Property

Property Get Make() As String
  Make = mstrMake
End Property

Property Get Speed() As Integer
  Speed = mintSpeed
End Property

Property Get Clean() As Boolean
  Clean = mboolClean
End Property
```

Notice that only the Make property is read/write. Both the Speed and Clean properties are modified by methods in the clsCar2 class module, so there is no need to add Property Let procedures for these properties.

Adding the Color Property Procedures

Listing 11.7 shows the property procedures for the Color property in clsCar2. The Property Get procedure is rather obvious but the Property Let requires a bit of explanation.

In this case, the incoming property value is passed in as the strColor argument. strColor is first converted to all lowercase characters with the VBA LCase function. Converting the incoming value to all lowercase characters means that the incoming value does not have to be case-correct to exactly match the comparison values in the body of the If..End If.

Listing 11.7. The Property Let for the Color property allows only one of six colors to be assigned to the Color property.

```
Property Get Color() As String
  Color = mstrColor
End Property

Property Let Color(strColor As String)
  strColor = LCase(strColor)
  If strColor = "black" _
  Or strColor = "blue" _
  Or strColor = "green" _
  Or strColor = "red" _
  Or strColor = "white" Then
    mstrColor = strColor
  Else
    mstrColor = "other"
  End If
End Property
```

The compound If..End If conditional then compares the value of strColor to several valid values such as "black", "blue", and "red". If a match is found the value of strColor is assigned to mstrColor, the private variable used to store the car object's Color property. If strColor does not match any colors in the list, a default value of "other" is assigned to the mstrColor property.

Adding the Year Property Procedures

The Year property is somewhat more challenging than the Color property discussed in the last section. The Property Get and Property Let for the Year property are shown in Listing 11.8. Retrieving the Year property value with a Property Get is simple enough, but the Property Let is much more complex.

Listing 11.8. The Property Let for the Year property bulletproofs the stored value.

```
Property Get Year() As String
  Year = mstrYear
End Property
```

```
Property Let Year(strYear As String)
  On Error GoTo Year_Error
  strYear = strYear & ""
  If CInt(strYear) >= 1990 _
     And CInt(strYear) < 2000 Then
    mstrYear = Trim(strYear)
  Else
    mstrYear = CStr(DatePart("yyyy", Date))
  End If
Year_Exit:
  Exit Property
Year_Error:
  mstrYear = CStr(DatePart("yyyy", Date))
  Resume Year_Exit
End Property
```

The `Property Let Year` procedure bulletproofs the private `strYear` variable used to store the `Year` property value. Because a text box is used on `frmCar2` to input the `Year` value, almost anything can be passed in, including strings containing alphabetic characters, numeric digits, and punctuation. Therefore, extensive error trapping is included in `Property Let Year` to avoid the obvious type conversion problems that would otherwise occur.

Next, the incoming value is tested to make sure it falls within the years 1990 to 2000. The `CInt` function converts the incoming string to an integer value, which is then compared to the years 1990 and 2000. As long as the converted integer value falls within these years, the value is assigned to `mstrYear` without future complications.

If, however, the year does not fall within the 1990 to 2000 range, the current year is determined by the `DatePart` function and is assigned to `mstrYear` after being converted to a string.

Adding Simple Methods to `clsCar2`

The `clsCar2` class module includes several simple methods. These methods are virtually the same as those in the `clsCar1` module documented earlier in this chapter. The methods shown in Listing 11.9 simply set the private variables used to store the related properties within the class module.

Listing 11.9. `clsCar2` includes several simple methods.

```
'StopCar method
Public Sub StopCar()
  mintSpeed = 0
End Sub

'Wash method
```

continues

Listing 11.9. Continued.

```
Public Sub Wash()
  mboolClean = True
End Sub
```

Enhancing the `Decelerate` Method

The `Decelerate` method for `clsCar2` is shown in Listing 11.10. This method is similar to the `Decelerate` method in `clsCar1` with one exception. An `If..End If` construct has been added to set the `mboolClean` property to `False` based on the value of a random number. The `Rnd` function returns a floating-point number between 0 and 1. This value is compared with 0.1 and, if less than this value, the private `mboolClean` Boolean variable is set to `False`. In this way, the car's `Clean` property becomes `False` every 10th time (on average) the `Decelerate` method is run.

Listing 11.10. The `Decelerate` method occasionally makes the car dirty.

```
Public Sub Decelerate()
  mintSpeed = mintSpeed - 10
  If mintSpeed < 0 Then
    mintSpeed = 0
  End If
  If Rnd < 0.1 Then
    mboolClean = False
  End If
End Sub
```

Enhancing the `Accelerate` Method

The `Accelerate` method in `clsCar2` (see Listing 11.11) is considerably different than the equivalent method in `clsCar1`. At the very top of this method, the value of the `mboolEngineOK` variable is checked to see whether the method should be allowed to run. If the variable is set to `False`, the method is aborted by the `Exit Sub` statement. Otherwise, the method is allowed to run.

Listing 11.11. The `Accelerate` method penalizes the driver when the maximum speed is exceeded.

```
Public Sub Accelerate()
  Static OverRevCount As Integer

  If Not mboolEngineOK Then
    Exit Sub
  End If
```

```
      mintSpeed = mintSpeed + 10
    If mintSpeed > pintMaxSpeed Then
      OverRevCount = OverRevCount + 1
      If OverRevCount >= 3 Then
        mintSpeed = 0
        mboolEngineOK = False
      Else
        mintSpeed = pintMaxSpeed
      End If
    End If
    If Rnd < 0.1 Then
      mboolClean = False
    End If
End Sub
```

Notice the static `OverRevCount` variable declared within the `Accelerate` method. This variable is used to count how many times the car exceeds its maximum speed, which is specified by the `pintMaxSpeed` constant. After the third incident, the car's speed is set to 0 and the `mboolEngineOK` variable is set to `False`. These settings emulate the car's engine blowing up. After the engine is ruined, the car will not move because the `Accelerate` method will not run. After all, in a real car, exceeding its maximum speed can result in a failed engine.

Near the bottom of this method, you'll see the same logic for setting the private `mboolClean` variable as used in the `Decelerate` method.

Using the Enhanced Object Class

Figure 11.4 shows `frmCar2`, a form included in the `Objects.vbp` project. This form exposes the properties and methods of the `clsCar2` class module. We won't examine every bit of code behind `frmCar2` because much of the programming behind this form is obvious, but several event procedures and other routines deserve our attention.

FIGURE 11.4.
The `frmCar2` *form uses the* `clsCar2` *object class.*

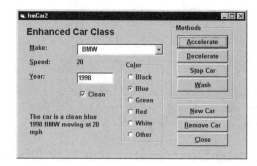

Filling the Form with Data

The frmCar2 form supports a single car object. That object's properties are displayed on the form by the FillForm sub, shown in Listing 11.12. One of the biggest differences between frmCar1 and frmCar2 is the option group for selecting the car's color added to frmCar2. This option group restricts the car's color to one of several different values and does not allow invalid colors to be selected.

In Listing 11.12, notice how the option group is managed by FillForm. A Select Case construct sets only one option button to True, depending on the car object's Color property value.

Listing 11.12. The FillForm procedure fills the form with data from the car object.

```
Private Sub FillForm()
  Dim i As Integer
  cboMake = mCar.Make
  txtYear = mCar.Year
  txtSpeed = mCar.Speed
  chkClean.Value = IIf(mCar.Clean, 1, 0)

  Select Case mCar.Color
    Case "black": optColor(1).Value = True
    Case "blue":  optColor(2).Value = True
    Case "green": optColor(3).Value = True
    Case "red":   optColor(4).Value = True
    Case "white": optColor(5).Value = True
    Case "other": optColor(6).Value = True
  End Select

  lblDescription.Caption = _
    "The car is a " _
    & IIf(chkClean, "clean ", "dirty ") _
    & mCar.Color & " " _
    & mCar.Year & " " _
    & mCar.Make _
    & " moving at " & mCar.Speed & " mph"
End Sub
```

Near the end of FillForm, the Caption property of lblDescription is set to a narrative description of the car. The description is updated any time the FillForm sub procedure is called, keeping the user informed of the car's status.

Creating and Destroying the Car Object

The frmCar2 form effectively manages creating new car objects and removing existing car objects from memory. Listing 11.13 shows the Click event procedures for the New

Car and Remove Car buttons on frmCar2. Notice how the New Car button's Click event procedure sets the initial Color, Make, and Year properties. The Clean and Speed properties are indirectly set by invoking the object's Wash and StopCar methods. As a final step, the New Car button makes sure all the buttons in the control button array (cmdMethods) supporting the object's methods are enabled.

Listing 11.13. frmCar2 includes these routines to create and destroy the car object.

```
Private Sub cmdNewCar_Click()
  Set mCar = New clsCar2
  mCar.Wash    'Makes car clean
  mCar.Color = "blue"
  mCar.Make = "New Car"
  mCar.StopCar    'Sets speed to 0
  mCar.Year = DatePart("yyyy", Date)
  Call FillForm
  cmdMethods(1).Enabled = True
  cmdMethods(2).Enabled = True
  cmdMethods(3).Enabled = True
  cmdMethods(4).Enabled = True
End Sub

Private Sub cmdRemoveCar_Click()
  Set mCar = Nothing
  cmdMethods(1).Enabled = False
  cmdMethods(2).Enabled = False
  cmdMethods(3).Enabled = False
  cmdMethods(4).Enabled = False
  Call FillForm
End Sub
```

The Remove Car's Click event procedure performs pretty much the opposite actions of those in the cmdNewCar_Click procedure. The existing car object is set to Nothing, destroying the object and removing it from memory. This statement also invokes the object's Class_Terminate event procedure. The method's buttons are then disabled and the FillForm procedure is invoked to refresh the data display on the form.

Setting the Car's Color

The option group on frmCar2 restricts the car's Color property to just a few valid values. The Click event procedure for this option group is shown in Listing 11.14. Any of several other types of controls, such as a Combo Box or List Box, could have been used on frmCar2, but the option group shows at a glance all the valid Color settings. It would not be practical to display dozens of different color options this way. If more than a few property-setting options are to be displayed, a combo box or list box is probably a better choice.

Listing 11.14. The Color property is set through this control array of option buttons.

```
Private Sub optColor_Click(Index As Integer)
  Select Case Index
    Case 1: mCar.Color = "black"
    Case 2: mCar.Color = "blue"
    Case 3: mCar.Color = "green"
    Case 4: mCar.Color = "red"
    Case 5: mCar.Color = "white"
    Case 6: mCar.Color = "other"
  End Select
  Call FillForm
End Sub
```

Making the Clean Check Box Read-Only

Finally, take a look at the Clean check box on frmCar2. There is no easy way to make this control read-only. Check boxes are normally used to display True and False values. On frmCar2, a check mark in this control indicates the car is clean (the Clean property is True) whereas an unchecked box means the car is dirty (the Clean property is False). Unfortunately, the behavior of a check box means that clicking the check box toggles its value between True and False, which could lead to misinterpretation of its actual value.

To prevent the check box from assuming a new value, the code shown in Listing 11.15 is attached to the check box's Click event. The immediate If (IIf) forces the check box to display the actual value of the car's Clean property.

Listing 11.15. The check box 's Click event procedure forces the check box to display the actual value of the Clean property.

```
Private Sub chkClean_Click()
  chkClean.Value = IIf(mCar.Clean, 1, 0)
End Sub
```

Using the Object Browser

Class modules and the objects created from them can be quite complex. It's important to properly use the properties and methods supported by the class module. Otherwise, the application using the class module's objects won't operate correctly or will generate runtime bugs.

Visual Basic provides a handy tool that makes it easy to delve into the interior of a class module without having to scan through all the module's code. The Object Browser, opened with the F2 key or View, Object Browser, provides the quickest and easiest way to decipher a class module's architecture.

Figure 11.5 shows the Object Browser open to the clsCar2 class module in Objects.vbp. The project has been selected from the Project/Library drop-down list in the upper-left corner of the Object Browser. This list contains the names of all the libraries referenced in the References dialog box. (You'll see how to use this dialog box in Chapters 20, "Integrating with Microsoft Office 97," 21, "Integrating with Microsoft Outlook 97," and other places in this book.)

Project/Library list

FIGURE 11.5.
The Object Browser provides a peek into a class module's architecture.

Class list

Members list

Description area

The class list along the left side of the Object Browser shows the names of all the classes defined within the Objects.vbp project. Selecting one of the classes, such as clsCar2, displays all the properties, methods, and other members of the class. The description of the class member is viewed in the bottom panel of the Object Browser after selecting the member in the Members list to the right of the Object Browser.

Notice that the Object Browser shows even the private members of the class. In Figure 11.5, you see the private variables such as mboolClean, and mstrColor used to store the property values within the clsCar2 class module. The descriptions of these variables tell you they are private members of clsCar2. The descriptions of the public members such as Color and Year are also displayed at the bottom of the Object Browser.

In other places in this book, you'll see the Object Browser used to determine which properties and methods of various objects are available for use in your programs.

Understanding Collections

An obvious enhancement is to allow tracking of more than one car object. Objects.vbp is limited in that it provides for just one object to be created from any of its classes at a time. Chapter 12, "Working with Objects and Collections," discusses the concept of object *collections*, objects that are actually aggregates of several other objects. Conceptually, a collection is a bag of objects. The objects within the collection can be all the same type or any number of different types.

A Visual Basic collection provides several properties and methods that are required to manage the objects contained within the collection. These properties and methods let you determine how many objects are in the collection, add new objects to the collection, and remove objects from the collection.

In the case of our car class, you might think of the corresponding Cars collection as the garage where the car objects are kept. Individual cars can be taken out of the garage one at a time and used in the application. New cars can be added at any time, and an existing car can be removed from the Cars collection when it is no longer needed.

Visual Basic collections are dynamic. Unlike arrays, you don't have to dimension them to any particular size. New items can be added to a collection at any time, and the only limit on the number of objects that can be added depends on the amount of memory and disk space available on the computer.

Collections are also very efficient. Unlike arrays, you needn't dimension the number of elements in a collection at the time the collection is declared. Additionally, you never have to redimension the memory used by a collection like you do for dynamic arrays. Collections act as infinitely expandable dynamic arrays of objects.

The full discussion of collections, including how to build custom collections for your Visual Basic applications, is deferred until Chapter 12.

Summary

Objects are often stored in collections containing a number of similar objects. Chapter 12, "Working with Objects and Collections," explains how to use the generic collection object as a container for objects as well as custom collections that extend the basic functionality of the collection object.

You'll revisit the topic of objects and object collections in the chapters in Part IV, "Accessing Data." As you'll see in this part of the book, Visual Basic's database capabilities are built around several object hierarchies and collections. These objects and collections contain the means to create, open, and manipulate databases and the data they contain.

Working with Objects and Collections

In Chapters 10 and 11 you saw how Visual Basic's object-oriented programming capabilities can ease the task of programming large projects by breaking program functionality into object components. You then use those objects by adding them to the application and manipulating their properties and methods.

The only problem not addressed in Chapters 10 and 11 was how to create more than one of the same object in an application. For example, an inventory control program is the ideal candidate for object-oriented programming. Each item in inventory becomes an object, and each object includes properties such as wholesale and retail prices, location in the warehouse, and quantity. The previous chapters did not suggest how you can create multiple instances of an inventory object and manage them in the application.

This chapter introduces Visual Basic *collections*, a special type of object that actually contains other objects within it. As you'll soon see, Visual Basic provides a catch-all Collection object that holds any type of object you add to it. Later in this chapter you learn how to create custom collections that hold only a single type of object, perhaps the car object you saw in Chapters 10 and 11 or an inventory object described in the previous paragraph. In many cases, you'll find it most convenient, and certainly more powerful, to create a custom collection to hold the objects you add to your applications. Because you build a custom collection in VBA code, you can provide the collection with its own properties and methods that help you perform work on the objects contained within the collection.

Collections are infinitely expandable. There is no predetermined limit to the number of objects that can be added to a collection. In fact, the only practical limit to the size of a collection is the amount of memory available on the computer running the application. Although the sample projects accompanying this chapter use collections containing just a few objects, large applications can manage collections containing thousands or even millions of objects. The same principles apply regardless of the size of the collection or the size of the objects contained within the collection.

Using Collections

A *collection* is a group of objects gathered together and treated as a single object. Usually the objects in the collection are of the same type (much as a garage might hold several car objects) but collections can also contain dissimilar objects (just as a garage might hold cars, trucks, and buses). A collection is itself an object specially designed to serve as a container for other objects.

Virtually all collections support four operations:

- Add objects to the collection
- Reference objects contained in the collection
- Determine how many objects are in the collection
- Remove objects from the collection

Each built-in collection discussed in this chapter supports these operations, as do all the custom collections found in the `Collect.vbp` project accompanying this chapter.

Visual Basic supports a special Collection object specifically designed to be used as a general-purpose container for Visual Basic objects. In addition to serving as a simple warehouse for objects, the Collection object can also be used to build custom collections. Both of these uses are described later in this chapter.

By default, the name of a collection is the plural of the name of the individual objects contained within the collection. For example, a collection of car objects should be named `Cars`. Each built-in Visual Basic collection follows this convention. Although it's not absolutely necessary for your custom collections to conform to this naming convention, your code will be easier to understand if you do. After all, one of the primary reasons for using Visual Basic's object-oriented features is to make your code easier to understand and maintain. There is no reason not to use the well-established convention of naming a collection as the plural of the individual objects contained within it.

Examining Built-In Visual Basic Collections

Visual Basic includes several built-in object collections. In each case, these collections provide an easy way to deal with many important types of objects. You'll find the built-in collections the easiest way to perform operations on several objects at a time.

Looking at the Forms Collection

The first of the built-in object collections we'll examine is the Forms collection. As its name implies, the Forms collection contains all the open forms in a Visual Basic application. Forms that might be part of the Visual Basic project but are not currently in use will not be included in the Forms collection. A form is added to the Forms collection as soon as it is opened. The Forms collection, therefore, is very dynamic and constantly changes in size and composition as forms are opened or closed.

We'll use the Forms collection to introduce many of the programming concepts you apply to any Visual Basic collection. Even when you've produced a custom collection to hold the objects you've created for your application, you'll use virtually the same code you see in this section to add new objects to the collection, reference objects within the collection, and remove objects from the collection.

Drilling Into the Forms Collection

It is important to know that the Forms collection is unique in many ways. For example, there are several ways to open forms in your Visual Basic applications. Not all of these methods are applicable to all types of objects added to their respective collections. Although this section ignores some of these techniques, keep in mind that this section does not cover the only way to open, access, and close Visual Basic forms.

The Forms collection is global throughout the application. Any reference to the Forms keyword in a Visual Basic application refers to the built-in Forms collection. Visual Basic automatically recognizes the word *Forms* to mean a reference to the Forms collection.

The project accompanying this chapter, `Collect.vbp`, includes code demonstrating how to work with the Forms collection. Running the `Collect.vbp` project reveals the form you see in Figure 12.1. The code behind the button labeled Open Forms is shown in Listing 12.1. This event procedure opens three identical forms. As the forms are opened, they are automatically added to the application's Forms collection.

FIGURE 12.1.
The frmForms *form is part of the* Collect.vbp *project.*

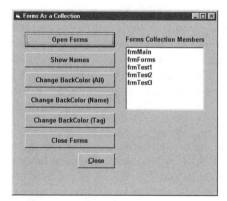

Listing 12.1. Opening a form with the Show method adds it to the Forms collection.

```
Private Sub cmdOpenForms_Click()
    frmTest1.Show
    frmTest2.Show
    frmTest3.Show
End Sub
```

After the forms are open, they can be referenced as members of the Forms collection. The code in Listing 12.2 shows how to display the names of all the forms in the Forms collection. The code in Listing 12.2 is behind the Show Names button on frmForms.

Listing 12.2. Enumerating the members of a collection is easy.

```
Private Sub cmdShowNames_Click()
  Dim i As Integer
  lstNames.Clear
  For i = 0 To Forms.Count - 1
    lstNames.AddItem Forms(i).Name
  Next i
End Sub
```

The code in Listing 12.2 is called whenever forms are opened or closed by the buttons on frmForms. You can also manually close forms and click the Show Names button to see how the number of forms in the Forms collection changes dynamically as an application runs.

Manipulating the Forms Collection

Notice the references to Forms.Count in Listing 12.2. The Count property, which is universal to all collections, reports the number of elements in the collection. The collection itself is treated as an array of form objects in the For..Next loop. The loop counter i is used as the index referencing the individual members of the Forms collection.

The For..Next loop in Listing 12.2 starts at 0 (zero) and walks up to Count - 1. The Forms collection, like all arrays by default, is zero-based. The first element of the Forms collection is index 0, and each element is numbered sequentially in the order in which it was added to the collection, up to Forms.Count - 1. Therefore, if there are five forms in the collection, the first form is index 0 and the last form is index 4. Unlike arrays, however, you cannot set a collection's index to start at 1 or any number other than 0.

> **Tip:** Do not assume that the indexes of all collections start at zero. As you'll soon see, collections built with the Collection object start at index number 1. This fact often leads to off-by-one errors when using collections in VBA code. You should, therefore, use the VBA techniques that avoid using specific numeric indexes when referencing objects in the collection.

The code behind the Change BackColor (All) button on the frmForms form is shown in Listing 12.3. This code changes the BackColor property of all forms in the Forms collection to magenta.

Listing 12.3. Use the Forms collection to manipulate properties of all forms as a single operation.

```
Private Sub cmdChangeAll_Click()
  Dim frm As Form
  For Each frm In Forms
    frm.BackColor = RGB(255, 0, 255)
  Next frm
End Sub
```

Again, this code uses a different type of loop to walk through the Forms collection. In this case, the loop uses the For Each type of loop, described later in this chapter in the section "Understanding the Controls Collection." In the meantime, notice how a Form object variable is declared and used to walk through the Forms collection, changing the BackColor property of every member of the Forms collection.

> **Tip:** Using the For Each..Next looping construct is the ideal way to avoid off-by-one index referencing issues. Because members of the collection are not referenced by a numeric index, there is no chance the wrong object will be retrieved from the collection when using For Each..Next.

A slightly different approach to manipulating form properties is shown in Listing 12.4. (This code is the Click event procedure of the button labeled Change BackColor (Name) on frmForms.) In this case, the BackColor is changed only on forms whose names begin with frmTest. It is quite easy to selectively manipulate properties on certain forms.

Listing 12.4. Manipulating members of the Forms collection by the form name.

```
Private Sub cmdChangeName_Click()
  Dim frm As Form
  For Each frm In Forms
    If Left(frm.Name, 7) = "frmTest" Then
      frm.BackColor = RGB(255, 255, 0)
    End If
  Next frm
End Sub
```

The code in Listing 12.4 works well but might be inconvenient in some cases. For example, if the application is partially or completely built, it might not be possible to manipulate the members of the Forms collection by name alone. Many applications contain dozens of forms. Think of all the code that would have to be changed if the forms had to be renamed so that the code in Listing 12.4 could be used. It'd be nice to have some other form property that can be easily changed at any time to indicate the form is a candidate for manipulation.

The Tag property perfectly fits the requirements outlined in the preceding paragraph. The Tag property is frequently used to store a flag value that indicates that some operation should be applied to the form. (The same principle applies to text boxes, command buttons, and any other type of control.) Listing 12.5 shows how to use the Tag property to indicate the form's BackColor property should be changed.

Listing 12.5. Using the Tag property to change the BackColor property of members of the Forms collection.

```
Private Sub cmdChangeTag_Click()
  Dim frm As Form
  For Each frm in Forms
    If InStr(frm.Tag, "Cyan") Then
      frm.BackColor = RGB(0, 255, 255)
    End If
  Next frm
End Sub
```

Notice that the code in Listing 12.5 uses the InStr function to test whether the flag value "Cyan" appears in each form's Tag property. The syntax of InStr is as follows:

InStr(*StringToSearch, SearchString*)

InStr returns the starting position of *SearchString* in *StringToSearch*. If *SearchString* is not found, zero is returned instead. Therefore, the expression returns a nonzero (true) value only when "Cyan" actually appears in the form's Tag property.

When working with the Forms collection, what's important to understand isn't the fact that you can open, close, and manipulate forms without running code behind the forms, although these are all useful operations. What's most important is the fact that you can perform operations on a form by virtue of its membership in the Forms collection found in every Visual Basic application. You don't even need to know the form's exact name. It's enough to know something about the form that distinguishes it from the other forms in the Forms collection. Using Forms(*index*).*PropertyName* is as valid as referencing the property using the form's exact name (*FormName.Property*).

Understanding the Controls Collection

Each form in a Visual Basic application includes a Controls collection that contains all the controls on the form. The Controls collection on most forms consists of several different control types, such as command buttons, text boxes, and combo boxes. Therefore, in any operations that affect all the members of a form's Controls collection, it is important to make sure only the intended controls are affected.

For example, assume you have a form with many different types of controls on it. The Collect.vbp project includes frmControls, shown in Figure 12.2. This form has a wide variety of controls on it, including command buttons, text boxes, option buttons, and frame controls.

FIGURE 12.2.

The frmControls *form features a variety of different kinds of controls.*

Earlier in this chapter, you read about the For Each..Next construct, which is useful for walking through all the members of a collection. The For Each loop applies to a form's Controls collection just as it did to the Forms collection. But, in the case of a form such as frmControls, you must be very careful that you're addressing exactly the controls you intend to when modifying properties.

All forms in a Forms collection are pretty much treated alike, except for the name given to each form, the controls on the form, and other specifics relating to each form. Almost every form shares a large number of properties and other attributes with every other form.

Controls, on the other hand, have very little in common with each other. The properties for a text box are quite different than those for an option button. A command button, for example, does not have a ForeColor property, and trying to set a command button's ForeColor causes a runtime error.

You must, therefore, make sure you're working with the correct type of control when sweeping through the Controls collection, setting properties, or making other changes. The code in Listing 12.6 shows how this is done. The code in Listing 12.6 is behind the Change Labels command button on the frmControls form.

Listing 12.6. Be sure to check the object type of controls before making property changes.

```
Private Sub cmdLabels_Click()
  Dim ctl As Control
  For Each ctl In Me.Controls
    If TypeOf ctl Is Label Then
      ctl.ForeColor = GetForeColor
      ctl.BackColor = GetBackColor
      ctl.FontName = GetFontName
      ctl.FontSize = GetFontSize
    End If
  Next
End Sub
```

The code in Listing 12.6 sets the ForeColor, BackColor, and other appearance properties of the labels on frmControls. The TypeOf operator is used to verify the object type of each control before the property values are assigned. If the control is not a label, the code simply ignores the control and goes on to the next control in the Controls collection.

The syntax of the TypeOf operator is

```
If TypeOf Object Is ClassName Then...
```

The TypeOf operator is valid only within an If..End If statement and can be used any time the class of an object must be verified.

You could also use the TypeName function to return the class name of the controls in the Controls collection. The code in Listing 12.7 is the Click event procedure for the button labeled Change Text Boxes on frmControls in the Collect.vbp project.

Listing 12.7. Be sure to check the object type of controls before making property changes.

```
Private Sub cmdTextBoxes_Click()
  Dim ctl As Control
  For Each ctl In Me.Controls
    If TypeName(ctl) = "TextBox" Then
      ctl.ForeColor = GetForeColor
      ctl.BackColor = GetBackColor
      ctl.FontName = GetFontName
      ctl.FontSize = GetFontSize
    End If
  Next
End Sub
```

A second approach to setting properties for all the controls in a Controls collection is shown in Listing 12.8. In this case, a runtime error is generated each time an invalid property assignment is made. This code is behind the Change All button on frmControls.

Listing 12.8. Sometimes it's more efficient to simply ignore the inevitable errors that occur.

```
Private Sub cmdAll_Click()
  Dim ctl As Control
On Error Resume Next
  For Each ctl In Me.Controls
    ctl.ForeColor = GetForeColor
    ctl.BackColor = GetBackColor
    ctl.FontName = GetFontName
    ctl.FontSize = GetFontSize
  Next
End Sub
```

The code in Listing 12.7 sweeps through the entire Controls collection, setting the ForeColor, BackColor, and other properties of all the controls on the form. However, the form includes controls such as command buttons and frames that have no ForeColor property. Attempting to set the ForeColor property of one of these controls generates a runtime error. The On Error Resume Next statement instructs Visual Basic to simply ignore any runtime errors that occur and to continue processing at the next executable statement. (Handling errors is discussed in Chapter 9, "Handling Runtime Errors.")

Surveying Other Built-In Collections

Visual Basic includes several other important built-in collections. In Chapter 18, "Mastering Jet DAO," you learn about managing data using the special DAO (Data Access Objects) syntax found in all VBA systems like Visual Basic. Chapter 19, "Using Advanced Data Access Methods," discusses ADO (ActiveX Data Objects), Microsoft's latest object-oriented syntax for data access. Both DAO and ADO feature object hierarchies that define data in terms of data sources (databases), data sets (records), and data values (fields). Understanding these hierarchies is critical when building database and data-driven applications with Visual Basic.

Using the Collection Object

So far you've learned collections in pretty general terms and have looked at several built-in Visual Basic collection objects. You'll study more general-purpose collections created for the sole purpose of holding objects created within a Visual Basic application.

Recall that a collection supports several operations:

- Adding objects to the collection (the Add method)
- Referring to objects within the collection (the Item method)
- Counting the number of objects in the collection (the Count property)
- Removing objects from the collection (the Remove method)

The following discussions refer to the generic Collection object included in Visual Basic 6. The Collection object supports all the operations in the preceding list. In all cases, the operation is actually performed by triggering a method of the Collection object or reading a property of the Collection object.

Let's go back to the car object defined in Chapter 10, "Creating Objects and Classes." This object supports the properties and methods listed in Table 12.1.

Table 12.1. Properties and methods of the car object class.

Name	Type	Description
Color	Property	Color of the car
Clean	Property	Cleanliness state of car
Make	Property	Car's manufacturer
Speed	Property	Current speed of car
Year	Property	Model year of car
Accelerate	Method	Makes car go faster
Decelerate	Method	Makes car go slower
StopCar	Method	Sets car's speed to zero
Wash	Method	Sets car's Clean property to True

Chapter 10 explained how to create individual car objects and manipulate the object's properties and methods. In Chapter 11, "Advanced Class Concepts," you enhanced the Car objects by adding read-only and write-only properties and adding a few methods. Now you create a collection to hold several car objects and learn how the collection can be used to store and manage the objects within the collection.

This chapter is accompanied by Cars.vbp, a Visual Basic 6 project that contains the code discussed in the following sections. The main form in Cars.vbp is frmCars, shown in Figure 12.3.

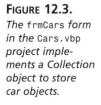

FIGURE 12.3.

The frmCars *form in the* Cars.vbp *project implements a Collection object to store car objects.*

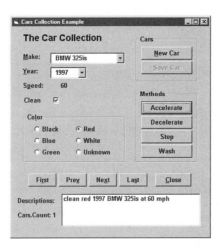

New cars are added to the application with the New Car button. After the properties of the new car are set using the form's controls, the Save Car button adds the new car to the Cars collection. The list box at the bottom of the form displays the properties of all the car objects in the Cars collection.

Creating a Collection

There is only one `Car` object behind `frmCars`, and only one collection object named `Cars`. The syntax for creating the `Car` object from the `clsCar` class is

```
Private Car As New clsCar
Set Car = New clsCar
```

After the `Car` object has been defined and instantiated, its properties and methods can be used anywhere in the code behind `frmCars`. The next step is to create the collection using the `Collection` object. The syntax required to create a collection is

```
[Public│Private│Dim│Static] CollectionName As Collection
Set CollectionName = New Collection
```

In the instance of the `clsCar` object class, the following syntax is used:

```
Private Cars As New Collection
```

The `New` keyword instructs Visual Basic to create the `Collection` object as soon as the `Cars` object is defined. Alternatively, you could declare the `Collection` object and instantiate it as a separate step:

```
Private Cars As Collection

'Later in the program:
Set Cars = New Collection
```

The second approach provides more flexibility. You don't have to instantiate the `Collection` object until it is needed by your application.

Adding Objects to the Collection

After the `Car` object has been created and its properties set, the object is ready to add to the Cars collection. The `Click` event procedure of the Save Car button is shown in Listing 12.9.

Listing 12.9. Car objects are added to the Cars collection with the Add method.

```
Private Sub cmdSaveCar_Click()
  'Write properties from form into Car object.
  Car.Make = cboMake
  Car.Year = cboYear

  'Set the Car object's color
  Select Case True
    Case optBlack.Value: Car.Color = "Black"
    Case optBlue.Value:  Car.Color = "Blue"
    Case optGreen.Value: Car.Color = "Green"
    Case optRed.Value:   Car.Color = "Red"
```

continues

Listing 12.9. Continued.

```
    Case optWhite.Value: Car.Color = "White"
    Case Else: Car.Color = "Unknown"
  End Select

  'Add this car to the cars collection
  Cars.Add Car

  cmdMethods(1).Enabled = True
  cmdMethods(2).Enabled = True
  cmdMethods(3).Enabled = True
  cmdMethods(4).Enabled = True

  Call FillForm
  cmdSaveCar.Enabled = False
End Sub
```

There is a lot more going on in Listing 12.9 than adding car objects to the Cars collection. Most of the code in cmdSaveCar_Click is involved in taking data off frmCars and putting the data into the Car object to keep it updated. Other statements in cmdSaveCar_Click manage the user interface, enabling and disabling the command buttons on the form. The only statement in Listing 12.9 that actually involves the Cars collection is

```
Cars.Add Car
```

This statement invokes the Add method of Cars, passing it the Car object that is available throughout frmCars. As soon as the Car object is added to Cars, the Count property of Cars is incremented by 1.

The general syntax of the Add method is as follows:

```
CollectionName.Add ObjectName, [Key], [Before], [After]
```

The Add method includes some interesting optional parameters not used by frmCars. For example, the Key parameter is a text string value attached to each object added to the collection. Later on, the object's Key string can be used to retrieve the object from the collection. Because the Key parameter is used to identify objects in the collection, each Key value must be unique within the collection.

The Before and After parameters are used when you want to insert an object into the collection at a specific point. If a numeric value is provided as either of these parameters, Visual Basic interprets the number as an index into the collection and inserts the new object before or after that index position. If the Before or After parameters are strings, Visual Basic assumes the string matches a Key value already added to the collection and inserts the new object relative to that object in the collection. Either the Before or After parameter can be specified, but not both at the same time.

Because of the simplicity of the Cars collection, none of the optional parameters (*Key*, *Before*, and *After*) are used in frmCars. The collections you create might be more complex than this example. For example, your applications might store binary objects in a collection. When retrieving objects from such a collection, it'd be difficult to examine a property of the binary objects to determine which of the objects to return. In such a case, you might want to provide the *Key* parameter (such as a filename, serial number, or other identifier) to make it easy to retrieve the correct object.

Alternatively, if your collection requires keeping objects sorted within the collection, the *Before* and *After* parameters might be exactly what you need.

> **Note:** Programmers familiar with other languages such as C, C++, and Pascal will recognize a collection as a type of linked list. The major difference between a Visual Basic collection and a linked list is that Visual Basic takes care of maintaining the items in the list. When programming linked lists in a language such as C++ or Pascal, the programmer must use code to manage all the connections between items in the list. Collections in Visual Basic are certainly much more efficient and easier to work with than traditional linked lists.

Counting the Number of Items in the Collection

Notice near the bottom of frmCars in Figure 12.3 a label reporting the number of car objects in the Cars Collection. The code setting this label's Caption property occupies a single statement:

```
lblCount.Caption = _
   "Cars.Count: " & Cars.Count
```

This statement uses the Count property of the Cars collection to report the number of Car objects in the Cars collection.

You read earlier in this chapter that the index into a Forms or Controls collection is zero-based. When using numeric values to reference members of the Forms and Controls collections, counting begins at 0 and progresses to Count - 1. The situation changes when using the Collection object. The first object in a collection created from the Collection object is always number 1 and the last object is index number Count. frmCars includes a list box displaying a description of all the car objects in the Cars collection. One approach to filling this list box is shown in Listing 12.10

Listing 12.10. The Count property can be used to list the members of a collection.

```
Dim i As Integer
For i = 1 To Cars.Count
```

continues

Listing 12.10. Continued.

```
  lstDescription.AddItem _
    IIf(chkClean, "clean ", "dirty ") _
    & Cars(i).Color & " " _
    & Cars(i).Year & " " _
    & Cars(i).Make & " at " _
    & Cars(i).Speed & " mph"
Next i
```

Unlike working with the Forms collection, an attempt to reference `Cars(0)` generates an error.

Because of the need to keep track of a numeric reference in Listing 12.10, the actual code filling the `lstDescription` list box near the bottom of `frmCars` is shown in Listing 12.11.

Listing 12.11. It's easy to enumerate the members of the Cars collection.

```
lstDescription.Clear
For Each Car In Cars
  lstDescription.AddItem _
    IIf(chkClean, "clean ", "dirty ") _
    & Car.Color & " " _
    & Car.Year & " " _
    & Car.Make & " at " _
    & Car.Speed & " mph"
Next Car
```

The code in Listing 12.11 is much easier to maintain. There's no need to remember or guess when a collection is zero-based or 1-based.

Retrieving Objects from the Collection

You've already seen an example or two of referencing `Car` objects in the Cars collection. Listings 12.10 and 12.11 both retrieve objects from the Cars collection using different techniques. Visual Basic is flexible when it comes to retrieving objects from collections. The three fundamental techniques involve the following indexing methods:

- `Ordinal value`
- `Key`
- `Name`

The general syntax for referencing an object in a collection is as follows:

```
CollectionName.Item(IndexValue)
```

The *IndexValue* can be a number representing the numeric index of an object in the collection (the *ordinal value* method), a string matching the optional Key parameter passed to the Add method as the object was added to the collection (the key method), or the object's name (the Name method). The Name method is applicable only where the object has a Name property and where care has been taken to ensure that the name is unique within the collection.

The full syntax for referencing an item by ordinal value is as follows:

```
CollectionName.Item(OrdinalValue)
```

The Item method of a collection returns an item from within the collection. Passing a numeric value as the *OrdinalValue* parameter returns the item whose index matches the ordinal value. A Subscript Out of Range error occurs if the numeric value is either less than 1 or more than the collection's Count property.

Every member of a collection has a specific position within the collection. Unlike eggs in a carton that can be mixed in any order, the elements in a collection are added to a collection in a specific order as the collection is constructed. As an item is added to a collection, Visual Basic assigns it a unique number that indicates the item's ordinal position within the collection, much like the index number of an item in an array. The only way to change an element's ordinal number is to delete another item in the collection or to remove the item from the collection and add it back again.

Using an object's ordinal number is often the fastest way to reference the object because Visual Basic does not have to interpret the object's Name (or other) property.

If a string value is passed as the index, Visual Basic assumes it matches the option Key argument passed to the Add method. If Visual Basic cannot find the key value within the collection, an error occurs. The key value must be a literal string surrounded by quotes or a string variable that has been assigned a valid key value.

The Name method is seldom used. In most cases, the objects added to a collection do not have a Name property. It is actually much easier to use the Key argument, passing some identifier that you are sure uniquely identifies the objects you're adding to the collection.

One situation in which the name-referencing technique works well is when referring to forms in the Forms collection. The following statement sets the BackColor property of the frmCars form to gray:

```
Forms("frmCars").BackColor = RGB(192,192,192)
```

Visual Basic easily locates a form named frmCars in the Forms collection and makes the property assignment.

Removing Items from the Collection

After an item has been located in a collection, its properties and other characteristics can be accessed and exploited by the application. The object also can be removed from the collection with the Remove method of the Collection object. The syntax of the Remove method is as follows:

```
CollectionName.Remove IndexValue
```

The *IndexValue* parameter is exactly the same as you read in the preceding section. The *IndexValue* can be numeric, in which case it must match the index of an object currently within the collection.

If the *IndexValue* is a string, Visual Basic assumes it is the key value of an item in the collection and removes that item. If the string value does not match the key of an existing object, an Invalid Procedure Call or Argument error is generated.

An interesting characteristic of Visual Basic collections is that the index values of the items in the collection might change as items are removed from the collection. For example, consider the code in Listing 12.12. This code is located in frmFruits in the Collect.vbp project (see Figure 12.4). The cmdAddItems_Click event procedure adds several Fruit objects to the Fruits collection. (The Name property is the only property of the Fruit object.)

FIGURE 12.4.

The frmFruits *form in* Collect.vbp *demonstrates a common problem with collections.*

Listing 12.12. The Fruit object is very simple.

```
Dim Fruits As New Collection
Dim Fruit As New Fruit

Private Sub cmdAddItems_Click()
  Set Fruit = New Fruit
  Fruit.Name = "Apples"
  Fruits.Add Fruit, "Apple"
  Set Fruit = Nothing
  'Sequence repeated for a number
  'of different types of fruit...
End Sub
```

Later, the code behind the Delete Item #3 button (see Listing 12.13) runs, removing the item at index 3 from the Fruits collection.

Listing 12.13. The `cmdDelete1_Click` event procedure uses one of several indexing techniques to remove the third item in the Fruits collection.

```
Private Sub cmdDelete1_Click()
  Fruits.Remove 3
  Call cmdRefresh_Click
End Sub
```

Finally, the items in the Fruits collection are displayed by the `cmdRefresh_Click` event procedure (see Listing 12.14). The text box on `frmFruits` displays the `Name` property of the fourth item in the Fruits collection. Each time the Delete Item #3 button is pressed, the `txtFruit.Text = Fruits(4).Name` statement retrieves a different object from the Fruits collection.

Listing 12.14. Be careful when referencing items by ordinal value.

```
Private Sub cmdRefresh_Click()
  Dim f As Fruit

  lstCollection.Clear
  For Each f In Fruits
    lstCollection.AddItem f.Name
    Debug.Print f.Name
  Next f

  txtFruit.Text = Fruits(4).Name
End Sub
```

Visual Basic dynamically adjusts the indexes pointing to a collection object, adjusting the numbers each time an object is removed or added to the collection. Be aware that you cannot rely on an index number to point to the correct object as the contents of the collection are changed.

Destroying the Collection

A collection can be destroyed and all its contents discarded by executing either of the following statements:

```
Set CollectionName = Nothing
Set CollectionName = New Collection
```

In the first case, the collection is removed from memory, destroying any objects the collection contains. The second statement removes the collection's contents by pointing the object reference to a new instance of the collection object.

Use whichever of these techniques is most appropriate for the application you're building. If you intend to use the collection over and over again, putting different objects into it each time, the second syntax is probably the best. It is faster to set a collection object to a new instance than it is to first destroy it by setting it to Nothing, then re-instantiating it a second time.

Optimizing Object References

When working with collections, it's easy to write code that is inherently inefficient. For example, the code in Listing 12.15 is fairly inefficient.

Listing 12.15. Repeated references to an object's properties are inefficient.

```
Dim strDescription As String
For Each Car In Cars
  strDescription = _
    IIf(chkClean, "clean ", "dirty ") & _
    Car.Color & " " & _
    Car.Year & " " & _
    Car.Make & " at " & _
    Car.Speed & " mph"
Next Car
```

The code in Listing 12.15 asks Visual Basic to locate the Car object in the Cars collection and set its properties over and over again. Each reference to Car causes Visual Basic to rereference the current Car object and its properties. A much faster way to retrieve the properties of the Car object is shown in Listing 12.16.

Listing 12.16. The With construct optimizes the references to the Car object.

```
Dim strDescription As String
For Each Car In Cars
  With Car
    strDescription = _
      IIf(chkClean, "clean ", "dirty ") & _
      .Color & " " & _
      .Year & " " & _
      .Make & " at " & _
      .Speed & " mph"
  End With
Next Car
```

The With Car statement instructs Visual Basic to grab hold of the Car object, cache it in memory, and use it repeatedly until the End With statement is encountered.

You can use the With..End With any time you are referencing an object or its properties and methods multiple times within a few lines of code. In most cases, using With..End With makes the code easier to understand and it is much less trouble to write than to repeatedly type the same full object.

Building the Case for Custom Collections

So far in this chapter we've been using the built-in Collection object to create collections to store custom objects such as the Car and Fruit objects. There are several problems with using the built-in Collection object for this purpose:

- There is no control over the type of object added to the collection. Any type of object can be added to the collection without causing an error.

- Operations on the collection must be conducted by the collection's consumer. This means that any changes to the collection's objects must be performed in the code using the collection, rather than by the collection itself.

You might never encounter either of these problems in your applications. But if you, like most other Visual Basic programmers, begin using objects and collections more and more often in your applications, you'll want to consider adding custom collection objects to your programs.

Understanding Wayward Objects

The first of these problems requires a bit of explanation. The Collection object is just a container for holding objects, much as a shoe box is a container for objects such as marbles, baseball cards, and pencils. There is nothing about a Collection object or a shoebox to restrict the types of objects added to it (other than the obvious limitations of memory and physical dimensions, respectively). Therefore, even if a collection is intended to hold the Fruit object, there is nothing to prevent another type of object from being added to the collection, much as there is nothing to prevent a pencil from being added to a shoebox intended to hold baseball cards.

The Cars.vbp project includes the form shown in Figure 12.5. This form demonstrates the problem that occurs when no controls are put on the types of objects added to a Collection object.

The frmProblem1 form contains much of the code you saw earlier in this chapter for adding car objects to the Cars collection. The biggest difference is the Click event procedure for the Add Problem button (see Listing 12.17).

FIGURE 12.5.

The `frmProblem1` *form demonstrates a dangerous problem with the* `Collection` *object.*

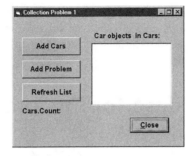

Listing 12.17. Nothing stops you from adding the wrong kind of object to the Cars collection.

```
Private Sub cmdProblem_Click()
  Dim ctl As Control
  For Each ctl In Me.Controls
    Cars.Add ctl
  Next ctl
  lblCount = "Cars.Count: " & Cars.Count
  Set ctl = Nothing
End Sub
```

The code in Listing 12.17 loops through the Controls collection on `frmProblem1` and adds each control to the Cars collection. A control, after all, is just a type of object much as a fruit is a type of object.

After the bogus `Car` objects have been added to the Cars collection, the `Click` event of the Refresh List button fails. Listing 12.18 shows the code behind the Refresh List button.

Listing 12.18. This code fails as soon as an invalid `Car` object is encountered in the Cars collection.

```
Private Sub cmdRefreshList_Click()
  Dim Car As clsCar

  lstCollection.Clear
  For Each Car In Cars
    lstCollection.AddItem Car.Make
    Debug.Print Car.Make
  Next Car
  lblCount = "Cars.Count: " & Cars.Count
End Sub
```

The `cmdRefreshList_Click` procedure expects only `Car` objects in the Cars collection. As soon as one of the control objects is encountered, Visual Basic fails with a Type Mismatch error in the middle of the `For Each` loop.

A custom collection can simply refuse to add the bogus object to the collection. Later in this chapter, you learn how to create custom collections and add the code necessary to protect the collection from errant additions.

Encapsulating Functionality

The second issue with using the generic Collection object is more subtle and conceptual than the first. Using a Collection object to manage the objects in an application neglects one of the primary motivations for using Visual Basic's object-oriented programming features. In Chapter 10, you learned that one of the principle advantages of object-oriented programming is that a well-designed object encapsulates functionality as a single, reusable object.

Consider the code you see in Listing 12.19.

Listing 12.19. Painting all the Car objects requires manipulating the object.

```
Private Sub cmdPaint_Click()
  Dim Car As clsCar
  For Each Car In Cars
    Car.Color = "Red"
  Next Car
End Sub
```

The code in Listing 12.19 is found behind the Paint the Cars button on frmProblem2 in the Cars.vbp project. This form is shown in Figure 12.6.

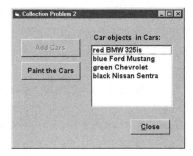

FIGURE 12.6.

The frmProblem2 *form demon-strates a common collection-related task.*

There is nothing wrong with the code in Listing 12.19. It works effectively to change the Color property of all the cars in the Cars collection. But what if this task must be performed in dozens of different places in a large Visual Basic application? A less skilled programmer will put paint code in multiple locations within the program. Each time the code is written small syntactical differences might creep in. Some of the paint routines might run more slowly than others, and so on. Furthermore, if a change must be made to the paint routine, there will be multiple locations where the code has to be updated.

A good programmer, on the other hand, puts the paint routine in a public module and calls it from wherever it is needed in the program. The second approach means only one copy of the code must be updated if the requirements of the paint routine change. Moving the routine into a public module vastly improves the situation, but it still requires a public approach to supporting the paint requirement.

A much better approach is to include the paint routine as a method of the collection storing the Car objects. In other words, the best solution is to encapsulate the paint functionality as part of the Cars collection.

There are numerous ways to benefit from this third approach. For example, a common task of many inventory control applications is to periodically depreciate the value of the oldest items in inventory. Using a Collection object means the task of maintaining the inventory's value is taken out of the inventory collection and moved to the mainstream program. Changes to the way old inventory is depreciated means hunting through the code looking for the depreciation routines. It'd be much easier to maintain the depreciation routine by including it as a method of a custom inventory collection object.

Creating Custom Collections

It shouldn't come as much of a surprise that a custom collection object is built around a Collection object. The custom collection object is based on a class module that has a Collection object at its center. The Collection object actually contains the objects managed by the custom collection. The custom collection itself is a wrapper object around the Collection object. The wrapper object contains the special properties and methods added to the custom collection object.

In the case of the Cars collection described earlier in this chapter, it's easy to see the sort of functionality that could be added to a custom collection object:

- Support methods such as Paint and Wash that apply to all Car objects in the custom Cars collection.
- Support a method such as RemoveAll that removes all the car objects from the Cars collection.
- Support special properties such as BlueCount that returns the count of the blue cars.

The custom collection will be implemented as a class module. The class module will contain a private Collection object and several properties and methods.

Beginning the Collection Class

The first step is to add a class module to the project. In the Cars.vbp project the collection class is named clsCars. The collection class contains the following declaration:

```
Private mColCars As Collection
```

The hidden Collection object, mColCars, is managed by clsCars. It will be used to contain the Car objects added to the collection created from clsCars. The mColCars object is instantiated in the Class_Initialize procedure in clsCars. Listing 12.20 initializes the private-scope mColCars collection object inside the clsCars class module.

Listing 12.20. The private Collection object is instantiated in the clsCars initialization routine.

```
Private Sub Class_Initialize()
  Set mColCars = New Collection
End Sub
```

Because mColCars is private to clsCars it cannot be seen outside the class module. The only interface to mColCars is through the properties and methods in the class module.

Earlier in this chapter, you read that all collections have the following methods and properties:

- A Count property, which returns the number of objects in the collection
- An Item method for referencing objects contained within the collection
- An Add method for adding new items to the collection
- A Remove method for removing items from the collection

The properties and methods in this list are added one at a time to clsCars. Of these, the Count property is easiest to implement. All the Count property passes the Count property of mColCars. Listing 12.21 shows the Property Get for the Count property. Because Count is a read-only property, there is no need for a Property Let.

Listing 12.21. The Property Get for the Count property returns the Count property of the mColCars collection.

```
Property Get Count() As Long
  Count = mColCars.Count
End Property
```

The following sections describe adding each of these properties and methods. In addition, a Paint method that changes the color of all the cars in the collection will be added to the collection class. A final addition will be a BlueCount property that returns the number of blue cars in the collection. These latter additions demonstrate how useful it is to encapsulate collection operations within the collection class, rather than leave it up to the collection's consumer to perform these tasks.

Adding the Item Method

The Item method references an individual item in the collection (see Listing 12.22). The Item method always requires a unique index of one type or another to locate the item in the private collection.

Listing 12.22. The Item method uses the Item method of the private mColCars collection.

```
Public Function Item(Index As Variant) As clsCar
  On Error Resume Next
  Set Item = mColCars.Item(Index)
End Function
```

The Item method returns a reference to a clsCar object because that is the type of object stored in the mColCars collection.

Notice that the Index parameter is a variant. Using a variant here permits the calling routine to pass either a numeric value serving as the ordinal position of the object in the collection or a string that is the key to an item in the collection.

The On Error Resume Next statement is required to prevent runtime errors from stopping the execution in the middle of the Item method. If an invalid Index value is passed to Item, an error is not generated in the class module; the code simply continues execution at the End Function statement.

Programming the Add Method

An essential method of any collection is an Add method. After all, without an Add method, there is no way to get new elements into the collection. The Add method is the collection's primary way of ensuring that only valid objects are added to mColCars.

One approach to insulate the mColCars collection from the outside world is to simply create the clsCar object inside the Add method and return a pointer to the new object. Listing 12.23 illustrates this approach. Notice that the Add method in Listing 12.23 is a function returning a clsCar object.

Listing 12.23. The Add method creates a new clsCar object and adds it to mColCars.

```
Public Function Add() As clsCar
  Dim Car As clsCar
  Set Car = New clsCar
  Set Add = Car
End Function
```

The Add method in Listing 12.23 requires rewriting the references in existing code. Using this Add method requires the following syntax in the collection class's consumer:

```
Dim Car As clsCar
Set Car = Cars.Add
```

In some applications this might mean dozens or hundreds of changes in existing code. It'd be better to come up with an Add method for the Collection class that accommodates existing code. The syntax of the Add method actually implemented in clsCars is shown in Listing 12.24.

Listing 12.24. The Add method in clsCars verifies the data type of the object passed to it.

```
Public Sub Add(Car As Variant)
  If TypeName(Car) <> "clsCar" Then
    Exit Function
  Else
    mColCars.Add Car
  End If
End Sub
```

Notice the use of the TypeName function to verify that only valid clsCar objects are passed into the Add method. If any other type of object is passed, the Exit Sub statement is executed, gracefully ignoring the erroneous object. In this way, no items are added to mColCars that are not valid clsCar objects.

Because the Add method in Listing 12.24 does not return a value, unlike the previous Add method example in Listing 12.23, it is declared as a Sub.

You've already seen the syntax for using the new Add method. Listing 12.25 shows the proper and complete syntax for using the enhanced Add method.

Listing 12.25. The improved Add method uses the syntax discussed earlier in this chapter.

```
Dim Car As clsCar
Set Car = New clsCar
'Set the Car object's properties
'Then, add Car to the Cars collection:
Cars.Add car
```

Implementing the Remove Method

The last of the standard collection methods programmed into clsCars is the Remove method. Not surprisingly, the clsCar Remove method invokes the Remove method of the mColCars collection. The Remove method in clsCars is shown in Listing 12.26.

Listing 12.26. The Remove method simply calls the Remove method of mColCars.

```
Public Sub Remove(Index As Variant)
  On Error Resume Next
  mColCars.Remove (Index)
End Sub
```

The Remove method includes the same On Error Resume Next statement that helps avoid runtime errors in the class module. The calling routine must handle the error that occurs if an invalid index value is passed to Remove.

Implementing the Paint Method

You've already seen the code for the Paint method. All that is needed is to enumerate the items in the mColCars collection, changing the Color property of each item. Listing 12.27 shows the implementation of the Paint method in the clsCars collection class.

Listing 12.27. The Paint method changes the Color property of all car objects to the Color parameter's value.

```
Public Sub Paint(Color As String)
  Dim Car As clsCar
  For Each Car In mColCars
    Car.Color = Color
  Next Car
  Set Car = Nothing
End Sub
```

There is really nothing special about the Paint method. Notice that Paint requires a Color parameter. The clsCar class module is already designed to ensure an appropriate color is assigned to each object in clsCars. Just as a review, the syntax of the Color property in clsCar is shown in Listing 12.28.

Listing 12.28. The Color Property Let in clsCar does not allow invalid color values to be assigned to the Color property of a clsCar object.

```
Property Let Color(strColor As String)
  strColor = LCase(strColor)
  If strColor = "black" _
  Or strColor = "blue" _
  Or strColor = "green" _
  Or strColor = "red" _
  Or strColor = "white" Then
    mstrColor = strColor
```

```
   Else
      mstrColor = "other"
   End If
End Property
```

The `Color` property procedure in `clsCar` is fully explained in Chapter 10.

Programming the `BlueCount` Property

The `BlueCount` property procedure enumerates the car objects in `mColCars` and increments a counter if the car object's `Color` property is blue. Listing 12.29 shows the complete syntax of `BlueCount`.

Listing 12.29. The `BlueCount` property counts the cars with their `Color` property set to blue.

```
Public Property Get BlueCount() As Long
   Dim i As Integer
   Dim Car As clsCar
   For Each Car In mColCars
      If UCase(Car.Color) = "BLUE" Then
         i = i + 1
      End If
   Next Car
   BlueCount = i
End Property
```

Notice the use of the `UCase` function to convert the `Color` property to uppercase characters. This step is required because of the string comparison in that statement. When comparing strings, Visual Basic sees `"Blue"`, `"blue"`, and `"BLUE"` as different values. Converting the `Color` value to uppercase ensures an accurate comparison will be done on the `Color` property.

The `BlueCount` property procedure could be extended slightly to count any color. Listing 12.30 shows how `ColorCount` might work. Notice that `ColorCount` accepts a parameter specifying the color value to count in `mColCars`.

Listing 12.30. The `ColorCount` property accepts a parameter specifying the color to count in the `mColCars` collection.

```
Public Property Get ColorCount(Color As String) As Long
   Dim i As Integer
   Dim Car As clsCar
   For Each Car In mColCars
      If UCase(Car.Color) = UCase(Color) Then
```

continues

Listing 12.30. Continued.

```
      i = i + 1
    End If
  Next Car
  ColorCount = i
End Property
```

The `ColorCount` property is nearly identical to `BlueCount`. The main difference is that the color is passed in as a parameter and both the `Car.Color` property and the `Color` parameter are converted to uppercase for the comparison.

The syntax of using the `ColorCount` property is slightly different from other properties you've seen so far. The following statement is an example of using the `ColorCount` property:

```
Count = Cars.ColorCount("blue")
```

Notice that the parameter must be enclosed in parentheses. An Argument Not Optional runtime error occurs if the parentheses are omitted.

Wrapping Up the Collection Class

The collection class built in this section is demonstrated in the form `frmColClass` (see Figure 12.7) in `Cars.vbp`. This form uses `clsCars` to define a collection object named `Cars`. Most of the code behind `frmColClass` is identical to the code behind `frmCars`, the form using the simple `Collection` object.

FIGURE 12.7.

The clsCars *collection class is demonstrated in* frmColClass.

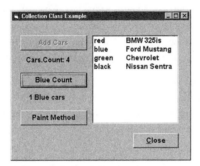

One small problem crops up when using the code directly from `frmCars`. In `frmCars`, the following statement runs without error:

```
lstDescription.AddItem Cars(Index).Year _
    & " " & Cars(Index).Make
```

This statement is actually shorthand for the following:

```
lstDescription.AddItem Cars.Item(Index).Year _
    & " " & Cars.Item(Index).Make
```

The `Item` method returns the item from the Cars collection designated by the `Index` value. Omitting the `Item` method reference works because `Item` is the default method of the Visual Basic `Collection` object. There is no corresponding default method in our custom `clsCars` collection class, so we must use the full syntax when referencing a property or method of an item stored in `clsCars`.

To designate a property or method such as `Item` as the default for the `clsCars` collection class, use the Procedure Attributes dialog box (see Figure 12.8). Open this dialog with the Tools, Procedure Attributes menu command.

FIGURE 12.8.

Designate the collection class's default property or method procedure with the Procedure Attributes dialog box.

Notice the drop-down list at the top of the Procedure Attributes dialog box. Select the procedure in `clsCars` you want to work with. When a procedure is selected (`Item` in Figure 12.8), use the drop-down list labeled Procedure ID and select Default from the list. From this point on Visual Basic will treat the `Item` method as the default member of the `clsCars` collection class.

Summary

This chapter has taken a look at the important topic of using collections to store the objects created in your Visual Basic applications. A collection is a storage device for virtually any type and number of objects. Visual Basic comes with several predefined collections such as Forms and Controls. The built-in collections make certain management tasks easier and more efficient than individually programming the operations.

Custom collection classes extend the concept of Visual Basic collections to include bulletproof and intelligent collection objects. With a bit of clever programming you can add collection classes that perform much of their own maintenance, extending the object-oriented concept of encapsulation to include collection objects.

PART III

Creating Printed Output

Using the Printer Object

In the first two sections of this book, you saw how to use Visual Basic to create Windows programs that contain many types of controls and features for the user to work with. You looked at how to handle any problems that might occur while the program is running and how to find and fix those problems before they happen. Although you have learned quite a bit about how Visual Basic works, everything you have done was geared toward getting information into your program and then processing it. If you want to have the information displayed, you must be able to create reports for the user to read. The term *reporting* is used to refer to printed reports as well as to onscreen information displayed in or on forms.

Although this chapter focuses on producing paper reports, the techniques you learn can be applied to onscreen reports. You can produce reports from a Visual Basic program by using either the Printer object, which is an integral feature of Visual Basic, or by using Crystal Reports, which is a reporting product included on the Visual Basic CD-ROM. Most applications include some type of printed reports even if they are the easiest, most visual programs around, proving that there is no substitute for the printed page.

Using the techniques in this chapter, you can create any type of report in Visual Basic that you might need. The key is in the design, layout, and testing of the report. However, there is no visual report designer that you can use, leaving you to the tried and true method of *code and test*.

Printing Information

The Printer object and its associated methods are probably the most forgotten feature in Visual Basic; they enable you to communicate directly with a printer installed on your computer. In this age of fancy database report designers, this leftover from the DOS days of computers is not used very often. To see what the fuss is all about, let's take a look at what is required for you to produce a printed report using the Printer object.

When you use the Printer object, you must decide when to start a new page, how wide the report will be, and even whether the user can cancel the printout. This might not sound like a lot of work, but think about it. When should you start a new page? After 50 lines or maybe 60 lines? Even that is not so simple. You must know the answer to many design questions including the following:

- What is the paper size?
- What font and font size should be used?
- How many characters can fit on a line?
- How many lines can fit on a page?
- What is the default printer?
- What features does the printer support?

In addition to these questions about the final report, you might have other questions, such as the following:

- How do I print a picture?
- How are columns defined in the report?

As you can see, the Printer object requires a great deal of thought to use it correctly. The more complex the report design, the more complicated the print code is. Okay, now that I put some fear in you about the Printer object, let's take a closer look at how to use it.

Following a Simple Print Routine

To produce a printout using the Printer object, you must first lay out the report on paper. This enables you to create the proper code to produce the report. As an example, you will create a simple print routine that you can then use later to produce reports from within your Visual Basic programs. To start, you must define several variables in the program for this routine to use. Table 13.1 lists the required variables and their descriptions.

Table 13.1. Print routine variables.

Variable Name	Type	Description
Line_Count	Integer	Counts the number of lines that have been printed to a page
Character_Count	Integer	Counts the number of characters that are on the current line
Total_Print_Cnt	Long	Loop through the data until there is nothing left to print
Print_Line	String	Hold the information that will be printed to the report

In the simplest form, the print routine resembles Listing 13.1.

Listing 13.1. PRINTEX1.TXT—Using the Printer object to print information.

```
Public Sub Print_Routine()
Total_Print_Cnt = 360
Line_count = 0
For I = 1 to Total_Print_Cnt
    Print_Line = "This is a demo of the Printer Object"
    Printer.Print Print_Line
    Line_Count = Line_Count + 1
    If Line_Count > 60 then
        Printer.NewPage
        Line_Count = 0
    End If
Next I
Printer.EndDoc
End Sub
```

As you can see from the code in Listing 13.1, the actual print routine is simple—the information you must keep track of is what makes it complex. Even the line count value changes for different paper sizes and printers. This routine does not deal with the width of the printed line or with more than one string being printed on a line. To handle these and other issues, you must modify the properties of the Printer object at runtime.

Using the Printer Object's Methods

The most important of the Printer object properties is the `Print` method. In its simplest form, the `Print` method specifies the information you want to have printed. The statement in Listing 13.1 prints the data in the variable `Print_Line` to the printer, as follows:

```
Print_Line = "This is a demo of the Printer Object"
```

When used this way the `Print` method prints a single piece of data and then goes to the next line of the printer. The `Print` method would not be very useful if you could print only one item at a time. However, you can print multiple items to the printer using the `Print` method. To print more than one item, you place the items in the print list, separating each item with either a comma or a semicolon. If you separate two items with a comma, the second item is printed in the next print zone. A print zone is defined as 14 characters wide in the print area. If you use a semicolon, the second item is printed immediately following the first item, with no spaces between them. To see how this works, start a new project and add a command button to the default form. Then place the code in Listing 13.2 in the command button's `Click` event.

Listing 13.2. PRINTEX2.TXT—Printing in fixed or variable columns.

```
Dim strLine1 As String
Dim strLine2 As String
```

continues

Listing 13.2. Continued.

```
strLine1 = "Demo string 1"
strLine2 = "Demo string 2"
Printer.Print strLine1; strLine2
Printer.Print
Printer.Print strLine1, strLine2
```

When you execute the code in Listing 13.2, the output should resemble Figure 13.1. In order to show you the spacing of the strings, I have printed them to the default form instead of to the printer.

FIGURE 13.1.
Multiple items can be printed to the Printer object.

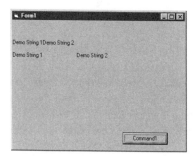

> **Warning:** Remember that the Printer object doesn't automatically support word wrapping. You must keep track of the number of characters being printed and deal with it in the program code.

If this were the only way to position the information on a report, the Printer object would not be very useful. Fortunately, you can specifically place text on a report by embedding spaces and tabs using the Spc and Tab functions.

The Spc function places a specified number of spaces in the printout. This enables you to add a specific amount of space between two items in the print list. The following line of code is an example of how to use the Spc function. In this code, 40 spaces are placed between the two strings:

```
Printer.Print "First String"; Spc(40); "Second String"
```

> **Note:** When using the Spc function, always use the semicolon as the separator. This prevents the spaces from starting in the next print zone.

The Spc function is useful only when you are printing information that is fixed in length. If you are printing variable-length information use the Tab function. The Tab function also enables you to create columns in a report by causing the printing to start at a specific location on the print line. The syntax of the Tab function is similar to that of the Spc function, but instead of specifying the number of spaces, you specify the column to tab to. The following line of code prints the second string in column 40 of the printout:

```
Printer.Print "First String"; Tab(40); "Second String"
```

The big difference between the Spc and Tab functions is how the data will line up on the report. Figure 13.2 shows how the two functions will print the information.

FIGURE 13.2.

In this example, the Spc and Tab functions are printed to a form.

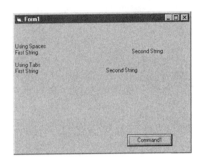

Almost any function available in Visual Basic can be used in conjunction with the Printer object to produce a report. Additionally, you can use the Format function to format the information exactly as you need it to appear in the final report.

After you lay out the report and start to print it, you must tell the printer when to perform tasks, and you need to know how much space on a line the information takes. There are several methods that you can use to work with the Printer object.

The NewPage method enables you to inform the Printer object when to go to a new page. Of course, you must track the number of lines that have been printed and issue this method when needed. Otherwise, you will print right off the bottom of the page. If you look back at the simple print routine, you will notice that the routine checks the number of lines printed and issues the NewPage method when the specified number of lines has been reached. The routine then resets the line counter (refer to Listing 13.1).

> **Note:** When the NewPage method is used to advance to the next page, it automatically increments the Printer object's Page property by 1.

After you send the information to the printer using the Print method, you must tell the printer that it is time to actually print the report. The EndDoc method is used to tell the Printer object to terminate the print operation and release the document to the print device or spooler.

When printing large reports you should enable the user to cancel the printout before it is actually sent to the printer. The KillDoc method is used to terminate the current print job. You can modify the simple print routine to enable the user to cancel the printout after every page is printed. It is really up to you when and how often you want the user to be able to cancel the printout. Listing 13.3 is the simple print routine modified with the KillDoc method.

Listing 13.3. PRINTEX3.TXT—Using the printer methods to perform printing functions.

```
Public Sub Print_Routine()
Total_Print_Cnt = 360
Line_count = 0
For I = 1 to Total_Print_Cnt
    Print_Line = "This is a demo of the Printer Object"
    Printer.Print Print_Line
    Line_Count = Line_Count + 1
    If Line_Count > 60 then
        Printer.NewPage
        Line_Count = 0
        If MsgBox("Do you want to Cancel the PrintOut?", _
                    vbQuestion + vbYesNo, App.Title) = vbYes Then
            Printer.KillDoc
            Exit For
        End If
    End If
Next I
Printer.EndDoc
End Sub
```

> **Warning:** If the Print Manager is handling the print job, KillDoc deletes the current print job before the printer receives any information. However, if the Print Manager is not handling the print job, some or all of the data might be sent to the printer before the KillDoc method can take effect.

To find the width or height of the text you want to print, use the TextWidth and TextHeight methods to determine the size of the text you are printing. Both of these methods return values expressed in terms of the ScaleMode property setting or Scale method that is in effect for the Printer object. As an example, the following line of code would calculate the width of a text string to be printed:

```
Character_count = TextWidth(Print_Line)
```

Controlling the Printer

So far, everything we have done with the Printer object has assumed that the printer was set up and ready to print anything we send to it. For the most part this is true; however, there are several properties that you can use to modify the way the information is printed. Most of these can be modified while your report is being created. Some of the things you can do are to set the orientation of the printer and specify the number of copies to print. Although the printer's default settings are fine for most jobs, you do have quite a bit of control over the way the printer is set up. The properties of the Printer object can be modified as needed. Table 13.2 lists the properties that you can use and the effects they will have on your printouts. Keep in mind that some of the properties listed do not apply to every printer.

Table 13.2. The Printer object's properties.

Property Name	Description
Copies	Tells the printer how many copies of each page to make.
Duplex	Determines whether the printout will be on one side of a page or both sides. If the printout is on both sides of the page, this property also determines whether the second side assumes a horizontal or vertical flip of the page.
FontTransparent	Determines whether background text of graphics shows through text printed on the page.
Orientation	Determines whether the page is in Portrait or Landscape mode.
Page	Tells your program the current page number.
PaperBin	Determines which paper bin of a printer will be used. This property is also used to tell the printer to wait for manual insertion of each page to be printed. This is very useful for handling preprinted forms.
PaperSize	Sets the size of paper for the printout. This property can be set to one of several default paper sizes. The property can also be set to allow a user-defined paper size, in which case you must define the Height and Width properties of the page.
PrintQuality	Sets the printer resolution to draft-, low-, medium-, or high-quality.
Zoom	Sets a percentage by which the size of the printout is scaled up or down. Setting the Zoom property to 50% would cause the report to be printed half-size.

You usually enable the user to change these properties by using the Common Dialog control included with Visual Basic. The Common Dialog control (see Figure 13.3) prompts the user for the different information for the printer, and that information is used to set the appropriate properties.

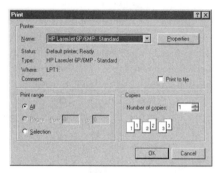

For more information on these properties, see the Visual Basic Help topics for the individual property.

Using the Printer Collection

The Printer collection enables you to gather the information on all the available printers installed on your computer so you can specify a default printer for your application. In Chapter 12, "Working with Objects and Collections," you learned that collections are arrays of objects and how you can use them in your programs. The Printer collection enables you to inspect the different properties of each printer and decide which one you want your application to use. As an example, you might want to find which available printer supports duplex printing. Listing 13.4 searches all the available printers to locate the first printer that supports duplex, and then sets it as the default printer.

Listing 13.4. PRINTEX4.TXT—Setting printer properties.

```
Dim myPrinter As Printer
For Each myPrinter in Printers
    If myPrinter.Duplex = vbPRDPHorizontal Then
        ' Set the default printer
        Set Printer = myPrinter
        Exit For
    End If
Next
```

The code in Listing 13.4 can be used to search or display the information about any printer defined on the computer. In addition, if your program needs to know whether any printer is installed on the computer you can use the Count property of the Printer collection as follows:

```
If Printers.Count <= 0 Then
    MsgBox "There are no printers installed on the Computer!", vbInformation
End If
```

> **Warning:** The Printer collection can access the properties only as read-only. To read and modify the properties of a printer, you must first set that printer as the default printer for the application.

Summary

In this chapter you have seen how much work is involved in creating and printing reports using the Printer object that comes with Visual Basic. You are in complete control of everything that is printed, and more importantly, you control how it is printed. By modifying the properties of the Printer object and using its methods, you can create some very complex reports or some very simple ones. As you will see in Chapter 14, "Using Crystal Reports," if you want to create very complex reports for your program you should use a tool designed to help you. The Printer object should be used only for simple list style reports; anything more complex than that is too difficult to maintain for different printers.

Using Crystal Reports

In Chapter 13, "Using the Printer Object," you saw how to send information to a printer from within a Visual Basic program. However, creating great-looking reports requires a unique program designed specifically for that purpose. Crystal Reports is a complete reporting tool included on the Visual Basic product CD-ROM. By using this reporting tool, you can create professional-looking reports to display onscreen with your application or send to a printer.

Now that you know how to use the Printer object, you will learn how to use the Crystal Reports product to design and create professional-looking reports to add to your Visual Basic program. In addition, you are going to learn how to run the reports from within the Visual Basic program using the Crystal Reports Custom control.

Explaining Crystal Reports

Before learning how to create a report, you must know what Crystal Reports is and what features and tools are available to you when using it. By knowing and understanding the tools, features, and options available to you in Crystal Reports, you can design the reports you need for your application. Crystal Reports is a powerful program for creating custom reports, lists, and labels from the data in your application database. When Crystal Reports connects to the database, it reads the values from the fields you selected and places them into a report, either as-is or as part of a formula that generates more complex values. Crystal Reports is designed to work with the different types of data that can be found in a database, such as the following:

- Numbers
- Currency
- Text
- Dates
- Boolean

A wide range of built-in tools can be used to manipulate data to fit the requirements of the report. These tools enable you to

- Create calculations
- Calculate subtotals and grand totals
- Convert data from one type to another
- Calculate averages
- Count the total number of records in a query
- Test for the presence of specific values
- Filter database records
- Perform date calculations

The data from your database can be placed wherever you need it on the report and can be highlighted by changing the fonts or font sizes. Using Crystal Reports, your reports can be as simple or as complex as your needs require. After you have designed a report for your application, you can use it within the application or as a template to create other similar reports. Crystal Reports was created to enable both technical and nontechnical users to create customized reports quickly and easily from a variety of databases. Although most database systems include their own report generators, they are usually too difficult for nontechnical people to use, and they generally require a good understanding of how that database works.

> **Note:** No matter how much you change the data in a report, it will not be changed in the database.

Crystal Reports connects to almost any database system available today. Actually, there are two unique methods used to connect to a database: Data File and SQL/ODBC. The Data File method is designed for the smaller, PC-based databases, such as dBase and Microsoft Access. The SQL/ODBC method uses an ODBC (Open Database Connectivity) connection, which connects to any database that supports it. Some databases in this group are Microsoft Access, Oracle, Sybase, and Microsoft SQL Server.

> **Note:** Although ODBC and the newer OLE/DB connections are generally used for complex server databases, they can also be used to access Paradox and, if needed, Microsoft Access.

Taking a Quick Tour

When you start Crystal Reports, you see the main application window (see Figure 14.1). After you begin working with a report, the main window contains two separate tabbed windows that you use to design and preview the report you are working on. Both the Design and Preview windows are actually included in a child window within the Crystal Reports application. These windows have their own unique features and functions that enable you to work with your report design in slightly different ways.

FIGURE 14.1.

The Crystal Reports main window is used to design and modify a report.

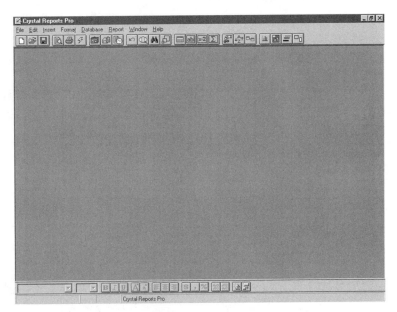

In the next several pages, you will see the different work areas of Crystal Reports and the tools that are available to you. After you have a working knowledge of these features, you will create a simple report and then run it from a Visual Basic program.

Using the Design Window

The Design window (see Figure 14.2) is separated into two sections that provide onscreen information which helps you design a report. The large white area of the Design window is the Edit box. This is where you design and format your report. The horizontal lines in the Edit box separate the report into several sections. As you add new data groups to your report, more sections appear in the Edit box. The gray area to the left of the Edit box displays additional information to assist you in placing the data and other objects on the report. The horizontal lines extend into the gray area, identifying which section is which.

Several common features are incorporated into Crystal Reports that you have probably used in other applications. These include a ruler that can be displayed to assist in the placement of data on the form and a Snap-to-Grid feature like the one in the Visual Basic development environment, which assists in lining up objects on the report. Crystal Reports functions and features are accessed via the toolbar at the top of the main window, the main menu, or by using the pop-up menus directly on the report. Crystal Reports also provides wizards to help you add the following objects to the report:

- Column totals
- Selection conditions
- Data groups
- Formulas (calculated fields)
- Sort orders

FIGURE 14.2.

You access the Design window through the Design Window tab in the main window.

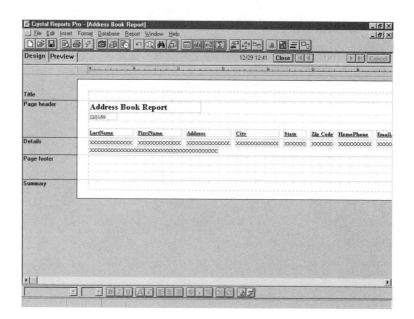

The right-click pop-up menus provide access to a selected object's related functions. Some of these options are as follows:

- Changing font styles
- Formatting the data
- Adding borders
- Changing colors
- Browsing the data from the database
- Adding conditions

After you select your database, the Design window is displayed to enable you to insert and format the data you need in your report. When you start a new report, the five sections listed in Table 14.1 are created automatically in the Design window.

Table 14.1. Section types found in the Design window.

Section Name	Description
Title	Displays the report title, data, and any other information that must appear at the top of the report. Information displayed here is shown only once.
Page Header	Similar to the Title section; this information is displayed at the top of every page.
Details	Displays the detail information from a query.
Page Footer	Usually displays the page number and any other information that you want at the bottom of each page.
Summary	Displays information only on the last page of your report.

You build reports by inserting data fields, formulas, and other information into the Details section of the Design window. You use the Insert menu to select or build the fields you want to insert on the report. You add subtotals and other group values by selecting a field and then building the conditions to generate the new subtotal or group value. These group sections are created as needed, and the values are placed in the associated group section. If you want the value to be some place else on the report, you simply select it and drag it there.

Using the Preview Window

You can see how your report will look when it is displayed or printed by switching to the Preview window. Whenever you select this tab, Crystal Reports retrieves the data from the database, performs any defined calculations, and then displays the report (see Figure 14.3). After the data is displayed, you can review the positioning and formatting of all the information on the report. Additionally, you can see the results of all summaries, calculations, and filters. In effect, this is what the final report looks like.

While on the Preview window, you can still modify the format of your report without having to return to the Design window. The Preview window does have a different look and feel than the Design window. Each field in the database can contain hundreds of values, depending on the number of records in the database. When you place a field in the report on the Design window, a single field box is displayed that represents all those values. When you select this field, sizing handles appear, and the border changes color (see Figure 14.4).

On the Preview tab, you are working with the actual data. Instead of a box with 9s or Xs in it, the data values are displayed. When you select a field, a sizing box appears around every value from the selected field. Despite the difference in look and feel, the process of building and modifying the report is the same in both windows.

FIGURE 14.3.
Use the Preview tab to view a report during the design process.

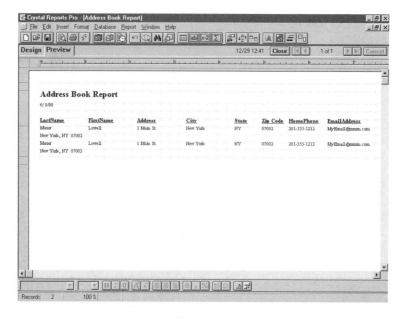

FIGURE 14.4.
Although you can't see the yellow border in this figure, you will see it when working with the report.

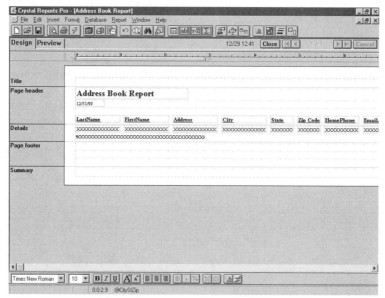

Working with the Crystal Reports Wizards

Crystal Reports contains several wizards you can use when creating reports. When you start a new report by choosing File, New, the Create New Report dialog box is displayed as shown in Figure 14.5.

FIGURE 14.5.
The Create New Report dialog box displays the available report wizards.

The series of buttons in the Create New Report dialog box represents the different report wizards from which you can choose. Each wizard takes you through the steps required to create that style of report. If you want to build a new report based on an existing one, click the Another Report button. The program will make a duplicate of the original report that you can modify as needed to create the new report. If you want to build a report from scratch, click the Custom button. Several Report Type and Data Type buttons appear at the bottom of the Create New Report dialog box (see Figure 14.6).

FIGURE 14.6.
Custom report buttons enable you to create a new report.

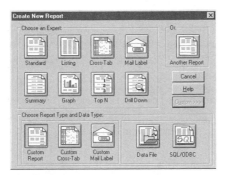

Adding Custom Formulas to a Report

Crystal Reports uses formulas and functions to do the kind of processing and data manipulation that is required for advanced database reporting. Choose Edit, Formula and use the Edit Formula dialog box to create the calculated fields in the report (see Figure 14.7).

The Edit Formula dialog box enables you to work with both formulas and functions. A *formula* is a set of instructions that calculate the information you can't directly receive from the database. If a database record has two fields, Unit Price and Quantity Sold, but you need the total sales price, you would have to multiply the two fields to calculate the total sales price. This process is accomplished by using a formula that you place in the report.

FIGURE 14.7.

Both simple and complex formulas are defined using the Edit Formula dialog box.

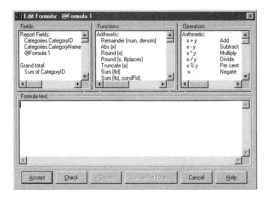

This type of formula is simple because it uses the standard arithmetic operators. However, not all the calculations you need are simple formulas. At times you might require complex calculations or manipulations of the database fields. If you want to display the average monthly sales for the previous year, rounded to the nearest unit, you need a mathematical formula. The functions required to perform these activities involve a fair amount of data manipulation. Whereas some of this can be done using only Crystal Reports operators, many types of manipulations can't be done without the use of functions.

Functions are built-in procedures or subroutines that are used to evaluate, calculate, or transform data from the database. The Edit Formula dialog box is divided into four sub-windows that are used to create the calculation (refer Figure 14.7). The Fields window lists all the database fields that are available to you, based on the tables you have previously selected. The Functions window lists all the functions you can use to create a calculated field. The Operators window lists all the operators you can use. The largest window is the Formula Text window, where you build the actual calculation. You can use the different windows to select items, or if you know the correct syntax, type directly into the Formula Text window.

You can combine fields, functions, operators, and other calculations to create complex calculated fields. This enables you to create complex calculations in steps (small calculated fields) and then combine them to form the finished calculation.

Selecting the Required Records

When you select a field for the report, every row or query in the table is printed. However, in many cases you need only specific rows of data from the database. For example, you might want only New York customer data, or only invoices that fall within a particular range of dates. Crystal Reports includes four options on the Report menu used to select the data in your report; the options are listed in Table 14.2.

Table 14.2. Available report selection menu options.

Menu Option	Description
Select Records	Enables you to limit the number of records in your report based on a condition (or conditions) specified using the Selection Formula dialog box.
Edit Record Selection Formula	Uses the Formula Editor to enable you to modify the selection condition.
Select Groups	Enables you to limit your report to a specific group or groups, based on a condition or conditions specified using a Selection Formula dialog box.
Edit Group Selection Formula	Uses the Formula Editor to enable you to modify the selection condition.

Even though you will be able to create professional-looking reports after completing this chapter, there are many more features included in Crystal Reports than can be covered. In the next section, you will see how to create a report by using the Crystal Reports program and then learn how to access the report from a Visual Basic application.

Creating a Report

As with anything else in the program design process, reports require both your time and analysis before you actually create them. For each report that you are creating, you should answer the following questions:

- What is the purpose of the report?
- What information should be included in it?
- Does it require selection capabilities?
- What is the layout of the report?

If you have the answers to these questions, your reports will perform well. Before starting Crystal Reports, you should sketch out what the report will look like and list the fields needed for the report. After you have listed the required fields, sketch the layout of the report. After you are satisfied with both the field list and the layout, you can take the next step, which is to start Crystal Reports. You are then placed in the main window (refer to Figure 14.1).

Starting the Design Process

To start the process, choose File, New from the menu to open the New Report dialog box. For the sample report you will be using the standard report format; however, Crystal Reports can assist you in creating many different styles of reports from this dialog box:

- Standard—Creates a standard report with rows and columns. It often has summary information at the bottom of the columns.

- Listing—Creates a simple row and column listing of the information in a record-set.

- Cross-Tab—Inverts the order of a standard columnar report. It is often used to obtain a quick summary view of a more complex set of data.

- Mail Label—Creates items such as mailing labels or name tags from the information in your database.

- Summary—Presents summary information about the data, such as total and average sales or the number of attendees.

- Graph—Shows the information in a graphical form.

- Top N—Shows only a specified number of the top records in the recordset. For example, this report style can be used to show the top five salespeople in the company.

- Drill Down—Shows the supporting information, or detail information, for each record.

After selecting the Standard report option and clicking OK, the related Report Wizard is automatically started. For the style selected, seven steps are involved in creating the initial report (see Figure 14.8).

FIGURE 14.8.

The Report Wizard steps you through the creation process.

Choosing a Database

The logical starting point of any report is to select the database tables required for the report. The first tab of the wizard displays the data access choices and any tables already included in the report. To select the data source for the report you are building, select the Data File button to display the Choose Database File dialog box (see Figure 14.9).

FIGURE 14.9.
Choose the database for the report.

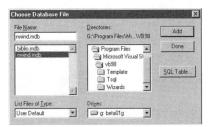

> **Note:** For the purposes of this discussion, you will be using the Northwind database (...\Microsoft Visual Studio\VB98\NWIND.MDB), which is included with Visual Basic.

Setting the Relationships

After you select the database, all the tables and queries available in the database are added to the report. If you see the wizard in the background, you will see the tables and queries listed. Click the Done button to return to the wizard. You are then automatically taken to the wizard's second tab.

> **Warning:** If you are using an ODBC/SQL database, you will be shown a list of tables and queries from which to select. Only the tables and queries that you select will be included in the report.

The Links tab of the Report wizard enables you to modify the join information that is already defined in the database. Because the Northwind database already has the join information defined, the joins are displayed (see Figure 14.10). On this tab, a message is displayed, enabling you to add more tables if needed.

Selecting the Fields for the Report

If the joins are correct, click the Next button to continue to the Fields tab. The Fields tab (see Figure 14.11) enables you to select the fields from each of the tables you need in the report.

FIGURE 14.10.
Define or modify the joins for a report.

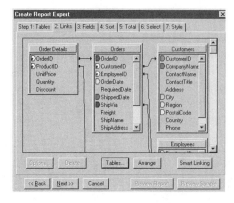

FIGURE 14.11.
Select the data fields from the included tables and queries.

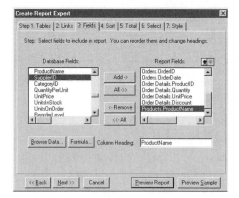

You add the fields to the report data list by double-clicking each field in the Database Fields list or by highlighting the fields you want and clicking the Add button. In addition, you can position the fields in the report. For each field selected, you can also enter a custom column heading in the text box below the list. Select the fields listed in Table 14.3 and add them to the fields list for the report.

Table 14.3. Database fields for the sample report.

Table	Field
Customers	CustomerID
	CompanyName
	ContactName
	Address
	City
	Region
	PostalCode

Table	Field
Orders	OrderID
	OrderDate
Order Details	ProductID
	Quantity
	UnitPrice
	Discount
Products	ProductName

Adding Calculations

During the design of a report, you will sometimes require some manipulation to be done to some of the fields you have selected, either by performing some mathematical or string process. The Fields tab contains the Formula button, which enables you to enter formulas for calculated fields. The report you are creating needs two calculated fields, so click the Formula button to add the fields included in Table 14.4.

Table 14.4. Adding the custom formulas to the report.

Field Name	Custom Formula
Extended Price	Order Details.Quantity * Order Details.UnitPrice
Discounted Price	Extended Price – (Extended Price * Order Details.Discount)

When you add the calculated fields, you should notice that they have an @ at the beginning of the name. This symbol indicates that the field is a formula. You will also see that the calculated fields are listed in a new section called Report Fields in the Database Fields window. They still must be added to the report like any other field. After you have added all the fields to the report, you can either preview the report or continue refining it by adding other options.

Other Options

Before you preview the report, look at the other available options on the other tabs of the Create Report Expert. These options are summarized in the following list:

- Sort tab—Specifies an order by which the lines of the report are sorted.
- Total tab—Determines whether subtotals and grand totals of numerical data are included on the report.
- Select tab—Specifies a selection criteria for the report. Choose it to produce only a subset of the recordset that is the source of the data. Use of a subset increases the processing speed of the report.

- Style tab—Specifies a specific style of the report, such as placing lines after each record or making the entire report appear as a table. It also enables you to add pictures to the report.

Now click the Next button to add the sorts required for this report. When you click the Next button, the Sort tab is displayed (see Figure 14.12).

FIGURE 14.12.
Choose the fields and order to sort by.

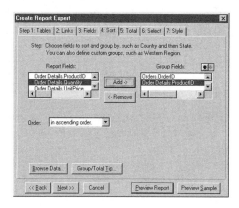

The Sort tab enables you to select the fields you want to sort and the order or direction of the sort. In this report, the following fields should be used to sort in the listed order:

- `Customers.CustomerID`
- `Orders.OrderID`
- `[Order Details].ProductID`

After specifying the sort criteria, click Next to add any subtotals to the report. The wizard's Total tab displays a tab for every field in the report for which you have specified a sort (see figure 14.13).

FIGURE 14.13.
Defining the totals for a report.

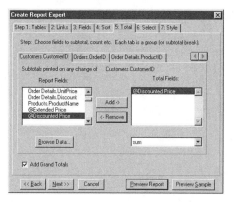

By removing any unnecessary fields from the Total Fields list, you can add the totals listed in Table 14.5 to the report.

Table 14.5. Totaling the correct report values.

Tab Name	Field to Sum
Customers.CustomerID	@Discounted Price
Orders.OrderID	Order Details.Quantity
[Order Details].ProductID	None

When you are satisfied with your selections, click Next twice to proceed to the Style tab.

> **Tip:** Although the Select tab is not used in this example, it enables to you to easily set up conditions that Crystal Reports will use when retrieving data from the database. Using this tab, you can build standard conditions. However, if you need more complex conditions, you should create your own selection formulas.

The Style tab (see Figure 14.14) enables you to choose from a list of default styles for your report. In addition, you can add a title to your report using this tab.

FIGURE 14.14.
Set the style of the report.

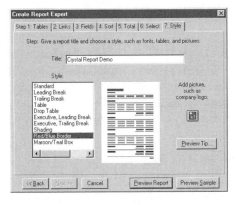

Choose the Standard style and enter Customer Order Report as the title of the report. To complete the creation process, click the Preview Report button. You should now be in the Preview window (see Figure 14.15).

As you can see from this preview, the report needs some formatting to make it look more professional. Some of the numeric fields need to be formatted, and the following items need to be added to the report:

- A page header
- A system date
- Page numbering

FIGURE 14.15.
The report displayed in the Preview window.

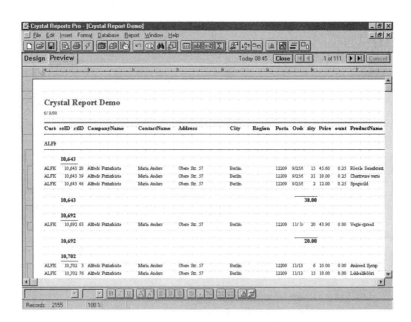

These items can be added to the report by using the Special Fields option on the Insert menu. Right-clicking any field to label gives you a pop-up menu that lists all the editing options available for the selected object. In addition to these changes, you probably want to move the fields around to arrange them in the style of an invoice. After all these changes are completed, the report could resemble the one shown in Figure 14.16.

After you have completed the design of the report, save it as a report file so that you can access it from your Visual Basic program.

Although you can run the reports you create from within Crystal Reports, you'll probably want to access them from within your Visual Basic program. You can do so by using the Crystal Reports Custom control, which is one of the controls installed with Crystal Reports. The Crystal Reports Custom control provides a link between the Crystal Reports engine and the reports you create with the report designer.

Using the Crystal Reports Custom Control

The first step in accessing Crystal Reports is to make the control available to your program. If Visual Basic is not started, start it and then create a new project. Now you must add the Crystal Reports Custom control to your Visual Basic toolbox using the Components dialog box (see Figure 14.17). To open the Components dialog box choose Project, Components. In this dialog box, you can specify which custom controls are available in your project.

FIGURE 14.16.
The final report includes formatting in the style of an invoice.

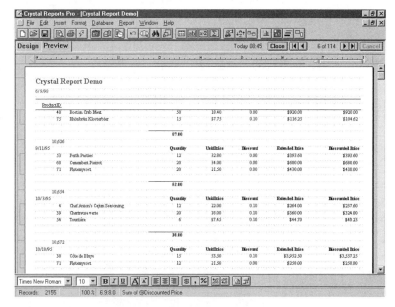

FIGURE 14.17.
Adding the Crystal Reports Custom control to the project.

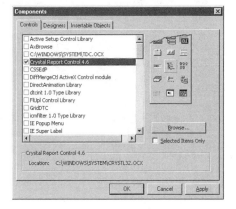

Tip: The Components dialog box can also be displayed by right-clicking the toolbox and selecting Components from the pop-up menu.

After the Crystal Reports control is available in your toolbox, you can use it in your program. To gain access to the control, simply select it from the toolbox and place it on the form where you will access the reports from. Because the Crystal Reports control is not visible at runtime, it appears only as an icon on your form. After the control is on the form, you can set the properties that access the reports you create with the report designer. Additionally, you should change the Name property to reflect your program's use of the control. For this example, set the Name property to crReport.

Selecting the Report to Run

The key property you must specify is the ReportFileName property. This property specifies the actual report that you will run from your program. You can easily set this property using the Property Pages dialog box. Click the ellipsis button that appears to the right of the property in the Properties window as shown in Figure 14.18. From this page, you can specify the name of the report and the report's destination.

FIGURE 14.18.
Specify the report filename and destination on the Custom Controls Property page.

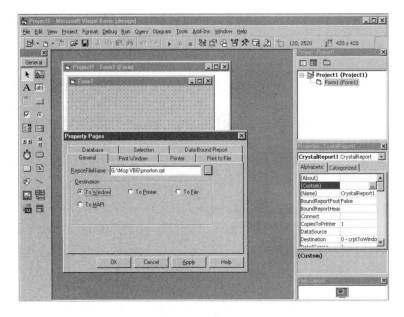

On the General tab of the Property Pages dialog box, either type the name of the report into the field for the ReportFileName property, or select the report from a file dialog box by clicking the ellipsis button on the Property Pages dialog box. Selecting the ReportFileName is the minimum requirement for Crystal Reports to run a report. The other tabs on the Properties page enable you to customize the report by specifying the following options for the report:

Print Window	Sets the properties of the Print display window
Printer	Sets the number of copies to print
Print to File	Sets the filename and file type when printing a report to the printer
Database	Enables you to enter the user ID and connection info for a database
Selection	Enables entry of the `SelectionFormula` and `GroupSelectionFormula`
Data-Bound Report	Sets the heading for a database report

Modifying the Optional Properties

Although the `ReportFileName` is the only required property for the report, you can choose to set several optional properties for the report. The first of these properties is the `SelectionFormula` property. This property enables you to limit the number of records that will be included in the report. The `SelectionFormula` property is similar to the `Where` clause of an SQL statement, but it uses its own particular format to enter the information. To specify the `SelectionFormula`, you must specify the name of the recordset and the field to be compared. You must express this recordset/field combination in dot notation and enclose it in curly brackets. After specifying the recordset and field, you must specify the comparison operator and the value to be compared. The final result is an expression like the following:

```
{MemberShipList.OrgCode}=1
```

You also can use multiple expressions by including the `And` or `Or` operators.

> **Note:** For a short discussion on SQL, see Chapter 17, "Creating Queries in Visual Basic."

> **Warning:** If you enter a `SelectionFormula` when you're designing your report, any formula you enter in the `SelectionFormula` property of the Crystal Reports control provides an additional filter on the records.

The `CopiesToPrinter` property enables the user to specify how many copies of the report are needed. This property can be set to any integer value.

Activating the Custom Control

After you have added the Crystal Reports control to your form and set the properties, you are almost ready to start printing. The final step is to have the Visual Basic code tell Crystal Reports when it should print the report. This is done by adding a single line of code to initiate the report. The following line of code sets the Action property of the Crystal Reports control to 1, which is the value that starts the printing process:

```
crReport.Action = crRunReport     'This is a constant with the value of 1
```

> **Tip:** To make it easier to understand your code, you should define a constant to use in place of the number when requesting Crystal Reports to run a report.

In the project, add a command button to the default form and place the previous line of code in its Click event routine. Now run the program and click the command button to run the report. The report you specified in the Properties page is then executed and displayed in its own window (see Figure 14.19).

FIGURE 14.19.
Display the specified report to the screen from a Visual Basic program.

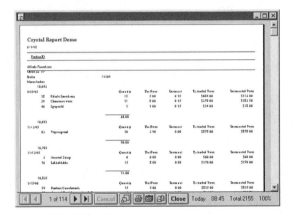

Remember that this was just a simple example of displaying a report from a program. There are many more options, properties, and methods you can access that enable you to customize how the report looks when it is displayed.

Changing the Properties at Runtime

What you have just completed is the quickest way to execute a report from Crystal Reports. However, in most applications there is usually more than one report that the users will need to display or print, so you will need to change the Crystal Reports control's properties at runtime. Otherwise, you would need to place a separate report control for each report you supply to the user. All the major properties of the Crystal Reports control, such as ReportFileName and SelectionFormula, are available at runtime. The following sample code sets up the Crystal Reports control for a new report and specifies a selection criteria based on user input:

```
crReport.ReportFileName = "AddrList.rpt"
crReport.SelectionFormula = "{EntryList.State}=" & txtStateCd
crReport.action = crRunReport   'This is a constant for the value 1
```

The other property you might need to set at runtime is the `DataFiles` property. This property is not available at design time. It specifies the name of the database file that is used by the report. Unless the user installs your application in exactly the same directory that you have on your computer, you will need to tell the Crystal Reports control the location of the database file on the user's PC.

The `DataFiles` property is actually an array with the first element number of zero. If you're using more than one database in your report, you must set the value of each `DataFiles` array element for each database. For most of your reports, however, you will be using only a single database. The following line of code shows you how to set the value of the `DataFiles` property for the database. This line assumes that the database file is in the same folder as your application:

```
crReport.DataFiles(0) = App.Path & "\AddressBook.mdb"
```

Creating a Report Selection Interface

In most Visual Basic applications that have many reports associated with them, a good report-selection interface is required for the user to be able to select a report easily. In addition, the user should be able to modify the report's options and specify selection criteria. In an application that I developed, a Visual Basic form was used with several controls in conjunction with an input table to generate the report manager (see Figure 14.20).

FIGURE 14.20.
A complete report manager used by a Visual Basic application.

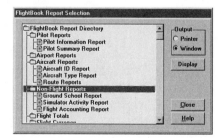

This report manager displays report descriptions in a TreeView control with headings for each group of reports added to the list. It also uses the CommonDialog control to display the Printer dialog box. Using a TreeView control requires copious amounts of code to populate and control it. You could create a simpler version of this interface by replacing the TreeView control with a List Box control (see Figure 14.21).

FIGURE 14.21.
Another simpler version of the report manager.

These are only two of the many different managers that you could create using Visual Basic controls and the Crystal Reports Custom control. The only real limitation is your own imagination.

Summary

In this chapter, you learned how to use Crystal Reports to create professional-looking reports with very little effort. In addition, you added the Crystal Reports Custom control to a Visual Basic application and used it to run and then display a report in a window. What you have accomplished in this chapter has only scratched the surface of what the Crystal Reports product is capable of. However, you now have a solid foundation to build on when adding complex reporting to your application.

PART IV

Accessing Data

Reading and Writing Text Files

This chapter begins the subject of data handling in Visual Basic. You begin your study of Visual Basic data access methods by examining the lowest common denominator in data storage; that is, the text file. Although more sophisticated data storage methods are available, the text file remains the most universal and, in some ways, the easiest way to share data among diverse computer systems. For example, text files are one of the few ways to share data between obsolete computer systems, computer programs that are no longer supported by their vendors or whose vendors have gone out of business, and situations in which direct connection between computer systems is not possible.

This chapter discusses several different formats frequently encountered when working with text files. As you will see later in this chapter, there are just a few different popular formats for storing data in text files. This chapter explains the Visual Basic commands required to open, retrieve data from text files, and display that data on Visual Basic forms. In later chapters in this section of the book, you will see how to take that data, or any data, and store it in database files. This chapter is intended to get you started thinking about how Visual Basic works with data.

Understanding Text Files

Most corporations have such a mix of data sources and machines that it's hard to get all the data together in one place for processing and comparison. A company might have an IBM 3090 mainframe, an AS/400 mid-range system, a couple of UNIX boxes, and a bunch of PCs all networked together (see Figure 15.1). That's where client/server, one of the key buzzwords of the '90s, comes in. Information systems departments are trying to find a way to use their mainframe hardware investment along with the power of today's desktop computers. A whole new product line has been developed by software vendors, creating "middleware" applications and database gateways, whose sole purpose is to connect different types of data. Many other vendors have started offering support for their back-end products out of the box.

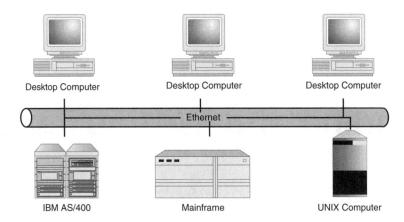

FIGURE 15.1.
*Diverse computers
must coexist in
modern business
environments.*

Desktop Computer   Desktop Computer   Desktop Computer

Ethernet

IBM AS/400   Mainframe   UNIX Computer

Suppose you work for Acme Widgets, Inc., which has been in business for 20 years. In those 20 years, Acme has amassed an impressive arsenal of computing hardware. Its order-entry system runs on "big iron" IBM mainframes. Its sales/marketing application runs on an AS/400. Now Acme has decided to build an executive information system (EIS) on its DEC Alpha NT Server using Visual Basic. Your job is to bring the most pertinent information from each system together into one place and make that data easy to understand for the decision makers at Acme. Where do you start? Plan your strategy for each component of the application and each platform you are supporting. Don't begin coding or make promises until you know the job can be done.

As a Visual Basic programmer, you might be overwhelmed by the challenge of integrating data from such a wide variety of data sources. Because of the differences in hardware and software architectures used in businesses today, there is no standardized way of moving data freely back and forth between Windows, UNIX, mainframe, and other computer systems. When you add the complexity of acquiring data across the Internet, legacy data stored in obsolete file formats, and other data sources frequently encountered in business, the task is truly daunting.

Fortunately, one reasonable solution is at hand. The lowest common denominator of data transfer has always been the text file. All computer systems and most software programs are capable of exporting data in text formats. Many mainframe and midrange systems routinely store their data in text files that can be read by any other application that has access to it. Although text files are very different from database tables in that a text file does not feature data validation, fancy storage capabilities, or other capabilities that are frequently found in database systems, almost all types of data can be stored in some text format or other. This chapter looks at two of the most common text file storage formats and shows how to read those text files into a Visual Basic program and display the data on a Visual Basic form.

Downloading the Data

Many software vendors are aware of the problems facing IS shops today. Tools are quickly becoming available to connect desktop computers to almost any platform (see Figure 15.2). Improved network communications and data transmission speeds are also making host connections more practical. Companies like Attachmate and Wall Data have built their businesses on connectivity. They provide software packages for terminal emulation, ODBC connections, and download functions for most of the popular hosts. Of course you can still use a co-ax connection with a 3270 emulation board in your workstation to connect to a mainframe as well.

FIGURE 15.2.
Middleware can be an important part of data sharing plans.

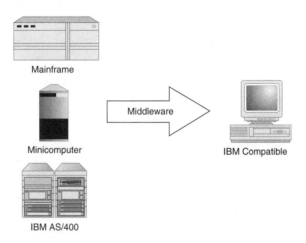

Mainframe

Minicomputer

Middleware

IBM Compatible

IBM AS/400

The key to success in one of these applications is finding a tool with scripting capabilities that enable you to schedule your downloads at regular intervals and react to errors when they occur. For example, Attachmate's Tools for Microsoft Office Professional lets you make API calls from your VBA procedures to automate routines.

This chapter is not about moving data between a mainframe or midrange system and desktop computers. Because there are so many different hardware and software systems out there, it's not possible to generalize how to go about migrating data between machines. You're on your own when it comes to getting the data off the remote machine. However, after the text data is resident on a Windows computer, Visual Basic has all the tools necessary to get it into the programs you write.

Reviewing Database Terminology

Although you will read much more about database terminology in later chapters of this book, before you can proceed much farther with the topic of text files it is important to establish the basic terminology used when working with data stored in databases. A basic assumption in this chapter is that you have been assigned the task of extracting data from text files and putting that data into a Visual Basic application. In this chapter, you will not store the data in a real database file and will leave that task to a later chapter. Working with database files is discussed in Chapters 18, "Mastering Jet DAO," and 19, "Using Advanced Data Access Methods." Instead, in this chapter you'll learn how to pull data out of text files and use that data on Visual Basic forms.

The data in a database table is arranged in rows and columns. Each column, called a *field*, contains the same type of data. For example, a field might contain string data such as names, addresses, and phone numbers. Another column might contain numeric information such as quantities, units on order, sales figures, and currency values. Another field in the table might contain date and time information.

Each row of the database table is called a *record* and contains several different fields. A record represents a single entity, such as an employee, customer, or order.

Figure 15.3 shows an example of a typical database table. This particular example is the Products table from the Northwind Traders sample database that comes with Visual Basic.

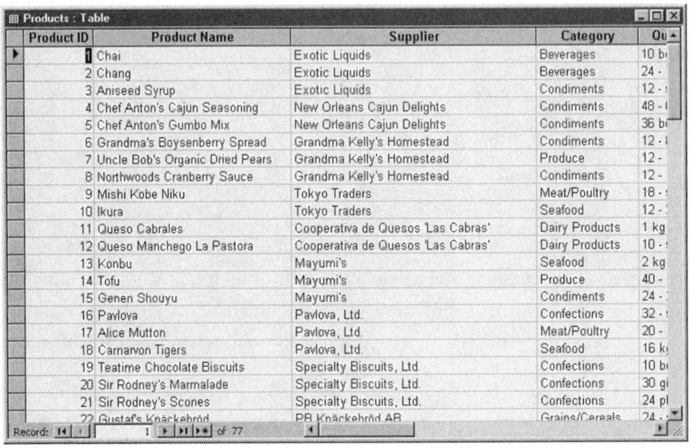
Products : Table

Product ID	Product Name	Supplier	Category	Qu
1	Chai	Exotic Liquids	Beverages	10 b
2	Chang	Exotic Liquids	Beverages	24 -
3	Aniseed Syrup	Exotic Liquids	Condiments	12 -
4	Chef Anton's Cajun Seasoning	New Orleans Cajun Delights	Condiments	48 -
5	Chef Anton's Gumbo Mix	New Orleans Cajun Delights	Condiments	36 b
6	Grandma's Boysenberry Spread	Grandma Kelly's Homestead	Condiments	12 -
7	Uncle Bob's Organic Dried Pears	Grandma Kelly's Homestead	Produce	12 -
8	Northwoods Cranberry Sauce	Grandma Kelly's Homestead	Condiments	12 -
9	Mishi Kobe Niku	Tokyo Traders	Meat/Poultry	18 -
10	Ikura	Tokyo Traders	Seafood	12 -
11	Queso Cabrales	Cooperativa de Quesos 'Las Cabras'	Dairy Products	1 kg
12	Queso Manchego La Pastora	Cooperativa de Quesos 'Las Cabras'	Dairy Products	10 -
13	Konbu	Mayumi's	Seafood	2 kg
14	Tofu	Mayumi's	Produce	40 -
15	Genen Shouyu	Mayumi's	Condiments	24 -
16	Pavlova	Pavlova, Ltd.	Confections	32 -
17	Alice Mutton	Pavlova, Ltd.	Meat/Poultry	20 -
18	Carnarvon Tigers	Pavlova, Ltd.	Seafood	16 k
19	Teatime Chocolate Biscuits	Specialty Biscuits, Ltd.	Confections	10 b
20	Sir Rodney's Marmalade	Specialty Biscuits, Ltd.	Confections	30 g
21	Sir Rodney's Scones	Specialty Biscuits, Ltd.	Confections	24 pl
22	Gustaf's Knäckebröd	PB Knäckebröd AB	Grains/Cereals	24 -

Record: 1 of 77

FIGURE 15.3.
Database tables consist of rows and columns of data.

In Figure 15.3, the fields contain information such as the product names, unit price, and units in stock. Each row of the database table in Figure 15.3 contains all the information about a single product. For example, the second row in Figure 15.3 tells you the name of the product is Chang, its product ID is 2, and it costs $19.00 per unit. Each of these bits of information (Product Name, Product ID, and Unit Price) makes up the fields of the record describing the Chang product.

In most cases, the text files you might work with in Visual Basic look similar to the table in Figure 15.3. At the very least, the data in a text file is arranged as lines of text, each line (the *records*) containing several different data values (the *fields*) that are needed by the application. Our Visual Basic program will read the text file one line at a time, breaking the lines of data into the individual data values.

Looking at Text File Formats

There are two common text file formats: fixed-width and delimited. Most database systems are capable of outputting data in both of these formats.

Fixed-width files are arranged as columns of data. Figure 15.4 shows a portion of a fixed-width file named `Fixed2.txt` containing data from the Northwind Traders sample database that comes with Visual Basic. Notice how each column starts at exactly the same position in every row. (`Fixed2.txt` can be found on this book's CD-ROM.)

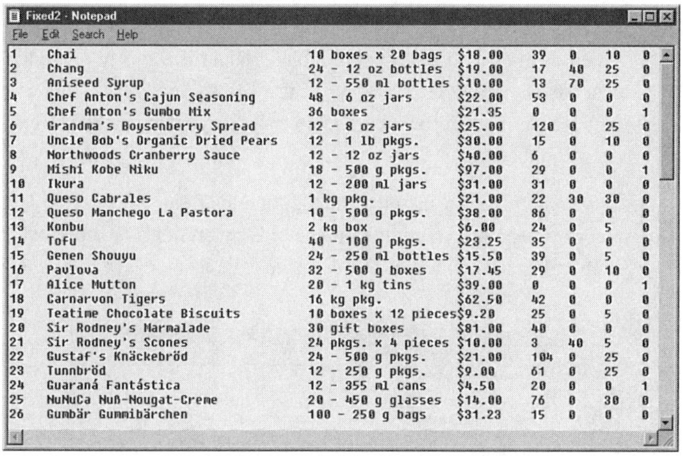

```
Fixed2 - Notepad
File  Edit  Search  Help
1    Chai                             10 boxes x 20 bags  $18.00   39   0    10   0
2    Chang                            24 - 12 oz bottles  $19.00   17   40   25   0
3    Aniseed Syrup                    12 - 550 ml bottles $10.00   13   70   25   0
4    Chef Anton's Cajun Seasoning     48 - 6 oz jars      $22.00   53   0    0    0
5    Chef Anton's Gumbo Mix           36 boxes            $21.35   0    0    0    1
6    Grandma's Boysenberry Spread     12 - 8 oz jars      $25.00   120  0    25   0
7    Uncle Bob's Organic Dried Pears  12 - 1 lb pkgs.     $30.00   15   0    10   0
8    Northwoods Cranberry Sauce       12 - 12 oz jars     $40.00   6    0    0    0
9    Mishi Kobe Niku                  18 - 500 g pkgs.    $97.00   29   0    0    1
10   Ikura                            12 - 200 ml jars    $31.00   31   0    0    0
11   Queso Cabrales                   1 kg pkg.           $21.00   22   30   30   0
12   Queso Manchego La Pastora        10 - 500 g pkgs.    $38.00   86   0    0    0
13   Konbu                            2 kg box            $6.00    24   0    5    0
14   Tofu                             40 - 100 g pkgs.    $23.25   35   0    0    0
15   Genen Shouyu                     24 - 250 ml bottles $15.50   39   0    5    0
16   Pavlova                          32 - 500 g boxes    $17.45   29   0    10   0
17   Alice Mutton                     20 - 1 kg tins      $39.00   0    0    0    1
18   Carnarvon Tigers                 16 kg pkg.          $62.50   42   0    0    0
19   Teatime Chocolate Biscuits       10 boxes x 12 pieces$9.20    25   0    5    0
20   Sir Rodney's Marmalade           30 gift boxes       $81.00   40   0    0    0
21   Sir Rodney's Scones              24 pkgs. x 4 pieces $10.00   3    40   5    0
22   Gustaf's Knäckebröd              24 - 500 g pkgs.    $21.00   104  0    25   0
23   Tunnbröd                         12 - 250 g pkgs.    $9.00    61   0    25   0
24   Guaraná Fantástica               12 - 355 ml cans    $4.50    20   0    0    1
25   NuNuCa Nuß-Nougat-Creme          20 - 450 g glasses  $14.00   76   0    30   0
26   Gumbär Gummibärchen              100 - 250 g bags    $31.23   15   0    0    0
```

FIGURE 15.4.
Fixed-width files are common in many environments.

You won't be able to tell much about the data or how it will be used just by looking at Figure 15.4. A clear and precise definition of the data is necessary before the text file can be imported into a Visual Basic application. Table 15.1 defines the columns you see in Figure 15.4. You'll need this information later in this chapter as you begin working with the data in the `Fixed2.txt` file.

Table 15.1. Data definition for `Fixed1.txt`.

Column Number	*Field Name*	*Data Type*
1	`ProductID`	`Long`
2	`ProductName`	`String`
3	`QuantityPerUnit`	`String`
4	`UnitPrice`	`Currency`

continues

Table 15.1. Continued.

Column Number	Field Name	Data Type
5	UnitsInStock	Integer
6	UnitsOnOrder	Integer
7	ReorderLevel	Integer
8	Discontinued	Boolean

Although fixed-width records are easy to work with in Visual Basic, there is a danger that data in a fixed-width table has been corrupted. The length of each row of a fixed-width table is the same throughout the table. Data stored in the field must fit in the width allowed by that field. If the data is wider than will fit into the field, the data is simply truncated and shortened to fit the available width.

When dealing with fixed-width tables, Visual Basic is not able to determine when the data has been truncated. Because Visual Basic looks for a field day to begin at a particular position in each row, there is no way for your programs to know when a field has been chopped off.

A *delimited* file, on the other hand, contains fields of different lengths. Each field in a record is separated from the other fields by commas or other delimiters that indicate the start and finish of the field. A delimited file is shown in Figure 15.5.

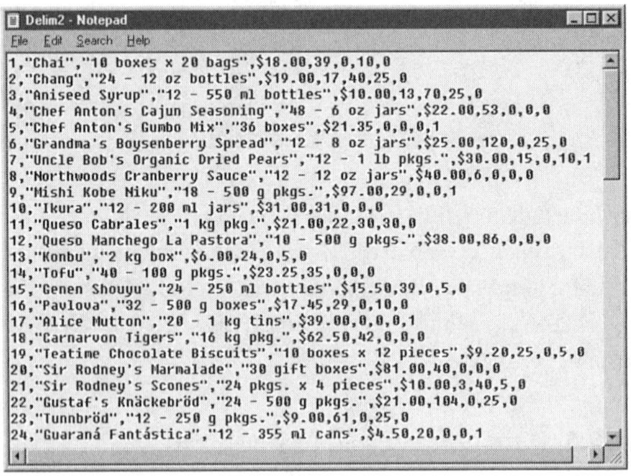

FIGURE 15.5.
The fields in
Delim2.txt *are*
separated by
commas.

The fields in the file in Figure 15.5 are separated by commas. Notice also that the text fields, such as the product name, are surrounded by double-quote characters, and numeric values are not surrounded by any character other than the commas separating them from the other fields. Each field and row of data in Delim2.txt is a different length than the other fields and rows in the table. The Delim2.txt file is also located on this book's CD-ROM.

The fields in delimited text files are usually separated by commas, but tab characters, square brackets, and other characters are sometimes used.

Understanding Data Access Methods

A file is nothing more than a series of bytes stored on the computer's disk. The arrangement of the bytes varies greatly, from completely unstructured and seemingly random to highly structured and well organized. A file containing a bitmap image appears to Visual Basic as a random sequence of bytes, whereas a fixed-width text file is more ordered and structured.

Visual Basic provides for three different types of data access: sequential, random, and binary. You must know how the data was stored in the file before attempting to read the data stored within it in a coherent fashion.

Sequential File Access

The *sequential* access method is appropriate for data stored in text files. Each byte within the file represents a character of data. As you have already seen, in a fixed-width table each record begins and ends at a predictable position within the file because each record is the same length as every other record within the file. When working with delimited text files, the length of each record, and the length of each field within each record, varies according to the data stored in the record and fields.

In either case, when working with text files, each line or record of data is terminated by a newline character. When Visual Basic works with a sequential file the newline characters are significant and are not ignored.

Random File Access

The *random* access method, on the other hand, assumes that each record is exactly the same length as every other record in the file. You must specify the length of the records in the random access file at the time the file is opened so that Visual Basic knows what to expect as you retrieve records from the files. When reading data from the file, you must tell Visual Basic the position of the record within the file. Then, based on the record length, Visual Basic knows how far into the file it must go to locate the desired record. Although it's difficult to see, each of the records in the dBASE table displayed in Figure 15.6 are all the same length. Text fields are padded with spaces to make them all the same size and numeric fields occupy as much space as required by the Numeric data type.

Random access files are most often used for data contained in user-defined data types created in a Visual Basic program. In a user-defined type, each record is exactly the same size as every other record. Listing 15.1 shows the definition of a user-defined data type for holding customer data.

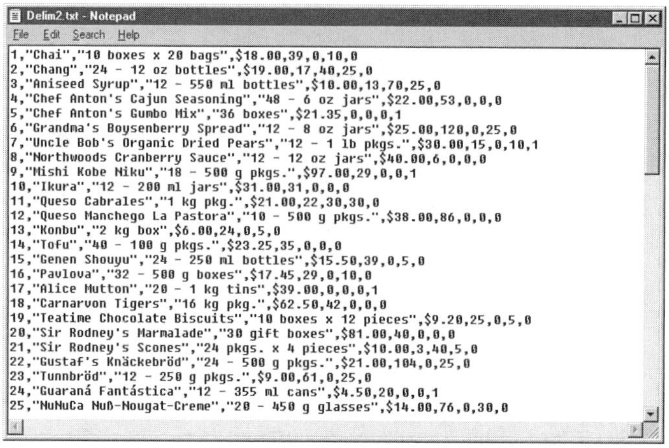

FIGURE 15.6.
The dBASE database tables are stored in random-access format.

Listing 15.1. User-defined types are a handy way to hold data.

```
Type Customer
   CustomerID As Long
   LastName As String * 20
   FirstName As String * 15
   Address As String * 25
   City As String * 15
   State As String * 2
   Zip As String * 10
End Type
```

Later in the program the declaration of a customer variable using the `Customer` data type would be as follows:

```
Dim Cust As Customer
```

In the case of the `Customer` user-defined type, each record is exactly 91 bytes long. Table 15.2 shows how this figure is derived.

Table 15.2. Calculating the size of a user-defined type.

Field	Data Type	Bytes
CustomerID	Long	4
LastName	String * 20	20
FirstName	String * 15	15
Address	String * 25	25
City	String * 15	15
State	String * 2	2
Zip	String * 10	10

Adding up the byte size column yields the 91-byte figure for each record. When using the `Customer` user-defined type in a random access file you'd specify a record length of 91.

Binary File Access

Binary access is by far the most difficult and challenging to implement. When opened for binary access, Visual Basic makes no assumptions about the arrangement of the bytes within the file. You must know exactly how the data is arranged in order to retrieve it correctly.

Because binary file formats vary so much, it is impossible to suggest a generalized method for opening and reading binary data. Binary data is often stored in a proprietary, unpublished format, making it very difficult for a Visual Basic developer to successfully open and read the data stored in the file. The `.MDB` file produced by Microsoft Access is an example of a proprietary binary format file.

The data access method you choose depends on how the data was stored in the file. In the case of the text files described earlier in this chapter, the sequential access method is most appropriate. When working with sequential access files, Visual Basic pays attention to newline characters, and every byte is treated as an ANSI character. The majority of this chapter explains the Visual Basic commands and functions necessary to create, write, and read sequential text files.

Opening Text Files

When reading text files Visual Basic reads one line of data at a time and *parses* it into its constituent fields. For example, reading the first line of either `Fixed2.txt` or `Delim2.txt` should result in data shown in Table 15.3. (We're using the table's definition provided in Table 15.1.)

Table 15.3. Field values in first row of `Fixed2.txt` and `Delim2.txt`.

Field Name	Value
ProductID	1
ProductName	Chang
QuantityPerUnit	10 boxes x 20 bags
UnitPrice	$18.00
UnitsInStock	39
UnitsOnOrder	0
ReorderLevel	10
Discontinued	False

It is your job, then, to ensure that your Visual Basic program reads the first line of data from `Fixed2.txt` and `Delim2.txt` and accurately returns the values you see in Table 15.3.

The following shows the basic syntax for reading text files in sequential mode in Visual Basic:

```
Open FileName For Mode As [#]FileNumber [Len=BufferSize]
```

Where

- *FileName* is the path to the text file.

- *Mode* is either Input, Output, Append, Binary, or Random. (See the following discussion about the Mode parameter.)

- *FileNumber* is a required integer from 1 to 511 that provides a handle on the open text file.

- *BufferSize* is an optional parameter that tells Visual Basic how many bytes to read each time the file is accessed.

The Open mode of a text file can be any of the following:

- Input—The text file is being opened on a read-only basis. Data cannot be written out to a text file opened for input. An error occurs if a nonexistent file is opened for input.

- Output—This is the opposite of the Input mode. In this case, the file is created on the disk and data is output to it from Visual Basic. If the data file already exists and the intention is to simply add new data to it, open the file in Append mode.

- Append—The file is opened only to add new records. You cannot read records from a file opened for append operations.

- Binary—The Binary mode option instructs Visual Basic to treat each byte of the file the same as every other byte. This means that special characters, such as carriage returns, are not seen as indicating the end of lines of data.

- Random—The random-access method has already been discussed. Random access is applicable to files specifically prepared to hold structured data. Each record is the same length as every other record, and the record length is usually provided at the time the file is opened. Random is the default Open mode for all files.

The code in this chapter opens text files in sequential Input mode. Each line of text in the files is read into Visual Basic, and the data in the line is separated into different fields.

An attempt to open a nonexistent text file for Input generates a runtime error. Trying to open a nonexistent file for Output or Append results in the creation of that file.

Notice the *FileNumber* parameter in the Open statement syntax. After you have a text file open, your code uses the file number to reference the file. Listing 15.2 shows how the file number is used in Visual Basic code.

Listing 15.2. User-defined types are a handy way to hold data.

```
Dim strData As String

Open "Fixed2.txt" For Input As #1

Do
  Line Input #1, strData
  Debug.Print strData
Loop Until VBA.EOF(1)

Close #1
```

The `Fixed2.txt` file is opened as a sequential-access input file and assigned #1 as its file number. Later in the code, the file is referenced as #1 as data is read from the file. At the very end of Listing 15.2, the file is closed.

A file is not a variable. The only reference to the file in a project is through its file number. Most of the Visual Basic file-management commands, such as `Line Input` and `Close`, require the file number as the target of the operation.

In Listing 15.2, the file number is hard-coded into the program. This is not always appropriate because in many applications there will be an arbitrary number of files open at the same time. It is an error to try to open a file that is already open or to fail to close a file that has been opened. If you're not sure what file number to use in a statement, the `FreeFile` function returns the next available file number. Listing 15.3 shows how to use `FreeFile` to obtain a file number at runtime.

Listing 15.3. `FreeFile` returns the next available file number.

```
Dim strData As String
Dim FileHandle As Integer

FileHandle = FreeFile()
Open "Fixed2.txt" For Input As #FileHandle

Do
  Line Input #FileHandle, strData
  Debug.Print strData
Loop Until VBA.EOF(FileHandle)

Close #FileHandle
```

The `FreeFile` function returns numbers between 1 and 255 if no argument is provided. If 1 is passed as the argument, `FreeFile` returns numbers between 256 and 511.

If you've opened a file for `Input` or `Append`, you must close the file before performing other operations on it. Pass the file number to the `Close` statement to ensure you're closing the correct file.

Reading Fixed-Width Text Files

The syntax required to read sequential text files varies depending on whether the data is arranged as fixed-width or delimited fields. For example, assume the following is a line of data from a fixed-width file (this data is from the Fixed1.txt file on the book's CD-ROM):

```
1          Davolio          Nancy    5/1/92 0:00:00    4000
```

As always, a short description of each field in Fixed1.txt is required before code can be written to use this data. Table 15.4 lists the fields found in Fixed1.txt.

Table 15.4. Descriptions of the fields in Fixed1.txt.

Field Name	Start Position	Width
EmployeeID	1	11
LastName	12	20
FirstName	32	10
HireDate	42	19
Bonus	61	5

You'll see that the width of the bonus column is 5 characters even though only 4 characters can be seen in the sample line of data from Fixed1.txt. Although you can't see it, there is an extra space following the Bonus column to accommodate bonuses greater than $9,999.

Figure 15.7 shows frmFixed1, included in the TextFile.vbp project accompanying this chapter. This form extracts the first line of data in the Fixed1.txt data file and displays it in the text boxes on the form's surface.

FIGURE 15.7.

The frmFixed1 form includes simple text file processing code.

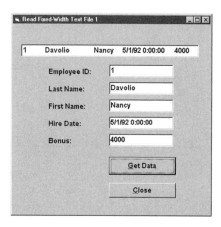

The code behind the Get Data button on frmFixed1 is shown in Listing 15.4. Each line of this procedure is numbered to aid the discussion following the listing.

Listing 15.4. This code behind frmFixed1 reads a single line of fixed-width data and displays the data in text boxes on the form.

```
 1 Private Sub cmdGetData_Click()
 2   Dim strData As String
 3   Dim FileHandle As Integer
 4
 5   FileHandle = FreeFile()
 6   Open App.Path & "\Fixed1.txt" For Input As #FileHandle
 7
 8   Line Input #FileHandle, strData
 9   Debug.Print strData
10
11   Close #FileHandle
12
13   txtData = strData
14   txtEmployeeID = Trim(Mid(strData, 1, 5))
15   txtLastName = Trim(Mid(strData, 12, 19))
16   txtFirstName = Trim(Mid(strData, 32, 10))
17   txtHireDate = Trim(Mid(strData, 42, 14))
18   txtBonus = Trim(Mid(strData, 61, 5))
19 End Sub
```

The file handle (or file number, if you prefer) is assigned in line 5 with the FreeFile function. In line 6, the Fixed1.txt file is opened for Input. Notice that App.Path is appended to the filename to ensure opening the file in the application's working directory.

In line 8, a single line of data is read into the String variable named strData and output to the Debug window in statement 9. The data file is closed in line 11. Line 13 displays the line of data in a text box on frmFixed1.

Lines 14 through 18 use the Mid and Trim functions to pull data out of strData and trim off any stray leading or trailing spaces. Notice that the arguments for the Mid function are hard-coded into each of these statements. You could, with enough work, use code to determine the beginning and end of the columns of data, or enable the user to select the column widths, but this flexibility would require considerable programming.

Also, if the format of the data file changes in the future and the column widths, number of columns, or other characteristics of the data file change, the code parsing the data (statements 14 through 18) must be updated.

Reading Delimited Text Files

As you saw in the previous section, reading data in fixed-width text files is fairly simple. The Mid function is easy to use and returns data from any predictable position in the data string. Working with delimited text files, by contrast, is quite challenging.

Figure 15.8 shows Delim1.txt, a simple delimited text file located on this book's CD-ROM. Delim1.txt contains exactly the same data as Fixed1.txt, except that the data is delimited rather than fixed-width. The fields in Delim1.txt are separated by commas and there are no secondary delimiters, such as quotes, around text values. Parsing the data in Delim1.txt, therefore, involves locating the beginning and the end of each field, based on the positions of the commas in the data string.

FIGURE 15.8.

Delim1.txt *contains comma-delimited text data.*

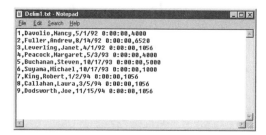

Other delimited files might wrap text data in double quotes or other characters. The advantage of enclosing string values in quotes is that the fields can then include commas (or whatever delimiting character the file uses). In the case of Delim1.txt, a comma included within a field (such as Acme Widgets, Inc.) causes the Visual Basic code reading the file to misinterpret the width of the field, ruining the data extraction process.

Listing 15.5 shows the Click event procedure of the Get Data button on frmDelim1 in the TextFile.vbp project. The code required to open the Delim1.txt sequential text file and read a line of data is identical to what you see in Listing 15.4. The biggest difference is how the data string is parsed. Instead of using Mid and Trim, Listing 15.5 uses the InStr function to locate commas in strData.

Listing 15.5. Parsing delimited text data is more complex than working with fixed-width data.

```
Private Sub cmdGetData_Click()
  Dim strData As String
  Dim FileHandle As Integer
  Dim iBegin As Integer
  Dim iEnd As Integer

  FileHandle = FreeFile()
  Open App.Path & "\Delim1.txt" For Input As #FileHandle
```

```
Line Input #FileHandle, strData
Debug.Print strData

Close #FileHandle

txtData.Text = strData

iBegin = InStr(1, strData, ",")
iEnd = InStr(iBegin + 1, strData, ",")
txtEmployeeID = Left(strData, iBegin - 1)
txtLastName = Mid(strData, iBegin + 1, iEnd - iBegin - 1)

iBegin = InStr(iEnd, strData, ",")
iEnd = InStr(iBegin + 1, strData, ",")
txtFirstName = Mid(strData, iBegin + 1, iEnd - iBegin - 1)

iBegin = InStr(iEnd, strData, ",")
iEnd = InStr(iBegin + 1, strData, ",")
txtHireDate = Mid(strData, iBegin + 1, iEnd - iBegin - 1)

iBegin = InStr(iEnd, strData, ",")
iEnd = InStr(iBegin + 1, strData, ",")
txtBonus = Mid(strData, iBegin + 1, Len(strData))
End Sub
```

Two integer variables are used to mark the beginning and end of each field in strData. The beginning (designated by iBegin) is determined by the location of the comma just preceding the field of data. The end of each field (iEnd) is located by the first comma that comes after the comma that begins a field of data.

After the beginning and ending of the field is located the Mid function returns the portion of the data string designated by the iBegin and iEnd variables. The end of the very last data item (Bonus) is determined by the length of the data string. There will not be a comma designating the end of the last item in the data string, so the length of the string marks the end of the last field in the data string.

Looking at More Complex Examples

Admittedly, the previous examples were pretty simple. For the most part, all that was needed was opening the text file, reading lines of text from the file, and using the Mid and InStr functions to parse the data. Because the data in Delim1.txt was so simple, there was no need to accommodate double quotes or other characters. Virtually every character, other than the commas and spaces between fields in both the Fixed1.txt and Delim1.txt files, was data.

The TextFile.vbp project includes two more complex text file examples. These files are perhaps more typical of the kind of text files you'll work with in Visual Basic 6.0 than those you've seen so far in this chapter.

Reading Complex Fixed-Width Files

Figure 15.9 shows `frmFixed2`, part of the `TextFile.vbp` project. This form opens the fixed-width text file you saw back in Figure 15.4. The eight columns of data in `Fixed2.txt` were defined in Table 15.1.

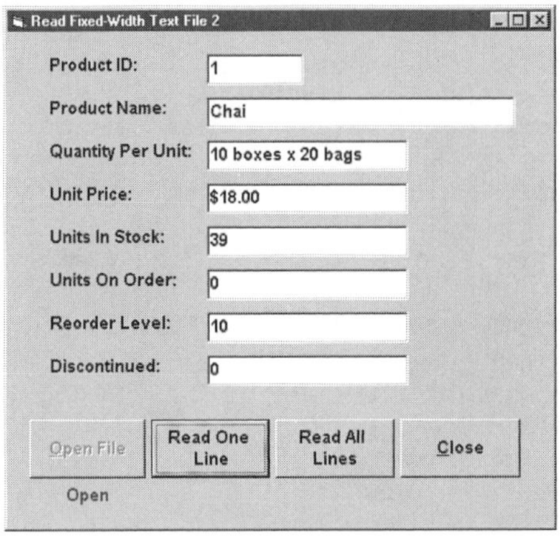

FIGURE 15.9.

The `frmFixed2`
form features a
more complex
approach to
reading text files.

The buttons along the bottom of the form control how the form interacts with the `Fixed2.txt` file. These buttons give you the choices of opening the `Fixed2.txt` file, reading a single line from the file, reading all lines from the file, and closing the form. The Read One Line and Read All Lines buttons are grayed out until the Open File button has been pressed. As soon as the file is open, the Read buttons are enabled and the Open File button is disabled. After the last line of data is read from the `Fixed2.txt` file the Read buttons are grayed out again and the Open File button is enabled.

Simple user-interface paradigms, such as the one described in the previous paragraph, go a long way toward making an application easy to use. The user of `frmFixed2` doesn't have to know which buttons are available or make sense to use. Because the `Enabled` property is modified to suit the state of the data file, only a subset of the buttons is available at any time.

Listing 15.6 shows how little code is required to open the `Fixed2.txt` file and manage the user interface on `frmFixed2`. Notice the three lines of code enabling or disabling the Read buttons and the Open File button.

Listing 15.6. Very little code is required to manage the user interface on `frmFixed2`.

```
Private Sub cmdOpenFile_Click()
On Error Resume Next
  Open App.Path & FILENAME For Input As #1
  lblStatus.Caption = "Open"
```

```
        cmdReadAllLines.Enabled = True
        cmdReadOneLine.Enabled = True
        cmdOpenFile.Enabled = False

        txtProductID.Text = ""
        txtProductName.Text = ""
        txtQuantityPerUnit.Text = ""
        txtUnitPrice.Text = ""
        txtUnitsInStock.Text = ""
        txtUnitsOnOrder.Text = ""
        txtReorderLevel.Text = ""
        txtDiscontinued.Text = ""
End Sub
```

Following the button property adjustments are several lines of code setting all the text boxes on the form to empty strings. The code setting the text boxes to empty strings in Listing 15.6 could be replaced with the For..Next loop shown in Listing 15.7.

Listing 15.7. Removing the specific text box references results in more efficient code.

```
For Each ctl In Me.Controls
  If TypeOf ctl Is TextBox Then
    ctl.Text = ""
  End If
Next ctl
```

This little bit of code enumerates the Controls collection on the form, searching for text box controls and sets each text box's Text property to an empty string. This code is very useful when there are a large number of text box controls on the form, or when the names of the text boxes might change during development. It is a good idea to write generic code such the code in Listing 15.7 whenever possible. The code in Listing 15.7 won't have to be changed every time a text box is added or removed from frmFixed2, reducing the form's maintenance requirements.

You might have noticed the reference to the FILENAME constant in Listing 15.7. FILENAME is declared at the top of the form's module:

```
Const FILENAME = "\Fixed2.txt"
```

Although it's tempting to concatenate the App.Path property to the literal filename in the FILENAME constant declaration, Visual Basic does not let you use anything other than a constant value as the constant's assignment. App.Path changes every time the application is used in a different directory on the computer, so it is considered a variable value.

Listing 15.8 shows the Click event procedure for the Read One Line button. Notice that cmdReadOneLine_Click() performs the Line Input statement on the open file, retrieving

a line of data as strData. strData is then passed to the FillForm sub, also shown in
Listing 15.8. For good measure the line of data is also displayed in the Debug window by
the Debug.Print statement.

Listing 15.8. This code reads and displays a single line of data from the
open data file.

```
Private Sub cmdReadOneLine_Click()
  Dim strData As String
  Line Input #1, strData
  Debug.Print strData
  Call FillForm(strData)
  If EOF(1) Then
    Call CloseFile
  End If
End Sub

Private Sub FillForm(strData As String)
  txtProductID.Text = Trim(Mid(strData, 1, 5))
  txtProductName.Text = Trim(Mid(strData, 6, 35))
  txtQuantityPerUnit.Text = Trim(Mid(strData, 41, 20))
  txtUnitPrice.Text = Trim(Mid(strData, 61, 10))
  txtUnitsInStock.Text = Trim(Mid(strData, 71, 5))
  txtUnitsOnOrder.Text = Trim(Mid(strData, 76, 5))
  txtReorderLevel.Text = Trim(Mid(strData, 81, 5))
  txtDiscontinued.Text = Trim(Mid(strData, 86, 1))
End Sub
```

Notice how FillForm uses the Mid function to pull fields of data from the strData text
string. The Trim function removes stray leading or trailing spaces. The trimmed fields are
then assigned to the text boxes on frmFixed2.

The code attached to the Click event of the Read All Lines command button is very similar to Listing 15.8. The only difference in Listing 15.9 is that the Fixed2.txt file is read
and processed one line at a time until the EOF function returns True, signaling the end of
the text file.

Listing 15.9. Reading all the lines in a text file is quite simple.

```
Private Sub cmdReadAllLines_Click()
  Dim strData As String

  Do
    Line Input #1, strData
    Call FillForm(strData)
    DoEvents
    Debug.Print strData
```

```
      Loop Until EOF(1)
      Call CloseFile
   End Sub

   Private Sub CloseFile()
      Close #1
      cmdReadAllLines.Enabled = False
      cmdReadOneLine.Enabled = False
      lblStatus.Caption = "Closed"
      cmdOpenFile.Enabled = True
   End Sub
```

Listing 15.9 also shows the CloseFile routine that is called near the end of the cmdReadAllLines_Click event procedure. This routine simply closes the file, sets the Enabled property of the Read buttons to False, changes the message displayed in the status label under the Open File button, and enables the Open File button. The interaction between the procedures behind frmFixed2 enables the user to repetitively read and display the contents of Fixed2.txt.

All in all, the code behind frmFixed2 is simple. Just open the file, read in a line of data, and parse the fields contained in the string. The next section discusses how to add the same flexibility to a routine reading a delimited text file.

Reading Complex Delimited Files

The preceding section discussed a few issues involved when adding more complexity to the task of reading fixed-width text files. Although somewhat more code was involved than the fixed-width example earlier in this chapter, the additional complexity in the code behind frmFixed2 is mostly the result of enabling and disabling the command buttons on the form, blanking the text boxes when no valid data has been read, and other user interface issues. Reading fixed-width text files remains a relatively simple process, relying on the Mid function to pick out a section of a text string and assign that substring to a variable.

Reading Delim2.txt is somewhat more complex than the delimited text file example (Delim1.txt) shown in Figure 15.8. Delim2.txt (see Figure 15.10) contains a mix of text values, currency, and numeric values, all separated by commas. Text values are surrounded by double quotes, complicating the task of locating fields in this file.

If the VBA code is written to simply search for commas as field delimiters, the data will not be read properly. For example, given the delimited text parsing technique shown earlier in this chapter in Listing 15.5, the following line of data will not parse correctly:

```
1,"Chai, Deluxe","10 boxes x 20 bags",$18.00,39,0,10,0
```

Notice the comma that appears in the middle of the product name. This extra comma, which is valid data, upsets the search applied by Listing 15.10. In the BadRead subroutine, after a comma beginning a field has been located the next comma in the line of data is assumed to terminate the field.

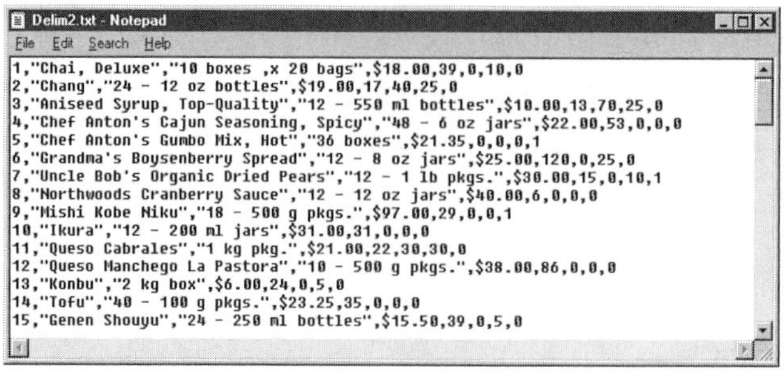

FIGURE 15.10. *The `frmDelim2` form reads a more complex delimited text file.*

Listing 15.10. The `BadRead` routine does not correctly read the `Delim2.txt` file.

```
Private Sub BadRead()
  Dim strData As String
  Dim FileHandle As Integer
  Dim iBegin As Integer
  Dim iEnd As Integer

  FileHandle = FreeFile()
  Open App.Path & "\Delim2.txt" For Input As #FileHandle

  Line Input #FileHandle, strData
  'Debug.Print strData

  Close #FileHandle

  'Example data:
  '1,"Chai, Deluxe","10 boxes ,x 20 bags",$18.00,39,0,10,0

  iBegin = InStr(1, strData, ",")
  iEnd = InStr(iBegin + 1, strData, ",")
  Debug.Print "Product ID:         " _
     & Left(strData, iBegin - 1)
  Debug.Print "Product Name:       " _
     & Mid(strData, iBegin + 1, iEnd - iBegin - 1)

  iBegin = InStr(iEnd, strData, ",")
  iEnd = InStr(iBegin + 1, strData, ",")
  Debug.Print "Quantity Per Unit: " _
     & Mid(strData, iBegin + 1, iEnd - iBegin - 1)

  iBegin = InStr(iEnd, strData, ",")
  iEnd = InStr(iBegin + 1, strData, ",")
  Debug.Print "Unit Price:         " _
     & Mid(strData, iBegin + 1, iEnd - iBegin - 1)

  iBegin = InStr(iEnd, strData, ",")
  iEnd = InStr(iBegin + 1, strData, ",")
```

```
Debug.Print "Units In Stock:    " _
    & Mid(strData, iBegin + 1, Len(strData))

iBegin = InStr(iEnd, strData, ",")
iEnd = InStr(iBegin + 1, strData, ",")
Debug.Print "Units On Order:    " _
    & Mid(strData, iBegin + 1, Len(strData))

iBegin = InStr(iEnd, strData, ",")
iEnd = InStr(iBegin + 1, strData, ",")
Debug.Print "Reorder Level:     " _
    & Mid(strData, iBegin + 1, Len(strData))

iBegin = InStr(iEnd, strData, ",")
iEnd = InStr(iBegin + 1, Len(strData))
Debug.Print "Discontinued:      " _
    & Mid(strData, iBegin + 1, Len(strData))
End Sub
```

The output of the BadRead subroutine is shown in Figure 15.11. Notice how the product name has been spread across more than one field. The Quantity Per Unit field is reported as Deluxe. Another problem is that the double quote marks surrounding the product name, quantity per unit, and other data are included in the fields. Correctly parsing this data means removing the double quote marks and ignoring commas that are part of the text data.

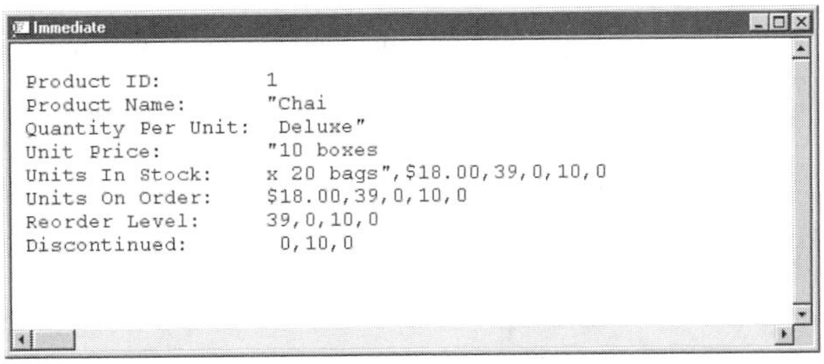

FIGURE 15.11.

The extra comma ruins the parsing technique in the BadRead *procedure.*

```
Immediate
Product ID:         1
Product Name:       "Chai
Quantity Per Unit:  Deluxe"
Unit Price:         "10 boxes
Units In Stock:     x 20 bags",$18.00,39,0,10,0
Units On Order:     $18.00,39,0,10,0
Reorder Level:      39,0,10,0
Discontinued:        0,10,0
```

A more robust approach is outlined in Listing 15.11. Line numbers have been added to this listing to make it easier to explain the logic in this code fragment. The comma indicates the start of a field in line 1. iBegin therefore points to the beginning of a field.

In line 3, the character following the comma is examined to see whether it is a double-quote character (Chr(34)). If so, the code assumes the field is a text field and sets bText (a Boolean variable) to True in line 4. The end of the field is then indicated in line 5 by the position of the very next double quote character. If the iBegin + 1 character is not a double quote, the field must be Numeric or Date or another nontext data type, and bText is set to False (line 7) and a comma is used to locate the end of the field in line 8.

Listing 15.11. Reading delimited text can be challenging.

```
 1 iBegin = InStr(1, strData, ",")
 2
 3 If Mid(strData, iBegin + 1, 1) = Chr(34) Then
 4   bText = True
 5   iEnd = InStr(iBegin + 2, strData, Chr(34))
 6 Else
 7   bText = False
 8   iEnd = InStr(iBegin + 1, strData, ",")
 9 End If
10 If bText Then
11   txtProductName.Text = _
12     Mid(strData, iBegin + 2, iEnd - iBegin - 2)
13 Else
14   txtProductName.Text = _
15     Mid(strData, iBegin + 2, iEnd - iBegin - 3)
16 End If
```

After the beginning and end of the field are selected, the `If..End If` construct at the bottom of Listing 15.11 (lines 10 through 16) examines the value of `bText`. If `bText` is `True`, the statement in lines 11 and 12 take the field data (`txtProductName` in this case) by excluding the double-quote characters at the beginning and end of the field. Otherwise, the field is processed just as in Listing 15.5.

Because there are so many different ways to output delimited data, it is impossible to generalize a parsing technique that works on every delimited text file. This section is intended to suggest one way of dealing with one particular type of delimited file. Surely the code you see in Listing 15.11 could be written any number of ways.

If the delimited files you are working with include delimiters around date fields, currency characters, and other nondata characters, you might have to customize your code to manage these characters. In any case, be sure to test your routines against every possible combination of data that might be found in the delimited text files you work with.

Taking a Closer Look at File Commands

This chapter has made liberal use of several Visual Basic file-handling commands. The `Open`, `Line Input`, and `Close` commands are all part of the VBA language syntax enabling Visual Basic to open and read sequential text files. This section discusses several important VBA commands related to file operations you should be familiar with.

Open

The Open statement was discussed earlier in this chapter. The Open statement prepares a file for input and output operations and is used for more than just sequential file access. Consult the section "Opening Text Files" for more details on the Open statement.

Line Input

After the file is open, the Line Input statement reads a line of data into a String variable (often referred to as a *string buffer* or *buffer variable*). Line Input uses the following syntax:

```
Line Input #FileNumber, VariableName
```

The *FileNumber* parameter refers to an open file handle. If the file number is not currently in use, an error occurs. The *VariableName* parameter references a String variable large enough to accept the data returned by the Line Input statement.

Line Input recognizes carriage return characters (Chr(13)) and carriage return-linefeed sequences (Chr(13)+Chr(10)) as the end of the lines of data in the text file. These end-of-line markers are not included in the data assigned to the String variable receiving the data returned by Line Input.

Input

The Input statement is somewhat different from Line Input. Instead of reading a line of data from a file as a single text string, Input reads the line of data and assigns it to several variables as a single operation. The Input statement uses the following syntax:

```
Input #FileNumber, VariableList
```

where *FileNumber* is the number of an open file and *VariableList* is a comma-delimited list of variables accepting the data read by the Input statement. In most cases, the text file being read with Input is a comma-delimited file with double quotes surrounding text data. The variable list cannot be an array or object variable but can include a user-defined data type or object variable property.

Input works only with files opened in Input or Binary mode. Usually the file read with Input is created from data written to the file with the Write statement.

The Write statement imbeds special delimiters around data fields that are recognized by the Input statement. These delimiters ensure that the Input statement correctly reads data output by the Write statement. Be sure to read the section on the Write statement to see how these delimiters look in a data file.

The Input statement avoids the issue of having to interpret each bit of data as it is read from the text file. Because of the special formatting and delimiters applied by the Write statement, the Input statement correctly interprets the data type and value of each variable as it is read.

The variables must appear in the variable list in the order in which they appear in each line of data in the data file. The Input statement generates an error when assigning a value to an inappropriate variable data type. For example, under most circumstances it would be an error to assign a text string to a Date variable. Numeric variables are assigned zero if the data in the file is not numeric.

The Input statement uses the special delimiters described in Table 15.5 to determine the data types of the variables in each line of data in the file.

Table 15.5. Delimiters recognized by the Input statement.

Data	Value
Comma or blank line	Empty
#NULL#	Null
#TRUE#, #FALSE#	True or False (Boolean)
#yyyy-mm-dd hh:mm:ss#	Date and time represented by the expression
#ERROR errornumber#	Variant containing error number

If a double-quote mark must appear within a text string, it must appear as two double quotes together.

Figure 15.12 shows frmWrite, a form included in TextFile.vbp that demonstrates the Input and Write statements.

FIGURE 15.12.

The frmWrite *form demon-strates alternative file input/output routines.*

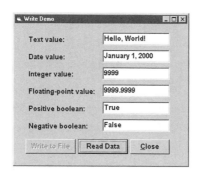

The code behind the Read Data button on frmWrite is shown in Listing 15.12. The first several lines declare some variables used by this procedure and clear the text boxes on the form. Then a data file named Write.txt is opened for input and the data read from Write.txt with the Input statement. Notice how the variables are passed as parameters to the Input statement.

Listing 15.12. Reading formatted text files is easy with the `Input` statement.

```
Private Sub cmdReadData_Click()
  Me.Caption = "Input Demo"
  Dim strText As String
  Dim dtmDate As Date
  Dim intInteger As Integer
  Dim dblDouble As Double
  Dim boolPositive As Boolean
  Dim boolNegative As Boolean
  txtText.Text = ""
  txtDate.Text = ""
  txtInteger.Text = ""
  txtDouble.Text = ""
  txtPositive = ""
  txtNegative = ""

  MsgBox "Click on OK when ready to continue:"

  Open App.Path & "\Write.txt" For Input As #1
  Input #1, strText, dtmDate, intInteger, _
    dblDouble, boolPositive, boolNegative
  Close #1

  txtText.Text = strText
  txtDate.Text = dtmDate
  txtInteger.Text = intInteger
  txtDouble.Text = dblDouble
  txtPositive = boolPositive
  txtNegative = boolNegative
  cmdReadData.Enabled = False
  cmdWrite.Enabled = True
End Sub
```

The `Write.txt` data file itself is shown in Figure 15.13. The data in `Write.txt` is carefully formatted with commas between each bit of data, double quotes around text items, and pound signs (#) around dates and Boolean values. `Write.txt` was created with the Visual Basic `Write` statement, which is discussed a little later in this chapter in the section titled "Creating Delimited Text Files."

FIGURE 15.13.

`Write.txt` *contains data formatted with the Visual Basic* `Write` *statement.*

Creating Text Files

Obviously there must be some way to get data into a text file from Visual Basic. After all, Visual Basic wouldn't be much of a data management development system if there were no way to output data in text formats.

Outputting Fixed-Width Data to a File

Use the Print statement to create fixed-width sequential text files. You can separate data with spaces or tabs and specify exactly the position in the output file for each column of data. The general syntax of the Print statement is as follows:

```
Print #FileNumber, [OutputList]
```

The *FileNumber* parameter is the number of an open file; the *OutputList* consists of data you want put into the text file. The *OutputList* consists of a mix of data and positioning arguments that compose the line to be added to the file. The *OutputList* for the Print statement uses the following format:

```
[{Spc(n) ¦ Tab[(n)]}] [Expression] [CharacterPosition]
```

Spc and Tab are keywords that instruct Visual Basic where to position data. *Expression* is the data itself. Table 15.6 shows the two primary positioning statements added to the output list. The *CharacterPosition* parameter is either a Tab or Spc keyword telling Visual Basic where to put the next bit of data. If *CharacterPosition* is omitted Visual Basic inserts a newline sequence (Chr(10)+Chr(13)) into the file, indicating the end of a line of data. A semicolon can be used as the *CharacterPosition* parameter to instruct Visual Basic to put the next bit of data in the next available print zone (usually every 15 characters).

Table 15.6. Output specification arguments for the Print statement.

Specifier	Description
Spc(*n*)	Inserts a number of space characters in the output string. The *n* parameter specifies how many spaces to insert.
Tab[(*n*)]	Positions the output in the column indicated by the *n* parameter. A tab with no argument instructs Visual Basic to insert the data at the next available print zone.

Here are some examples of the Print statement and how the data looks in the output file:

Statement:

```
Print #1, "One"; Tab(10); "Two"; Tab(20); "Three"
```

Output:

```
One     Two     Three
```

Statement:

```
Print #1, "One"; Tab; "Two"; Tab; "Three"
```

Output:

```
One        Two        Three
```

Statement:

```
Print #1, Tab(10); "Hello"; " "; "World"
```

Output:

```
Hello World
```

Because the Tab keyword can be used to designate a specific column position in the output file, the Print statement is ideal for creating fixed-width text files. Figure 15.14 shows frmPrint in the TextFile.vbp project on this book's CD-ROM. This form demonstrates two different uses of the Print statement to create sequential text files.

FIGURE 15.14.

The frmPrint *form demonstrates how to use the* Print *statement to output text data in a variety of formats.*

Listing 15.13 shows the code behind the Print This Data to File button on the frmPrint form. This button's code takes the data off the form and prints it into a text file using several different Print statement arguments.

Listing 15.13. The Print statement outputs text data in a variety of formats.

```
Private Sub cmdPrint_Click()
  strText = CStr(txtText.Text)
  dtmDate = CDate(txtDate.Text)
  intInteger = CInt(txtInteger.Text)
  dblDouble = CDbl(txtDouble.Text)
  boolPositive = CBool(dtmDate = dtmDate)
```

continues

Listing 15.13. Continued.

```
    txtPositive = boolPositive
    boolNegative = CBool(dtmDate = #1/1/1900#)
    txtNegative = boolNegative

    Open App.Path & "\Print.txt" For Output As #1
    Print #1, strText
    Print #1, strText; Tab; dtmDate
    Print #1, strText; " "; strText
    Print #1, Spc(10); strText
    Print #1, Tab(15); strText; Tab(25)
    Print #1, intInteger; Tab(10); dblDouble; Tab(20)
    Print #1, boolPositive; Tab; boolNegative

    Close #1
    cmdDisplay.Enabled = True
    cmdWrite.Enabled = False
End Sub
```

The data file prepared with Listing 15.13 is shown in Figure 15.15. Notice how the data is output in helter-skelter fashion in each line of this file. Although Visual Basic has carefully prepared this file from the Print statements in Listing 15.13, the data doesn't line up well and displays an inconsistent number of spaces between fields in each line.

FIGURE 15.15.

It's easy to end up with inconsistent results when misusing the Print *command.*

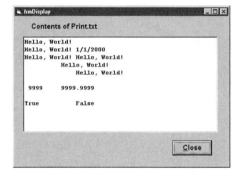

Figure 15.15 convincingly illustrates how careful you must be when using the Print command to output text data. Mixing different output specifiers (Spc and Tab) with a variety of position data results in a mess in the output file. Listing 15.14 does a much better job of producing a fixed-width text file than Listing 15.13. In this case the data output to the fixed-width table is from the Northwind Traders sample database. (cmdNWind_Click is found behind the frmPrint form in the TextFile.vbp project.)

Listing 15.14. Use consistent tab locations in the Print statement to create fixed-width text files.

```
Private Sub cmdNWind_Click()
  Dim intEmployeeID As Integer
  Dim strLName As String
  Dim strFName As String
  Dim dtmHireDate As Date
  Dim curBonus As Currency

  Open App.Path & "\NWind.txt" For Output As #1

  intEmployeeID = 1
  strLName = "Davolio"
  strFName = "Nancy"
  dtmHireDate = #5/1/92#
  curBonus = 4000

  Print #1, intEmployeeID; _
            Tab(10); strLName; _
            Tab(25); strFName; _
            Tab(35); dtmHireDate; _
            Tab(45); curBonus

  Print #1, "2"; _
            Tab(10); "Fuller"; _
            Tab(25); "Andres"; _
            Tab(35); "8/14/92"; _
            Tab(45); 6520

  Print #1, "3"; _
            Tab(10); "Leverling"; _
            Tab(25); "Janet"; _
            Tab(35); "5/1/92"; _
            Tab(45); 4000

  Close #1   ' Close file.
End Sub
```

The file created with the code in Listing 15.14 is shown in Figure 15.16. Notice how nicely the columns line up. The data in NWind.txt is a good candidate to be read with the Line Input statement and parsed with the Mid function.

Notice also that the data in the first line is indistinguishable from the data in the other lines in the NWind.txt file. The first line was created from data contained in variables; the values in the other lines were hard-coded into the Print statements. Visual Basic doesn't care how data is sent to the file when the Print statement is being used.

Figure 15.16.
Consistently for-matted fixed-width data is easily output with the Print *statement.*

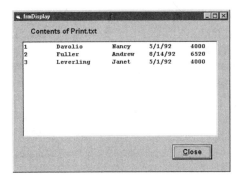

In Figure 15.16 notice the following:

- No commas or other delimiters are used to set off fields of data.
- Text data is not delimited with quotes.
- Dates are displayed in Short Date format. The exact format of date data depends on the Regional settings established in the computer's Control Panel.

The Print statement is the best choice when creating fixed-width text files. If you intend to build a delimited text file, the Write statement is the best option.

Creating Delimited Text Files

Fixed-width files might be easier to work with when it comes to reading data, but delimited files are more powerful. Because the data in a delimited file is separated by delimiting characters, each field can be as large as necessary to hold the data required by the field. Also, as you saw in the case of the Input statement, delimited files do not have to be difficult to read, in spite of the fact that they contain such varied data.

The Write statement is the ideal choice when preparing delimited text files. The Write statement automatically inserts the appropriate delimiters around each data field in the text file, providing as much room in the output file as the data requires.

The Write statement uses the following syntax:

```
Write #FileNumber, [OutputList]
```

The *FileNumber* parameters, as you have seen before, references an open text file. The *OutputList* in this case is a comma-delimited list of numeric or string values to output to the text file. In most cases, the data files created with the Write command are read with the Input statement.

Back in Figure 15.12 you saw frmWrite, a form included in the TextFile.vbp project on this book's CD-ROM. This form includes the code shown in Listing 15.15, which shows the Click event procedure behind the Write To File button on frmWrite. This procedure takes the data off the form and writes it into a file named Write.txt (see Listing 15.15).

Listing 15.15. The `Write` statement adds delimited lines of data to a sequential text file.

```
Private Sub cmdWrite_Click()
  Me.Caption = "Write Demo"
  strText = CStr(txtText.Text)
  dtmDate = CDate(txtDate.Text)
  intInteger = CInt(txtInteger.Text)
  dblDouble = CDbl(txtDouble.Text)
  boolPositive = CBool(dtmDate = dtmDate)
  txtPositive = boolPositive
  boolNegative = CBool(dtmDate = #1/1/1900#)
  txtNegative = boolNegative

  On Error Resume Next
  Kill App.Path & "\Write.txt"
  On Error GoTo 0

  Open App.Path & "\Write.txt" For Output As #1
  Write #1, strText, dtmDate, intInteger, dblDouble, boolPositive,
boolNegative
  Close #1
  cmdReadData.Enabled = True
  cmdWrite.Enabled = False
End Sub
```

`Write.txt` is shown in Figure 15.17. Notice the commas delimiting the fields of data in this file and the secondary delimiters such as double-quote characters and pound signs (#) around other fields in the line of data in this file.

FIGURE 15.17.
Write.txt *contains delimited data produced with the* Write *statement.*

It is important to understand how the `Write` statement delimits data:

- Text fields are always surrounded with double quotes. If a double-quote character must appear within a field, it must be included as two double-quote characters.

- Numeric data is not surrounded by secondary delimiters. In Figure 15.17 notice that the numbers 9999 and 9999.9999 are not surrounded by quotes or other characters.

- Dates are always displayed in yyyy-mm-dd format. Microsoft calls this the *universal date format.*

- Boolean values are surrounded by pound signs.
- If the data is truly null, and not just empty, #NULL# is written into the file.

The Write and Input statements are tailor-made for each other. The Input statement correctly interprets the delimiters and special formatting conventions applied by the Write statement. Unfortunately, not all systems output data in the carefully delimited format supported by the Write statement. You might have considerable programming ahead of you when working with delimited files produced by other systems.

Understanding Visual Basic's String Functions

You might have noticed that there are two syntaxes for using the Mid function: one with a dollar sign (Mid$) and one without (Mid). In case you're wondering, the Mid$ function returns a string; the Mid function returns a variant. The same rule applies to Left$, Right$, and most other string handling functions.

Although the difference between Mid$ and Mid is not often important, use Mid$ in situations in which you are sure the target of the Mid$ function is a string and Mid in other situations. One place where Mid is important is when the data source is unreliable and the data item might be missing. In this case, the Mid function (without the dollar sign) can return a Null variant. The IsNull function immediately identifies the missing data.

In this chapter the Mid, Left, and other string functions returning variants are used throughout. The code listings do not contain the statements required to validate the incoming data, but these lines of code are easily added.

Looking at Other File Operations

Obviously, a file must be open before performing most operations on it such as Input or Append. However, there are other ways you might work with text files on the computer. The TextFile.vbp project includes frmFileOps, shown in Figure 15.18.

FIGURE 15.18.

The frmFileOps *form demonstrates important file operations in Visual Basic 6.0.*

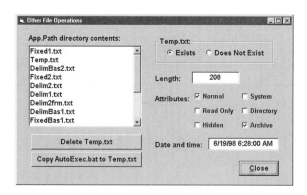

The frmFileOps form demonstrates some of the more common file operations described in the next several sections.

Deleting Files

If it is important to remove an existing file and replace it with another, you should use the Kill statement to first delete the existing file; then use either Open or Append and let Visual Basic create it anew. The Kill uses the following syntax:

```
Kill PathName
```

The Kill statement removes the file designated by the PathName parameter. No verification of this action is required. Kill removes the file without confirmation.

An error is generated if a file is not found at the path's location. The Kill statement is frequently wrapped with On Error statements as shown in Listing 15.16. The On Error Resume Next statement directs Visual Basic to simply ignore errors and proceed with execution at the statement following the Kill, while On Error GoTo Error_Handler directs execution to the procedure's error handling routine (see Listing 15.16).

Listing 15.16. Wrap the Kill statement in error traps to avoid the runtime error that occurs if the target file does not exist.

```
'Visual Basic statements here
On Error Resume Next
'Error occurs on next statement
'if TempFile.txt does not exist:
Kill "TempFile.txt"
On Error GoTo Error_Handler
'More Visual Basic statements here
```

Listing the Contents of a Folder

The Dir function returns the directory contents of a file, directory, or drive volume matching the path specification passed as an argument. Dir uses the following syntax:

```
Dir[(PathName[, Attributes])]
```

Notice that the PathName is not optional the first time Dir is called. The path specification can be omitted in subsequent calls if you intend to use the same path and retrieve additional filenames matching the path. Listing 15.17 shows an example of using the Dir command.

Listing 15.17. Dir is a useful function for returning filename information.

```
Private Sub DoDirFunction()
  Dim strDir As String
  ' Return first *.TXT file in current application path.
  strDir = Dir(App.Path & "\*.TXT")
  txtDir = strDir & vbCrLf
  'Loop until all .TXT file names have been retrieved.
  Do
    strDir = Dir
    txtDir.Text = txtDir.Text & strDir & vbCrLf
  Loop Until (strDir = "")
End Sub
```

One oddity about the Dir function is that only the first call to Dir can contain the parentheses, unless you intend to change the filename pattern specification. The first call to the Dir function includes the path and filename pattern (such as "*.txt") you want to search for and returns only the first file matching the pattern. If you intend to look for multiple files matching the pattern, call Dir without an argument (and without parentheses) to retrieve the next file matching the pattern.

By default, the Dir function returns every file matching the *PathName* specification. You can narrow the search considerably by specifying a value for the Dir function's Attributes parameter. Table 15.7 lists the valid values for the Attributes parameter. Notice that you can find the names of hidden, read-only, and other special files.

Table 15.7. Parameter values for the Dir function.

Constant	Description
vbNormal	Normal.
vbHidden	Hidden.
vbSystem	System file.
vbVolume	Volume label. If vbVolume is specified, all other attributes are ignored and the disk's volume name is returned.
vbDirectory	Directory or folder.

The Attributes parameters can be combined to yield highly selected results. For example, the following statement returns only hidden normal files with a .txt filename extension:

```
Dir("*.txt", vbNormal + vbHidden)
```

Detecting the End of a File

The end of a data file is indicated by the EOF function. EOF returns True when the end has been reached and False all other times. The code in Listing 15.18 shows how to use EOF to read all the data from a sequential text file.

Listing 15.18. The EOF function notifies you when the end of a file has been reached.

```
Do
  Line Input #1, strData
  Call FillForm(strData)
  'Process strData
Loop Until EOF(1)
```

The EOF function requires the file number of an open file and remains False until the end of that file is reached. When outputting data to files, EOF is always True.

Copying a File

The FileCopy statement copies an existing file to a new file. You must specify both the source file (the existing file) and the destination file. FileCopy uses the following syntax:

```
FileCopy SourceFile, DestinationFile
```

The *SourceFile* parameter is the path to an existing file; *DestinationFile* specifies the path and name of the new file created by the copy action. The source file must not be open during the copy or an error occurs. No value is returned by FileCopy, so you might want to check that the copy succeeded. For example, use FileLen to verify that the new file is the same length as the old file.

Determining a File's TimeStamp

The FileDateTime function returns a date variant reporting the date and time the file was created. FileDateTime uses the following syntax:

```
FileDateTime(FilePath)
```

The frmFileOps form uses the FileDateTime function to fill the Date and Time text box in its lower-right corner.

Determining the Size of a Closed File

The FileLen returns the length (in bytes) of a file that is not currently open. The name of this function emphasizes the fact that Visual Basic treats files as linear sequences of bytes on the disk, rather than as structured data. FileLen returns a long integer value.

You can run FileLen against open files. In this case, FileLen returns the size of the file before it was opened. Therefore, if any operations performed on the file while it was opened added to the size of the file, FileLen returns an invalid file size. Use the LOF function to return the accurate size of a file currently open.

Determining the Size of an Open File

You might need to examine the size of a file that is currently open. Perhaps you are adding data to a file and you want to make sure you don't exceed the size permitted by the available disk space or an email system. The LOF (length of file) function returns the number of bytes an open file occupies. You can run the LOF function any time the file is open. You needn't close the file before running LOF.

LOF uses the following syntax:

LOF(*FileNumber*)

The *FileNumber* parameter must be a handle to an open file.

Getting a File's Attributes

Most files are available for read and write operations at all times. There are files, however, that are restricted to certain operations such as reading or writing. A file with attributes that include the read-only flag cannot be deleted or opened for output. You might have to check a file's attributes before performing read or write operations on that file.

The GetAttr function provides a look at a file's attributes and reports which attributes have been set on the file. GetAttr uses the following syntax:

GetAttr(*PathName*)

where *PathName* is the path to an existing file.

GetAttr returns an integer value number that is the sum of all the attributes applied to the table. Each attribute is represented by an intrinsic constant. Table 15.8 lists the attribute values for systems running Microsoft Windows.

Table 15.8. GetAttr attribute parameter values.

Constant	Value	Description
vbNormal	0	Normal
vbReadOnly	1	Read-only
vbHidden	2	Hidden
vbSystem	4	System
vbDirectory	16	Directory or folder
vbArchive	32	File has changed since last backup

Interpreting the number returned by GetAttr can be tricky. You must use the And operator to perform a bitwise comparison of each of the intrinsic constants against the value returned by GetAttr. To understand bitwise comparisons, consider a value of 35 returned by GetAttr when run against a certain file. You can figure out that 35 is the sum of 1 + 2

+ 32, or vbReadOnly + vbHidden + vbArchive. But, how do you write Visual Basic code so that the computer can figure this out?

When used for bitwise comparisons, the And operator uses the following syntax:

```
TestValue And ConstantValue = SomeNewValue
```

The *SomeNewValue* obtained when And is used to combine *TestValue* and *ConstantValue* is either 0 or the same as *ConstantValue*. It is the same as *ConstantValue* when *ConstantValue* is part of *TestValue*. For example, the result of 35 And vbArchive is 32.

Using this principle, frmFileOps uses the code shown in Listing 15.19 to set the check boxes reporting the file's attributes.

Listing 15.19. The GetAttributes procedure uses the And operator to perform bitwise comparisons on the value returned by GetAttr.

```
Public Sub GetAttributes()
  Dim Attr As Integer
  Attr = GetAttr(App.Path & "\Temp.txt")
  chkNormal = IIf((Attr And vbNormal) = vbNormal, 1, 0)
  chkReadOnly = IIf((Attr And vbReadOnly) = vbReadOnly, 1, 0)
  chkHidden = IIf((Attr And vbHidden) = vbHidden, 1, 0)
  chkSystem = IIf((Attr And vbSystem) = vbSystem, 1, 0)
  chkDirectory = IIf((Attr And vbDirectory) = vbDirectory, 1, 0)
  chkArchive = IIf((Attr And vbArchive) = vbArchive, 1, 0)
End Sub
```

The immediate if (IIF) functions in GetAttributes sets the value of each check box to 1 (checked) or 0 (unchecked) if the corresponding attribute is set on the Temp.txt file.

Setting a File's Attributes

The SetAttr statement is the opposite of GetAttr. In this case, SetAttr sets an attribute (or several attributes, for that matter) on a file. SetAttr is useful for protecting data files from accidental erasure or removal from a system. SetAttr uses the following syntax:

```
SetAttr PathName, Attributes
```

PathName is the path to an existing file while *Attributes* is an attribute constant or a number of constants added together. For example, the following statement sets the hidden attribute on a file named Temp.txt:

```
SetAttr Temp.txt, vbHidden
```

The next example not only hides Temp.txt, but also makes Temp.txt read-only:

```
SetAttr Temp.txt, vbHidden + vbReadOnly
```

Use the intrinsic constants listed in Table 15.8 when using SetAttr. These constants are easily understood in VBA code and will not be as confusing as using their numeric equivalents.

Summary

This chapter has taken a look at the task of reading and writing data in text files. In most businesses, data comes from several different sources, including mainframe and midrange computer systems, desktop applications, and online locations such as Internet ftp sites. In many situations, the only way to move data between systems is by importing and exporting text files.

Visual Basic offers excellent capabilities to import and export fixed-width and delimited text files. In this chapter, you learned the VBA code necessary to read lines of text data, parse those lines into discrete fields, and display those fields on Visual Basic forms.

Later in this part of this book, you'll learn how to store data in real database files. When working with the special-purpose binary files produced and used by the Jet database engine (the relational database system built into Visual Basic) you won't have to worry about reading and parsing lines of data. Instead, you'll run queries that extract and manipulate data stored in Jet database format. Often the data you store in Jet databases started out as simple text files that were opened and processed with the VBA commands you read about in this chapter.

But first, you'll take a look at the Visual Basic Data control, a special type of control that can be added to any Visual Basic form, providing database capabilities to that form. Later you'll see how to write queries that return just the data you want, regardless of the database source attached to your Visual Basic program. After that you'll learn some truly advanced data access techniques.

Mastering the Visual Basic Data Control

Visual Basic was designed to allow you to create database applications for the Windows environment quickly and easily. If you have an existing database that you want to access, Visual Basic makes it easy for you to write a complete data management application with almost no programming. You just need to drop a few controls on a form and set the properties. In fact, Visual Basic makes it so easy that it can even create the data forms for you. The component that makes all these capabilities possible is the Data control, which is used to access the database along with the data-bound controls that display the data. With these controls, you can create a wide range of applications, from simple to complex.

Of course, as your applications become more complex, you'll need to add code to the application. However, the Data control enables you to create more full-featured applications that give you a high degree of control over the data in the database. The Data control is used to create applications that can display, edit, and update information from any database supported by the Microsoft Jet database engine.

Introducing the Data Control

Before building complex applications, however, you should learn how to use the Data control and manipulate it from within your Visual Basic code. In the next several sections, you learn how to work with the Data control and its associated properties and methods. Then you see how to create a simple, codeless program that accesses the Northwind database that comes with Visual Basic. By itself, the Data control can perform the following tasks without the use of code:

- Connect to a local database.
- Open a specified database table or define a set of records based on a Structured Query Language (SQL) query in that database.
- Pass data fields to bound controls, where you can display or change the values.
- Add new records or update a database based on any changes you make to data displayed in the bound controls.

- Trap errors that occur as data is accessed.
- Close the database.

To create a database application, add the Data control to your forms just as you would any other Visual Basic control. You can have as many Data controls on your form as needed; however, one Data control is generally used for each database table you need to access. The simplest of database applications can be created by performing the following:

1. Add a Data control to a form.
2. Set its properties to indicate the database and table from which you want to get information.
3. Add bound controls (such as text boxes, list boxes, and other controls that you bind to the Data control).
4. Set the properties of the bound controls to indicate the data source and data field to be displayed.

When you run the application, these bound controls automatically display fields from the current record in the database. Like all Visual Basic controls, the Data control has some properties that must be set in the Properties window at design time. Many of these properties can also be set at runtime by your program code as needed.

Using the Data Control

You control what the Data control will access and how it behaves by setting its properties as needed. To use the Data control, you must first place a Data control on the form, then set the DatabaseName and RecordSource properties. After you have set the DatabaseName property, Visual Basic will retrieve the names of all tables and available queries in the database and display them in the drop-down list for the RecordSource property. Try using the Data control by starting a new project and adding a Data control to the default form. Using the Properties window, select the Northwind database by clicking the button on the DatabaseName property to display the Windows Open dialog box. Then choose the Employees table from the RecordSource properties drop-down list as shown in Figure 16.1.

If you execute the program, you do not really see anything happening, because nothing is on the form but the Data control. Basically, the Data control links to the database but requires data-bound controls to be placed on the form to display the information. By default, the Data control creates a dynaset-type recordset from one or more tables in your database.

The Data control also provides built-in record-navigation functions that you can use to access the data. With these buttons (see Figure 16.2), users can move to the first or last record in the recordset, or to the next or previous record in the recordset. The button design is similar to the buttons on a VCR or CD player, making the buttons easy to understand.

FIGURE 16.1.

Selecting a table or query from the RecordSource *drop-down list.*

FIGURE 16.2.

Adding the Data control to a form also adds the default navigation buttons.

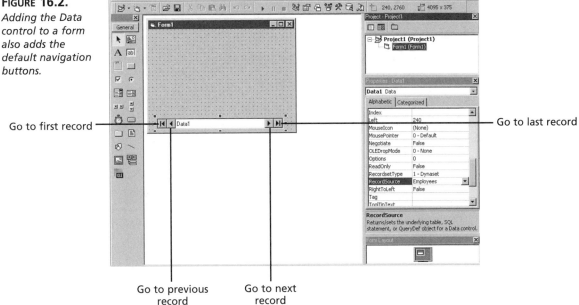

Go to first record

Go to last record

Go to previous record

Go to next record

The Data control also has a Caption property that you can use to display any important information, such as the last name of the address record you're browsing. Unfortunately, you can't set the Caption property automatically; it can be done only with code, which is discussed later in this chapter. Before adding controls to the form to display the data accessed by the Data control, look at a few of the more important properties of the Data control.

Understanding the Data Control Properties

By default, the Data control creates a dynaset-type recordset when you specify the RecordSource property. However, you can also create a snapshot-type recordset, or a table-type recordset to access a table directly. Each of the three recordset types is described in the following list. To change the RecordsetType property, select the desired type from a drop-down list in the Properties window.

- Table-type recordset —Creates a set of records that represent a single database table that you can use to add, change, or delete records.

- Dynaset-type recordset—Creates a dynamic set of records that represent a database table or the results of a query containing fields from one or more tables. You can add, change, or delete records from a dynaset-type recordset, and the changes will be reflected in the underlying tables.

- Snapshot-type recordset—A static copy of a set of records that you can use to find data or generate reports. A snapshot-type recordset can contain fields from one or more tables in a database but can't be updated.

You might want to change the RecordsetType for better performance. For example, if you don't need to edit a recordset, you can use a snapshot-type recordset, which provides faster access than a dynaset. Or, you might want to use a table so that you can change the order in which the data is displayed by selecting an index of the table because indexes are supported only by the table-type recordset.

Knowing the Current Record

A recordset contains a pointer that keeps the position of the current record. Only one current record exists for a given Data control at any time. A recordset also has two special positions known as beginning of file (BOF) before the first record and end of file (EOF) after the last record. Because there's no current record when the record pointer is positioned at either of these, problems can occur.

By default, the Data control prevents these problems by setting the record pointer to the first record when the beginning of the file is reached or by setting the pointer to the last record when the end of the file is reached. This way, there's always a current record for viewing or editing. However, sometimes you must know when you've actually reached the BOF or EOF position while using the Data control. You can control what the Data control does by setting the control's BOFAction and EOFAction properties.

The BOFAction property tells the Data control what action to take when the beginning of the file is reached. This property has two settings:

- 0—Move, the default setting, executes the MoveFirst method to set the record pointer at the first record and the BOF flag to False.

- 1—BOF sets the BOF flag to True.

The EOFAction property tells the Data control what action to take when the end of the file is reached. This property has three possible values:

- 0—Move Last, the default setting, executes the MoveLast method to set the record pointer to the last record and the EOF flag to False.
- 1—EOF sets the EOF flag to True.
- 2—Add New executes the AddNew method to prepare for the addition of a new record.

Note: The BOF and EOF actions are triggered only when users reach the beginning or end of the file by using the Data control's navigation buttons. They have no effect if you're using any of the Move methods (such as MoveNext) in your code.

If you choose to set either of these properties so that the respective flag is set, you will need to add code to handle the errors.

Using Data-Bound Controls

Data-bound controls are the data-aware controls through which you will access the information in the databases. When you add a Data control on a form, you must add one or more bound controls to connect to the Data control to easily access the data. Many controls that come with Visual Basic are set up to work with the Data control and can be used to create database applications. Each bound control is connected to a Data control and to a single field in the recordset specified by the Data control. The bound control automatically displays the data in the specified field for the current record. As you use the navigation buttons to move from one record to another, the data in the bound controls is updated to reflect the current record.

However, the bound controls aren't limited to displaying the data in the record; they can also be used to modify the data. This is done by editing the contents of the control. Then, when the current record is changed or the form is closed, the data in the database is automatically updated to reflect the changes.

Note: Only controls with an editable area can be used to update data.

To see how this works, add a couple of text box controls to the form you created earlier, as shown in Figure 16.3.

To get a bound control to work, you must set only a few properties, depending on the control. Most bound controls use two main properties to control the access: DataSource and DataField. When you select the DataSource property for a bound control, you'll see a list of the Data controls on the form. To set DataSource, select a control from the list.

In this example, only one Data control should be in the list. Select it for each bound control that you placed on the form.

FIGURE 16.3.
*Adding bound
controls to access
data from the
Data control.*

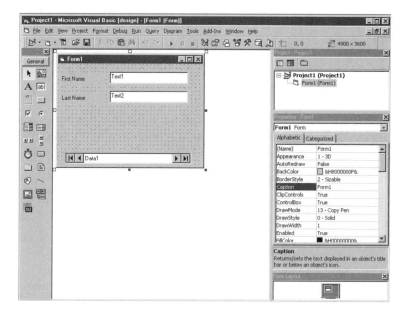

Note: You can have more than one bound control for a particular field, but you do not need to provide a bound control for each field in the table. Neither the Data control nor the bound controls need to be visible, so you can incorporate data access capabilities into any form you design, manipulating the Data control "behind the scenes" with your program code.

Although the DataSource property tells the bound control which Data control to use, you still must tell the bound control what data to retrieve. The DataField property tells the control which field of the recordset to retrieve. To set the DataField property, select it in the Properties window to display the list of fields available from the associated Data control. Then select a field from the list. Now, run the application again; you should see that data is now being displayed in the controls that you've added to the form, as shown in Figure 16.4.

Try using the Data control's navigation buttons to move around the recordset. As you can see, you've created a usable data access application without writing any code at all. As simple as this application is, you can even change the data shown in the text boxes to update the database. However, in most complex database applications, you'll need to manipulate the data that's accessed with the Data control.

FIGURE 16.4.

Displaying data from the database without code by using the Data control and bound controls.

Manipulating the Data Control at Runtime

The Data control offers a great deal of functionality that you can use without writing any code at all—simply by setting and manipulating its properties and adding data-bound controls to provide a user interface. There will be occasions, however, when you will want to extend the functionality of the Data control in Visual Basic code that you write yourself. Visual Basic provides this functionality by allowing you to manipulate the Data control and the recordset objects it creates.

For example, if you want to write code to move to the last record in the recordset, you can treat the recordset as an object and then apply the MoveLast method to it:

```
Data1.Recordset.MoveLast
```

Or, if you want to check the value of a specific field in the current record, you could write

```
MyString = Data1.Recordset.Fields("Title").Value
```

The syntax you are using in this section is the same as the syntax used by the Data Access Objects discussed in Chapters 18, "Mastering Jet DAO," and 19, "Using Advanced Data Access Methods."

Programmed Access Using Events

To manipulate the data accessed by a Data control, you add code to the events for the Data control and possibly for the bound controls. The following are some ways that you can use code with the Data control:

- Change the properties of the Data control or the bound controls during program execution.
- Add code to the Validate or Reposition events of the Data control (discussed in the next section).
- Provide capabilities that the Data control doesn't have by using the recordset methods.

Like any other control, you can change the properties of the Data control and bound controls at runtime. You can choose to change the DatabaseName, RecordSource, and RecordsetType properties of the Data control for one or both of these reasons:

- To allow users to specify the database to use.
- To set specific conditions on the data users want to see. This can take the form of changes to the Where clause or sort order, or your application might have the conditions set as part of an access control scheme.

If you need to set the properties at runtime, simply set the properties with code:

```
DtaMyDatabase.DatabaseName = "c:\program files\Microsoft Visual Studio\
➥VB98\Nwind.mdb"
DtaMyDatabase.RecordSource = "Employees"
DtaMyDatabase.RecordsetType = vbRSTypeTable
DtaMyDatabase.Refresh
```

After setting the properties, the Data control's Refresh method is used to apply the changes and requery the database, as shown in the last line of the code. The changes to the Data control take effect only after the Refresh method is invoked.

> **Note:** When a form is loaded, any Data controls on the form are initialized with the settings assigned at design time. To modify them before the Data control is initialized, place the code that modifies the control's properties in the form's Initialize event routine.

You can also set the properties of the bound controls at runtime. The DataSource of the bound control can be changed to access a different Data control on the form. You can also change the setting of the DataField property to have the control display the contents of a different field in the recordset.

You can use three key events to manipulate the way the Data control performs:

- Validate processes any data before the record is updated.
- Error is triggered for any data-access error.
- Reposition is used to perform calculations based on data in the current record or to change the form in response to data in the current record.

Although most of the Data control's actions are handled automatically, these events can help you add enhanced capabilities to your application.

Using the Validate Event

You use the Validate event to check or validate the data before the database is updated. The Validate event is triggered just before the record pointer is moved. This event occurs when users process a navigation button on the Data control or when the form containing the Data control is unloaded.

When the Validate event is triggered, the Data control checks all the controls bound to it to see whether any data has been changed. Two parameters are then used by the Validate event: Save, which specifies whether any data has been changed, and Action, which contains the reason the Validate event was triggered. The Save parameter can be True or False, whereas the Action parameter can be one of 12 values listed in Table 16.1. By checking the Action parameter, you can perform different processes depending on the type of action taken against the Data control.

Table 16.1. Action parameter values for the Validate event.

Constant	Value	Description
vbDataActionCancel	0	Cancels the current action
vbDataActionMoveFirst	1	MoveFirst
vbDataActionMovePrevious	2	MovePrevious
vbDataActionMoveNext	3	MoveNext
vbDataActionMoveLast	4	MoveLast
vbDataActionAddNew	5	AddNew
vbDataActionUpdate	6	Update
vbDataActionDelete	7	Delete
vbDataActionFind	8	Find
vbDataActionBookmark	9	Sets a bookmark
vbDataActionClose	10	Uses the Close method of the Data control
vbDataActionUnload	11	Unloads the form

The code you place in the Validate event can be as complex as you need. An example Validate routine follows:

```
Private Sub log_db_Validate(Action As Integer, Save As Integer)
    If Save Then
        If Not IsDate(txtDate.Text) Then
            MsgBox "The Flight date you entered is Invalid" & _
                    vbCRLF & "Please Re-enter!", vbCritical, App.Title
            Action = vbDataActionCancel
            txtDate.DataChanged = False
            txtDate.Text = "??/??/??"
        End If
    End If
End Sub
```

This code checks the Save parameter to see whether any data in the bound controls has been changed. If changes have been made, the txtDate field is checked to see whether it contains a valid date. If it doesn't, the Action is canceled, the bound control's DataChanged property is set to False, and a message is displayed explaining the error.

Using the Error Event

The Data control's Error event is triggered only when an error occurs during an automated process, such as the following:

- The Data control is loaded.
- A navigation button is clicked.
- The database specified in the DatabaseName property can't be found.

When the event is triggered, two parameters, DataErr and Response, are set. The DataErr contains the error number for the error that triggered the event. The Response parameter sets the action to be taken by your application. If the parameter is set to vbDataErrContinue, an attempt is made to continue with the next line of code. If the parameter is set to the default, vbDataErrDisplay, an error message appears. When you write the code for the Error event, you can set the Response parameter to vbDataErrContinue for those errors that can be corrected in your code, or to vbDataErrDisplay for all the other errors that might occur.

Using the Reposition Event

The Reposition event is triggered whenever the current record pointer is moved to another record. You can use this event to control the movement of related Data controls on a form or to modify the display of data as mentioned earlier in this chapter. The Caption property can be set in this event using the following code:

```
dtaMyDatabase.Caption = dtaMyDatabase.Recordset.Fields("First Name")
```

Also, if you're creating an order entry display and select a new customer, you might want to change the recordset of the order's Data control by changing the RecordSource property and then invoking the Refresh method for the second Data control.

Navigating the Data Control in Code

In addition to changing the Data control properties and modifying its behavior in the associated events, you can use several Data control methods in your application code to navigate around the data.

Navigating refers to moving around or changing the current record in a recordset. You have already seen how to move from record to record using the arrow buttons on the Data control. These arrows correspond to recordset object methods that you can use to carry out these same actions in code. The single arrows on the Data control correspond to the MoveNext and MovePrevious methods, whereas the double arrows correspond to the MoveFirst and MoveLast methods.

Even though the Data control provides the standard navigation buttons, at some point in your career with Visual Basic you will want to hide the actual Data control and provide them yourself.

Moving Around the Recordset

To move forward or backward in a recordset, you use the MoveNext and MovePrevious methods, respectively. The MoveNext method makes the next record in the recordset current. Generally, MoveNext is used to step through a recordset's rows to extract data on a record-by-record basis.

If the Data control is positioned at either the first or last record of the recordset, any further movement toward the beginning or end will set the BOF (beginning of file) or EOF (end of file) flags to True. If the BOFAction and EOFAction properties of the Data control are set to 1 (BOF and EOF, respectively), you will no longer have a valid current record at this point, and the bound controls will be cleared. If you use a Move method that moves beyond BOF or EOF, Visual Basic generates a trappable error. The MovePrevious method makes the previous record current. This method works like the MoveNext method, except that it moves the current record pointer toward the front of the recordset.

To see how this works, add two command buttons to the form as shown in Figure 16.5.

FIGURE 16.5.
Replacing the automatic navigation buttons with custom command buttons and code.

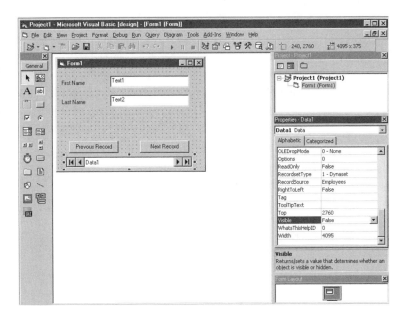

Also set the Data control's Visible property to False. Then add the following code to the form replacing the Forward and Backward function of the Data control:

```
Private Sub cmdNext_Click()
    MyDyn.MoveNext
End Sub


Private Sub cmdPrevious_Click()
    MyDyn.MovePrevious
End Sub
```

> **Note:** Even though the Data control's `Visible` property is `False`, you will still see it on the form at design time.

You can also add the capability to move to the beginning or end of the recordset by using the `MoveFirst` and `MoveLast` methods. Now execute the application and try using the command buttons that you just added. You should be able to move around the records in the dynaset. You'll still have to deal with one problem, however, when you try to move past the beginning or end of the recordset. You should get an error message as shown in Figure 16.6.

FIGURE 16.6.

Trying to move past the beginning or end of a record results in an error.

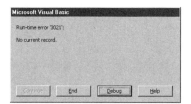

To prevent this from happening, check the `EOF` and `BOF` properties of the recordset when moving forward or backward in the recordset. Listing 16.1 shows the additional code needed for this function.

Listing 16.1. DATACTRL.TXT—Checking for errors when navigating the Data control recordset.

```
Private Sub cmdNext_Click()
    MyDyn.MoveNext
    If MyDyn.EOF Then
        MsgBox "Last record displayed", vbInformation, App.Title
        MyDyn.MoveLast
    End If
    Call DisplayFields
End Sub

Private Sub cmdPrevious_Click()
    MyDyn.MovePrevious
    If MyDyn.BOF Then
        MsgBox "First record displayed", vbInformation, App.Title
        MyDyn.MoveFirst
    End If
    Call DisplayFields
End Sub
```

Although the `Move` methods allow you to navigate through a recordset one record at a time, you might want to search for a specific record. To locate specific records, you can use the `Find` methods with dynaset- and snapshot-type `Recordset` objects, and the `Seek` method with table-type `Recordset` objects.

Using the `Find` Methods

The following methods can be used to locate a record in a dynaset- or snapshot-type `Recordset` object:

- The `FindFirst` method finds the first record satisfying the specified criteria.
- The `FindLast` method finds the last record satisfying the specified criteria.
- The `FindNext` method finds the next record satisfying the specified criteria.
- The `FindPrevious` method finds the previous record satisfying the criteria.

When you use the `Find` methods, you specify the search criteria, typically an expression equating a field name with a specific value. For example, the following code shows how to find the first record in the Employee table where the STATE field equals `'NY'`:

```
Data1.Recordset.FindFirst "STATE = 'NY'"
```

After the first record is found, the `FindNext` method can be used to move forward looking for each subsequent occurrence of the search value. You can also locate the matching records in reverse order by finding the last occurrence with the `FindLast` method and then use the `FindPrevious` rather than the `FindNext` method.

By using the `Find` methods, you can give the user the capability to search the database for a specific employee. To see how this would work, add the controls in Table 16.2 to the form (enlarging the form if needed) as shown in Figure 16.7.

Table 16.2. Controls required to add a search function to the data access example.

Control	Property	Value
Textbox	Name	txtSearchStr
CommandButton	Name	cmdSearch
	Caption	Begin Search
Label	Caption	Enter a Search String

Now, the only thing you must add is a single line of code to the `cmdSearch` `Click` event routine as shown here:

```
dtaMyDatabase.FindFirst "Name = '" & txtSearchStr & "'"
```

In the preceding code, the single quotes are required by the syntax of the `Find` method. Try running the program to see how this works. As you can see, this allows the user to go directly to a given record in the database. However, the recordset still contains all the records, regardless of whether the user needs them.

FIGURE 16.7.

Adding the controls to provide a Search *function to the data form.*

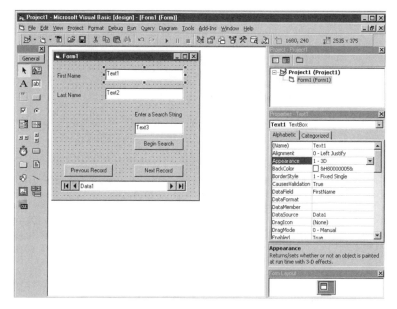

To further enhance this program, you can have the user enter a specific string and then modify the `RecordSource` property to reduce the number of records returned in the recordset. To include this function, place the controls in Table 16.3 on the form as shown in Figure 16.8.

Table 16.3. Controls required to add the filter function.

Control	Property	Value
Textbox	Name	txtFilterBy
CommandButton	Name	cmdRequery
	Caption	ReFresh
Label	Caption	Enter Ending Birth Date

With this function, as shown on Figure 16.8, you would need to perform a little editing on the input string before modifying the `RecordSource` property. You are actually modifying the SQL statement the `RecordSource` property is using by appending a WHERE clause to it. However, if the filter text box is empty, you do not want to change the Data control. The following code should be placed in the `cmdRequery` Click event to enable this function:

```
If Len(txtFilterBy.Text) > 0 Then
    dtaMyDatabase.RecordSource = _
        "Select * From Employees Where BirthDate <= #" & txtFilterBy.Text &
"#"
End If
```

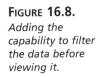

FIGURE 16.8.
Adding the capability to filter the data before viewing it.

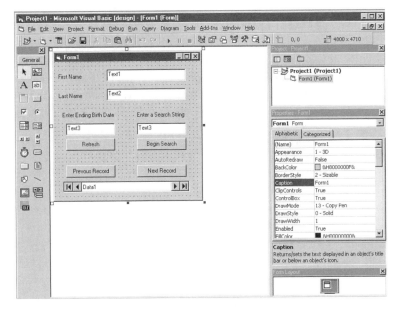

Of course, in an actual application you should also check to ensure that the text entered is a valid date. As you can see with these few examples, by using the available properties, methods, and events, you can create a sophisticated database program while writing very little code.

Note: To learn more about coding SQL statements, see Chapter 17, "Creating Queries in Visual Basic."

Unique Data Control Methods

Besides these methods, there are two other methods that you can use specifically with the Data control. They are the UpdateRecord and UpdateControls methods.

The UpdateRecord method forces the data in the bound controls to be saved to the recordset. Typically, you would have a Save or Update button on the form to execute this method, so users can save their work on the current record without having to move to another record.

The UpdateControls method is the reverse of the UpdateRecord method. UpdateControls redisplays the data from the current record in the bound controls. This method cancels any changes that users might have made but haven't saved yet.

Summary

In this chapter, you've seen how to add the Data control to your program to enable automatic access to a database. In addition, you learned how to manipulate this control in your code to provide additional functionality to the user. You also saw how to add bound controls to a form and bind them to the Data control on the form to automatically display, modify, and delete information in the associated recordset. In the next few chapters, you are going to learn what SQL is all about and how to apply this knowledge to combine the Data control with Data Access Object coding to enhance the database access in your program.

Creating Queries in Visual Basic

Earlier you learned how to access information in a database by using the Visual Basic Data control and to create reports that display information from the database. What you might not have realized is that you were using SQL to specify what information was needed from the database. A strong working knowledge of SQL programming is important if you plan to access information from a database in your program. This chapter provides you with an understanding of what SQL is and how you can use it to your advantage in a Visual Basic program.

Defining SQL

First, take a look at what SQL is and what it will let you do. Structured Query Language (SQL) is the language that every computer program uses to access a relational database. Learning to use SQL is like learning to use any other programming language. SQL was created and designed so that after you know how to use it, you can access any database that supports SQL access. Just as Visual Basic conforms to standards and each command or statement has a certain syntax, so does SQL. SQL is actually divided into two types of statements:

- One used to define the database itself is called *data-definition language* (*DDL*).

- The other, used to access the database, is called *data-manipulation language* (*DML*).

Because of the differences in how data-definition languages are supported and processed by different databases, this chapter focuses on the data-manipulation language encompassed by SQL. SQL is a specialized set of programming commands that enable you to perform the following tasks:

- Retrieve data from one or more tables in one or more databases

- Manipulate data in tables by inserting, deleting, or updating records

- Obtain summary information about the data in tables, such as totals; record counts; and minimum, maximum, and average values

Note: The SQL syntax shown in this chapter is designed to work with the Microsoft Jet database engine and is ANSI SQL compatible. However, there are some minor differences between Microsoft SQL and ANSI SQL, as there are with most other database systems. Read the related documentation before starting to design SQL for a particular database.

SQL statements allow you to perform processing in one line or a few lines of SQL code that would take you many lines of BASIC code to perform. SQL statements create queries that define the fields, tables, and ranges of records needed in a particular process. When a query is processed, the data is usually returned in a recordset. A recordset contains a collection of pointers to the data. SQL statements consist of the following three sections:

- *Parameter declarations* are optional parameters passed by the program code to the SQL statement.

- *Manipulative statements* tell the database engine what kind of process it will perform.

- *Options declarations* define and filter conditions, groupings, or sorts that must be applied to the data being processed.

The following is the syntax for a standard SQL statement:

```
[Parameters] Manipulative statement [Options]
```

This section reviews one of the manipulative statements and a few of the options that you can use to access data. SQL statements can perform a wide variety of tasks. These mirror the actions that users would need to perform on their data. These actions fall into one of four distinct manipulative statements:

- SELECT is used to retrieve a group of records from the database and place them into a dynaset.

- INSERT INTO adds a group of records to a table.

- UPDATE updates the values in a table.

- DELETE FROM removes the specified records from the database.

Although the manipulative statement instructs the database engine to perform a given action, the options declarations tell it what fields to process.

Warning: You can't use SQL statements directly in a Visual Basic application. They're used with Data controls or Data Access Objects.

Using the SELECT Statement

In most applications, the SQL statement most often used is the `SELECT` statement. This statement is used to retrieve records from the database and place them into a dynaset for access by the application code. The syntax of the `SELECT` statement is as follows:

```
SELECT [predicate] fieldlist FROM tablelist [table relations]
     [range options] [sort options] [group options]
```

Although you can create complex SQL statements, as you can see from the syntax, the simplest form of the `SELECT` statement retrieves all fields from a table. The following statement retrieves all fields and rows from the Customers table as shown in Figure 17.1:

```
SELECT * FROM Customers
```

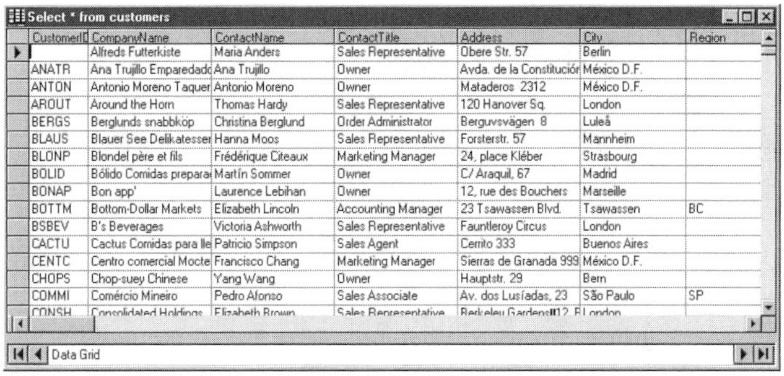

Select * from customers

CustomerID	CompanyName	ContactName	ContactTitle	Address	City	Region
	Alfreds Futterkiste	Maria Anders	Sales Representative	Obere Str. 57	Berlin	
ANATR	Ana Trujillo Emparedado	Ana Trujillo	Owner	Avda. de la Constitución	México D.F.	
ANTON	Antonio Moreno Taquer	Antonio Moreno	Owner	Mataderos 2312	México D.F.	
AROUT	Around the Horn	Thomas Hardy	Sales Representative	120 Hanover Sq.	London	
BERGS	Berglunds snabbköp	Christina Berglund	Order Administrator	Berguvsvägen 8	Luleå	
BLAUS	Blauer See Delikatesser	Hanna Moos	Sales Representative	Forsterstr. 57	Mannheim	
BLONP	Blondel père et fils	Frédérique Citeaux	Marketing Manager	24, place Kléber	Strasbourg	
BOLID	Bólido Comidas prepara	Martín Sommer	Owner	C/ Araquil, 67	Madrid	
BONAP	Bon app'	Laurence Lebihan	Owner	12, rue des Bouchers	Marseille	
BOTTM	Bottom-Dollar Markets	Elizabeth Lincoln	Accounting Manager	23 Tsawassen Blvd.	Tsawassen	BC
BSBEV	B's Beverages	Victoria Ashworth	Sales Representative	Fauntleroy Circus	London	
CACTU	Cactus Comidas para lle	Patricio Simpson	Sales Agent	Cerrito 333	Buenos Aires	
CENTC	Centro comercial Mocte	Francisco Chang	Marketing Manager	Sierras de Granada 999	México D.F.	
CHOPS	Chop-suey Chinese	Yang Wang	Owner	Hauptstr. 29	Bern	
COMMI	Comércio Mineiro	Pedro Afonso	Sales Associate	Av. dos Lusíadas, 23	São Paulo	SP
CONSH	Consolidated Holdings	Elizabeth Brown	Sales Representative	Berkeley Gardens#12 B	London	

Data Grid

Figure 17.1.
Retrieving all the fields from the Customers table.

The asterisk (*) serves as a wildcard for the field list section of the `SELECT` statement. The field list defines the fields included in the output recordset. The field list can include all fields in a table, only selected fields, or calculated values based on fields in the table. Also, by using the `AS` clause you can rename a field to be used in the recordset.

Note: Renaming fields doesn't affect the actual database field name, only the name used by the application to access that field in that particular recordset.

Because SQL enables you to retrieve data from multiple tables, you must specify from which table a field should be retrieved. The syntax of the field list section allows you to do this as follows:

```
[tablename.]field1 [AS alt1][,[tablename.]field2 [AS alt2]]
```

You usually need only a few fields from a table. By using the field list, you can specify which fields should be retrieved with the SELECT statement. Within the field list, the individual fields are separated by commas.

> **Tip:** A recordset created with specified fields is more efficient than one created with the wildcard (*), in both the size of the recordset and in database processing. As a general rule, limit your queries to the smallest number of fields that can accomplish your purpose.

By using the field list, you can retrieve only the first and last name of a contact (see Figure 17.2), as follows:

```
SELECT [CompanyName], [ContactName] from Customers
```

> **Warning:** If a field name contains blanks, you must enclose it in brackets.

FIGURE 17.2.
Obtaining only the needed fields.

Accessing Multiple Tables

Because data can be placed in many different tables, you must have a way to define the relationships between these tables. When you retrieve this data, you want to see all the information from the related tables. SQL allows you to gather information from these various tables into a single recordset. To create this recordset from multiple tables, you must specify three things:

- The tables from which to retrieve the field
- The fields that need to be retrieved
- The relationship between the tables

When specifying the fields to be retrieved, you must place the table name and a period in front of the field name as shown earlier. If you must retrieve some fields from one table and all fields from another, you can still use the wildcard character (for example, `Contact.[First Name], Sales.*`). The next step is to specify the tables you're using in the `FROM` clause of the `SELECT` statement. Finally, the relationship between the tables is specified by using one of two methods:

- `JOIN`—Combines two tables based on the contents of specified fields in each table and the type of join.
- `WHERE`—Usually used to filter the records returned by a query; however, it can be used in place of an `INNER JOIN`.

The final SQL statement using the `WHERE` clause would look like this:

```
SELECT Customers.[CompanyName], Customers.[ContactName], Orders.*
➥FROM Customers,
     Orders WHERE Customers.CustomerID = Orders.CustomerID
```

or when using the `JOIN` clause, it would look like this:

```
SELECT Customers.[CompanyName], Customers.[ContactName], Orders.*
➥FROM Customers,
     Orders, Customers INNER JOIN Orders ON Customers.CustomerID =
     ➥Orders.CustomerID
```

Both statements retrieve the first and last name from the Contact table and all the related sales information from the Sales table as shown in Figure 17.3.

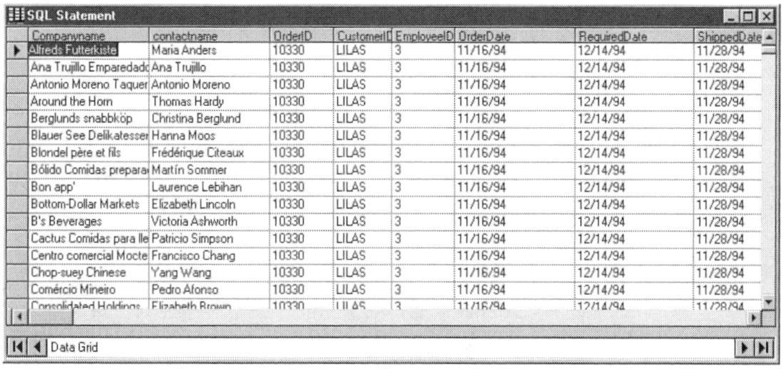

SQL Statement

Companyname	contactname	OrderID	CustomerID	EmployeeID	OrderDate	RequiredDate	ShippedDate
Alfreds Futterkiste	Maria Anders	10330	LILAS	3	11/16/94	12/14/94	11/28/94
Ana Trujillo Emparedadc	Ana Trujillo	10330	LILAS	3	11/16/94	12/14/94	11/28/94
Antonio Moreno Taquer	Antonio Moreno	10330	LILAS	3	11/16/94	12/14/94	11/28/94
Around the Horn	Thomas Hardy	10330	LILAS	3	11/16/94	12/14/94	11/28/94
Berglunds snabbköp	Christina Berglund	10330	LILAS	3	11/16/94	12/14/94	11/28/94
Blauer See Delikatesser	Hanna Moos	10330	LILAS	3	11/16/94	12/14/94	11/28/94
Blondel père et fils	Frédérique Citeaux	10330	LILAS	3	11/16/94	12/14/94	11/28/94
Bólido Comidas prepara	Martín Sommer	10330	LILAS	3	11/16/94	12/14/94	11/28/94
Bon app'	Laurence Lebihan	10330	LILAS	3	11/16/94	12/14/94	11/28/94
Bottom-Dollar Markets	Elizabeth Lincoln	10330	LILAS	3	11/16/94	12/14/94	11/28/94
B's Beverages	Victoria Ashworth	10330	LILAS	3	11/16/94	12/14/94	11/28/94
Cactus Comidas para lle	Patricio Simpson	10330	LILAS	3	11/16/94	12/14/94	11/28/94
Centro comercial Mocte	Francisco Chang	10330	LILAS	3	11/16/94	12/14/94	11/28/94
Chop-suey Chinese	Yang Wang	10330	LILAS	3	11/16/94	12/14/94	11/28/94
Comércio Mineiro	Pedro Afonso	10330	LILAS	3	11/16/94	12/14/94	11/28/94
Consolidated Holdings	Elizabeth Brown	10330	LILAS	3	11/16/94	12/14/94	11/28/94

Data Grid

FIGURE 17.3.
Accessing data from multiple tables in the database.

> **Tip:** Table names can be omitted from the field list as long as the field name is unique within the tables listed.

Adding Calculated Fields

In the preceding SQL example, the sales-related information for each contact is retrieved. Suppose that you also need to work with the average sale made for that contact. You can calculate this value by dividing the two values in your program code, or you can define a calculated field directly in the `SELECT` statement. A calculated field can be the result of an arithmetic operation or a string operation. In addition to the standard arithmetic and string operations, each database supports many operations and functions unique to that database. For example, Microsoft Access enables you to use the same set of functions as Visual Basic, such as `MID$` or `UCASE$`. The following SQL statement shows how to get the average sale made for the contact as part of the query, and the results are shown in Figure 17.4:

```
select customers.companyname, customers.contactname, orders.orderid,
    [order details].[unitprice] * [order details].[quantity] as [Total Sale],
    [order details].* from customers, orders, [order details]
    where customers.customerid = orders.customerid and
    orders.orderid = [order details].orderid
```

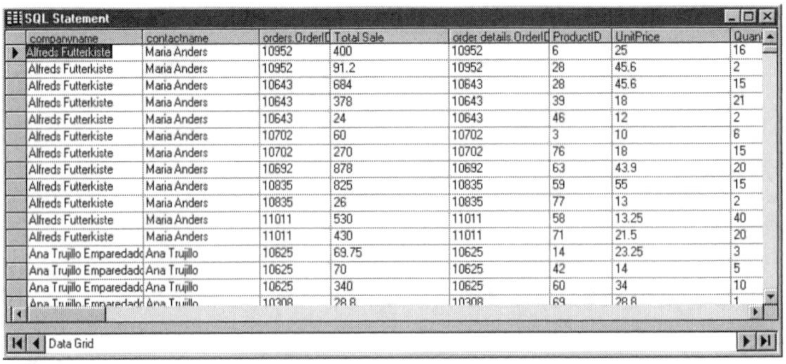

companyname	contactname	orders.OrderID	Total Sale	order details.OrderID	ProductID	UnitPrice	Quan
Alfreds Futterkiste	Maria Anders	10952	400	10952	6	25	16
Alfreds Futterkiste	Maria Anders	10952	91.2	10952	28	45.6	2
Alfreds Futterkiste	Maria Anders	10643	684	10643	28	45.6	15
Alfreds Futterkiste	Maria Anders	10643	378	10643	39	18	21
Alfreds Futterkiste	Maria Anders	10643	24	10643	46	12	2
Alfreds Futterkiste	Maria Anders	10702	60	10702	3	10	6
Alfreds Futterkiste	Maria Anders	10702	270	10702	76	18	15
Alfreds Futterkiste	Maria Anders	10692	878	10692	63	43.9	20
Alfreds Futterkiste	Maria Anders	10835	825	10835	59	55	15
Alfreds Futterkiste	Maria Anders	10835	26	10835	77	13	2
Alfreds Futterkiste	Maria Anders	11011	530	11011	58	13.25	40
Alfreds Futterkiste	Maria Anders	11011	430	11011	71	21.5	20
Ana Trujillo Emparedad	Ana Trujillo	10625	69.75	10625	14	23.25	3
Ana Trujillo Emparedad	Ana Trujillo	10625	70	10625	42	14	5
Ana Trujillo Emparedad	Ana Trujillo	10625	340	10625	60	34	10

FIGURE 17.4.
Adding calculations to a SQL statement.

You can also assign a name to any field in the field list by including the `AS` clause and the new name after the definition of the field as shown in the preceding SQL statement. Although this SQL statement creates a recordset that you can update, any calculated field in the recordset is read-only. In addition, if you update the original data used to create the field, the changes are not reflected in the calculated field.

> **Tip:** If you use a calculated field with a Data control, it is a good idea to use a label control to display the contents of that field. This prevents the user from attempting to update the field and causing an error.

Because of the length of the table names you're using, the SQL statement could get very long when supplying them in the field list. To prevent this and to simplify the SQL code, you can assign a short name to any table in the statement, in much the same way that you can rename a field in the field list. By using aliases in the `FROM` clause, you can assign to each table a name that makes sense to you. For example, the preceding SQL statement could be rewritten as follows:

```
SELECT CT.[First Name], CT.[Last Name], SA.*,
      SA.[Sale Total] / SA.[Sale Units] as [Avg Sale]
      FROM Contact as CT, Sales as SA WHERE CT.ID = SA.ID
```

As you can see, this approach makes the SQL statement a bit easier to read. When accessing the database, you usually want to retrieve all the records that meet a specified criterion. You do this by specifying the ALL predicate in front of the field list or by omitting the predicate altogether (ALL is the default). Therefore, the following two statements would be processed the same way:

```
SELECT * FROM Customers
SELECT ALL * FROM Customers
```

Sometimes, you might require only the unique values of the fields. To do this, you would use the DISTINCT or DISTINCTROW predicate. DISTINCT acts on the created recordset and tells the database engine to retrieve only one record with a specific set of field values, no matter how many duplicates might exist. For a record to be rejected by DISTINCT, its values for all the selected fields must match those of another record. For example, you can retrieve several people with the last name of Doe, but you wouldn't get multiple occurrences of John Doe.

If you want to eliminate records that are completely duplicated in each table before the recordset is created, use the DISTINCTROW predicate, which compares the values of all the fields in the table, regardless of whether they are selected.

> **Warning:** The DISTINCTROW predicate has no effect if the query is on a single table.

Specifying the Filter Criteria

One powerful feature of SQL is its capability to control the range of records to be processed by specifying a filter condition. You can use many types of filters, such as [Last name] = "Smith", Units > 20, or [Order Date] between #5/1/98# and #5/31/98#.

> **Note:** Although the SELECT statement is being discussed, filtering can be used in all other SQL statements, such as DELETE and UPDATE.

Filter conditions in a SQL command are specified in the WHERE clause. The syntax of the WHERE clause is as follows:

```
WHERE logical-expression
```

Four types of logical statements define the condition that you can use with the WHERE clause:

- A comparison is used to compare a field to another field or a given value (for example, [Sales Quantity] > 20).

- LIKE compares a field to a specified pattern (for example, JO*).
- IN is used to compare a field to a list of acceptable values (for example, State IN ("NY", "NJ", "CT")).
- BETWEEN is used to compare a field to a value range (for example, [Order Date] BETWEEN #01/01/98# and #02/28/98#).

Each predicate has many different options and wildcard values that you can use. Because some of them vary depending on the database, I suggest that you review these options for the database with which you're working.

The WHERE clause lets you specify multiple conditions to filter on more than one field at a time. Each individual condition follows the syntax discussed earlier but can be combined by using the logical operators AND and OR. By using multiple-condition statements, you can find all the contacts in New York and New Jersey, or you can find anyone whose first name begins with Rich:

```
SELECT * FROM Contact WHERE State IN ('NY', 'NJ') or
    [First Name] = LIKE 'RICH*'
```

The preceding example uses another predicate to check for a specified string pattern. The LIKE predicate lets you make comparisons such as last names starting with S, titles containing VISUAL, or five-letter words starting with B and ending with C. The wildcard characters, * and ?, are used to create the required patterns. The actual conditions for the previous examples would be

- Lastname LIKE 'S*'
- Titles LIKE '*VISUAL*'
- Word LIKE 'B???C'

The syntax of the LIKE predicate is as follows:

expression LIKE *pattern*

In addition to specifying the records to be retrieved, you can also use the SELECT statement to specify the order in which you want the records to appear in the dynaset. To sort the records, you would use the ORDER BY clause of the SELECT statement. You can specify the sort order with a single field or with multiple fields. If you use multiple fields, the individual fields must be separated by commas. When specifying a sort, the default direction is ascending; to change the sort order for a given field, you use the DESC keyword after the field name. To sort contact information alphabetically by state and then by last name in a descending order, use the following SQL statement:

```
SELECT * FROM Contact WHERE State IN ('NY', 'NJ') ORDER BY State,
    [Last Name] DESC
```

Working with SQL can be frustrating at times, but it also makes your life as a programmer easier because of the functions it performs for you. Without SQL and relational databases, every data-access function would need to be coded within your application. This review was only for the SELECT statement and a few of the many possible actions that you can perform with SQL. In the next few sections, you learn how to use SQL while designing the data forms and data-access processes in your application.

Aggregating the Data

You can also use the SELECT statement to perform calculations on the data in your tables as it is being selected from the database by using SQL aggregate functions. To perform these calculations, define them as a field in your SELECT statement, using the following syntax:

```
function(expression)
```

The expression can be a single field or a calculation based on one or more fields, such as Quantity * Price. The COUNT function can also use the wildcard * as the expression because Count returns only the number of records. Table 17.1 lists the aggregate functions available in Microsoft SQL.

Table 17.1. Available aggregate functions in SQL.

Function	Description
Avg	The arithmetic average of the field for the records that meet the WHERE clause
Count	The number of records that meet the WHERE clause
Min	The minimum value of the field for the records that meet the WHERE clause
Max	The maximum value of the field for the records that meet the WHERE clause
Sum	The total value of the field for the records that meet the WHERE clause
First	The value of the field for the first record in the recordset
Last	The value of the field for the last record in the recordset
StDev	The standard deviation of the values of the field for the records that meet the WHERE clause
StDevP	The standard deviation of the values of the field for the records that meet the WHERE clause
Var	The variance of the values of the field for the records that meet the WHERE clause
VarP	The variance of the values of the field for the records that meet the WHERE clause

The aggregate functions will operate only on the records that meet the filter criteria specified in the WHERE clause. In addition, the Aggregate functions are unaffected by sort order and return a single value for the entire recordset unless the GROUP BY clause (described in the following section) is used. If GROUP BY is used, a value is returned for each record group. The following SQL code shows the SELECT statement used to calculate the minimum, maximum, average, and total sales amounts, as well as the total item volume from the Sales table in the sample case. Figure 17.5 shows the output from this query.

```
select min(OD.quantity * OD.unitprice) as MinSale,
       max(OD.quantity * OD.unitprice) as MaxSale,
       avg(OD.quantity * OD.unitprice) as AvgSale,
       sum(OD.quantity * OD.unitprice) as TotSale,
       sum(OD.quantity) as TotVol
from [order details] as OD
```

FIGURE 17.5.
Results of running the aggregate SQL statement example.

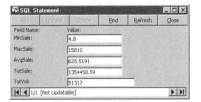

Grouping the Data

When you access information from the database, you sometimes must group like information together to make displaying or processing it that much easier. Record groups let you create a recordset that has only one record for each occurrence of a specified field. For example, if you group the Customers table by state, you would get one output record for each state. Grouping the records is especially useful when combined with the calculation functions described in the previous section. When groups are used with aggregate functions, you can easily get summary data by state, salesperson, or any other desired field.

Usually, the groups that you create will be based on a single field. You can, however, specify several fields in the GROUP BY clause. If you do specify several fields, a record is returned for each unique combination of field values. This technique can be used to obtain sales data by salesperson and item code. Multiple fields in a GROUP BY clause are separated with commas. The following SQL statement uses aggregates with a GROUP BY added on the SalespersonID. The result of this new query is shown in Figure 17.6.

```
select ORD.customerID,  min(OD.quantity * OD.unitprice) as MinSale,
       max(OD.quantity * OD.unitprice) as MaxSale,
       avg(OD.quantity * OD.unitprice) as AvgSale,
```

```
      sum(OD.quantity * OD.unitprice) as TotSale,
      sum(OD.quantity) as TotVol
from [order details] as OD, orders as ORD
where ORD.[orderid] =OD.[orderid]
Group by ORD.CustomerID
```

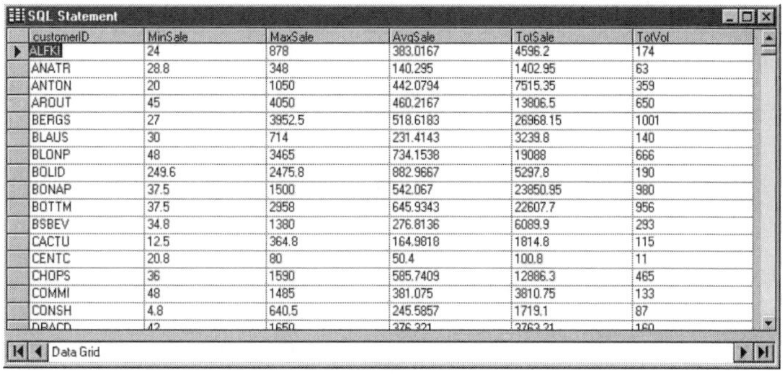

FIGURE 17.6.

The results of the GROUP BY clause being added to the SQL statement.

The GROUP BY clause can also include an optional HAVING clause. The HAVING clause works like the WHERE clause except that it only examines the field values of the returned records. The HAVING clause determines which of the selected records to display, whereas the WHERE clause determines which records to select from the database tables.

Using SQL Statements with the Data Control

The Visual Basic Data control uses the RecordSource property to create a recordset when the form that contains the Data control is loaded at runtime. The RecordSource can be a table, a SELECT statement, or a predefined query in the database. By changing the RecordSource property at runtime and then refreshing the Data control, you can change the data contained in the recordset that is accessed by the Data control as follows:

```
dbMyDataControl.RecordSource = SELECT SL.SalesID, _
    Min(SL.Quantity * RT.Retail) AS Minsls, _
    Max(SL.Quantity * RT.Retail) AS Maxsls, _
    Avg(SL.Quantity * RT.Retail) AS Avgsls, _
    Sum(SL.Quantity * RT.Retail) AS Totsls, _
    Sum(SL.Quantity) AS Totvol _
FROM Sales AS SL, [Retail Items] AS RT _
WHERE SL.[Item Code]=RT.[Item Code] _
GROUP By SL.SalesID
dbMyDataControl.Refresh
```

Testing the SQL

When you create and test your SQL statements, you can add them directly to your code and then run the program to see whether the SQL works. This can be tedious and frustrating, especially if you are creating complex statements. An alternative way to test your

SQL is to use the Visual Data Manager. The Visual Data Manager is a Visual Basic add-in that enables you to create and modify databases for your Visual Basic programs. It also has a window that enables you to enter and debug the SQL statements you are creating. In addition, if you don't want to create the SQL statements yourself, the Data Manager includes a query builder that helps you through the process.

To start the Visual Data Manager, simply select the Visual Data Manager item from the Add-Ins menu of Visual Basic. Then open a database by choosing File, Open Database from the menu. A dialog box appears that enables you to open a database. When the database is open, a list of the tables and queries available in the database appears in the left window of the application. Figure 17.7 shows the Visual Data Manager with the Northwind database open.

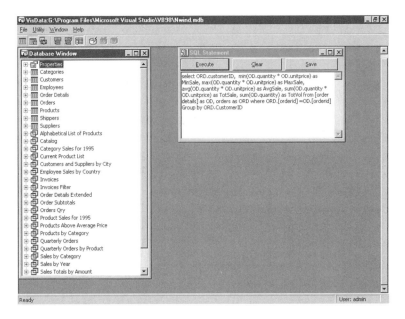

FIGURE 17.7.
Working with the Northwind database in the Visual Data Manager.

To develop and test SQL statements, you would enter the SQL statement in the text box of the SQL dialog box (the one on the right of Figure 17.7). Then when you're ready to test the statement, click the Execute button. If you're developing a retrieval query, a dynaset is created, and the results are displayed in a grid as shown in Figure 17.7 or a data entry form if the statement has no errors. If you're developing an action query, a message box appears telling you that the execution of the query is complete (again, assuming that the statement is correct). If you have an error in your statement, a message box appears informing you of the error.

Note: All the SQL results shown in this chapter were created using the Visual Data Manager.

Summary

This chapter has only taught you the basics of creating and using SQL statements. You have seen how to select records and how to limit the selection by using the WHERE clause. In addition, you have also seen how SQL statements are used to modify the structure of a recordset by using the other features of the SQL language, such as GROUP BY and ORDER BY. A single chapter cannot show you everything you need to know about SQL; however, it is enough to get you started. In the next couple of chapters, you see how to use what you learned in this chapter to directly manipulate the database using both Data Access Objects and ActiveX Data Objects.

Mastering Jet DAO

Jet is a funny thing if you're not used to it. You can't find Jet on your start menu and you can't launch it from your Windows Explorer, but just about everything you use on your desktop is capable of using Jet. When you develop applications in Visual Basic you will find that most of your development efforts will use Jet in some way.

So what is Jet? It's an application-independent database engine that can be used by Microsoft Excel, Word, Access, C++, Visual Basic, and others. The tool used to communicate with Jet is called Data Access Objects (DAO).

The original purpose for Jet was a Microsoft project called Omega, a single-user database engine that was not released. An early version of the Jet engine was released as part of the WinLogin program for Windows for Workgroups. It handled the user names, file locations, and other administrative tasks of a workgroup before Microsoft System Management Server was introduced. This version of Jet was not widely used in this incarnation.

Understanding How Jet Began

In November 1992, Microsoft released Access 1.0 with Jet 1.0 serving as its data engine. Jet handled the standard database functions such as data definition, querying, data manipulation, maintenance and security, and some that were never before seen on a desktop. Jet broke new ground with its updateable views (dynasets), nested queries, and its capability to gather data from many different sources at the same time.

This version of Jet could not be addressed or controlled in any programmatic way; you had to have Microsoft Access in order to get Jet to do anything. This caused many developers to consider Jet to be a part of Microsoft Access and not the standalone, independent database engine it was and is.

The release of Jet 1.1 brought with it the implementation of Data Access Objects v1.1. This version enabled developers in Visual Basic 3.0 to use the Data Definition Library to control Jet and harness its power directly.

Jet 2.0 saw an improved hierarchical object model for DAO. Programmers now had nearly complete access to all of Jet's underlying services from security to data definition and transactions. It also provided referential integrity, which is the capability to make sure that a database does not have records in one table without a related record in another table. (For example, referential integrity would be violated if there were order details in the Order Details table, but no order in the Orders table.) The cascading of updates and deletes was another major addition to the engine's services. Cascading updates and deletes enabled a user to change or delete an item, like a customer, and have all related records in the database automatically change or be deleted. This greatly improved the maintainability of the data.

Today, the Jet engine is a 32-bit implementation with substantially improved performance over its earlier versions. It now offers replication and data synchronization to help solve many problems caused by databases being located in different locations or from their being disconnected from the network periodically.

DAO first appeared as an unnamed, limited, forward-only access tool for Visual Basic 2.0 to use through ODBC. It also worked behind the scenes in Access 1.0 to provide an interface to the table and query structures and other objects to represent dynasets and recordsets. Visual Basic 3.0 saw the introduction of `TableDef`, `QueryDef`, and `Field` to the programmatic interface. The exposure of these structures in DAO 2.0 marks the start of DAO as we know it today. Since then nearly the entire object model of DAO has been exposed for programmatic access. Today DAO has an extensive object model replete with methods and properties and it can support many hosts from Excel to Visual C++.

It's important to remember that Jet and DAO are not the same thing. Jet is a database engine that provides a set of services, and DAO is a programmatic interface to Jet.

What Jet Does

Jet is a database management system (DBMS). The generally accepted standard holds that a DBMS should provide seven basic functions to its users. These basic functions are as follows:

- Definition—The system should provide a way to create and modify structures for the data, such as tables and fields.
- Integrity—The system should have the capability to enforce rules regarding the entry or editing of data.
- Storage—A DBMS must be able to contain data as defined by its structure and according to its rules.
- Manipulation—Users of the system must be able to append new data, edit existing data, and delete data from the system.
- Retrieval—Users must be able to retrieve and view data from the system.

- Data Sharing—More than one user should be able to access the data at the same time.

- Security—The system should be able to prevent corruption of the data and protect it from unauthorized uses.

All Microsoft Jet objects are stored in a single database file with a default extension of MDB (for example, NWind.mdb). The MDB file contains the structure of the data as well as the actual data. This is true unless you are using Microsoft Jet to access data in some other type of database such as FoxPro, Excel, or an ODBC source. In these cases, the data and the data structure are contained in accordance with those applications' specifications. From this point forward, I will treat all references to databases as meaning Jet databases unless otherwise noted.

Jet Tables

Tables are the repositories of data in a Jet database. Jet offers great flexibility in storing data. A Jet database can have tables that are native to Jet or they can be linked from other sources—all at the same time.

Tables are made up of one or more fields or columns. Jet provides for the following field types:

- Text
- Date
- Auto number
- Yes/No
- Memo
- Object

Jet Storage

These fields and the data contained in them comprise the storage aspect of the database. In Access, storage is in the form of Indexed Sequential Access Method (ISAM). This means records are ordered by their index or in the order of entry if there is no index; records are stored in a variable-length method by default on a data page scheme where the pages are 2KB in size. Several records can fit on one page, but a record cannot span more than one page. Large fields such as Memo or Object are stored in separate pages, but the developer does not have to control this. However, you should be aware that MDB files grow overly large when there has been a lot of data entry or importing. This is because there is slack in the data storage to accommodate the way Jet handles the data pages and new records.

Jet stores this data on disk by using a method known as *variable-length fields* by default. This means that it uses only as much space as is needed by the actual data you are storing. Microsoft Jet supports up to 255 fields in a table.

Jet Indexes

Indexes are presorted values tied to each record in a table. An index is set while designing the table in order to speed searches and guarantee the uniqueness of a record. The telephone book is a list indexed by name. When you must search for a phone number you must search through only a few pages. If the telephone numbers were arranged in the order they were assigned, the phone book would be useless. But because the phone book is alphabetized, searching is easy.

The index can be one field or a combination of fields, and the fields can require unique values or not. If an index requires a unique value, it is called a *unique index*. If it does not require a unique value, it is called a *clustered index*. An index can be created through DAO or SQL. Records in a table are actually sorted by their index as they are entered. Because an index might force a record to be inserted into the middle of a table, too many indexes can actually slow the data entry process.

Jet Relations

Relations are a vital part of how Jet works. Microsoft Jet is a *relational database* engine. In a relational database, data can be spread out among several tables to prevent repetition and ensure integrity. A relational database also enables you to get useful information out of data coming from different sources. For example, your phone bill arrives every month with every call you have made for the preceding month. The only problem is you can't remember every number on the phone bill and the bill doesn't come with subtotals by number or day. If you put the phone bill into a relational database as one table and join it by the phone number to a list of phone numbers from your telephone directory, you can get some useful information.

A relational database can provide you with the names of all the people you called and how much time and money you spent on those calls. Jet enables you to define the relationships between tables as you design your database, or you can assign ad hoc relationships later through queries. You can also institute referential integrity between tables and enforce it with cascading updates and deletes.

Microsoft Access provides an effective visual representation for relationships. It enables the user to draw a line between the related fields in tables or queries (see Figure 18.1).

Jet Queries

Queries handle the bulk of the data retrieval tasks for Jet. Queries are instructions to the database to present or manipulate data in a way described by a Structured Query Language (SQL) statement. The SQL statements can select data based on criteria or they can append, update, or delete data from the database. SQL statements can also be used to alter the structure of the database and its objects. DAO can also be used to manage data and manipulate Jet databases, but SQL is often more efficient. We will examine both approaches (DAO and SQL) in this chapter.

FIGURE 18.1.
Relationships as represented in Microsoft Access.

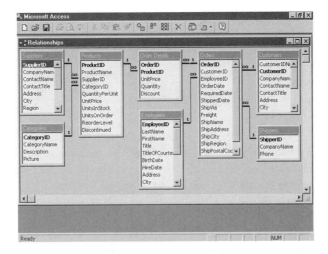

Using Jet in the World of Database Applications

To use Jet effectively, you must understand what kind of database it is, how it expects to have its data structured, and how applications using Jet should be configured.

Of all the different ways to arrange data, the most popular are as follows:

- ISAM
- Network-model
- Hierarchical
- Relational

The differences are significant and to program and manage these different types of systems require that you understand the concepts that lay behind them.

Understanding Relational Databases

Jet is a relational database engine. The relational database model was conceived in the early 1970s by Codd and Date as a way to reduce repetition in data, thereby reducing the chances for errors, reducing the need for storage, and easing the burden of entry and post-entry processing. In a relational database, data is stored economically in simple tables and these simple tables are related to one another through a set of similar data items called keys. A key identifies a record and can relate that record to another record or records in another table or tables.

In this chapter, you work with a sample database that is included with Visual Basic, NWind.mdb (Northwind). In Northwind, there is a table of customers that contains some very simple information about the customer. Figure 18.2 is a sample of the customer data.

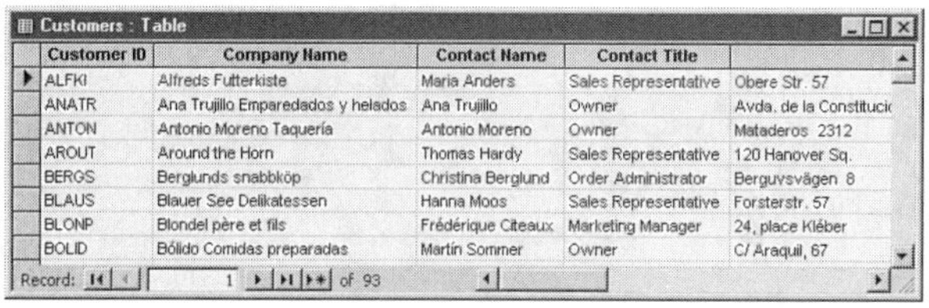

Customers : Table

Customer ID	Company Name	Contact Name	Contact Title	
ALFKI	Alfreds Futterkiste	Maria Anders	Sales Representative	Obere Str. 57
ANATR	Ana Trujillo Emparedados y helados	Ana Trujillo	Owner	Avda. de la Constituci
ANTON	Antonio Moreno Taquería	Antonio Moreno	Owner	Mataderos 2312
AROUT	Around the Horn	Thomas Hardy	Sales Representative	120 Hanover Sq.
BERGS	Berglunds snabbköp	Christina Berglund	Order Administrator	Berguvsvägen 8
BLAUS	Blauer See Delikatessen	Hanna Moos	Sales Representative	Forsterstr. 57
BLONP	Blondel père et fils	Frédérique Citeaux	Marketing Manager	24, place Kléber
BOLID	Bólido Comidas preparadas	Martín Sommer	Owner	C/ Araquil, 67

Record: 1 of 93

FIGURE 18.2. *Customer data from the Customer table.*

Notice there is no information in the table about what the customer purchased. Although this is important information, it is not kept with the customer data. If we kept the customers in the same table as their addresses and phone numbers, we would have to repeat those items every time something was purchased. This would result in a lot of needless duplication. Instead, the data for orders are kept in two other tables: Orders and Order Details (see Figure 18.3).

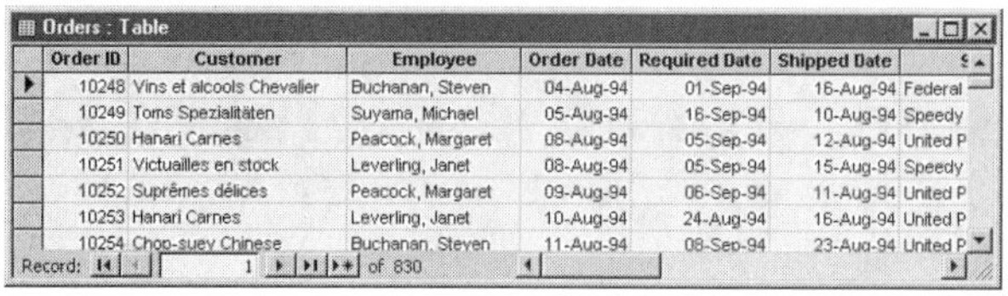

Orders : Table

Order ID	Customer	Employee	Order Date	Required Date	Shipped Date	S
10248	Vins et alcools Chevalier	Buchanan, Steven	04-Aug-94	01-Sep-94	16-Aug-94	Federal
10249	Toms Spezialitäten	Suyama, Michael	05-Aug-94	16-Sep-94	10-Aug-94	Speedy
10250	Hanari Carnes	Peacock, Margaret	08-Aug-94	05-Sep-94	12-Aug-94	United P
10251	Victuailles en stock	Leverling, Janet	08-Aug-94	05-Sep-94	15-Aug-94	Speedy
10252	Suprêmes délices	Peacock, Margaret	09-Aug-94	06-Sep-94	11-Aug-94	United P
10253	Hanari Carnes	Leverling, Janet	10-Aug-94	24-Aug-94	16-Aug-94	United P
10254	Chop-suey Chinese	Buchanan, Steven	11-Aug-94	08-Sep-94	23-Aug-94	United P

Record: 1 of 830

FIGURE 18.3. *The Orders table from* `NWind.mdb`.

The Orders table contains the higher-level information about the order such as the customer information, the shipping information, the salesperson information, and so on. Because most orders consist of more than one item being purchased, the listing of the items is kept in a separate Orders Detail table.

In the Order Details table (see Figure 18.4), the item, the quantity, the unit price, and any discount can be listed without repeating any unnecessary data.

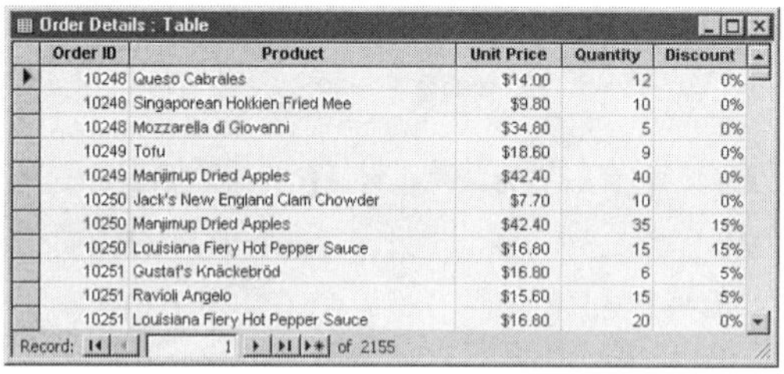

Order Details : Table

Order ID	Product	Unit Price	Quantity	Discount
10248	Queso Cabrales	$14.00	12	0%
10248	Singaporean Hokkien Fried Mee	$9.80	10	0%
10248	Mozzarella di Giovanni	$34.80	5	0%
10249	Tofu	$18.60	9	0%
10249	Manjimup Dried Apples	$42.40	40	0%
10250	Jack's New England Clam Chowder	$7.70	10	0%
10250	Manjimup Dried Apples	$42.40	35	15%
10250	Louisiana Fiery Hot Pepper Sauce	$16.80	15	15%
10251	Gustaf's Knäckebröd	$16.80	6	5%
10251	Ravioli Angelo	$15.60	15	5%
10251	Louisiana Fiery Hot Pepper Sauce	$16.80	20	0%

Record: 1 of 2155

FIGURE 18.4. *The Order Details table contains the data you don't want to appear in the Orders table.*

The Order Details records are related to the Orders table by way of a field called `OrderID`. In the Order table, `OrderID` is a *primary key*. This means it can exist for only one record and can't be duplicated. The Order Detail table has this same field. Here it is called a *foreign key* because it is related to the `OrderID` field in the Orders table, and that field is a *key field*. In the Order Details table, the `OrderID` can be repeated as many times as necessary.

With this kind of system, you can always find out what your customers have bought from you because they are related to their orders and their orders are related to the order details. Not only does this approach cut down on duplication, but also if it is done properly, it can be very efficient because the primary and foreign keys can be searched more quickly than entire names in a traditional flat file.

> **Note:** A flat file is produced when data dealing with lots of details are kept in one place. You might have seen these types of arrangements in spreadsheet databases. If you took all the information needed to track exactly what your customers ordered in Northwind and kept it in Excel, you would probably have a record for every single item ordered, and you would have to repeat all customer information (name, address, account, and so on) and all the order information (salesperson, delivery address, and so on) for each item purchased.
>
> It's easy to see how this scheme would jeopardize the quality of the data because a user or the system would have to accurately copy lots of information many times just to sell an item.
>
> Another way to create a flat file would be to repeat certain columns many times. To capture the data needed in Nwind a flat file might repeat order information fields (for example, Order Item1, Order Item2, and so on). Fields would also have to repeat for each order.
>
> Repeating fields makes it difficult to find exactly what is being searched for because you don't always know that a certain product is listed in Order Item1 or Order Item2.

Understanding Normalization

The process of putting data into this relational model is called *normalization*. There isn't enough room in this chapter to cover normalization or the five levels of normal form. However, there is a simple rule of thumb: whenever data is repeating in a table, there is probably an opportunity to break that table into two or more separate and related tables.

Like most rules, there are times when normalization is not the best form—even in a relational database. If you are querying massive amounts of data through a join of nonindexed keys, you might want to consider performing that search once (or infrequently) and creating a flat file to search against locally. This might improve performance for the users, but the data should still be stored in a normalized form.

Database applications can be divided into two basic types (see Figure 18.5):

- Client/server
- Remote

The basic difference is in where the database engine resides and where the data resides. In a client/server system the data and the engine reside together and the clients access the data from many different locations. In this situation, the single engine handles all the users and all the disk issues at the same time.

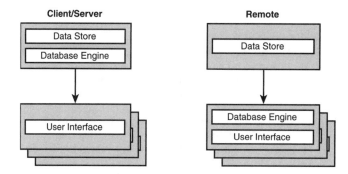

FIGURE 18.5.
*Comparing
client/server con-
figuration and
remote database
configuration.*

In the remote configuration, the data resides on a file server and the database engine lives on the desktops. They independently fetch data from the data store (the MDB file in Jet's case) and process it locally.

Jet is a remote multiuser implementation. Jet is not a data server like Oracle or Microsoft SQL Server. Because the file server controls the environment, locking and concurrence management are ultimately limited by the file server. In client/server systems, the database actually runs in something like its own operating system. For these reasons these systems have the capability to handle hundreds or thousands of users, whereas a Jet database can effectively manage a few dozen. However, with smart design and good coding, it is possible to have a very effective database system with several dozen users and tens of thousands of records using Jet.

Understanding DDL and DML

In order to be successful with Jet, you must know the data definition language (DDL) and the data manipulation language (DML) of Jet. These are not two separate languages, but rather they are two broad categories of the same sets of tools dealt with in this chapter.

DDL addresses the capability to create and alter storage structures, institute relationships, establish indexes, and enforce validation for the data. Traditionally, this structure is called the *schema*. Defining the database is typically done only once, and Jet stores all that information with the data, so you don't need to call a separate data dictionary when you use Jet. Everything there is to know about your database is there when you call it.

DML lets you get at your data so you can put it to good use through tables and queries. Like so many other things about Jet, this is complicated. There is more than one way to approach DML in Jet. You can use SQL statements to manage some aspects of data definition or you can use DAO. Likewise, DDL can be accomplished with either SQL statements or with DAO.

Although SQL is usually the best way to get useful information out of your database, you'll find that a solid foundation in DAO's DDL capabilities can greatly enhance your ability to get what you want out of Jet. SQL and DAO both deal with the structure and content of your data, but SQL is best suited for dealing with the content (DML). DAO is best suited for dealing with structure (DDL).

Understanding DAO Collections, Classes, and Objects

Jet and DAO become much easier to understand when you understand some terms and structures.

The most basic term is the *class*. A class is a blueprint for something that is waiting to be made. So the idea of a table, with its fields and indexes, its name and relationships to other tables is a class.

After you actually make something from its class, it is called an *object*. The object is the physical representation of the class. In other words, an object is a real table or a real form. All these things are kept in *collections*.

A collection is simply a gathering of similar items. All the fields in a table constitute that table's field collection. All the tables in your database make up its tables collection and so on. There are no relationships in the index collection, and there are no forms in the tables collection. Everything in a collection comes from the same class as everything else in that collection. The only thing a collection does is hold other objects and collections.

Collections, classes, and objects can be grouped together in a hierarchical structure as illustrated in Figure 18.6.

FIGURE 18.6.
The DAO hierarchical object model.

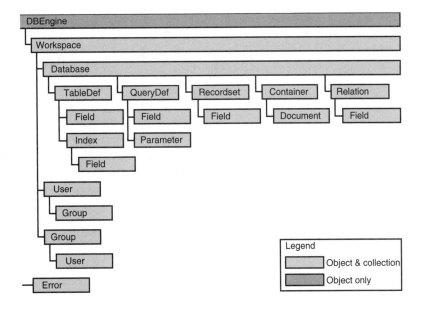

DAO is really a hierarchy of collections. (Collections are named with the plural of the classes they contain, so a field is contained in the Fields collection.) The only object that is not a collection and is not contained within another container is the DBEngine.

A single instance of Jet can contain several workspaces (usually used to accommodate different users) and multiple databases. The rest of the object model does double-duty as both objects and collections.

Addressing DAO's structure requires some unusual phrasing. The objects in a collection are numbered starting with 0. The objects also have names, but you'll find the numbering scheme very useful later.

In order to get to anything in the object model, you must employ a path from the top of the hierarchy to the object you seek to affect. In order to get to a table's `Customers` field, the path would look something like this:

```
DBEngine.Workspaces(0).Databases(0).TableDefs(0).fields("Customers")
➥-literal reference
DBEngine.Workspaces(0).Databases(0).TableDefs(0).fields(strCustomers)
➥-variable reference
DBEngine.Workspaces(0).Databases(0).TableDefs(0).fields(1)
➥-using the field's index number
```

Fortunately, Jet recognizes that certain things are needed more often than others. Most of the objects have default collections, so the paths to get to what you want can be much shorter. For example, the Fields collection is the default collection for tabledefs and recordsets, so you don't have to refer to the Fields collection between the name of the tabledef and the field you want. It would look like this:

```
MyRecordset!Customer
```

Instead of like this:

```
MyRecordstet.Fields!Customer
```

When you refer to the thing you want explicitly (for example, `MyRecordset!Customer`) use the (`!`) bang and when you refer to it through its collection use the (`.`) dot.

Getting Started with Jet and DAO

The only way to truly understand Jet and DAO is to use it. In this chapter you perform a few simple exercises to better understand DAO, and then you put those techniques to good use in a simple database application running against Northwind.

The first step is to actually open a database. In Visual Basic it takes only a few lines of code to have access to a Jet database. Then, complete the following steps:

1. In a new project, select the Project menu and choose References.
2. In the References dialog box (see Figure 18.7), check Microsoft 3.5 DAO Object Library and click OK. This reference must be in place in order to use DAO.

Figure 18.7.

Choose the reference to Microsoft 3.5 DAO Object Library to use DAO in this VB project.

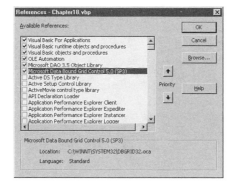

3. Create a new module and enter the following variables in the declarations section:

```
Global wrk As Workspace
Global gdb As Database
```

These global variables are going to serve as the representatives of the objects you are going to create from the DAO class hierarchy. You are going to have a workspace within Jet to use your database and you will be able to open a database within that space. You will always refer to the workspace and the database through these variables.

Now you can create the function to open the database.

4. Choose Add Module from the Project menu to create a new module in your project.

5. Click Open on the resulting dialog box (see Figure 18.8). You now have a blank module sheet to type your module onto. Type the following:

```
Function GetData() As Boolean
    Dim stDBName As String
    On Error GoTo OpenError
    Set wrk = DBEngine.Workspaces(0)
    stDBName = "C:\Program Files\DevStudio\VB\Nwind.mdb"
    Set gdb = wrk.OpenDatabase(stDBName)
    Set rs = gdb.OpenRecordset("Select * from Customers",
    ➥dbOpenDynaset)
    GetData = True
Exit Function
OpenError:
GetData = False
End Function
```

6. Save the module as DAO_Module. Later you put more functions and subroutines in here to build your application.

Note: Working in the Immediate window is a good way to see how DAO works.

FIGURE 18.8.
Creating a new module.

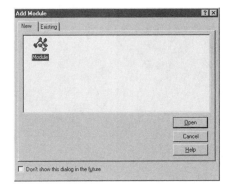

7. From the View menu, select Immediate Window and enter ?GetData() (see Figure 18.9).

FIGURE 18.9.
Use the Immediate window to run the function

If everything is correct with the function, you should have True as the return value. This means you have successfully opened Jet's NWind database.

Enter the following path into the Immediate window:

```
?workspaces(0).databases(0).tabledefs(2).fields(3).name
```

This give you the name of the fourth field in the third table of the current database in the current workspace (Title).

As you typed the command, you probably noticed that Visual Basic was offering you the next applicable methods and properties to guide you through the hierarchy of DAO. At this point in the Immediate window you can only affect the structure of the database. You can't create recordsets in the Immediate window because it would require the assignment of an object variable. However, you can manipulate some objects and observe others from the Immediate window.

The GetData() function also creates a recordset of the Customers table. You can view that recordset from the Immediate window.

Enter the following line into the Immediate window:

```
?rs.recordcount
```

You should get a result of about 90 records. Although you can't see it, Jet has loaded those customer records into memory.

Try the following command and you will see some data. This command presents the data from the second column of the first record.

```
?rs.fields(1)
```

It is also possible to navigate the records with DAO. There are essentially four navigation methods:

```
.MoveFirst
.MovePrevious
.MoveNext
.MoveLast
```

You can try these in the Immediate window. Use the `?rs.fields(1)` to watch the data change from one record to another as you move through the recordset.

Changing the Data Structure

DAO is also a data manipulation language. You can use it to change the structure of the data when necessary. It is best to make all the data structure decisions at design time, but sometimes there is a need to dynamically construct a table or query at runtime. DAO accommodates this very nicely.

You are going to add a field to the Customers table, and then you are going to fill it with data as you loop through the records of the Customers table. This gives you the opportunity to use the DDL capabilities and the DML capabilities at the same time.

Write the function (see Listing 18.1) in the DAO_Module.

Listing 18.1. `CreateField.txt` This function creates a new field in the Customers table of the database and fills that field with data.

```
Sub CreateField()
    Dim db As Database
    Dim strTblName As String
    Dim strFldName As String
    Dim tbldef As TableDef
    Dim fldCustIDNum As Field
    Dim i As Long

    strTblName = "Customers"
    strFldName = "CustomerIDNumber"

    'Open the database
    Set db = OpenDatabase("C:\Program Files\DevStudio\VB\Nwind.mdb")
```

continues

Listing 18.1. Continued.

```
'Set an object variable to a table in the database
Set tbldef = db.TableDefs(strTblName)

'Crate a field in that table with a data type of long integer
Set fldCustIDNum = tbldef.CreateField(strFldName, dbLong)

'Set it to be the first field in the table
fldCustIDNum.OrdinalPosition = 0

'Append the new field to the fields collection of the table - otherwise _
'it won't be persistent
tbldef.Fields.Append fldCustIDNum


'Open a recordset of the table to manipulate the data
Set rs = db.OpenRecordset(strTblName, dbOpenTable)

i = 1


While Not rs.EOF
    rs.Edit                     'Prepare the recordset for changes
    rs(strFldName) = I    'Assign a value to the field
    i = i + 1                   'Increment the value
    rs.Update                 'Commit the record
    rs.MoveNext              'Move to the next record
Wend
rs.Close
Set tbldef = Nothing
db.Close

End Sub
```

Execute this code from the Immediate window by entering the following code:

```
CreateField
```

Then from the Add-Ins menu, select Visual Data Manager. From here you'll be able to see the changes to the structure of the table and the new data in the table.

From its File menu, Open the C:\Program Files\DevStudio\VB\Nwind.mdb database. Double-click the Customers node and a small window opens displaying the field you created through DAO and the values you entered with another set of DAO methods (see Figure 18.10).

FIGURE **18.10.**

The Customer table after the new field has been added with data.

In one routine, you addressed the hierarchy from workspace to field data type and entered data into each of the records in the table.

Now you'll see how to put DAO to work in a real application. You will also see how and when to use SQL with Jet.

Creating an Application

The database application will be very simple, but it will cover several important aspects of developing with Jet:

- Using DAO
- Using SQL
- Errors
- Working with forms
- Explicit and Implicit references
- TableDefs
- QueryDefs
- Recordsets

The application consists of two forms and one module. One form is used to browse the Customer data, and the other form presents order history on a data grid for whichever customer is currently active on the customer form.

You can start with a new form. Select Add Form from the Project menu to open a blank form. Add 12 text controls and a label for each one. Also add nine buttons along the bottom of the form so you can program their Click() events later. The form should look something like Figure 18.11.

FIGURE **18.11.**
*The Customer
form in Design
view.*

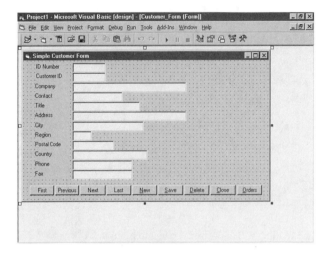

> **Note:** You can align the controls neatly by selecting them as a group and using
> the Format menu's Align, Vertical Spacing, and Horizontal Spacing commands.

The label captions are not important, but they should be easy to read and fit in the space
provided. However, you can employ a simple naming convention trick to make it easier
to get data on and off this form. Name the text controls with the same name as the field
they represent. In order to do this you must be sure you have the spelling correct. Use the
Data Manager to ensure this (see Figure 18.12).

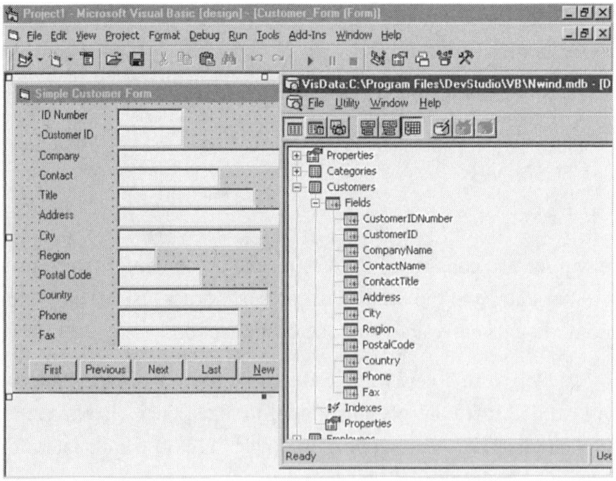

FIGURE **18.12.**
*View of field
names from
Customer table.*

Choosing the Visual Data Manager from the Add-Ins menu opens the Data Manager. Opening the database is simple because you've already done it. Checking the File menu should reveal the path as the last database opened. Selecting it will bring you to Northwind. Expanding on the Customers table and then the Fields collection reveals all the fields. You can copy the fields' names into the Name properties of the controls to ensure that they match exactly.

The command buttons should also be named according to a convention. Naming the command buttons makes it easier to disable and enable buttons depending on the context of the form. Table 18.1 lists the command button names and captions. The caption is especially important for the Close button because you are going to change the caption to reflect what is happening on the form.

Table 18.1. Button names and captions.

Button Name	Button Caption
CmdFirst	First
CmdPrevious	Previous
CmdNext	Next
CmdLast	Last
CmdNew	&New
CmdSave	&Save
CmdDelete	&Delete
CmdClose	&Close
CmdOrders	&Orders

You already created the connection to the database with GetData(). That's going to stay as it is. Moving data around on an interface requires that you park some data in memory somehow while you do other things.

Global variables are the easiest way to accomplish this. However, global variables are not the preferred technique for running VB interfaces. Global variables can be changed by any routine or function in the application; they consume memory the entire time you are running your application, and sometimes they conflict with other variables you import from other projects.

A better technique would be to use *class objects* or other object-oriented techniques, but these are beyond the scope of this chapter. For now, use global variables and concentrate on handling Jet interactions with DAO and SQL.

Dimensioning two more global variables in the declarations section of the DAO_Module gives the application all the variables it needs to run:

```
Global rs As Recordset
Global frm As Form
```

Because the controls on the form have the same name as the fields in the Customers table, you can write a very simple function to populate the form:

```
Function PopulateForm()
    On Error Resume Next
    Dim cntrl As Control
    Set frm = Customer_Form
    'Assigning the field values to the form
    'This simple function is why it's worth
    'adopting a naming convention
    For i = 0 To rs.Fields.Count
        frm(rs.Fields(i).Name) = rs.Fields(i)
    Next

End Function
```

Now you have a routine to fetch data from the database and another one to put that data on the form. These two routines will often be called together to refresh the form after changes have been made; therefore you should create one subroutine for the sake of simplicity:

```
Sub RefreshForm()
    GetData
    PopulateForm

End Sub
```

Preparing the form helps keep you focused as you continue to develop the application, so get some housekeeping out of the way by taking care of the button settings. The settings in this case are simple. The following functions in the General Declarations section of the form take care of it.

ResetButtons() sets the buttons as they should be when the application starts. DataBeingEntered disables the New, Delete, and Orders buttons; it activates the Save button and changes the caption of the Close button to Cancel. These changes are appropriate when data is being entered into the database.

```
Sub ResetButtons()
    cmdFirst.Enabled = True
    cmdPrevious.Enabled = True
    cmdNext.Enabled = True
    cmdLast.Enabled = True
    cmdNew.Enabled = True
    cmdDelete.Enabled = True
    cmdOrders.Enabled = True
    cmdSave.Enabled = False
    cmdClose.Caption = "&Close"
End Sub

Sub DataBeingEntered()
    cmdFirst.Enabled = False
```

```
    cmdPrevious.Enabled = False
    cmdNext.Enabled = False
    cmdLast.Enabled = False
    cmdNew.Enabled = False
    cmdDelete.Enabled = False
    cmdOrders.Enabled = False
    cmdSave.Enabled = True
    cmdClose.Caption = "&Cancel"
End Sub
```

Starting the Application

Starting the application requires only a few steps. First make sure the Customer_Form is selected as the Startup Object under Project Properties. If that's the case, then placing the following lines of code in the Form_Load event starts the application as Visual Basic loads the Customer_Form:

```
Private Sub Form_Load()
    RefreshForm
    ResetButtons
    Customer_Form.Show
End Sub
```

To make this form open when the project's code is executed, you must set this form as the project's Startup Object. This is done through the Project Properties dialog box (see Figure 18.13). Select Project1 Properties from the Projects menu to set this property.

FIGURE 18.13.

The Project Properties dialog box.

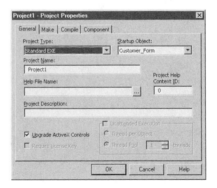

The RefreshForm subroutine opens the connection to the data and creates a recordset of the dynaset type. The dynaset type is one of the most flexible recordset types. It enables you to move through the data backward and forward and to update the data using the Edit and AddNew methods with the Update method. The data can be presented and updated as a single table or as a set of joined tables or queries.

However, as it is currently constructed, the application displays only the first record and then you are stuck looking at it. You must have a way to move around the recordset and have the form's display updated with each move.

Because you opened a recordset as a dynaset and stored it as a global variable, you can execute move methods against it from the form. This means you must program the movement buttons.

Installing these functions in the DAO_Module makes them easy to maintain and move around:

```
Sub MoveLast()
    rs.MoveLast
    PopulateForm

End Sub

Sub MoveFirst()
    rs.MoveFirst
    PopulateForm

End Sub

Sub MoveNext()
    'If we are at the End of File then don't bother
    If Not rs.EOF Then
        rs.MoveNext
        PopulateForm
    End If

End Sub

Sub MovePrevious()

    'If we are at the Beginning of File then don't bother
    If Not rs.BOF Then
        rs.MovePrevious
        PopulateForm
    End If

End Sub
```

Notice how you must run the PopulateForm after each move. This is because the recordset you are manipulating is in memory and has no relationship with the form unless you grab the data with GetData and put it into the form controls with PopulateForm. Putting these two functions together in one routine saves typing and ensures a consistent result.

Next, you must program the Click() events of the First, Previous, Next, and Last buttons in the same fashion. Keeping the form light of code helps with larger and more complicated interfaces and it also makes it much easier to know what's going on. There is no doubt what these buttons are doing and how they get it done.

Running the application after the buttons are programmed gives you a fully functional data browser. You can move through the recordset forward and backward and jump from the first record to the last. Now you must be able to add new records, edit incorrect or changed records, and delete records from the database. These are larger and more complicated tasks, but they are very manageable with the structure you have already built.

Adding a Record

Clicking the New button clears the form and enables you to enter a new record. It should also disable the Delete, Orders, and New buttons. It doesn't have to do anything else at this point. Because you have opened a dynaset recordset type, you can enter new records at any time. The Save button does the hard work of adding your new data to the database. The New button only takes care of the cosmetics.

This next function clears the form. You are using your omnipresent recordset again to guide your processes. A very simple function can accurately take care of your form:

```
Sub ClearForm()
    On Error Resume Next

    Dim cntrl As Control

    Set frm = Customer_Form

    For i = 0 To rs.Fields.Count
        frm(rs.Fields(i).Name) = ""
    Next

End Sub
```

Changing the status of the buttons has already been programmed, so all that's left is to program the `Click()` event of the New button. Clear the form and change the status of the buttons; the rest can wait:

```
Private Sub cmdNew_Click()
    ClearForm
    DataBeingEntered

End Sub
```

Saving the Record

Saving the record is slightly more complicated. When you were getting ready to enter the record, you cleared the form by using the recordset to guide you, and you disabled some buttons on the form. In this instance, you are again going to use the recordset to guide you and set the buttons back the way they were originally. By using the recordset to drive the process, it's almost as if you have the recordset vacuum the data into the database. This is much easier than feeding data to the recordset or pushing them into a SQL statement and worrying about syntax and order. Tapping into the DDL capabilities of DAO simplifies all the previous tasks.

In order to pass new values to the recordset you must alert it that you intend to add a record. The recordset is notified by the AddNew method. After the recordset sees AddNew, it is able to accept one new record but doesn't commit the record permanently to the table until it gets an Update method.

After the new record has been added, you refresh the form so that the new record can be seen in the interface (see Listing 18.2). This is important because the recordset you are working with reflects the state of the data at the time you created the recordset. If it is not refreshed, you could be out of sync with what others are seeing and doing with the data.

Listing 18.2. SaveRecord.txt This function saves a new or edited record in the Customers table of the database.

```
Sub SaveRecord()
 On Error Resume Next

    Dim cntrl As Control
    Dim fldval As Variant
    Dim starter As Integer

    'Prepare the recordset for append or edit
    'and decide where to start gathering data
    If Customer_Form!CustomerIDNumber = "" Then
        rs.AddNew
        starter = 0
    Else
        rs.Edit
        starter = 1
    End If

    'Prepare to move through all the fields for new records
    'and all except the first for edited records.
    'If the field name matches the control name
    'then pass the value to the recordset
    For i = starter To rs.Fields.Count

        fldval = frm(rs.Fields(i).Name)

        'Don't bother with empty fields
        If Not 0 = Len(fldval) Then
            rs.Fields(rs.Fields(i).Name) = fldval
        End If

    Next

On Error GoTo 0

    'Commit the record
    rs.Update
```

```
        RefreshForm

End Sub
```

The `cmdSave` button should have a `Click()` event as follows:

```
Private Sub cmdSave_Click()
    SaveRecord
    ResetButtons

End Sub
```

Working with SQL

Handling input and editing is easy with DAO, but Jet offers other tools for managing data besides DAO. SQL is a powerful way to manipulate data and, at times, to change structure. Following are just a few of the many advantages of SQL:

- It's a standard. Even though Jet's version of SQL probably won't run on other computer systems, the differences to human beings are slight. A developer of VB applications can understand SQL statements from other systems easily and the same is true the other way around.

- Changing the way an application behaves or changing where it gets its data is easy to do when using SQL as the data manipulation method. A few changes to the statements equals the rewriting of entire DAO routines.

- SQL is faster than DAO for most DML tasks. The Jet engine is optimized for SQL because SQL is the language of databases. Therefore, SQL runs faster than most DAO code. This is especially true if a stored query or stored procedure is run. Stored queries in Access and stored procedures on Oracle or Microsoft SQL Server have already created execution plans to enhance their performance. DAO cannot create an execution plan.

- It's easier to upsize the database to Microsoft SQL Server or Oracle when SQL is used to accomplish the DDL tasks because these routines do not have to be completely re-created from noncompatible DAO code.

Using SQL takes some study and practice. You are going to use SQL statements in a couple of different ways: to delete records and to use a stored query to retrieve records after changing the criteria in its SQL statement.

The simplest way to use SQL in an application is to create a SQL string and execute it against the database. This is how to delete records in the current database:

```
Sub DeleteRecord()
    Dim strSQL As String
    If MsgBox("Are you sure you want to permanently delete this record?",
    ➥vbYesNo) Then
```

```
        strSQL = "Delete * from Customers where CustomerID = " & Chr(39) _
        & frm!CustomerID & Chr(39)
        gdb.Execute strSQL
        RefreshForm
    End If
End Sub
```

Putting the `DeleteRecord` subroutine in the DAO_Module and calling it from the Delete button is a good approach because it keeps the code off the form and in one place. This makes it easier to work with it in the rest of the exercise. After the user confirms that he or she wants to delete the current record, a SQL string is constructed with the `CustomerID` taking its proper place in the criteria.

> **Note:** Notice the use of `Chr(39)` instead of a single quotation mark. Quote marks are hazardous to the health of a SQL statement. If a value is passed for inclusion in the criteria and it has a single quote or apostrophe in it, a simple concatenation with single quotes won't work. `Chr(39)` is more reliable in such situations.

After the string is built, it is simple to execute. It's similar to quickly building a query, executing it, and destroying it in Access.

The Delete button's `Click()` event should have the following statement:

```
Private Sub cmdDelete_Click()
    DeleteRecord

End Sub
```

Referential integrity rules in the data will not allow you to delete customers who have orders. For simplicity's sake in this example, you have not trapped that error (Error 3200). To see the function work, enter a record and then use the Delete button to delete it.

Working with the Data Bound Control

The Orders button uses a different technique for handling SQL statements and getting data from the database. For this functionality, employ a `QueryDef` object or a saved SQL statement in Access. To use this technique you must build another form to display the result.

Selecting the Add Form command from the Projects menu gives you a new form to display the order history for each customer. The form by itself can't be bound to data, nor can it display any data. Use the Data Bound control to maintain a connection to your database. The Microsoft Data Bound Control 5.0 (SP3) must be referenced by your project. The data grid was the easiest way to get this data onto a form. Selecting this tool from the References dialog box automatically brings it onto your toolbar.

Binding a Data control to a data source is the fastest way to get data into your VB application, but you lose some control and performance when you use it. In this case, because you are only going to retrieve a few records, the performance is more than adequate. Given how easy it is to incorporate this feature into your application, it makes sense to use the Bound Data control.

Creating a Data control on the form is like creating any other control, but the settings are a little different (see Figure 18.14). There are five properties you must be concerned with:

- `Connect`—What kind of database are you connecting to? In this case it's Access.
- `Database Name`—You can browse for it or you can enter the same string the `GetData()` function uses.
- `Default Type`—2-UseJet.
- `Recordset Type`—2-Snapshot.
- `RecordSource`—VBQry; you will have to type this in yourself.

FIGURE 18.14.
The Data control properties.

Setting the `Recordset` type to Snapshot helps you get better performance from the application. Snapshots reflect a particular moment in time for the data and they are read-only. Unlike the more flexible Dynaset, Jet doesn't need to devote time and resources to create and manage cursors or deal with locking issues. For these reasons, Snapshots can be built quickly and are ideal for viewing data when no editing or additions are appropriate.

With these properties set, you can move on to displaying the records handled by the Data control. To do this, you are going to use the Data Bound Grid control.

Displaying Related Records with a Data Grid

The Customer form you have built can display only one customer record at a time. However, each customer is likely to have several orders and each order will have several records comprising the order details. One of the best ways to display these records to the user is to use a data grid.

A data grid arranges multiple records like a table view in Access or a range in Excel. By using a data grid you can view several related records at one time without having to navigate through a recordset.

In order to use the data grid, it must be a registered component in the project. The steps needed to register a component are similar to the steps needed to make a reference.

You can place the data grid onto your toolbar by choosing Components from the Project menu. In the resulting dialog box, search the list for the Microsoft Data Bound Grid Control (see Figure 18.15). Select it and click OK.

FIGURE 18.15.
Registering the Data Bound Grid control in the project.

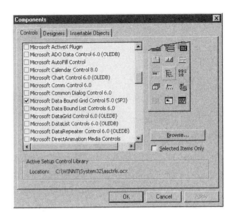

Your toolbar should now have a new tool (see Figure 18.16).

FIGURE 18.16.
Selecting this tool enables you to create a data grid on the form and then bind it to the Data control you've already created.

Create a grid large enough to display several rows of data and three fields. Name the grid GrdDataGrid.

In the grid's Property window, set its Data Mode property to 0-Bound. Now the Data Source property can be set to the name of the Data control (datPrimaryRS). That's all there is to it. VB carries the data to the form and the Grid control receives it and places it into its matrix without any further intervention from you.

All you must do now is trigger the event that creates the correct query and loads the form.

Listing 18.3 shows the function that rewrites the SQL statement and tries to change the existing query's SQL property. It rewrites the SQL statement with a new customer ID in the Where clause. If it can't find the query, it creates a new one using the CreateQuerydef() method.

The CreateQuerydef() method has four parts:

- The querydef object variable that represents the query object you are creating.
- The object representing the open database or connection that will contain the query object you are creating.
- An optional string to use as the name of the query object you are creating.
- An optional string representing the SQL statement for the query object. The SQL statement can be assigned or change at any time.

After the query is created or updated, the subroutine opens the form with the bound Data control and data grid to display the order history for the customer who was selected on the Customer_Form at the time.

Listing 18.3. GetOrderHistory.txt This subroutine retrieves the order history for the selected customer by changing or creating a query in the Jet database.

```
Sub GetOrderHistory(IDField As String)
    Dim qdOrdHist As QueryDef
    Dim strSQL As String

    On Error GoTo GetOrderHistory_Error

    'This is the SQL Statement to find a customer's order history
    strSQL = "SELECT Orders.OrderDate, Products.ProductName,
    ➥[Order Details].Quantity" _
    & " FROM Products INNER JOIN ((Customers INNER JOIN Orders ON
    ➥Customers.CustomerID = Orders.CustomerID)" _
    & " INNER JOIN [Order Details] ON Orders.OrderID =
    ➥[Order Details].OrderID)" _
    & " ON Products.ProductID = [Order Details].ProductID" _
    & " Where (((Customers.CustomerIDNumber) = " & IDField & "))" _
    & " ORDER BY Orders.OrderDate, Products.ProductName;"
    'Try to change the existing query's sql statement
    gdb.QueryDefs("VBQry").SQL = strSQL
    'Open the form and let the Data Control and Grid do the rest of the work
    Load frmVBQry
    frmVBQry.Show

    Exit Sub
GetOrderHistory_Error:
```

continues

Listing 18.3. Continued.

```
'Couldn't find the query, so make a new one
If Err = 3265 Then
    Set qdOrdHist = gdb.CreateQueryDef("VBQry", strSQL)
    Resume Next
End If
End Sub
```
The cmdOrders button on the Customer_Form needs to have this line inserted
➥into the Click() event.
```
Private Sub cmdOrders_Click()
    GetOrderHistory CustomerIDNumber

End Sub
```

Finally, you must call this function from the cmdOrders button. In the Click() event of
the cmdOrders control enter the following function:

```
Private Sub cmdOrders_Click()
    GetOrderHistory CustomerIDNumber

End Sub
```

Executing the project now opens the Jet database, creates a dynaset as a global variable,
and populates a form with one record of data. The form also enables you to browse,
append, edit, and delete that data easily. The frmVBQry enables you to view the ordering
history of any customer in the data by dynamically creating or altering a query in the
Northwind database and presenting the results. You've also seen how the DAO hierarchy
enables you to tap into a wealth of information about your data and its structure to make
programming database applications easier and more reliable.

This is only a small part of what Jet can do when approached with DAO or SQL. There
are hundreds of collections, objects, properties, and methods in the DAO object model at
your disposal so you can make your applications robust and effective.

Summary

This chapter has explored just a few things you can do with a Jet database using DAO
and SQL. Jet exposes a well-developed and highly detailed object model to DAO which
empowers you to do just about anything you need to a database's data or structure. As if
that were not enough, Jet also offers SQL functionality for greater compatibility and
upsizing potential. Taken together, these tools can satisfy most of your Jet database
needs.

The next chapter goes further in database management with an exploration of ADO
(Active Data Objects), OLE_DB, transactions, parameter queries, and open database connectivity. These tools enable you to build powerful applications across the enterprise.

19

Using Advanced Data Access Methods

ActiveX Data Objects, Microsoft's new data-access model, promises to be the method of choice for future database development within Visual Basic. ADO is a fast, high-level interface into the OLE DB application-programming interface (API). ADO's benefits include next-generation, data-access specification with the ease of an interface similar to the Data Access Objects (DAO) syntax you learned in Chapter 18, "Mastering Jet DAO." The differences between syntax and method for ADO and DAO are so minimal that novice DAO programmers can make an easy transition into the next phase of data access.

So what is so grand about this new data-access method and what necessitates leaving DAO behind? Well, Microsoft has openly stated that ADO will eventually replace DAO, Remote Data Objects (RDO, a component of earlier versions of Visual Basic) and all other data-access models currently supported by Microsoft. Microsoft's position makes it clear that sooner or later you are going to have to make the change to ADO. Now ADO is still a developing technology and currently does not support all the functionality of the Data Access Objects. However, the soon-to-be-released version of ADO 2.0 will not only contain a superset of DAO but also RDO. To make ADO even more enticing you really have to examine the new OLE DB API.

Understanding OLE DB

OLE DB introduces a universal data-access paradigm that is not restricted to Jet, ISAM, or even relational data sources. OLE DB is capable of dealing with any type of data regardless of its storage method or format. This access even includes an ADO data provider into ODBC so that you can use it with your ODBC data sources. It is important to note that OLE DB does not replace ODBC because they each feature completely independent APIs. However, OLE DB is expected to surpass ODBC in ease of use and functionality in the near future.

Using ADO to build enterprise solutions has the following primary advantages:

- High speed
- Low memory overhead

- Ease of use
- Small disk footprint

ADO has many key features for building client/server and Web-based applications.

Independently Created Objects

You no longer have to navigate through a hierarchy to create an object derived from the root object of the class. Creating a recordset object in DAO meant first opening a connection to the database through a database object and creating a recordset object from the database object. Now you can skip the connection and simply declare whatever you need such as the recordset object. This process results in fewer ADO objects, letting you manage and track only the objects you actually need. ADO also introduces a new data-access paradigm made up of dissociate resultsets managed independently of specific data sources or connections.

Different Cursor Types

A cursor is a pointer into a set of records. A database engine uses cursors to determine which records are scheduled for some operation. ADO provides several different cursor types, which introduces the potential for support of back-end-specific cursors.

If the recordset object supports batch updating, you can cache multiple changes to one or more records locally until you call the UpdateBatch method. This dramatically increases the performance of updating multiple records by only updating the server once instead of on each record.

Using the ADO Library

To use the ADO Library inside a Visual Basic 5.0 project, follow these steps:

1. Install the OLE DB SDK 1.5, which will register all associated DLLs and update all the clients installed on the machine.

2. Go to Project from the VB Main toolbar and select Project. Scroll down until you get to References and then click to bring up the project References dialog box (see Figure 19.1).

3. In the References dialog box, scroll down until you see Microsoft ActiveX Data Objects 2.0 Library and make sure that the check box is checked. If the item does not appear in the list you can click the Browse button and try to find the file yourself. The ADO library DLL is named MSADO15.DLL and should be in Program Files\Common Files\System\ADO directory.

4. Click OK and the ADO library is loaded into the system.

All available ADO objects and functions are then made available to the project.

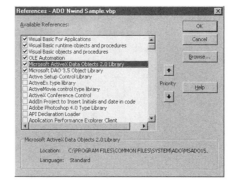

FIGURE 19.1.

*Insert the ADO
2.0 Library into
your project.*

Looking into the ADO Object Model

The ActiveX data object model is a flattened version of both DAO and RDO. For this reference we will stick to the comparison's held between the ADO model and the DAO model. Although the two models share much commonality, DAO code will not port over to ADO without some conversion.

There are seven objects in the ADO hierarchy (see Figure 19.2). Although ADO objects can be created outside the scope of a hierarchy, the objects exist within hierarchical relationships. At any time you can create an independent object, such as a recordset with or without the Connection object. This reduces the objects that must be handled throughout the life of the program.

FIGURE 19.2.

*The ADO model
and its relation-
ships.*

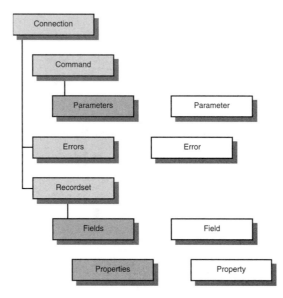

Most DAO programmers still find it beneficial to make a single public Connection object and derive child objects from that. Making only one connection throughout the application speeds up performance and frees you from having to deal with connection issues continually.

Let's take a look at each of the seven objects and how they are going to impact your data-access code:

- Command—Contains information about a command such as parameter definitions, query string, or other such data relevant to a command. The Command object is most useful when executing stored procedures or if there is a need to define query parameters. Recordset objects can be derived from command execution or through straight SQL statements applied to the recordset object. If you plan to run execute queries, you might want to use the Connection object instead of loading the Command object into memory.

- Connection—Contains connection information with the data provider. The Connection object is the root of the ADO model. From this, all the other six objects can be derived. The Connection object also contains functionality for executing SQL statements directly or handling transaction accounting.

- Error —Holds extended error information about an error condition raised by the data provider. Because single statements can generate more than one error, the Errors collection can have multiple Error objects. (This is only for provider-specific errors not handled by ADO.) The trappable ADO errors are specific events that can be handled by and returned to the Visual Basic Err object.

- Field—Contains information about a single column in a recordset object. The recordset object contains a Field collection that contains all the Field objects for that recordset.

- Parameter—A single parameter for a parameterized command, the Command object contains a Parameter collection to contain all its Parameter objects. These objects can either be defined or returned from the data provider.

- Property—A provider-defined characteristic of an ADO object.

- Recordset—Used to manipulate data at the record level of a data provider. Recordsets can be created from queries or table names without explicitly opening a Connection object first. However, if you want to orchestrate more than one recordset from a single connection, it is recommended that you provide a single Connection object to that data provider.

All these features and benefits of using objects are wrapped up in what Microsoft calls the Component Object Model (COM). The main objective of the COM philosophy is reusability: create an object once and use it in many applications. Following the COM principles, applications are constructed from several object components that are bound together with a programming language like Visual Basic.

Establishing ADO Connections

The ADO `Connection` object enables you to create a connection to a data provider of OLE DB. As soon as a connection has been established you can build your enterprise solutions from the wide range of functionality supplied from the `Connection` object.

The `Connection` object enables you to programmatically customize the connection to the database, initiate local transactions, get schema information, set timeouts, and handle errors through the `Errors` collection object.

First you check out the connection string so you can connect to a data provider and begin exploring the possibilities of the ADO `Connection` object.

Using a Connection String

Using a connection string in ADO is simple. Its syntax is the same as the syntax that connects an ODBC data source through DAO for ODBC connections. If you are used to using DAO's `OpenDatabase` method then you are going to have to make a few modifications to apply the new methods. Listings 19.1 and 19.2 show you the basics for declaring the object and attaching to an ODBC data source, an Access database, and a SQL database using the OLE DB type connection string.

Listing 19.1. Declaring an object and attaching it to an ODBC data source.

```
Dim adCN As New ADODB.Connection

'ODBC Style Connection String
adCN.Connectionstring = "DSN=anySql;UID=sa;PWD=;"
adCN.Open

'Typical Access Style Connection String
ConnectString = _
    "DRIVER={Microsoft Access Driver (*.mdb)};" _
    & "DefaultDir=" & App.Path _
    & "UID=admin;PWD=;" _
    & "DBQ=Nwind.mdb;"
adCN.Open ConnectString

'OLE DB Style Connection String
adCN.Connectionstring = "Provider=SQLOLEDB; _
    & DataSource=anySql;User ID=sa;Password='''"
adCN.Open
```

Listing 19.2. Connecting to a Jet database using DAO.

```
Public Sub OpenDAOConnection()
  Dim strConnect As String
  Dim strErrorMsg As String
```

continues

Listing 19.2. Continued.

```
sOn Error GoTo Error_Enumerator

  'Set String Variables
  strConnect = App.Path & "\NWind.mdb"

  'Connect and Execute Query
  Set ws = DBEngine.Workspaces(0)
  Set db = ws.OpenDatabase(strConnect, False)

  Exit Sub

Error_Enumerator:
  strErrorMsg = "Error Number : " & Err.Number _
      & vbCrLf & "Description : " & Err.Description
  Call MsgBox(strErrorMsg, vbCritical)

End Sub
```

Notice that you can either set up the ConnectString property of the Connection object or simply pass the connection string when you execute the Open method. The results are the same, so it is a matter of taste when selecting the exact sequence. The documentation from Microsoft concerning ADO connections varies slightly from those displayed in Listing 19.1; however, these methods have been proven to work effectively.

Connection Object Methods and Properties

Now that you have accomplished a very basic connection to the Northwind database, let's explore some of the more detailed methods and properties of the Connection object. The first set defines some of the parameters to which ADO actually connects to the database. These properties include the following:

- Command Timeout—Sets or returns a Long integer specifying in seconds the amount of time to wait for a command to execute. If the time exceeds the specified value, ADO returns an error in the Visual Basic Error object and cancels the command. If you set the value to 0 (zero) ADO waits indefinitely for the command to execute.

  Default Value: 30

- Connection Timeout—Sets or returns a Long integer specifying, in seconds, the amount of time before the connection is abandoned. Use this for connections that involve network routing over a slow or busy network connection. Setting the value to 0 makes the system wait indefinitely for a connection.

  Default Value: 15

- Cursor Location—Sets or returns a Long integer specifying the cursor location. The constants for this are adUseClient or adUseServer. This property enables you to choose between various cursor libraries accessible to the provider.

Setting the value to adUseClient might allow features that driver-side cursors do not provide.

Using adUseServer enables cursors that are sometimes very flexible and also allows for some additional sensitivity to reflecting changes that others make to the actual data source.

Default Value: adUseServer

- Isolation Level—Sets or returns one of the following IsolationLevelEnum intrinsic constants:

adXactChaos—You cannot overwrite pending changes from more highly isolated transactions.

adXactBrowse—From one transaction you can view uncommitted changes in other transactions.

adXactCursorStability—From one transaction you can view changes in other transactions only after they've been committed.

adXactRepeatableRead—From one transaction you cannot see changes made in other transactions, but querying again can bring new recordsets.

adXactIsolate—Transactions are conducted in isolation from other transactions.

Default Value: adXactCursorStability

- Mode—Sets or returns the access permissions in use by the provider on the current connection. You can set the Mode only when the State property of the Connection object is closed. Possible ConnectModeEnum intrinsic values are as follows:

adModeUnknown—Indicates that the permissions have not yet been set or cannot be determined.

AdModeRead—Indicates read-only permissions.

AdModeWrite—Indicates write-only permissions.

AdModeReadWrite—Indicates read/write permissions.

adModeShareDenyRead—Prevents others from opening the connection with read permissions.

AdModeShareDenyWrite—Prevents others from opening the connection with write permissions.

adModeShareExclusive—Prevents others from opening the connection.

adModeShareDenyNone—Prevents others from opening the connection with any permissions.

Default Value: adModeUnknown

As you can see, there are many options to choose from when establishing how the ADO Connection object interfaces with a data provider. Let's generate some code and employ some of the properties to make a completely customized connection to the Northwind database (see Listing 19.3).

Listing 19.3. A customized connection to the Northwind database.

```
Public ws As Workspace
Public db As Database

Public adoConn As ADODB.Connection

Public Sub OpenComplexADOConnection()
  Dim strConnect As String
  Dim strErrorMsg As String

On Error GoTo Error_Enumerator

  'Set connection string variable
  strConnect = _
      "DRIVER={Microsoft Access Driver (*.mdb)};" _
      & "DefaultDir=" & App.Path _
      & "UID=admin;PWD=;DBQ=Nwind.mdb;"

  'Set Connection Properties and Execute Connection
  Set adoConn = New ADODB.Connection
  With ado.Conn
    .CommandTimeout = 45      'Setting for SLOW Network
    .ConnectionTimeout = 25   'Setting for SLOW Network
    .CursorLocation = adUseServer
    .IsolationLevel = adXactCursorStability
    .Mode = adModeShareExclusive
    .ConnectionString = strConnect
    .Open
  End With
  Exit Sub

Error_Enumerator:
  'Format and display error information
  strErrorMsg = "Error opening ADO connection " _
      & "Error Number : " & Err.Number vbCrLf & _
      & "Description : " & Err.Description
  Call MsgBox(strErrorMsg, vbCritical, "ADO Connection Error")
End Sub
```

Using `BeginTrans`, `CommitTrans`, and `RollbackTrans`

Next look at a set of items for the `Connection` object that shows transaction accountability, schema analysis, and execute methods. You apply these methods to the Northwind database to demonstrate some of the possibilities available.

Many database structures that are accessed by more than one individual require the capability to track changes made to the database and the capability to either accept or decline those modifications. The three methods that the ADO Connection object incorporates to facilitate these requirements are BeginTrans, CommitTrans, and RollbackTrans.

From the Connection object, you are also able to run update queries that modify or input data into data objects. This is done from the .Execute method and has syntax equivalent to normal SQL statements. A typical Execute statement's syntax for updating would be similar to the following:

```
"UPDATE tblTable SET colColumn = 'New Value' WHERE colColumn = 'Old Value'"
```

The value of tblTable is the name of a table structure existing in the data object; colColumn is the name of a column in the table structure and the values consistent with the column data type.

The Northwind database contains a table named Employees, which, as the table name suggests, contains information about employees at Northwind. This table includes data such as the employee's last name, first name, date of birth, and title. For this exercise you are going to focus on the column named Title. The human resources department at Northwind has decided that the sales staff should have more politically correct titles. This decision requires changing the old Sales Representative title to Sales Coordinator. Imagine that the department representatives have come to you and asked you to make this simple change for them.

Listings 19.4 and 19.5 demonstrate two approaches to complying with this user request. Listing 19.4 is a DAO solution for this problem, and Listing 19.5 shows how to solve this problem with ADO. Both of these listings execute the same query, but less code is required to work with the flattened ADO object model than with DAO. The ADO solution also assumes that you execute the previous Sub OpenComplexADOConnection.

Listing 19.4. Performing an update query with DAO.

```
Public ws As Workspace
Public db As Database

Public Sub OpenDAOConnection()
  Dim strConnect As String
  Dim strErrorMsg As String
  Dim strQry As String

On Error GoTo Error_Enumerator

  'Set String Variables
  strConnect = App.Path & "\NWind.mdb"
  strQry = "UPDATE Employees " _
        & "SET Title = 'Sales Coordinator' " _
        & "WHERE Title = 'Sales Representative'"

  'Connect and Execute Query
```

continues

Listing 19.4. Continued.

```
  Set ws = DBEngine.Workspaces(0)
  Set db = ws.OpenDatabase(strConnect, False)

  ws.BeginTrans        'Begin transaction
  db.Execute strQry    'Execute query
  ws.CommitTrans       'Commit transaction
  Exit Sub

Error_Enumerator:
  strErrorMsg = "Error Number : " & Err.Number _
      & vbCrLf & "Description : " & Err.Description
  Call MsgBox(strErrorMsg, vbCritical)
End Sub
```

Listing 19.5. Performing an update query with ADO.

```
Public Sub UpdateEmployeeInfo1()
  Dim errADO As ADODB.Error
  Dim strQry As String

On Error GoTo Error_Enumerator

  strQry = "UPDATE Employees " _
        & "SET Title = 'Sales Coordinator' " _
        & "WHERE Title = 'Sales Representative'"

  adoConn.BeginTrans
  adoConn.Execute strQry

  If MsgBox("Save changes?", vbYesNo) = vbYes Then
    adoConn.CommitTrans      'Commit transaction
  Else
    adoConn.RollbackTrans    'Rollback transaction
  End If

  Exit Sub

Error_Enumerator:
  If adoConn.Errors.Count > 0 Then
    For Each errADO In adoConn.Errors
      Call MsgBox("Error: " & errADO.Number _
                & vbCrLf & errADO.Description)
    Next errADO
  End If
End Sub
```

With ADO's simplified object model, you probably noticed in Listing 19.5 that it was not necessary to reference DAO's WorkSpace object to control transactions. Instead, all this base functionality has been rolled up into the ADO Connection object. The most current release of ADO supports functionality that is only a subset of DAO. There are still things that DAO can accomplish which ADO cannot. Microsoft reports that the functionality of future versions of ADO will be superior to both DAO and RDO.

In Listing 19.5 (using ADO) you use a vbYesNo message box to see whether the user would like to commit the transaction to the Northwind database. Both the ADO and DAO coding parameters are the same for beginning, committing, and rolling back transactions. The main difference is the object that handles the functionality. When working with transaction tracking to build solutions that must use nested transactions, please adhere to the parameters specified from the data provider for nested transactions. In most cases, the data provider requires that you handle the current transaction in order to resolve any higher level transactions.

An example of this would be if you decided to execute the BeginTrans method again in Listing 19.5 and ran another update query before either the CommitTrans or RollbackTrans lines were reached. After a second query, there are two levels in this nested transaction and the second level must be closed before the first level can. You still have the ability of committing or rolling back changes to any level in the nested loop without it affecting the other levels.

Using the Error Object

Each ADO Error object represents a specific provider error, not an ADO error. ADO errors are exposed to the runtime exception handling mechanism. For example, in Microsoft Visual Basic, the occurrence of an ADO-specific error triggers an Error event and appears in the Err object.

Use the Error object to deal with provider errors. By initiating a new request to the Collection object the Error object count is cleared and then set according to the number of errors returned that were not handled by the ADO object library. To get all the errors returned, examine the Errors collection's Count property, and then loop through the object to display all current errors. The Errors collection holds the numbers and descriptions of the errors that have occurred. This information can be retrieved by using the syntax of the Error_Enumerator code (refer to Listing 19.5). The ADO Error object is equivalent to the DAO Workspace's Error object.

Database design information is also accessible from ActiveX data object as it was with data access objects. Remember, the ADO object model is less complicated so the functionality has switched from a subordinate DAO object to the top-level ADO Connection object. Listing 19.6 uses ADO to analyze the table structure of the Northwind database and return all table-type objects' names to a list box on a form.

Listing 19.6. Using ADO to analyze the Northwind database table structure.

```
Public Sub GetSchema(ByRef lstTables As ListBox)
  Dim rst As ADODB.Recordset
  Dim strTableName As String

On Error GoTo Err_Handler

  lstTables.Clear 'Clear the list box for clean insertion

  'If Connection object is closed, start a new session
  If adoConn.State = adStateClosed Then
    OpenComplexADOConnection
  End If

  'OpenSchema field returns all table-type objects
  Set rst = adoConn.OpenSchema(adSchemaTables)

  Do Until rst.EOF
    strTableName = "Table name: " & rst!TABLE_NAME & " " _
             & "Table type: " & rst!TABLE_TYPE
    'Add table's name to list box
    lstTables.AddItem strTableName
    rst.MoveNext
  Loop

  rst.Close   'Closes recordset after input is complete
  Exit Sub

Err_Handler:
  If adoConn.Errors.Count > 0 Then
    For Each errADO In adoConn.Errors
      Call MsgBox("Error: " & errADO.Number _
                 & vbCrLf & errADO.Description)
    Next errADO
  End If
End Sub
```

The ADO `Collection` object is powerful and broad in its functionality. The `Collection` object unifies several objects previously applied to the DAO model and adds a subset of the DAO `Connection` object. The basis for beginning any data manipulation from a data object is establishing a connection to the data source. After that connection is made, the features of ADO become apparent.

Understanding the Basics of the ADO Recordset Object

The ADO Recordset object is very similar to the DAO Recordset object. The base definition of the Recordset object still holds true: It is a set of records from a base table or the results of an executed command or query. Manipulating records in ADO is as simple as it was in DAO, with the exception of one new object, the Command object.

You can still open a recordset by executing a SQL statement, typing the particular table or query name, or using the ADO Command object's functionality. The Command object is a definition of a specific command that you intend to execute against a data source. While it is not required to create a recordset, you might find it useful for controlling key points of recordset creation.

Creating a Recordset

Before you delve into creating a recordset without the use of the Command object, create one with it. The Command object is versatile and easy to use as far as available methods and properties are concerned. The normal sequence of events for Command object creation and usage is to set the Command object's ActiveConnection, CommandType, CommandText, properties, and then use the Execute method to produce the recordset.

Go back to the Northwind database and open the Employee table through DAO Listing 19.7. Then use ADO (see Listing 19.8) to get an idea of the proper syntax for the Command object and how it can benefit the basic DAO programmer.

Listing 19.7. Opening the Employee table with DAO.

```
Public Sub OpenTableDAO()
  Dim rst As Recordset
  Dim strConnect As String
  Dim strErrorMsg As String

On Error GoTo Error_Enumerator

  'Set String Variables
  strConnect = App.Path & "\NWind.mdb"

  'Connect and Execute Query
  Set ws = DBEngine.Workspaces(0)
  Set db = ws.OpenDatabase(strConnect, False)

  Set rst = db.OpenRecordset("Employees", dbOpenDynaset)

  rst.MoveLast
  rst.MoveFirst
  rst.Close
  Exit Sub
```

continues

Listing 19.7. Continued.

```
Error_Enumerator:
  strErrorMsg = "Error Number : " & Err.Number _
      & vbCrLf & "Description : " & Err.Description
  Call MsgBox(strErrorMsg, vbCritical)
End Sub
```

Listing 19.8. Opening the Employee table with ADO.

```
Public Sub OpenTableADO()
  Dim rst As ADODB.Recordset
  Dim cmd As ADODB.Command
  Dim strConnect As String
  Dim errADO As Error

  On Error GoTo Err_Enumerator

  'Set connection string variable
  strConnect = "DRIVER={Microsoft Access Driver (*.mdb)};" _
      & "DefaultDir=" & App.Path & ";" _
      & "UID=admin;PWD=;DBQ=Nwind.mdb;"

  'Set Connection Properties and Execute Connection
  Set adoConn = New ADODB.Connection
  adoConn.IsolationLevel = adXactCursorStability
  adoConn.ConnectionString = strConnect
  adoConn.Open

  'Set up the Command object for execution
  Set cmd = New ADODB.Command
  Set cmd.ActiveConnection = adoConn
  cmd.CommandType = adCmdTable
  cmd.CommandText = "Employees"

  'Create the recordset from the Command ojbect
  Set rst = cmd.Execute
  rst.Close
  Exit Sub
Err_Enumerator:
  'Cycle through error objects
  If adoConn.Errors.Count > 0 Then
    For Each errADO In adoConn.Errors
      Call MsgBox("Error: " & errADO.Number _
                & vbCrLf & errADO.Description)
    Next errADO
  End If
End Sub
```

Adding a New Record

Opening the recordset proves to be similar for both DAO (see Listing 19.9) and ADO (see Listing 19.10). Now let's see how the Recordset property behaves when you add a new employee to the Employees table. First, open a Recordset object, and then use the AddNew method followed by the Update method.

Listing 19.9. Adding a new record with DAO.

```
Public Sub AddNewEmployeeDAO()
  Dim rst As Recordset
  Dim strConnect As String

  'Set String Variables
  strConnect = App.Path & "\NWind.mdb"

  'Connect and execute query
  Set ws = DBEngine.Workspaces(0)
  Set db = ws.OpenDatabase(strConnect, False)

  Set rst = db.OpenRecordset("Employees", dbOpenDynaset)

  ws.BeginTrans

  With rst
    .AddNew
    !LastName = "Maddich"
    !FirstName = "Nick"
    !Title = "Supervisor"
    !BirthDate = "3/13/64"
    !HireDate = Format(Now, "Short Date")
    !Address = "1234 Any Street"
    !City = "Pittsburgh"
    !Region = "PA"
    !PostalCode = "32817"
    !Country = "USA"
    !HomePhone = "919-555-1212"
    !Extension = "5132"
    !Notes = "New Hire, no more info at this time."
    .Update
  End With

  ws.CommitTrans      'End Transaction

  rst.Close   'Close Recordset
  db.Close    'Close Database
  ws.Close    'Close WorkSpace
End Sub
```

Listing 19.10. Adding a new record with ADO.

```
Public Sub AddNewEmployeeADO()
  Dim rst As ADODB.Recordset
  Dim cmd As New ADODB.Command

  'If the Connection object is closed, start a new session
  If adoConn.State = adStateClosed Then
    OpenComplexADOConnection
  End If

  Set cmd.ActiveConnection = adoConn
  cmd.CommandType = adCmdTable
  cmd.CommandText = "Employees"
  Set rs = cmd.Execute

  adoConn.BeginTrans

  With rst
    .AddNew
    !LastName = "Maddich"
    !FirstName = "Nick"
    !Title = "Supervisor"
    !BirthDate = "3/13/64"
    !HireDate = Format(Now, "Short Date")
    !Address = "1234 Any Street"
    !City = "Pittsburgh"
    !Region = "PA"
    !PostalCode = "32817"
    !Country = "USA"
    !HomePhone = "919-555-1212"
    !Extension = "5132"
    !Notes = "New Hire, no more info at this time."
    .Update
  End With

  adoConn.CommitTrans
  rst.Close
  adoConn.Close
End Sub
```

As far as adding, editing, or retrieving values from Recordset columns, ADO and DAO syntax are similar. It starts to get frustrating for the DAO programmer when digging into the DAO toolbox and finding out that some favorite methods are gone. Methods such as FindFirst, FindNext, FindLast, or even Seek are not present in the ADO (Version 1.5) Recordset object. In ADO Version 2.0, the ADO Recordset object has added the method Find. The method requires you to input criteria (string) and lets you set the search direction, records to skip, and which direction to search the recordset. Be careful when working with this new method because it is very easy to let necessary steps slip by, which causes you to miss needed data. Some common mistakes associated with this new method include not moving to the first record when you want to find the first instance of a particular record matching the search criteria; doing a find when you are already at the Recordset.EOF, and forgetting to specify the proper search direction.

The DAO programmer has a few coding-style options. One choice is to start to create temporary tables that contain only the necessary data that fulfills all specified criteria. The second choice is to create some custom functions to add the missing pieces of the ADO Recordset object. The third and final option is to wait until subsequent releases of ActiveX data objects appear and then begin to port your code over from DAO to ADO.

Creating Temporary Tables

Temporary table creation from existing Recordset objects is simple, and for the most part, beneficial for the day-to-day programmer. Although in the beginning you might miss some of the DAO search methods, you will find new strength (and speed) in using these tables for data acquisition. The basics for setting up a temporary table are easy. Listing 19.11 shows how you create a temporary table from an existing recordset using DAO. Listing 19.12 shows how to create the table using ADO.

To demonstrate this method, look at the Northwind database. Your human resources department is at it again. They have diligently entered all the data using a form you designed earlier that employed the AddNew method. Now that they've entered the data, they want to start running some basic queries to the database. The first query that comes from the HR director's lips is to see how many personnel are living in London. Apparently they are taxed differently and she needs to have this data right away.

Listing 19.11. Creating temporary tables with DAO.

```
Public Sub FindLocationDAO()
  Dim rstEmp As Recordset
  Dim rstLoc As Recordset
  Dim strConnect As String
  Dim strSQL As String
  Dim lRecordCount As Long

  'Set String Variables
  strConnect = App.Path & "\NWind.mdb"

  'Connect and Execute Query
  Set ws = DBEngine.Workspaces(0)
  Set db = ws.OpenDatabase(strConnect, False)
  Set rstEmp = db.OpenRecordset("Employees", dbOpenDynaset)

  strSQL = "City = 'LONDON'"
  rstEmp.Filter = strSQL
  Set rstLoc = rstEmp.Open
```

continues

Listing 19.11. Continued.

```
With rstLoc
  If .RecordCount > 0 Then
    .MoveLast
    .MoveFirst
    lRecordCount = .RecordCount
  Else
    lRecordCount = .RecordCount
  End If
End With
rstEmp.Close
rstLoc.Close
End Sub
```

Listing 19.12. Creating temporary tables with ADO.

```
Public Sub FindLocationADO()
  Dim rstEmp As ADODB.Recordset
  Dim rstLoc As ADODB.Recordset
  Dim cmd As New ADODB.Command
  Dim strSQL As String
  Dim lRecordCount As Long

  'If Connection object is closed, start a new session
  If adoConn.State = adStateClosed Then
    OpenComplexADOConnection
  End If

  Set cmd.ActiveConnection = adoConn
  cmd.CommandType = adCmdTable
  cmd.CommandText = "Employees"
  Set rstEmp = cmd.Execute

  strSQL = "City = 'LONDON'"
  rstEmp.Filter = strSQL
  Set rstLoc = rstEmp.Open

  'Opens Recordset and determines RecordCount
  With rstLoc
    If Not .EOF And Not .BOF Then
      If .RecordCount = -1 Then
        lRecordCount = 0
        Do
          lRecordCount = lRecordCount + 1
        Loop Until .EOF
      Else
        lRecordCount = .RecordCount
      End If
    End If
```

```
    End With
    rstEmp.Close
    rstLoc.Close
End Sub
```

Both ADO and DAO have their own idiosyncrasies when it comes to determining how many records exist in a newly created `Recordset` object. DAO must move to the last record in the recordset before determining an accurate count with the `RecordCount` property. ADO states that if it receives a record count of –1 it is unable to determine how many records are in that recordset. This can be frustrating for DAO programmers who rely on record counts for populating objects such as combo boxes or the `MSFlexGrid` control with data. So again you must move from the beginning to end of the recordset to determine an accurate record count. ADO actually moves through the recordset more quickly, but it is still an annoying task that must be performed. In ADO 2.0, Microsoft fixed the `Recordcount` bug. Upon creation of the ADO recordset, it returns an accurate record count and also moves immediately to the first record. This is a definite plus in ADO's favor when deciding which data access collection to choose.

Human resources finally compiled the numbers they need, and now they want to make it a little more interesting. They want to see all the people who live in London whose last name begins with a D, arranged alphabetically. Sure, no problem. For this you are going to create one recordset with a SQL statement. Oh, and one more thing: the London office is closing and the affected employees are moving to South Hampton. First, look at the original code in DAO Listing 19.13. Listing 19.14 shows the same code converted to ADO.

Note: The listings from this point to the end of the chapter do not show how to connect to a database. Refer to the listings earlier in this chapter to see how this is done.

Listing 19.13. Opening a DAO recordset with a SQL statement.

```
Public Sub ChangeAddressDAO()
    Dim rstEmp As Recordset
    Dim strSQL As String

    strSQL = "SELECT * FROM Employees " _
        & "WHERE LastName LIKE 'D*' " _
        & "AND City = 'LONDON' " _
        & "ORDER BY LastName"

    Set rstEmp = db.OpenRecordset(strSQL, dbOpenDynaset)
```

continues

Listing 19.13. Continued.

```
With rstEmp
  If .RecordCount > 0 Then
    Do
      .Edit
      !City = "South Hampton"
      .Update
      .MoveNext
    Loop Until .EOF
  End If
End With
rstEmp.Close
End Sub
```

Listing 19.14. Opening an ADO recordset with a SQL statement.

```
Public Sub ChangeAddressADO()
  Dim rstEmp As ADODB.Recordset
  Dim strSQL As String

  strSQL = "Select * from Employees " _
         & "WHERE LastName LIKE 'D*' " & _
         & "AND City = 'LONDON' " _
         & "ORDER by LastName"

  rstEmp.Open strSQL, adoConn, , , adCmdTable

  With rstEmp
    If Not .BOF And Not .EOF Then
      Do
        !City = "South Hampton"
        .MoveNext
      Loop Until .EOF
      .UpdateBatch adAffectAll
    End If
  End With
  rstEmp.Close
End Sub
```

With just a basic SQL statement, you were able to solve the problem that human resources presented. You created a Recordset object from a SQL statement, a basic SQL statement but an SQL statement none the less. The point to this exercise was to show you how you can create ADO Recordset objects from SQL statements. Your talents will soon encompass the knowledge of a strong SQL skillset, which you can leverage against the Recordset object to complete solutions to simple problems as Listing 19.14 as well as to complex data analysis stemming from INNER and OUTER joins with multiple criteria. There are no limits to the number of statements that you can construct, but make sure that each SQL statement follows current structured query language syntax and verbiage.

Accessing Parameter Queries and Stored Procedures

Many ADO providers support *parameterized* commands. These are commands where the desired action is defined once, but variables (or parameters) are used to alter the details of the command. The number of parameters can range from one to many and can include different types of data for each parameter. To handle parameterized commands, ADO has instituted the Parameter object.

You use the Parameter object collection in conjunction with the ADO Command object to run stored procedures or parameterized commands. Before using the Parameter object, examine its following properties and methods:

- Attributes—Indicates how the Parameter object handles the parameter value. There are three possible options for this property:

  adParamSigned—Indicates that the parameter accepts assigned values.

  adParamNullable—Indicates that the parameter accepts NULL values

  adParamLong—Indicates that the parameter accepts long binary data.

  Default: adParamSigned

- Direction—Tells whether the parameter represents an input parameter, an output parameter, or both, or whether the parameter is the return value from a stored procedure. Possible values and their corresponding meanings are as follows:

  adParamInput—Indicates an input parameter.

  adParamOutput—Indicates an output parameter.

  adParamInputOutput—Indicates both an input and an output parameter.

  adParamReturnValue—Indicates a return value.

  Default: adParamInput

- Name—Assigns or retrieves the name of a parameter. For names not yet appended to the Parameters collection, this property is read/write. However, after the parameter is added to the Parameters collection, its Name property becomes read-only. The Name property of a parameter is not required to be unique, so be careful when creating new parameters.

- NumericScale—Determines how many numbers to the right of the decimal point will be used to represent a value for a numeric parameter.

- Precision—Indicates the degree of precision to apply to a parameter value. Sets or determines the maximum number of digits used to represent a numeric value.

- Size—Used to determine the maximum size for values read or written from the Value property of the Parameter object. If setting a parameter type to adVarLength, you must set the Size property before appending it the Parameters collection or an error occurs.

- Type—Sets or returns the parameter type as specified in the DataTypeEnum values collection. The collection is large, but it is necessary to show all possible values because at any time you might want to create or need to interact with a parameter containing on of the DataTypeEnum values here:

adArray—OR'd together with another type to indicate that the data is a safe-array of that type.

adBigInt—An 8-byte signed integer.

adBinary—A binary value.

adBoolean—A Boolean value.

adByRef—OR'd together with another type to indicate that the data is a pointer to data of the other type.

adBSTR—A null-terminated Unicode character string.

adChar—A String value.

adCurrency —A Currency value. Currency is a fixed-point number with four digits to the right of the decimal point. It is stored in an 8-byte signed integer scaled by 10,000.

adDate—A Date value. A date is stored as a double, the whole part is the number of days since December 30, 1899, and the fractional part is the fraction of a day.

adDBDate—A Date value (*yyyymmdd*).

adDBTime—A Time value (*hhmmss*).

adDBTimeStamp—A date-timestamp (*yyyymmddhhmmss* plus a fraction in billionths).

adDecimal—An exact numeric value with a fixed precision and scale.

adDouble—A double-precision floating point value.

adEmpty —No value was specified.

adError—A 32-bit error code.

adGUID—A globally unique identifier (GUID).

adIDispatch—A pointer to an IDispatch interface on an OLE object.

adInteger—A 4-byte signed integer.

adIUnknown—A pointer to an IUnknown interface on an OLE object.

adLongVarBinary—A long binary value.

adLongVarChar—A long String value.

adLongVarWChar—A long null-terminated String value.

adNumeric—An exact numeric value with a fixed precision and scale.

adSingle—A single-precision floating point value.

adSmallInt—A 2-byte signed integer.

adTinyInt—A 1-byte signed integer.

adUnsignedBigInt—An 8-byte unsigned integer.

adUnsignedInt—A 4-byte unsigned integer.

adUnsignedSmallInt—A 2-byte unsigned integer.

adUnsignedTinyInt—A 1-byte unsigned integer.

adUserDefined—A user-defined variable.

adVarBinary—A binary value.

adVarChar—A String value.

adVariant—An Automation variant.

adVector—OR'd together with another type to indicate that the data is a DBVECTOR structure, as defined by OLE DB, that contains a count of elements and a pointer to data of the other type.

adVarWChar—A null-terminated Unicode character string.

adWChar—A null-terminated Unicode character string.

- Value—Sets or returns the value of a parameter. The type of value returned is predicated by the type set for the specific parameter in the Parameters collection.

The Parameter object contains several properties and only one method: the AppendChunk method. AppendChunk usage and creation is order specific. The first AppendChunk call on a Parameter object writes data to the parameter, overwriting any existing data. Future AppendChunk calls on a Parameter object add to existing parameter data. An AppendChunk call that passes a Null value generates an error; you must manually set the Value property of the Parameter object to a zero-length string ("") in order to clear its value.

Using the Parameter Object

To see how to use the Parameter object in an ADO solution, return to the shipping department of the Northwind Company. A new mandate by recent labor unions in the shipping industry has caused an inflated pricing paradigm involving packages that have a shipping destination outside the USA. A complete breakdown is needed on all packages whose shipping cost rose above the mandated $60.00 ceiling. The mandated ceiling is expected to rise based on the results of this query and will need to be rerun in the future to reflect the current ceiling. Because this number is dynamic, a parameter query, as shown in Listing 19.15, works well as the solution. These results are to be presented in a list box on the calling form shown in Figure 19.3. The parameter query result output appears in Figure 19.4.

FIGURE 19.3.
The results of a parameterized query.

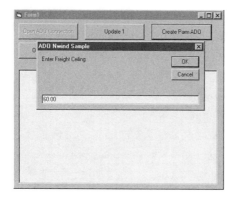

Listing 19.15. Creating parameters with ADO.

```
Public Sub CreateParameterADO(ByRef lstShip As ListBox)
   Dim cmdFreight As New ADODB.Command      'Command object
   Dim rstFreight As New ADODB.Recordset    'Freight RS
   Dim rstEmployee As ADODB.Recordset       'Employee RS
   Dim prmFreight As ADODB.Parameter        'Freight parameter
   Dim curFreight As Currency               'Cost from user input
   Dim strSQL As String                     'SQL for Employee RS
   Dim sListEntry As String                 'Temp string

   'Open Command object with one parameter
   cmdFreight.CommandText = _
       "SELECT * FROM Orders " _
     & "WHERE Freight > ? " _
     & "ORDER BY Freight"
   cmdFreight.CommandType = adCmdText

   'Set parameter value from user input
   curFreight = Trim(InputBox("Enter freight ceiling:"))
   Set prmFreight = cmdFreight.CreateParameter( _
      "Freight_Ceiling", adCurrency, adParamInput)
   cmdFreight.Parameters.Append prmFreight
   prmFreight.Value = curFreight

   'Execute Command to create recordset
   Set cmdFreight.ActiveConnection = adoConn
   Set rstFreight = cmdFreight.Execute
   strSQL = "SELECT * FROM Employess"
   rstEmployee.Open strSQL, adoConn, , , adCmdTable

   'Loop through return values and populate list box
   With rstFreight
     If Not .BOF And Not .EOF Then
        Do
           'Filter returns only one unique record
```

```
        rstEmployee.Filter = "EmployeeID = " & !EmployeeID
        sListEntry = !ShipName & " ordered by " _
                   & rstEmployee!LastName & ", " _
                   & rstEmployee!FirstName _
                   & " for the amount of $" _
                   & !Freight
      lstShip.AddItem sListEntry
      .MoveNext
    Loop Until .EOF
  End If
End With


  rstEmployee.Close
  rstFreight.Close
End Sub
```

FIGURE 19.4.
The parameter query result output.

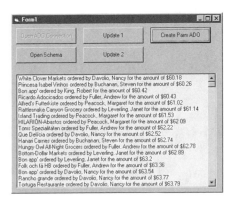

Executing Parameter-Driven Stored Procedures

Executing parameter-driven stored procedures is a similar task. For this example we are going to have to assume a connection to a SQL Server 6.5 running a database similar to that of the Northwind database. On the Northwind device, there is a stored procedure named `OrderDates` that expects two parameters to be given: `dtBegin` and `dtEnd`. This SP (stored procedure) returns a recordset with all the orders placed between the two dates input through the parameters (see Listing 19.16). Listing 19.17 shows the same parameter-driven query written in ADO.

Listing 19.16. Parameter-driven stored procedures with DAO.

```
Public Sub OrderDateSP_DAO()
  Dim rst As Recordset    'Query RS
  Dim qdf As QueryDef     'QueryDef object
  Dim prm1 As Parameter   'Parameter BeginDate
  Dim prm2 As Parameter   'Parameter EndDate
```

continues

Listing 19.16. Continued.

```
  'Set QueryDef and Parameter objects
  Set qdf = db.QueryDefs("OrderDates")
  Set prm1 = qdf.Parameters!dtBegin
  Set prm2 = qdf.Parameters!dtEnd

  'Set Parameter values
  prm1 = #2/10/96#
  prm2 = #2/12/96#

  'Execute QueryDef to produce a DAO recordset
  Set rst = qdf.OpenRecordset(dbOpenForwardOnly)

  'Close the Recordset object
  rst.Close
End Sub
```

Listing 19.17. Parameter-driven stored procedures with ADO.

```
Public Sub OrderDateSP_ADO()
  Dim cmd As New ADODB.Command
  Dim rst As ADODB.Recordset
  Dim prm1 As ADODB.Parameter
  Dim prm2 As ADODB.Parameter

  'Set Command object type and connection object
  Set cmd.ActiveConnection = adoConn
  cmd.CommandType = adCmdStoredProc
  cmd.CommandText = "OrderDates"

  'Declare the BeginDate parameter
  With prm1
    .Type = adDate              'Data Type is Date
    .Name = "dtBegin"           'Parm Name
    .Direction = adParamInput   'Input Parameter
    .Value = #2/10/96#          'Value applied
  End With

  'Append parameter to the Command object's Parameters collection
  cmd.Parameters.Append prm1

  'Declare the EndDate parameter
  With prm2
    .Type = adDate              'Data Type is Date
    .Name = "dtEnd"             'Parm Name
    .Direction = adParamInput   'Input Parameter
    .Value = #2/12/96#          'Value applied
  End With
```

```
'Append parameter to the Command object's Parameters collection
cmd.Parameters.Append prm2

'Execute the Command object to construct a Recordset
Set rst = cmd.Execute

'Close the Recordset object
rst.Close
End Sub
```

More code is put in place to execute the ADO parameter-driven stored procedure, as shown in Listing 19.16 than the DAO parameter-driven stored procedure shown in Listing 19.17. However, you will find that ADO handles these procedures more efficiently than DAO can because of the nature of underlying libraries. ADO is accessing the OLE DB API, whereas DAO is routing through the Jet Engine.

Multiple Resultset Stored Procedures

Another area of interest when it comes to stored procedures is multiple resultset stored procedures. This situation comes about when you execute a stored procedure that is intended to return more than one recordset. With ADO, the first recordset returned is automatically closed as soon as you move on to the next recordset. In future releases, the recordset is supposedly going to stay open until you programmatically close it.

This exercise, shown in Listing 19.18, is generated from SQL statements similar to those working on a traditional back-end server, so you can see what is being created and what is expected back, as far as the Recordset object. From the SQL statement, you determine the number of records that met the specified criteria for each recordset.

Listing 19.18. Using a multiresultset recordset with ADO.

```
Public Sub MulitRS_ADO()
  Dim rst As ADODB.Recordset
  Dim strSQL As String
  Dim lFirstCount As Long
  Dim lSecondCount As Long

  'SQL to create two ADO recordsets
  strSQL = "SELECT * FROM Orders " _
        & "WHERE Freight > 15 AND Freight < 30;" _
        & "SELECT * FROM Orders " _
        & "WHERE Freight => 30 AND Freight < 50;"

  'Opens the first Recordset
  rst.Open strSQL, adoConn
```

continues

Listing 19.18. Continued.

```
'Loop to determine record count
With rst
  If Not .EOF And Not .BOF Then
    If .RecordCount = -1 Then
      lFirstCount = 0
      Do
        lFirstCount = lFirstCount + 1
        .MoveNext
      Loop Until .EOF
    Else
      lFirstCount = .RecordCount
    End If
  End If
End With

'Closes the first Recordset and opens the Second
Set rst = rst.NextRecordset

'Loop to determine recordcount
With rst
  If Not .EOF And Not .BOF Then
    If .RecordCount = -1 Then
      lSecondCount = 0
      Do
        lSecondCount = lSecondCount + 1
        .MoveNext
      Loop Until .EOF
    Else
      lSecondCount = .RecordCount
    End If
  End If
End With

'Close the recordset
rst.Close
End Sub
```

Executing stored procedures from ADO saves a lot of processing time on the client side because the procedures are all stored on the data server and cached into the server's memory. The client-side application developed from stored procedures benefits not only in application data retrieval times, but also with the stability and data integrity ability of the stored procedures that are employed.

The Recordset and Parameter objects have changed slightly between the DAO and ADO as with the methods available to them. With the previous examples, you should be able to analyze your DAO code and convert it to ADO without too much of a headache. No quick conversion utility is available, but the benefits of ADO should be weighed before employing it as a solution for your programming needs.

Summary

ADO is a streamlined version of DAO boasting greater speed, enhanced flexibility with independent object creation, and a new, less complicated object model. Due to ADO's powerful relationship with OLE DB, ADO definitely has potential to be the data access method of choice. ADO's viability as a replacement for DAO is somewhat questionable due to many problems existing from the ongoing development of this new data access tool.

ADO 2.0, found in Visual Interdev 6.0, is definitely a step in the right direction when compared to version 1.5. Many of the problems inherent in ADO 1.5 have all but vanished. Although it is not a true superset of DAO, most of the DAO methods are available in one of ADO's seven objects. Relational database support is seamlessly handled through the ADO object and so is the handling and management of available objects derived from or created independently of the ADO Connection object.

If you are trying to be on the cutting edge and need to show that you can handle the latest technology that Microsoft has to offer, you should make the transition to ADO. However, if you have incorporated many of the programming methodologies adopted from DAO and those programs are working, you should consider leaving them as DAO applications. Visual Basic 6 supports DAO, and it is likely that future versions of Visual Basic will continue supporting DAO for some time to come. Waiting for future releases of the ADO library would be a wise decision unless you need some of the functionality that ADO can provide and DAO cannot.

In reference to the changes in coding syntax and object handling and creation, you will not have much of a learning curve. Coding changes must reflect not only new objects but also a change in existing ones accessed through the DAO method. All in all, you should be able to jump right into programming with the ADO data access model and reap the benefits from its increased speed and smaller size. With future releases of ADO the functionality will continue to grow and eventually outperform that of DAO.

PART V

Integrating with Other Applications

Integrating with Microsoft Office 97

This chapter examines the interesting and powerful capabilities of Automation with applications such as Microsoft Word, Excel, and Access. Automation provides the Visual Basic developer with the capability to exploit the features and utilities of commercial Windows applications. With Automation, you can add features such as spell-checking, graphing, and document preparation by controlling Word, Excel, or Access.

Understanding ActiveX

Automation is part of the ActiveX initiative sponsored by Microsoft and is supported by all Microsoft Office applications. This chapter describes several uses of Automation applicable to your Visual Basic programs.

Automation provides a way to leverage the substantial capabilities built into Word, Excel, and many other Windows applications. These applications have been carefully engineered and built at great expense by their vendors. Instead of trying to duplicate the capabilities of these applications using Visual Basic code, you're much better off simply hooking into those applications with Automation and using their features from within your Visual Basic programs.

For example, suppose two companies make word processing applications. One company (Company A) produces a mediocre word processor, but its spell checker is great. The other company (Company B) has a great word processor, but the spell checker is lacking in functionality. Using Microsoft's OLE standards and concepts, Company A might release only its spell checker and by exposing its methods make it available to Company B's word processing application through OLE Automation.

This provides the best of both worlds. Not only does the user get a great word processor and spell checker, but he or she doesn't lose a lot of hard-disk space by having two word processors or two spell checkers.

For example, Microsoft Word is an extremely powerful word processor. Word provides many capabilities not available with Visual Basic's built-in report writer, Crystal Reports. It is possible to use Word as a report writer from within a Visual Basic application, taking advantage of all the capabilities such as color text, tables, multiple columns, and the other features Word users have enjoyed for a long time.

ActiveX includes much more than Automation. ActiveX is a blanket technology promoted by Microsoft that defines a communications standard between applications. ActiveX includes such things as custom controls you buy commercially or create yourself with Visual Basic 6 or another development system such as Visual C++. ActiveX communication also includes the dialog between ActiveX objects on a Web page and Web browsers. In its most advanced implementation, ActiveX technology can be used for communication between applications running on different computers on a network or across the Internet.

ActiveX is a major component of Microsoft's *component object model* (COM). The component object model is based on the concept of an application built from several different components. The components can be commercially acquired or built from scratch using development systems such as Visual Basic. The components are bound together with a programming language such as Visual Basic (see Figure 20.1). ActiveX is the technology that Microsoft intends to become the binding element of the COM applications.

FIGURE 20.1.
Microsoft's COM philosophy is an important technology for Visual Basic developers.

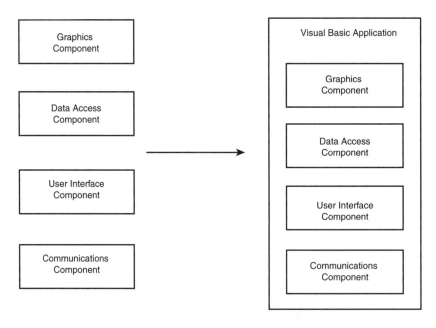

Figure 20.1 is perhaps slightly misleading. Figure 20.1 makes it appear that the components are actually bound together in a single .EXE file. This is not necessarily the case. Often, the actual application architecture is more like you see in Figure 20.2. In this case, several components (perhaps Visual Basic object classes) are bound into the .EXE, whereas other components exist as independent mini-applications bound into the application with Automation.

FIGURE 20.2.

Components can be utilized in a Visual Basic application through Automation.

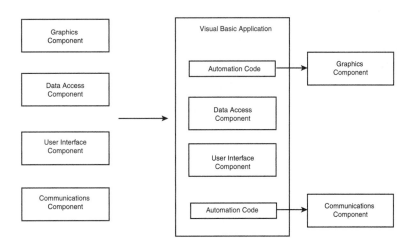

The Automation pathways shown in Figure 20.2 are part of the ActiveX category of technologies.

This chapter is all about using Automation to control other applications such as the graphics and communications components you see in Figure 20.2. Specifically, this chapter is about using Automation to connect to Microsoft Word from the Office 97 package. You'll see how to use these programs for mail merge, document preparation, and graphing data. Chapter 21, "Integrating with Microsoft Outlook 97," explains how to use Microsoft Outlook for scheduling and email tasks.

Understanding Automation Concepts

ActiveX Automation is based on a dialog between two Windows applications running under Windows 95 or Windows NT. During the dialog, the applications can share data, commands, and other resources such as database files, ActiveX controls, and other information.

In an Automation scenario, one of the applications serves as the *server* and provides services and resources. When Microsoft Excel is the server, the resources might include the Excel Graph Wizard. The other application is the *controller* that uses the services and resources provided by the server. In most cases, Visual Basic serves as the controller, whereas other applications such as Word or Excel act as servers. There are other uses for Visual Basic in Automation scenarios, as described in the next section.

Figure 20.3 diagrams how Automation works. The Visual Basic application on the left connects to the Automation server through object variables declared within the Visual Basic code. After the objects are connected through object variables, the properties and methods of the server's objects are accessible to the Visual Basic program.

FIGURE 20.3.

An Automation server exposes objects that are incorporated into Visual Basic applications through object-oriented programming principles.

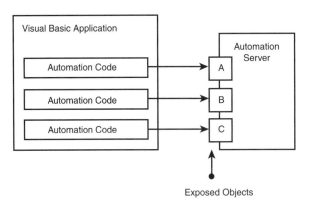

Figure 20.3 is a bit like the radio in a car. The radio is the server component, and you are the Visual Basic program. The radio exposes its functions through various knobs and buttons and other exposed objects. Turning a knob is like running a method of the radio object, and looking at the dial to see the frequency is like reading a property of the radio object.

Writing Automation code in Visual Basic involves these steps:

1. Declare object variables.
2. Hook the variables into the server's objects.
3. Manipulate the objects through their properties and methods.

The next several sections dive right into the Visual Basic 6 code required to implement Automation. In these sections, you see what is required to successfully exploit the features and capabilities of Word, Excel, and Microsoft Access.

Looking at a Short Example

This chapter is accompanied by several different projects. The first project examined is Word1.vbp, which demonstrates Automation from Visual Basic to Word 97. One of the forms in Word1.vbp is frmRomeo, shown in Figure 20.4.

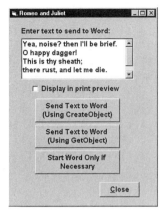

FIGURE 20.4.

The frmRomeo *form demonstrates Automation to Word 97.*

The frmRomeo form includes a large text box near the top of the form and four command buttons. Each of the three large command buttons in the center of the form implements a different approach to attaching to Word and delivering the contents of the text box to Word. The check box, when selected, instructs Visual Basic to display the text in Print Preview mode in Word.

The Click event procedure for the top command button is shown in Listing 20.1. Line numbers have been added to this listing to make it easier to document the important statements in this procedure. (Listing 20.1 is part of the Word1.vbp project accompanying this chapter.)

Listing 20.1. Automation requires very little code.

```
1 Private Sub cmdCreateObject_Click()
2   Dim wrd As Word.Application
3   Dim doc As Word.Document
4
5   Set wrd = CreateObject("Word.Application")
6
7   With wrd
8     .Visible = True
9     .Application.WindowState = wdWindowStateMaximize
10    Set doc = .Documents.Add
11
12    With wrd.Selection
13      .Text = txtMessage.Text
14    End With
15    If chkPrintPreview = 1 Then
16      .ActiveDocument.PrintPreview
17    End If
18  End With
19 End Sub
```

The Automation code starts in line 3 of Listing 20.1. A variable named wrd is established as a Word.Application object. Word.Application is part of the Word object model, a representation of the objects Word exposes to Automation controllers. We'll come back to the important topic of object models a bit later in this chapter.

Line 5 in Listing 20.1 actually invokes the Automation server. In response to the CreateObject command, Windows searches through the System Registry, looking for the application supporting the Word.Application object. Assuming that the object and its application are located somewhere in the Registry, Windows starts up the server (Microsoft Word) on the computer system. When the server application has been loaded into memory and started, Windows returns a pointer to the application, satisfying the wrd object variable definition.

In lines 7 through 18, you see the Visual Basic code using the properties and methods of the wrd object. You've seen object variables in many other chapters in this book. An object variable is very much unlike a simple variable such as an integer or string. An object variable contains much more depth and information than just a number or character string. In Listing 20.1, an entire hierarchy of large and small objects is attached to the Word.Application definition applied to the wrd variable.

For example, line 12 in Listing 20.1 references the Selection object that is subordinate to the Application object connected to the wrd variable. A rigorous description of each of the Word objects is far beyond what can be covered in this book. Word contains more than 200 exposed objects, each of which includes several properties and methods, and in many cases, the exposed objects include other objects that are not directly accessible to Visual Basic.

Referencing the Automation Server

An important line of code in Listing 20.1 is as follows:

```
Dim wrd As Word.Application
```

This is an object variable declaration, of course. But what's interesting is that the Word.Application object is not built into Visual Basic, yet Visual Basic does not generate a compile-time or runtime error when this statement is encountered. Where, then, does Visual Basic get the definition of Word.Application so that the reference to this object does not generate a compile-time error?

Simply put, a reference has been established in the Word1.vbp project, pointing to an object library describing the Word Automation objects. You add a reference to the Word 8.0 Object library in the References dialog box (see Figure 20.5).

FIGURE 20.5.

Select the object library from the References dialog box.

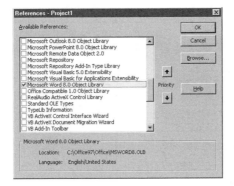

You open the References dialog box by selecting Project, References from the Visual Basic menu. With the dialog box open, search for Microsoft Word 8.0 Object Library in the list and select its check box. With its check box marked, the object definitions contained in the object library are available to your Visual Basic application. Without this reference, Visual Basic refuses to compile any references to the Word objects.

The Word object library is added to the computer when Microsoft Office 97 is installed. Because Microsoft has built the Office 97 applications to be Automation-compliant, several different object library files are added to the system so that developers can use the Office Automation features in their applications. There are object libraries for Word, Excel, Access, PowerPoint, and Outlook.

Understanding Object Models

Product by product, Microsoft has defined an *object model* that conforms to OLE specifications. Each part of the application is defined as an object that can be isolated and used independently of the other parts of the application. The object model for each application follows a direct hierarchy, with the `Application` object being the highest level (parent), and all other objects being children or grandchildren below it. Excel, for example, exposes itself as an `Application` object, its worksheets as `Worksheet` objects, and its ranges within worksheets as `Range` objects. These objects can be used within Excel or called from any OLE-compliant server application.

Figure 20.6 shows the object model for Microsoft Outlook. (You learn how to program the object model in Outlook in Chapter 21, "Integrating with Microsoft Outlook 97.")

FIGURE 20.6.
Understanding the object model of the Auto-mation server is an important step in creating Automation appli-cations.

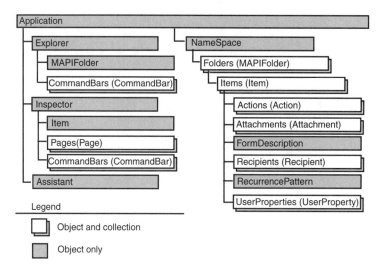

At the top of the Outlook object model is the `Application` object, which represents the running instance of Outlook. Below the `Application` object are the `Explorer`, `Inspector`, `Assistant`, and `NameSpace` objects. Of these subordinate objects, only the `NameSpace` object contains interesting data. All the Outlook email messages, contacts, appointments, and other items are contained in the `Folders` collection under the `NameSpace` object.

Each Office application has an object model similar to Figure 20.6. Later in this chapter are sections describing how to control Word and Excel through their object models. In each of these sections, you see a picture of the application's object model.

Hooking into an object model is not difficult. You first declare an object variable and then attach it to an instance of the server application. You've already seen this happen in Listing 20.1:

```
Dim wrd As Word.Application
Set wrd = CreateObject("Word.Application")
```

Windows provides the intelligence to connect the `wrd` object variable to the `Word.Application` object definition, using the System Registry to locate Word on the computer. Visual Basic takes its definition of `Word.Application` from the Word object library. All in all, it's an elegant system.

Integrating with Word 97

Microsoft Word has a rich object model. Figure 20.7 illustrates just the top-level objects in Word 97. An entire book could be written describing the more than 200 top-level and subordinate objects in the Word object hierarchy, each of which has several properties and methods. Virtually every aspect of Word documents and the Word environment is revealed in its object hierarchy. Word features a truly amazing object model.

FIGURE 20.7.
Word 97 features a sophisticated object model.

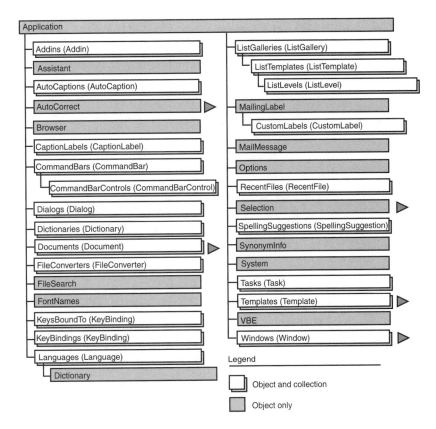

We'll be working mostly with the `Application` object and `Documents` collection in the Word object hierarchy. Do take a moment, though, and get an appreciation for the depth and completeness of the other objects available in the Word object model.

Opening a Document in Word 97

You've already seen the code for starting Word from Visual Basic. Now we'll take a look at opening a document and printing it. Listing 20.2 shows the code required to start Word and load a document named `R&J.doc`.

Listing 20.2. Loading a document into Word.

```
Private Sub cmdOpenDocument_Click()
  Set wrd = CreateObject("Word.Application")
  With wrd
    .Visible = True
    .Application.WindowState = wdWindowStateMaximize
    .Documents.Open filename:=App.Path & "\R&J.DOC"

  End With
End Sub
```

The wrd object is declared as a private module-level variable in frmWord2 in the Word2.vbp project. Therefore, the wrd object is available throughout frmWord2.

Printing the R&J document is simple and is shown in Listing 20.3.

Listing 20.3. Printing a Word document.

```
Private Sub Command1_Click()
  wrd.Application.PrintOut
End Sub
```

As long as frmWord2 is open, the wrd object and any documents contained in Word are available. At the conclusion of the experiment, Word is closed with the code in Listing 20.3. Notice that the wrd object is released and set to Nothing:

```
Private Sub cmdCloseWord_Click()
  wrd.Quit   ' Close Word
  Set wrd = Nothing
Set wrd = Nothing
```

Learning the Word Commands to Use

So how does a developer learn which commands to use in Word? If Word is so complicated, how is it possible to make sense of its sophisticated and extensive object model?

The easiest way to learn Word or any other Automation server, for that matter, is to turn on its macro recorder (assuming there is a macro recorder, of course!) and perform whatever actions you want to automate with VBA code. You locate the Word macro recorder by choosing Tools, Macro, Record New Macro from the Word menu. Word asks you for the name of the new macro (see Figure 20.8).

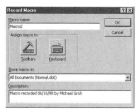

FIGURE 20.8.

The name assigned to the Word macro is irrelevant.

A little toolbar pops up showing you that the Word macro recorder is in operation (see Figure 20.9). From this point on, any action you perform in Word will be recorded by the macro recorder. For example, simply open a document and then click on the Print button. When your recording is complete, click on the Stop button on the macro recorder toolbar.

Next, open the macro you just recorded in the Word macro editor. Choose Tools, Macro, Macros and select the macro from the list that appears (see Figure 20.10). Click the Edit button to open the macro in the editor. Figure 20.11 shows the macro recorded that opens and prints the R&J.doc document.

FIGURE 20.9.
Use the Stop button to end the macro recording.

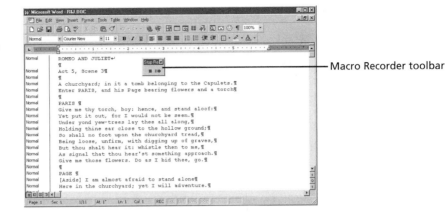

Macro Recorder toolbar

FIGURE 20.10.
Select the macro from the Macros dialog box and click the Edit button.

FIGURE 20.11.
The Word macro contains a lot of superfluous code.

Most of what you see in the code editor is irrelevant. When the recorder converts your actions to Word VBA code, all optional arguments are provided with default values. Fortunately, the recorder includes the names of all the arguments, making it easy for you to determine which arguments are relevant to your program. You'll have to consult the Word VBA help file to understand each of the commands recorded by the macro recorder.

Listing 20.4 shows the macro produced by the Word macro recorder, slightly rearranged. The relevant commands in this macro are `Documents.Open` and `Application.Printout`.

Listing 20.4. The macro produced by the Word macro recorder.

```
Sub Macro2()
  ChangeFileOpenDirectory _
     "F:\books\_PNVB6\Chap20\Project\Word2\"
  Documents.Open FileName:="R&J.DOC", _
     ConfirmConversions:=False, ReadOnly:= _
     False, AddToRecentFiles:=False, _
     PasswordDocument:="", _
     PasswordTemplate:= "", Revert:=False, _
     WritePasswordDocument:="", _
     WritePasswordTemplate:="", _
     Format:=wdOpenFormatAuto
  Application.PrintOut FileName:="", _
     Range:=wdPrintAllDocument, _
     Item:= wdPrintDocumentContent, _
     Copies:=1, Pages:="", _
     PageType:=wdPrintAllPages, _
     Collate:=True, Background:=True, _
     PrintToFile:=False
End Sub
```

What's missing in Listing 20.4 is the reference to the Application object. But it's safe to say in most cases that all that's needed in any of the commands recorded by the macro recorder is to add a reference to the Word.Application object when migrating the Word macro code to a Visual Basic application. For example, Listing 20.5 is the Visual Basic code equivalent to Listing 20.4.

Listing 20.5. Converting Word macros to Visual Basic is generally easy.

```
Private Sub OpenAndPrint
  Dim wrd As Word.Application
  Set wrd = CreateObject("Word.Application")

  wrd.ChangeFileOpenDirectory _
     "F:\books\_PNVB6\Chap20\Project\Word2\"
  wrd.Documents.Open FileName:="R&J.DOC", _
     ConfirmConversions:=False, ReadOnly:= _
     False, AddToRecentFiles:=False, _
     PasswordDocument:="", _
     PasswordTemplate:= "", Revert:=False, _
     WritePasswordDocument:="", _
     WritePasswordTemplate:="", _
     Format:=wdOpenFormatAuto
  wrd.Application.PrintOut FileName:="", _
     Range:=wdPrintAllDocument, _
     Item:= wdPrintDocumentContent, _
```

```
        Copies:=1, Pages:="", _
        PageType:=wdPrintAllPages, _
        Collate:=True, Background:=True, _
        PrintToFile:=False
    wrd.Quit
    Set wrd = Nothing
End Sub
```

Finally, removing the default arguments and other superfluous commands from the previous code example leaves us with Listing 20.6. This is certainly not much code for all the work performed for us!

Listing 20.6. Removing default argument values considerably reduces the Automation procedure.

```
Private Sub OpenAndPrint
  Dim wrd As Word.Application

  Set wrd = CreateObject("Word.Application")

  With wrd
    .ChangeFileOpenDirectory _
      "F:\books\_PNVB6\Chap20\Project\Word2\"
    .Documents.Open FileName:="R&J.DOC"
    .Application.PrintOut
    .Quit
  End With
  Set wrd = Nothing
End Sub
```

Unfortunately, not every Automation server includes a macro recorder as accommodating as Word 97. In many cases, you'll have to spend considerable research time figuring out how to control the server from your Visual Basic code.

Displaying a Word Document in Print Preview

Another common task is to display a document in Print Preview mode. The ActiveDocument object, which is owned by Word.Application, is a reference to the document currently open in Word. The following statement puts the current document in Print Preview mode in Word:

```
wrd.ActiveDocument.PrintPreview
```

The assumption in the preceding example, of course, is that wrd is attached to Word.Application. Listing 20.7 shows a more complete example of using Print Preview.

Listing 20.7. Users might want to see the Word document in Print Preview.

```
Private Sub PrintPreview
  Dim wrd As Word.Application
  Dim doc As Document

  Set wrd = CreateObject("Word.application")
  With wrd
    .Visible = True
    .Application.WindowState = wdWindowStateMaximize
    .Documents.Open filename:=App.Path & "\R&J.DOC"
    .ActiveDocument.PrintPreview
  End With

  MsgBox "Press OK to close Word"
  wrd.Quit
  Set wrd = Nothing
End Sub
```

The code in Listing 20.7 opens Word, loads the R&J document, and displays it in Print Preview mode in Word. Word stays open until the user dismisses the message box near the bottom of Listing 20.7. In the meantime, however, the user can print the document, return it to Edit view in Word, and perform other operations on the document. Word is closed and removed from memory by the last several statements in Listing 20.7. Figure 20.12 shows the R&J document in Word Print Preview.

FIGURE 20.12.
The user can work with this document in Word.

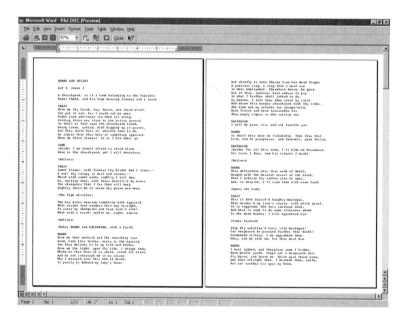

Creating a New Word Document

You've already seen an example of creating a new Word document. Listing 20.1 creates a new document but creates the document using the default Normal template. You might want to specify a document template to use as the basis of the new document. Listing 20.8 shows how to specify the name of a document template to use for the new document.

Listing 20.8. Specifying a document template to use with a new document.

```
Private Sub CreateNewDocument()
  Dim wrd As Word.Application
  Dim doc As Document

  Set wrd = CreateObject("Word.application")
  With wrd
    .Visible = True
    .Application.WindowState = wdWindowStateMaximize
    Set doc = .Documents.Add("Memo.dot")

    With wrd.Selection
      .Text = "This is some added text"
    End With
    'Make changes to document
    ' Save under a new name
    .ActiveDocument.SaveAs (App.Path & "\Memo.doc")
  End With
  wrd.Quit
  Set doc = Nothing
  Set wrd = Nothing
End Sub
```

Notice that SaveAs is used to save the document. (SaveAs is described in the next section.) Because the document is brand new, it can't be saved with its name until the SaveAs command has been executed. After the Save As command has been run, the Save command can be used to save subsequent revisions of the document.

Saving a Word Document

It's easy to save a document that is open in Word. Listing 20.9 shows how to open and then save a document under a new name. txtName.Text is a text box on frmWord2 in the Word2.vbp project.

Listing 20.9. Opening the document and saving it as a new name.

```
Private Sub cmdOpenSave_Click()
  Dim wrd As Word.Application

  If txtName.Text = "" Then
    Do
      txtName.Text = InputBox("Please enter the new file name:")
    Loop Until txtName.Text <> ""
  End If

  Set wrd = CreateObject("Word.application")

  With wrd
    .Visible = True
    .Application.WindowState = wdWindowStateMaximize
    .Documents.Open filename:=App.Path & "\R&J.DOC"
    .ActiveDocument.SaveAs (App.Path & "\" & txtName.Text)
  End With

  MsgBox "Press OK to close Word"

  wrd.Quit
  Set wrd = Nothing

End Sub
```

Notice that Listing 20.9 uses the `ActiveDocument.SaveAs` method. This is the same as choosing File, Save As in Word to save a document under a new name. The alternative is to do a simple `ActiveDocument.Save` to save the document with its current name.

Using Automation in Visual Basic Projects

Using Automation in Visual Basic projects is not the only use of Automation in Visual Basic 6 applications. Although it is possible to create custom Automation servers with Visual Basic 6, this advanced topic is beyond the scope of this book.

One such Automation server created with Visual Basic 6 might be a data acquisition program that automatically logs on to a mainframe computer, downloads selective information from the mainframe, and formats the data in such a way that it is easily used by other Windows applications. Such an Automation server would hide the complexity of the mainframe data accessing processes from the applications using the services of the Automation server.

Any Automation-compliant application would be able to use the services provided by the Visual Basic Automation server. Furthermore, if the business rules change for selecting data from the mainframe, the only changes necessary would be to the Automation server, not to each of the programs using the Automation server. These *multitier* business applications have become popular in the last several years because of the way they encapsulate functionality into discrete layers of programming.

Summary

This chapter explored using Automation from Visual Basic to control Microsoft Word. Word has a rich and varied object model and allows you to perform many different operations on documents. Microsoft Excel, PowerPoint, and Access can all be controlled through Automation using the techniques described in this chapter.

The next chapter examines controlling Microsoft Outlook through Automation. Outlook is an exciting and powerful personal information manager and scheduler for office users. As you'll see in that chapter, it is easy to get Outlook to create and save many different types of contacts, email messages, notes, and other items managed by Outlook.

Integrating with Microsoft Outlook 97

Microsoft Outlook is arguably one of the most interesting applications in the Office suite (see Figure 21.1). It is a general-purpose personal information manager (PIM) designed to handle appointments, contacts, email, and task lists. Outlook also includes workgroup features such as meeting scheduling and group calendar management.

FIGURE 21.1.
Microsoft Outlook is an important part of Office.

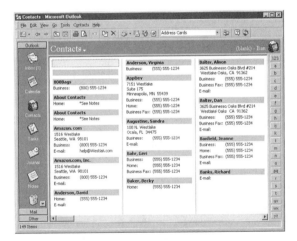

Microsoft Outlook is an ambitious and sophisticated program. In fact, Outlook is frequently criticized for being a bit *too* sophisticated and more complex than many users require. At the same time, however, Outlook has a tremendously well-developed object model that is easily adapted to Automation schemes. The next section describes the Outlook object model and explains where to find the particular object you want to control from Visual Basic.

Understanding the Outlook Object Model

The Outlook object model is deceptively simple. Figure 21.2 shows the diagram of the Outlook object model. This figure includes only objects and object collections. It does not include any properties or methods associated with any of the objects indicated.

FIGURE 21.2.
Outlook's object model is robust and flexible.

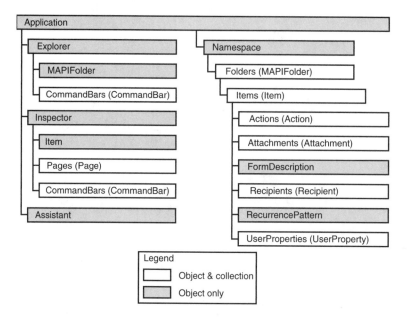

Notice how the Outlook object model is divided in two main branches. The most interesting Outlook objects are located in the branch headed NameSpace. All the appointments, contacts, and email messages are stored under the NameSpace branch along with any other information. The branch to the left contains the Outlook interface components and is not studied in this chapter. Table 21.1 provides an explanation of the NameSpace branch of the Outlook object model.

Table 21.1. The NameSpace branch contains the Outlook data items.

Object Name	Description
Application	The Application object is the parent of all other objects in the Outlook hierarchy.
NameSpace	Owns all the Folder objects in an Outlook installation.

Object Name	Description
Folder	All the Outlook data is stored in `Folder` objects. For example, the items in the Outlook Inbox folder are `MailItem` objects. Folders can be recursively nested within other folders.
Items	The `Item` objects contain the actual data managed by Outlook.
Actions	All Outlook `Item` objects have several actions associated with them. An `Action` object for a mail message might be `Send` or `Reply`.
Attachments	The `Attachments` collection contains all the objects attached to a mail message.
FormDescription	Outlook forms can be customized. A form's properties are stored in the `FormDescription` object.
Recipients	A mail message can be sent to any number of recipients. The recipient addresses are stored in the `Recipients` collection.
RecurrencePattern	Contains the type of recurrence pattern (daily, weekly, monthly, and so on) assigned to appointments or tasks.
UserProperties	Stores custom properties.

Most of the objects shown in Figure 21.2 have several subordinate objects within them. For example, the `Items` collection object (located under `Application`, `NameSpace`, `Folders`) contains several important types of objects. Table 21.2 lists the objects found in the `Items` collection.

Table 21.2. The `Items` collection includes several important Outlook objects.

Object Name	Description
AppoinmentItem	An `AppoinmentItem` is an item in the Calendar folder. Appointments can be a meeting, a one-time appointment, or a recurring appointment or meeting.
ContactItem	A contact managed by the Outlook Contacts folder.
JournalItem	An Outlook journal entry.
MailItem	A mail message contained in the Outlook Inbox folder.
MeetingRequestItem	See the discussion following this table.
NoteItem	`NoteItem` is an item in the Outlook Notes folder. Unlike several other object types, the `NoteItem` does not include a large number of properties or methods.

continues

Table 21.2. Continued.

Object Name	Description
PostItem	A PostItem is a special type of public email message. It is posted in a public Outlook folder and can be browsed by any user on the system.
RemoteItem	A RemoteItem mail item is created by Outlook when you specify a remote access system (RAS) connection.
ReportItem	A ReportItem is generated by Outlook when email delivery fails. The ReportItem contains the text of the email failure message.
TaskItem	A TaskItem is located in the Tasks folder. Tasks can be self-imposed or assigned by another user.
TaskRequestItem	This is another object that cannot be created. Outlook creates a transient TaskRequestItem when a user delegates a task to another user on the system. The TaskRequestItem is converted to a TaskItem as it is added to the other user's Outlook task list.

The MeetingRequestItem requires a bit of explanation. This object cannot be created. It is actually a special type of email message in the user's Outlook inbox. Outlook prepares this message when another user initiates a meeting by filling out a meeting request form (see Figure 21.3) and sending it to another user. Meeting requests are discussed in the section, "Adding Appointment Items," later in this chapter.

FIGURE 21.3.
A meeting request results in a special type of email message.

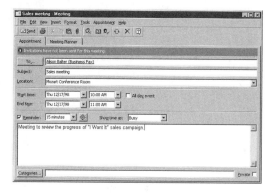

The processes of creating several different types of item objects such as contacts, appointments, and notes are described later in this chapter. Creating these items is discussed in the sections titled "Creating Outlook Contact Items," "Adding Appointment Items," and "Creating Outlook Note Items" near the end of this chapter.

Microsoft has carefully engineered Outlook for maximum flexibility and extensibility. You can definitely have it your way in Outlook. Schedule+, in many ways the predecessor to Outlook, had a clumsy nonstandard Automation interface that complicated everything programmers wanted to do with Schedule+. Microsoft did the right thing by abandoning Schedule+ and designing an entirely new system in Outlook. Thankfully, we do not have to deal with leftover hacks and workarounds when controlling Microsoft Outlook from Visual Basic.

Controlling Outlook

Outlook 97 is a multidimensionally programmable system. Not only can you build forms within Outlook and automate those forms with VBScript (a programming language similar to Visual Basic), Outlook exposes its elegant object model to Automation controllers created with Visual Basic and other 32-bit development systems.

Before you can hook into the Outlook object model from a controller created with Visual Basic, you must load the Outlook reference library. You'll also want the Outlook VBA Help file on hand.

The Outlook object library is named `msoutl8.olb`. Normally this object library is found in the Office 97 folder on your system. To add this library to your project, open the References dialog box (under the Tools menu). Make sure the Microsoft Outlook 8.0 Object Library entry is selected (see Figure 21.4) and press OK.

FIGURE 21.4.

`msoutl8.olb` *must be referenced or VB will not understand the Outlook object references in your code.*

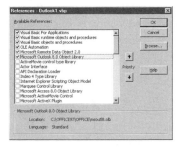

The Outlook VBA Help file is not installed in either the custom or typical installation profiles you use when installing Office 97. You must manually copy the Outlook VBA Help file from the Office 97 CD-ROM disk to your computer. Look in the ValuPack\MoreHelp folder and copy `VBAOutl.hlp` and `VBAOutl.cnt` to the Office 97 directory. If asked whether to overwrite existing files with these names, go right ahead; you're not losing anything of value.

Outlook has one of the most sophisticated and refined object models in the Office suite. Outlook exposes objects and their properties and methods for almost every aspect of

Outlook, its environment, and the data managed by Outlook. This chapter examines only a portion of the total object model for the mail, contacts, appointments, tasks, and several other items stored in Outlook, but you'll get a notion of the total size and depth of the fascinating Outlook object hierarchy.

At the very top Outlook has two major objects named `Application` and `NameSpace`. The `Application` object is the parent of everything else in Outlook, including the user interface, options, folders, and forms. The `NameSpace` object provides a handle on the Outlook data repository. The `NameSpace` object owns all the Outlook folders. Without a `NameSpace` object in your application, you are unable to read the Outlook contacts, schedules, journal entries, and other information stored in the folders within Outlook. In this chapter, we deal primarily with the `NameSpace` object.

The `NameSpace` object points only at MAPI data, so from the Automation perspective, all Outlook folders are actually MAPI folders. Be aware that you need to look for "MAPIFolder" instead of simply "folder" in the Outlook VBA Help. Many of the Outlook folder and folder item objects have properties and methods that map directly to the equivalent MAPI objects and methods.

It's possible that the `NameSpace` object in future versions of Outlook will access more than MAPI data. Imagine the power of an Outlook that could directly read Jet `.MDB` database files. Unfortunately, we're not there yet, but the potential does exist.

This chapter is accompanied by a Visual Basic 6.0 project named `Outlook1.vbp`. You'll find this project on the book's CD-ROM. This project includes the form you see in Figure 21.5. This form contains a series of command buttons that execute the individual functions you see throughout this chapter. `Outlook1.vbp` is there just for you to practice working with the Outlook object model and controlling Outlook from a Visual Basic application through Automation.

Figure 21.5.

`Outlook1.vbp` *includes all the functionality necessary to email-enable your Visual Basic applications without Outlook 97.*

Understanding Outlook Folders

Just about everything (that is, every *data* thing) in Outlook is either a folder or contained within a folder. Think of a folder as a filing drawer that can handle several different objects. Usually, a folder contains a certain type of object. Therefore, the Contacts folder contains `ContactItem` objects and the Inbox folder contains `MailItem` objects.

Microsoft Outlook 97 comes with nine built-in folders: Calendar, Contacts, Inbox, Journal, Notes, Tasks, Outbox, SentMail, and DeletedItems. You can add as many custom folders to your Outlook installation as you want (see Figure 21.6).

FIGURE 21.6.
Outlook lets you add as many folders as you want to the Folders collection.

Folders can be nested. So you can have a folder of project correspondence, and within that folder have subfolders of product specification memos, email with vendors, and meeting notes.

In this chapter, you'll be working with the Inbox folder, the default home of mail messages and other mail-type items. Depending on how you have Outlook set up on your computer your new email messages will end up in either the Inbox folder and sent immediately or in the Outbox folder for transfer to a mail server at a later time.

The code described in this chapter prepares a new message, addresses it for sending to a valid email account, and sends it by whatever method you have set up on your computer.

Creating an Outlook Instance

The form module in the main form in `Outlook1.vbp` includes the module-level variables in Listing 21.1.

Listing 21.1. Several object variables are declared in the main form's declaration area.

```
Dim mOutlookApp As Outlook.Application
Dim mNameSpace As Outlook.NameSpace
Dim mFolder As Outlook.MAPIFolder
Dim mItem As Outlook.MailItem
```

The CreateObject function in Listing 21.2 creates a running instance of Outlook on the local computer. This function assumes that you have Office 97 installed on your machine.

Listing 21.2. The CreateObject function starts up an invisible instance of Outlook.

```
Function GetOutlook() As Boolean
On Error Resume Next
  GetOutlook = False

  Set mOutlookApp = _
    CreateObject("Outlook.Application.8")
  If Err Then
    MsgBox "Could not create Outlook object", _
      vbCritical
    Exit Function
  End If

  Set mNameSpace = _
    mOutlookApp.GetNamespace("MAPI")
  If Err Then
    MsgBox "Could not create NameSpace object", _
      vbCritical
    Exit Function
  End If

  GetOutlook = True

End Function
```

In the GetOutlook() both the mOutlookApp and mNameSpace objects are module-level variables. Because this is a Visual Basic application and because this code is behind the main form, as long as the form remains open you have a handle on the Outlook object. If Outlook happens to be running at the time this function executes, the mOutlookApp hooks into that running Outlook instance.

If Outlook is not currently available, Windows silently starts up Outlook and runs it as a background process. You do not see the background instance of Outlook on the Windows 95 taskbar nor is it visible as you Alt+Tab from process to process. Yet the background instance is visible in the Windows 95 task list, which you see when you execute an Alt+Ctrl+Del keystroke combination. Keeping Outlook invisible to the user is a pretty neat trick. Just as Excel developers have known for years, you can use an Automation server running in the background to do all sorts of sophisticated work for you without the user ever being aware that it's running. When running as a background process, the Outlook user interface does not become visible until you instruct it to.

Notice the `"Outlook.Application.8"` syntax in the function `GetOutlook()`. This syntax references the Office 97 version of Outlook. You can achieve more version independence by dropping the `.8` from this string (`"Outlook.Application"`) to achieve the `"Version Independent Program ID"`. This information is stored in the Windows System Registry and is interpreted by Windows at runtime. Either syntax is acceptable.

Making Outlook Visible

After you have an Outlook instance running on your desktop, making it visible is relatively easy. In fact, Listing 21.3 is how you reveal the user's inbox Outlook folder on the Windows 95 desktop.

Listing 21.3. Outlook remains invisible until you ask to see a folder.

```
Private Sub cmdInboxFolder_Click()
  Set mFolder = _
    mNameSpace.GetDefaultFolder(olFolderInbox)
  mFolder.Display
End Sub
```

This code is a little misleading. Outlook contains several different types of folders. Each folder type is indicated by one of the intrinsic constants listed in Table 21.3. You'll frequently use these intrinsic constants. In fact, any time you want to access an Outlook folder you must tell Outlook what kind of folder you want to open and work with. Many Outlook object methods have similar lists of intrinsic constants that influence how the methods work. Use the Object Browser (a feature in all the 32-bit Microsoft development systems) to see which constants are available for the methods you want to use.

Table 21.3. The Outlook intrinsic constants for referencing folder types.

Folder Type	Intrinsic Constant
Calendar	olFolderCalendar
Contacts	olFolderContacts
Deleted Items	olFolderDeletedItems
Inbox	olFolderInbox
Journal	olFolderJournal
Notes	olFolderNotes
Outbox	olFolderOutbox
Sent Mail	olFolderSentMail
Tasks (To-Do List)	olFolderTasks.

The GetDefaultFolder method returns the default folder of the designated type, rather than a global default folder. The Display method actually displays the folder in the Windows environment. In many cases, there is no need to reveal the Outlook folders to your users. Instead, write your code in such a way as to create and manipulate the Outlook folders as required by your application's features.

Creating a Mail Message in Outlook

An Outlook email message is represented by the MailItem object. MailItem objects live in the Outlook folders (usually the Inbox folder) and are created by the Outlook Application object. MailItem objects have a large number of properties that define every possible parameter associated with email and a number of methods necessary to send, receive, and reply to mail messages.

An email message is a simple thing. Like a letter delivered by the US Postal Service, all that is needed is the recipient's address and a message. An Outlook MailItem object is a bit more complex. There are 59 different properties (most of which you'll never use) and 13 methods for the Outlook MailItem object. Table 21.4 shows some of the most important MailItem properties, and Table 21.5 describes the MailItem methods.

Table 21.4. Important MailItem properties.

Property	Data Type	What It Does
Attachments	RO	Contains a collection of attachments to this MailItem object.
BCC	RO	Returns the list of blind carbon-copy names for the message.
Body	R/W	Contains the free-text body of the mail message.
CC	RO	Contains the carbon-copy names.
Categories	R/W	Contains the string array of the categories assigned to this MailItem object.
CreationTime	RO	Enters the creation date and time of the mail item.
ExpiryTime	R/W	Enters the date and time at which the mail item becomes obsolete.
LastModificationTime	RO	Lists the date and time the Outlook object was last modified.
ReceivedByName	RO	Names the person who received the message.
ReceivedTime	R/W	Lists the date and time the message was received.

Property	Data Type	What It Does
Recipients	RO	Returns a pointer to the collection of recipients of the message.
Saved	RO	True if item has not been changed since it was last saved.
SentOn	RO	Lists the date and time the message was sent.
Size	RO	Lists the size of the message.
Subject	R/W	Names the subject of the message.
To	RO	Creates the semicolon-delimited list of recipients of the mail message.
UnRead	RO	True if the message has not been opened for reading.

Table 21.4 shows only a portion of the properties for Outlook MailItem objects. Many other properties are available (consult the VBAOutl.hlp file for information on the properties not listed here).

Most of the properties in Table 21.5 are shown in the user interface when creating or receiving email messages.

Table 21.5. Outlook 97 MailItem methods.

Method	What It Does
ClearConversationIndex	If the message is part of a thread, this method clears the thread index.
Close	Closes the mail message. This is not the same action as the Save method.
Copy	Creates and returns a copy of the MailItem. You should move or save the copied MailItem object after it has been created by the Copy method.
Delete	Deletes the MailItem object.
Display	Displays the MailItem object (makes it visible in the Windows 95 user interface).
Forward	Forwards the message to another user. You should add the new recipient's address to the MailItem object's Recipients collection.
Move	Moves the MailItem to another folder.
PrintOut	Prints the MailItem with all defaults selected.

continues

Table 21.5. Continued.

Method	What It Does
Reply	Creates a reply message already addressed to the sender of the original message.
ReplyAll	Same as Reply, except creates the reply to all recipients of the original message as well as the sender.
Save	Saves the MailItem object
SaveAs	Saves the message as a disk file in one of a number of different formats (such as MSG, DOC and RTF).
Send	Sends the message

Actually creating the message is simple. The Outlook Application object includes a CreateItem method that lets you create virtually any type of Outlook object. The olMailItem intrinsic constant instructs Outlook to create a new MailItem. The new MailItem is automatically stored in the Inbox folder. The other lines in the cmdCreateMail_Click() event procedure simply set a few of the properties required to send an email message (see Listing 21.4).

Listing 21.4. Create an email item with the CreateItem method.

```
Private Sub cmdCreateMail_Click()
  Dim pRecip As Recipient

  Set mItem = mOutlookApp.CreateItem(olMailItem)
  Set pRecip = _
     mItem.Recipients.Add("mgroh@austin360.com")
  mItem.Subject = "Email created by Visual Basic"
  mItem.Body = "Email message created by " _
           & "Visual Basic on " _
           & Date & " at " & Time()
  mItem.Save
End Sub
```

The Save method at the bottom of this event procedure forces Outlook to save the new message in its Inbox folder. Until the message is explicitly saved, you risk losing the message in the event of a hardware or software failure. The new message created with the cmdCreateMail_Click event procedure is shown in Figure 21.7.

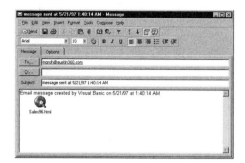

FIGURE 21.7.
This message was created with the code presented in this chapter.

Attaching an Object to a Mail Message

The `MailItem` object includes an `Attachments` property that returns a handle on the collection of objects attached to the mail message. Unlike simpler email systems, MAPI messages enable you to attach multiple objects to a single message. You could, for example, generate a report in Access or Visual Basic, convert the report to HTML or RTF format, and attach the resulting file to your Outlook email message.

You attach objects to the mail message with the `Add` method of the Attachments collection. The event procedure in Listing 21.5 adds a file to an existing mail message. Notice how an `Attachments` object is used to reference the `MailItem`'s Attachments collection.

Listing 21.5. Attach an object to an email item by adding the object to the mail item's Attachments collection.

```
Private Sub cmdAttach_Click()
  Dim pAttachments As Attachments
  Set pAttachments = mItem.Attachments
  pAttachments.Add _
    "C:\SharedDatabases\Sales96.html", olByValue
End Sub
```

Binary objects are encoded before mailing by whatever method you've designated in the Outlook Services dialog box (select Tools, Services, General, and then click the Message Format button). Usually you'll want MIME encoding, which permits multiple attachments containing binary data.

Sending the Message

Sending the message is incredibly simple. Use the `MailItem` object's `Send` method to instruct Outlook to deliver the message to the local mail handler. On my machine, I have

Outlook set up so I can read and write mail messages offline. Because I must dial into my ISP to pick up or send email, I'd rather not stay connected any longer than necessary. (I use the same phone line for sending and receiving faxes and browsing the World Wide Web in addition to sending and receiving email.)

The event procedure in Listing 21.6 is triggered when the Send Message button is clicked in `Outlook1.vbp`.

Listing 21.6. Use the `Send` method of the mail item to prepare it for sending.

```
Private Sub cmdSend_Click()
On Error GoTo Send_Error
  mItem.Send
  MsgBox "Message Sent"
Send_Exit:
  Exit Sub
Send_Error:
  MsgBox "Error sending message"
  Resume Send_Exit
End Sub
```

This subroutine simply moves the message to the Outbox folder. I still must press the F5 key to instruct Outlook to actually dial up my ISP and exchange email. Although I'm sure I could automate this process I'd rather reserve this action for manual control and send several email messages as a single batch.

Closing Outlook

As with any object variables you really should set all the Outlook objects to `Nothing` before shutting down your application. Even though Visual Basic (and Access 97) normally destroy all object variables when the application ends, good programming practice dictates that you should explicitly destroy these objects to free up the memory they occupy (see Listing 21.7).

Listing 21.7. Be sure to set all object variables to `Nothing` when you are finished.

```
Private Sub cmdClose_Click()
  mOutlookApp.Quit
  Set mNameSpace = Nothing
  Set mFolder = Nothing
  Set mItem = Nothing
  Set mOutlookApp = Nothing
End Sub
```

The last line of cmdClose_Click() invokes the Quit method of the Outlook application, which forces Outlook to remove itself from the computer's memory. If your application has been using a visible instance of Outlook you see the Please Wait While Outlook Exits message as Outlook stops running. A background instance of Outlook stops silently and unobtrusively.

Creating Outlook Items

Creating and sending email via Outlook has been presented as an example of a typical Automation programming exercise. The following sections look at some other programming tasks that can be accomplished by controlling Outlook with ActiveX Automation.

Most of the following examples involve creating Outlook objects through the Automation interface. Similar syntax is used regardless of the type of object being created:

```
Set ItemName = AppObject.CreateItem(ItemConstant)
```

The Outlook item constants are listed in Table 21.6. Each of these items corresponds to some item visible in the Outlook user interface.

Table 21.6. olItems constants.

Constant	Value	Description
olMailItem	0	Creates a mail message.
olAppointmentItem	1	Adds an item to the Outlook calendar.
olContactItem	2	Adds a new contact to the Contacts list.
olTaskItem	3	Adds a new task to the task list.
olJournalItem	4	Makes a new entry into the Outlook journal.
olNoteItem	5	Adds a Note to the Outlook notes area.
olPostItem	6	Adds a PostItem to the Outlook data.

Looking at Common Properties

The next several sections detail how to create each of the types of items you see in Table 21.6. Virtually every object type in Outlook has a large number of read-only and read/write properties that your code can utilize. Many of these properties are found in most of the Outlook object types, and the use of these properties is the same for each of the objects using those properties.

Table 21.7 lists several of the most common properties and describes how these properties might be used in your Visual Basic programs.

Table 21.7. Common Outlook object properties.

Property Name	Data Type	Description
Actions	RO	Actions. See following discussions.
Application	RO	Application. The Outlook application containing the object.
Attachments	RO	Attachments. Collection of attachments to the item.
CreationTime	RO	Date. The date and time the object was created.
EntryID	RO	String. See following discussions.
FormDescription	RO	FormDescription. The Outlook form used to display the item.
GetInspector	RO	Inspector. A handle to the window used to display the item.
Importance	RW	olImportance. See following discussions.
LastModificationTime	RO	Date. Date and time item was last modified.
Mileage	RW	String. Mileage required to complete this item.
NoAging	RW	Boolean. Whether to age this item or not.
OutlookInternalVersion	RO	String. Build number of the Outlook version.
OutlookVersion	RO	String. Outlook version (such as 8.0) for the item.
Parent	RO	Object. Parent object of the item.
Recipients	RO	Recipients. Collection of Contacts to receive this item.
Saved	RO	Boolean. Has item been saved since last modification?
Sensitivity	RW	olSensitivity. See following discussions.
Size	RO	Long. Size in bytes of the item.
UnRead	RW	Boolean. Reports whether item has been opened.
UserProperties	RO	UserProperties. Collection of custom properties assigned to item.

Some properties require a bit more explanation than what's given in Table 21.7. The following sections detail several of the more interesting properties listed in Table 21.7.

Actions

Most Outlook objects have a variety of actions that can be performed on it. For example, you can reply to or forward a `MailItem` object. The `Actions` object is a collection containing the `Action` objects that are applicable to the object.

EntryID

Every object in an Outlook installation is assigned a unique identifier by Outlook at the time the object is created. The `EntryID` of an object is its read-only identifier.

Importance

`Importance` refers to the importance assigned to the Outlook item. Use one of the `olImportance` constants in Table 21.8 to specify the importance of the item.

Table 21.8. Values for the `Importance` property.

Constant	Value
olImportanceLow	0
olImportanceNormal	1
olImportanceHigh	2

Sensitivity

The `Sensitivity` property indicates the confidentiality of the item. This does not imply that Outlook secures the item. Instead, the item is marked as confidential, personal, or private, depending on what value has been assigned to its `Sensitivity` property. The Outlook constants in Table 21.9 are used to set the `Sensitivity` property.

Table 21.9. Values for the `Sensitivity` property.

Constant	Value
olNormal	0
olPersonal	1
olPrivate	2
olConfidential	3

Notice that many of the common properties are read-only. In many cases, this means that Outlook assigns the value to the property and the property value cannot be modified except by Outloook. Read-only does not imply that the value will never change, however. Outlook updates a property such as `LastModificationTime` when the data in the object or any of its properties change.

Creating Outlook Contact Items

The `ContactItem` object has an exceptional number of properties that describe the person represented by the object, the person's address, phone number, and other contact information. Outlook is exceptionally capable when it comes to managing contact information. Table 21.10 lists some of the more than 130 properties associated with the `ContactItem` object.

Table 21.10. `ContactItem` properties.

Property	Type
Anniversary	Date
AssistantTelephoneNumber	String
Birthday	Date
BusinessAddress	String
BusinessAddressCity	String
BusinessAddressCountry	String
BusinessAddressPostalCode	String
BusinessAddressState	String
BusinessAddressStreet	String
BusinessFaxNumber	String
BusinessHomePage	String
BusinessTelephoneNumber	String
CarTelephoneNumber	String
Children	String
CompanyName	String
CustomerID	String
Department	String
Email1Address	String
FirstName	String
FullName	String
Gender	olGender
Hobby	String
JobTitle	String
Language	String
LastName	String
ManagerName	String
MiddleName	String
NickName	String

Property	Type
OfficeLocation	String
PagerNumber	String
PersonalHomePage	String
Profession	String
Spouse	String
WebPage	String

Most `ContactItem` properties are self-explanatory. Several properties, such as `FullName`, are constructed by Outlook from the `FirstName`, `MiddleName`, and `LastName` properties.

Keep in mind that the properties listed in Table 21.10 are just part of the total number of properties available for the `ContactItem` object. Be sure to check the Outlook VBA online help to see a complete list of properties.

Listing 21.8 is a code example showing how to create a new contact via automation to Outlook 97.

Listing 21.8. Contact items have many different properties to set.

```
Dim objApp As Outlook.Application
Dim objContact As Outlook.ContactItem

Set objApp = _
   CreateObject("Outlook.Application")
Set objContact = _
   objApp.CreateItem(olContactItem)
With objContact
  .CompanyName = "Acme Widgets"
  .BusinessAddressStreet = "123 Main Street"
  .BusinessAddressCity = "Anytown"
  .BusinessAddressState = "IN"
  .BusinessAddressCountry = "USA"
  .BusinessAddressPostalCode = "52240"
  .BusinessTelephoneNumber = "(317) 555-1234"
  .BusinessFaxNumber = "(317) 555-1234"
  .WebPage = "www.acme.com"
  .FullName = "Jack O'Brien"
  .JobTitle = "Chairman and CEO"
  .Gender = olMale
  .Email1Address = "JackO@acme.com"
  .Save
  .Display ' Optionally display
End With
Set objApp = Nothing
```

Figure 21.8 shows the form created from the previous code sample.

FIGURE 21.8.

The frmContact *form creates a new contact from data entered on the form.*

The Outlook contact created from the data on frmContact is shown in Figure 21.9.

FIGURE 21.9.

Example of a new contact item.

Adding Appointment Items

The process of creating an Outlook appointment is similar to the other examples you've seen in this chapter. The general syntax of creating an appointment is as follows:

```
Set objItem = myOlApp.CreateItem(olAppointmentItem)
```

The AppointmentItem is another object type with a lot of different properties. Table 21.11 lists a few of the most important of these properties.

Table 21.11. AppointmentItem properties.

Property	Type
AllDayEvent	Boolean
BusyStatus	Status
Duration	Long
End	Date
Location	String
MeetingStatus	olMeetingStatus

Property	Type
OptionalAttendees	String
ReminderMinutesBeforeStart	Long
ReminderPlaySound	Boolean
ReminderSoundFile	String
RequiredAttendees	String
Start	Date
Subject	String

The code in Listing 21.9 creates an appointment at 1:30 p.m. on July 14, 1999 in the Mozart conference room.

Listing 21.9. Creating an `AppointmentItem` follows the general pattern you've seen so far in this chapter.

```
Dim objApp As Outlook.Application
Dim ApptItem As Outlook.AppointmentItem

Set objApp = CreateObject("Outlook.Application")
Set ApptItem = objApp.CreateItem(olAppointmentItem)
With ApptItem
  .Start = "07/14/1999 13:30"
  .Duration = 90 ' Minutes
  .Location = "Mozart Conference Room"
  .Subject = "Sales Meeting"
  .Body = "Second quarter wrap-up"
  .AllDayEvent = False
  .BusyStatus = olBusy
  .Save
  .Display ' Optionally display the appointment
End With
Set objApp = Nothing
```

Notice the `BusyStatus` property. When setting up appointments, several different values can be applied to this property. These values are listed in Table 21.12 and correspond to the Show Time As text box you see in Figure 21.10.

Table 21.12. `olBusyStatus` constants.

Constant	Value
olFree	0
olTentative	1
olBusy	2
olOutOfOffice	3

Figure 21.10 shows the Appointment item that was created via the previous code example.

FIGURE 21.10.

Example of a new Appointment item.

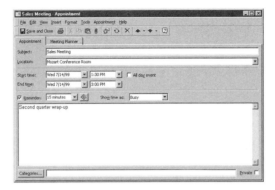

Earlier in this chapter you read about the special MeetingRequestItem Outlook object. At that time the MeetingRequestItem was described as a special type of email message. Listing 21.10 shows how to create such a message and send it to several users. This meeting request includes one required and one optional attendee.

Listing 21.10. A MeetingRequestItem creates an appointment for other users.

```
Set objItem = myOlApp.CreateItem(olAppointmentItem)
With objItem
  .MeetingStatus = olMeeting
  .Subject = "Strategy Meeting"
  .Location = "Conference Room B"
  .Start = #9/24/97 1:30:00 PM#
  .Duration = 90
  End With
  Set objReq = _
      objItem.Recipients.Add("Darby Giles")
  objReq.Type = olRequired
  Set objOpt = _
     objItem.Recipients.Add("Regis McGuigan")
objOpt.Type = olOptional
Set myResourceAttendee = _
    objItem.Recipients.Add("Conference Room B")

myResourceAttendee.Type = olResource
objItem.Send
```

Creating Outlook Note Items

The code in Listing 21.11 is an example of creating a new note item in Outlook.

Listing 21.11. Very little code is required to create notes in Outlook.

```
Dim objApp As Outlook.Application
Dim myNote As Outlook.NoteItem
Set objApp = CreateObject("Outlook.Application")
Set myNote = objApp.CreateItem(olNoteItem)
With myNote
  .Body = "Give Joe a call about inventory control"
  .Color = olYellow
  .Save
  .Display ' Optionally display
End With
Set objApp = Nothing
```

Outlook provides a large number of properties applicable to NoteItem objects. Because the note appears in the user interface, many of these properties influence where the note appears and how it looks to the user. Table 21.13 lists a few of the NoteItem properties available to your applications.

Table 21.13. NoteItem properties.

Property	Type
Body	String
Categories	String
Color	olNoteColor
Height	Long
Left	Long
MessageClass	String
Top	Long
Width	Long

Figure 21.11 shows the output from the code example in Listing 21.11.

FIGURE 21.11.
Notes are useful additions to Outlook.

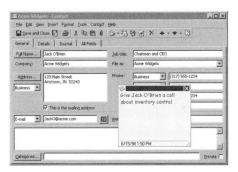

Creating a Journal Entry

Another interesting Outlook feature is the capability to log the activity of certain applications on the user's computer. By default Outlook logs the activity of all the other Office applications (Word, Excel, Access, and PowerPoint). The start and stop times are recorded in a hierarchical manner by Outlook as shown in Figure 21.12.

FIGURE 21.12.
Outlook's Journal feature provides a handy way to track events.

In Figure 21.12, the Journal items are indicated by the icons in the wide band in the center of the figure. In this particular case, the Outlook Journal is displaying the Microsoft Word activity for the period May 5 through May 11, 1998. The icons indicate individual Word sessions and identify the Word document being edited in each session. Double-clicking an icon reveals the details of the session such as the starting and ending times and the duration of the editing session.

You can use Outlook to log other events just as you see in Figure 21.12. The Outlook JournalItem object can be created exactly as you've seen other Outlook item objects created in this chapter. Listing 21.12 shows the code that logs a new Journal event into the Consulting Jobs entry type category. This category is just like the Microsoft Word entry type in Figure 21.12.

Listing 21.12. Use Outlook's Journaling feature to log special events.

```
Private Sub cmdJournalItem_Click()
  Dim objApp As Outlook.Application
  Dim objJournal As Outlook.JournalItem
```

```
     Set objApp = CreateObject("Outlook.Application")
     Set objJournal = objApp.CreateItem(olJournalItem)
     With objJournal
       .Type = "Consulting Jobs"
       .Subject = "Peterson Report"
       .Body = "Peterson Personnel Project"
       .Start = #6/1/99 12:00:00 PM#
       .End = #6/1/99 3:00:00 PM#
       .Duration = 180   'Minutes
       .Close (olSave)
       .Display ' Optionally display
     End With
     Set objApp = Nothing
End Sub
```

Notice the `Type` property specifies the entry type for the new Journal item. The `Duration`
property is a long value indicating how many minutes were consumed by the new journal
item. Figure 21.13 shows the Journal item created with the code in Listing 21.12.

FIGURE 21.13.

*This Journal entry
was created with
the code in
Listing 21.12.*

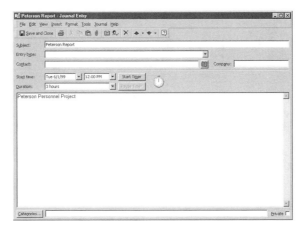

The Journal item includes many different properties, only a few of which are used in
Listing 21.12. Table 21.14 lists the most common Journal item properties you'll work
with in Outlook.

Table 21.14. Journal item properties.

Property	Type
Attachments	Attachments (RO)
BillingInformation	String
Body	String

continues

Table 21.14. Continued.

Property	Type
Categories	String
Companies	String
ContactNames	String
DocPosted	Boolean
DocPrinted	Boolean
DocRouted	Boolean
DocSaved	Boolean
Duration	Long
End	Date
MessageClass	String
Mileage	String
Recipients	Recipients
Saved	Boolean
Start	Date
Subject	String
Type	String
UnRead	Boolean
UserProperties	UserProperties

Creating Outlook Task Items

The last Outlook entry we'll examine is the Task item. An Outlook task is often described as a "to-do" item in other personal information managers. An Outlook task includes the description and due date for the task, an area for a long explanatory note about the task, and other information frequently required by this type of entry.

Listing 21.13 shows the code required to create an Outlook task item. This procedure follows the pattern shown elsewhere in this chapter. A reference is made to the Outlook Application object and the CreateItem of the Application object is used to create the Task item. Then a few properties of the new Task item are set and the new item is saved.

Listing 21.13. The Outlook Task item includes a few properties not seen in other item types.

```
Private Sub cmdTaskItem_Click()
  Dim objApp As Outlook.Application
  Dim objTask As Outlook.TaskItem
```

```
Set objApp = CreateObject("Outlook.Application")
Set objTask = objApp.CreateItem(olTaskItem)
With objTask
  .Subject = "Send Disk"
  .Body = "Send Betty the sample code disk"
  .DueDate = "05/14/1997"
  .Status = olTaskCompleted
  .Importance = olImportanceHigh
  .Save
  .Display ' Optionally display
End With
Set objApp = Nothing
End Sub
```

The task created with the code in Listing 21.13 is shown in Figure 21.14. Notice how the properties set in Listing 21.13 are translated into the settings you see in this figure.

FIGURE 21.14.
Outlook Task items are a handy way to manage a dynamic to-do list.

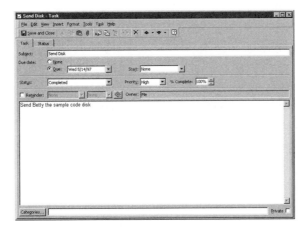

As with the other Outlook item types, the Task item includes a large number of properties not used in Listing 21.13. Table 21.15 shows some of these properties.

Table 21.15. `TaskItem` properties.

Property	Type
ActualWork	Long
BillingInformation	String
Body	String
CardData	String
Categories	String
Companies	String

continues

Table 21.15. Continued.

Property	Type
Complete	Boolean
Contacts	String
DateCompleted	Date
DelegationState	olTaskDelegationState (RO)
Delegator	String (RO)
DueDate	Date
EntryID	String (RO)
Importance	olImportance
IsRecurring	Boolean (RO)
MessageClass	String
Ordinal	Long
Owner	String
Ownership	olTaskOwnership
PercentComplete	Long
Recipients	Recipients
ReminderOverrideDefault	Boolean
ReminderPlaySound	Boolean
ReminderSet	Boolean
ReminderSoundFile	String
ReminderTime	Date
ResponseState	olTaskResponse
Role	String
Saved	Boolean
SchedulePlusPriority	String
Sensitivity	olSensitivity
StartDate	Date
Status	olTaskStatus
StatusOnCompletionRecipients	String
StatusUpdateRecipients	String
Subject	String
TeamTask	Boolean
TotalWork	Long

The properties listed in Table 21.15 emphasize how useful the Task item is to business environments. There are properties enabling you to set the reminder options, delegation information, billing specifics, and other important aspects of typical to-do list items.

Summary

Automation is an important technology for Visual Basic developers to master. Many people feel there is no need to know how to send email messages with Outlook. After all, each of the Office 97 applications all have a Send command in the File menu that permits you to deliver the current document via email in many different formats. But, as you discovered in this chapter, working with the Outlook object model is fun and efficient. Using Automation to create email messages and control Outlook provides much more flexibility than you'll ever get using the Send command in the Office 97 application File menus.

The Outlook object model is elegant, sophisticated, and refined. Notice how few lines of code are needed to create and manage email messages through the Outlook object model. None of the procedures presented in this chapter are more than a dozen lines long. Outlook provides a lot of power with very little work.

The next section of this book discusses how to create Internet-enabled applications with Visual Basic 6.0. In those chapters you'll learn how to apply your Automation skills to Internet Explorer, use the Web browser ActiveX control built into Internet Explorer 4.0, and exploit the other Internet capabilities of Visual Basic 6.0.

PART VI

Developing for the Internet

Integrating with Internet Explorer

The power and flexibility of the Internet are changing the way people think, affecting people's private and professional lives. The World Wide Web is an incredible research tool and an unparalleled method of communication. The most commonly used application for navigating the constantly changing and expanding Web is the Web browser.

By employing a Web browser you can locate common or obscure pieces of information, and you can view such information in a collage of still graphics, moving video, audio, and text. Using the Automation capabilities of Microsoft's Internet Explorer 4, you can add Web browsing functionality to your own applications.

Using Automation with Internet Explorer

Internet Explorer 4 is, like most current Microsoft products, an Automation server. Using Visual Basic, it's easy to add functionality to your application to control Internet Explorer by manipulating its object model.

The object model of Internet Explorer is simple compared to object models of other applications such as Word. The Internet Explorer object model consists of a single object and a handful of properties, methods, and events.

Referencing the Internet Explorer Automation Server

The Internet Explorer Automation object is found in the file SHDOCVW.DLL. This DLL is used just like any other Automation server; you must set a reference to the Automation server before you can manipulate its object.

> **Note:** The SHDOCVW.DLL file is installed on a computer only when Internet Explorer 4 is installed; you cannot distribute this file. To use the Web browsing functionality you add to your application, users must have a copy of Internet Explorer 4 installed on their computers.

To enable your application to automate Internet Explorer, simply choose Project, References from the menu to display the References dialog box (see Figure 22.1) and then scroll down to select Microsoft Internet Controls in the list of available references.

FIGURE 22.1.
Select the library from the References dialog box.

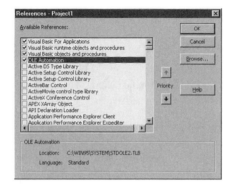

Referencing an Internet Explorer Automation Object

The one and only object in the Internet Explorer object model is the InternetExplorer object. After the Internet Explorer library is referenced in your project, you can create object variables to hold references to instances of the InternetExplorer object. By manipulating the object variable, you manipulate an instance of Internet Explorer.

In previous chapters, you learned how to create object variables and reference objects. The same principles apply with Internet Explorer. You must create an object to hold the reference, then you must assign an object reference to that variable. You can do this in one of two ways. First, you could dimension an object variable as InternetExplorer and then instantiate a new object for the variable using the Set statement:

```
Dim objIE as InternetExplorer
...
Set objIE = New InternetExplorer
```

Alternatively, you could perform both steps in a single statement using the New keyword:

```
Dim objIE As New InternetExplorer
```

> **Note:** Throughout the rest of this chapter, the variable name objIE is used to denote a reference to an instance of the Internet Explorer object just as the previous two code listings have illustrated. For example, when discussing the Visible property, you will see code such as objIE.Visible = True.

Hiding and Showing Internet Explorer

As soon as you create a reference to a new Internet Explorer Automation object using the New keyword, a new instance of Internet Explorer is started. This new instance is not visible, however, so you must explicitly show the instance if you want the user to see it. You can fully manipulate Internet Explorer while it is hidden, but most often you will probably want the user to see Internet Explorer. If you plan on manipulating Internet Explorer while it's hidden, you should still consider displaying Internet Explorer while debugging your application. If you attempt to debug your Automation code while Internet Explorer is hidden, tracking down problems in your code might prove to be difficult because not only can't you see what Internet Explorer is doing, Internet Explorer's error messages are suppressed when Internet Explorer is not visible.

To display the hidden instance of Internet Explorer, simply set its Visible property to True:

```
ObjIE.Visible = True
```

Shutting Down Internet Explorer

When a client application using objects from an Automation server is shut down, the objects created by that client are released and destroyed—usually resulting in the server application closing. This is not the case with Internet Explorer. Any and all open windows of Internet Explorer created through Automation remain open after your application terminates. To close Internet Explorer and all its windows, you must explicitly invoke the Quit method of the Internet Explorer Automation object:

```
objIE.Quit
```

Browsing a Specific Page or Document Using the Navigate Method

Navigating to specific Web sites is accomplished by using, intuitively enough, the Navigate method. The Navigate method enables you to browse and display any valid document supported by Internet Explorer. All that is required to browse to a document or Web page (keeping in mind that a Web page is simply a type of document) is the URL of the document. The URL (Uniform Resource Locator) is the address and name of the document, as you'll see.

Note: In addition to the Navigate method, Internet Explorer also has a Navigate2 method. This method exposes additional functionality of the Internet Explorer object but unfortunately this additional functionality cannot be used from within Visual Basic, only from C++.

As you can see by the following syntax of the Navigate method, you can exert some additional control over how Internet Explorer navigates to a URL by supplying values for some optional parameters.

The full syntax of the Navigate method is as follows:

```
explorerobject.Navigate url, [flags], [TargetFrameName], _
[PostData], [Headers]
```

The URL is the only required parameter, and it's often the only parameter used. The URL is simply the full address and filename of the document to browse. For example, to navigate to the main certification page at Microsoft's Web site, you would use the Navigate method:

```
objIE.Navigate "http://www.microsoft.com/train_cert/Internet Explorer0.htm"
```

To display the default document at a domain, simply provide the full address to the domain but do not provide a document name. For example, to navigate to the default home page at odintechnologies.com, you would use a statement such as this:

```
objIE.Navigate "http://www.odintechnologies.com"
```

As you might know from previous experience using Internet Explorer, Internet Explorer maintains a history list (sometimes called a resource list) of the most recently browsed pages and documents. This list makes the navigation buttons, Back and Forward, in the browser possible. The optional *Flags* parameter can be used to control how the currently displayed page or document is handled in the history list. The *Flags* parameter can also be used to force Internet Explorer to display the specified URL in a new window. The possible values for *Flags* are listed in Table 22.1.

Table 22.1. Possible values for the *Flags* parameter of the Navigate method.

Constant Name	Value	Description
navOpenInNewWindow	1	Open the resource or file in a new window.
navNoHistory	2	Do not add the document or file to the history list. The new page replaces the current page in the list.
navNoReadFromCache	4	Do not read from the disk cache for this navigation.
navNoWriteToCache	8	Do not write the results of this navigation to the disk cache.

If you want to use the named constants of the *Flags* parameter, instead of using the literal numbers, you must manually add them to your project:

```
Const navOpenInNewWindow =  1
Const navNoHistory = 2
Const navNoReadFromCache = 4
Const navNoWriteToCache = 8
```

Using the *Flags* parameter is simple. For example, to display Microsoft's home page in a new window, leaving the currently viewed page in its window, you could use a statement such as this:

```
objIE.Navigate "www.microsoft.com", navOpenInNewWindow
```

By default, whenever you navigate from one page to another, Internet Explorer adds to the history list the page from which you are navigating. If you do not want the page added to the history list, simply use the navNoHistory constant:

```
objIE.Navigate "http://www.odintechnologies.com", navNoHistory
```

Web pages are often large and complex, and even with fast modems, downloading a lot of text, graphics, and audio can take some time. To help minimize the amount of time required to display a page or document, Internet Explorer stores to its cache the components of recently viewed Web sites. When you attempt to navigate to a Web page, Internet Explorer first looks at its cache. If the page and its elements are stored in the cache, it uses them to display the document—almost instantly. Although this is a cool feature and can greatly reduce the amount of time needed to display a page or document, there are times when this behavior is undesirable. For example, some Web pages are built dynamically—such as those used to display current stock quotes. If Internet Explorer were to display these dynamic pages from information stored in its cache, you'd run the risk of displaying outdated information to the user.

You can tell Internet Explorer not to use information stored in its cache when displaying a page or document by specifying the navNoReadFromCache value in the *Flags* parameter:

```
objIE.Navigate "http://www.odintechnologies.com", navNoReadFromCache
```

The navNoReadFromCache parameter works great, but for sensitive pages where the user must always see the most accurate information, it might not always be enough. For example, suppose you display a page using the navNoReadFromCache setting. The user then decides to navigate to a different page directly using Internet Explorer's address bar. Finally, the user clicks the Back button to redisplay the page you originally specified. Because you are not programmatically displaying the page, you cannot control the cache behavior, and Internet Explorer might attempt to display the page using information in its cache. For such sensitive pages and documents, use the navNoWriteToCache parameter when displaying the URL. This prevents Internet Explorer from storing the page's information in its cache, forcing it to load the page from the original site the next time the page is viewed.

It is possible to combine multiple values using the OR parameter. For example, to display Microsoft's home page, forcing Internet Explorer to load the page from Microsoft's site—not from its cache—while preventing Internet Explorer from storing the site's information in its cache, you could use the following statement:

```
objIE.Navigate "http://www.microsoft.com/train_cert/Internet Explorer0.htm", _
navNoReadFromCache Or NavNoWriteToCache
```

Whereas frames were once a fringe feature of Web sites and could be displayed only by the most current browsers, frames are now an integral part of most Web sites. Using frames, a Web site can display many different HTML documents simultaneously. Web sites commonly use one frame to display a site navigation document while another frame displays a document selected by the visitor (see Figure 22.2). If you want to display a Web site in a specific frame instead of displaying it in the entire browser window, specify the desired frame's name in the *TargetFrameName* parameter.

FIGURE 22.2.

Frames add diversity to Web pages, and you can control what document displays in any specific frame.

Note: The *PostData* and *Headers* parameters require knowledge of HTML, and therefore only a short description of their application is offered here.

The *PostData* parameter is data to send to the server during the HTTP POST transaction. The POST transaction is most often used to send data gathered by an HTML form. If this parameter does not specify any post data, the Navigate method issues an HTTP GET transaction. This parameter is ignored if the URL is not an HTTP URL. This parameter is not often used because Web pages themselves can post data as necessary.

The *Headers* parameter is used to enter a value that specifies additional HTTP headers to send to the server. These headers are added to the default Internet Explorer headers and can specify such things as the action required of the server, the type of data being passed to the server, or a status code. This parameter is ignored if the URL is not an HTTP URL. Like the *PostData* parameter, the *Headers* parameter is an advanced HTML technique not often used when adding simple browsing capabilities to an application.

Navigating the History List

The Forward and Back buttons in Internet Explorer are used to navigate the history list—a list of the most recently browsed sites. You can achieve the same functionality in your applications by using the GoForward and GoBack methods of the Internet Explorer object, respectively.

To navigate back one page or document in the history list, use the GoBack method:

```
objIE.GoBack
```

To navigate one page or document forward in the history list, use the GoForward method:

```
objIE.GoForward
```

Displaying the User's Home Page or Search Page

In addition to duplicating the functionality found in Internet Explorer's Forward and Back buttons, you can also reproduce the behavior of Internet Explorer's Home and Search buttons. Internet Explorer's Home button allows the user one-click access to any Web site or document that she designates as her home page (sometimes referred to as *Start page* because it is the first page displayed when Internet Explorer is started). Users designate this page on their Internet Explorer's Options dialog box (see Figure 22.3).

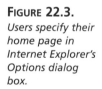

FIGURE 22.3.
Users specify their home page in Internet Explorer's Options dialog box.

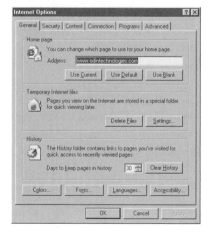

To display the Web page designated as the user's home page, invoke the GoHome method:

objIE.GoHome

To emulate Internet Explorer's Search button, which displays a Web site used to search the Internet, use the GoSearch method:

objIE.GoSearch

Using the Properties of the Internet Explorer Object

The Internet Explorer Automation object exposes several properties. Some of these properties are used to adjust the appearance of Internet Explorer, whereas others are used to extract information about the currently displayed document.

Changing the Appearance of Internet Explorer

Although you don't have total control over the appearance of Internet Explorer (for example, you can't add your own toolbars), you can alter the general appearance using properties of the Internet Explorer object. Table 22.2 lists the properties that affect the appearance of Internet Explorer.

Table 22.2. Appearance properties of the Internet Explorer object.

Property	Use
AddressBar	Returns or sets a value that determines whether Internet Explorer's URL address bar is visible or hidden.
FullScreen	Determines whether Internet Explorer appears in full-screen or normal window mode. When Internet Explorer is in full-screen mode, the title bar, borders, status bar, shortcut bar, and address bar of Internet Explorer are all hidden to dedicate as much space as possible to displaying the current page or document (see Figure 22.4).
TheaterMode	Performs the same functionality as FullScreen.
OffLine	Returns or sets a value indicating whether Internet Explorer is currently operating in offline mode. In offline mode, Internet Explorer is forced to read HTML pages from the local cache rather than from the source document.
MenuBar	Determines whether the Internet Explorer menu bar is visible or hidden.
StatusBar	Determines whether the Internet Explorer status bar is visible or hidden.
StatusText	Sets or returns the text for the status bar.
Toolbar	Determines whether the Internet Explorer toolbar is visible or hidden.

FIGURE 22.4.

When in full-screen mode, Internet Explorer uses as much screen space as possible to display Web pages and documents.

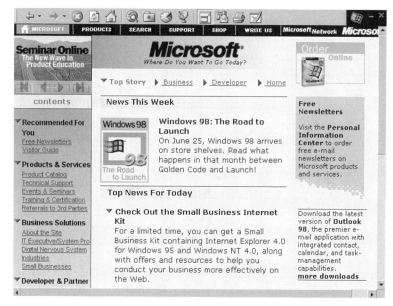

Getting the Path and Filename of Internet Explorer

At times, you might find it desirable to know the exact location in which Internet Explorer is installed on a user's computer. The Internet Explorer Automation object makes this easy by exposing the `FullName` property, which returns the path and executable name of Internet Explorer. For example, to display the full path and filename of Internet Explorer in a message box, you could use the following code:

```
MsgBox objIE.FullName
```

Gathering Information About the Currently Displayed Document

Internet Explorer is all about viewing documents. The various navigational methods give you control over displaying specific documents, but they don't give you any information about a document already displayed in the browser. You can gather specific information about the location and type of the currently displayed document using the properties listed in Table 22.3.

Table 22.3. Document information properties of Internet Explorer.

Property	Description
LocationName	Returns a string that contains the name of the page or document that Internet Explorer is currently displaying. If the page or document is an HTML page on the World Wide Web, the name is the title of that page.

continues

Table 22.3. Continued.

Property	Description
LocationURL	Returns a string that contains the URL of the page or document that Internet Explorer is currently displaying. If the page or document is a folder or file on the user's network or local computer, the name is the UNC or full path of the folder or file.
Type	Returns a string expression that specifies the type name of the contained document. Note: If Internet Explorer has not finished displaying the page, you will get an Automation error when you attempt to reference the Type property, so be sure to use error trapping when reading the Type property.

For example, review the code shown in Listing 22.1.

Listing 22.1. Retrieving document information.

```
Private Sub Command1_Click()
Dim objIE As New InternetExplorer
objIE.Visible = True
objIE.Navigate "http://www.microsoft.com"
Debug.Print objIE.LocationName
Debug.Print objIE.LocationURL
Debug.Print objIE.Type
End Sub
```

Listing 22.1 prints the following output:

```
Welcome to Microsoft's Homepage
http://www.microsoft.com/Internet Explorer0.htm
Microsoft HTML Document 4.0
```

Determining Whether Internet Explorer Is Busy

As you probably know, navigating to and displaying a Web page or document can take some time. There are many reasons for this, including busy servers, large bitmaps that must be downloaded, and so on. Fortunately, Internet Explorer runs in an asynchronous mode, meaning that it actually divides and allocates its processing time to display all the elements of a page or document and to accept user input. If Internet Explorer didn't performed these tasks asynchronously, it wouldn't be capable of responding to any user input until all elements of a page or document had been downloaded and displayed.

The Internet Explorer object includes a property that you can use to determine whether the Internet Explorer is engaged in a navigation or downloading operation: the Busy property. To determine whether Internet Explorer is busy, simply check the Busy property using code such as this:

```
If objIE.Busy Then
    ...
Else
    ...
End If
```

Using the WebBrowser Control

Although you can use Automation to control Internet Explorer, there might be times when you want to integrate Web browsing functionality directly on your own forms within your application. For example, you might want to create a limited browser that lets the user view only specific documents—perhaps help files for your application. Or perhaps you're a network administrator and you want to create a browser that keeps a log file of every page a user visits. In either of these cases, you might prefer to provide a simple browsing application that you've created and that gives you the control you want instead of having users work with the full Internet Explorer product. Using the Internet Explorer Automation object gives you control of Internet Explorer, but it does not allow you to embed a Web browser on your forms. Microsoft has created an ActiveX component specifically for this purpose: the WebBrowser control.

The WebBrowser control is simply a wrapper around the Internet Explorer Automation object, with a visual browser interface. With the WebBrowser control, you get capability to embed a Web browsing interface directly on any form in your application. You also get easy access to several events that give you even finer control of your custom browser.

> **Note:** The events of the WebBrowser control are also available when using the Internet Explorer Automation object, but using them requires advanced knowledge of Automation servers and is beyond the scope of this book.

Without the WebBrowser control, you could create a browser interface in your applications only by manually coding an application to decipher HTML documents on the Internet and display them visually—a massive undertaking. Because Microsoft has already done all this work, it's advantageous that it has exposed the functionality in an easy-to-use ActiveX control. The WebBrowser control, however, is not limited to displaying simple HTML files. The WebBrowser control can display any type of document that Internet Explorer can display because it is merely a wrapper around the Internet Explorer functionality. The WebBrowser control is also capable of displaying the following:

- Standard HTML and HTML enhancements, such as floating frames and cascading style sheets
- Other ActiveX controls
- Most Netscape plug-ins

- Scripting, such as Microsoft Visual Basic Scripting Edition (VBScript) or JavaScript Java applets
- Multimedia content, such as video and audio playback
- Three-dimensional virtual worlds created with Virtual Reality Modeling Language (VRML)
- ActiveX documents
- Microsoft Excel spreadsheets, Microsoft Word documents, and Microsoft PowerPoint presentations

Note: If Microsoft Office is not installed, the runtime viewers of each of these documents (Microsoft Excel spreadsheets, Microsoft Word documents, and Microsoft PowerPoint presentations) must be installed to view the document in the WebBrowser control.

In addition to viewing Web-related documents, the WebBrowser control can be used to browse folders on a local hard disk or on a local area network by simply entering a path in the URL field of the address bar. The WebBrowser control even maintains a history list that users can navigate to view previously browsed sites, folders, and documents (see Figure 22.5).

FIGURE 22.5.
The WebBrowser control can be used to browse local and network hard disk drives.

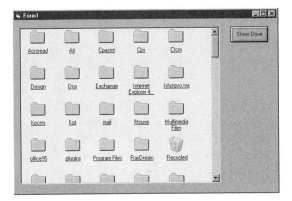

The WebBrowser control is located in the same DLL as the Internet Explorer Automation library: SHDOCVW.DLL. To add the WebBrowser control to a project, follow these steps:

1. Open the project to which you want to add the WebBrowser control.
2. Choose Project, Components to display the Components dialog box.

3. Locate and select the check box next to the Microsoft Internet Controls item (see Figure 22.6).

4. Click OK.

After you've added the control to the project, the WebBrowser appears as a globe in the toolbox. Figure 22.7 shows what the WebBrowser tool looks like once added to the toolbox.

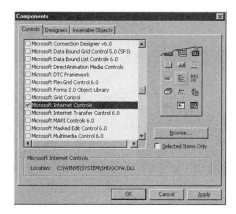

FIGURE 22.6.
The WebBrowser control is part of the Microsoft Internet Controls component.

FIGURE 22.7.
The WebBrowser control appears as a globe icon in the toolbox.

Although the WebBrowser control is a wrapper around the Internet Explorer Automation object, it does not expose all the functionality of the Automation object. As a result, several properties appear in the Properties window that don't actually affect the WebBrowser control. You can change these properties in code or in the Properties window, but changing them will not affect the appearance of the WebBrowser control.

The properties that do not affect the WebBrowser control are as follows:

- AddressBar
- FullScreen
- MenuBar

- StatusBar
- TheaterMode
- Toolbar

> **Note:** The property `StatusText` is completely unavailable for the WebBrowser control. Attempting to reference the `StatusText` property will generate a run-time error.

Understanding the WebBrowser Events

The WebBrowser control has several events to keep you informed and in control of what is happening as a user of your application browses and downloads files and documents. Table 22.4 lists the custom events of the WebBrowser control.

Table 22.4. Custom events of the WebBrowser control.

Event	Description
BeforeNavigate2	Occurs when the WebBrowser control is about to navigate to a new URL.
CommandStateChange	Occurs when the enabled state of a command changes.
DocumentComplete	Occurs when the document being navigated to is finished loading.
DownloadBegin	Occurs when a navigation operation is beginning, shortly after the BeforeNavigate event.
DownloadComplete	Occurs when a navigation operation is finished.
OnFullScreen	Occurs when the FullScreen property changes.
OnMenuBar	Occurs when the MenuBar property changes.
OnStatusBar	Occurs when the StatusBar property changes.
OnTheaterMode	Occurs when the TheaterMode property changes.
OnToolbar	Occurs when the ToolBar property changes.
OnVisible	Occurs when the Visible property changes.
NavigateComplete2	Occurs after the browser has successfully navigated to a new URL.
NewWindow2	Occurs when a new window is to be created for displaying a page or document.
ProgressChange	Occurs when the progress of a download is updated.
TitleChange	Occurs when the title of a document in the WebBrowser control becomes available or changes.

> **Note:** As Microsoft releases updates to the WebBrowser control, it continues to add new events. Often, these new events parallel existing events but have added functionality. Because it is against the basic principles of COM to change the interface of a property, method, or event, these new events must be given new names. These enhanced events have been given the names of the events they were based on, ending in the number 2. For example, the WebBrowser has an enhanced `BeforeNavigate` event called `BeforeNavigate2`.

Although some of the events are intuitive, such as the `On...` events that fire when a property changes, others require some explanation and are therefore explored in detail in the following sections.

The `BeforeNavigate2` Event

The `BeforeNavigate2` event occurs when the WebBrowser control is about to navigate to a different URL. All the data related to navigating to the Web page or document is passed into this event. If you want to stop the WebBrowser control from navigating to this new page or document, set the `Cancel` property of the event to `True`.

The code in Listing 22.2 shows a simple child protection filter implemented using the `BeforeNavigate2` event. It assumes that a URL with XXX in it is an adult site and prevents the browser from displaying the specified URL.

Listing 22.2. Code to implement a simple child protection filter.

```
Private Sub WebBrowser1_BeforeNavigate2(ByVal pDisp As Object, _
URL As Variant, Flags As Variant, TargetFrameName As Variant, _
PostData As Variant, Headers As Variant, Cancel As Boolean)

If (InStr(1, URL, "xxx") <> 0) Then
   MsgBox "Access denied to URL: " & URL
   Cancel = True
End If

End Sub
```

The `CommandStateChange` Event

The `CommandStateChange` event occurs when the enabled state of a command changes. The following is the declaration of the `CommandStateChange` event:

```
Private Sub WebBrowser1_CommandStateChange(ByVal Command As Long,
➡ByVal Enable As Boolean)
```

The three possible values for `Command` are listed in Table 22.5.

Table 22.5. Possible values of Command in the CommandStateChange event.

Constant	Value	Meaning
CSC_UPDATECOMMANDS	-1	The enabled state of a toolbar button might have changed; the Enable parameter should be ignored.
CSC_NAVIGATEFORWARD	1	The enabled state of the Forward button has changed.
CSC_NAVIGATEBACK	2	The enabled state of the Back button has changed.

You can use the CommandStateChange event to enable and disable command buttons in your application used to perform these functions. For example, if you've created a custom browser by embedding a WebBrowser control on a form, you will need your custom Forward and Back buttons to enable and disable appropriately as the user browses Web sites. Sample code used to do this is shown in Listing 22.3.

Listing 22.3. Dynamically enabling and disabling custom navigational buttons.

```
Private Sub WebBrowser1_CommandStateChange(ByVal Command As Long,
➥ByVal Enable As Boolean)
Const CSC_UPDATECOMMANDS = -1
Const CSC_NAVIGATEFORWARD = 1
Const CSC_NAVIGATEBACK = 2

Select Case Command
   Case Is = CSC_NAVIGATEFORWARD
      cmdForward.Enabled = Enable
   Case Is = CSC_NAVIGATEBACK
      cmdBack.Enabled = Enable
End Select

End Sub
```

The DownloadBegin Event

The DownloadBegin event occurs when a download operation begins. This event is fired shortly after the BeforeNavigate event unless the navigation is canceled. The DownloadBegin event is a great place to put any animation or "busy" indication to show the user a download is in progress. All DownloadBegin events have a corresponding DownloadComplete event, as discussed in the next section.

The DownloadComplete Event

The DownloadComplete event occurs when a download operation has finished, was halted, or failed. Unlike NavigateComplete2, which is fired only when a URL is successfully navigated to, this event is always fired after a navigation starts. You can use this event to update any status information or animation that you initialized in the DownloadBegin event.

The NavigateComplete2 Event

The NavigateComplete2 event occurs after the WebBrowser control has successfully navigated to a new location. The page or document might still be downloading (and in the case of HTML pages, images might still be downloading), but at least part of the document has been received from the server, and the viewer for the document has been created.

The NewWindow2 Event

By default, navigating to a new page or document causes the WebBrowser control to display the new page in the current browser window, replacing the currently viewed URL. Under the circumstances listed in the following list, Web pages can be displayed in a new window, leaving the current page in its own window. The NewWindow2 event occurs when a new window is created to display a document instead of the document replacing the one currently being viewed.

A new window is created under the following circumstances:

- A user Shift-clicks a link.
- A user right-clicks a link and selects Open in new window.
- A navigation is targeted to a frame name that does not exist.

The ProgressChange Event

The ProgressChange event occurs when the progress of a download operation is updated. Use the ProgressChange event to display the status of an operation. The ProgressChange event passes you two parameters: a Progress parameter and ProgressMax parameter. The Progress parameter is the amount of progress to show, whereas the ProgressMax parameter specifies the maximum progress value. The Progress parameter will be -1 when the progress is fully complete.

For example, if a user downloads a file from a Web site, the ProgressChange event will fire periodically as the file is downloaded. The ProgressMax value will be the total number of bytes to download and will not change. However, the value of the Progress parameter will change to reflect the number of bytes downloaded. The code in Listing 22.4 uses the Progress and ProgressMax parameters to compute a percentage complete of the operation and displays this percentage in a label's caption.

Listing 22.4. Code to display the percentage progress of a download.

```
Private Sub WebBrowser1_ProgressChange(ByVal Progress As Long,
➥ByVal ProgressMax As Long)

Label1.Caption = (Progress * 100) / ProgressMax
DoEvents' Let the label update

End Sub
```

The `TitleChange` Event

The `TitleChange` event fires when the title of a page or document changes. Although not immediately apparent, titles of Web pages almost always change as you download them. For example, while downloading an HTML Web page, the title of the page is set to the URL of the page. After the real title is parsed from the HTML document (sometime during the download of the page), the title is changed to reflect the actual title and the `TitleChange` event fires.

The code in Listing 22.5 is all the code necessary to create the simple Web browser shown in Figure 22.8. To create the Web browser, add the controls listed in Table 22.6 to a form; then enter the code shown in Listing 22.5 to the form's module. (The sample browser exists in its entirety on the accompanying CD-ROM.)

FIGURE 22.8.

A custom Web browser is easily created using the WebBrowser control.

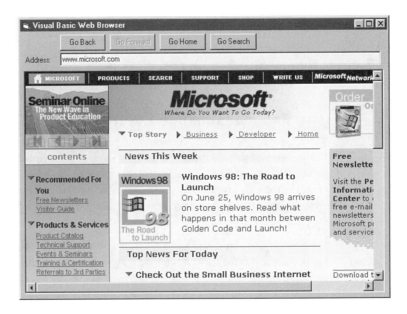

Table 22.6. Controls for a simple Web browser.

Control	Name
Command button	cmdGoBack
Command button	cmdGoForward
Command button	cmdGoHome
Command button	cmdGoSearch
Label	Label1
Text box	txtAddress
WebBrowser	WebBrowser1

Listing 22.5. Complete code for a simple Web browser.

```
Private Sub cmdGoBack_Click()
   WebBrowser1.GoBack
End Sub


Private Sub cmdGoForward_Click()
   WebBrowser1.GoForward
End Sub


Private Sub cmdGoHome_Click()
   WebBrowser1.GoHome
End Sub

Private Sub cmdGoSearch_Click()
   WebBrowser1.GoSearch
End Sub


Private Sub txtAddress_KeyPress(KeyAscii As Integer)
   If KeyAscii = 13 Then
      WebBrowser1.Navigate txtAddress.Text
   End If
End Sub


Private Sub WebBrowser1_CommandStateChange(ByVal Command As Long,
➥ByVal Enable As Boolean)
   Const CSC_NAVIGATEFORWARD = 1
   Const CSC_NAVIGATEBACK = 2
```

continues

Listing 22.5. Continued.

```
Select Case Command
   Case Is = CSC_NAVIGATEFORWARD
      cmdGoForward.Enabled = Enable
   Case Is = CSC_NAVIGATEBACK
      cmdGoBack.Enabled = Enable
End Select

End Sub
```

The WebBrowser control lets you easily add robust Web browsing capabilities to your applications. Remember, however, that you cannot distribute the WebBrowser control to other users. For the WebBrowser control to be used within your application, users of the application must have the full version of Internet Explorer installed on their computers.

Summary

The power of ActiveX gives you the capability to create powerful Web browsing functionality for your applications. The purpose of this functionality is left up to you. You might want to give users easy access to your Web site for sales support reasons, or you might want to include online HTML help files with your application and give users a controlled environment for viewing those files; the possibilities are vast, and the decisions are up to you.

Whether you choose to automate Internet Explorer or use the WebBrowser control directly within your program, Visual Basic and Internet Explorer make it easy to add robust Web functionality to any application.

Web Development with Visual Basic 6

With the direction that programming is taking these days, everyone is at least aware of the importance of the Internet. Whether through true understanding or media hype, businesses want to get on the Web in increasing numbers. The problem is that getting applications running on the Internet is not as simple as recompiling and deploying. The process of how everything works together must be entirely rethought. This chapter, together with the next, gives you some of the basis for that thought.

In this chapter, you explore the creation of ActiveX controls for Web use. Before Visual Basic 5, it was difficult to build components for use on the Web. But, first with the Control Creation edition of Visual Basic 5 and then the full version, a programmer no longer had to learn C, C++, or Delphi to create components. Now the average Visual Basic programmer need only be versed in a few additional skills to be able to create entirely portable and reusable ActiveX components for use on the Web.

Although this chapter deals primarily with creating ActiveX components for use on the Web, you also learn how to use the component you create in a Web page and how to interact with that control using VBScript. You learn more about VBScript in the next chapter, but a few words of introduction are given here.

To take advantage of the examples in this chapter, you need Visual Basic and an ActiveX-enabled Web browser. At this time, that means you need Microsoft's Internet Explorer.

Understanding Scripting Versus Components

When you create an ActiveX control in Visual Basic, or any other language for that matter, you are creating a self-contained object of specific behavior and capability. Whether the control is a simple type of button or a complicated engineering engine, the control is essentially an encapsulated operation.

The control usually accepts input of one type or another, it might perform some action, and it makes results available or calls other controls. Throughout all this—and it has been simplified here—you do not get into the innards of the control or interact with it in an undefined manner. One advantage to controls of this type is that you can get them from someone else, drop them on your project—be it Web site or program—and just use the controls without having to understand all the nuances of what they are doing. The disadvantage is that rarely do controls come out of the box exactly as you want them. It is at this point that the scripting comes into play.

Using VBScript to interface with and adjust the settings of your ActiveX controls, you can modify their behavior and use their result to create applications that act as you want them to. Microsoft has billed VBScript as the glue needed to assemble applications out of various objects, be they user created, system inherent or purchased from third parties.

Understanding the Difference Between ActiveX Controls and Visual Basic Documents

In addition to creating ActiveX controls, Visual Basic can also be used to create Visual Basic documents for use within the context of a container, such as the Internet Explorer Web browser. Just as a word processing document must be viewed within a word processor to be used, a Visual Basic document must be viewed or used within an appropriate container. The difference between a document and a control is that the document represents the entire program, not just a single encapsulated operation. The difference between a Visual Basic document and a Visual Basic standalone EXE, other than the way they are compiled, is that the standalone EXE needs no other program to run.

Creating an ActiveX Control for the Web

To create an ActiveX control for the Web, as with all programming projects, you should make a few decisions first. These include

- What the component is to do
- What its interface will look like
- What methods, properties, or events it will expose

For this chapter, you are going to create a control called SimpleCalc. It will have a Label control that will display an integer value, two buttons for adding or subtracting one from the number, one method for setting the number's initial value, and one property—the value of the number. This is an extremely basic control with no real useful purpose, but it demonstrates all the steps you must go through to create a real deployable component.

Creating the New Control

Start Visual Basic and select ActiveX Control to create a new control. The control pad
icon displayed in the selection screen is one that you will see later when you use your
control (see Figure 23.1).

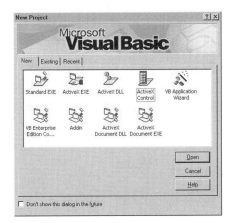

FIGURE 23.1.
*The Visual Basic
opening screen
gives you the
chance to estab-
lish what type of
project you are
creating.*

You will have one user control named `UserControl1`. Before going any further, make
sure that the control is selected; go to the properties for `UserControl1` and set the name
to `SimpleCalc`. Your environment should now look something like Figure 23.2.

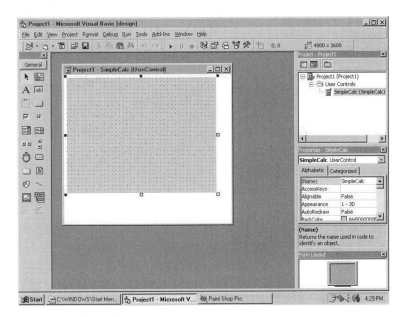

FIGURE 23.2.
*Other than the
indication of
controls in the
Project window,
there is little dif-
ference in the ini-
tial programming
environment for
an ActiveX control
from that of a
normal program.*

Now complete the following steps to create the new control:

1. Put a command button on the control and change the button's name to cmdCountUp.

2. Change the button's caption to Count Up.

3. Put a second command button on the control and change the button's name to cmdCountDown.

4. Change the button's caption to Count Down.

5. Drop a label control on the form.

6. Change its name to lblValue and its caption to 0.

Take the opportunity to save your project. Click the Save button and save your control as SimpleCalc.ctl and the project as SimpleCalc.vbp. Your project should now resemble the one in Figure 23.3.

FIGURE 23.3.
The user interface of your ActiveX control is now complete.

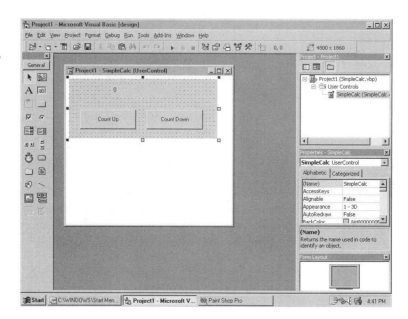

Now you can add the code behind this form.

Adding the Code Behind the Form

When you begin adding code, first add just a bit of initialization code. Because this is a simple control, make sure that the label control does in fact contain the number 0. To do this, double-click any open area of the control. This takes you to the code window with the Initialize routine. You will be adding only one line of code, so the entire subroutine will read

```
Private Sub UserControl_Initialize()
    lblCount.caption = cstr(0)
End Sub
```

Before moving on, look at the manner in which that subroutine is declared. Remember that by declaring it private, it can be used only internally and cannot be accessed by a programmer trying to manipulate the control.

Next, get to the code window for the cmdCountUp button. You can do this by double-clicking on the cmdCountUp button or by selecting the appropriate control in the drop-down box of the code window. You should be taken to the Click event of the button, the button's default value. One line of code will go in this event:

```
lblCount.caption = cstr(cint(lblCount.caption) +1)
```

In the same way, set the code for the cmdCountDown button. The code will be the same except that it will subtract one from the value of lblCount. It should read

```
lblCount.caption = cstr(cint(lblCount.caption) -1)
```

You still have not added the properties or methods to the control, but now is a good time to test, so click the Save button.

Because controls cannot be run alone, to test the control you must add a standard EXE project, close your control's windows, and place an instance of the control on a form of the new EXE project. Either choose File, New or select Add Standard EXE Project from the button bar.

Make sure that you have closed the windows for your simple control. Do not remove the project or anything, just close the window. As soon as you do, the icon for your simple control should appear on the bottom of your toolbar. Click and drop an instance of the control onto Form1 of your new project and resize as necessary. Your project should now look something like Figure 23.4.

FIGURE 23.4.

You can see your control used on the new form, as well as the icon representing it.

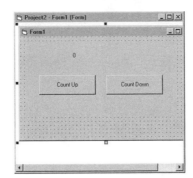

Now run the new project to see your component in action. The label should have a count of 0 to start with and then increment or decrement by one every time the appropriate button is clicked.

At this point, you have a fully functional control; however, it has no contact with the outside world. In other words, there is no way for other programs to set or inquire about the control's value. To do this, you must create a property that can be used to get the value of the component and a method that can be used to set the value of the component. Now go back to the control and add a property to be seen.

Adding Properties and Methods to Your Web Control

As with many things in Visual Basic, there are many ways to create methods and properties. The one you learn here is one of the more simple and dependable methods.

To start, complete the following steps:

1. Choose Add-Ins, Add-In Manager from the menu. From that screen, make sure that VB Active X Control Interface Wizard is checked. If not, check it now.

2. Click OK to return to the main screen and then choose the Add-In menu again. You can now select the new menu choice of Active X Control Interface Wizard, which should be available.

3. After starting the wizard, you see a general information dialog box. Clicking the Next button takes you to a screen where you can select interface members for your control. These are properties of elements in your control that you can choose to expose to other programs or scripting. For our purposes, we want none of these, so clear the list by clicking the button that looks like two less-than signs to move everything from the Selected Names list to the Available Names list (see Figure 23.5). Then click the Next button to proceed.

FIGURE 23.5.

Using the Select Interface Members dialog box, you can map properties and methods of controls used in your control directly to your interface.

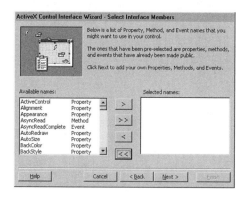

4. On the page to add your one property and method, first click the New button.

5. From the Add Custom Member dialog box, type `Value` in the text box and click that this is a property; then click OK. Next add another new member named `SetValue`. `SetValue` should be a method.

6. On the next page, you could map a property, method, or event directly to one of the same type on a control. In this, case you want the value function to return a filtered value of the txtCount's caption property. Because this takes only a little bit of code manipulation after the wizard is complete, you should do the mapping here. First, highlight the Value line in the list; then select Maps to control lblCount and Member caption. Then click Next.

7. On the Set Attributes page, you can specify the values accepted and returned by the SetValue method. Because the Value property takes its specifications from the caption property of lblCount, it does not appear here (see Figure 23.6).

FIGURE 23.6.

Establishing property and method interfaces is simple with the wizard interface.

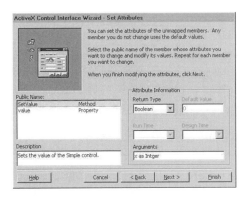

8. For the SetValue method, set the Return Type to Boolean. This will be used to determine whether the value was set correctly.

9. Set the arguments to x as Integer because an integer will be passed to set the value.

10. Enter some description of the function purpose in the Description field.

11. Click the Next button to go to the next screen. This displays the final action of the wizard, which is to create a report of what is done to finish creation of an ActiveX control. Although this is an odd place to put this information, and we have gone over most of it here, it is useful to save, print out, and read at least once. I say only once because the report is always the same and contains no information specific to your control.

12. Save your project, and then go to the code window for the control.

By using the wizard, a good deal of code has been added for you. The most important code is the SetValue function and the Value function. Notice that both of these are declared as public. That means that other controls, code, or script can interface with your control through these properties and methods.

As helpful as the wizard is, there is one danger. If you use the wizard after you have already created code for events, properties, or methods of a control, that code can be altered or deleted by the wizard. So either do not reuse the wizard after you have made changes, or save those changes elsewhere so they can be reapplied through copy and paste if they are lost.

Changing the Code Functionality

To make the code functionality work the way you want, though, you must first make some changes to this code. Find the function that reads

```
Public Property Get Value() As String
    Value = lblCount.Caption
End Property
```

This would be fine except that you want the Value property to return the integer value of the control, which is the result of the calculation. To do this, simply change the code line to read

```
Value = CInt(lblCount.Caption)
```

Because you want the Value property to be accessed only through the SetValue method and not written to directly, delete the Public Property Let Value function.

Finally, add the code for the SetValue function. This function accepts an integer, sets the value of the control, and then passes back a Boolean value indicating whether the operation was a success. The code for this is as follows:

```
Public Function SetValue(x As Integer) As Boolean
    SetValue = False 'set initial return value
    lblCount.Caption = CStr(x) 'set the value of the label control
    If CInt(lblCount.Caption) = x Then   'test to see if it worked
        SetValue = True 'if it worked return true
    End If 'if not the initial false value will be returned
End Function
```

As commented, the code basically accepts a value, converts it to a string, and assigns it to the label control. A test is then performed to see whether it worked and either a True or False value is passed back.

To test that this all works, go back to your EXE project and add two buttons and a text box to the form. Name the text box txtValue and the buttons cmdSetValue and cmdGetValue.

In the code for cmdSetValue, add these lines:

```
Private Sub cmdSetValue_Click()
    If SimpleCalc1.SetValue(CInt(txtValue.Text)) Then 'convert and then
    ➥pass the value of the text box to the control
        MsgBox ("Succeeded") 'if the action is successful, say so
```

```
    Else
        MsgBox ("Failed") 'if not, say it failed
    End If
End SubTest it all
```

This simply takes whatever value you type into the text box, converts it to a value, and passes it to your SimpleCalc control. Notice that because the properties and methods of your control are exposed, Visual Basic's Intellisense even kicks in with the proper information on the control. With this code, you are also checking to see whether the action succeeds and displays an appropriate message box.

In the code for cmdGetValue, add this single line:

```
txtValue.Text = CInt(SimpleCalc1.Value)
```

This simply gets the value through the property you created and assigns it to the text box.

Your test application should now look something like Figure 23.7, and now it is time to save and test. The application is not complex, but it does show how the interaction with the ActiveX control works. When a value is entered into the text box and then the Set Value button is clicked, that value is transferred to the control where it can be added to or subtracted from. The result can then be retrieved into the text box by clicking the Get Value button.

FIGURE 23.7.
Your control and test applications are now fully functional.

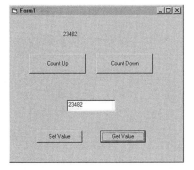

In real life, other than the fact that there would not be much use for such a simple control, you would want to add error checking and much more. But for this chapter, the control serves its purpose.

Deploying Your Web Control

Now comes the moment you have been waiting for—the time when you get to send your control off to live on the Web. In one sense, this is simple. The installed control is referenced on a page, and there it is. On the other hand, this doesn't address the issues of installing the control or identifying it after it is there. To accomplish these tasks, you must compile the control, package it up, and deploy it.

The compile is basically the same as compiling a Visual Basic EXE. Make sure that the control project is selected in Visual Basic and then choose File, Make Simplecalc.ocx from the menu. You can select the name of the resulting OCX when you do this, and you can click the Options button to set up some things about the OCX. Because most of the options have been covered elsewhere, the most important one for controls to be deployed over the Web is on the Compile tab. Pay particular attention to optimizations depending on your audience (see Figure 23.8).

FIGURE 23.8.
Through the options of the OCX compile, you can fine-tune the OCX to your delivery environment.

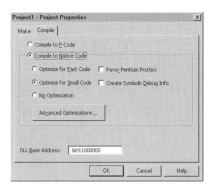

Compiling Your Control

If your control will be used over an intranet where you must have a lot of bandwidth and know the target machines, you might select to optimize for speed and favor Pentium Pros. However, over the open Internet, it usually makes more sense to optimize for size, to reduce download time, and not favor a particular machine or processor.

After you have selected your options, click OK and compile your OCX. You now have an OCX ready to go somewhere, and you just need the transport.

Creating the Setup for Your Control

To provide transport, you must create an installation file. For the next steps, you must get out of Visual Basic and use the Setup program. Exit Visual Basic, but before starting the Application Setup Wizard, create a location on your system to store the setup files. For this example, create a new folder called C:\VB23.

After you have created the folder, run the Application Setup Wizard, which should be located in your Visual Basic group, and follow these steps:

1. Skipping the Introduction screen takes you to the Select Project and Options screen. Click the Browse button and select the project file you created for this chapter. This should be `simple.vbp`.

2. In the Options section, select Create Internet Download Setup. This tells the Setup Wizard to package your files in a manner that can be distributed over the Web.

3. Specify the directory you created as the destination for the setup files to be placed. If there is an existing setup of the same name in that directory, you are asked to confirm that those files should be overwritten.

4. On the next screen (see Figure 23.9), you specify where to get the additional run-time components of your control. You can select to have these components down-loaded from the Microsoft site, the Web site on which your component resides, or a third-party site. The advantages of each are listed in Table 23.1. For this exam-ple, you want the components downloaded from your site, so click the Use Alternate Location button, but leave the location field blank.

FIGURE 23.9.

Depending on your deployment environment, you can have support-ing files down-loaded from your site, Microsoft's site, or a third party's site.

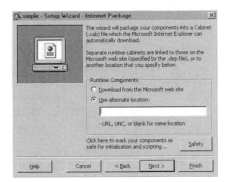

Table 23.1. Component download selection option.

Site	Advantages	Disadvantages
Microsoft	Most Current	Slow over some lines
Component site	Faster for intranet	Not always the most
	Known version of	current
	component	Additional maintenance
	May be the only	and space required
	choice if you are	
	behind a firewall	
Third party	May be the source	Unpredictable behavior
	if from that party	Could still be slow over
	Could be faster	some lines
	than a busy	
	Microsoft site	

5. Also in Figure 23.9 is an important button that is almost hidden. By clicking the Safety button, the component developer can mark the packaged components as safe for initialization and scripting. This is the message that gets passed to the browser when the component is loaded. Because the developer is on the honor system to label these settings correctly, it is important to know what they mean.

There has been much concern both in the media and among actual users about the behavior of controls acting on a PC. By specifying that your controls are safe, you are personally guaranteeing that your control will not do things such as read or write to the user's hard drive with a scripted filename, send commands to other applications, read or write to script-defined locations in the Windows Registry, or call script-defined or potentially volatile Windows API functions.

Basically, you are assuring a user that not only did you not create a hostile control, but that your control cannot be used by someone else in a hostile manner. Although this can be difficult to ensure, it is important to honestly do your best to do so.

6. On the next screen, the Setup Wizard identifies any additional server components on which your control might be dependent. Also, if it missed any, you could add those dependencies here.

7. After going to the next screen, the wizard begins assessing all the files that must be included in the setup file. While doing so, it asks whether you want to include the Property Page DLL. This DLL should be included if you expect anyone to use your control in design time, not just runtime. For most installations it is best to include the DLL, so answer Yes.

8. Now all the files that must be included in the setup are shown. This is your last chance to include any additional files that might be needed or to check that no extraneous files are included. You can also check the path to which each file will be installed by clicking File Details. The total number and size of all files included in the setup distribution can be checked by clicking the Summary Details button (see Figure 23.10).

FIGURE 23.10.
The File Summary screen tells you the size of the final setup you will be deploying.

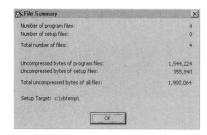

9. On the next screen, you can then save the template for the setup project. This is a good thing to do, even if you think this particular setup will never be used again, because invariably some file gets left out or some modification must be made to the ActiveX control. If you have saved the template for the setup, you can simply walk through the entire wizard accepting the defaults and make short work of the entire process.

10. Clicking the Finish button completes the creation of your setup distribution and also creates a sample Web page to test your control. As the setup program warns, if you are going to distribute your control, always scan it for viruses before distribution.

After you have finished creating the setup for your control, you should test it.

Testing Your Control in a Web Page

Now that you have a Web page with your control imbedded, let's take a look at it. Start Internet Explorer and browse to the location where your distribution setup was created. If you followed the preceding example, this should be C:\VB23. When you look in that directory, there should be two files and a subdirectory (see Figure 23.11). The `simple.cab` file is the actual setup file. It contains your ActiveX control and the installation instruction. The `simple.htm` file is the test Web page. The subdirectory contains the uncompressed version of all the files in the `simple.cab` file.

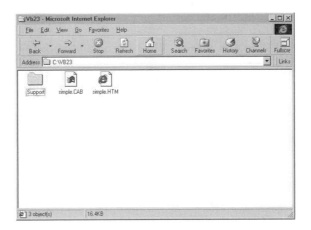

FIGURE 23.11.
The setup program creates an HTM page to test your installation from, as well as the CAB installation file.

Double-clicking the `simple.cab` file loads your test page into the browser (see Figure 23.12). You should see your control, just as it appeared in Visual Basic, waiting for you to click buttons to add and subtract numbers. If you transferred this page and the `simple.cab` file up to a Web server, you could make this wonderful application available to anyone hitting your page. To understand what is happening, you must look at the source code behind the page, though.

Enabling a Control Through Script

We will save the full discussion of scripting for the next chapter, but let's look at what this simple page does. In your browser, choose View, Source from the menu, and the code in Listing 23.1 should be displayed.

FIGURE 23.12.
Your control is now fully capable of being used in Web pages.

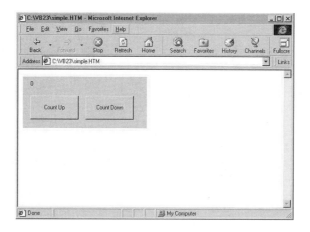

Listing 23.1. The code generated by the setup program includes the necessary object calls to your ActiveX control.

```
<HTML>
<!-- If any of the controls on this page require licensing, you must
     create a license package file. Run LPK_TOOL.EXE to create the
     required LPK file. LPK_TOOL.EXE can be found on the ActiveX SDK,
     http://www.microsoft.com/intdev/sdk/sdk.htm. If you have the Visual
     Basic 5.0 CD, it can also be found in the \Tools\LPK_TOOL directory.

     The following is an example of the Object tag:

<OBJECT CLASSID="clsid:5220cb21-c88d-11cf-b347-00aa00a28331">
    <PARAM NAME="LPKPath" VALUE="LPKfilename.LPK">
</OBJECT>
-->

<OBJECT ID="ctlSimple" WIDTH=269 HEIGHT=107
CLASSID="CLSID:F91E3149-0452-11D2-9FAC-DC3150775865"
CODEBASE="simple.CAB#version=1,0,0,0">
</OBJECT>
</HTML>
```

Although a full HTML tutorial is not appropriate here, a few words of explanation are necessary. All Web pages are created using code called Hypertext Markup Language, or HTML. HTML consists of codes that tell a browser how to interpret what is presented on a page. HTML is made up of pairs of tags. All tags open with a keyword between brackets, such as <HTML>, and close with the same keyword preceded by a slash character between brackets, such as </HTML>. Certain tags take modifiers to elaborate on the formatting. For example, a paragraph tag <P> can take an alignment modifier to specify how the text should be aligned, such as <p align="CENTER">. Everything between the two tags is interpreted as the tags dictate. Table 23.2 lists some of the most important tags.

Table 23.2. Commonly used HTML tags.

Tag Pair	Function
`<HTML></HTML>`	Marks the beginning and end of a Web page.
`<TITLE></TITLE>`	The text between these tags does not appear on the page but becomes the title of the page that appears in the browser title bar.
`<BODY></BODY>`	Marks the beginning and end of the text area of a Web page.
`<P></P>`	Marks the beginning and end of a paragraph.
`<!--><-->`	Marks the beginning and end of a comment section that will not display on the page. Note the exception to the closing backslash rule.
`<OBJECT></OBJECT>`	Marks the definition of an object on the page.
`<SCRIPT></SCRIPT>`	Marks the beginning and end of a script section. The script itself is not displayed on the page, only whatever results are dictated.

If you look back now at the source code of your test page, you will notice that lines 2 through 13 are all comments. Even though an object tag is imbedded within those lines, it will be ignored because the entire block has been marked as a comment.

What you are concerned with right now starts at line 15. This is the declaration of your SimpleCalc control. Notice that an ID of `ctlSimple` is specified. This is the same as the name of a control in Visual Basic, and you use it the same way in the next section. After the ID is a specification of the viewable interface of the control. By default, this is set to the exact size the control was created.

Next, a `CLASSID` is specified. This ID is a unique identifier generated when the control was compiled. No two controls will ever have the same identifier. This means that when you deploy your control to the Internet, it is uniquely identifiable. Never change this ID manually; always let a program, such as the Setup Wizard, insert it, and if you must move it, use copy and paste. Your page or application is guaranteed to crash if this `CLASSID` is even slightly messed up. Finally, you will see the `CODEBASE`. This specifies what distribution file and version is used to create the control. This is how a browser that doesn't have the control already knows how to go get the control. All this object definition ends with the closing object tag.

With this page, your control appears on a Web page. Notice no other text is on the page; not even a body section. In other words, your page does nothing but display the control. In the next section, you learn how to interact with the control.

Interacting with Your Control in a Web Page

Now that your control is on the page, you can use the property and method you develop to interact with it. To do so, you add just a few simple lines of VBScript.

First, establish a body section in your HTML. After the closing </OBJECT> tag on your simple.htm page, you must insert both opening and closing body tags.

After that, between the two body tags, you should open a scripting area, set the value of the control, and then test to see whether the value was set correctly and write the appropriate message out to the screen. To do all of this, you must modify your simple.htm page to Listing 23.2. Notice that the comment area has been deleted for clarity.

Listing 23.2. By adding simple VBScript to the code created by the setup program, you can interact with your control.

```
<HTML>
<OBJECT ID="ctlSimple" WIDTH=269 HEIGHT=107
CLASSID="CLSID:F91E3149-0452-11D2-9FAC-DC3150775865"
CODEBASE="simple.CAB#version=1,0,0,0">
</OBJECT>
<body>
<script language="VBSCRIPT">
document.open
document.write "<P>"
if ctlSimple.setvalue(23) then
    document.write "Succesfully set Value to " & ctlSimple.value
else
    document.write "Didn't work. Value is still" & ctlSimple.value
end if
document.write "</P>"
document.write "Done"
document.close
</script>
</body>
</HTML>
```

Starting after the body is declared, notice that the next line is a script declaration. Here, you let the browser know that the following lines are script and what language the script is written in. The next command, document.open, enables writing to the document area of the browser. This should be done before trying to write to the screen. The following line, document.write "<P>", starts a paragraph using the tag specified in Table 23.2.

On the line starting with the condition, you are using the control's ID and SetValue method to establish a value for the control. Notice that this is exactly as it would be done in standard Visual Basic and that you use the Boolean return value to test for the success of the operation. If the operation was a success, a line is written to the screen that shows the current value of the object. Again, you use the control ID and the name of the property you created earlier. If for some reason the SetValue method returns an error, you write a line out to the screen indicating that. Then you close your If...then...Else statement with an End If.

The next two lines again write directly to the browser screen. The first one simply writes out the word Done, and the second closes out the paragraph opened a few lines before. Remember that paragraph tags, like all other HTML tags, come in pairs, and you must close what you open. Finally, you also close the </SCRIPT> command.

After saving your changes, click the Refresh button in your browser. The control comes up along with an indication of your success (see Figure 23.13). Again, although this is not a complicated, or even very useful, application of the technology, it does demonstrate what you can accomplish with ActiveX controls in an intranet application.

FIGURE 23.13.
You have now created a fully interactive Web page using an ActiveX control programmed in Visual Basic.

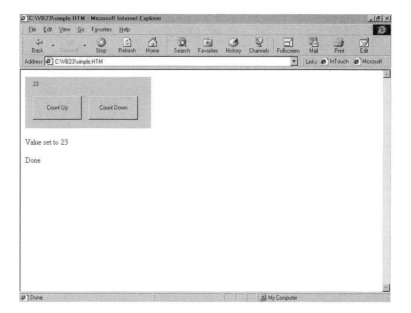

Summary

In this chapter, you learned how to create a fully functional ActiveX control for use on the Web. Additionally, you saw how that control can be deployed and used in a Web page. In the next chapter, you will gain a broader understanding of scripting and learn how you can decide what the browser displays even before it is sent from the server.

Creating Intranet Applications

Until recently—most of the short history of the World Wide Web—Web pages were static pages of formatted information. For the most part, what one person saw on a page was exactly the same as what the next person saw. It didn't matter whether the people spoke different languages, used different types of computers, lived in different countries, or had different interests. If they went to the same page, they saw the same thing. This was nice in a way, but not very exciting after the second or third trip. Scripting changed all this.

With scripting you can have active pages. What you see on your Web browser can be tailored to you. What you see can be tuned to the version of the browser you are using, a question you have answered, or even what time of day it is—either in your location or where the server resides. Although some of this capability has been available for a while through the use of UNIX scripts and CGI programs, not until recently did scripting of pages reach a level where non-UNIX gurus could feel comfortable doing it. With the development of JavaScript and VBScript, scripting has moved into the arena of the average programmer.

This chapter explores how you can use VBScript to enhance and control the presentation of information to a Web browser. VBScript, a subset of VBA, is directly related to Visual Basic, and all your hard-earned skills will pay off here. In addition, the common notions of client/server technology are familiar here, though pieces of the pie have changed plates slightly. At the end of the chapter, you also get an introductory glance at using ActiveX Data Objects (ADO) to pull database information into your Web pages with VBScript. These basic scripts are the foundation of a full-blown application that you should feel comfortable exploring after you have finished.

Comparing Client-Side and Server-Side Scripting

The scripting of what a browser displays can happen in basically two different places, the server or the client. If the scripting takes place on the server, then the script is actually run by the server, and only the results are passed down to the client browser. If the script is run on the client, then the server totally ignores the script and simply hands it off to the browser to be run.

In the preceding chapter, all the scripting done to the ActiveX control was performed on the client. If you know that a page performs scripting but do not know whether it is server side, there is one easy way to tell. Simply go to the menu of your browser and choose View, Source. If you see the source code for the script, then it is client side. If you do not see the code, then it was executed on the server.

One advantage of server-side scripting is that it can be essentially browser independent. If you write a script to be executed by the client, you must be aware that the browser will execute the script and take its interpretation—or lack of it—into account. For example, at the moment, only Microsoft Explorer can execute VBScript. Therefore, if you craft your entire page around VBScript and someone with Netscape attempts to view your page, all your hard work will fail.

On the other hand, if the script is interpreted by the server, all that must be transferred to the client is standard HTML. In the case of VBScript, you can use Microsoft's Internet Information Server or Personal Web Server with Active Server Page Extensions to create pages that query databases and use server-side objects. The results of all that code can then be presented to the client with no scripting at all.

An advantage of client-side scripting, however, is that all the action takes place locally. Because no transaction goes across the wires, bandwidth and line speed are not problems. But, if a database is on a server, total client-side scripting is not possible. What you often see then is a combination of the two. In a single application, server scripting might be used for the actual database routines, whereas client-side scripting might be used for formatting or input validation. Input validation is a good use of client-side scripting because the mass of data is not transferred across the network until it is in a format to be accepted.

Understanding Client-Side Scripting

As discussed in the preceding chapter, if you wanted to create a page in standard HTML that simply displayed Hello World, then the HTML would look something like this:

```
<html>
<body>
Hello World
</body>
</html>
```

This is simplified to some extent, but what you are basically doing is telling the browser that HTML is coming, saying that the body of the text is coming, displaying the body of the text, saying that the body is finished (with the </BODY>), and saying that the HTML code is finished (with the </HTML>). If you put this into a text file and look at it with a browser, it will work.

To do this in VBScript, the code would be similar:

```
<html>
<body>
<script language="vbscript">
document.open
document.write "Hello World"
document.close
</script>
</body>
</html>
```

What changes here is how the text Hello World actually gets written. Looking at the code starting with the third line, you see that a script is declared, and the language of the script is VBScript. The next line opens the document window for writing. The next line writes the actual text to the screen. The sixth line closes the document window, and the seventh line closes the script.

Using ASP with Microsoft Web Servers

Server-side scripting is used with Microsoft Web servers through Active Server Pages, also known as ASP. These are basically HTML pages that contain script and are saved with an extension of .ASP rather than .HTM or .HTML. That extension lets the server know to run the page through a preprocessor scripting engine before sending the page to the client. To use ASP with Microsoft servers, the only ones that support ASP at this time, you must install the ASP extensions to the server. This can be done through the Microsoft FrontPage extensions or the Internet Information Server tools.

Although a full explanation of the installation of ASP is beyond the scope of this chapter, there is one important consideration when establishing the locations of your ASP. For any directory that contains Active Server Pages, you must make sure that the Web permissions are set so that programs can be executed. If you are using FrontPage Explorer for your Web management, you do this by right-clicking the folder and checking the box labeled Allow Scripts or Programs to Be Run (see Figure 24.1).

FIGURE 24.1.

You must set a directory to allow scripts to be run using an administration tool, such as FrontPage, before Active Server Pages will run.

Creating an ASP Page

If you take the code written in the "Client-Side Scripting" section to display Hello World and rewrite it for server-side scripting, it might look something like this:

```
<html>
<body>
<% language="vbscript"
response.write "Hello World"
%>
</body>
</html>
```

This is similar to the previous example but with a few differences. First, instead of the keyword SCRIPT, a percent sign is used to open and close the script. Although not required, this is a shorthand often used to make for easier typing. More important, notice that instead of using a document object you are using a response object. Also notice that with a response object you do not open or close the object. This is all due to the fact that the server is assembling a response and that it handles all those actions.

Glimpsing at Database Access with ADO

Now that you have had an introduction to server-side scripting, let's create a small but useful application. The application will be used to track events and could be used for a corporate or even club calendar. The application will use a Microsoft Access database with one table. Table 24.1 lists the fields in that table. For the purpose of this example, assume the database is created as C:\DATABASE\EVENTS.MDB.

Table 24.1. Layout of table EVENT in the EVENTS.MDB database.

Field Name	Type	Length
ID (Primary Key)	Counter	n/a
Name	Text	30
Description	Text	255
City	Text	20
State	Text	10
ContactName	Text	30
ContactEmail	Text	30
ContactPhone	Text	13
BeginDate	Date/Time	n/a
DateAdded	Date/Time	n/a

After you have set up that database and table, you must go into 32-bit ODBC in your Control Panel and set up a data source that points to it. To do this, complete the following steps:

1. Go to the Control Panel and double-click on 32-bit ODBC. Next, and this is very important, make sure that you select the System DSN tab. If you make your entry under the User DSN tab, your Web server will not be able to see the entry.

2. Click the Add button and then select Microsoft Access Driver from the list.

3. Click Finish to take you to the screen to fill in the Data Source Name, which should be MSEvents. You can also add a description of the database.

4. Click the Select button in the database section and point the DSN to the Access database you created (see Figure 24.2).

FIGURE 24.2.
*Use the 32-bit
ODBC setup in the
Control Panel to
establish a data-
base connection
for a System DSN.*

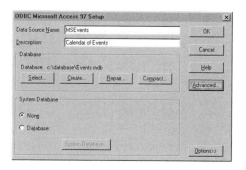

For this application, you use one of the newest methods of database access, the ActiveX Data Object (ADO). ADO is Microsoft's next step beyond DAO and RDO. Although most of the language constructs are similar to DAO or RDO, there are some differences in declaration methods and usage. Without too much detail, these are explained as you go through the sample code.

Creating the Default Application Screens

This application appears in your browser in two frames. *Frames* are independently controllable regions within your browser's window. The smaller top frame is used as a menu area to control the application. The lower larger frame is used as the interaction and display area. An illustration of this can be seen in Figure 24.3.

FIGURE 24.3.

The main screen of the application shows the menu frame at the top with a list of events in the lower frame.

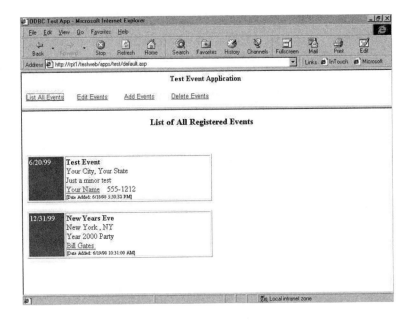

To establish a framed interface like this, you must have a default page that establishes each frame with a name and positioning information. In Listing 24.1, you see that two frames are established—one named Header and the other named Application. When the page is first called, the file THEAD.HTM is displayed in the Header frame, and the LIST.ASP page is displayed in the Application frame.

If you happened to use a browser that doesn't support frames—not likely these days—you would get the NoFrames code, which would simply tell you that frames are required for this and that you are, unfortunately, out of luck.

Listing 24.1. DEFAULT.ASP—This file, though not directly seen in the browser, controls the appearance of the frames in your application.

```
<html>

<head>
<title>ODBC Test App</title>
</head>

<frameset rows="76,*">
  <frame name="header" scrolling="no" noresize target="main" src="thead.htm">
  <frame name="application" src="list.asp">
  <noframes>
  <body>
  <p>This page uses frames, but your browser doesn't support them.</p>
  </body>
```

```
  </noframes>
</frameset>
</html>
```

The header is a small area that appears in the top frame and provides a menu for the application. The four available selections are List Events, Edit an Event, Add an Event, or Delete an Event. The header simply provides hyperlinks to the ASP page for each of these procedures. Listing 24.2 shows the code for the header.

In Listing 24.2, you see the title of the page and a declaration of where pages called from this header should appear. By declaring the target as Application, it means that pages called by clicking on a link in this page will be displayed in the frame named Application by the default page. That would be the larger bottom frame on the screen.

Listing 24.2. HEADER.HTM—The header frame provides a menu of the functions in your application.

```
<html>
<head>
<title>Event Application Header</title>
<base target="application">
</head>
<body topmargin="5">
<p align="center"><strong>Test Event Application</strong></p>
<p><small><font face="Arial">
<a href="list.asp">List All Events</a>
     
<a target="application" href="edit.asp">Edit Events</a>
       
<a href="add.asp">Add Events</a>
       
<a href="delete.asp">Delete Events</a>
</font></small></p>
</body>
</html>
```

The   codes are the code for a nonbreaking space. These are used simply to space the various links apart. Finally, the links themselves are just references to each of the pages for the list, add, edit, or delete functions.

Listing the Records

The third piece of the Default view is the main window or List view. In this window, the events are simply listed out in table format. This is where you first encounter the ADO code to access the database. Beginning with the tenth line, you first declare a variable called Events to be used as your recordset object. On the next line, that object is instantiated as an ADO database recordset with the `Server.CreateObject` command. Next, the recordset is populated with the `Open` method using a SQL string and system DSN. As you can see, ADO is actually simple. In many ways, it is more straightforward than DAO or RDO.

Now that the recordset is established, you simply step through it using a `Do...While` loop. Although you are not at the end of file, you will write out records, move to the next record, and then loop. Notice that to write out a record in ADO, you simply use the format `RECORDSET("FIELDNAME")`. Also, notice that you do not need to do a `MoveFirst` before you start the loop. Unlike some other methods, in ADO when you open a recordset, you are automatically placed on the first record.

Listing 24.3. `LIST.ASP`—This page contains script that will open the database and step through each record to create a list of events.

```
<html>
<head>
<title>List of All Events</title>
</head>
<body>
<p align="CENTER"><big><strong>List of All Registered
Events</strong></big></p>
<p> </p>
<% @ LANGUAGE="VBSCRIPT"%>
<%
Dim Events
Set Events = Server.CreateObject("ADODB.Recordset")
Events.Open "Select * from Event Order by BeginDate", "DSN=MSEvents"
Events.MoveFirst
do while not Events.EOF 'loop through all records
    response.write "<table border='1' width='400'>"
    response.write "<tr ><td width='75' valign='top' bgcolor='BLUE'>
➥<font color='WHITE'><b>" & Events("BeginDate") & "</FONT></td>
➥<td>  <b>" & Events("Name") & "</b><br>"
    response.write Events("City") & ", " & Events("State") & "<br>"
    response.write Events("Description") & "<br>"
    if Events("ContactEmail") > " " then
        response.write "<a href='mailto:"&Events("ContactEmail") & "'>" &
        ➥Events("ContactName") & "</a>    
        ➥"& Events("ContactPhone")&"<br>"
    else
        response.write Events("ContactName") &"    " &
        ➥Events("ContactPhone")&"<br>"
    end if
    response.write "<font size='-2'>[Date Added: " & Events("DateAdded") &
    ➥"]</font><br></td></tr>"
    response.write "</table></br>"
    Events.MoveNext
```

```
loop 'end loop
%>
<p> </p>
</body>
</html>
```

Adding a Record

The add form, shown in Figure 24.4, is not even an ASP form; it is a simple HTML form. Because none of the fields are prefilled with information from the database, there is no need to script the creation of this page. This will not be the case with the editing screen you will create later.

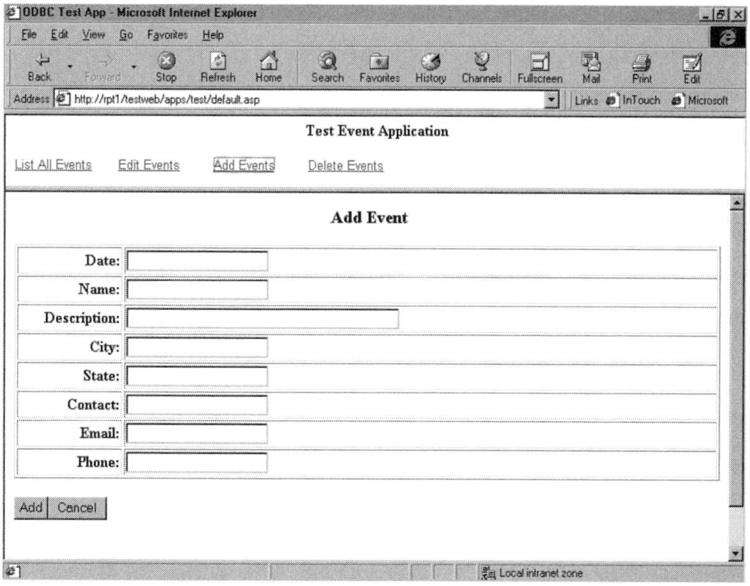

FIGURE 24.4.
The Add Event form is a simple HTML-based form (not ASP-based).

This form takes the information of the new event and passes it as parameters to the ACONFIRM.ASP page, which does the actual addition of the record to the database. Although it looks complicated, this is only because the fields of the form are contained within a table. This lends to the visual formatting of the page but has no material effect on the contents of the data.

You will see that with the <FORM> and </FORM> labels are several <INPUT> fields. These take parameters of the type of field, the name, and the size. All the fields on this page are simple text fields bearing the names of the database fields they represent.

Immediately before the ending <FORM> label is a line that establishes two buttons on the page. The first button appears with the word Add on it and has a value of Submit. When this button is clicked, it invokes the Post method specified in the opening <FORM> label. This posts the contents of the fields to the ACONFIRM.ASP page. The second button, labeled Cancel, simply resets all the fields on the page to their original, in this case empty, values.

Listing 24.4. ADD.HTM—The form for adding new records is a standard HTML page that could easily be created in FrontPage.

```
<html>
<head>
<title>Add Events</title>
</head>
<body>
<p align="CENTER"><big><strong>Add Event</strong></big></p>
<form method="POST" action="aconfirm.asp">
  <table border="1" width="100%">
    <tr>
      <td width="15%" align="right"><strong>Date: </strong></td>
      <td width="85%"><input type="text" value name="BeginDate"
      ➥size="20"></td>
    </tr>
    <tr>
      <td width="15%" align="right"><strong>Name: </strong></td>
      <td width="85%"><input type="text" value="  " name="Name"
      ➥size="20"></td>
    </tr>
    <tr>
      <td width="15%" align="right"><strong>Description:</strong></td>
      <td width="85%"><input type="text" value="  "
      ➥name="Description" size="40"></td>
    </tr>
    <tr>
      <td width="15%" align="right"><strong>City: </strong></td>
      <td width="85%"><input type="text" value="  " name="City"
      ➥size="20"></td>
    </tr>
    <tr>
      <td width="15%" align="right"><strong>State: </strong></td>
      <td width="85%"><input type="text" value="  " name="State"
      ➥size="20"></td>
    </tr>
    <tr>
      <td width="15%" align="right"><strong>Contact: </strong></td>
      <td width="85%"><input type="text" value="  "
      ➥name="ContactName" size="20"></td>
    </tr>
    <tr>
```

```
      <td width="15%" align="right"><strong>Email: </strong></td>
      <td width="85%"><input type="text" value="   "
      ➥name="ContactEmail" size="20"></td>
    </tr>
    <tr>
      <td width="15%" align="right"><strong>Phone: </strong></td>
      <td width="85%"><input type="text" value="   " name="ContactPhone"
      ➥size="20"></td>
    </tr>
  </table>
  <p><input type="submit" value="Add" name="B1"><input type="Reset"
  ➥value="Cancel" name="B2"></p>
</form>
<p> </p>
</body>
</html>
```

The actual addition of the record occurs on the ACONFIRM.ASP page (see Listing 24.5).
Notice that when the recordset is created this time, it is created in the same way as when
you opened the set for the listing, but now some parameters are added. The parameters,
specified as the constants adOpenStatic, adLockOptimistic, and adCmdText, enable the
addition of a record using optimistic record locking. After the recordset is open, an
AddNew method is called; then each of the fields is given the value passed from the
ADD.HTM form. These are passed as Request objects that have the name assigned to them
on the form.

Listing 24.5. ACONFIRM.ASP—This page takes the data passed to it from the
ADD.HTM page and posts it to the database.

```
<html>
<head>
<title>Confirm Event Addition</title>
</head>
<body>
<p align="CENTER"><big><strong>Confirm Event Addition</strong></big></p>
<% @ LANGUAGE="VBSCRIPT"%>
<%
' Declare the Open method constants
Const adOpenStatic = 3
Const adLockOptimistic = 3
Const adCmdText = 1
On Error Resume Next
Set Events = Server.CreateObject("ADODB.Recordset")
Events.Open "Select * from Event", "DSN=MSEvents",
adOpenStatic, adLockOptimistic, adCmdText
'Add a record to the database
```

continues

Listing 24.5. Continued.

```
Events.AddNew
'Replace each field with the new contents
Events("Name") = Request("Name")
Events("ContactName") = Request("ContactName")
Events("ContactEmail") = Request("ContactEmail")
Events("BeginDate") = Request("BeginDate")
Events("Description") = Request("Description")
Events("City") = Request("City")
Events("State") = Request("State")
Events("ContactPhone") = Request("ContactPhone")
Events("DateAdded") = Now()
'Update the database
Events.Update
'Check for update errors
if Err = 0 then
    On Error Goto 0
    response.write Request("Name") & " Added Successfully"
else
    On Error Goto 0
    response.write "Add Failed"
end if
%>
<p> </p>
</body>
</html>
```

After each field is assigned the appropriate value from its corresponding `Request` object, an `Update` method is called. By checking for errors at this point, you can establish whether the addition was successful and respond with the appropriate screen message. Remember also that there is an ID field in the database that, although not updated directly, received a unique sequential value when the record was added. This is the ID you will use to identify the record for edits or deletion.

Editing an Existing Record

The form for editing an existing record, seen in Figure 24.5, is somewhat more complicated than the addition form for three reasons:

- A record must be selected to edit.
- The fields on the editing form must be populated with the existing data.
- The correct record must receive the changes.

FIGURE 24.5.

The initial display of the Edit Event form displays a list of events with radio buttons to indicate the selection.

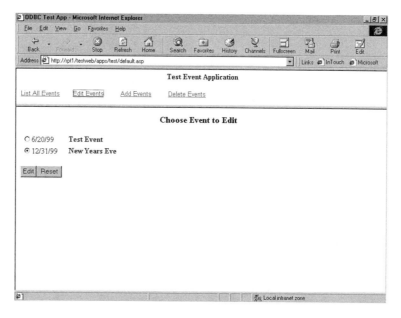

In Listing 24.6, you see that the majority of the page is enclosed by a large `If...Then...Else` statement. The `If` statement looks at the value for the `EventID` `Request` object for the form. If the `EventID` has a value, then that event is displayed for editing. If the `EventID` has no value, then a list of events is displayed to choose from.

Starting with the latter scenario, you will see that the code to present the list of events is basically the same as on the `LIST.ASP` page. The difference here is driven by the need to identify one of the events and pass that choice back. To accomplish this, the entire list of events is surrounded by a form. Within that form, each event gets a radio button. These radio buttons behave as expected in that only one can be selected at a time. This is how the record to edit will be identified.

Looking at the code for the radio button, notice that it is made up of the type of input *radio*, the value, which is set to each event's ID, and the name of `EventID`. Remember that `EventID` is being checked when the page is called to see whether it has a value. When one of these radio buttons is checked and the Submit button is clicked, the form reloads itself and sends itself the `EventID` that has been checked. This prompts the first part of the `If....Then...Else` statement to be executed instead of the list.

After a record to be edited has been selected, another form is created (see Figure 24.6). This time the form contains each of the fields in the record, and they have been prefilled with the current contents of the record. This is done by assigning each Text input box a `Value` equal to the field through string concatenation. After all the fields are filled, the form is displayed for editing. When the Submit button is clicked now, the `Post` method is called, which loads the `ECONFIRM.ASP` page and passes it the values of all the fields.

FIGURE 24.6.

After an event has been selected to edit, the Edit Event form displays a form containing the values for that record.

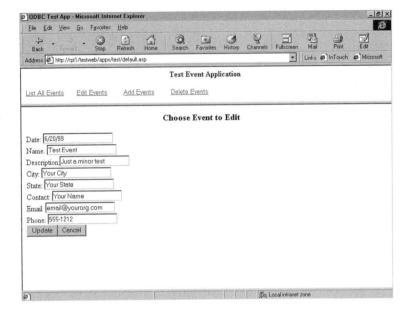

Listing 24.6. EDIT.ASP—Unlike the record addition page, the edit page contains script to set the initial values of the fields. If a record has not been selected yet, a list of records is presented.

```
<html>
<head>
<title>Edit Events</title>
</head>
<body>
<p align="CENTER"><big><strong>Choose Event to Edit</strong></big></p>
<% @ LANGUAGE="VBSCRIPT"%>
<%
Set Events = Server.CreateObject("ADODB.Recordset")
if request("EventID") > "0" then
    Events.Open "Select * from Event where ID=" & request("EventID"),
    ➥"DSN=MSEvents"
    response.write "<form method='POST' action='econfirm.asp'>"
    response.write "<input type='hidden' value='"& Events("ID") &"'
    ➥name='EventID'>"
    response.write "Date:        <input type='text' value='"&
    ➥Events("BeginDate")   &"' name='BeginDate'><br>"
    response.write "Name:        <input type='text' value='"&
    ➥Events("Name")        &"' name='Name'><br>"
    response.write "Description:<input type='text' value='"&
    ➥Events("Description")&"' name='Description'><br>"
    response.write "City:        <input type='text' value='"&
    ➥Events("City")        &"' name='City'><br>"
    response.write "State:        <input type='text' value='"&
```

```
    ➥Events("State")        &"' name='State'><br>"
    response.write "Contact:     <input type='text' value='"&
    ➥Events("ContactName") &"' name='ContactName'><br>"
    response.write "Email:       <input type='text' value='"&
    ➥Events("ContactEmail")&"' name='ContactEmail'><br>"
    response.write "Phone:       <input type='text' value='"&
    ➥Events("ContactPhone")&"' name='ContactPhone'><br>"
    response.write "<input type='submit' value='Update' name='B1'>
    ➥<input type='Reset' value='Cancel' name='B2'></form>"
else
    Events.Open "Select * from Event", "DSN=MSEvents"
    Events.MoveFirst
    response.write "<form method='POST' action='edit.asp'>"
    response.write "<table width='400'>"
    do while not Events.EOF 'loop through all records
        response.write "<tr><td width='95'><input type='radio' value='"&
        ➥Events("ID") &"' checked name='EventID'>" & Events("BeginDate")
        ➥ & "</td><td><b>" & Events("Name") & "</b><br></td></tr>"
        Events.MoveNext
    loop 'end loop
    response.write "</table>"
    response.write "<p>"
    response.write "<input type='submit' value='Edit' name='B1'>
    ➥<input type='Reset' value='Reset' name='B2'></form>"
end if
%>
<p> </p>
</body>
</html>
```

The ECONFIRM.ASP page in Listing 24.7 works much the same as the ACONFIRM.ASP page except that instead of using an AddNew method, a search is done using the EventID passed in. That EventID is combined into a SQL statement that is run against the database and creates an editable recordset of the one record that you are editing. Unlike DAO or RDO, you are using ADO here and so do not need to call an Edit method.

Using the same syntax as when the record was added, you simply assign values to each field. When the values are assigned, you call the Update method and check for errors. Depending on the error status, you then get either a success or failure message.

Listing 24.7. ECONFIRM.ASP—Much like the ACONFIRM.ASP page, this page takes the values passed to it and posts those changes to the database.

```
<html>
<head>
<title>Confirm Event Change</title>
</head>
```

continues

Listing 24.7. Continued.

```
<body>
<p align="CENTER"><big><strong>Confirm Event Change</strong></big></p>
<% @ LANGUAGE="VBSCRIPT"%>
<%
' Declare the Open method constants
Const adOpenStatic = 3
Const adLockOptimistic = 3
Const adCmdText = 1
On Error Resume Next
Set Events = Server.CreateObject("ADODB.Recordset")
Events.Open "Select * from Event where ID=" & request("EventID"),
➥"DSN=MSEvents", adOpenStatic, adLockOptimistic, adCmdText
'Replace each field with the new contents
Events("Name") = Request("Name")
Events("ContactName") = Request("ContactName")
Events("ContactEmail") = Request("ContactEmail")
Events("BeginDate") = Request("BeginDate")
Events("Description") = Request("Description")
Events("City") = Request("City")
Events("State") = Request("State")
Events("ContactPhone") = Request("ContactPhone")
'Update the database
Events.Update
'Check for update errors
if Err = 0 then
    On Error Goto 0
    response.write "Update Successful"
else
    On Error Goto 0
    response.write "Update Failed"
end if
%>
<p> </p>
</body>
</html>
```

Deleting an Existing Record

The delete function is simple. Listing 24.8 uses the same method of listing the events for selection as was used in the EDIT.ASP page. The page is even less complicated here, though, because no editing must be done after the selection. The radio buttons are set up in the same manner as before, and when an event is selected, that EventID is passed to the DCONFIRM.ASP page. To see what this page looks like, see Figure 24.7.

FIGURE 24.7.

The Delete Event form, like the Edit Event form, displays a list of events with radio buttons for selection.

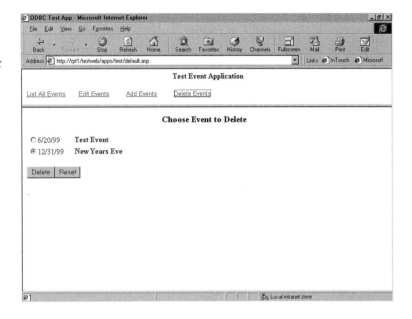

Listing 24.8. DELETE.ASP—This code steps through the database to create a form with a list of all the records in the database.

```
<html>
<head>
<title>Delete Event</title>
</head>
<body>
<p align="CENTER"><big><strong>Choose Event to Delete</strong></big></p>
<% @ LANGUAGE="VBSCRIPT"%>
<%
Set Events = Server.CreateObject("ADODB.Recordset")
Events.Open "Select * from Event", "DSN=MSEvents"
Events.MoveFirst
response.write "<form method='POST' action='dconfirm.asp'>"
response.write "<table width='400'>"
do while not Events.EOF 'loop through all records
response.write "<tr><td width='95'><input type='radio' value='"& Events("ID")
➥&"' checked name='EventID'>" & Events("BeginDate") & "</td><td><b>" &
➥Events("Name") & "</b><br></td></tr>"
Events.MoveNext
loop 'end loop
response.write "</table>"
response.write "<p>"
response.write "<input type='submit' value='Delete' name='B1'>
➥<input type='Reset' value='Reset' name='B2'></form>"
%>
<p> </p>
</body>
</html>
```

The actual deletion might be one of the simplest actions of all (see Listing 24.9). After a
record is selected on the DELETE.ASP page, the EventID passed to the DCONFIRM.ASP page
is used to create a SQL statement that returns a recordset with that one record to be
deleted. Then the ADO Delete method is called and, again, error checking is performed.
The record could have been deleted directly from the SQL statement, but using the ADO
method provides for cleaner trapping of errors and clearer error messages if needed. The
results can be seen in Figure 24.8.

Listing 24.9. DCONFIRM.ASP—This page accepts the ID of the record to be
deleted and uses the Delete method to remove the record from the database.

```
<html>
<head>
<title>Confirm Event Deletion</title>
</head>
<body>
<p align="CENTER"><big><strong>Confirm Event Deletion</strong></big></p>
<% @ LANGUAGE="VBSCRIPT"%>
<%
' Declare the Open method constants
Const adOpenStatic = 3
Const adLockOptimistic = 3
Const adCmdText = 1
On Error Resume Next
Set Events = Server.CreateObject("ADODB.Recordset")
Events.Open "Select * from Event where ID=" & request("EventID"),
➥"DSN=MSEvents",,adOpenStatic, adLockOptimistic, adCmdText

'Update the database
Events.Delete
'Check for update errors
if Err = 0 then
    On Error Goto 0
    response.write "Delete Successful"
else
    On Error Goto 0
    response.write "Delete Failed"
end if
%>
<p> </p>
</body>
</html>
```

FIGURE 24.8.
The result of a successful deletion is a simple confirmation message.

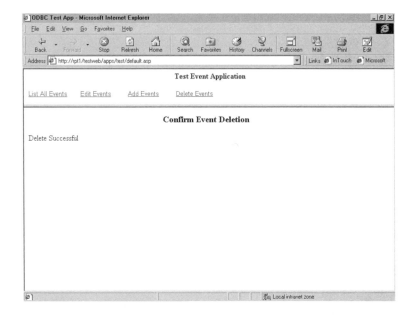

Summary

In this chapter, you learned how to create Active Server Pages that, although requiring Microsoft server technology, can be used to interact with almost any breed of browser. The application you created also shows how to use the newest database access method, ADO.

Although the application you created is usable in its present form, to be a robust application you should add error checking, security, and perhaps additional fields to it. Although not covered here, all these additions are straightforward and should be viewed as a necessity for a fully deployable application.

One of the nice things about this application is its scalablity. First, it works on a small intranet or the worldwide Internet. In fact, I have deployed a more fully developed version on both. Second, by simply changing the database that the DSN points to, you could upgrade this from an Access application to a SQL Server or Oracle application. All the code would remain the same. And nothing would need to be redeployed or distributed to the client. That is the beauty of Internet programming.

PART VII

Advanced Topics

Mastering the Windows API

Visual Basic helps you develop powerful applications. There's no question that Visual Basic is the most powerful, fastest development platform available for general-purpose Windows applications. However, in spite of its power and complexity, Visual Basic alone can't always get the job done.

Windows is a complicated operating system. It includes services such as system management, networking, printing, and security that are only partially implemented in Visual Basic or are absent from the VBA language. The Windows application programming interface (API) provides you with hooks into all the facilities provided by Windows. Programming these hooks provides your Visual Basic applications with all the features available in Windows itself.

Using the Windows API, you can take full advantage of the Windows graphical user interface to create your own windows (forms), dialog boxes (message boxes), list boxes, combo boxes, command buttons, and so on. These are the objects that make your application a *Windows* application, and that's what this chapter is about.

Although this chapter concentrates on the API calls included with 32-bit Windows, the concepts are applicable to many other API calls. These API functions include the Open Database Connectivity (ODBC) API, the Messaging Application Programming Interface (MAPI), and the Telephony Application Programming Interface (TAPI). After you learn the principles of programming the Windows API, you can take this skill and apply it to any other published API. Visual Basic does not include documentation for anything other than the Windows API, so you must look to these other products and technologies to learn their API secrets.

Defining the Windows API

The Windows API is a set of built-in code libraries providing the features built into Microsoft Windows. Visual Basic makes these code libraries available to you and simplifies their use. The API libraries include functions that enable you to create windows, check system resources, work with communications ports, send messages to applications, control .INI files, and access the Registry, among other things.

These functions are hooks into the internal workings of Windows. Although Visual Basic lets you reach a great many of these hooks transparently, there are still some you can't get to without writing your application in C or referencing the Windows API directly. Visual Basic gives you everything you need to tap into this collection of hundreds of functions. You must know only how they work and what to look for.

The API functions are written in libraries that can be dynamically linked to Windows applications. Typically, they are contained in dynamic link libraries (almost always abbreviated DLL), but they can also be placed in EXEs, DRVs, and OCXs. For example, USER.EXE and GDI.EXE were two of the Windows 3.1 libraries, but their Windows 95 32-bit equivalents are USER32.DLL and GDI32.DLL, respectively.

Understanding Dynamic Linking

Dynamic linking is a method of making functions available to your applications without hard-coding them into the executable. In many compiled languages, the code referenced by an application during development is included in the final product when the executable (EXE) is produced. This is called *static* linking. (Another common term is *early binding* because the libraries are bound into the executable early in the executable's life.) It makes for tightly integrated code, but it can also be difficult to manage. The same type of function might be included in several applications, which can take up space on your user's hard drive. In addition, if you must update or enhance your application you must replace the entire EXE, making those enhancements more difficult to execute. This process is illustrated in Figure 25.1.

FIGURE 25.1.
Traditional programming environments made inefficient use of library services.

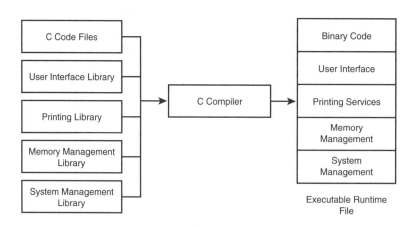

In Figure 25.1 notice how several different libraries are bound together by the compiler as a single EXE file. At runtime the EXE executed and the library functions bound into the EXE were loaded into memory. Often the libraries on the left side of this figure were platform-specific. Therefore, the user-interface library for a Sun Microsystem UNIX computer usually contained a different set of functions than an equivalent library for an HP UNIX system. Managing the libraries needed for cross-platform development was a major challenge for developers working with traditional development tools.

A less obvious problem is the inherent inefficiency of the arrangement diagrammed in Figure 25.1. On multitasking operating systems like UNIX, it is possible to start up multiple applications at the same time. Each application loads its own set of bound libraries into memory, taxing the computer system with redundant program information.

Dynamic linking, on the other hand, enables you to store a library of code in one place—a dynamically linked library or DLL—and reference functions from that library only when they are needed at runtime. (Dynamic linking is sometimes called *late binding* because the library routines are bound to the executable late in the executable's life.) Dynamic linking is diagrammed in Figure 25.2.

FIGURE 25.2.
Windows programming makes efficient use of shared resources.

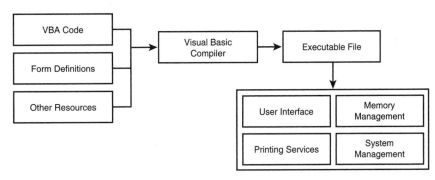

DLLs provided by Windows

Using DLLs has several advantages. First, it keeps unneeded code out of memory. When calling a function from a dynamic link library, the code takes up memory only when it is being used. In fact, after a library is loaded it can be used by more than one Windows application at a time. After loading, the memory is reclaimed when the called function is unloaded and the memory released.

Second, as a Visual Basic developer you can create a variety of applications. Rather than include the same code in each of these applications, you can use Visual Basic to compile the code into a reusable DLL. Later you can include only one copy of the DLL with your applications and call the functions from all your applications. This gives your applications a smaller footprint. Finally, it also enables you to update or enhance just the DLL, without replacing all the applications that use its code.

As you'll see later in this chapter, calling functions stored in the Windows DLLs involves following certain rules. Generally you must declare a Windows API call before using it in your code, and most API functions are fussy about the parameters used in the VBA statements calling them. However, over all the benefits to be gained from using the API functions greatly outweigh the relatively short learning curve necessary to master them.

Why Use the Windows API?

There are many reasons why you should consider using the Windows API (and other application programming interfaces). The following sections discuss some of these reasons.

Accessing a Common Code Base

Microsoft has done a lot for programmers. In establishing the Windows API, Microsoft has made a common library of code available to your Visual Basic applications. You can count on the fact that if some 32-bit version of Windows is installed, the Windows API and its 500-plus functions are available. You don't have to distribute or check for these code modules because they exist on every Windows machine. You also know that any time Microsoft adds functionality to one of its DLLs that functionality is available to all your applications.

Using Tested and Proven Code

If you develop applications professionally, then you know that time is everything. Getting your application to market before a competitor or getting an application running on your company's network can give your company a competitive edge. Every module of code you or the other programmers in your team produce takes time to develop and time to test. The functions included in the Windows API libraries are already tested and proven. They exist on hundreds of thousands, even millions, of machines all over the world.

A good example is the function `GetPrivateProfileString`. This function retrieves an entry from an application's `.INI` file. Yes, the VBA programming language has tremendous string manipulation and file I/O capabilities, but why waste time writing and testing a function to do what `GetPrivateProfileString` already does? Let the API take some of the burden from your programming staff and enable them to concentrate on more important business issues. As you'll see later in this chapter, `GetPrivateProfileString` is easy to use—much easier than writing an equivalent function in Visual Basic's implementation of VBA.

Gaining Cross-Platform Compatibility

Microsoft's strategy for the future of its operating systems includes the convergence of its code base. Windows NT, NT Workstation, and Windows 9x all use the Win32 API, which makes the applications you write for one platform portable to others. Almost all Win32 API declarations are available across all platforms, which gives you an extended user base and keeps you from rewriting much of your code to fit each kind of installation.

Achieving a Smaller Application Footprint

As mentioned earlier, using the dynamic link libraries included with Windows keeps you from distributing the same code within your applications. This keeps the size of your applications smaller. Users appreciate the consideration you put into helping them manage their hardware resources.

Using DLL Documentation

Most Windows DLLs are contained in a collection of C functions. Windows ships with a large number of DLLs, and most application vendors distribute their own DLLs with their applications. Microsoft has documented the core Windows DLLs so that developers can experience the advantages listed previously. Of course, this strategy has benefited Microsoft as well. By making it easier for programmers to write applications for Windows, Microsoft has made Windows the most popular development platform.

Not every vendor documents its DLLs, however. Many consider the DLLs distributed with their applications as proprietary property and do not make the interfaces to them available to the public. If a vendor does not formally release documentation for its libraries, it is usually not good practice to try to use the DLLs in your applications, even if some outside documentation exists. A vendor could remove or change functions within a library without notification, making any applications you have based on them unreliable at best, unusable at worst.

Finding Documentation

Microsoft has released software development kits (SDKs) for many of its products, including ODBC, MAPI, and of course Win32, the programmer's interface to the 32-bit versions of Windows. These kits contain not only general product information but also documentation for the core DLLs included in the products. They comprise a wealth of resources, documenting each function, argument, return value, data type, and so on. They can be purchased directly from Microsoft, or if you are a member of the Microsoft Developer Network they are included with the MSDN library.

Deciphering the Documentation

The good news is, Microsoft releases documentation of its API calls. The bad news is that the documentation is cryptic and designed primarily to be used by C and C++ programmers. Most of Microsoft's high-level product documentation assumes you're already an experienced developer. The "official" API documentation from Microsoft is not for the faint of heart, but the following hints should help you understand what you find. The end of this chapter also documents several useful functions and gives you examples of how they are used.

Understanding API Data Types

The hardest part of understanding API documentation is deciphering data types. Many books, articles, and the Microsoft documentation have standards for referring to data types. After you know what kind of data type is being referred to and how that type translates to Visual Basic, the battle is almost over.

C contains several data types, most of which have Visual Basic equivalents. Occasionally the arguments included with API functions are structures composed of several different data types. Table 25.1 shows each C data type, its size, and its Visual Basic VBA equivalent.

Table 25.1. C data types and their VBA equivalents.

C Type	Size	VBA Data Type
BOOL	32 bits	Boolean
BYTE	8 bits	Byte
char	8 bits	String * 1
double	64 bits	Double
DWORD	32 bits	Long
float	32 bits	Single
HANDLE	32 bits	Long
int	32 bits	Long
long	32 bits	Long
LPTSTR	32 bits	No equivalent
LPCTSTR	32 bits	No equivalent
short	16 bits	Integer
UINT	32 bits	Long
ULONG	32 bits	Long
USHORT	16 bits	Integer
UCHAR	8 bits	String * 1
WORD	16 bits	Integer

These equivalents are important when you are examining both the SDKs and other API references for Visual Basic. You must know what kind of data type the function is expecting and match it with a compatible type in your Visual Basic applications. Listing 25.1 shows how the `GetPrivateProfileString` function is declared in the API reference of the Win32 SDK and how to decipher each argument declared.

Listing 25.1. The Windows SDK reference for `GetPrivateProfileString`.

```
DWORD GetPrivateProfileString(
  LPCTSTR  lpszSection,      // points to section name
  LPCTSTR  lpszKey,          // points to key name
  LPCTSTR  lpszDefault,      // points to default string
  LPTSTR   lpszReturnBuffer, // points to destination buffer
  DWORD    cchReturnBuffer,  // size of destination buffer
  LPCTSTR  lpszFile          // initialization file name
);
```

Listing 25.1 is not found in `WinAPI.vbp`. It is provided strictly to show you the difference between C-style API declarations and the VBA declarations you'll see later in this chapter.

Listing 25.2 shows the same declaration using Visual Basic syntax instead of C syntax. Notice how the C data types are converted to their VBA equivalents.

Listing 25.2. Visual Basic declaration for `GetPrivateProfileString`.

```
Declare Function GetPrivateProfileStringA Lib "Kernel32" _
   (ByVal sSection As String, _
    ByVal sKey As String, _
    ByVal sDefault As String, _
    ByVal lReturnBuffer As Long, _
    ByVal lReturnBuffer As Long, _
    ByVal sFile As String) As Long

'Here's an alternative VBA declaration syntax:

Declare Function GetPrivateProfileStringA& Lib "Kernel32" _
   (ByVal sSection$, _
    ByVal sKey$, _
    ByVal sDefault$, _
    ByVal lReturnBuffer&, _
    ByVal lReturnBuffer&, _
    ByVal sFile$)
```

Listing 25.2 is not found in `WinAPI.vbp`. The discussions of reading and writing INI files occur in Chapter 26, "INI Files and the System Registry." You'll see these declarations in that chapter.

The second syntax shown here uses the dreaded single-character shortcuts for declaring the variable data types. Unless you feel *very* comfortable with these shortcuts, you should avoid using them. It's too easy to mistake the data type of a variable, leading to all kinds of problems later.

> **Warning:** When you use the Windows API you must declare the correct data types in your applications. Failure to do so can result in the dreaded General Protection Fault. If you don't declare variables of the proper size, your function calls might try to overwrite memory locations allocated by other applications. Using inappropriate data types as parameters to API functions is the most common cause of problems when using the Windows API.

In the previous example, notice the prefix attached to each argument passed to the functions. These standard prefixes are used throughout most of the API documentation. Some of the common prefixes are shown in Table 25.2.

Table 25.2. Equivalent prefixes for API arguments.

Prefix	C Data Type	VBA Data Type
lpsz	long pointer to a null-terminated string	string
dw	DWORD	Long
w	WORD	Integer
hwnd	HANDLE	Long
b	BOOL	Long
l	LONG	Long

You might encounter situations in which a function uses a data type you aren't familiar with or might not have even heard of. Most likely, the parameter being passed is a *data structure*, which is a fancy name for a user-defined data type. If that term sounds familiar, then you're probably thinking about the Visual Basic Type statement. Data structures are usually a collection of fields allocated contiguously (next to each other in memory). The Type statement in Visual Basic is compatible with its Struct counterpart from C, as long as the fields declared within the structure are compatible. Listing 25.3 shows the data structure passed in the GetVersionEx API and its Visual Basic equivalent.

Listing 25.3. OSVERSIONINFO structure.

```
'C-type OSVERSIONINFO structure syntax
typedef struct _OSVERSIONINFO{
    DWORD dwOSVersionInfoSize;
```

```
    DWORD dwMajorVersion;
    DWORD dwMinorVersion;
    DWORD dwBuildNumber;
    DWORD dwPlatformId;
    TCHAR szCSDVersion[ 128 ];
} OSVERSIONINFO;

'VBA-typedef for OSVERSIONINFO
Private Type OSVERSIONINFO
  lVersionInfo As Long
  lMajorVersion As Long
  lMinorVersion As Long
  lBuildNumber As Long
  lplatformID As Long
  sVersion As String * 128
End Type
```

Only the VBA-style `Type` declaration you see in Listing 25.3 can be found in the
`basDeclares` module in `WinAPI.vbp`. Don't bother looking for the C-style declaration
because it is provided here so that you can see the differences between these two languages.

Moving from Windows 3.1 to Win32

This section is intended primarily for developers moving to Visual Basic 6 from one of
the older 16-bit versions of Visual Basic. Both Visual Basic 3.0 and Visual Basic 4.0-16
enabled you to make extensive use of the Windows 3.1 API and will continue to do so in
Windows 9x and NT with no problem. However, you'll run into problems when you convert old 16-bit Visual Basic applications to Visual Basic 6. It seems that as long as
Windows 3.1 API functions are called from compiled 16-bit Windows applications they
run fine on the 32-bit platforms. However, you can't call 16-bit API calls from 32-bit
applications; the following sections explain some of the reasons why.

Taking Advantage of Architectural Differences

The first reason is specific to the whole reasoning behind 32-bit operating systems.
Win16 made developers go through all kinds of contortions because it ran on top of MS-
DOS, a 16-bit operating system. Although the Intel 80x86 chip architecture gave developers the ability to address memory using 32-bit registers, the operating system did not.
It's somewhat like putting a race car engine in a Chevette. Applications were being
choked by the 16-bit limitations of the operating system. (That's where the 64KB barrier
in the USER and GDI Windows resources comes from.) The 16-bit integer data type was
used extensively in Win16 applications because it fit the 16-bit memory model.

One of the main advantages of Windows NT and Windows 95 is the capability to address
32-bit registers without all the workarounds and other manipulations. A 32-bit data type

is the most efficient type in a 32-bit operating system, so Microsoft expanded the integer data type to 32 bits in Windows 95. That meant every API call that used a 16-bit integer data type in Windows 3.x had to be changed during the development of Windows 95.

> **Tip:** Although Microsoft expanded the Integer data type from 16 bits to 32 bits in its operating system, the Integer data type in Visual Basic 6.0 still refers to a 16-bit data type. Be sure to convert `int` API declarations in 16-bit API calls to the VBA `Long` data type.

Finding New Homes for API Functions

The second reason really goes with the first: When Microsoft changed the API calls to reflect the operating system it recompiled the libraries and moved several of the functions to different libraries. For example, `KERNEL.EXE` is now `KERNEL32.DLL`; `USER.EXE` is now `USER32.EXE`; `GDI.EXE` is now `GDI32.EXE`; and the Registry functions have now been moved from `SHELL.DLL` to `ADVAPI32.DLL`. Many DLLs included with Windows 95 were not included in Windows 3.1. For example, `WFWNET.DLL`, which contains network API functions, was included with Windows for Workgroups but not Windows 3.1, so the network functions were not available to all programmers. Because Windows 95 is being promoted for its networkability, the network API calls are included with each copy of 32-bit Windows.

The library names are important because you must specify the name of the DLL containing the function call you're making in your code. Windows will not hunt down a Windows API procedure called from a Visual Basic application because there are so many different procedures in the Windows API. Also, the API call you're making might be included in an application DLL and would, therefore, not be known to Windows.

Learning New API Function Names

Third, when the API functions were changed and moved they also were renamed. Unless you break up the include files (`.H` files) that come in the Windows SDK included with Visual C++ or take the time to read deeply into the SDK documentation, you couldn't know this. Many of the API functions mentioned in the Win32 documentation refer to migrated API calls using the same function names as their 16-bit predecessors. For example, `GetPrivateProfileString` from Windows 3.1 is documented in the Win32 API reference as `GetPrivateProfileString`. However, you will probably use `GetPrivateProfileStringA` in your applications.

Because of the expansion of software vendors into the international community, many API functions are using an expanded character set called *Unicode*. The standard 8-bit ANSI character set did not have enough room for all the special characters used in languages around the world. The Unicode character set, a set of characters based on 16-bit values, is being incorporated into a lot of software, especially operating systems. The

Win32 API functions reflect this change by giving you the option of using either ANSI or Unicode when making your function calls. If you are using ANSI character sets you call `GetPrivateProfileStringA`, but if you're using Unicode you call `GetPrivateProfileStringW`. Both functions achieve the same result, which is the same as the Windows 3.1 `GetPrivateProfileString` function, so that's how they're documented. Not all API calls reflect this change, but many of the API functions dealing with character strings do.

> **Note:** One of the changes made most frequently to applications as they are converted from older versions of Visual Basic to Visual Basic 6.0 is to update the API calls in the old code. You'll discover, for example, that `GetPrivateProfileString` does not exist in the 32-bit Windows DLLs, and a `Declare` statement referencing `GetPrivateProfileString` can't be used by Visual Basic 6.0. Make sure you are using an up-to-date API reference when you use 32-bit API functions in your applications.

Accounting for Changes to API Calls

Fourth, some of the API functions have been expanded to reflect changes in how Microsoft wants Windows to run, and some have even been removed because they weren't needed anymore. A good example is the INI file functions mentioned previously. INI files were used extensively by software vendors (including Microsoft) in previous versions of Windows. As you know, INI files are used to store application settings. However, INI files are not very flexible, so Microsoft expanded its use of the System Registry within Windows 95 and Windows NT and is encouraging software vendors to abandon INI files in favor of the Registry. To reflect this change, the Registry API functions have been expanded and are much more powerful than they were in Windows 3.1.

Microsoft has recognized, however, that old habits die hard, so it has included INI file functions such as `GetPrivateProfileString` in the Win32 API. Both types of API functions are covered in this chapter. You should become comfortable with using the System Registry instead of INI files because INI support might disappear completely from future versions of Windows.

Using the Windows API

If you've made it this far, congratulations. The concept of API functions can be a little intimidating. When you understand the concepts, however, using them is as easy as calling any other function or subroutine from Visual Basic.

> **Warning:** Whenever you're working with API functions you should save your work frequently. Because you are working deep within the Windows system, application errors can occur, especially when you are first learning how to make these calls.

Understanding the `Declare` Statement

In order to use an API in your Visual Basic application, you must first tell Visual Basic the name of the API function and where to find it. You do this within the (declarations) section of a module using the `Declare` statement. A prototype `Declare` statement is shown in Listing 25.4. The `Declare` statement has several parts, each of which is discussed in the following sections.

Listing 25.4. The `Declare` statement prototype.

```
Declare [Function¦Sub] FunctionName Lib "LibraryName" _
     Alias "AliasName" (ArgumentList) As DataType
```

Function **or** Sub

API calls can be in the form of a function or a subroutine, just like Visual Basic procedures. A *function* returns a value back to the calling code, whereas a *subroutine* does not. When an API function returns a value, good programming practices require the calling procedure to check the return value to verify that the function completed as expected. You'll see examples of both API functions and subroutines later in this chapter.

FunctionName

The function name you specify can be one of two things:

- The actual name of the API function you will be using as declared in the library. For example, if you were going to use `GetPrivateProfileString` listed previously, you would declare *FunctionName* as `GetPrivateProfileStringA`.
- The name of the function as you would like to use it within your code. `GetPrivateProfileStringA` is a long function name, especially if you are going to be using the function frequently within your code. You might want to shorten its name to `GetString` instead. You can do this by using the `Alias` parameter discussed in the "`Alias 'AliasName'`" section of this chapter.

Lib "*LibraryName*"

The library name is simply the name of the DLL that contains the API function or subroutine you are declaring. This parameter tells Visual Basic where to find the function. If the DLL is not one of the standard Win32 DLLs, or it has been moved to another location, you must specify the complete path of the DLL.

Note: The *LibraryName* parameter must be enclosed in quotations but is not case-sensitive.

Alias "*AliasName*"

If you wanted to call an API function by another name in your Visual Basic program, you could. In such a case, the *FunctionName* parameter would be the new name you assigned to the function. However, you still must tell Visual Basic the real name of the function as it exists within the library. The GetPrivateProfileString example has been used several times in this chapter. I stated in the section "Moving from Windows 3.1 to Win32" that the name of the function had been changed to GetPrivateProfileStringA in the Win32 API. This is a good example of when you might want to use an alias. In your code, you could use the standard API name as the *FunctionName* parameter and the real name as the alias. Listing 25.5 shows how you would use an alias.

Listing 25.5. Using an API function alias.

```
Declare Function GetPrivateProfileString lib "Kernel32" _
     Alias "GetPrivateProfileStringA"
```

Listing 25.5 is not found in WinAPI.vbp. A similar declaration is discussed in Chapter 26, "INI Files and the System Registry."

In some situations you must use an alias within your Visual Basic modules. Occasionally, you will encounter API functions that begin with an underscore, such as _lopen or _lread. Visual Basic identifiers such as procedure names can't begin with an underscore, so you must alias these functions. Another reason to alias your function names is to avoid the possibility of declaring a function using a name that already exists in your Visual Basic application or in its libraries. If you try to declare a function with a name that already exists, you will receive an error: Ambiguous Name Detected: *FunctionName*.

Note: Like library names, aliases must always be enclosed in quotations.

The project accompanying this chapter (WinAPI.vbp) is full of code. The code includes a large number of Windows API calls and custom procedures written for the project. To make it easier for you to tell which procedure calls are API functions, all the API calls in WinAPI.vbp have been aliased by prefixing api to the procedure names. Therefore, apiGetCommandLine is a reference to an API call whereas GetCommandLine is a custom procedure written just for WinAPI.vbp.

ArgumentList

The ArgumentList is composed of the elements the function expects to receive from you in order to do its job. When you declare a function you must declare the same number of arguments in the function declaration that the function's documentation specifies. If you do not, you will receive a runtime error 49: Bad DLL calling convention. The same error will occur if you pass API function arguments that are incompatible with what it is expecting. That's a best-case scenario—you could end up with a General Protection Fault that crashes the application, crashes Visual Basic, and possibly crashes Windows.

It's important to realize that the arguments in the argument list are only placeholders. It doesn't matter what you name them, although most developers assign them the same name the SDK documentation does. The argument list simply tells Visual Basic what to expect when the function is called, so that it can type check and argument check. In other words, it's for your own good. Visual Basic does not check the type declarations against the actual library, so it's up to you to assign the correct data types to your arguments.

ByVal or ByRef?

When you assign arguments to a declaration statement, you must decide how the API expects to receive the arguments. By default, when Visual Basic passes an argument it does so by reference, or ByRef. This means that Visual Basic passes the memory address of the variable to the function it is calling. When a function receives the address of an argument, it can change the value stored at that address, which might or might not be desirable.

When you pass an argument by value, or ByVal, you are telling Visual Basic to pass to the function only the value of what's in the variable. In other words, you pass a copy of the variable rather than the variable itself. When a function receives only the value of an argument, it can use only that value to do its job. Passing an argument by value is usually desirable because it ensures that the variables used in your application keep a consistent value. Listing 25.6 shows an example of using the ByVal keyword.

Listing 25.6. Using the ByVal keyword.

```
Declare Function GetTempPath _
   Lib "Kernel32" _
   Alias "GetTempPathA" _
  (ByVal lBufferSize As Long, _
   ByVal sReturnBuffer As String) As Long
```

Listing 25.6 is not found in WinAPI.vbp as you see here. Instead, look for apiGetTempPath as shown in Listing 25.23.

There is always an exception to a rule, and the exception in this case is string variables. Visual Basic and C handle strings differently. C expects to receive pointers to strings that are terminated with a null value; Visual Basic does not. In order to format a string in the method expected by most API functions, you must pass the string by value (ByVal). As stated previously, passing an argument by value passes the data stored in the variable instead of the memory address—except when you pass strings. When you pass a string using the ByVal option you pass the address of the variable, which means the function can change the value passed to it by manipulating what's stored at the memory address.

In the case of API calls, that's a good thing. An API function can't return a string value, so you must give the function permission to alter a memory location in order to retrieve a string value from an API. You do this by specifying that the argument is to be passed by value. Notice that in Listing 25.6 sReturnBuffer is a pointer to a string that GetTempPath uses to place the path Windows uses for temp files. It is being passed as an address. Buffersize, on the other hand, is only passing the value of a variable that contains the length of the string being passed in sReturnBuffer.

A final note on passing strings: Many API functions expect to receive addresses to string values. Most of the time, these functions expect a minimum number of bytes to be allocated for the string value. In order to fulfill these requirements you must know in advance how many bytes the function expects the string to be, and you must expand your string variables to that length before passing the string. You can do this using the String$() function in Visual Basic. The string function fills a string variable with a character for a desired length:

```
Dim strMyString As String
strMyString = String$(20," ")
```

The previous code fills the string variable strMyString with 20 spaces. You can achieve the same result by declaring the string with the number of characters already allocated:

```
Dim strMyString * 20
```

If you do not allocate enough space for an API function to write a string, it could end up writing over another application's data, causing a General Protection Fault (GPF). It's very difficult to know how many characters an API call will accept, so a safe way to declare your string variables is to allocate 255 characters to them. Most functions will not pass a string any larger than 255 characters. This is, however, inefficient in that you are probably using more memory than you need. If you can, try to find the exact string length your function expects.

DataType

Any API call that is a function returns a value. A subroutine does not. Therefore, a subroutine does not need a return value data type specified. The value returned by a function is usually a value you expect to use in your application, or it is an error number. For example, many functions return zero or ERROR_SUCCESS if the function completes successfully. If the value returned is a nonzero value, you should provide an error-handling routine to deal with the function's failure. Other functions, such as GetPrivateProfileString, return the number of characters copied into a string buffer.

Therefore, if GetPrivateProfileString completes successfully, you use its return value and the Left() function to extract the returned string from a string buffer:

StringVar = Left(*StringBuffer, ReturnValue*).

If the value returned by GetProfileString is 0, it means that no string was found in the INI file.

Another difference between 16-bit versions of Visual Basic and Visual Basic 6 is that Windows API calls from Visual Basic 6 are case-sensitive. In previous versions of Visual

> **Note:** The data type specified for the return value must be compatible with the data type specified in the API function's documentation.

Basic, API function names did not have to honor the case of the stored function. In Visual Basic 6 you must declare your function names with the proper case. Be sure to carefully check the API call's documentation and verify you're using proper case in your API declarations.

Understanding Windows Handles

When working in Visual Basic, you reference forms by their Name property. The Name property, however, is simply a bit of information that Visual Basic uses to keep track of the forms in your projects. Windows doesn't know anything about a form's name. In fact, because you can run multiple programs at one time under Windows, you'd have name collisions if two windows with the same name were open at the same time. Instead, Windows uses a *handle* to keep track of application objects.

A handle is a long (32-bit) integer value that Windows assigns to the graphical objects on the screen. Every button, text box, menu bar, and form has its own unique handle. The handle is assigned by Windows to the object as the application creates the object (for example, when a form is opened in a Visual Basic program) and persists as long as the object is available. The handle assigned to an object is unique, which means no other object in Windows has the same handle value. The handle does not change during program execution and will be different each time the application is restarted. The handle persists even if the object is momentarily hidden behind another object or if the application is minimized and is not currently being used. Long integer values are needed as handles because of the large number of objects that can be open at one time.

In Visual Basic you access the Windows handles through the hWnd property. The following statement references the handle of a form named frmMain:

```
frmMain.hWnd
```

> **Tip:** Because Windows handles do not change during program execution, you might consider using public long integer variables to hold the handles of objects you frequently reference in your applications. Retrieving the handle of an
>
> *continues*

> object takes a bit of time. You'll find it faster to assign the handle's value to a variable and use that variable in your code instead of referencing an object's handle repeatedly.

In the `WinAPI.vbp` project you'll see many instances where a form's handle is passed to an API routine. In all cases, you can think of the handle as a long integer value that uniquely identifies the form or other object.

Taking a Look at `WinAPI.vbp`

Here comes the fun part. At the beginning of the chapter I listed several different uses for the Windows API. From here to the end of the chapter you'll see some examples of different types of API functions, how to declare them, what you would use them for, error messages you might encounter, and so on. All the examples are included on your companion CD-ROM in the `WinAPI.vbp` sample project. The declarations themselves are contained in a public module named `basDeclares`. Each API function declaration has been made public to the entire application, making it easy for each API call to be used anywhere in the application. Each form in the application contains the code necessary to support the API calls demonstrated on the form. All the API declarations are prefixed with `api` to make it easy for you to differentiate the API calls from the other procedure calls in `WinAPI.vbp`.

`WinAPI.vbp` starts out with the switchboard form you see in Figure 25.3. Each of the buttons on this form leads to a form demonstrating some aspect of programming the Windows API.

FIGURE 25.3.

`WinAPI.vbp` includes five forms in all, including this switchboard form.

Getting Application Information

The Windows API provides many functions that help you manage and control your applications at runtime. As you read through the next section, notice that many API calls are duplicated by simple Visual Basic property changes whereas other API calls have no Visual Basic equivalents. Obviously, it's easier to set or retrieve a built-in Visual Basic property than it is to set up and use an API function. However, the examples you see here should give you a feel for employing API calls in your applications.

The WinAPI.vbp project includes the form you see in Figure 25.4. This form contains several controls that display information about the application.

Each of the controls you see in Figure 25.4 uses a Windows API call. The following sections describe the code found behind frmAppInfo and explain how frmAppInfo retrieves the information displayed in the form's controls.

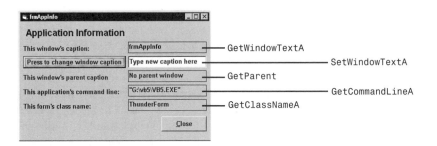

Figure 25.4.

frmAppInfo con-
tains all the code
you see in this
part of this chap-
ter.

GetWindowTextA

The GetWindowTextA function returns the title bar text of a window (see Listing 25.7). Here is an example of an API function that duplicates capabilities built into Visual Basic. In fact, Visual Basic likely uses this exact API function to return the Caption property of a window. The biggest difference here is that you provide the window's handle rather than the window's name. Remember that apiGetWindowText is the alias used in WinAPI.vbp to reference the Windows function named GetWindowTextA. Because GetWindowsTextA is our first foray into API programming, this section contains a bit more detail than you'll see in the rest of this chapter.

Listing 25.7. The GetWindowTextA API function prototype.

```
Declare Function apiGetWindowText _
    Lib "user32" _
    Alias "GetWindowTextA" _
  (ByVal hWnd As Long, _
    ByVal sCaption As String, _
    ByVal lCaptionSize As Long) As Long
```

The parameter list for GetWindowTextA includes the following:

- hWnd: The handle to the window.
- sCaption: The string that will accept the window's caption.
- lCaptionSize: The length of the caption.

Oddly enough, instead of simply returning the window caption (which would make GetWindowTextA a function returning a string rather than a long), GetWindowTextA actually returns the length of the string found in the window's title bar. But, aren't we required to pass that information in as a parameter (lCaptionSize in Listing 25.7)? Yes, you are correct—working with the Windows API can be confusing and contrary at times.

Because GetWindowTextA requires the length of the window's title bar text, the Windows API conveniently provides a function that does just that. GetWindowTextLengthA (see Listing 25.8) returns the length of the text in a window's title bar as a Long integer value.

Listing 25.8. GetWindowTextLengthA API function prototype.

```
Declare Function apiGetWindowTextLength _
    Lib "user32" _
    Alias "GetWindowTextLengthA" _
    (ByVal hWnd As Long) As Long
```

The only argument to GetWindowTextLengthA is the handle of the window to examine. In WinAPI.vbp these two APIs are used by a function named GetCaption behind the form named frmAppInfo (see Listing 25.9).

Listing 25.9. The GetCaption function serves as a wrapper for apiGetWindowTextLength.

```
Function GetCaption(WhWnd As Long) As String
    'WhWnd: The hWnd of the window
    Dim lLength As Long
    Dim sCaption As String
    Dim lRetValue As Long

    'Get the length of the window's caption
    lLength = apiGetWindowTextLength(WhWnd) + 1

    'Create a string of blanks to pass into apiGetWindowText
    sCaption = String$(lLength + 1, " ")

    'Now get the window caption in sCaption
    lRetValue = apiGetWindowText(WhWnd, sCaption, lLength)
    GetCaption = Left$(sCaption, lLength)
End Function 'GetCaption
```

There are a couple of things to notice about `GetCaption`:

- `lLength` is assigned to the value returned by `apiGetWindowTextLength`.
- `sCaption` is set to a string of blanks before being used in the `apiGetWindowsText` function. The length of the blank string is set to `lLength` plus one. This ensures we have a clean string of the maximum possible length of the windows caption.
- `lLength` is then passed into `apiGetWindowsText`, the alias for the `GetWindowTextA` API function.
- At the conclusion of the function the caption is returned in the `sCaption` string. `sCaption` is then assigned to the value of the `GetCaption` function.

The process you see here (setting up local variables, setting initial values, passing those variables into the API function, and returning interesting information) is repeated time and again when you work with API calls. A function like `GetCaption` acts as a *wrapper* around the API call, simplifying your programming. After `GetCaption` has been written, a very simple statement such as the following is all that's needed to use the API call:

```
sRetValue = GetCaption(Me.hWnd)
```

The `GetCaption` wrapper function does all the rest.

SetWindowTextA

Now that you've seen how to get the title bar text of a window, wouldn't it be nice to be able to set the text to anything you want? You can use the `SetWindowTextA` function to change the caption displayed in a given window's title bar. It's much like altering the `Caption` property of a form. The prototype for the `apiSetWindowText` function is shown in Listing 25.10. As you've seen elsewhere in this chapter `apiSetWindowText` is an alias for the Windows API function named `SetWindowTextA`.

Listing 25.10. The `SetWindowTextA` API function prototype.

```
Declare Function apiSetWindowText _
  Lib "User32" _
  Alias "SetWindowTextA" _
  (ByVal hWnd As Long, _
   ByVal sCaption As String) As Long
```

`SetWindowTextA` requires two parameters:

- `hWnd`: The handle to the window to be changed.
- `sCaption`: The text to use in the window's title bar.

`SetWindowTextA` returns a long value that indicates whether the function was able to successfully change the text in the window's title bar. A 0 (zero) indicates the title bar text was not changed; 1 indicates success.

Because `SetWindowTextA` always returns a value, the wrapper function shown in Listing 25.11 is used in `WinAPI.vbp` to absorb the return value, making `SetWindowTextA` easier to use in this project.

Listing 25.11. Using `SetWindowText` to change the text in a window.

```
Sub ChangeCaption(WhWnd As Long, _
    sNewCaption As String)
  Dim lRetValue As Long
  lRetValue = apiSetWindowText(WhWnd, sNewCaption)
End Sub 'ChangeCaption
```

`ChangeCaption` is used behind `frmAppInfo` to change the caption of the form. When the user types a new caption into the text box on `frmAppInfo` (see Figure 25.4) and presses the button labeled Press to Change Window Caption, the event procedure in Listing 25.12 runs.

Listing 25.12. Call `ChangeCaption` from the `cmdCurrentTitle` command button.

```
Private Sub cmdCurrentTitle_Click()
  Call ChangeCaption(Me.hWnd, txtNewCaption)
End Sub
```

This subroutine calls `ChangeCaption`, passing in the handle to `frmAppInfo` as well as the text typed into `txtNewCaption` on the form. `ChangeCaption` in turn calls `SetWindowTextA`, which actually changes the form's caption. The value returned by `SetWindowTextA` is simply ignored by `ChangeCaption`.

This is much more work than simply setting `frmAppInfo.Caption` to the value in `txtNewCaption`, but it is more flexible. If you can get the handle of any other window or form that happens to be open in Windows, you can change its title bar text. The window does not have to be a Visual Basic application, for example.

GetParent

The `GetParent` API function returns a handle to the current window's parent window. In an MDI application you'll get a handle on the MDI parent form, whereas in an SDI application `GetParent` returns a `Null` value because there is no parent window in an SDI application. For example, you might combine `GetParent` with `GetWindowsTextA` to return the title bar text of an MDI parent window. Listing 25.13 shows the `Declare` for the `GetParent` API function in `WinAPI.vbp`.

Listing 25.13. The `GetParent` API function prototype.

```
Declare Function apiGetParent _
   Lib "user32" _
   Alias "GetParent" _
   (ByVal hwnd As Long) As Long
```

When passed a valid window handle, `GetParent` retrieves the handle of the child window's parent. `GetParent` returns a 0 value if there is no parent window or if the call is unsuccessful. The only argument to `GetParent` is the handle to the child window. In fact, this logic is supported by the `Form_Load` event procedure behind the `frmAppInfo` form in `WinAPI.vbp`. Listing 25.14 shows a portion of the code from the `Form_Load` procedure in `frmAppInfo`.

Listing 25.14. A portion of `frmAppInfo`'s `Form_Load` procedure.

```
lHandle = apiGetParent(Me.hWnd)

If lHandle = 0 Then
  txtParentCaption = "No parent window"
Else
  txtParentCaption = GetCaption(lHandle)
End If
```

The first statement calls `apiGetParent`, `WinAPI.vbp`'s alias for the `GetParent` API function. Then, depending on the value returned in `lHandle`, the `If...Then...Else` statement assigns the `No Parent Window` message or the caption of the parent window to the text box named `txtParentCaption`. Because `WinAPI.vbp` has been written as an SDI application, you'll never see the parent window's caption. However, you can use this logic in an MDI application to grab the parent window's title bar text.

GetCommandLineA

All Windows applications are started by some command-line statement even when the user clicks a program icon or selects an item from the Start | Programs menu. Windows uses the command line, which includes the path to the executable file, to locate the program and start it up.

The `GetCommandLineA` function retrieves the command line used to start the current process. The command line is returned wrapped in quotation marks. Listing 25.15 shows the `apiGetCommandLine` function prototype in `WinAPI.vbp`.

> **Note:** When GetCommandLineA is run from Visual Basic during the development process, it returns the full path, including the executable name, for Microsoft Visual Basic. When run from a compiled runtime EXE, the path to the executable EXE is returned.

Listing 25.15. The GetCommandLineA API function prototype.

```
Declare Function apiGetCommandLine _
   Lib "Kernel32" _
   Alias "GetCommandLineA" () As String
```

In WinAPI.vbp the GetCommand function uses the apiGetCommandLine function prototype to return the path to Visual Basic. This information is then displayed in txtCommandLine on frmAppInfo (refer to Figure 25.4). Listing 25.16 shows how frmAppInfo in WinAPI.vbp uses GetCommandLine.

Listing 25.16. Using the GetCommandLine API function.

```
Function GetCommand() As String
  GetCommand = apiGetCommandLine()
End Function
```

In Chapter 26, you'll see the path used to create application-specific INI files. In most cases, an application-specific INI file should be stored in the same directory as its application.

GetClassNameA

Finally, as you learned earlier in this book, all Visual Basic objects are members of some class that defines the object. It should come as no surprise, then, that the Windows API provides a way to return the class name of an object. Listing 25.17 shows the Declare for the GetClassNameA API function used in WinAPI.vbp.

Listing 25.17. The GetClassNameA API function prototype.

```
Declare Function apiGetClassName _
   Lib "User32" _
   Alias "GetClassNameA" _
   (ByVal hWnd As Long, _
   ByVal sClassName As String, _
   ByVal lClassSize As Long) As Long
```

GetClassName returns the class name of a given window. The window's handle is passed as an argument (hWnd), and the function places the window's class name in the string sClassName. If GetClassNameA successfully determines the class name of the window, the function returns the number of characters copied to the string buffer in the lClassSize parameter. Otherwise, lClassSize is set to zero.

The frmAppInfo form in WinAPI.vbp uses the GetClassName wrapper function (see Listing 25.18). You've seen all the logic in this function before in Listing 25.9 where GetCaption served as a wrapper for apiGetWindowTextLength.

Listing 25.18. The GetClassName API function prototype.

```
Function GetClassName(lHandle As Long) As String
  Dim sClassName As String * 255
  Dim lSize As Long
  Dim lRetValue As Long

  sClassName = String(255, " ")
  lSize = Len(sClassName)
  lRetValue = apiGetClassName(lHandle, sClassName, lSize)
  GetClassName = Left$(sClassName, lRetValue)
End Function
```

GetClassNameA returns the length of the class name in the lRetValue variable. The GetClassName wrapper function effectively hides this detail from any routine or statement that requires the class name of a form.

Getting Windows Information

Visual Basic 6 applications run under any 32-bit version of Windows (except Windows CE). At runtime you must know which version of Windows is hosting the application. It could be Windows 95 or Windows 98, or it could be Windows NT Workstation or NT Server in any of the current versions of these operating systems (3.51, 4.0, 5.0). The Windows API provides a quick and easy way to check for detailed Windows information, including the version number, the platform (95, 98, or NT), and the location of the Windows and Windows system directories.

The WinAPI.vbp sample project includes the form shown in Figure 25.5. All the code discussed in this section, with the exception of the API declarations, is contained behind this form.

There is very little event code behind frmWinInfo. The Form_Load procedure taps into the wrapper functions behind this form and plugs the values returned by the wrappers into text boxes on the form.

Figure 25.5.
frmWinInfo *returns interesting and valuable information about the Windows installation on the local computer.*

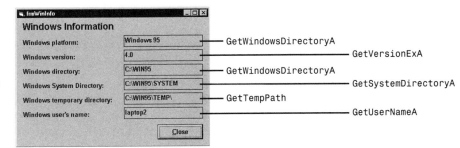

```
Private Sub Form_Load()
  txtWinDir = GetWinDir()
  txtSysDir = GetSysDir()
  txtTempDir = GetTempDir()
  txtWinVer = GetWinVerInfo()
  txtPlatform = GetPlatform()
  txtUser = GetUser()
End Sub
```

The following sections explain how each of the API calls implemented behind frmWinInfo work.

GetWindowsDirectoryA

The GetWindowsDirectoryA function retrieves the path to Windows and stores it in a string buffer. The return value of this function is the length of the string copied into the buffer. If the buffer isn't long enough, the return value is the length required. If the function fails, the return value is zero. The declaration for GetWindowsDirectoryA used in WinAPI.vbp is shown in Listing 25.19.

Listing 25.19. The GetWindowsDirectory API function prototype.

```
Declare Function apiGetWindowsDirectory _
  Lib "Kernel32" _
  Alias "GetWindowsDirectoryA" _
  (ByVal sReturnBuffer As String, _
  ByVal lBuffSize As Long) As Long
```

The GetWinDir function (see Listing 25.20) serves as a wrapper to apiGetWindowsDirectory. GetWinDir uses a global constant named MAX_PATH to establish the sWinDir string. The longest path of any file or directory under any version of Windows is 260, so this is an appropriate size. MAX_PATH is defined in basDeclares in WinAPI.vbp.

Listing 25.20. GetWinDir is a wrapper for the apiGetWindowsDirectoryA API function.

```
Function GetWinDir() As String
  Dim sWinDir As String * MAX_PATH 'MAX_PATH = 260
  Dim lWinDirSize As Long
  Dim lRetValue As Long

  'Create string of MAX_PATH spaces
  sWinDir = String(MAX_PATH, " ")
  lWinDirSize = Len(sWinDir)
  lRetValue = apiGetWindowsDirectory(sWinDir, lWinDirSize)
  GetWinDir = Left$(sWinDir, lRetValue)
End Function
```

The frmWinInfo form uses GetWinDir to plug the Windows path into a text box named txtWinDir.

GetSystemDirectoryA

In addition to the Windows directory, you might need the path to the Windows system directory. Most DLLs, ActiveX components, and other system resources are kept in the Windows system directory, and you might need this path to reference those resources. The GetSystemDirectoryA API function returns the path to the Windows system directory. Listing 25.21 shows the Declare statement used in WinAPI.vbp for the GetSystemDirectoryA API function.

Listing 25.21. The GetSystemDirectory API function prototype.

```
Declare Function apiGetSystemDirectory _
   Lib "Kernel32" _
   Alias "GetSystemDirectoryA" _
  (ByVal sReturnBuffer As String, _
   ByVal lBufferSize As Long) As Long
```

GetSystemDirectory returns the Windows system directory for the current machine in the sReturnBuffer parameter. Upon success, the function returns the number of characters contained in the lReturnBuffer argument. It returns zero if unsuccessful.

As you've seen elsewhere in this chapter, WinAPI.vbp uses a wrapper function to hide the complexity of the GetSystemDirectoryA function call. GetSysDir (see Listing 25.22) is included in the frmWinInfo form and provides a clean interface to the API call. Notice that GetSysDir uses the MAX_PATH global constant to set up the sSysDir string used to retrieve the Windows system directory path.

Listing 25.22. Retrieving the system directory with `GetSystemDirectory`.

```
Private Function GetSysDir() As String
  Dim sSysDir As String * MAX_PATH 'MAX_PATH = 260
  Dim lSize As Long
  Dim lRetValue As Long

  'Create string of MAX_PATH spaces
  sSysDir = String(MAX_PATH, " ")
  lSize = Len(sSysDir)
  lRetValue = apiGetSystemDirectory(sSysDir, lSize)
  GetSysDir = Left$(sSysDir, lRetValue)
End Function
```

GetTempPath

Another useful path to know is the path to the Windows temporary directory. Although Windows makes extensive use of this directory to store temporary files, there is no reason your application couldn't do the same thing. The path to the Windows temporary directory is returned by the `GetTempPath` API function (see Listing 25.23).

Listing 25.23. The `GetTempPath` API function prototype.

```
Declare Function apiGetTempPath _
   Lib "Kernel32" _
   Alias "GetTempPathA" _
  (ByVal lBufferSize As Long, _
   ByVal sReturnBuffer As String) As Long
```

This function retrieves the path to the directory where temp files are stored and places it in a string buffer (`sReturnBuffer`). The return value is the length of the returned string. Like `GetWindowsDirectory`, if the buffer isn't long enough the return value is the length required. But if the function fails, the return value is zero.

The `GetTemp` function (see Listing 25.24) provides the wrapper for `apiGetTempPath`. `GetTempDir` returns the path to the Windows temporary directory as a string.

Listing 25.24. Finding the Windows temporary directory with the `GetTempPath` API function.

```
Private Function GetTempDir() As String
  Dim sTempDir As String * MAX_PATH
  Dim lSize As Long
  Dim lRetLength As Long
```

continues

Listing 25.24. Continued.

```
'Create string of MAX_PATH spaces
sTempDir = String(MAX_PATH, " ")
lSize = Len(sTempDir)
lRetLength = apiGetTempPath(lSize, sTempDir)
GetTempDir = Left$(sTempDir, lRetLength)
End Function
```

GetVersionExA

Things are more complicated when you want to retrieve information about Windows. Windows provides a rather complicated data structure called an OSVERSIONINFO data type to return the Windows information. The structure of OSVERSIONINFO is shown in Listing 25.25.

Listing 25.25. The GetVersion function prototype.

```
Private Type OSVERSIONINFO
  lVersionInfo As Long
  lMajorVersion As Long
  lMinorVersion As Long
  lBuildNumber As Long
  lplatformID As Long
  sVersion As String * 128
End Type
```

frmWinInfo uses this structure to return a variety of different information about Windows. This information is returned from Windows with the GetVersionExA API call (see Listing 25.26). The only argument to GetVersionExA is the OSVERSIONINFO structure.

Listing 25.26. The GetVersion function prototype.

```
Declare Function apiGetVersion _
   Lib "Kernel32" _
   Alias "GetVersionExA" _
   (ByRef osVer As OSVERSIONINFO) As Long
```

This particular API comes in two different forms: GetVersion and GetVersionEx. GetVersion was migrated from the Win16 API, but GetVersionEx is new to the API collection. There are advantages to using GetVersionEx rather than the older GetVersion. First, it seems that many people had problems getting accurate information out of GetVersion. It used bit comparisons (AND/OR) to manipulate bits within a value to retrieve information, and these conversions weren't very straightforward. GetVersionEx uses a data structure to store each different part of the version information, which is easier to use. A second reason to use GetVersionEx is portability. GetVersion runs on Windows 95 but not on the NT platform. If your application is expected to operate on Windows NT, you must use GetVersionEx.

The OSVERSIONINFO can be interpreted like this: lVersionInfo is the length, in bytes, of the data structure. lMajorVersion would be 4 in Windows 95 and 3 in Windows 3.1. The lMinorVersion is the minor version release of the operating system. In Windows 95 this is always 0; in Windows 3.1 it's always 1.

The build number (dwBuildNumber) is a number that is mostly used by Microsoft internally, but might be important when debugging a problem that appears to be build-specific. lPlatformID is a long integer representing the platform on which the application is running. Windows 3.1 running Win32s is 0, Windows 95 is 1, and Windows NT is 2. They are declared as the constants in Listing 25.27, which appear in basDeclares in WinAPI.vbp.

Listing 25.27. Constant declarations to use with the GetVersion API call.

```
Public Const VER_PLATFORM_WIN32S = 0
Public Const VER_PLATFORM_WIN32_Windows = 1
Public Const VER_PLATFORM_WIN32_NT = 2
```

WinAPI.vbp on the CD-ROM uses the GetVersionEx function to display the current version of Windows in the system information using the following two wrapper functions. GetVerInfo retrieves a string representing the major and minor version numbers, whereas GetPlatform retrieves the platform number. Both of these routines are shown in Listing 25.28.

Listing 25.28. Getting the Windows version and platform information with API calls.

```
Private Function GetWinVerInfo() As String
  Dim lRetVal As Long
  Dim VersionNo As OSVERSIONINFO
  Dim lngVer As Long
  Dim Version As String

  VersionNo.lVersionInfo = 148
  lRetVal = apiGetVersion(VersionNo)
  GetWinVerInfo = _
     VersionNo.lMajorVersion & "." & _
     VersionNo.lMinorVersion
End Function

Private Function GetPlatform() As String
  Dim lRetVal As Long
```

continues

Listing 25.28. Continued.

```
Dim VersionNo As OSVERSIONINFO

VersionNo.lVersionInfo = 148
lRetVal = apiGetVersion(VersionNo)
Select Case VersionNo.lplatformID
  Case VER_PLATFORM_WIN32S
      GetPlatform = "Windows 3.x"
  Case VER_PLATFORM_WIN32_Windows
      GetPlatform = "Windows 95"
  Case VER_PLATFORM_WIN32_NT
      GetPlatform = "Windows NT"
  Case Else
      GetPlatform = "Unknown"
End Select
End Function
```

GetUserNameA

The last bit of information we'll look at is how to get the name the user entered into the Windows login dialog box. This data can be used to validate a user, load a user profile, or personalize the application. Listing 25.29 shows the declaration in `WinAPI.vbp` referencing `GetUserNameA`.

Listing 25.29. The `GetUserName` API function prototype.

```
Declare Function apiGetUserName _
   Lib "Advapi32" _
   Alias "GetUserNameA" _
   (ByVal sBuffer As String, _
    lBufferSize As Long) As Long
```

This function retrieves the name of the user currently logged on to the system and places it in the `sBuffer` string buffer. If `GetUserNameA` is successful, it returns a `True` value, and the length of the returned string is placed in the `lBufferSize` variable.

The `GetUser` function in `frmWinInfo` (see Listing 25.30) serves as the wrapper function for `GetUserNameA`. This wrapper works exactly as the other wrappers you've seen in this chapter.

Listing 25.30. Getting user information with the `GetUserName` API function.

```
Private Function GetUser() As String
  Dim sUserName As String * 255
  Dim lNameSize As Long
  Dim lRetValue As Long
```

```
      sUserName = String(255, " ")
      lNameSize = Len(sUserName)
      lRetValue = apiGetUserName(sUserName, lNameSize)
      GetUser = Left$(sUserName, lNameSize - 1)
End Function
```

Getting Hardware Information

You open the Windows System Information dialog box (see Figure 25.6) from the Visual Basic Help | About dialog box. The System Information dialog box contains useful information about the computer and its resources.

FIGURE 25.6.
The Windows System Information dialog box contains useful information.

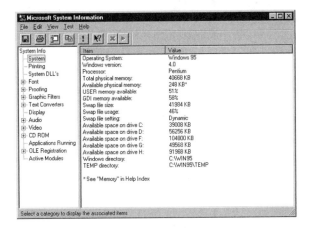

The code behind frmSysInfo (see Figure 25.7) contains some of the information you see in the System Information dialog box. The frmVolumeInfo form you'll see in the next section contains information that is specific to the hard disk volumes on your computer.

FIGURE 25.7.
frmHdwInfo *contains some of the information that is available in the Windows System Information dialog box.*

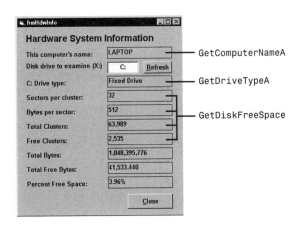

The Windows API provides several functions you'll find useful for retrieving information about the Windows system, the hardware, and other software that might be running on the computer. This information is often useful for avoiding problems like running out of disk space or trying to write data to a CD-ROM drive. These functions also provide handy information, like the location of the Windows and temporary directories.

In Figure 25.7, notice the text box and command button on frmHdwInfo. Filling in the drive designation of one of the hard disks on your computer or on the network and pressing the Refresh button causes the form to display the drive information for that hard disk. The following sections explain how frmHdwInfo uses these API calls to return the information you see in Figure 25.7.

GetComputerNameA

Every computer on a Windows network has a unique name. This name is useful to identify the computer and its resources. The GetComputerNameA API function (see Listing 25.31) retrieves the Windows name for the location computer in the sBuffer argument.

Listing 25.31. The GetComputerNameA API function prototype.

```
Declare Function apiGetComputerName _
   Lib "Kernel32" _
   Alias "GetComputerNameA" _
   (ByVal sBuffer As String, _
    lBufferSize As Long) As Long
```

GetComputerNameA retrieves the name of the current system. If the function fails, its return value is 0 (false). Otherwise, the return value is nonzero and is interpreted as true. The lBufferSize argument returns the number of characters copied to the sBuffer string variable. The GetComputer function in WinAPI.vbp (see Listing 25.32) provides a wrapper for the apiGetComputerName declaration.

Listing 25.32. GetComputer is the wrapper for the apiGetComputerName function.

```
Function GetComputer() As String
  Dim sComputerName As String * 255
  Dim lSize As Long
  Dim lName As Long

  lSize = Len(sComputerName)
  lName = apiGetComputerName(sComputerName, lSize)
  GetComputer = Left$(sComputerName, lSize)
End Function
```

GetDriveTypeA

frmHdwInfo includes a text box reporting the type of disk present in the computer. The GetDriveTypeA function (see Listing 25.33) returns a long integer value that indicates the type of disk that has been passed.

Listing 25.33. The GetDriveTypeA API function prototype.

```
Declare Function apiGetDriveType _
   Lib "Kernel32" _
   Alias "GetDriveTypeA" _
   (ByVal sPath As String) As Long
```

You pass the function the path to the drive you want to test (for example, C:), and GetDriveTypeA returns a long integer value representing the drive type. The constants in Listing 25.34 can be used to determine the drive type.

Listing 25.34. Constant values to use with GetDriveType.

```
Const DRIVE_UNKNOWN = 0
Const DRIVE_NOT_AVAILABLE = 1
Const DRIVE_REMOVABLE = 2
Const DRIVE_FIXED = 3
Const DRIVE_REMOTE = 4
Const DRIVE_CDROM = 5
Const DRIVE_RAMDISK = 6
```

The GetTypeDrive function (see Listing 25.35) uses a Select Case statement to determine the description of the drive passed in as the sPath argument. GetDriveType is a string function returning the description of the drive type.

Listing 25.35. Getting drive information with the GetComputerName API function.

```
Function GetTypeDrive(sPathName As String) As String
  Dim lRetValue As Long

  lRetValue = apiGetDriveType(sPathName)

  Select Case lRetValue
    Case DRIVE_UNKNOWN
      GetTypeDrive = "Unknown"
    Case DRIVE_NOT_AVAILABLE
      GetTypeDrive = "Not Available"
```

continues

Listing 25.35. Continued.

```
  Case DRIVE_REMOVABLE
    GetTypeDrive = "Removable Drive"
  Case DRIVE_FIXED
    GetTypeDrive = "Fixed Drive"
  Case DRIVE_REMOTE
    GetTypeDrive = "Network Drive"
  Case DRIVE_CDROM
    GetTypeDrive = "CD-ROM Drive"
  Case DRIVE_RAMDISK
    GetTypeDrive = "RAM Drive"
  Case Else
    GetTypeDrive = "Unknown"
  End Select
End Function
```

GetDiskFreeSpaceA

Another common application requirement is checking the amount of available free disk space on the computer. There is no reason to try to write a lot of data to a disk file unless there is adequate space for it. The GetDiskFreeSpaceA function call (see Listing 25.36) returns the information necessary to determine how much of a disk is available.

Listing 25.36. The GetDiskFreeSpace API function prototype.

```
Declare Function apiGetDiskFreeSpace _
  Lib "Kernel32" _
  Alias "GetDiskFreeSpaceA" _
  (ByVal sPath As String, _
  lSectors As Long, _
  lBytes As Long, _
  lFreeClusters As Long, _
  lClusters As Long) As Long
```

GetDiskFreeSpace uses the sPath argument to determine which disk is to be examined. If the sPath argument is Null, the function returns the amount of free space remaining in the current path. The number of sectors per cluster, bytes per sector, total clusters, and clusters remaining are all returned, enabling you to determine free and used space for a particular drive. If the function is successful, it returns a nonzero (true) value; if it is unsuccessful, it returns 0 (false).

The GetDiskInfo wrapper subroutine (see Listing 25.37) accepts a valid pathname as an argument and returns a lot of information on the disk indicated by the path. Notice that with this API function you get more than just the free disk space.

Listing 25.37. GetDiskInfo returns a lot of interesting information about the computer's disk.

```
Sub GetDiskInfo(sPathName As String)
  Dim iRetValue As Integer
  Dim lSectorsPerCluster As Long
  Dim lBytesPerSector As Long
  Dim lFreeClusters As Long
  Dim lTotalClusters As Long
  Dim lFreeBytes As Long
  Dim lTotalBytes As Long

  iRetValue = apiGetDiskFreeSpace( _
      sPathName, _
      lSectorsPerCluster, _
      lBytesPerSector, _
      lFreeClusters, _
      lTotalClusters)

  lFreeBytes = _
      Format((lSectorsPerCluster * lBytesPerSector) * lFreeClusters, "#,##0")

  lTotalBytes = _
      lTotalClusters * lSectorsPerCluster * lBytesPerSector

  DiskInfo.SectorsPerCluster = lSectorsPerCluster
  DiskInfo.BytesPerSector = lBytesPerSector
  DiskInfo.TotalClusters = lTotalClusters
  DiskInfo.FreeClusters = lFreeClusters
  DiskInfo.TotalBytes = lTotalBytes
  DiskInfo.FreeBytes = lFreeBytes
End Sub
```

GetDiskInfo uses a structure to capture the disk information. The DiskInfo structure is shown in Listing 25.38.

Listing 25.38. The DiskInfo structure returns just about everything you'd ever want to know about your computer's disks.

```
Private Type DiskInfoType
  SectorsPerCluster As Long
  BytesPerSector As Long
  FreeClusters As Long
  TotalClusters As Long
  TotalBytes As Long
  FreeBytes As Long
End Type
```

The `DiskInfo` structure is not part of the Windows API. Instead, it is a custom data type established just for `WinAPI.vbp`. After the `DiskInfo` structure has been filled in by `GetDiskInfo`, the `FillForm` subroutine (see Listing 25.39) plugs the data into the `frmHdwInfo` form. Notice that `FillForm` calls the other hardware information routines (`GetComputer`, `GetTypeDrive`, and so on) in the `WinAPI.vbp` project.

Listing 25.39. The FillForm procedure calculates important information about the computer's hard drive.

```
Sub FillForm()
On Error Resume Next
  lblDrive.Caption = txtDrive & " Drive type:"
  txtComputerName = GetComputer()
  txtDriveType = GetTypeDrive(txtDrive)
  Call GetDiskInfo(txtDrive)
  txtSectorsPerCluster = _
    Format(DiskInfo.SectorsPerCluster, "#,0")
  txtBytesPerSector = _
    Format(DiskInfo.BytesPerSector, "#,0")
  txtTotalClusters = _
    Format(DiskInfo.TotalClusters, "#,0")
  txtFreeClusters = _
    Format(DiskInfo.FreeClusters, "#,0")
  txtTotalBytes = _
    Format(DiskInfo.TotalBytes, "#,0")
  txtFreeBytes = _
    Format(DiskInfo.FreeBytes, "#,0")
  txtPercentFree = _
    Format(DiskInfo.FreeBytes / DiskInfo.TotalBytes, _
    "Percent")
End Sub
```

Filling a new disk designator into the text box near the top of `frmHdwInfo` and clicking the Refresh button runs the `FillForm` subroutine. This simple technique provides you with a way to examine each of the disks on the computer in turn without hard coding the disk designation.

Getting Disk Volume Information with `GetVolumeInformationA`

The Windows API also provides detailed information about the disk and file systems on your computer. This information is collectively referred to as *volume* information. Each root directory on a disk is considered a volume of the file system. Because of the complexity of 32-bit Windows systems, a single computer might have any number of different file systems on it, including FAT and NTFS. Although it is unlikely your applications will need this information, this section demonstrates how complete the Windows API is.

The `WinAPI.vbp` project includes `frmVolInfo` (see Figure 25.8). Keep in mind that this is only part of the information that is available to you through the Windows API.

FIGURE 25.8.

`frmVolInfo` *reports detailed information about the file structures on your comput-er's disks.*

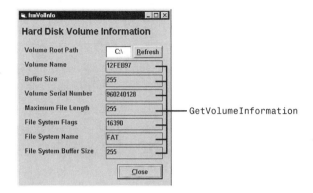

Form `frmVolInfo` includes a text box that contains the drive designation of the root directory on a hard disk connected to the computer (`C:\` by default) and a button to refresh the volume information displayed on the form. Any local drive or network drive mapped into the local computer's directory structure can be examined with `frmVolInfo`.

Interestingly, all the information you see in Figure 25.8 is provided by a single API call. `GetVolumeInformationA` (see Listing 25.40) returns a variety of information in the arguments passed to this routine.

Listing 25.40. The `GetVolumeInformation` API function prototype.

```
Declare Function apiGetVolumeInformation _
   Lib "Kernel32" _
   Alias "GetVolumeInformationA" _
  (ByVal sPath As String, _
   ByVal sNameBuffer As String, _
   ByVal lVolumeNameSize As Long, _
   lVolSerialNo As Long, _
   lMaxFileLength As Long, _
   lSystemFlags As Long, _
   ByVal sSysNamebuffer As String, _
   ByVal lSysNameBufSize As Long) As Long
```

This function returns information about the file system and volume information for a valid path. `lMaxFileLength` is the maximum number of characters allowed for a filename on the particular file system. `lSystemFlags` is a long integer value that indicates whether the volume is compressed, whether filenames are case-sensitive, and whether the volume supports file-based compression. The return value of `GetVolumeInformationA` is non-zero (true) if successful and 0 (false) if not.

The wrapper function for GetVolumeInformationA is shown in Listing 25.41. Notice that GetVolumeInfo uses a structure variable named mVolInfo.

Listing 25.41. Retrieving information about a disk volume with apiGetVolumeInformation.

```
Sub GetVolumeInfo(sPathName As String)
  Dim lRetValue As Long

  mVolInfo.sVolName = String(255, " ")
  mVolInfo.sFileSysName = String(255, " ")

  mVolInfo.lBufferSize = Len(mVolInfo.sVolName)
  mVolInfo.lFileSysBufSize = Len(mVolInfo.sFileSysName)

  lRetValue = apiGetVolumeInformation( _
     sPathName, _
     mVolInfo.sVolName, _
     mVolInfo.lBufferSize, _
     mVolInfo.lVolumeSerialNumber, _
     mVolInfo.lMaxFileLength, _
     mVolInfo.lFileSysFlags, _
     mVolInfo.sFileSysName, _
     mVolInfo.lFileSysBufSize)
End Sub
```

mVolInfo is not part of the Windows API. Instead, mVolInfo is a custom structure created just for the WinAPI.vbp project. Listing 25.42 shows how mVolInfo is laid out.

Listing 25.42. The mVolInfo data structure stores the data returned by the apiGetVolumeInformation function.

```
Private Type VolumeInfoType
  sVolName As String * 255
  lBufferSize As Long
  lVolumeSerialNumber As Long
  lMaxFileLength As Long
  lFileSysFlags As Long
  sFileSysName As String * 255
  lFileSysBufSize As Long
End Type

Dim mVolInfo As VolumeInfoType
```

The data in the mVolInfo structure is filled into the frmVolInfo form with the FillForm subroutine shown in Listing 25.43. This form is identical in action to the FillForm routine behind frmHdwInfo.

Listing 25.43. FillForm plugs the data in the mVolInfo structure variable into form frmVolInfo.

```
Sub FillForm()
  Call GetVolumeInfo(txtVolume)
  txtVolName = mVolInfo.sVolName
  txtBufferSize = mVolInfo.lBufferSize
  txtVolSerialNumber = mVolInfo.lVolumeSerialNumber
  txtMaxFileLength = mVolInfo.lMaxFileLength
  txtFileSysFlags = mVolInfo.lFileSysFlags
  txtFileSysName = mVolInfo.sFileSysName
  txtFileSysBufSize = mVolInfo.lFileSysBufSize
End Sub
```

Summary

In this chapter you looked at how you can go beyond the limits of Visual Basic by digging into the guts of Windows. The Windows API is a great way to add extra functionality to your applications. Almost 1,000 different functions are built into Windows that enable you to control your application settings, communications, Registry settings, and network functions.

Chapter 26, "INI Files and the System Registry," sheds light on the subject of utilizing the system registry and INI files to store application information. In this chapter you'll find the explanations and code samples necessary to add multiple levels of security to your applications to ensure the safety and integrity of the data stored there.

INI Files and the System Registry

Many programs need some way to preserve information from session to session. Many games, for example, store the highest score, a player's nickname, or other parameters between game sessions. You might want to store a directory path, user preference information, or a user's name in a way that won't get changed if another user runs the same program. Although you could use the data storage techniques described in Part IV, "Accessing Data," creating a database with tables and fields is overkill in most cases.

What you really want in these cases is a quick and easy way to indelibly record this information on the user's computer. Traditionally most Windows applications have stored configuration information in *initialization files* that are read as the application starts up. Initialization files all have an .INI filename extension and can be stored in several different locations, including the Windows directory, the Windows system directory, and the application's runtime location.

An application's INI file is a simple text file saved on the computer's disk. The configuration information in the INI file is read by the application each time it is started on the computer. New or updated information can be written to the INI file as the application runs. Because the information saved in the INI file is permanently stored in a file, the application's configuration is available any time the application is started.

The structure of an INI file is quite simple. Figure 26.1 shows the INI file for the ODBC manager. Notice how the data in the file is divided into several *sections* (ODBC Data Sources, MS Access Databases, FoxPro Files, and so on) each containing several *keys* (MS Access Databases) and *values* (Access Data (*.mdb)).

All INI files follow this pattern. There is no limit to the number of sections in an INI file, and each section can contain many keys and values.

Visual Basic does not contain any built-in functions or subroutines specifically designed to create or read INI files. You could expend considerable effort to write the code and succeed in programming the functions necessary to perform these tasks. Alternatively, you could use the Windows API functions specifically designed to create and read INI files and their contents. The "Manipulating INI Files" section near the end of this chapter describes how to use the API calls in your programs. `Registry.vbp` is a sample Visual Basic project that includes all the code and techniques described in that section and the others in this chapter.

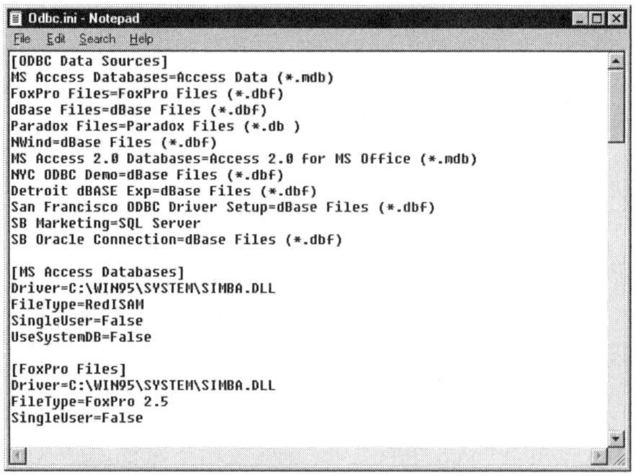

```
[ODBC Data Sources]
MS Access Databases=Access Data (*.mdb)
FoxPro Files=FoxPro Files (*.dbf)
dBase Files=dBase Files (*.dbf)
Paradox Files=Paradox Files (*.db )
NWind=dBase Files (*.dbf)
MS Access 2.0 Databases=Access 2.0 for MS Office (*.mdb)
NYC ODBC Demo=dBase Files (*.dbf)
Detroit dBASE Exp=dBase Files (*.dbf)
San Francisco ODBC Driver Setup=dBase Files (*.dbf)
SB Marketing=SQL Server
SB Oracle Connection=dBase Files (*.dbf)

[MS Access Databases]
Driver=C:\WIN95\SYSTEM\SIMBA.DLL
FileType=RedISAM
SingleUser=False
UseSystemDB=False

[FoxPro Files]
Driver=C:\WIN95\SYSTEM\SIMBA.DLL
FileType=FoxPro 2.5
SingleUser=False
```

FIGURE 26.1. *INI files are divided into sections containing keys and values.*

For several reasons, INI files might not be the ideal repository for initialization and configuration information. Because INI files are simple ASCII files they can be edited by Notepad or any suitable editor. This means, of course, that making direct changes to the contents of a INI file is easy, but it also means that INI files are exposed to tampering. Also, because the INI file is not protected by Windows, the file might be deleted or overwritten due to accident or malicious behavior on the part of the computer's users. Furthermore, there is only one level of organization in an INI file. The keys and values are all contained within the sections of the INI file, and you can't nest sections. Therefore, the data stored in INI files is fairly simple. Finally, all the values stored in INI files are strings. Any numeric values must be read in as strings and converted to the appropriate numeric value, complicating the task of programming these files.

For all these reasons, Microsoft engineered the *System Registry* to serve as the primary repository of program settings information. The System Registry is a single file in the Windows directory that acts as a hierarchical database of configuration data. The System Registry is not an ASCII file and can't be edited with Notepad or any other simple editor. You must use the specially designed Regedit program built into Windows to edit the System Registry. Regedit is discussed in the "Using Regedit" section of this chapter. Because INI files are the older technology, discussion of programming INI files is deferred until the Registry has been thoroughly explored.

> **Note:** The terminology involved with the Registry changes somewhat as you work with Regedit, the built-in VBA Registry functions, and the Windows API calls designed to program the Registry. Each approach to the Registry has its own unique terminology that is different from the others in minor ways.

Understanding the Registry

Unlike an INI file, which is basically a simple arrangement of information with only one level of organization, the data in the Registry is arranged in a hierarchical manner. The data structure in the Registry is similar to the Windows file system, although instead of folders, think of Registry *keys*. Under Windows 95, all these keys are grouped into six top-level categories. Table 26.1 names these categories and provides a description of each one.

Table 26.1. Registry top-level sections.

Section Name	Description
HKEY_CLASSES_ROOT	Stores information about object classes and file associations
HKEY_CURRENT_USER	The configuration information for the current user
HKEY_LOCAL_MACHINE	Detailed information about the computer and its software
HKEY_USERS	Generic user information not specific to a particular user
HKEY_CURRENT_CONFIG	General configuration information about the computer and its software
HKEY_DYN_DATA	Temporary storage during a Windows session

Under each of these top-level keys are several *subkeys*, each of which might have any number of subkeys. At any level, a key can contain a mixed number of *value* entries and more subkeys. This hierarchical arrangement allows an immense amount of data to be stored in the System Registry.

Figure 26.2 shows a small portion of the System Registry open to details about the IBM Voice Type, a voice recognition package installed on this particular computer. (The next section explains how to use Regedit, the application you see open in Figure 26.2.) The plus sign to the left of some of the keys in Figure 26.2 indicates that there are subkeys arrayed under those keys.

In Figure 26.2, the IBM Voice Type program has several configuration parameters stored under a key named MAIN. Each parameter is a *value* in Registry parlance. These values include size and state. The data associated with the size value is "0,0,239,101" while state is "NORMAL". Both of these values are strings, but they could be binary or long integer values or any of a number of the other data types described in the section "Programming the Registry" later in this chapter.

The Registry key hierarchy looks a lot like the folders in the Windows directory system. In fact, you can think of a key as a folder that holds other keys (or folders) and key values. In this chapter, the expression *folder* refers to a key that holds subkeys or key values within it.

Key   Value   Data

FIGURE 26.2.
Registry keys are arranged in a hierarchical fashion.

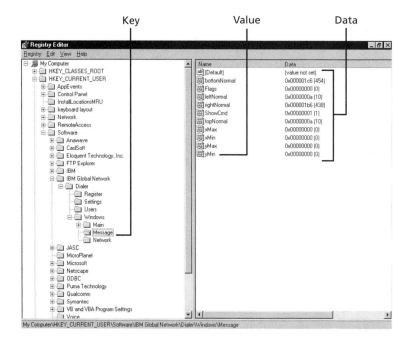

Note: When working with VBA, the items referred to as *values* by Regedit are called *keys*. When working with VBA calls, you create *keys* that contain *values*. (You'll see these functions in the "Programming the Registry" section later in this chapter.)

Because each computer running any 32-bit version of Windows has its own registry, it is easy to store user-specific and installation-specific configuration information in the Registry. This is true even if multiple users invoke a single copy of an application running on a network file server. Also, the location and availability of the Registry is in doubt because it is closely integrated into Windows.

Using Regedit

Under Windows 95 and 98, you use REGEDIT.EXE to get a look into your Registry. Under Windows NT, the corresponding program is REGEDT32.EXE. This program enables you to view existing Registry keys and their values as well as edit the keys and value data.

Warning: If you change the wrong key you could make it impossible to start Windows and be faced with reinstalling all your software—including Windows.

> **Note:** You can't edit or repair the Registry from outside Windows, so Windows must be in working order to make changes. Breaking the Registry can mean breaking Windows in a big way.

Using Regedit is easy. Select the Run option from the Start menu and enter REGEDIT.EXE or REGEDIT (case is not important—regedit.exe works just fine) in the Open dialog box when the Run dialog box appears (see Figure 26.3).

FIGURE 26.3.
The Run dialog box.

> **Tip:** If you find that you use Regedit often, create a shortcut to it on your desktop or Start menu.

A few seconds after clicking OK, the Registry Editor appears (see Figure 26.4). The Registry Editor's main window is divided into two panes. In the left pane you select the key you'd like to examine; the values and the data contained within the key appear in the right pane. For example, in Figure 26.4 Regedit is open to the owner registration information for a product produced by the Acme company. Acme sells two types of products, Widgets and Gadgets. This owner has apparently installed a copy of both the standard and deluxe versions of Widgets on his computer. The Registry entries you see in Figure 26.4 were added by the Acme applications as they were installed on the user's computer.

FIGURE 26.4.
The Registry Editor at work.

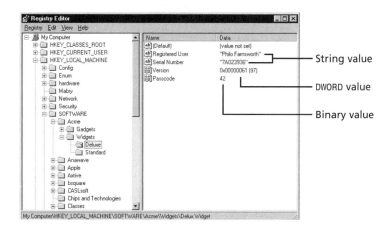

The values for the Deluxe Widgets product include two strings (Registered User and Serial Number) and one DWORD (long integer) value (Version). The Passcode is a binary value. Figure 26.4 illustrates one advantage of using the System Registry for storing configuration data. Simple INI files store only strings, whereas the Registry stores a variety of data types.

Notice that the Registry keys in Figure 26.4 are arranged in a hierarchical manner, much as the Windows 95 files and folders are organized. A plus sign in a folder icon indicates that subordinate folders exist within that folder. Double-clicking a folder tagged with a plus sign, or selecting a folder and pressing the plus key on your computer's keyboard, opens the folder to reveal the folders at the next lower level.

Editing Registry Values

Changing data in the Registry is dangerously easy. In the right pane, simply double-click the value you'd like to change or highlight the value and select Edit | Modify from the Registry Editor's menu bar. The Edit String dialog box shown in Figure 26.5 opens, permitting you to change the key's value.

FIGURE 26.5.
String values are easy to change.

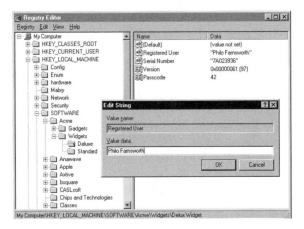

Registry entries contain more than just text data. As you see in Figure 26.6, a Registry key can contain binary or long integer values. Each of these entries is handled differently in Regedit, although the principles of managing Registry keys are identical for all three types of keys.

Because it's so easy to assign an unworkable value to a key, it's best not to experiment with Registry entries unless you're sure you know what you're doing. Many of the Registry entries determine the most fundamental Windows 95 functions and operations. Invalid entries could destroy your ability to reliably run Windows 95 and the applications you've installed on your system.

FIGURE 26.6.

Registry entries include DWORD (left) and binary (right) values.

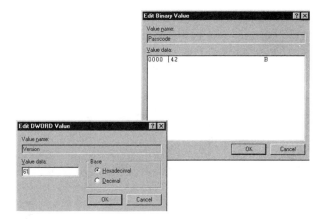

> **Note:** Improper changes to the Registry can impair your ability to use the peripherals attached to your computer.

Adding New Registry Values

Using Regedit to add new keys and new values to the Registry is not difficult. Open the top-level key categories to the desired location by double-clicking the keys in succession. For example, if you want to add the four required keys to the Acme Gadgets key and you previously added Acme as a key under HKEY_LOCAL_MACHINE / Software and the Gadgets subkey under Acme, right-click Gadgets to reveal the shortcut menu you see in Figure 26.7. Alternatively, use Regedit's menu bar to select Edit | New | Key.

FIGURE 26.7.

Regedit's shortcut menu includes all the commands necessary to manage Registry entries.

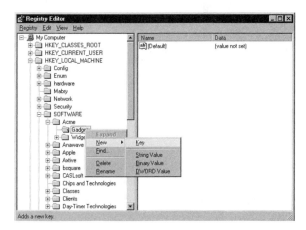

Regedit adds a new subkey to the selected folder as shown in Figure 26.8. The key's name is available for editing, so type whatever you want as the key name. Key and value names can include spaces, but should not include punctuation. In Figure 26.8, a new sub-key named Professional has been added to the Gadgets key under the Acme key.

Figure 26.8.

Assign a meaning-ful name to the new key.

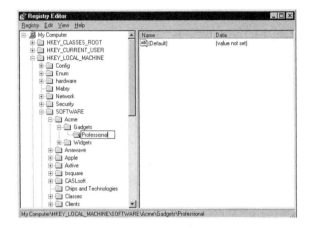

Adding values to the key is a continuation of adding keys. The main difference is that you select a data type for the new value from the shortcut menu that opens in response to the right-click. Figure 26.9 shows how this works.

Figure 26.9.

Specifying a data type from the shortcut menu adds a value of that type to the selected key.

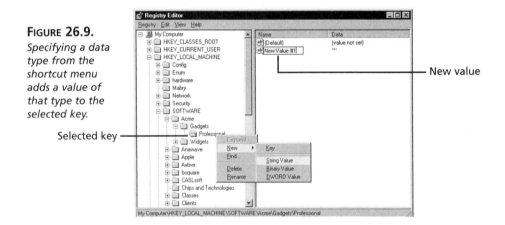

Figure 26.9 actually shows two different steps. The first step is the right-click on the folder name to open the shortcut menu so you can select the data type. The second step is entering the name of the new value under the key in the right side of the Regedit screen. The value name (Registered User) has not yet been typed into the value's name area.

Adding the other values (Serial Number, Version, and PassCode) is a process of repeating the steps required to enter the Registered User value. The only difference is selecting the correct data type for each value. If you select the wrong data type for a value, highlight the value name by clicking it and press the Delete button to remove the value from the Registry. You can't change the data type of a Registry key after the key has been added to the Registry. The "Programming the Registry" section of this chapter explains how to read values from the Registry.

> **Warning:** The System Registry Editor (Regedit) does not support an Undo feature, so be sure to verify the value you intend to remove before pressing Delete.

Programming the Registry

Windows 3.1 had a Registry, but few people paid attention to it. It primarily was used to keep up with OLE information, which few people used, so it was mentioned only when something went wrong. Windows 95 and Windows NT keep up with everything about your PC using the System Registry. Your hardware settings—user preferences (color, desktop, background), the software you have installed on your PC—all have entries in the Registry.

When you're manipulating the Registry, there are standards you should follow. Your application's entry should follow a pattern. It's a hierarchy that starts with the HKEY_LOCAL_MACHINE key, then moves to SOFTWARE, then to the software vendor's name, the application name, followed by the current version entry, and then any setting you want to make. HKEY_LOCAL_MACHINE is the key that tracks what software is installed on the machine. If you wanted to make any user-specific settings, you would also add an entry to the HKEY_CURRENT_USER key. Refer to Table 26.1 for descriptions of the data stored in the top-level keys of the Registry.

> **Note:** If you place a key in the Registry, make plans to remove it. In other words, plan an uninstall program that removes any traces of your software from the Registry. This isn't required, but it's good programming practice.

As you'll see in the following sections, there are two distinct approaches to programming the system Registry. The first utilizes built-in VBA calls; the second requires API functions to manipulate the Registry. Each has its own limitations and requirements but they both get the job done. Therefore, you can choose whether to program the Registry directly with VBA functions or go to the trouble and effort required to include the appropriate API calls in your programs.

Using VBA Calls to Program the Registry

The VBA language includes several calls designed to create new Registry keys, add values to the keys, and modify the values after they are set. You can also delete keys when you are finished with them, perhaps as part of an uninstall routine.

The main limitation of using the VBA Registry statements is that they operate on one specific key in the system Registry. Any Registry keys created through these VBA statements are added to the following key:

```
HKEY_CURRENT_USER\Software\VB and VBA Program Settings
```

You can't use the VBA Registry statements to manipulate keys in any other location in the System Registry.

A second restriction is that all Registry key values created with the VBA statements are string values. You can't explicitly write a numeric value to the Registry using these commands. All values you pass as arguments are converted to strings, regardless of their native data types.

The VBA statements for managing the Registry are presented in Table 26.2.

Table 26.2. The VBA Registry functions.

Function Name	Description
SaveSetting	Creates a new key and value or modifies an existing key value
GetSetting	Retrieves a key's value from the Registry
DeleteSetting	Removes a key from the Registry
GetAllSettings	Returns a list of all keys and values from a section of the Registry

Of these statements, you'll use SaveSetting and GetSetting the most. SaveSetting creates a new key and establishes the key's initial value. If the key already exists, SaveSetting simply updates the key's value. GetSetting brings back a value from the Registry to use in your program. Therefore, if you're saving program configuration data in the Registry, you'll set up the keys and fill them with data with SaveSetting and read them back during the next program session with GetSetting.

DeleteSetting is a one-time command. After you delete a key you can't recover it, so you'll use this statement mostly for maintenance or when it's time to uninstall an application.

The following sections detail the use of these VBA statements in your Visual Basic applications. Be sure to notice that some of the VBA commands are simple statements that do not return a value, whereas others are functions that either return the value you're looking for or return a code that indicates how well the function performed.

SaveSetting

The syntax of SaveSetting is as follows:

```
SaveSetting(ApplicationName, Section, KeyName, KeyValue)
```

ApplicationName is the name of the application that's writing to the Registry. This becomes the subkey immediately under the HKEY_CURRENT_USER\Software\VB and VBA Program Settings key in the system Registry.

Section is the name of a subkey folder under the application's key in the Registry. For example, if your application is named Acme, you might have a section folder named User Preferences under the Acme key. Within this folder you'll store all the keys and values that specify the user's preferences when working with the Acme application.

KeyName and *KeyValue* go hand-in-hand. For example, assume you want to save the position of the main form as the user shuts down the application so that you can open the form in the same location on the screen the next time the program is started. You'll need to preserve the Left and Top values under the User Preferences section. These two statements perform this task:

```
SaveSetting "Widget", "User Preferences", "MainFormLeft", frmMain.Left
SaveSetting "Widget", "User Preferences", "MainFormTop", frmMain.Top
```

Notice that even though a form's Left and Top properties are integer values the SaveSetting statement writes these values into the Registry as strings.

If, at a later time, the following statements are executed, the new values overwrite whatever happens to be stored in the Registry:

```
SaveSetting "Widgets", "User Preferences", "MainFormLeft", 100
SaveSetting "Widgets", "User Preferences", "MainFormTop", 100
```

> **Tip:** If you're like most other developers, you like to watch the product of your efforts as you work on a project. The most direct way to see the result of the SaveSetting statement is to have Regedit open to the Visual Basic program key area while you run this code. But, you won't be able to see the effect of SaveSetting until you run the View | Refresh menu command from the Regedit menu bar or press F5 to force Regedit to refresh its display.

It is not an error to overwrite an existing value and you are not notified that values have been overwritten. If it's important to know in advance whether SaveSetting will overwrite existing data, you should first use the GetSetting statement to attempt to retrieve the value. An error is generated if GetSetting fails to find the specified key. This error serves as your indication that the key has not yet been written into the Registry.

The Visual Basic online help does not mention how to create nested keys using SaveSetting. In fact, it appears that SaveSetting is designed to provide a single level of keys under the application folder. The fact is that you can easily create nested keys by including the nested key in the Key argument you pass to SaveSetting. The following statement creates a subkey named Widgets under the Acme application folder. Deluxe is the name of the Registry section and MainFormLeft is the name of the value key:

```
SaveSetting "Acme\Widgets", "Deluxe", "MainFormLeft", 100
```

Alternatively, the nesting could be performed on the section parameter. The following statement is equivalent to the preceding example:

```
SaveSetting "Acme", "Widgets\Deluxe", "MainFormLeft", 100
```

The sample project accompanying this chapter (Registry.vbp) uses one level of sub-folder under the Acme application folder, but you should keep in mind that it's easy to nest folders if necessary. Registry.vbp includes frmSaveSetting (see Figure 26.10). This form contains the code necessary to save the four Registry values displayed on the form.

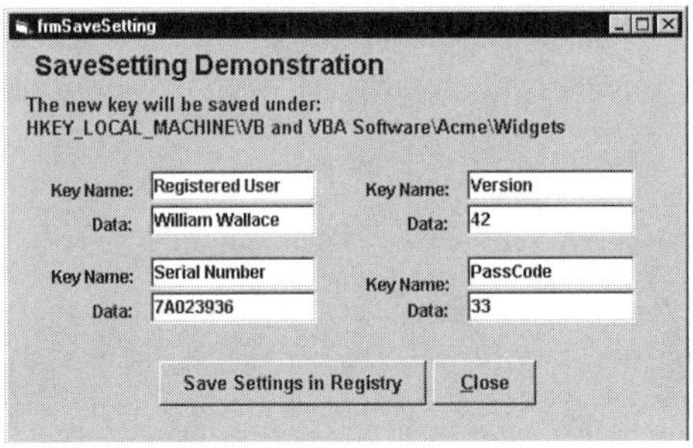

FIGURE 26.10.

frmSaveSetting *contains all the code necessary to save Registry keys using VBA calls.*

GetSetting

The syntax of the GetSetting function is very similar to SaveSetting:

```
GetSetting(ApplicationName, Section, KeyName, [Default])
```

Most of the parameters to GetSetting are self-evident. The only new argument is the *Default* value at the end. If GetSetting tries to retrieve a nonexistent key value, the default is applied. An empty string is assumed if *Default* is omitted.

> **Tip:** When you use GetSetting you should always include the default value because there's a chance the key value is an empty string.

The following statement returns the Version value from the Acme\Widgets Registry folder and stores it in the iVer variable (an integer data type). The built-in CInt function is used to convert the string Version value stored in the Registry to an integer after the data is retrieved from the Registry.

```
iVer = CInt(GetSetting("Acme", "Widgets", "Version"))
```

Listing 26.1 shows how you can use the default argument to determine when the key value has not been assigned.

Listing 26.1. Your code should always check to make sure the Registry values have been successfully returned by the GetSetting function.

```
iVer = CInt(GetSetting("Acme", "Widgets", "Version", 99))
If iVer = 99 Then
  MsgBox "Version has not yet been set"
End If
```

Your programs should not unwisely assume a particular setting has been saved in the Registry; so you'll write fail-safe Registry code in most cases.

The Registry.vbp project includes frmGetSettings (shown in Figure 26.11). This form intelligently checks for the Registry values that have been saved on frmSaveSetting and informs the user (through code such as you see in Listing 26.1) when the Registry settings can't be found.

FIGURE 26.11.

frmGetSetting *retrieves values from the System Registry.*

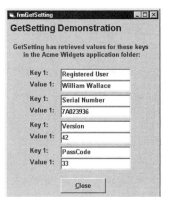

DeleteSetting

The DeleteSetting statement is simple:

```
DeleteSetting ApplicationName[, Section][, KeyName]
```

Notice that both the *Section* and *KeyName* parameters are optional. If these arguments are omitted, the entire application folder tree is removed. The following statement removes the Acme application folder and all subfolders under it:

```
DeleteSetting "Acme"
```

Similarly, if a section is provided the section folder and all its keys are removed. The following statement removes the Widgets key folder in the Acme application folder. Any other key folders in the Acme application are not removed or modified.

```
DeleteSetting "Acme", "Widgets"
```

Finally, providing all three arguments removes just one key within one section folder under the application's folder:

```
DeleteSetting "Acme", "Widgets", "PassCode"
```

> **Warning:** Deletions performed using `DeleteSetting` are permanent and are performed as soon as the statement executes. You cannot undo the effect of the `DeleteSetting` statement.

Contrary to what the Visual Basic online help tells you, an error is generated if the application folder, section folder, or key do not exist. An error 5 (Invalid procedure call or argument) is triggered if you run `DeleteSetting` against a nonexistent key or folder. Therefore, your code should always include appropriate error handling when working with `DeleteSetting`. The `Registry.vbp` project includes code that follows the pattern shown in Listing 26.2.

Listing 26.2. A procedure using the `DeleteSetting` statement should contain appropriate error handling.

```
Private Sub cmdDelPasscode_Click()
On Error GoTo Err_cmdDelPasscode_Click
  DeleteSetting "Acme", "Widgets", "Passcode"
Exit_cmdDelPasscode_Click:
  Exit Sub
Err_cmdDelPasscode_Click:
  MsgBox "An error has occurred: " & vbCrLf _
      & "Number: " & Err.Number & vbCrLf _
      & "Description: " & Err.Description
  Resume Exit_cmdDelPasscode_Click
End Sub
```

`Registry.vbp` includes `frmDeleteSetting` (see Figure 26.12) that steps through the Registry keys set up for the Acme Widgets project, deleting first the Passcode key value, then the Widgets folder, and finally the Acme folder. At each step of the way, `frmDeleteSetting` shows you the command line it's about to execute.

Notice that you can't delete the top-level folder until the subordinate folders under it have been removed. For example, the button to delete the Widgets folder is kept disabled until the Delete Passcode Key button has been clicked. The VBA registry commands give you considerable control over how the Registry settings you've established are managed.

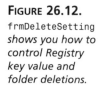

FIGURE 26.12.

frmDeleteSetting *shows you how to control Registry key value and folder deletions.*

GetAllSettings

The last VBA registry command we'll look at is GetAllSettings. This function returns a list of all the keys and their settings within a Registry folder. The syntax of GetAllSettings is as follows:

```
vName = GetAllSettings(ApplicationName, Section)
```

vName is a variant that accepts the values returned by GetAllSettings. You treat *vName* as a two-dimensional array to display or use the Registry key values. The first column of the array contains the key names, whereas the second column contains the key values. Using a variant is convenient because you can't know beforehand how many or what kind of values will be returned.

The Registry.vbp project includes a form (frmGetAllSettings) that demonstrates how to use GetAllSettings. In practical terms, however, you will almost always be working with one setting at a time and will not want to use an array to handle Registry values.

If there are no key values in the ApplicationName\Section folder, GetAllSettings returns an empty value. Listing 26.3 shows how to test for this condition. This code is derived from the frmGetAllSettings form in the Registry.vbp project. You can see this form in Figure 26.13.

Listing 26.3. GetAllSettings returns an empty value when no key values are found in the specified Registry folder.

```
Private Sub Form_Load()
    Dim i As Integer
    Dim v As Variant
```

continues

Listing 26.3. Continued.

```
On Error GoTo Err_Form_Load
  v = GetAllSettings("Acme", "Widgets")
  If IsEmpty(v) Then
    MsgBox "There are no key values in this section"
    GoTo Exit_Form_Load
  End If
  For i = LBound(v, 1) To UBound(v, 1)
    lstKeys.AddItem v(i, 0) & Chr(9) & v(i, 1)
  Next i
Exit_Form_Load:
  Exit Sub
Err_Form_Load:
  MsgBox "There is a problem getting values from this section"
  Resume Exit_Form_Load
End Sub
```

FIGURE 26.13.

frmGetAllSettings *retrieves all the settings found in the Acme Widgets Registry folder.*

Using the Windows API to Program the Registry

This section details all the API calls you must make to create a Registry entry, set the value of a subkey, query the subkey, and then remove it from the Registry. The Registry.vbp project contains all the code shown in this section.

One of the biggest problems with using the built-in VBA calls to program the Registry is that the only section you can write to in the Registry is HKEY_CURRENT_USER\Sofware\VB and VBA Program Settings. You might want to manipulate Registry keys found in other sections of the Registry from your programs, but the statements and functions you've seen so far in this chapter don't provide the features that enable you to do that.

The Windows API functions provide complete access and control over the System Registry. Obviously, you must be careful when programming the Registry with API calls. A simple misspelling or incorrect value can damage the Registry because there are no safeguards when working with API calls.

Unlike the VBA calls, the API functions work with a variety of data types. All the VBA Registry commands read or write string values from and to the Registry. The API calls, on the other hand, work with a variety of different data types. Table 26.3 shows the data types you most often work with when using the API Registry functions.

Table 26.3. System Registry data types.

Data Type	Description
REG_BINARY	Binary value
REG_DWORD	32-bit integer
REG_SZ	String value
REG_NONE	Unidentified

Table 26.3 is not an exhaustive list of Registry data types but is adequate for most Visual Basic applications. A complete list can be found in the *Visual Basic 5.0 Programmer's Guide to the Win32 API* by Daniel Appleman. This book, published by Ziff-Davis Press, is a good reference for the most commonly used API functions.

The Windows API provides a variety of functions for working with the Registry. Table 26.4 contains a complete list of these functions. We will not be discussing all of these functions, but it's important that you know these API calls are available to you. The API functions in Table 26.4 are arranged in alphabetical order rather than in the sequence that you'll normally use them.

Table 26.4. API functions for controlling the Registry.

Function	Description
RegCloseKey	Closes a key that is currently open
RegConnectRegistry	Opens a Registry key on another computer
RegCreateKey, RegCreateKeyEx	Creates a new Registry key
RegDeleteKey	Deletes an existing Registry key
RegDeleteValue	Removes a value from a key
RegEnumKey, RegEnumKeyEx	Enumerates (reports) the subkeys of a key
RegEnumValue	Enumerates the values of a key
RegFlushKey	Writes changes to a key to disk
RegGetKeySecurity	Retrieves the security information of a key
RegLoadKey	Loads information from a file into the Registry
RegNotifyChangeKeyValue	Notifies an application when the value of a key changes
RegOpenKey, RegOpenKeyEx	Opens a key

continues

Table 26.4. Continued.

Function	Description
RegQueryInfoKey	Retrieves information about a key
RegQueryValue, RegQueryValueEx	Retrieves value information
RegReplaceKey	Replaces Registry information with data stored in a disk file
RegRestoreKey	Restores the Registry from information stored in a disk file
RegSaveKey	Saves Registry information in a disk file
RegSetKeySecurity	Sets security on a key
RegSetValue, RegSetValueEx	Sets a key's value
RegUnLoadKey	Disconnects a Registry key on a remote computer

Using the Windows API involves more work than exploiting the built-in VBA commands. However, you gain a lot more control over where the information is stored in the Registry and the format of the data that is stored. The following sections discuss the most commonly used API calls that deal with the Registry.

RegCreateKeyEx

The RegCreateKeyEx function writes a new Registry key and is roughly equivalent to the SaveSetting statement. Listing 26.4 shows its function declaration.

Listing 26.4. The RegCreateKeyEx API function declaration.

```
Declare Function RegCreateKeyEx Lib "Advapi32" _
    Alias "RegCreateKeyExA" _
    (ByVal lKey As Long, _
    ByVal sSubKey As String, _
    ByVal lReserved As Long, _
    ByVal sClass As String, _
    ByVal lOptions As Long, _
    ByVal lDesired As Long, _
    lSecurityAttributes As Long, _
    lResult As Long, _
    lDisposition As Long) As Long
```

RegCreateKeyEx creates a key in the Registry. If the key already exists, then RegCreateKeyEx opens it. This enables you to use only one function to either create or open a key for reading. Use RegOpenKeyEx (explained in the following section) if you simply want to open an existing key. However, if you use only RegOpenKeyEx, you must perform error-checking to test whether the key exists. RegCreateKeyEx returns 0 if successful.

The arguments for RegCreateKeyEx are complex, so they're explained one at a time:

- lKey is a top-level key, such as HKEY_LOCAL_MACHINE, and can be represented using one of the constants shown in Table 26.5. These constants are located in the basPublics module in the Registry.vbp project.
- sSubKey is a string containing the complete path of the subkey below the top-level key. Use backslash characters to separate keys and subkeys.
- lReserved is reserved, so it is set to 0. (Be sure not to set it to any other value.)
- sClass is a string value containing the class name you want to use for the key—if you are using one. Normally you'll leave this as an empty string (" ").
- lOptions can be used to specify whether the key is volatile (the key is not saved when the computer system is shut down) or nonvolatile (the key is permanently added to the Registry). Use the public constant REG_OPTION_VOLATILE (value is 1) to indicate that the key is temporary and REG_OPTION_NON_VOLATILE (value is 0) to make the new key permanent.
- lDesired pertains to security access for the key. Security access can be represented using the constants defined in Listing 26.5.
- lSecurityAttributes is the address of a security structure, which is an optional parameter. The lSecurityAttributes parameter is used only by Windows NT. If you aren't using the structure, pass this argument a 0. A complete discussion of lSecurityAttributes is beyond the scope of this book.
- The handle to the new key is returned in the lResult parameter.
- lDisposition returns a value indicating whether a new key was created (REG_CREATED_NEW_KEY, value is 1) or an existing key was opened (REG_OPENED_EXISTING_KEY, value is 2) .

Table 26.5. Constants defined in basPublics in Registry.vbp to use when navigating the Windows 95 Registry.

Constant Name	Constant Value
HKEY_CLASSES_ROOT	&H80000000
HKEY_CURRENT_USER	&H80000001
HKEY_LOCAL_MACHINE	&H80000002
HKEY_USERS	&H80000003
HKEY_CURRENT_CONFIG	&H80000005
HKEY_DYN_DATA	&H80000006

Listing 26.5. Security constant values to use with `RegCreateKeyEx`.

```
Const KEY_QUERY_VALUE = &H1&
Const KEY_SET_VALUE = &H2&
Const KEY_CREATE_SUB_KEY = &H4&
Const KEY_ENUMERATE_SUB_KEYS = &H8&
Const KEY_NOTIFY = &H10&
Const KEY_CREATE_LINK = &H20&
Const READ_CONTROL = &H20000
Const KEY_READ = READ_CONTROL _
   Or KEY_QUERY_VALUE _
   Or KEY_ENUMERATE_SUB_KEYS _
   Or KEY_NOTIFY
Const KEY_WRITE = READ_CONTROL _
   Or KEY_SET_VALUE _
   Or KEY_CREATE_SUB_KEY
Const KEY_EXECUTE = KEY_READ
Const KEY_ALL_ACCESS = KEY_QUERY_VALUE _
   And KEY_ENUMERATE_SUB_KEYS _
   And KEY_NOTIFY _
   And KEY_CREATE_SUB_KEY _
   And KEY_CREATE_LINK _
   And KEY_SET_VALUE
```

The following sample creates (or opens) a key in which an application's title setting will be stored. In this case the key will be created in HKEY_LOCAL_MACHINE\Software\Acme\Widgets instead of the usual location for Visual Basic application keys. Listing 26.6 is taken from the `frmAPICreate` form in `Registry.vbp` (see Figure 26.14).

Listing 26.6. Using `RegCreateKeyEx` to create a new Windows 95 Registry key.

```
Function CreateKey(sKeyName As String) As Long
   Dim sSubKey As String
   Dim sClass As String
   Dim lOptions As Long
   Dim lRegSam As Long
   Dim lSecAttrib As Long
   Dim lResult As Long
   Dim lDisposition As Long
   Dim lRetVal As Long

   sSubKey = "Software\Acme\Widgets" & sKeyName
   lOptions = 1
   lRegSam = KEY_ALL_ACCESS
   lSec_Attrib = 0
   lRetVal = RegCreateKeyEx(HKEY_LOCAL_MACHINE, _
        sSubKey, 0, "", lOptions, lRegSam, _
```

```
            lSecAttrib, lResult, lDisposition)
      OpenKey = lRetVal
End Function
```

FIGURE 26.14.

frmAPICreate *uses the Windows API to store these values in the System Registry.*

> **Warning:** RegCreateKeyEx writes a new key into the absolute location in the Registry that you indicate in this function's arguments. You can easily overwrite an existing key or insert a key into the middle of another program's Registry settings.

RegOpenKeyEx

Making API calls to manipulate the System Registry is a more complicated process than using the equivalent VBA functions. You must explicitly open an existing key to manipulate that key or its values. After you have a handle on that key you can perform virtually any task necessary on the key, including changing its value or data type. The RegOpenKeyEx API call opens a key and returns a handle to the key to the calling routine. Listing 26.7 shows the function declaration for RegOpenKeyEx.

Listing 26.7. The RegOpenKeyEx API function declaration.

```
Declare Function RegOpenKeyEx _
   Lib "Advpi32.dll" _
   Alias "RegOpenKeyExA" _
  (ByVal lKey As Long, _
   ByVal sSubKey As String, _
   ByVal lOptions As Long, _
   ByVal lDesired As Long, _
   lResult As Long) As Long
```

RegOpenKeyEx returns 0 if the key was successfully opened, a nonzero result otherwise. The handle to the opened key is returned in the lResult parameter. Listing 26.8 shows the OpenKey function from Registry.vbp. OpenKey acts as a wrapper for the RegOpenKeyEx API call, hiding some of the complexity of the API function. OpenKey returns 0 if RegOpenKeyEx was unsuccessful, or the handle to the key folder indicated by sKeyName if RegOpenKeyEx was successful.

Listing 26.8. OpenKey is a wrapper function for RegOpenKeyEx.

```
Private Function OpenKey(sKeyName As String) As Long
  Dim lRetValue As Long
  Dim lResult As Long

  lRetValue = RegOpenKeyEx _
    (HKEY_LOCAL_MACHINE, sKeyName, _
     0, KEY_ALL_ACCESS, lResult)

  If lRetValue = 0 Then
    OpenKey = lResult
  Else
    OpenKey = 0
  End If
End Function
```

You've seen most of the arguments to RegOpenKeyEx in the RegCreateKeyEx discussion. The lOptions parameter is reserved and should not be set to any value other than 0. All the examples in this chapter set the lDesired parameter to KEY_ALL_ACCESS. A discussion of the other settings for this parameter is beyond the scope of this book. The handle to the opened key is returned in the lResult parameter.

RegSetValueEx

So far, you've seen how to create and open a new key. The next task is to set a key value under that key. The RegSetValueEx function creates a new key value and sets it to its initial value (see Listing 26.9). If the key already exists, its value will be reset to the lData parameter. Notice that you must provide a type parameter and tell Windows how long the data is that you're passing to the API function.

Listing 26.9. The RegSetValueEx API function declaration.

```
'Listing 26.
'The RegSetValueEx API function declaration.
Declare Function RegSetValueEx _
   Lib "Advapi32" _
   Alias "RegSetValueExA" _
  (ByVal lKey As Long, _
   ByVal sValueName As String, _
   ByVal lReserved As Long, _
   ByVal lType As Long, _
   ByVal sData As String, _
   ByVal lLenData As Long) As Long
```

There are several new parameters for the RegSetValueEx function:

- lKey is the address of an open key.
- sValueName is a string containing the name of the value you want to set. In an INI file, this would be the key name.
- lReserved should be set to 0.
- lType is a flag telling the Registry what type of data value to create. Listing 26.10 shows constants that can be used as symbolic constants for lType.
- sData is the value for the key you are setting.
- lData is the length (Len(sData)) of the value.

Listing 26.10. Constant values to use with RegSetValueEx.

```
Const REG_NONE = 0&
Const REG_SZ = 1&
Const REG_EXPAND_SZ = 2&
Const REG_BINARY = 3&
Const REG_DWORD = 4&
Const REG_DWORD_LITTLE_ENDIAN = 4&
Const REG_DWORD_BIG_ENDIAN = 5&
Const REG_LINK = 6&
Const REG_MULTI_SZ = 7&
Const REG_RESOURCE_LIST = 8&
Const REG_FULL_RESOURCE_DESCRIPTOR = 9&
Const REG_RESOURCE_REQUIREMENTS_LIST = 10&
```

RegSetValueEx returns 0 if successful.

Listing 26.11 shows the RegisterUser function, derived from frmAPICreate. You won't find this exact function in this form, but the logic shown in Listing 26.11 is the same as that used by frmAPICreate.

Listing 26.11. Setting the registered user key value in the Registry with RegSetValueEx.

```
Function RegisterUser() As Long
  Dim lRetValue As Long
  Dim sKeyName As String
  Dim sData As String
  Dim lLen As Long
  Dim lHandle As Long
  Dim lType As Long

  If CreateKey("Software\Acme\Widgets") <> 0 Then
```

continues

Listing 26.11. Continued.

```
    lHandle = OpenKey("Software\Acme\Widgets")
    If lHandle <> 0 Then
      'Set up Registered User key value
      sKeyName = "Registered User"
      lType = REG_SZ
      sData = "William Wallace"
      lLen = Len(sData)
      lRetValue = _
        RegSetValueEx(lHandle, sKeyName, _
          0, lType, sData, lLen)
      RegFlushKey (lHandle)
    End If
  End If
End Function
```

RegFlushKey

When a Registry key is created or altered, the changes are often cached in memory. To force the changes to be written immediately to the Registry, *flush* the key using RegFlushKey. RegFlushKey accepts the handle of an open key as an argument and returns 0 if successful. RegisterUser, from the previous section, creates the RegisteredUser setting, then uses RegFlushKey to commit the changes to the Registry. Listing 26.12 shows the declaration of the RegFlushKey function the basDeclares module in Registry.vbp.

Listing 26.12. The RegFlushKey API function declaration.

```
Declare Function RegFlushKey Lib "Advapi32" _
    (ByVal lKey As Long) As Long
```

RegQueryValueEx

Obviously, the Windows API must provide some way to get values back out of the Registry. RegQueryValueEx (see Listing 26.13) retrieves the value for an opened key.

Listing 26.13. The RegQueryValueEx API function declaration.

```
Declare Function RegQueryValueEx _
  Lib "Advapi32" _
  Alias "RegQueryValueExA" _
 (ByVal lKey As Long, _
  ByVal sValueName As String, _
  ByVal lReserved As Long, _
  lType As Long, _
  ByVal sData As String, _
  lSize As Long) As Long
```

1Key is the handle of an opened key. sValueName is a string that contains the key of the value you want to retrieve. 1Reserved should be set to 0. U1Type is a buffer that contains one of the symbolic constants listed earlier, which tells the function what kind of data it should expect to receive. sData is a buffer to receive the data, and 1Size is a buffer to receive the size of the returned value. RegQueryValueEx returns 0 if successful.

The next example accepts the handle of an open key and returns the value for the Registered User key in Acme Widgets Registry information. Listing 26.14 is a slight modification of the GetValue function in Registry.vbp. Look for this function behind the frmRegQueryValue form (see Figure 26.15).

Listing 26.14. Retrieving the setting of a Windows Registry key with RegQueryValueEx.

```
Function GetRegisteredUser() As String
  Dim lHandle As Long
  Dim sValue As String
  Dim lReserved As Long
  Dim sData As String * 128
  Dim lDataSize As Long
  Dim lDataType As Long
  Dim lRetVal As Long

  lHandle = OpenKey("Software\Acme\Widgets")
  If lHandle = 0 Then
    MsgBox "Cannot retrieve the Registered User information"
    Exit Sub
  End If

  sValue = "Registered User"
  lReserved = 0
  lDataType = REG_SZ
  sData = String(128, " ")
  lDataSize = Len(sData)
  lRetVal = RegQueryValueEx(lKey, _
      "Registered User", lReserved, _
      lDataType, sData, lDataSize)
  GetRegisteredUser = Left(sData, lDataSize - 1)
End Function
```

There are a few things to notice about using RegQueryValueEx. RegQueryValueEx requires a handle to an open Registry key. You must open the key with the RegOpenKeyEx API call. In Registry.vbp, the OpenKey function is a wrapper around this API call and returns either 0 if the key was not opened properly or a long value if the call to RegOpenKeyEx was successful.

Second, the Registry key you open is the register folder that contains the value you want returned from the Registry. Don't use RegQueryValueEx to retrieve an entire key. Instead, notice how the call to RegQueryValueEx specifies the Registered User value. The key that's been opened with the OpenKey function is HKEY_LOCAL_MACHINE\Software\Acme\Widgets, the folder that holds the Registered User value.

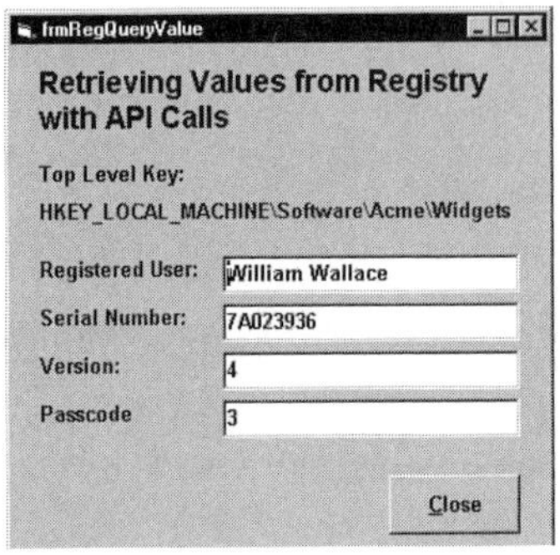

FIGURE 26.15.
frmRegQueryValue
uses the Windows
API to retrieve
data stored in the
System Registry.

RegCloseKey

Whenever you access a Registry key—whether you open it, query it, set the value, or remove it—you must close the handle of the key when you are finished with it. RegCloseKey accepts the handle of an open key as an argument and returns 0 if successful. The declaration for RegCloseKey is shown in Listing 26.15. You'll find this declaration in basDeclares in the Registry.vbp project.

Listing 26.15. The RegCloseKey API function declaration.

```
Declare Function RegCloseKey Lib "Advapi32" _
      (ByVal lKey As Long) As Long
```

The Registry.vbp project closes the HKEY_LOCAL_MACHINE\Software\Acme\ Widgets folder key with this simple statement:

```
lRetValue = RegCloseKey(lHandle)
```

RegDeleteValue

It's not difficult to delete a single value from the Registry. Once again, you need a handle to the Registry folder holding the key value; then specify which value in the folder is to be deleted. Listing 26.16 shows the declaration of the RegDeleteValue function.

Listing 26.16. The `RegDeleteValue` API function declaration.

```
Declare Function RegDeleteValue _
   Lib "Advapi32.dll" _
   Alias "RegDeletValueA", _
  (ByVal lKey As Long, _
   ByVal sValueName As String) As Long
```

`RegDeleteValue` returns 0 if the value was successfully deleted and some other nonzero value if the value was not deleted. A typical reason the value is not deleted is because it does not exist. Simply check for the value returned by `RegDeleteValue` to see whether the specific key value has been deleted.

RegDeleteKey

Whenever you alter the Registry, you should provide a way to remove the changes you have made. For example, you should provide a plan for uninstalling your application should the user choose to do so. `RegDeleteKey` removes a subkey from the specified parent key. It accepts a pointer to the top-level key (such as HKEY_CURRENT_USER) and the path of the subkey. It returns a 0 value if it is successful. Listing 26.17 shows the declaration found in `basDeclares` in the `Registry.vbp` project for the `RegDeleteKey` API call.

Listing 26.17. The `RegDeleteKey` API function declaration.

```
Declare Function RegDeleteKey Lib "Advapi32" _
     Alias "RegDeleteKeyA" _
    (ByVal lKey As Long, _
     ByVal sValue As String) As Long
```

Manipulating INI Files

In the past, software vendors and Microsoft have used INI files to control the settings of their applications. The `System.ini` and `Win.ini` files controlled almost everything about Windows 3.1. Usually, each application on your hard drive has an INI that contains sections, key names, and string values that relate to everything from screen color to network protocols. Although many vendors will still use application-specific INI files for their applications, Windows 95 and NT use the Registry for most settings. Microsoft is encouraging other software vendors to do the same. The change will be difficult for many people who are used to working with INI files, but Microsoft's Win32 API comes with all you need to control System Registry settings.

On the other hand, if you feel that storing data in INI files is appropriate for your applications there is no reason to feel compelled to use the System Registry. INI files have the undeniable advantage of flexibility. You could, for example, set up an INI file in an application's home directory. All the user must do to move the application to another computer system is copy the directory onto the other computer without having to worry about the application's Registry settings. (There might still be problems with custom controls, runtime DLLs, and other considerations, of course.) Additionally, skilled users can use Notepad or another ASCII editor to update an application-specific INI file without poking around in the System Registry with Regedit.

This section demonstrates the use of the Windows API INI functions to read and write INI files. All INI files follow this pattern:

```
[Section]
Key=String
```

The *section* might be something like Acme Widgets whereas the *key* could be something like Registered User. The *string* is the value assigned to that particular key and can be retrieved at any time.

The Windows API provides a large number of functions for reading and writing INI files. Because INI files tend to be simpler than the Windows System Registry, there are fewer of these functions. Table 26.6 shows the API functions involved with creating and maintaining INI files. Notice that these functions are divided into generic functions that always write to Win.ini (yes, Windows 95 has a Win.ini file just like Windows 3.1) and private functions that write into INI files associated with specific applications.

Table 26.6. API calls for managing INI files.

INI Function	Description
GetProfileInt	Gets an integer value from the Win.ini file
GetProfileSection	Gets an entire section from Win.ini
GetProfileString	Gets a string from Win.ini
WriteProfileSection	Writes an entire section into Win.ini
WriteProfileString	Writes a string value into Win.ini
GetPrivateProfileInt	Gets an integer from an application-specific INI file
GetPrivateProfileSection	Gets an entire section from an application-specific INI file
GetPrivateProfileString	Gets a string from an application-specific INI file
WritePrivateProfileSection	Writes a section into an application-specific INI file
WritePrivateProfileString	Writes a string into an application-specific INI file

Of these API calls, only the functions to read and write string and integer values are used with any regularity.

WriteProfileString

Because WriteProfileString works only with Win.ini, there is no need to specify the name of an INI file as an argument. The syntax of WriteProfileString is straightforward and is shown in Listing 26.18.

Listing 26.18. The WriteProfileString API function declaration.

```
Declare Function WriteProfileString _
    Lib "Kernel32" _
    Alias "WriteProfileStringA" _
    (ByVal sSection As String, _
    ByVal sKey As String, _
    ByVal sSetting As String) As Long
```

Like GetProfileString (discussed in the next section), this function works only on the Win.ini file. If the function completes successfully, the return value is True; if not, it returns False.

frmWriteProfileString in the Registry.vbp project (see Figure 26.16) contains the code necessary to write the string value you specify into the Win.ini file.

FIGURE 26.16.

frmWriteProfile-
String *writes any
string value into
any section in*
Win.ini.

Figure 26.17 shows the Win.ini file after frmWriteProfileString has completed its task. Repeat the code behind frmWriteProfileString for each value you want to store in Win.ini. If the value already exists, it is simply overwritten by the call to the WriteProfileString function.

You should be wary of constantly writing data into Win.ini. Because it is so easy to add sections and values to Win.ini, this file gets cluttered up with lots of information. Oddly enough, there are no API calls for removing data from Win.ini (or any other INI file for that matter). This odd fact helps explain why INI files are famous for cluttering up every Windows installation.

> **Note:** If you must remove entries from an INI file, low-level file editing techniques can be used.

GetProfileString

Retrieving a value from Win.ini is easily done with the GetProfileString API function. The declaration for GetProfileString is shown in Listing 26.19. Notice the sDefault parameter. If the string specified by sKey can't be found, sDefault is returned instead.

Listing 26.19. The GetProfileString API function declaration.

```
Declare Function GetProfileString Lib "Kernel32" _
    Alias "GetProfileStringA"_
    (ByVal sSection As String, _
    ByVal sKey As String, _
    ByVal sDefault As String, _
    ByVal sReturnString As String, _
    ByVal lReturnSize As Long) As Long
```

Form frmGetProfileString (see Figure 26.18) retrieves any string value from Win.ini. This form is part of the Registry.vbp project and can be used to retrieve any value from Win.ini.

The code behind the Get Value button on frmGetProfileSetting is shown in Listing 26.20.

Listing 26.20. The cmdGetValue_Click sub from frmGetProfileSetting in Registry.vbp.

```
Private Sub cmdGetValue_Click()
  Dim lSize As Long
  Dim lRetValue As Long
  Dim sValue As String

  sValue = String(128, " ")
  lSize = Len(sValue)

  lRetValue = _
     GetProfileString(txtSection, txtKey, "No user", sValue, lSize)

  txtValue = sValue
End Sub
```

Notice how the lSize parameter must be initialized before it is used. It can be set to any value that is longer than the longest string you expect to read out of Win.ini.

GetProfileInt

GetProfileInt is an API call that functions exactly like GetProfileString. In fact, GetProfileInt is so similar to GetProfileString that Registry.vbp does not include an example of this API call and no further discussion is required here. The GetProfileInt function declaration is shown in Listing 26.21.

Listing 26.21. The GetProfileInt API function declaration.

```
Declare Function GetProfileInt _
   Lib "kernel32" _
   Alias "GetProfileIntA" (ByVal _
   sSection As String, _
   ByVal sKey As String, _
   ByVal sDefault As Long) As Long
```

GetProfileInt returns the integer value retrieved from Win.ini. If the value specified by sKey can't be found, the value of sDefault is returned.

WritePrivateProfileString

WritePrivateProfileString writes information to a private (application-specific INI file). This function receives a section, key, default, and filename as arguments. It also

accepts the value you want to place in the INI file in the sSetting argument.
WritePrivateProfileString returns a nonzero value if it is successful, otherwise it
returns 0. Listing 26.22 presents the declaration for WritePrivateProfileString.

Listing 26.22. The WritePrivateProfileString API function declaration.

```
Declare Function WritePrivateProfileString Lib "Kernel32" _
    Alias "WritePrivateProfileStringA" _
    (ByVal sSection As String, _
    ByVal sKey As String, _
    ByVal sSetting As String, _
    ByVal sFilename As String) As Long
```

Figure 26.19 shows frmWritePrivateProfileString, included in Registry.vbp. This
form uses WritePrivateProfileString to write the data displayed in its text boxes into
the INI file specified on the form.

FIGURE 26.19.

frmWritePrivate-
ProfileString
uses
WritePrivate-
ProfileString
*to write informa-
tion into an
application-
specific INI file.*

Listing 26.23 shows how frmWritePrivateProfileString writes the registered user
information to an INI file named Widgets.ini in the C:\Acme directory on the local
computer.

Listing 26.23. Writing information into an INI file with
WritePrivateProfileString.

```
Private Sub cmdWrite_Click()
  Dim lRetValue As Long
  lRetValue = _
    WritePrivateProfileString(txtSection, txtKey, txtValue, txtPath)
  If lRetValue <> 0 Then
    MsgBox "Success!"
  Else
    MsgBox "Couldn't write to " & txtPath & "!"
  End If
End Sub
```

cmdWrite_Click performs rudimentary error checking. If the value returned by WritePrivateProfileString is not 0 a message box appears reporting Success!. Otherwise a simple error message is displayed. A more sophisticated approach would involve using VBA to create the Acme folder and the Widgets.ini file, and then trying to write the registered user information to the INI file.

GetPrivateProfileString

The GetPrivateProfileString API function retrieves a value from a private INI file. GetPrivateProfileString works exactly like the GetProfileString function you saw earlier in this chapter. It is passed the section, key, and complete path to an INI file and retrieves the value for the key. Listing 26.24 shows the declaration of the GetPrivateProfileString API call.

Listing 26.24. The GetPrivateProfileString API function declaration.

```
Declare Function GetPrivateProfileString Lib "Kernel32" _
    Alias "GetPrivateProfileStringA" _
    (ByVal sSection As String, _
    ByVal sKey As String, _
    ByVal sDefault As String, _
    ByVal sReturn As String, _
    ByVal lReturnSize As Long, _
    ByVal sFilename As String) As Long
```

If a Null value is passed as a key, all the entries for the section are retrieved. If a specified key is not found, the value passed as sDefault is returned. If the function is successful, GetPrivateProfileString returns the number of characters copied into the string buffer sReturnString.

Listing 26.25 uses GetPrivateProfileString to retrieve the registered user's name from the C:\Acme\Widgets.ini file.

Listing 26.25. Getting information from an INI file with GetPrivateString.

```
Private Sub cmdGet_Click()
  Dim lRetValue As Long
  Dim sReturn As String
  Dim sDefault As String
  Dim lSize As Long

  sDefault = "Not registered"
  lSize = 128

  lRetValue = _
```

continues

Listing 26.25. Continued.

```
    GetPrivateProfileString(txtSection, txtKey, _
        sDefault, sReturn, lSize, txtPath)

  If lRetValue <> 0 Then
    MsgBox "Success!"
    txtValue = sReturn
  Else
    MsgBox "Couldn't get " & txtPath & "!"
    txtValue = sDefault
  End If
End Sub
```

GetPrivateProfileInt

The GetPrivateProfileInt function is analogous to GetPrivateProfileString except that it returns an integer value from the application's INI file. The declaration for the GetPrivateProfileInt function is given in Listing 26.26.

Listing 26.26. The GetPrivateProfileInt API function declaration.

```
Declare Function GetPrivateProfileInt Lib "Kernel32" _
    Alias "GetPrivateProfileIntA" _
    (ByVal sSection As String, _
    ByVal sKey As String, _
    ByVal lDefault As Long, _
    ByVal sFilename As String) As Long
```

This function returns an integer value from an application-specific INI file. It accepts a section, key name, default, and filename like GetPrivateProfileString but does not accept a string buffer. If the function is successful it returns the integer value. Because GetPrivateProfileInt is so similar to GetPrivateProfileString, no example is given here and this function is not used in Registry.vbp.

Summary

Most applications need some way to store configuration information. As a Visual Basic developer, you have several different ways to permanently store information without having to resort to writing custom text files or using a database. VBA includes several functions and statements specifically designed to store and retrieve information from the System Registry. In addition, the Windows API contains a wide variety of functions to read and write to the System Registry as well as store and retrieve data in INI files.

As a developer, you can choose which of these methods you use in your applications. Microsoft wants all applications to store their configuration information in the System Registry. However, there are many practical reasons why it makes sense in some cases to store this information in application-specific INI files. The choice is yours.

Using the Package and Deployment Wizard

After you complete the development of your program and decide that it has been tested fully, you're ready to give it to friends or maybe even sell it. Now you must figure out how to distribute your program to others. How this is done has really changed since the first PC was introduced. Before Windows, many applications fit on one disk and were easy to distribute to users. You would copy the files onto the disk, and when users purchased the software, they would copy it onto their computers.

It's not that easy anymore. These days, Windows and Visual Basic make it a little more than just copying files onto disks. More support files must be installed with your application than you might realize. Even a small Visual Basic application requires many of the Visual Basic files that provide the access to the controls and database commands that your application uses.

Using the Distribution Wizard

To help you create a professional distribution package, Visual Basic 6 has included with it the Package and Deployment Wizard. This wizard replaces the older Application Setup Wizard included with Visual Basic since version 1. The Package and Deployment Wizard automates much of the work involved in creating and deploying the files needed for your program to run on another computer. The wizard has three options or functions that you use to create a product.

- Package option—Helps you package a project's files into .CAB files that can then be deployed, and in some cases the setup program that installs the .CAB files.

- Deploy option—Delivers your packaged applications to the appropriate distribution medium, such as disks, a network drive, or a Web site.

- Manage Scripts option—Lets you view and manipulate the scripts you have saved from the previous packaging and deployment sessions.

The Package and Deployment Wizard gives you the capability to create the distribution package in several different formats. These distribution methods include

- Disk
- CD-ROM
- Network access
- Internet or intranet access

Each of these methods requires a slightly different installation process. The two main steps that you need to perform for your application are as follows:

- Packaging—Your application must be packaged into one or more cabinet (.CAB) files that can be deployed to the location you choose.
- Deployment—The packaged application must be moved to a location from which users can install it. This might mean copying the package to disks or to a local or network drive, or deploying the package to a Web site.

Note: A .CAB file is a compressed file that is well suited to distribution on either disks or the Internet.

Working with the Wizard

The Package and Deployment Wizard helps you create professional-looking installation packages for your application. In addition to creating a standard installation process, it also includes the files and programs to allow users to uninstall your application if they want. An application package consists of the .CAB file or files that contain your compressed project files and any other files the user needs to install and use your application. You can create two kinds of packages: standard or Internet packages. If you plan to distribute the application on disk, network drive, or CD-ROM, you should create a standard package for the application. However, if you plan on distributing the application through an intranet or Internet site, you should create an Internet package.

No matter which type of package you choose, there are certain steps you must perform to create the package:

1. Select the package type you want to create.
2. Specify all the files you need to distribute.
3. Set the location to install the files on the user's computer.
4. Create the package.
5. Deploy the package.

When you start the Package and Deployment Wizard, you are taken through several steps that prompt you for the information needed to build the final installation package. You must do the following:

1. Specify your application's project and select whether you are packaging or deploying the application

2. Decide how you want to package your application

3. Set the destination for the completed package

4. Add any files that your application needs, such as the database file

5. Save the setup template and actually build the install program

When you finish the process, the Package and Deployment Wizard compresses all the selected files included with the application. It then copies these .CAB files as well as any required install program files to the specified destination. If you had chosen to create a disk installation, you would be asked for disks.

Starting the Wizard

You can start the Package and Deployment Wizard from the Windows Start menu as shown in Figure 27.1. From here, complete the following steps:

1. Specify which Visual Basic project you want to work with in the first dialog box of the creation process. You are presented with three options to choose from (see Figure 27.2):

    • Package

    • Deploy

    • Manage Scripts

FIGURE 27.1.
Starting the Package and Deployment Wizard from the Start menu.

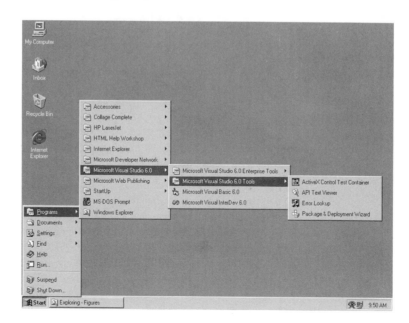

Figure 27.2.
Selecting the application project and choosing the processing option.

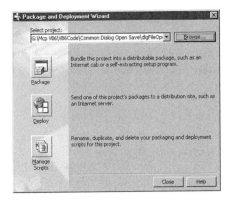

2. Use the Browse button to locate your application project on your computer. Select a project that you created during the course of this book.

3. After you have chosen the project, click the Package button to continue the process. The next dialog box (see Figure 27.3) asks you to choose the type of package you are creating.

Figure 27.3.
Choosing the packaging type for the application.

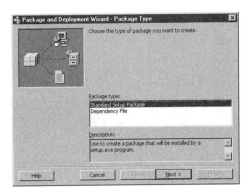

- If you're using any custom controls that you've created yourself, you should run the wizard's Package option, selecting the Dependency option for each control before you run the wizard for the actual application to create the dependency file for each control.

- If the package you are creating is a custom control you are selling, a dependency file needs to be created and included with the installation files so that people using the control will know whether they have all the required support files for it.

Note: The Package and Deployment Wizard uses a dependency file to determine which files are required by an .OCX, .DLL, or ActiveX component.

4. Select the Standard Setup package and click the Next button to continue. You are now prompted for the directory path to which you want to save the package files as shown in Figure 27.4.

FIGURE 27.4.
Specifying the build path for the application package files.

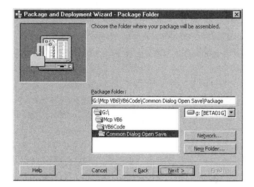

5. After specifying the directory path, click Next. Now consider the following:

- If your project accesses a database, you are asked which drivers to include in the package as shown in Figure 27.5.

FIGURE 27.5.
Selecting the required DAO system drivers.

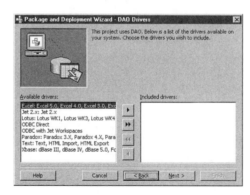

- If your application requires any of these drivers, select them and then click the Next button to continue the process. You then see all the components that your application requires to execute properly (see Figure 27.6).

Figure 27.6.

All the files for your application are listed on this dialog box.

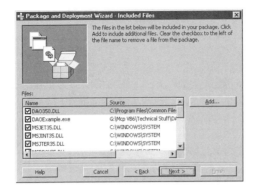

- If your application needs any other files, add them now. Some files that you might have to add are as follows:

    Online help files

    Database-related files

    ReadMe text files

    Any electronic documentation files

6. When you're finished checking the list of files to include, click the Next button to continue. You now must decide how you'll distribute your application. You can choose from the two distribution types, as shown in Figure 27.7.

    - Single cab—This creates a single cabinet file that can be copied to CD-ROM or a network drive for deployment.

    - Multiple cabs—This creates cabinet files that will fit on disks.

Figure 27.7.

Select the distribution type you want for your application in this dialog box.

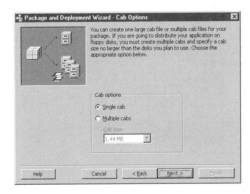

7. After selecting the distribution type, click Next to specify the title that will be seen on the installation screen.

8. After entering the title for your application, click Next to continue. The dialog box in Figure 27.8 allows you to define the Start menu group name and items in the group as well as the icons to be used. Some items you might want to put in your application Start group are as follows:

   - Help menu

   - ReadMe text file

   - Utility programs

FIGURE 27.8.

The Package and Deployment Wizard allows you to define exactly what the Start menu group contains and what icons are used.

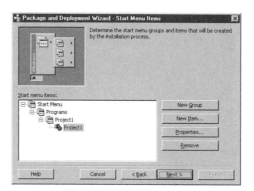

9. After you have set up the Startup group, click Next to continue. The dialog box shown in Figure 27.9 allows you to specify where each file in your application is installed. For most of the files, use the default locations. However, for any files specific to the application (for example, database files, help, or report files), you should verify the install locations.

FIGURE 27.9.

Verifying the location in which each file is installed on the user's computer.

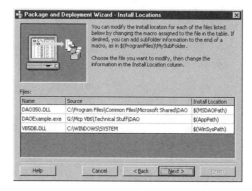

10. After you have done this, click Next to specify which files you are deploying can be shared or used by more than one program (see Figure 27.10). Specifying a file as shared prevents the file from being removed during an uninstall until every program that uses it is removed.

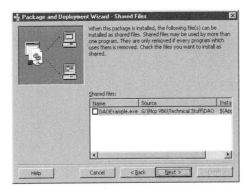

11. After selecting the shared files, click Next to continue. The final dialog box prompts you to name and save the packaging script for you to use at a later time when updating the installation package.

12. Click the Finish button to create the installation package.

At this point, you are returned to the main wizard dialog box.

Deploying the Package

Now that you have created an installation package for your application, you must specify the deployment strategy for the application. You can use the deployment option of the wizard to deploy your application to floppy disks, a local or network drive, or a Web site. Deploying your application requires you to take the following steps:

- Create a package for deployment.
- Select the package to deploy.
- Choose the deployment method.
- Select the files to deploy.
- Specify the deployment destination.

Starting from the main wizard dialog box, select the project for which you just created the package and click the Deploy button. This displays a dialog box that asks you which package for this project you want to deploy (see Figure 27.11).

This allows you to support different types of deployment by creating a package for each deployment type. Choose the package you created and click Next. You are now asked which type of deployment you want to perform. The three available deployment types are as follows:

- Floppy Disk
- Folder
- WebPost

Each of these requires certain information to process the package.

Figure 27.11.
Choosing the package for deployment.

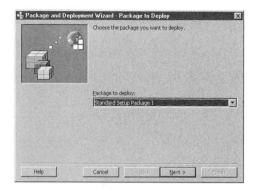

Floppy Disks

After you select Floppy Disks and click Next you are asked which disk drive to use. Then click the Next button to save the information as a script and click the Finish button to actually start copying the files to the diskettes.

Folders

By selecting Folder, you can distribute the package to a folder on either a local or network drive. Clicking Next displays a dialog box that asks you to specify the Folder name and location as shown in Figure 27.12.

Figure 27.12.
Deploying the package to a specific location on a hard drive.

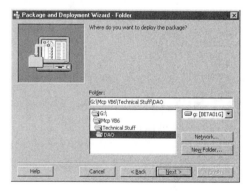

After setting the folder, click Next to save the deployment script; then click Finish to complete the process.

WebPost

This option enables you to deploy the application package across the Internet by posting the package to a Web server. Clicking Next displays the files included in the package as shown in Figure 27.13.

FIGURE 27.13.
Selecting the files to post to the Web site.

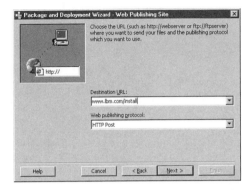

This enables you to select the files you want to deploy. After choosing the files, click Next to continue. The next dialog box lets you add other files or folders that you want to deploy along with the package. After you have added any other files or folders, click Next to continue. At this point, you are asked for the WebPost site to display the package to. Only sites registered on your computer PC appear in the drop-down list. To add a new site, click the New Site button. In the next series of dialog forms, you are asked for the following:

- A name for the new site
- The type of Web providers to use (that is, FTP, HTTP)
- The posting URL
- The base folder to set on the posting URL

After specifying this information, clicking the Finish button posts or copies all the information to the posting URL.

Managing Scripts

The third function the Package and Deployment Wizard provides is the capability to manage the scripts that you have saved for a project. By selecting a project on the main wizard dialog box and clicking Manage Scripts, a dialog box displays listing both the package and deployment scripts you have previously saved (see Figure 27.14).

FIGURE 27.14.
Managing the Package and Deployment scripts for your application.

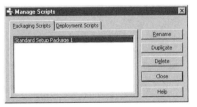

If you need to make modifications to any of the scripts, you can use this feature to either rename or duplicate a script before making changes to it.

> **Warning:** If you remove a packaging script, the deployment function does not recognize the package created from that script as one that it can deploy.

Testing the Installation

Now that you've finished the packaging and deployment process for your application, take the time to test the installation process by installing your application on a different PC. The PC that you use to test the install program shouldn't have Visual Basic installed on it; this would invalidate the test by already having the Visual Basic files on the PC. The purpose of the test is to ensure that all the required files for your application are included in the installation file set.

Summary

If you have used a PC for more than a day, chances are that you have purchased and installed applications on the computer. Each application that you install uses some variation of the deployment process you have just learned about in this chapter. With practice and time, Visual Basic even allows you to modify the Setup program to present the user with install choices such as you had when installing Visual Basic. Another method is to purchase one of the many commercial installation systems available. Whichever way you choose to create the install package, the process is basically the same. In the next chapter, you are presented with some topics and guidelines that show you what it takes to create a professional-looking application.

Professional Visual Basic Development

Designing and building a professional Visual Basic application is more difficult than it looks and at the same time, easier than you think. All it takes is time, patience, and some good standards to follow. This chapter explores what you must consider when deciding what type of application to create. You learn some of the things you must do to give the user a good application and some of the things you must take care of after the application has been created. Basically, in this chapter you learn that there are a great many issues that have nothing to do with Visual Basic.

Understanding What Makes a Professional Application

If you've read one or more Visual Basic books or have worked with Visual Basic for any length of time, you've probably created many small programs, trying out Visual Basic's different features. After you do this for a while, you've probably asked yourself, "What do I do now?" By using all the tools, controls, and objects that you've learned, you can really impress your friends and family with the things you can get the computer to do. To do anything useful on your computer, however, you must create larger and more complex programs, or groups of programs called applications. Whether the application you're creating is a small inventory program for the house, a personal phone book, or possibly a personnel tracking system for your office, many things go into creating it. If you look closely at most popular software programs on the market, such as Microsoft Money, you can see that many different related routines create the single application.

Whether you're a seasoned programmer or a newcomer to the industry, you probably dream of creating an application that you can sell. Next time you go into a computer store, look at the numerous software applications available; most of them started as one person's idea. If this is where you're heading, you need to know how to plan your application accordingly.

When developing an application, most programmers don't consider what happens when they're finished creating the application. If you're working for a company, the finished application is handled differently than if you're planning to sell the application yourself. Putting everything together into one package takes patience, time, imagination, a little luck, and lots of planning. If all goes well, the finished product looks good and works well.

Application Types

You might not realize it, but you can create three distinct types of applications. If you're just starting out as a developer, this might seem strange. Depending on where you work, the type of application you're creating, and the application's final audience, the package you create will be quite different.

You can create three types of applications: personal, internal, and retail:

- A *personal application* is one that you create for yourself and no one else. You probably won't create any help files or a manual for your own application. Also, because it's running on your own PC, you won't create any distribution disks. As you can see, a personal application is like keeping a private journal; no one else will ever know about it unless you tell them.

- When working for a company, most applications that you develop will probably be *internal* ones used by other employees of that company or by company clients (for example, home banking software). If the application is completely internal, you don't need to consider any issues that deal with marketing the application. However, you do need to create a help system and a manual because you aren't the only one who will be using the application. Users must have some type of documentation to refer to when using the application.

- If the application is for company clients or for retail distribution, marketing and advertising must be included in the overall process.

Picking the Right Application

Before jumping in and creating an application, decide what function the application will serve. This decision isn't as easy as it sounds. For every idea that you have, probably 10 other people have had the same idea. Depending on whether you're creating an application to learn more about programming, something that you want to use at home, or an application to sell, you must do some market research about what the application will do. If you're selling, it's important to understand the type of person who would use the application and how many you might sell. This helps you decide whether it makes any sense to go any farther with the idea.

Without doing market research, you might create a great product that nobody wants, or a product with so many competitors that your product gets lost in the crowd. If you find that too many other products of the same type are already on the market, you might decide to select a different type of application or to place the finished product into the realm of shareware (discussed later in this book). For example, you don't want to spend the time creating a word processing product with applications such as Word and WordPerfect already on the market.

In short, select an idea that's new, or at least different, and run with it. Also compare the cost of creating the product and advertising it versus your available cash and expected sales. After you decide on the application, however, jump in and start the process. You definitely want to get your product to the public as quickly as you can, with the best quality possible.

Following the Project Life Cycle

When creating an application, you must take several steps to ensure that it's done correctly. These steps are generally grouped together and called the *project life cycle*. Although the number of steps in this cycle can change depending on the complexity of the project, every project must take several universal steps. These steps, or standard life cycle (see Figure 28.1), allow you to plan each section of work and set goals to help verify that you're ready to move on to the next step.

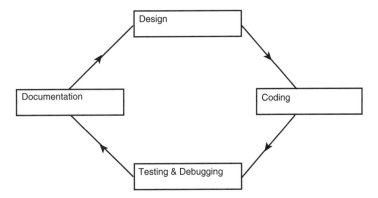

FIGURE 28.1.
The standard project life cycle used in the creation of most computer applications.

Many newer Windows programmers tend to sidestep this approach and prefer to start coding their application immediately. Doing so, however, usually causes problems later. If you don't plan or blueprint your application, you could wind up forgetting something important, thus having to redo large portions of your work just when you thought you were finished.

Determining the Design

The most difficult part of creating any application is deciding what it will do. When that's accomplished, the rest becomes relatively easy. The time you spend designing an application is the most important portion of the project. As mentioned earlier, some programmers like to jump right in and start coding. For every hour that you spend designing your application, you could wind up saving as much as a day of debugging time. If you start with a good design, you'll have considered many more of the situations that might cause problems later and resolve them before they occur.

> **Tip:** Fixing design problems on paper is always easier than fixing them after they're coded.

After you write down the functional definitions for your application, start translating them into a technical definition. As you move from one step to the next, you'll probably find things that you missed the first time; back up, rewrite that definition, and then continue forward again. In this way, when you start coding, it will be almost a line-for-line translation from your pseudocode to Visual Basic code.

If you think of designing an application the way a house is designed, you would get a good feel for the step-by-step approach you should set up before actually building the application. For example, you wouldn't put up the roof of the house before the walls, and you wouldn't put up the walls before the foundation is poured. You also wouldn't take a pile of lumber and just start nailing the wood together without a plan. If you did this, your house would not be habitable. It's the same with an application. The plan, or design, is the foundation of the application. If you start with a good foundation, your application will hold up, no matter how hard it is used.

To get a good design you must understand what the application will consist of. A house and an application must be built according to a carefully laid out series of steps. In a Visual Basic application, you don't want to create any code before you create the forms, or create the forms before you know what types of forms you need or their functions.

If you build the application in the wrong order or leave a part out, it will be that much harder to add the code when the rest of the application is finished. It could take longer to finish, or never work at all. To design an application correctly, you must first understand what you want it to do.

Finally, you must define the forms and reports you'll need according to the functions already defined. This is more difficult to do because there's really no set way of doing this type of design. You'll find many tips, concepts, and suggestions about form design (as covered later in this book); however, it really comes down to personal choice on how the forms will look.

With all that said, remember that the design you finally come up with isn't set in concrete. You can and should go back over the design several times, looking for possible problems before you start creating the actual application. This critical review of your plans is an important part of the design process.

Writing Code

Well, you've done it. You made it past the design phase of your project. Be proud that you did; more than half of all application projects never make it this far. Now you're ready to start coding, but don't bite off more than you can work on at a time. Treat the coding process like you're peeling an orange. Start by coding the main form of your application with the menu and button bar in place (see Figure 28.2). When you code your application, start with what the user will see when it's started.

FIGURE 28.2.

The main form of a sample application showing the skeleton of the user interface.

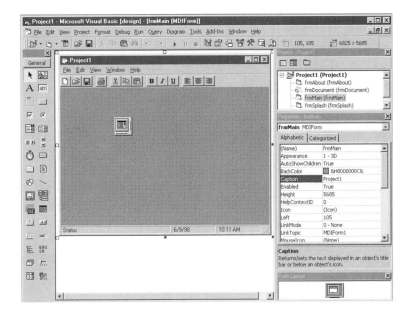

At this point, if you selected any menu or button options nothing much would happen because you haven't written any code related to those options. Writing code for the computer isn't as simple as writing a letter. The code placed in a Visual Basic application is organized hierarchically. An application generally consists of one or more modules, including form modules—one for each form in the application, standard modules for shared code, and possibly class modules. Determining which procedures belong in which module depends somewhat on the type of application you're creating.

There are certain ways or conventions for formatting and labeling everything in program code. Coding conventions are an attempt to standardize the structure and coding style of any application so that you—and more important, others—can easily read, understand, and maintain the code. Because most applications aren't as simple as the Hello World example most books use to teach programming, the organization or structure of your application code becomes very important. Depending on what a section of code does and where it's used, you would place it in different areas of your application. Code is placed in one of the following three areas:

- *Event procedures* are subprograms coded to execute in response to specific events in your application.

- *Standard code modules* are subprograms not related to a specific form or control that might be used by objects in different forms.
- *Class modules* contain code and data.

By structuring your code properly and following good coding conventions, your source code will be more precise, readable, unambiguous, and as intuitive as possible. Listing 28.1 is a before example of a coded function.

Listing 28.1. Sample routine before applying coding standards.

```
Private Sub save_but_Click()
Screen.MousePointer = 11
noupd_ent = False
If new_but.Enabled = False Then
Set logset = logdb.CreateDynaset("cdt_tbl")
logset.FindFirst "[first name] = '" & fname.Text & "' and [last name] =_
        '" & lname.Text & "'"
If Not logset.NoMatch Then
logset.Close
noupd_ent = True
Screen.MousePointer = 0
MsgBox "Duplicate Candidate Name Entered"
fname.SetFocus
Exit Sub
End If
logset.Close
End If
If data1.Recordset.EOF And data1.Recordset.BOF Then
norecs = True
Else
bk = data1.Recordset.BookMark
norecs = False
End If
If Len(lname.Text) = 0 Then
Screen.MousePointer = 0
MsgBox "You Must Enter a First and Last Name.", 32, setmsg
Exit Sub
End If
data1.Recordset.Update
loading = True
cdt_sel = data1.Recordset.Fields("cdt_id").Value
noupd_ent = False
Screen.MousePointer = 0
End Sub
```

When you enter code, the two easiest things that you can do are add comments to the code and consistently indent the code so that different logic blocks become obvious (for example, If...Then...Else...End If). Both conventions improve the overall readability of your code. To further the trend of commenting your application, you should have a brief comment box at the beginning of each procedure and function to describe what the item does (but not how). Any arguments passed to the procedure should be described when their usage isn't obvious or when a certain range of values is expected.

You've probably also read about the need for naming conventions. In a Visual Basic application, every object, constant, and variable must have a well-thought-out name. Each name should include a prefix that indicates the data type it's defined as. For example, strFirstname tells any programmer that the variable is defined as a string and that it's used to hold the first name for a data entry. To show you how all this helps, the preceding sample code has been rewritten with all these conventions used in Listing 28.2.

Listing 28.2. After applying conventions, the routine is easier to follow.

```
Private Sub cmdSaveRecord_Click()
'********
'* This routine will check to see if the person being added to
'* the database is already there. If it is not on the database then
'* it will complete the ADDNEW function by issuing an UPDATE against
'* the database.
'*
'* The variable vntBookMrk is used to pass the pointer to the current record.
'* The variable intNoRecords is used to inform the calling routine if the
'*                          Record was found or not.
'*
'********
  Screen.MousePointer = VBHourglass
'* If this is a new entry check to see if it already exists
  If cmdNewEntry.Enabled = False Then
      Set recLogRecord = dbLogBook.CreateDynaset("cdt_tbl")
      recLogRecord.FindFirst "[first name] = '" & txtFirstName & _
                          "' and [last name] = '" & txtLastName & "'"
      If Not recLogRecord.NoMatch Then
          recLogRecord.Close
          Screen.MousePointer = VBDefault
          MsgBox "Duplicate Candidate Name Entered", VBExclamation, App.Title
          txtFirstName.SetFocus
          Exit Sub
      End If
      recLogRecord.Close
  End If
'* If no records were found set intNoRecords to True
  If datLogEntry.Recordset.EOF And datLogEntry.Recordset.BOF Then
      intNoRecords = True
```

continues

Listing 28.2. Continued.

```
   Else
       vntBookMrk = datLogEntry.Recordset.BookMark
       intNoRecords = False
   End If
'* If the last name was not entered then display an error message
'* to the user and exit the routine
   If Len(txtLastName) = 0 Then
       Screen.MousePointer = VBDefault
       MsgBox "You Must Enter a First and Last Name.", VBExclamation,
       ➥App.Title
       Exit Sub
   End If
'* if you got this far update the record.
   datLogEntry.Recordset.Update
   intEntryKey = datLogEntry.Recordset.Fields("cdt_id").Value
   Screen.MousePointer = VBDefault
End Sub
```

As you can see from this final version of the routine, the code becomes very easy to follow. Related If...End If statements are easy to spot, and the comment box explains the routine's overall purpose.

In the routine, notice that two variables are global, meaning that they are defined outside the routine. The *scope* of your objects, constants, and variables are important. They should always be defined with the smallest scope possible. Global variables can make the logic of an application extremely difficult to follow. They also make it much more difficult to reuse functions or subprograms in other applications.

Testing and Debugging

After you start coding your application, you must start the process of testing the code to see whether it works and fixing, or debugging, the code that doesn't. Not everyone tests as thoroughly as he or she should, as is obvious by the number of fixes and upgrades to existing software. Then again, no matter how much you test, you will always miss some bugs. In addition to bugs that you didn't find in the first place are bugs introduced into an application whenever changes or other fixes are applied to the code. To prevent these types of bugs, you should perform *regression testing*, which is retesting everything that has been tested before.

You'll actually do two levels of testing:

- Unit testing—Testing individual routines or sections of code. For example, test just the code for the data-entry routine and nothing else.

- Integration testing—Testing all the different units as a single system.

When testing your application, try not to use data or input that you know will work. The real art in testing is to choose test data that most likely will cause errors. You also can try the "what-if" method: Ask yourself what would happen if the user does something unexpected, such as enter letters in a phone number text box. After you begin testing your code, errors will show themselves.

The other half of this team, *debugging*, is the process of identifying the cause of an error and correcting it. (*Testing*, on the other hand, is the process of detecting the error when it occurs.) On some projects, debugging occupies as much as half the total development time and, for many programmers, is the most difficult part of programming.

The testing and debugging process is long and arduous; however, Visual Basic comes with some great tools to help you. Pay close attention to the usability of the forms that you create for your application. Making sure that the application you've created is intuitive to use is part of the total testing process.

Documenting

No matter how great your forms are, sometimes users will need help. A help system for an application should include online help and a printed manual. It might also contain other features, such as ToolTips, status bars, What's This help, and wizards.

Online help is important for any application; it's usually the first place users go when they're having problems or have questions. Even a simple application should provide some type of help; not providing help assumes that your users will never have any questions.

Conceptual documentation, whether printed or provided in electronic format such as a Word document, is helpful for all but the simplest applications. It can provide information that might be difficult to convey in the shorter help topics. At the very least, you should provide documentation in the form of a ReadMe text file that users can print out if they want.

Application Performance

Making an application run better and faster is every programmer's goal. Performance is the second most important aspect of any application, right behind the application's usability and features. When people talk about performance in an application, however, the answer these days is usually, "Get a faster computer." In a perfect world, your application's users would have computers with the fastest possible processor, plenty of memory, and unlimited disk space.

Unfortunately, reality dictates that for most users, the actual performance of an application is affected by one or more of the preceding factors. In today's world of Pentium Pro processors and MMX technology, however, computer processing speed is quickly passing the 400 MHz range, meaning that users have come to expect better performance out of every application they install on their computers.

As your applications become larger and more complex, the amount of memory the application uses and the speed in which it executes become very important. To get your application to perform the best it can, you must understand the different code and techniques that affect performance. This is known as *optimizing and tuning* an application.

When you're optimizing the application code, you can use several techniques to increase performance. Some techniques help make your application faster, whereas others help make it smaller. One problem that you face when tuning your application is that the changes you make to the code might not always benefit you in the long run. Changes made to the application to improve its performance can cause the code to become more difficult to maintain or change in the future. Sometimes a change can actually decrease an application's performance. You must weigh the final performance of the application against the changes you make to affect it.

Creating the Right Impression

You know how important first impressions are. If your application takes a long time to start, it can annoy users and appear as though it's not working correctly. The larger and more complex the first form in the application is, the slower it will load. Any custom controls in the form also must be loaded at startup. And if the first form calls procedures in other modules, these modules must be loaded at startup time as well.

As you can see, performance can quickly become a domino effect. All these factors can cause the application to slow down. You can resolve the perceived problem by changing how the application is started. Rather than have the application's main form be the first one displayed, use a splash screen instead (see Figure 28.3).

FIGURE 28.3.

Present users with a splash screen to enhance startup performance.

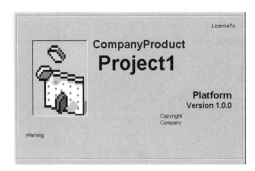

This splash screen should have the minimum amount of processing code in it. While the screen is displayed, the main form is loaded. Finally, when the main form is ready to appear, the splash screen is unloaded. The Application Wizard helps you set up the code for this to work, as follows:

```
Sub Main()
    frmSplash.Show
    frmSplash.Refresh
```

```
      Load frmMain
      Unload frmSplash

      frmMain.Show

End Sub
```

Letting Windows Work

Another reason that an application appears to slow down occurs when code routines processing large amounts of data don't have any commands that require calls to the Windows engine. This causes users to think that the computer has frozen or locked up. Windows can't process any user input, such as mouse clicks, unless a Visual Basic control command or Windows call is executed. To prevent this from becoming obvious, execute a DoEvents statement within the intensive processing code. This statement passes control to the operating system. After the operating system finishes processing the events in its queue and all keys in the SendKeys queue are sent, control is returned to your application.

Distracting the User

Another way to prevent the perceived impression of a slow application is to display the status of a process and add a little animation at the same time (see Figure 28.4). You can create a professional-looking status display that does several things: tells users that something is definitely being processed and, in most cases, shows users that the computer hasn't locked up.

Figure 28.4.
Progress bars and animations add a little spice when displaying the status of an application process.

Understanding an Application's Components

When you decide to create an application, you must consider many topics. Dealing properly with these topics or issues eventually helps you create a great application. Most product-related issues you'll deal with fall into one of the following categories:

- Program design
- Reporting
- Online help

- Performance
- Error handling
- Printed documentation

Make sure that you address each issue as you continue your application's design and development process.

Program Design

Deciding what your application will do and how it should look is the most demanding task in the creation process. Time spent in designing the application provides you with an easier task when coding the application. Because your application will run in the Windows environment, the overall look of the forms that you design should reflect the type of person who will use it.

Reports

When adding the reporting capability to your application, you must decide on the type of reporting to give your application's users. Unfortunately, the various reports that might be needed tend to evolve during the creation process. You generally don't know exactly what reports are really needed until the application is completed. However, reports, like weeds, keep popping up, even when you thought you had covered them all.

Online Help

The online help system included with the final application isn't a walk in the park to create. As you've already seen, designing and creating the help system is as difficult to do as the application design and creation. Designing the help system after the application is done only delays the final application, as you go back and add the help topic references to the application code and retest the application. You should really design the help system as you design the application, working with both of them at the same time.

Performance

Performance is a difficult topic to cover because the idea of performance is as fleeting as the most current PC on the market today. No matter how well you design your application, it will run differently on each and every computer that it's installed on. Because each computer is unique and there are many types and speeds of computer, the best you can hope for is to get your application to run as fast and efficiently as possible.

Error Handling

If everything worked the way it should, there would be no need for error handling in your application. However, we live in an imperfect world where mistakes happen, files are deleted, and hard disks still run out of space. If you have no error handling in your application, Visual Basic must handle any problems that happen. Unfortunately, Visual Basic isn't as forgiving as you might be when it comes to error handling. If an error occurs, Visual Basic displays a simple default error message and then stops the application's execution. It's your job to code enough error-handling routines to deal with any problems that you think might happen.

Printed Documentation

A good manual for your application is a difficult thing to produce. Deciding what to put into it and how detailed to be is complicated. You not only decide what topics are in the manual, but you also have to decide which forms and examples from the application should be placed in the manual. The starting point of any design is to assume that users won't be at the computer when reading the manual. You must balance the manual's content between text and figures as users read about what the application will do. A good manual usually contains the following sections:

- Table of contents
- Product introduction
- Getting started
- Using the product
- Troubleshooting
- Getting technical support
- Index

Each section of the manual should give users enough information to get started, figure out some of the simpler questions, and know where to find technical support. Again, look at other product manuals to see which features you like and which features you don't like. If your manual is well laid out and well written, with the online help file, the amount of support calls you receive from users should be fairly low.

Another way to produce a manual, without incurring the cost of printing, is by using a product such as Acrobat. Acrobat and products like it let you create an electronic form of your manual that you can include on your distribution disks. This way, users can view the manual on their computers or, if they want to, print it out themselves.

> **Note:** An online manual isn't an online help file. The manual can be read and searched, but there are no dynamic hyperlinks to other areas in the manual.

Designing Good Forms

Perhaps the most important concept to learn is simplicity. If the form design in your application looks difficult, it probably is difficult. Spending some time designing the forms can help you create an interface that works well and is easy to use. Also, from a visual point of view, a clean, simple design is always preferable. A common mistake of most programmers is to design the forms after their real-world paper versions. This creates some problems for the user. The size and shape of paper forms are different from the size and shape of a screen display; if you were to duplicate the paper form exactly, you would be limited to text boxes and check boxes. What's more, there is no added benefit to the user.

In Figure 28.5, you can see an entry form that uses several Visual Basic controls, which allows the form to remain on one screen.

FIGURE 28.5.

Advanced controls enable more information to be displayed on a single screen form with no scrolling required.

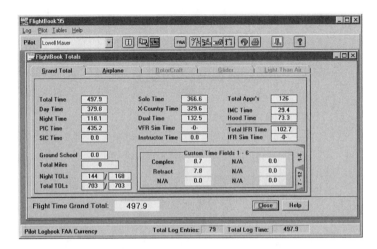

If this information were placed on the form all at the same time, not only would the user have to search for some of the fields, but he also would have to scroll to see every section of the form. When designing an application that is replacing a paper-based system, you could provide the user with a version of the input form that mirrors the original paper form and could be printed. Then, this would become a reporting issue, not a form design problem.

One thing a paper form cannot provide the user is a list of valid choices for some of the input areas. By using controls such as the list box, preloaded with choices, you can reduce the amount of typing that the user must do. In addition, you can simplify the application by moving rarely used functions to their own forms and displaying them only when needed.

With all that said, you can prevent many form problems or design issues by using the following design principles:

- Make the forms as consistent as possible within an application.
- Apply the same standards throughout the application.
- Place the command buttons on all forms in the same position and order, whenever possible.
- Use color to highlight important information.

- Don't clutter the forms with too much information.
- Group related information together on the form.
- Keep the data entry forms simple.

These design principles are not difficult to understand when you have either seen examples of them or have used an application that doesn't conform to them.

When designing a user interface, begin by looking at some of the applications already available. You will find that they have many design concepts and objects in common. Objects such as toolbars, status bars, ToolTips, menus, and tabbed dialog boxes are used to enhance the interface. Therefore, it should come as no surprise that Visual Basic provides you with the capabilities to add any or all of these objects to your application.

Making Use of Space

By using space effectively in your forms, you can emphasize different controls and improve the usability of your application. This concept is generally called *whitespace*. Whitespace doesn't have to be white; it really refers to the empty areas around and between the controls on a form. If you place too many controls on a form (see Figure 28.6), the form will look cluttered, making it difficult for the user to find any single field or control. By using some of the framing type controls, such as the Tab control, you can display only sections of the form in the same space, making the display less cluttered.

FIGURE 28.6.

Too many controls overpower the visual image of the form and make it difficult to use.

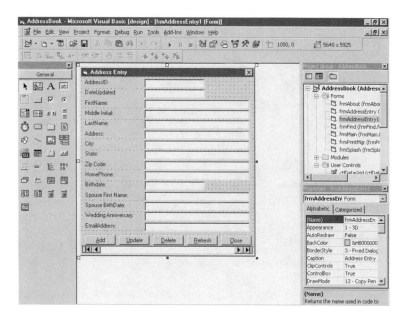

Consistency and Standards

Some objects in most forms that you will design will be more important than others.
When actually laying out the form, make sure that the more important objects are easily
recognized by the user. Because of the way you learned to read (left to right and top to
bottom) your eyes will be drawn to the upper-left portion of the screen first, so you
should place the most important objects there. Objects such as command buttons (OK or
Continue) should be placed in the lower-right portion of the screen because users won't
use those buttons until they have finished working with the form.

The way in which you group the different controls that you place on the forms is also
important. Grouping the controls in a logical order according to their function or relationship with other controls on the form enables the user to work with their data in the
same way. When entering name and address information, having all the fields placed in
the same area of a form is far better than scattering them all over the form. In many
cases, other controls such as the Frame control can be used to contain groups of controls,
reinforcing the relationship of these controls. Figure 28.7 shows a form that was not
designed using relationships and groupings. You can see that the input fields were placed
on the form as the designer thought of them.

FIGURE 28.7.

*Haphazard place-
ment of controls
on a form creates
confusion for the
user.*

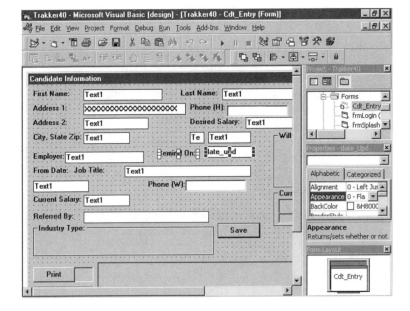

In Figure 28.8 the same form has been redesigned by placing the different input controls
into logical groupings. Immediately, you can see how much easier it is to use this
version of the form.

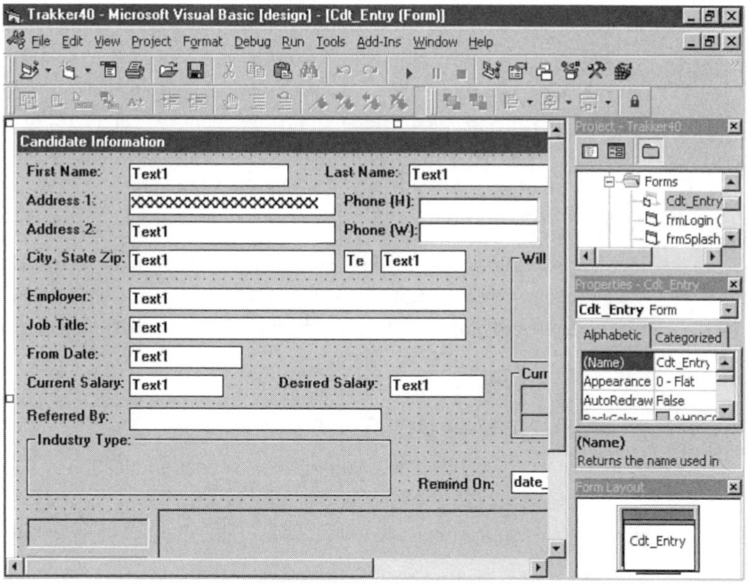

FIGURE 28.8.

Grouping the input controls creates an efficient-looking form.

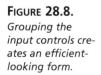

Also, because this form is used to enter date-related information, the data input field has been placed in the upper-left position of the form. If you decide on a style to use when designing your forms, stick with it. If all your forms have a consistent look to them, the user will find them easier to use.

Consistency enables you to create harmony in your application. When the user looks at your application, everything on the forms seem to fit together. On the other hand, inconsistency can be confusing and make your application appear disorganized. The best way to provide consistency in your application is to establish a strategy and style for your forms before you begin designing them. You must consider the following elements:

- Size of the controls (command buttons, text boxes, and so on)
- Font style, size, and properties
- Types of controls to use

Because Visual Basic comes with many different controls, using all of them in an application can be tempting for a developer. Try to avoid this by choosing the subset of controls that best fits your application design and image that you want to present. For example, the following controls are all used to present lists of data to the user. However, each one has specific reasons for you to select them:

- List view
- Combo box
- Grid
- Tree view

In most applications, the standard way to display a list from which to choose is by using a combo box. However, if you are displaying data from a database, the grid control is usually the control of choice. In addition, try not to use controls for a purpose for which they were not designed. Although text box controls can be set to read-only and used to display data, a label control is more normally used for this purpose. Not only is a label designed to display read-only information, it takes up less system resources than a text box control.

Keep the same styles as you move from form to form. Don't change fonts, colors, or control sizes on different forms; this only annoys the user. Finally, design your forms with some thought, and then step back and look at them. If you do not think they look good, a user probably won't either.

Using an About Box

Another form template that you can add to your application is the About dialog box. This is the same standard form that you see whenever you choose Help, About from most Windows applications (see Figure 28.9). This dialog box is usually shown only from the Help menu.

FIGURE 28.9.
Displaying infor-mation about the application in the About dialog box.

In addition, the About dialog box has a button on it that has code already in it that will execute the Microsoft System Information application, which displays many different types of system-related information (see Figure 28.10).

The information displayed on both of these forms can be retrieved directly from the application. The location of most of the information is the properties of the project. When you create your application project, you would enter the information shown in Figure 28.11. This information can then be accessed using the APP object properties in your code.

FIGURE 28.10.
The Microsoft System Information application displays important information about the programs that the computer is processing.

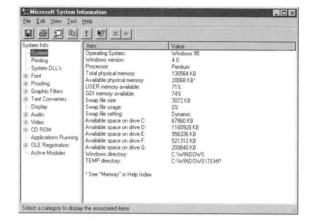

FIGURE 28.11.
Using the project properties to set the application's information.

The following code displays the related information from the application properties in the Label controls on the splash form:

```
lblVersion.Caption = "Version " & App.Major & "." & App.Minor & "."_
    & App.Revision
lblProductName.Caption = App.Title
lblCompany.Caption = App.CompanyName
```

The APP object has several other properties that can be used for display purposes.

> **Tip:** The About form is usually displayed as a modal form, which prevents the user from continuing until he clicks OK on the form to unload it.

Using the System Registry

Visual Basic now has a way of helping. Two new functions are available to you in your application.

When you must save application-execution information in between the times you run it, you can use the SaveSetting command to save the information in the user's System Registry file. Conversely, you can retrieve these settings from the Registry by using the GetSetting command. The syntax is basically the same for both, as you can see here:

```
SaveSetting appname, section, key, setting
GetSetting(appname, section, key[, default])
```

The following are the parameters for each of the commands:

- *appname*—String containing the name of the application or project whose key setting is requested.
- *section*—String containing the section name where the key setting is found.
- *key*—String containing the name of the key setting to return.
- *setting*—Expression containing the value to which the key is being set.
- *default*—The value to return if no value is set in the key setting.

When the user changes any of the colors or fonts, you should save them in the Registry. When the application is started, these settings should be retrieved during the form_ initialize routine to set the objects. Whenever you change the colors on the form, the changes are not saved anywhere. So when you close the application and restart it, the colors are reset to the defaults. You can use the SaveSetting and GetSetting functions to save the color change and then retrieve it when the application is started. The following line of code could be used in the Unload event routine of the program to save the changed settings:

```
SaveSetting "FileCopy", "Colors", "frmBackColor", frmDialog.BackColor
```

Then in the form's LOAD routine, the following line of code is an example of how to retrieve the settings:

```
frmDialog.BackColor = GetSetting("FileCopy", "Colors", "frmBackColor",_
    vb3DFace)
```

This line of code will get the color value and set the application's background color using it. Now when you run the application and change the color, it will be saved for future use. These two lines of code must be used for every color value or font-related value that you let the user change. In addition, you might want to set the original colors as constants in the application. By doing this, you can enable the user to reset the colors or fonts to the default settings.

Supporting the Users

Depending on who you talk to, support is different things to different people. This all depends on what the problem, question, or concern might be. When customers call the software company that created an application they use, they want their answers fast, and they want the answers to be correct. What happens when you call a company for support? Do you like the response that you get, or can they do better? Providing customers with a way of getting good application support is part of the overall application package that you must create.

No matter how hard you try, you'll never be able to satisfy everyone who buys your software. Don't be upset when someone returns the software because it doesn't do what she needs it to do. Most of the time, users call support only when they run out of all the other options they can think of. By the time they call you for support, they're annoyed with the product, and you have to work harder just to calm them down.

When considering the whole concept of support, there's more to this process than just having someone answer a phone when it rings. Consider the following issues when developing a plan for supporting your application:

- Easy access
- Questions and problems
- Application upgrades and fixes

You must plan for each of these issues when deciding how to give your users support. If you do this all correctly, your product will be well received by the people who use it.

Easy Access

The entire idea of easy access to technical support has changed over the last year or two. In the past, technical support was provided by telephone, fax, or mail. Now, with the increasing use of the Internet, most software providers give access to technical support through a page on their Web site. Depending on the time and money that you want to spend in this area, you can give your users one or all of the following options:

- Direct technical support phone number
- Toll-free technical support
- 24-hour technical support by fax
- Technical support email address
- Interactive Internet support Web page

Every option that you give users comes with its own unique set of problems and more important to you, cost. The best, most-used method of offering support to your users is over the phone. However, unless you plan to sit by the phone 24 hours a day, five to seven days a week, you need some type of answering machine or service to take phone messages. Of course, allowing users to fax in questions can be useful, but what if you have questions to ask them? The resolution process tends to become drawn out and frustrating for users. In my opinion, if you set a standard of getting back to your users within a range of six hours, users will get the impression that you care about the application and their use of it.

The hottest way to offer support these days is by using the World Wide Web. If you decide to use this method, you need to obtain space on a Web server, design and build the Web site itself, and then set up a method for checking messages that come into the site, in addition to updating the information on the site. You also can have any fixes or upgrades to your application available to your users on the Web for them to download when needed.

Deciding on the type of support that you want to supply to the users of your application really depends on your budget. However, you must choose one or more of these options and then implement them before you start distributing the application.

Questions and Problems

Now that you've given users a way of calling, faxing, or emailing their questions and problems to you, how will you handle them? You have to develop a way of tracking the user who sent the question or problem. This way, you can keep track of who your users are. It also allows you to know which questions are being repeated, so you can determine what needs to be changed in your application and whether it's part of the interface or the documentation.

Problems and questions should be dealt with a little differently. With questions that deal with how your application works, you can usually answer them quickly, with a simple answer or instructions on how to do something. With problems, however, you need to obtain enough information to allow you to resolve a problem. You often hear that a user started the application and then it *blew up*. This isn't a specific indication of what happened. You need to know what the user typed, which function keys were pressed, or which command buttons were clicked. These bits of information are important when you're trying to narrow down the possible problems.

Sometimes, when a problem is difficult to resolve, you might come up with a way around it. Called a *workaround*, this *stop-gap* solution doesn't fix a user's problem, but it allows that user to continue working with the application while you're revising it. Workarounds are important because sometimes a problem takes a long time to fix or can't be fixed without major changes to the application.

Application Upgrades and Fixes

When you decide that it's time to create the next version of your application, you must figure out what new features are to be added. Also, you need to think about how your current users will upgrade to this new version. You must give your users the capability to use the new release without having to input their data all over again. Think of how you would feel if you spent months learning and entering information into an application, only to receive the next release with no way of moving your preexisting data over to it. Keep this in mind; otherwise, you'll lose customers soon.

When designing an upgrade to your application, consider how you want to distribute it. If many things have changed in the application, you might consider creating a new set of distribution disks. If only a few things changed, you would want to distribute only the changes. Also, you'll want to have two separate sets of distribution disks: one for new users and one for current users upgrading to the new release. Generally, upgrades should contain fixes to problems that have popped up, as well as any new features and functions. This gives current users a good reason to buy the upgrade and new users a reason to try the application.

Owning Your Program

After working for many weeks, months, or years on designing, creating, and distributing your application, you want to make sure that you own everything about the application. This means dealing with several different legal issues related to the ownership of the application and the source code that you've written. This all might sound a bit daunting if you work at home. However, with the right amount of information, these issues aren't all that mysterious. You must consider the following:

- User registration of the application
- Software theft
- Trademark
- Application copyright

Having users register the purchase of the application and worrying about software theft are really two sides to the same coin. There's really no foolproof way of preventing someone from copying your application disks and giving them to someone else. However, if you require that users register the application with you to obtain technical support, you'll reduce the possibility of this theft from happening. Another way to help in the prevention of product theft is to have a serial number associated with each copy of the application that you produce. Although the serial number can be given with the disks, it makes it a little easier for you to keep track of who really owns a particular copy of the software.

The incentive for users to register the application with you is the availability of support and the notification of any upgrades, fixes, or new versions of the application. When you receive a call from users for support, you should first see whether they're already registered; if not, ask them for the serial number. If they can't tell you what the serial number is, you must decide whether to refuse to answer their question or to continue with the phone call. At the end of the day, if you do catch someone who doesn't own your software but has a copy of it, you must decide what course of action, legal or otherwise, you want to take.

Protecting Your Application Name

Protecting the name of your application requires you to trademark the name. The decision to trademark the name is the first step in a long legal process, however. Having a trademark for your application prevents someone else from legally using the name. For example, if someone designed a new operating system and wanted to call it Windows, Microsoft would have the legal right to prevent them from doing it. But before you jump into the trademark process, you should know that it takes time and money to get it done. Some developers decide to take a chance and not trademark their application. Unfortunately, if someone else decides to trademark the name, the developer would have to change the name of the application wherever it might appear in the application, documentation, and marketing.

As you can probably guess, this decision could be expensive. When applying for a trademark, you need to be aware of many rules. If you can afford it, you should really use a trademark lawyer because this type of lawyer does this type of work daily and knows what to watch for that might cause problems. If you decide to do it yourself, you should know that if the trademark is denied, you don't get your processing fee refunded. To get the information about the trademark process, call or write to the trademark office in Washington, D.C., as soon as you can:

> U.S. Department of Commerce
> Patent and Trademark Office
> Washington D.C. 20231
> (703) 308-4357

The process can take from three to six months if there are no delays or problems with the trademark submission.

Copyrighting Your Work

Another area that you need to protect yourself in is the possible theft of your idea, design, or implementation of your application. If you decide to copyright your application, you're protecting it from any unauthorized copying. Although you can copyright your source code, help files, and documentation, you can't copyright the actual idea or the forms design that your application uses. If you decide to copyright your application, however, apply for the copyright protection before you start selling your application. The actual protection afforded you by obtaining a copyright is directly proportional to your desire to take legal action against the person who has violated the copyright. For more information about obtaining a copyright, call or write the following:

> Publications Section
> LM-455
> Copyright Office
> Library of Congress
> Washington D.C. 20559
> (202) 707-3000

A copyright is considered effective on the date the copyright office receives all the required elements. A return receipt should be used when sending the application to the copyright office so that you know when it gets there.

Making the Final Decision

When choosing the way you want to sell your product, you have only three real choices:

- Sell your product yourself
- Sell with the help of another company
- Place your application into the wonderful world of *shareware*

Shareware is a different way to *sell* your product. Shareware products aren't sold through the use of advertising, direct mail, or catalogs; in fact, they aren't actually sold. They're instead placed in an area on the Internet or on an accessible download area of a service such as America Online (AOL). Anyone who wants to try your application can just copy it from one of these locations. If the user likes the application, he's supposed to send you the price of a copy of the software. Unfortunately, there's no real way to actually force anyone to pay for the product. To encourage people to pay for the shareware product if they decide to keep it, most shareware products use one of three methods:

- Use a *Nag* dialog box—Every time the shareware product is started, users are presented with a dialog box reminding them that the product isn't free and that they should pay the specified amount to get a registered copy and upgrades from the company.
- Build in a kill switch —After a shareware product has been used for a preset number of days or occasions, a *kill switch* causes the product to stop working.
- Disable several of the application's more interesting features—The only way users can use these features is to purchase the application, at which time you would send them an update of the executable file that would unlock the features.

One of the most successful products on the market today started as a shareware program. PKZIP was originally developed to address the issue of space on a computer disk. It allowed users to compress their files when they weren't needed and to decompress them when they were needed. Because of the way it worked, everyone who used it told everyone they knew about it, until the product became a requirement on a computer.

Many online services today, such as AOL, have areas for posting shareware products. And catalogs of shareware products have popped up over the years. Of course, the best part of selling your product as shareware is the small amount of money required to do so.

By comparison, the retail world is more costly and much more confusing. Retailing your application often consists of everything but programming. You can advertise your product through the following media:

- Magazines
- Newspapers
- Trade journals
- Direct mail
- Television

Each option has its own associated costs and concerns. You should also investigate paying a catalog service to advertise your product for you. If you have a small budget, this is probably one of the best methods of selling a product. The catalog company does all the advertising and order processing for you, at a price (generally, the company takes a percentage of the sale price for its services).

Summary

In this chapter, you've read about a lot of different issues that you must be concerned with when creating a Visual Basic application to distribute. In addition to what makes a good application program—the analysis, design, and layout of the screen forms—you have seen that there are many things to worry about that have nothing to do with programming the project. What I have attempted to do in this chapter is get you to think about these different issues. You probably never thought about standards or copyrighting your program. But, to protect yourself, you might want to consider it. Finally, you saw that retailing the application is not the only choice when it comes to selling the product. Shareware has become a very big business itself.

PART VIII

Appendixes

Glossary

accelerator key A combination of keystrokes (such as Alt+F) that performs some operation within an application. Accelerator keys cause the application to perform an action that would otherwise require several keystrokes or mouse clicks.

ActiveX A collective term applied to a family of Microsoft-sponsored technologies that permit communications and data sharing between Windows applications.

ActiveX components A name applied to applications that communicate with other Windows applications using ActiveX communications pathways. ActiveX components are part of the Component Object Model strategy promoted by Microsoft.

ActiveX controls A name applied to a special category of ActiveX component. An ActiveX control is intended to be included in Visual Basic applications and provides more intelligence and independent action than the built-in Visual Basic controls.

ActiveX Data Objects (ADO) The latest in Microsoft's data access technologies for desktop development systems such as Visual Basic. The ADO syntax abstracts the data sources and data structures retrieved from the data sources as an object hierarchy. ADO is the successor to the Data Access Objects (DAO) syntax. ADO differs from DAO in that the data sources are isolated from the data consumer by a *provider* layer whereas the DAO syntax directly references the Jet database engine.

ANSI An acronym for American National Standards Institute, a governing and standards organization responsible for specifying a number of important communications and encoding specifications. The most common ANSI standard in place for the English alphabet is ASCII, the American Standard Code for Information Interchange. The ASCII character sequence determines the number assigned to each digit and letter of the alphabet as well as many nonprintable characters.

API An acronym for Application Programming Interface, the method of utilizing the resources built into Microsoft Windows as part of a Visual Basic application. The API specifies the syntax of VBA calls made to the Windows DLLs (dynamically linked libraries) that support almost all of Windows functionality.

application A software program created with a development system such as Visual Basic. An application is normally designed to support a certain task or operation such as word processing, data acquisition, or graphics.

argument A parameter passed to a procedure. The argument is normally data in the form of a character string, object reference, or numeric value.

array A linear data structure consisting of a sequence of numeric, string, or object values.

ASCII The ordered sequence of numeric values assigned to the letters of the alphabet, numeric digits, and other characters. ASCII is an acronym for American Standard Code for Information Interchange.

Automation One of the ActiveX technologies permitting an application to control the activities of another application.

Automation controller The Windows application controlling the activities of another application.

Automation server An application providing services (such as document preparation or sound and video playback) in an Automation scheme.

BASIC An acronym for Beginner's All Purpose Symbolic Instruction Code, a language developed in the 1960s at Dartmouth College. BASIC began as an instructional language for computer science students but rapidly found acceptance on many different types of computer systems.

bitmap A binary data structure that contains the information necessary for Windows to render an image on the screen.

Boolean A data type that accepts only `True` or `False` values. `True` is stored internally as `-1`; `False` is stored as `0` (zero).

breakpoint A debugging construct that halts execution at a predetermined place in VBA code. Although the VBA language engine is engaged and operating, the program's execution is halted at the breakpoint, enabling the developer to examine the status of the program's execution.

check box A type of control that displays `True` or `False` values. When checked, a check box is considered to be `True`; when empty the check box is `False`.

client A broad term that refers to any program using the services of another program or hardware resource.

Clipboard A shared Windows resource that enables copying data or text to temporary storage in memory. The text or data item can then be copied from the Clipboard into another Windows application.

code A general term applied to the English-like words, numbers, and symbols that make up a computer program.

Code Editor The name applied to the Visual Basic window used to compose and modify VBA code.

column A single vertical column of data in a database table. A column is usually referred to as a field. Each column contains a single type of information such as an address or phone number.

COM See *Component Object Model*.

combo box A special type of control consisting of a text box combined with a drop-down list of acceptable values. Depending on how the combo box is designed the user might be confined to selecting an item from the list or able to enter new values by typing free text in the text box portion.

command button A Windows control that triggers a `Click` event when clicked with the mouse. Command buttons are frequently used to run code upon command from the user.

comment A statement within VBA code that has been inserted as an explanation of the code's operation. Comments are established by inserting a single-quote character in a VBA statement.

Common Dialog control A Visual Basic control that opens a number of standard Windows dialog boxes that can be used to perform different operations. The Common Dialog control can be used to open a File Find dialog box, a Save As dialog box, Color and Font selection dialog boxes, and so on.

compile The process of converting the various parts of a Visual Basic program into a single executable file.

Component Object Model (COM) An application design philosophy and technique whereby an application consists of a number of components bound together by a programming language such as Visual Basic.

concatenation The act of joining two text values together as a single value.

constant A reference to an unchanging value within an application. After the constant's value has been established, it cannot be modified.

container The term applied to an object that holds other objects. Generally speaking, a container holds only a single type of object.

control A graphical object added to a Visual Basic form. A control supports a single task, such as collecting information from the user, or displays the status of data within the application.

control array A set of controls treated as a single entity. The members of a control array are referenced through an index value that points unambiguously to only one member of the control array.

Control box A Windows-provided control found in the leftmost position of the title bar of most forms. The Control box is actually a button that reveals a menu of standard form operations such as Resize, Maximize, Minimize, and Close. The Control box can be suppressed on the forms in Visual Basic forms.

custom control Visual Basic comes with a large number of built-in controls that can be added to forms. In addition to the built-in controls, Visual Basic is able to accommodate a variety of special-purpose *custom controls* that are available from commercial sources or built with Visual Basic. In most cases, a custom control supports an operation that is not available through Visual Basic's built-in controls.

Data Access Objects (DAO) The DAO syntax abstracts the data access and management capabilities of the Jet database engine as an object hierarchy. In the DAO hierarchy Jet is the ultimate owner of all other data objects with the data contained in database fields at the very bottom. DAO is largely replaced with ADO in Visual Basic 6.

database A collection of data structures and other components designed to effectively store data.

database application An application specifically designed to support database activities. Most database applications include the database components plus a user interface that makes the database easy to use and programming code that adds intelligence and logic to the application.

database table The primary data structure in a database. A table consists of rows (also called *records*) and columns (the *fields*) of data.

debug, debugging The process of identifying and repairing errors in the logic or programming language syntax of a computer program.

Debug window A special window in the Visual Basic design environment that provides a way to run and test code. The Debug window enables the Visual Basic developer to run functions and subroutines and read and set the values of variables.

declaration section An area of a code module intended to contain the module-level variable and constant declaration. In a Public module the declarations section might contain global constant and variable declarations.

Design mode, Design view Visual Basic supports two distinctly different modes: design time and runtime. During design time the forms, code, and other parts of the application are seen in Design view, a special view that permits changes to the design of the application's objects.

design time The period of time spent designing and building an application. During design time the application is in an unfinished state and changes are being made to the program, its code, and its features.

DLL An abbreviation for dynamically linked library, a file that is loaded into memory when demanded by an application. A DLL is a shared resource under Windows. After a DLL is loaded into memory, it can be used by any number of applications, conserving memory and CPU cycles.

drag-and-drop An application technique whereby an object can be moved to a new location. Most Visual Basic controls are drag-and-drop–enabled.

embedding A technique whereby OLE data (see *OLE*) is contained within the application rather than being linked into the application. When data is embedded it travels with the application as the program is installed on different computers or sent to another location via email or on disk.

Empty The value of a variant variable that has not yet been assigned a value.

Enabled property A common property of most Visual Basic controls that makes the control available to the user (Enabled = True) or unavailable (Enabled = False). In most cases, a control that is not enabled features a grayed-out appearance.

error trapping The process of stopping errors that occur at runtime. Rather than allowing Windows to handle the error through its default error reporting mechanism, you can add VBA code to your Visual Basic programs that intercepts errors and handles them in a fashion most appropriate for the application.

event A change in the state of some aspect of the computer or its software. A Click event, for example, signals that the user has pushed a button on the computer's mouse.

event-driven A descriptive term applied to computer programs that respond to actions by the user or the computer. You write code in response to the events generated in response to the actions.

executable A file that can run outside of the Visual Basic design environment. Most often the programs you prepare with Visual Basic are compiled into an executable and distributed to its users.

expression A combination of values, variables, delimiters, and operators that yields a value.

field A single bit of information within a record in a database table.

focus The selected or highlighted object on the screen. Under Windows only one object can contain the focus and receive the user's input.

Frame control A type of Visual Basic control that serves as a container for other controls. A Frame control appears as a rectangle on a form surrounding the other controls.

global A term implying that the object is visible throughout the application. A global variable, for example, is usable by any procedure or routine anywhere in the application. The Global keyword has been superceded by the Public keyword.

HTML An abbreviation for hypertext mark-up language, a convention that specifies certain tags that are embedded in an otherwise plain-text document. The document must be read by some kind of interpreter such as a Web browser that converts the mark-up tags as font typeface changes, colors, and other appearance attributes.

index A numeric or text reference to a member of an array or collection of items. In most cases, the index assigned to an item must be unique within its collection.

instance An object created from a class definition. For example, each form in a Visual Basic application is an instance of a Form object.

instantiate The act of creating a new instance of an object from a class module. See *instance*.

Jet The name applied to the database engine built into Visual Basic. Jet is a resource shared with more than 20 other programs including Microsoft Access, Word, Excel, PowerPoint, and Project. Jet is a fully relational database engine and supports its own SQL syntax (see *SQL*), tables, queries, and other database features.

key When applied to a database table, a key is a field in the table used to identify the data contained in a single row (or record) in the table. See *field, record, relational*.

keyboard shortcut A Windows convention that makes applications easier to use. A keyboard shortcut is a single character, that, when pressed at the same time as the Ctrl, Alt, or Shift key, performs some action. Without shortcut keys the user has to rely on menu commands or other user-interface components.

keyword A word that has special meaning to Visual Basic. Keywords are often statements, reserved words that cannot be used as the name of an object or identifier within the application.

List Box control A type of control that consists of a scrolling list of text or numeric values.

method An attribute of an object that describes some action supported by the object. For example, all Visual Basic forms have a Show method that makes the form appear on the screen.

modal The state of a form that must be closed before the user can continue working with the application. While a modal form is open on the screen, processing is halted until the form is dismissed by the user.

modeless A state of a form that enables the user to move on to other parts of the application while the form is open. By default, all Visual Basic forms are modeless and do not restrict the user's movements throughout the application.

module A container for VBA code. A module consists of a declarations area within the General section and a number of procedures.

null The value of a variable that has no value or whose value is unknown.

object An entity within a Visual Basic application. All Visual Basic forms, controls, and many variables are objects. Most objects feature a number of *properties* and *methods*.

OCX controls Another name for *ActiveX controls*.

ODBC An abbreviation for Open Database Connectivity, a Microsoft-sponsored specification that describes a communications protocol for database applications. The ODBC specification describes how front-end applications, such as those produced with Visual Basic, communicate with back-end data sources such as SQL Server and Oracle.

OLE An acronym for *object linking and embedding*, a somewhat older communications and data-sharing protocol for Windows applications. The term OLE has been largely replaced by ActiveX, a broad collection of communications methods for Windows applications.

Option button A user-interface control that provides for selection from among a number of mutually exclusive values. Only one of the values can be selected at a time.

parameter A bit of data passed into a procedure.

parse A verb describing the process of locating constituent substrings within a larger string.

Private A keyword that implies limited visibility of a variable. When declared with the Private keyword, a variable can be seen only with the module in which it appears. The Private keyword cannot be used within a procedure.

program A compiled, executable collection of code contained within modules, form, controls, and other components. *Program* and *application* are practically synonymous, with the exception that the former emphasizes the computer code underlying the entity whereas the latter emphasizes the functionality of the entity.

property A descriptive attribute of an object. Properties can be read/write or read-only at runtime.

property page A special dialog box attached to some ActiveX controls that enables modification of custom properties of the control.

Public An expression that describes universal visibility of an object or variable in a Visual Basic application. The Public keyword has largely replaced the older Global keyword.

query A query extracts or manipulates data stored in a database file on the computer. Queries take a number of different forms in Visual Basic applications and can be as simple as an SQL statement (see SQL).

Radio button See *Option button*.

read-only An attribute of a file that makes it impossible to modify or delete the file.

record A single row in a database table. A row contains all the information describing a single entity such as a customer, employee, or patient. A record is made of a number of fields, each of which contains one data item about the entity such as an address or phone number.

recordset A set of records treated as a single entity. A recordset is much like a table and consists of a series of records, each of which is made up of a number of fields.

Registry A database of hardware and software configuration information managed by Windows. The Registry includes information such as the location of certain shared resources and the number and type of serial ports installed on the computer.

relational database A database design methodology whereby the data is stored in a number of related tables rather than a few large tables. The tables are related through key fields (see key).

row A record in a database table. See *record*.

runtime The application during the time it is running on a user's desktop. Runtime implies the application's development cycle is complete and all features are in place. See *design time*.

scrollbar An animated control for setting a variable property or setting a relative value of one sort or another. A scrollbar provides visual feedback of the setting. A scrollbar can be used, for instance, to set the intensity of a control's background color.

sequential file A file in which the data appears in a sequential fashion. Each new piece of data appears immediately after the preceding data. Sequential files can contain fixed-width data, in which each record is the same length as every other record, and delimited data in which each record varies in length depending on how much data is stored in the record.

shortcut key A Ctrl+key combination that triggers a specific action in an application.

source code The actual words and symbols making up the programming in an application. Source code is contained within modules in a Visual Basic application.

SQL An acronym for Structured Query Language, the English-like syntax passed to a database engine such as Jet (see *Jet*) to perform database operations such as querying data or modifying the structure of a table.

statement A sequence of Visual Basic keywords, commands, variable references, operators, and other information that acts as an executable unit. Most Visual Basic statements perform a single action within the program.

string A unit of data containing only letters of the alphabet, numeric digits, and punctuation marks.

syntax The rules that determine how VBA code is to be written. The syntax of a statement specifies how the VBA command is to be spelled, what arguments are required, and other requirements of the command.

tab order The sequence that controls on a form are visited as the user presses the Tab button.

Text Box control A control intended to display data or accept input from the user.

title bar The area at the very top of a form containing some identifier for the form, a Control Box button, and the Minimize, Maximize, and Close buttons.

toolbar A user interface construct that consists of an array of command buttons, most often featuring graphical icons. Each button performs a single action or invokes a more complex operation within the program.

toolbox A special window in the Visual Basic design environment that contains buttons representing each type of common Visual Basic control.

twip A unit of measure on a form or report. One twip is one-twentieth of a printer's point, or 1/1440th of an inch.

variable The name provided to a value within an application. The value assigned to the variable can change as the application runs.

VBA See *Visual Basic for Applications.*

Visible property A Boolean (`True` or `False`) property of a control that determines whether the control can be seen on the form (`Visible = True`) or is invisible to the user (`Visible = False`).

Visual Basic The name applied to the standalone development system using the VBA programming language. Visual Basic is a general-purpose development system, which means it is not restricted to producing database applications as with Microsoft Access, and can be used to produce virtually any type of computer program.

Visual Basic for Applications (VBA) The general term applied to the language found in Visual Basic 6.0 and many other applications. VBA is a descendent of the BASIC language found on many early desktop computers running the DOS operating system.

Windows Registry See *Registry.*

The Reddick VBA Naming Conventions

Version 5.0

Copyright© 1992-1997 by Gregory Reddick & Associates. All Rights Reserved.

The purpose of the Reddick VBA (RVBA) Naming Conventions is to provide a guideline for naming objects in the Visual Basic for Applications (VBA) language. Having conventions is valuable in any programming project. When you use them, the name of the object conveys information about the meaning of the object. These conventions attempt to provide a way of standardizing that meaning across the body of VBA programmers.

VBA is implemented to interact with a host application—for example, Microsoft Access, Microsoft Visual Basic, AutoCAD, and Visio. The RVBA conventions cover all implementations of the VBA language, regardless of the host application. Some of the tags described in this document may not necessarily have an implementation within some of the particular host programs for VBA. The word object, in the context of this document, refers to simple variables and VBA objects, as well as to objects made available by the VBA host program.

While I am the editor of these conventions, they are the work of many people, including Charles Simonyi, who invented the Hungarian conventions on which these are based, and Stan Leszynski, who co-authored several versions of the conventions. Many others, too numerous to mention, have also contributed to the development and distribution of these conventions.

These conventions are intended as a guideline. If you disagree with a particular part of the conventions, simply replace that part with what you think works better. However, keep in mind that future generations of programmers may need to understand those changes, and place a comment in the header of a module indicating what changes have been made. The conventions are presented without rationalizations for how they were derived although each of the ideas presented has a considerable history to it.

Changes to the Conventions

Some of the tags in the version of the conventions presented here have changed from previous versions. Consider all previous tags to be grandfathered into the conventions—you don't need to go back and make changes. For new development work, I leave it up to you to decide whether to use the older tags or the ones suggested here. In a few places in this document, older tags are shown in {braces}. As updates to this document are made, the current version can be found at `http://www.mcwtech.com`.

An Introduction to Hungarian

The RVBA conventions are based on the Hungarian conventions for constructing object names, named for the native country of the inventor, Charles Simonyi. The objective of Hungarian is to convey information about the object concisely and efficiently. Hungarian takes some getting used to, but once adopted, it quickly becomes second nature. The format of a Hungarian object name is

```
[prefixes]tag[BaseName[Suffixes]]
```

The square brackets indicate optional parts of the object name. These components have the following meanings:

Component	Meaning
Prefixes	Modify the tag to indicate additional information. Prefixes are all lowercase. They are usually picked from a standardized list of prefixes, given later in this document.
Tag	Short set of characters, usually mnemonic, that indicates the type of the object. The tag is all lowercase. It is usually selected from a standardized list of tags, given later in this document.
BaseName	One or more words that indicate what the object represents. The first letter of each word in the BaseName is capitalized.
Suffixes	Additional information about the meaning of the BaseName. The first letter of each word in the Suffix is capitalized. They are usually picked from a standardized list of suffixes, given later in this document.

Notice that the only required part of the object name is the tag. This may seem counter-intuitive; you may feel that the BaseName is the most important part of the object name. However, consider a generic procedure that operates on any form. The fact that the routine operates on a form is the important thing, not what that form represents. Because the routine may operate on forms of many different types, you do not necessarily need a BaseName. However, if you have more than one object of a type referenced in the routine, you must have a BaseName on all but one of the object names to differentiate them. Also, unless the routine is generic, the BaseName conveys information about the variable. In most cases a variable should include a BaseName.

Tags

You use tags to indicate the data type of an object, and you construct them using the techniques described in the following sections.

Variable Tags

Use the tags listed in Table B.1 for VBA data types. You can also use a specific tag instead of `obj` for any data type defined by the host application or one of its objects. (See the section "Host Application and Component Extensions to the Conventions" later in this document.)

Table B.1. Tags for VBA variables.

Tag	Object Type
bool {f}	Boolean
byte {byt}	Byte
cur	Currency
date {dtm}	Date
dec	Decimal
dbl	Double
int	Integer
lng	Long
obj	Object
sng	Single
str	String
stf	String (fixed length)
var	Variant

Here are several examples:

```
lngCount
intValue
strInput
```

You should explicitly declare all variables, each on a line by itself. Do not use the old-type declaration characters, such as %, &, and $. They are extraneous if you use the naming conventions, and there is no character for some of the data types, such as Boolean. You should always explicitly declare all variables of type Variant using the As Variant clause, even though it is the default in VBA. For example:

```
Dim intTotal As Integer
Dim varField As Variant
Dim strName As String
```

Constructing Properties Names

Properties of a class present a particular problem: should they include the naming convention to indicate the type? To be consistent with the rest of these naming conventions, they should. However, it is permitted to have property names without the tags, especially if the class is to be made available to customers who may not be familiar with these naming conventions.

Collection Tags

You treat a collection object with a special tag. You construct the tag using the data type of the collection followed by the letter s. For example, if you had a collection of Longs, the tag would be lngs. If it were a collection of forms, the collection would be frms. Although, in theory, a collection can hold objects of different data types, in practice, each of the data types in the collection is the same. If you do want to use different data types in a collection, use the tag objs. For example:

```
intsEntries
frmsCustomerData
objsMisc
```

Constants

Constants always have a data type in VBA. Because VBA will choose this data type for you if you don't specify it, you should always specify the data type for a constant. Constants declared in the General Declarations section of a module should always have a scope keyword of Private or Public, and be prefixed by the scope prefixes m and g, respectively. A constant is indicated by appending the letter c to the end of the data type for the constant. For example:

```
Const intcGray As Integer = 3
Private Const mdblcPi As Double = 3.14159265358979
```

Although this technique is the recommended method of naming constants, if you are more concerned about specifying that you are dealing with constants rather than their data type, you can alternatively use the generic tag con instead. For example:

```
Const conPi As Double = 3.14159265358979
```

Menu Items

The names of menu items should reflect their position in the menu hierarchy. All menu items should use the tag `mnu`, but the BaseName should indicate where in the hierarchy the menu item falls. Use `Sep` in the BaseName to indicate a menu separator bar, followed by an ordinal. For example:

```
mnuFile (on menu bar)
mnuFileNew (on File popup menu)
mnuFileNewForm (on File New flyout menu)
mnuFileNewReport (on File New flyout menu)
mnuFileSep1 (first separator bar on file popup menu)
mnuFileSaveAs (on File popup menu)
mnuFileSep2 (second separator bar on file popup menu)
mnuFileExit (on File popup menu)
mnuEdit (on menu bar)
```

Creating Data Types

VBA gives you three ways to create new data types: enumerated types, classes, and user-defined types. In each case, you will need to invent a new tag that represents the data type that you create.

Enumerated Types

Groups of constants of the *long* data type should be made an enumerated type. Invent a tag for the type, append a `c`, then define the enumerated constants using that tag. Because the name used in the `Enum` line is seen in the object browser, you can add a BaseName to the tag to spell out the abbreviation indicated by the tag. For example:

```
Public Enum ervcErrorValue
    ervcInvalidType = 205
    ervcValueOutOfBounds
End Enum
```

The BaseName should be singular, so that the enumerated type should be `ervcErrorValue`, not `ervcErrorValues`. The tag that you invent for enumerated types can then be used for variables that can contain values of that type. For example:

```
Dim erv As ervcErrorValue
Private Sub Example(ByVal ervCur As ervcErrorValue)
```

While VBA only provides enumerated types of groups of the long type, you can still create groups of constants of other types. Just create a set of constant definitions using an invented tag. For example:

```
Public Const estcError205 As String = "Invalid type"
Public Const estcError206 As String = "Value out of bounds"
```

Unfortunately, because this technique doesn't actually create a new type, you don't get the benefit of the VBA compiler performing type checking for you. You create variables that will hold constants using a similar syntax to variables meant to hold instances of enumerated types. For example:

```
Dim estError As String
```

Tags for Classes and User-Defined Types

A class defines a user-defined object. Because these invent a new data type, you will need to invent a new tag for the object. You can add a BaseName to the tag to spell out the abbreviation indicated by the tag. User-defined types are considered a simple class with only properties, but in all other ways are used the same as class modules. For example:

```
gphGlyph
edtEdit
Public Type grbGrabber
```

You then define variables to refer to instances of the class using the same tag. For example:

```
Dim gphNext As New gphGlyph
Dim edtCurrent as edtEdit
Dim grbHandle as grbGrabber
```

Polymorphism

In VBA, you use the *implements* statement to derive classes from a base class. The tag for the derived class should use the same tag as the base class. The derived classes, though, should use a different BaseName from the base class. For example:

```
anmAnimal (base class)
anmZebra (derived class of anmAnimal)
anmElephant (derived class of anmAnimal)
```

This logic of naming derived classes is used with forms, which are all derived from the pre-defined Form base class and use the `frm` tag. If a variable is defined to be of the type of the base class, then use the tag, as usual. For example:

```
Dim anmArbitrary As anmAnimal
Dim frmNew As Form
```

On the other hand, if you define a variable as an instance of a derived class, include the complete derived class name in the variable name. For example:

```
Dim anmZebraInstance As anmZebra
Dim anmElephantExample As anmElephant
Dim frmCustomerData As frmCustomer
```

Constructing Procedures

VBA procedures require you to name various items: procedure names, parameters, and labels. These objects are described in the following sections.

Constructing Procedure Names

VBA names event procedures, and you cannot change them. You should use the capitalization defined by the system. For user-defined procedure names, capitalize the first letter of each word in the name. For example:

```
cmdOK_Click
GetTitleBarString
PerformInitialization
```

Procedures should always have a scope keyword, `Public` or `Private`, when they are declared. For example:

```
Public Function GetTitleBarString() As String
Private Sub PerformInitialization
```

Naming Parameters

You should prefix all parameters in a procedure definition with `ByVal` or `ByRef`, even though `ByRef` is optional and redundant. Procedure parameters are named the same as simple variables of the same type, except that arguments passed by reference use the prefix `r`. For example:

```
Public Sub TestValue(ByVal intInput As Integer, ByRef rlngOutput As Long)
Private Function GetReturnValue(ByVal strKey As String, ByRef rgph As Glyph)
➥As Boolean
```

Naming Labels

Labels are named using upper and lower case, capitalizing the first letter of each word. For example:

```
ErrorHandler:
ExitProcedure:
```

Prefixes

Prefixes modify an object tag to indicate more information about an object.

Arrays of Objects Prefix

Arrays of an object type use the prefix a. For example:

```
aintFontSizes
astrNames
```

Index Prefix

You indicate an index into an array by the prefix i, and for consistency the data type should always be a long. You may also use the index prefix to index into other enumerated objects, such as a collection of user-defined classes. For example:

```
iaintFontSizes
iastrNames
igphsGlyphCollection
```

Prefixes for Scope and Lifetime

Three levels of scope exist for each variable in VBA: Public, Private, and Local. A variable also has a lifetime of the current procedure or the lifetime of the object in which it is defined. Use the prefixes in Table B.2 to indicate scope and lifetime.

Table B.2. Prefixes for scope and lifetime.

Prefix	Object Type
(none)	Local variable, procedure-level lifetime, declared with Dim
s	Local variable, object lifetime, declared with Static
m	Private (module) variable, object lifetime, declared with Private
g	Public (global) variable, object lifetime, declared with Public

You also use the m and g constants with other objects, such as constants, to indicate their scope. For example:

```
intLocalVariable
mintPrivateVariable
gintPublicVariable
mdblcPi
```

VBA allows several type declaration words for backwards compatibility. The older keyword "Global" should always be replaced by "Public", and the "Dim" and "Static" keywords in the General Declarations section should be replaced by "Private".

Other Prefixes

Table B.3 lists and describes some other prefixes:

Table B.3. Other commonly used prefixes.

Prefix	Object Type
c	Count of some object type
h	Handle to a Windows object
r	Parameter passed by reference

Here are several examples:

```
castrArray
hWndForm
```

Suffixes

Suffixes modify the base name of an object, indicating additional information about a variable. You'll likely create your own suffixes that are specific to your development work. Table B.4 lists some generic VBA suffixes.

Table B.4. Commonly used suffixes.

Suffix	Object Type
Min	The absolute first element in an array or other kind of list.
First	The first element to be used in an array or list during the current operation.
Last	The last element to be used in an array or list during the current operation.
Lim	The upper limit of elements to be used in an array or list. Lim is not a valid index. Generally, Lim equals Last + 1.
Max	The absolutely last element in an array or other kind of list.
Cnt	Used with database elements to indicate that the item is a Counter. Counter fields are incremented by the system and are numbers of either type Long or type ReplicationId.

Here are some examples:

```
iastrNamesMin
iastrNamesMax
iaintFontSizesFirst
igphsGlyphCollectionLast
lngCustomerIdCnt
varOrderIdCnt
```

File Names

When naming items stored on the disk, no tag is needed because the extension already gives the object type. For example:

```
Test.Frm (frmTest form)
Globals.Bas (globals module)
Glyph.Cls (gphGlyph class module)
```

Host Application and Component Extensions to the Conventions

Each host application for VBA, as well as each component that can be installed, has a set of objects it can use. This section defines tags for the objects in the various host applications and components.

Access 97, Version 8.0 Objects

Table B.5 lists Access object variable tags. Besides being used in code to refer to these object types, these same tags are used to name these kinds of objects in the form and report designers.

Table B.5. Access object variable tags.

Tag	Object Type
app	Application
chk	CheckBox
cbo	ComboBox
cmd	CommandButton
ctl	Control
ctls	Controls
ocx	CustomControl
dcm	DoCmd
frm	Form
frms	Forms
grl	GroupLevel
img	Image
lbl	Label
lin	Line
lst	ListBox
bas	Module
ole	ObjectFrame
opt	OptionButton
fra	OptionGroup (frame)
brk	PageBreak
pal	PaletteButton
prps	Properties

Tag	Object Type
shp	Rectangle
rpt	Report
rpts	Reports
scr	Screen
sec	Section
sfr	SubForm
srp	SubReport
txt	TextBox
tgl	ToggleButton

Some examples:

```
txtName
lblInput
```

For ActiveX custom controls, you can use the tag ocx as specified in Table B.5 or more specific object tags that are listed later in this document in Tables B.12 and B.13.

DAO 3.5 Objects

DAO is the programmatic interface to the Jet database engine shared by Access, VB, and VC++. The tags for DAO 3.5 objects are shown in Table B.6.

Table B.6. DAO object tags.

Tag	Object Type
cnt	Container
cnts	Containers
db	Database
dbs	Databases
dbe	DBEngine
doc	Document
docs	Documents
err	Error
errs	Errors
fld	Field
flds	Fields
grp	Group

continues

Table B.6. Continued.

Tag	Object Type
grps	Groups
idx	Index
idxs	Indexes
prm	Parameter
prms	Parameters
pdbe	PrivDBEngine
prp	Property
prps	Properties
qry	QueryDef
qrys	QueryDefs
rst	Recordset
rsts	Recordsets
rel	Relation
rels	Relations
tbl	TableDef
tbls	TableDefs
usr	User
usrs	Users
wrk	Workspace
wrks	Workspaces

Here are some examples:

```
rstCustomers
idxPrimaryKey
```

Table B.7 lists the tags used to identify types of objects in a database.

Table B.7. Access Database Explorer object tags.

Tag	Object Type
tbl	Table
qry	Query
frm	Form
rpt	Report
mcr	Macro
bas	Module

If you wish, you can use more exact tags or suffixes to identify the purpose and type of a database object. If you use the suffix, use the tag given from Table B.7 to indicate the type. Use either the tag or the suffix found along with the more general tag, but not both. The tags and suffixes are shown in Table B.8.

Table B.8. Specfic object tags and suffixes for Access Database Explorer objects.

Tag	Suffix	Object Type
tlkp	Lookup	Table (lookup)
qsel	(none)	Query (select)
qapp	Append	Query (append)
qxtb	XTab	Query (crosstab)
qddl	DDL	Query (DDL)
qdel	Delete	Query (delete)
qflt	Filter	Query (filter)
qlkp	Lookup	Query (lookup)
qmak	MakeTable	Query (make table)
qspt	PassThru	Query (SQL pass-through)
qtot	Totals	Query (totals)
quni	Union	Query (union)
qupd	Update	Query (update)
fdlg	Dlg	Form (dialog)
fmnu	Mnu	Form (menu)
fmsg	Msg	Form (message)
fsfr	SubForm	Form (subform)
rsrp	SubReport	Form (subreport)
mmnu	Mnu	Macro (menu)

Here are some examples:

```
tblValidNamesLookup
tlkpValidNames
fmsgError
mmnuFileMnu
```

When naming objects in a database, do not use spaces. Instead, capitalize the first letter of each word. For example, instead of Quarterly Sales Values Table, use `tblQuarterlySalesValues`.

There is strong debate over whether fields in a table should have tags. Whether you use them is up to you. However, if you do use them, use the tags from Table B.9.

Table B.9. Field tags (if you decide to use them) .

Tag	Object Type
lng	Autoincrementing (either sequential or random) Long (used with the suffix Cnt)
bin	Binary
byte	Byte
cur	Currency
date	Date/time
dbl	Double
guid	Globally unique identified (GUID) used for replication AutoIncrement fields
int	Integer
lng	Long
mem	Memo
ole	OLE
sng	Single
str	Text
bool	Yes/No

Visual Basic 5.0 Objects

Table B.10 shows the tags for Visual Basic 5.0 objects.

Table B.10. Visual Basic 5.0 object tags.

Tag	Object Type
app	App
chk	CheckBox
clp	Clipboard
cbo	ComboBox
cmd	CommandButton
ctl	Control
dat	Data
dir	DirListBox

Tag	Object Type
drv	DriveListBox
fil	FileListBox
frm	Form
fra	Frame
glb	Global
hsb	HScrollBar
img	Image
lbl	Label
lin	Line
lst	ListBox
mdi	MDIForm
mnu	Menu
ole	OLE
opt	OptionButton
pic	PictureBox
prt	Printer
prp	PropertyPage
scr	Screen
shp	Shape
txt	TextBox
tmr	Timer
uctl	UserControl
udoc	UserDocument
vsb	VScrollBar

Microsoft Common Control Objects

Windows 95 and Windows NT have a set of common controls that are accessible from VBA. Table B.11 lists the tags for objects created using these controls.

Table B.11. Microsoft Common Control Object tags.

Tag	Object Type
ani	Animation
btn	Button (Toolbar)

continues

Table B.11. Continued.

Tag	Object Type
btns	Buttons (Toolbar)
hdr	ColumnHeader (ListView)
hdrs	ColumnHeaders (ListView)
ctls	Controls
iml	ImageList (ImageList)
lim	ListImage
lims	ListImages
lit	ListItem (ListView)
lits	ListItems (ListView)
lvw	ListView (ListView)
nod	Node (TreeView)
nods	Nodes (TreeView)
pnl	Panel (Status Bar)
pnls	Panels (Status Bar)
prb	ProgressBar (Progress Bar)
sld	Slider (Slider)
sbr	StatusBar (Status Bar)
tab	Tab (Tab Strip)
tabs	Tabs (Tab Strip)
tbs	TabStrip (Tab Strip)
tbr	Toolbar (Toolbar)
tvw	TreeView (TreeView)
udn	UpDown (UpDown)

Other Custom Controls and Objects

Finally, Table B.12 lists the tags for other commonly-used custom controls and objects.

Table B.12. Tags for commonly-used custom controls.

Tag	Object Type
cdl	CommonDialog (Common Dialog)
dbc	DBCombo (Data Bound Combo Box)
dbg	DBGrid (Data Bound Grid)
dls	DBList (Data Bound List Box)

Tag	Object Type
gau	Gauge (Gauge)
gph	Graph (Graph)
grd	Grid (Grid)
msg	MAPIMessages (Messaging API Message Control)
ses	MAPISession (Messaging API Session Control)
msk	MaskEdBox (Masked Edit Textbox)
key	MhState (Key State)
mmc	MMControl (Multimedia Control)
com	MSComm (Communication Port)
out	Outline (Outline Control)
pcl	PictureClip (Picture Clip Control)
rtf	RichTextBox (Rich Textbox)
spn	SpinButton (Spin Button)

Summary

Using a naming convention requires a considerable initial effort on your part. The payoff comes when either you or another programmer has to revisit your code at a later time. Using the conventions given here will make your code more readable and maintainable.

Note: Greg Reddick is the President of Gregory Reddick & Associates, a software development company developing programs in Visual Basic, Microsoft Access, and C/C++. He leads training seminars in Visual Basic for Application Developers Training Company and is a co-author of the *Microsoft Access 95 Developer's Handbook*, published by SYBEX. He worked for four years on the Access development team at Microsoft. He can be reached at 71501. 2564@compuserve.com.

Index

SYMBOLS

* (asterisk), 417
, (comma)
  delimited text files, 366
  Print method, 329
  syntax errors, 215
; (semicolon), 329
!-- tag (HTML), 573
#Const compiler directive, 81-83, 221
#Else compiler directive, 82
#End If compiler directive, 82
#If compiler directive, 81-82
#If...Then compiler directive, 82
2000th year problems, troubleshooting, 93

A

About dialog box, 704-705
Accelerate method
  adding, 288-289
  code listing, 268
Access
  ISAM (Indexed Sequential Access Method),
    431
  object naming conventions, 734-735
accessing
  multiple projects, 44
  SQL (Standard Query Language) tables,
    418-419
  text files, 367
    binary method, 369
    random file method, 367-369
    sequential method, 367
ACONFIRM.ASP (Listing 24.5), 588

Action parameter
  Crystal Reports, 356
  Validate event, 407
Actions object, 509
Actions property (Outlook), 522-523
Activate event, 149
Active Server Pages (ASPs), 579-580
ActiveDocument.SaveAs method, 504
ActiveX controls, 490, 559-560
  automation, see automation
  COM (component object model), 490-491
  compiling, 568
  creating, 560-562
    codes, adding, 562-564
    functionality, changing, 566-567
    methods, 564-566
    properties, 564-566
  Setup, creating, 568-571
  testing, 571-575
  VB (Visual Basic) documents comparison, 560
ActiveX Data Objects, see ADO
adBSTR (Type property), 478
adByRef (Type property), 478
adChar (Type property), 478
adCurrency (Type property), 478
Add Class Module command (Project menu),
  265
Add Custom Member dialog box, 564
Add Form command (Project menu), 125, 452
Add MDI Form command (Project menu), 160
Add method
  collections, 303, 306
  custom collections, 318-319
  Outlook, attaching objects, 519
Add Watch command (Debug menu), 236
Add Watch dialog box, 236

ADD.HTM (lListing 24.4), 586-587
adDate (Type property), 478
adDBDate (Type property), 478
adDBTime (Type property), 478
adDBTimeStamp (Type property), 478
adDecimal (Type property), 478
adding
    Color property, 286
    methods, 288
    property procedures, 285
    records
        ADO, 472
        DAO, 471
    Year property, 286-287
AddItem method, 174
AddNew method, 403
adDouble (Type property), 478
AddressBar property (Internet Explorer), 546
adEmpty (Type property), 478
adError (Type property), 478
adGUID (Type property), 478
adIDispatch (Type property), 478
adInteger (Type property), 478
adIUnknown (Type property), 478
adLongVarBinary (Type property), 478
adLongVarChar (Type property), 478
adLongVarWChar (Type property), 478
AdModeRead (Mode property), 463
AdModeReadWrite (Mode property), 463
adModeShareDenyNone (Mode property), 463
adModeShareDenyRead (Mode property), 463
AdModeShareDenyWrite (Mode property), 463
adModeShareExclusive (Mode property), 463
adModeUnknown (Mode property), 463
AdModeWrite (Mode property), 463
adNumeric (Type property), 479
ADO (ActiveX Data Objects), 457
    cursors, 458
    databases, 580-581
        adding records, 585-588
        deleting records, 592-595
        editing records, 588-592
        frames, 581-583
        listing events, 583-585
    hierarchy, 460
    library, 458-459
    objects, 459-460

    Collection, 468
    Command, 477-479
    Connection, 461-467
    creating, 458
    Error, 467-468
    Parameter, 477-483
    Recordset, 469-477
    OLE DB, 457-458
    stored procedures, 483-484
ADO Northwind database analysis
    (Listing 19.6), 468
adParamInput (Direction property), 477
adParamInputOutput (Direction property), 477
adParamLong (Attributes property), 477
adParamOutput (Direction property), 477
adParamReturnValue (Direction property), 477
adSingle (Type property), 479
adSmallInt (Type property), 479
adTinyInt (Type property), 479
adUnsignedBigInt (Type property), 479
adUnsignedInt (Type property), 479
adUnsignedSmallInt (Type property), 479
adUnsignedTinyInt (Type property), 479
adUseClient (Cursor Location property),
    462-463
adUserDefined (Type property), 479
adUseServer (Cursor Location property),
    462-463
adVarBinary (Type property), 479
adVariant (Type property), 479
adVarWChar (Type property), 479
adVector (Type property), 479
advertising applications, 711-712
adWChar (Type property), 479
adXactBrowse (Isolation Level property), 463
adXactChaos (Isolation Level property), 463
adXactCursorStability (Isolation Level
    property), 463
adXactIsolate (Isolation Level property), 463
adXactRepeatableRead (Isolation Level
    property), 463
After parameter (Add method), 306-307
aggregate functions (SQL), 423-424
AliasName keyword, 611
aligning controls in forms, 168-169
Alignment property
    Label control, 171
    Option Button controls, 178

ALL predicate (SQL), 421
AllowCustomize property (toolbars), 207
API function alias (Listing 25.5), 611
apiGetCommandLine function, 621
apiGetComputerName function, 630
apiGetVolumeInformation function, 636
apiGetWindowsDirectory function, 623-624
APIs (application programming interfaces),
  Windows API, 599-600, 609-610
    compatibility, 603
    Declare statement, 610-614
    DLLs, 600-607
    handles, 614-615
    INI files, 666-672
    modules, 602
    pre-tested code, 602
    Registry, 654-665
    Win32 upgrades, 607-609
    see also WinAPI.vbp example
App.Path property, 377
appearance properties (Internet Explorer),
  546-547
Append mode (text files), 370
AppendChunk method, 479
Application object, 495, 508, 512
Application property (Outlook), 522
applications
    coding, 693
    creating, 26-27
      controls, 28-32
      debugging, 32-33
      forms, 28
    design, 698
    distribution, *see* distribution
    documentation, 699
    error handling, 698-699
    event-driven, 15
    forms, 699-701
      About dialog box, 704-705
      organizing, 702-704
      whitespace, 701
    internal, 688
    Jet DAO
      creating, 443-447
      records, 449-451
      starting, 447-449
    legal issues, 709

      copyrights, 710
      trademarks , 709-710
    market research, 688-689
    MDI (Multiple-Document Interface), 159-160
      child forms, creating, 160-161
      creating, 160
      startup forms, 161
    Menu and Toolbar Demo program, 211
    online help, 698
    performance, 695-698
    personal, 688
    professional, 687-688
    programming, 12
      DOS, 13
      Windows, 13-14
    project life cycle, 689
      coding, 690-694
      debugging, 694-695
      designing, 689-690
      documentation, 695
    redirecting execution, 231-232, 243
    Registry, 705-706
    reporting capabilities, 698
    runtime conversions, 33-34
    selling, 711-712
    support, 706-707
      access, 707-708
      tracking users, 708
      upgrades/fixes, 708-709
    toolbars, creating, 205-207
    see also listings
applying routine conventions (Listing 28.2),
  693-694
Appointment items, Outlook (Listing 21.9), 527
AppointmentItem object, 509, 526-528
argument lists, Declare statement, 612
arguments
    API (application programming interface)
      prefixes, 606
    compiler directives, 83
    GetDiskFreeSpace function, 632
    GetSystemDirectory function, 624
    named, 117-118
    optional, 116-117
    passing
      as controls, 189-190
      by reference, 115

by value, 115
  Windows API declarations, 612-613
Print statement, 386
RegCreateKeyEx function, 657
strColor, 286
see also parameters
array demonstration (Listing 4.13), 109
arrays, 107
  bounds, 108
  cmdMethods, 270-271
  controls, 187-189
  declaring, 107-108
  dynamic, 108-109
  fixed, 108-109
  menus, 200
  naming conventions, 731
  Preserve keyword, 109
  Redim statement, 108-109
AS clause (SQL), 420
ASPs (Active Server Pages), 579-580
asterisk (*), 417
Attach an object to an email item (Listing 21.5), 519
Attachmate, 363
Attachments object, 509
Attachments property (Outlook), 516, 519, 522
attributes
  GetAttr function, 396-397
  SetAttr function, 397-398
Attributes property (Parameter object), 477
automatic declarations, 67
automatic indents, 66
automatic members lists, 67
automatic syntax check, 67
automatic word completion, 65
automation (ActiveX), 489-492, 504-505
  frmRomeo example, 492-494
  Internet Explorer, 539
    referencing, 540-541
    shutting down, 541
    Visible property, 541
  object models, 495-496
  Outlook, 507
    AppointmentItem object, 526-528
    constants, 521
    ContactItem object, 524-526
    controllers, 511-512

  displaying, 515-516
  folders, 512-513
  items, creating, 521
  JournalItem object, 530-532
  NoteItem object, 528-529
  object model, 508-512
  properties, 521-523
  TaskItem object, 532-535
  variables, creating, 513-515
servers, referencing, 494-495
Word 97, 496-497
  commands, 498-501
  opening documents, 497-498
  Print Preview mode, 501-502
  saving, 503-504
  templates, 503
Automation code (Listing 20.1), 493
AutoRedraw property (Paint event), 150
Avg function (SQL), 423

B

b prefix (API arguments), 606
BackColor property, 131
  Forms collection, changing, 298-299
  Label control, 172
background compiles, 220
BackStyle property (Label control), 171
BadRead routine, 379-381
BAS files, 24
BaseName, Hungarian naming conventions, 726
basPublics (Registry.vbp), 657
BCC property (MailItem object), 516
Before parameter (Add method), 306-307
BeforeNavigate2 event (Internet Explorer), 552-553
beginning of file (BOF), 402-403
BeginTrans command, 465-467
binary access method (text files), 369
binary values (registry), 645, 655
binding
  controls, 192-193
  early binding, 600
BlueCount method, 321-322
BlueCount property (Listing 12.29), 321

Body property (MailItem object), 516
<BODY> tag (HTML), 573
BOF (beginning of file), 402-403
BOFAction property (Data controls), 402-403
bold font property, 132
bookmarks, 62-64
Bookmarks command (Edit menu), 63
Boolean variables, 88, 92
BorderStyle property, 127-129, 207
bound controls (Data controls), 403-404
bounds of arrays, 108
breakpoints, 226-229
   watches, 236
browsers, Object Browser, 292-293
BufferSize, 370
bugs
   implicit declaration variables, 98
   static variables, 105
build numbers (dwBuildNumber), 627
Busy property (Internet Explorer), 548-549
ButtonHeight property, 210
buttons
   ADO databases, 589
   Jet DAO application, 445
   Jet SQL, Delete, 452
   mouse events, 152
   toolbars, 204
      adding, 209
      captions, 210
      deleting, 207
      icons, 208
      moving, 209
      option controls, 210
      toggle controls, 209
      ToolTips, 207-208
Buttons collection, 210
buttons parameter (MsgBox function), 156-158
ButtonWidth property, 210
ByRef keyword, 612-613
Byte variables, 88-90
ByVal keyword, 115-116, 612-613

Call keyword, 51
call stack, 237-239
Call Stack command (View menu), 237
Call Stack dialog box, 238
calling procedures, 51
calls, Registry, 648
   DeleteSetting, 651-653
   GetAllSetting, 653-654
   GetSetting, 650-651
   SaveSetting, 649-650
   see also functions
Cancel property (Command Button control), 172-173
Caption property, 129, 262, 401
   Check Box control, 176
   Command Button control, 172
   Frame control, 178
   GetWindowTextA function, 616
   Label control, 171
   Menu Editor, 199
   naming controls, 29-30
   toolbar buttons, 210
Car collection Add method (Listing 12.9), 305-306
Car example
   Clean check box, 292
   collections, *see* collections
   Color property, 291-292
   FillForm event procedure, 290
   object classes, 289
   objects, creating/deleting, 290-291
Car example Color property (Listing 11.14), 292
Cars collection object restrictions (Listing 12.17), 314
Case Else clause, 75
Categories property (MailItem object), 516
CByte function, 107
CC property (MailItem object), 516
CCur function, 107
CDate function, 107
CDbl function, 107
CDec function, 107, 112
ChangeCaption function, 619
changing Control collection properties (Listing 12.6), 301-302
changing Forms collection by name (Listing 12.4), 299

C

CAB files, 676-677, 680
cache, Internet Explorer, 543
calculated fields (SQL), 419-421

CharacterPosition parameter, 386
characters, Unicode, 608
Chart control, 185
Check Box controls, 166
    properties, 176-177
    Read-Only property controls, 292
Checked property
    Menu Editor, 199
    menus, 203
checking syntax, 67
child forms, 159-161
child menus, 197-198
Choose Database File dialog box, 347
CInt function, 107
Circle method, 141
circular references (constants), 118
class module property declarations (Listing 10.1), 267
classes, 263
    Collection, 322-323
        custom collections, 316-317
    creating, 23, 264-266
    defaults, 282-284
    derived, 730
    error handling, 220
    initializing, 277-279, 284-285
    Jet DAO, 437
    methods, 264
        Accelerate, 288-289
        adding, 267-268, 287
        Decelerate, 288
    modules, 269-271, 278
    Object Browser, 292-293
    objects, 263
        collections, 294
        testing for, 280-281
    properties, 263-264
        adding, 266-267
    property procedures, 271-275
        adding, 285
        Color, 285-286
        invalid values, 275-276
        Year, 286-287
    terminating, 277-280
Class_Initialize event procedures, 277-279, 284-285
Class_Terminate event procedures, 277-280

clauses (SQL)
    AS, 420
    FROM, 420
    GROUP BY, 424-425
    HAVING, 425
    WHERE, 419-422
    see also statements
Clear All Breakpoints command (Debug menu), 227
ClearConversationIndex (MailItem object), 517
Click event, 151, 197
    Car example, 291
    Jet DAO, 448
    Jet SQL, 452
    procedures, 31, 86
client-side scripting, 578-579
    server-side comparisons, 577-578
client/server configuration, Jet database normalization, 436
CLng function, 107
Close method, 517
CloseFile routine, 379
closing
    Code window, 57
    Outlook, 520-521
Cls method, 143
clustered indexes, 432
cmdDelete1_Click event procedure (Listing 12.13), 311
cmdGo_Click event procedure, 90
cmdMethods control array, 270-271
cmdTestDecimal_Click event procedure, 112
cmdTestVariant_Click event procedure, 111
Cnt suffix (naming conventions), 733
code listings, *see* **listings**
Code window, 53-56
    automatic word completion, 65
    bookmarks, 62-64
    closing, 57
    color queuing, 59-60
    comment blocks, 65-66
    continuation characters, 57-58
    declarations, 67
    drag-and-drop editing, 68
    formatting, 69
    help, 67-68
    indents, 59, 66

keyboard shortcuts, 60-62
members lists, 67
mouse shortcuts, 62
opening, 56-57
outdents, 58-59
procedure separators, 68
Search and Replace, 60
syntax checks, 67
tabs, sizing, 68
variables, 67-68
views, 68
coding applications, 690-694
coercion, 106
Collect.vbp
Forms collection, 297-300
frmControls, 300-303
Collection class, 316-317
Collection object
collections, 296, 303-304, 468
Buttons, 210
controls, 191, 300-303
Count property, 307-308
creating, 305
custom, 313
Add method, 318-319
BlueCount property, 321-322
Collection class, 316-317, 322-323
encapsulation, 315-316
Item method, 318
Paint method, 320-321
Remove method, 319-320
restricting objects, 313-315
deleting, 311-312
Forms, 296-300
Jet DAO, 437
objects
adding, 305-307
retrieving, 308-309
Printer, 334-335
Remove method, 310-311
tags (naming conventions), 728
With statement, 312-313
color, customizing, 215
Color property
Car example, 291-292
procedures, adding, 285-286

Color Property Let in clsCar (Listing 12.28), 320-321
color queuing
bookmarks, 64
Code window, 59-60, 69
ColorCount property, 321-322
COM (component object model), 260-261, 490-491
Combo Box control, 166, 175-176
Command Button control, 166, 172-173
Command object (ADO), 460, 469, 477-479
commands
Debug menu
Add Watch, 236
Clear All Breakpoints, 227
Quick Watch, 234
Edit menu
Bookmarks, 63
Formula, 343
Modify, 644
File menu
Make, 33
New Project, 123
GetSetting, 706
Project menu
Add Class Module, 265
Add Form, 125, 452
Add MDI Form, 160
Components, 167, 353
References, 495, 540
Report menu
Edit Group Selection Formula, 345
Edit Record Selection Formula, 345
Select Groups, 345
Select Records, 345
SaveSetting, 706
Set Next Statement, 231-232
Tools menu
Macro, 498
Menu Editor, 198
View menu
Call Stack, 237
Code, 57
Immediate window, 232, 440
Properties window, 125
Refresh, 649
Toolbars, 225
Word 97, 498-501

CommandStateChange event, 552-554
comma (,)
    delimited text files, 366
    Print method, 329
    syntax errors, 215
comments, 52-53, 65-66
CommitTrans command, 465-467
common controls, naming convention tags,
    739-741
Common Dialog control, 180-181
Common Dialog Print dialog box, 334
compartmentalization, 114-115
compatibility, Windows API, 603
Compile on Demand, 220
Compile page (project properties), 46-47
compiler directives, 81-83
compiling
    ActiveX controls, 568
    backgroud compiles, 220
    Compile on Demand, 220
Components command (Project menu), 167,
    353
Components dialog box, 168
concatenation operator, 87
conditional branches, 70
    End If, 71
    If...Then, 70-72
    If...Then...Else, 72-73
    If...Then...Else If, 73-75
    If...Then...End If, 73-75
    Select Case, 75
conditional watches, 234, 237
configuring
    menus, 203-204
    printers, 333-334
    toolbars, 210
ConfirmDeletion() function, 221
Connection object (ADO), 460-464
    connection string, 461-462
    methods, 462-464
    properties, 462-464
    transaction commands, 465-467
Connection Timeout property (Connection
    object), 462
connectivity, 363
ConnectString property, 462
#Const compiler directive, 81-83, 221

constants, 118-119
    CommandStateChange event, 554
    Cursor Location property, 462-463
    Flag parameter, 542
    Isolation Level property, 463
    mconSize, 282
    mouse events, 152
    MsgBox function, 156-157
    Outlook, 521
        folders, 515-516
        Importance property, 523
        Sensitivity property, 523
    private, 284-285
    Read-Only property, 282
    RegCreateKeyEx function, 657-658
    RegSetValueEx function, 661
    tags (naming conventions), 728
    Validate event, Action parameter, 407
Contact items, Outlook (Listing 21.8), 525
ContactItem object, 509, 524-526
continuation characters, 57-58
control arrays, 188-189, 270-271
Control collection errors (Listing 12.8), 302
control's SetFocus method (Listing 6.12), 192
ControlBox property, 133
controllers
    automation, 491-492
    Outlook, 511-512
controls, 18, 166-167
    ActiveX, 559-560
        compiling, 568
        creating, 560-567
        Setup, 568-571
        testing, 571-575
        VB (Visual Basic) documents comparison,
            560
    applications, organizing, 702-704
    arguments, passing as, 189-190
    arrays, 187-189
    binding, 192-193
    Chart, 185
    Check Box, 176-177
    Code window, opening, 56
    collections, 191
    Combo Box, 175-176
    Command Button, 172-173
    Common Dialog, 180-181

copying, 187
creating, 28-29
Crystal Reports, 354-357
custom, 167
Data Bound Grid, 183
Data controls, *see* Data controls
DirListBox, 180
drag-and-drop, 193
DriveListBox, 180
event-driven code, attaching, 30-32
FileListBox, 180
FlexGrid, 183-184
forms
    adding to, 168
    aligning in, 168-169
    layout, 169-170
Frame control, 178
Jet DAO application, 444
keyboard events, 194-195
Label, 171-172
List Box, 173-175
Menu Editor, 199
menus
    keyboards, 202
    shortcut keys, 202-203
mouse events, 195
Multimedia, 185
naming, 186, 739-741
OLE Container, 182-183
Option Button, 177-178
Picture Box, 179
program execution, 231-232
Progress Bar, 185
properties, 29-30, 170-171
    TabIndex, 192
    TabStop, 192
referencing, 189-191
RichTextBox, 185
selecting multiple, 169-170
SetFocus method, 191-192
Slider, 185
Status Bar, 185
Tab, 184-185
Text Box, 178
Timer, 181-182
Toolbar, 205-207
toolbars, 208

toolbox, 165-166
TreeView, 185
WebBrowser, 549-558
With blocks, 189
Controls collection, 191, 300-303
conventions
    menus, 200-201
        ellipses, 201
        keyboard controls, 202
        shortcut keys, 202-203
    naming, 101
converting
    runtime conversions, 33-34
    string variable values, 105-106
    variable values, 105-107
    Word macros, 500-501
    see also coercion
Copies property (Printer object), 333
CopiesToPrinter property (Crystal Reports), 355
Copy method, 517
Copy shortcut key, 202
copying
    controls, 187
    files, 395
copyrights, 710
Count function (SQL), 423
Count property, 298, 303, 307-308
Count property in collections (Listing 12.10), 307-308
Create New Report dialog box, 342
Create notes in Outlook Listing 21.11), 529
CreateField.txt (Listing 18.1), 442
CreateItem method, Outlook (Listing 21.4), 518
CreateObject function, Outlook (Listing 21.2), 514
CreateQuerydef() method, 455
Creating and destroying Car objects (Listing 11.13), 291
Creating parameters with ADO (Listing 19.15), 480-481
CreationTime property
    MailItem object (Outlook), 516
    Outlook, 522
Cross-Tab reports, 346

Crystal Reports, 337-339
  Custom control, 352-354
    printing reports, 356
    properties, 354-357
    ReportFileName property, 354
  Design window, 339-341
  formulas, 343-344
  functions, 344
  Preview window, 341-342
  properties, 356
  report-selection interfaces, 357-358
  reports
    database tables, 347
    fields, 347-349
    formulas, 349
    linking data, 347-348
    previewing, 351-352
    sorting, 350
    styles, 346, 351
    totals, 350-351
  selecting data, 344-345
  wizards, 342-343
CSC_NAVIGATEBACK constant, 554
CSC_NAVIGATEFORWARD constant, 554
CSC_UPDATECOMMANDS constant, 554
CSng function, 107
CStr function, 107
Currency variables, 88, 91-92
CurrentX property, 140
CurrentY property, 140
Cursor Location property (Connection object), 462-463
cursors, 458
custom collections, 313
  Add method, 318-319
  BlueCount property, 321-322
  Collection class, 316-317, 322-323
  encapsulation, 315-316
  Item method, 318
  Paint method, 320-321
  Remove method, 319-320
  restricting objects, 313-315
Custom control (Crystal Reports), 352-354
  printing reports, 356
  properties, 354-355
    ReportFileName property, 354
    runtime changes, 356-357

customers, NWind.mdb, 434
customized Northwind database connection (Listing 19.3), 464
customizing
  projects, 44-47
  syntax color, 215
  toolbars, 207
Cut shortcut key, 203
CVar function, 107
CVErr function, 113

D

DAO (Data Access Objects), *see* **Jet DAO**
Data Bound Control (Jet SQL), 452-453
Data Bound Grid (DBGrid) control, 183
Data Bound Grid Control, 453-456
Data controls, 167, 192-193, 399-400
  bound, 403-404
  current records, 402-403
  properties, 400-402
  runtime, 405
    events, 405-408
    methods, 408-413
  SQL (Standard Query Language), 425
Data File method, 338
data grids, 453-456
Data Mode property, 454
Data Source property, 454
Data Tips, 67-68
data types
  arrays, 108
  documentation, 604-607
  OSVERSIONINFO, 626-627
  tags (naming conventions), 729
    enumerated, 729-730
    user-defined, 730
  user-defined text files, 367-369
  variables, 88-89
    boolean, 92
    byte, 89-90
    currency, 91-92
    Date, 92-93
    double, 91
    Integer, 90

long integers, 91
object, 95-96
single, 91
string, 94
variant, 96-97
Data-Bound Report (Crystal Reports), 355
data-definition language (DDL), 415, 436-437
data-manipulation language (DML), 415, 436-437, 441-443
Database (Crystal Reports), 355
database management systems (DBMS), 430-431
see also Jet DAO
DatabaseName property
Data control, 193
Data controls, 400
databases, 363-365
ADO (Access Data Objects), *see* ADO
Crystal Reports, 337-339
Design window, 339-341
formulas, 343-344
functions, 344
Preview window, 341-342
reports, *see* reports
selecting data, 344-345
wizards, 342-343
Data controls, *see* Data controls
EVENTS.MDB, 580
Jet DAO (Data Access Objects), 429-431
application, 443-451
classes, 437
collections, 437
DDL (data-definition language), 436-437
DML (data-manipulation language), 436-437, 441-443
hierarchy, 437-438
indexes, 432
normalization, 435-436
objects, 437
opening, 438-441
queries, 432
relational, 432-435
SQL (Standard Query Language), 451-456
storage, 431
tables, 431
relational, 432
server-side scripting, 580-581

adding records, 585-588
deleting records, 592-595
editing records, 588-592
frames, 581-583
listing events, 583-585
SQL (Structured Query Language), 415-417
aggregate functions, 423-424
AS clause, 420
calculated fields, 419-421
Data Control, 425
filters, 421-423
FROM clause, 420
GROUP BY clause, 424-425
HAVING clause, 425
JOIN statement, 419
multiple tables, accessing, 418-419
SELECT statement, 417-418
testing, 425-427
WHERE clause, 419-422
see also text files
DataErr parameter (Error event), 408
DataField property (Data control), 193, 404
DataFiles property (Crystal Reports), 357
DataSource property (Data control), 192, 403-404
Date variables, 88, 92-93
DBGrid control, 183
DblClick event, 151, 175
DBMS (database management systems), 430-431
see also Jet DAO
DCONFIRM.ASP (Listing 24.9), 594
DDL (data-definition language), 415, 436-437
Deactivate event, 149
Debug menu commands
Add Watch, 236
Clear All Breakpoints, 227
Quick Watch, 234
Debug toolbar, 225
Debug.Print statements, 223-224
debugging, 23-24, 213-214, 224-225
applications, 32-33, 694-695
breakpoints, 226-229
call stack, 237-239
comment blocks, 65-66
compiler directives, 81-83
Debug toolbar, 225

Debug.Print statements, 223-224
Immediate window, 232-233
Locals window, 233-234
logical errors, 214-217
modules, 219-220
MsgBox statements, 220-223
runtime errors, 217
stepping through code, 229-230
syntax errors, 214-216
variables
　　declaring, 218-219
　　static variables, 105
watches, 234-237
DEBUGGING compiler constant, 81
Decelerate method (Listing 11.10), 288
decimal variant variables, 112
declarations
ADO object, 461
arrays, 107-108, 119
Code window, 54, 67
constants, 118-119, 284-285
GetPrivateProfileString, 605
procedures, 51
properties, 266-267
RegCreateKeyEx function, 656
variables, 97-98
　　errors, 218-219
　　forcing, 100-101
　　implicit/explicit comparisons, 98-99
　　lifetimes, 103-105
　　private, 284-285
　　scope, 102-103
Windows API (application programming
　interface), 610
　　arguments lists, 612
　　ByVal keyword, 612-613
　　functions, 610-614
　　subroutines, 610
wrd object, 498
Declare statement (Listing 25.4), 610
Default parameter
Command Button control, 172
GetSetting function, 650
InputBox function, 158
DEFAULT.ASP (Listing 24.1), 583

defaults
Code window, 68
methods, 282-284
properties, 282-284
Delete button (Jet SQL), 452
DELETE FROM statement (SQL), 416
Delete method, 517
DELETE.ASP (Listing 24.8), 593
DeleteRecord subroutine, 452
DeleteSetting function, 648, 651-653
DeleteSetting statement (Listing 26.2), 652
deleting
bookmarks, 63
breakpoints, 227
Click event procedures, 291
collections, 311-312
comments, 66
files, 393
toolbar buttons, 207
watches, 235
Delim2.txt, 379-382
delimited text files
creating, 390-392
opening, 374-375, 379-382
delimiters, 384
deploying
ActiveX controls, 567-568
　　compiling, 568
　　Setup, 568-571
applications, Package and Deployment
　Wizard, 682-684
derived classes, naming, 730
DESC keyword, 422
Description property (Err object), 245
Design view, 56-57
Design window (Crystal Reports), 339-341
designing
applications, 689-690, 698
　　About dialog box, 704-705
　　copyrights, 710
　　forms, 699-704
　　legal issues, 709-710
　　Registry, 705-706
　　support, 706-708
　　tracking users, 708
　　upgrades/fixes, 708-709

reports, 346
database tables, 347
fields, 347-349
formatting, 351-352
formulas, 349
linking data, 347-348
previewing, 351-352
sorting, 350
styles, 351
totals, 350-351
DestinationFile parameter (FileCopy statement), 395
Details section, Crystal Reports Design window, 341
determining control types (Listing 6.10), 191
diagnostics, 23-24, 32-33
dialog boxes, 154
About, 704-705
Add Custom Member, 564
Add Watch, 236
Call Stack, 238
Choose Database File, 347
Common Dialog Print, 334
Components, 168
Create New Report, 342
Edit Formula, 343-344
Edit String, 644
error, 33
InputBox function, 158
Macros, 499
Make Project, 34
Menu Editor, 198
Message box, 155-158
Nag, 711
New Project, 123
New Report, 346
Options, 66-69, 215, 219-220
Outlook Services, 519
Project Properties, 45-47, 447
Property Pages, 354
References, 438, 495, 540
Selection Formula, 345
System Information, 629
Word Options, 122
Dim keyword, 86-87, 102
Dir function, 393-394
Direction property (Parameter object), 477

directives, 81-83, 221
Directory list box, 167
DirListBox control, 180
disk drives, WebBrowser control, 550
DiskInfo structure (Listing 25.38), 633
Display method
MailItem object (Outlook), 517
Outlook, 516
displaying
invisible menus, 203
Outlook, 515-516
DISTINCT predicate (SQL), 421
DISTINCTROW predicate (SQL), 421
distribution
Package and Deployment Wizard, 675-677
deploying applications, 682-684
script management, 684-685
starting, 677-682
testing, 685
preparing for, 25-26
DLLs (dynamic link libraries), 24, 600-602
MSVBVM60.DLL, 24-25
SHDOCVW.DLL, 539-540
Win32 API upgrades, 608
Windows API, 603
declarations, 610-611
documentation, 603-607
DML (data-manipulation language), 415, 436-437, 441-443
Do...Loop statements, 79-81
document.open command, 574
document.write command, 574
documentation
applications, 695, 699
Windows API DLLs, 603
data types, 604-607
finding, 603
DocumentComplete event (WebBrowser control), 552
documents
ActiveX controls comparison, 560
Internet Explorer properties, 547-548
Word 97, opening, 497-498
DOS, 13
double data type variables, 91
Double variables, 88

DownloadBegin event (WebBrowser control), 552-554

DownloadComplete event (WebBrowser control), 552, 555

downloading, 363

drag-and-drop
> Code window, 68
> controls, 193
> editing, 56

DragDrop event, 193

DragIcon property (controls), 193

DragMode property (controls), 193

DragOver event (controls), 193

drawing methods, 140
> Circle, 141
> Cls, 143
> Line, 141-142
> Picture Box control, 179
> Point, 143
> PSet, 142-143
> Refresh, 143
> SetFocus, 144
> Show, 144-145
> TextHeight, 143
> TextWidth, 143

Drill Down reports, 346

DriveListBox control, 167, 180

drivers, DAO, 679

Duplex property (Printer object), 333

dw prefixes (API arguments), 606

dwBuildNumber, 627

DWORD values (registry), 645, 655

dynamic arrays, 108-109

dynamic link libraries, *see* DLLs

dynaset-type recordsets, 402

E

early binding, 600

ECONFIRM.ASP (Listing 24.7), 592

Edit Formula dialog box, 343-344

Edit Group Selection Formula command (Report menu), 345

Edit menu commands
> Bookmarks, 63
> Formula, 343
> Modify, 644

Edit Record Selection Formula command (Report menu), 345

Edit String dialog box, 644

EDIT.ASP (Listing 24.6), 591

editing
> Code window, 53-56
>> automatic word completion, 65
>> bookmarks, 62-64
>> closing, 57
>> color queuing, 59-60
>> comment blocks, 65-66
>> continuation characters, 57-58
>> declarations, 67
>> default views, 68
>> drag-and-drop editing, 68
>> formatting, 69
>> help, 67-68
>> indents, 59, 66
>> keyboard shortcuts, 60-62
>> members lists, 67
>> mouse shortcuts, 62
>> opening, 56-57
>> outdents, 58-59
>> procedure separators, 68
>> Search and Replace, 60
>> syntax checks, 67
>> tabs, sizing, 68
>> variables, 67-68
> drag-and-drop, 56
> Menu Editor, 198-199
> Registry, 642-644
>> keys, adding, 645-647
>> values, 644-645
>> views, 643-644

ellipses, 201

Else clause, 72-73

#Else compiler directive, 82

Else If clause, 73-75

empty procedures, 56

Empty value, 113

Enabled property
> Menu Editor, 199
> menus, 204
> Timer control, 182

enabling custom navigational buttons (Listing 22.3), 554

encapsulation
custom collections, 315-316
objects, 260
End Function statement, 318
End If clause, 73-75
#End If compiler directive, 82
End If statements, 71
End keyword, 51
end of file (EOF), 402-403
EndDoc method, 331
EntryID property (Outlook), 522-523
enumerated data types, 729-730
enumerating collections, 298, 308
EOF (end of file), 402-403
EOF function, 394-395
EOFAction property (Data controls), 402
Err.Description property (Err object), 245-246
Err.Number property (Err object), 246
error dialog boxes, 33
Error event, 408
error handling, 244, 698-699
error logging (Listing 9.9), 254-255
Error object, 460, 467-468
Error value, 113
errors
breaking, 219-220
Err object, 245
Err.Description property, 245-246
Err.Number property, 246
help messages, creating, 246-248
logical, 214-217
memory, 217
modules, 219-220
null, 216
runtime errors, 217, 242-243
Bad DLL calling convention, 612
GoTo statement, 250
handling, 245, 252-254
logging, 254-255
On Error GoTo statement, 252
redirecting programs, 245
Resume statement, 249-252
trapping, 243-245, 248-249
syntax, 214-216
variables, declaring, 218-219
Event Monitor, 21-22
event procedures, 31

event processing of a menu array (Listing 7.1), 200
event-driven applications, 15, 20-22, 30-32
EventID Request object, 589
events, 147-148
Activate, 149
ADO databases
adding, 585-588
deleting, 592-595
editing, 588-592
listing, 583-585
Class_Initialize, 277-279, 284-285
Class_Terminate, 277-280
Click, 86, 197
Car example, 291
Jet DAO, 448
cmdGo_Click, 90
cmdTestDecimal_Click, 112
cmdTestVariant_Click, 111
Data controls, 405-406
Error, 408
Reposition, 408
Validate, 406-407
Deactivate, 149
drag-and-drop, 193
FllForm, 290
Form_Load, 447
GotFocus, 149
Initialize, 148
Internet Explorer, 552-558
keyboard, 153
controls, 194-195
KeyDown, 153-154
KeyPress, 154
KeyUp, 153-154
List Box control, 175
Load, 148, 270
LostFocus, 149
mouse, 150
Click, 151
controls, 195
DblClick, 151
MouseDown, 151-152
MouseMove, 153
MouseUp, 151-152
Paint, 150
QueryUnload, 149

Resize, 150
Terminate, 149
toolbars, 210-211
Unload, 149, 706
EVENTS.MDB database, 580
executables, 24
Make command, 33-34
runtime, 24-25
see also DLLs (dynamic link libraries)
execution, redirecting, 231-232
Exit For statement, 77-78
Exit Function statement, 77
Exit shortcut key, 202
exiting Code window, 57
ExpiryTime property (MailItem object), 516
explicit declarations (variables), 97
forcing, 100-101
implicit comparisons, 98-99
explicit declarations speed test (Listing 4.8), 99
Explicit variables (Listing 4.5), 98
expressions, watches, 234-237

F

Field object, 460
fields, 364
calculated, 419-421
Fixed1.txt, 372
Jet databases
indexes, 432
storage, 431
Report wizard, 347-349
SELECT statement, 417-418
text files
delimited text files, 366-367
random access method, 367
fields in Fixed1.txt (Listing 15.4), 372
Fields window (Crystal Reports), 344
File list box, 167
File menu commands
Make, 33
New Project, 123
FileCopy statement, 395
FileDateTime function, 395
FileLen function, 395
FileListBox control, 180

FILENAME, 377
FileName parameter (text files), 370
FileNumber (text files), 370
FileNumber parameter
Line Input statement, 383
text files, 370
files
BAS, 24
CAB, 676-677, 680
deleting, 393
Dir function, 393-394
distribution, 25-26
EOF function, 394-395
EXE, *see* executables
FileCopy statement, 395
FileDateTime function, 395
FileLen function, 395
flat, 435
FRM, 24
GetAttr, 396-397
Hungarian naming conventions, 733
initialization, *see* INI files
Input statement, 383-385
Line Input statement, 383
LOF (length of file), 396
MSVBVM60.DLL, 24-25
Open statement, 383
Outlook VBA Help, 511
SetAttr, 397-398
text, 361-362, 365
accessing, 367-369
delimited, 366-367
fixed width, 365-366
text, *see* text files
VBP, 24
see also projects
FillForm procedure (Listing 25.39), 634
filling frmVolInfo with mVolInfo structure (Listing 25.43), 637
filter function, 412
filters (SQL), 421-423
Find methods, 411-413
Find shortcut key, 202
finding documentation, 603
First function (SQL), 423
First suffix (naming conventions), 733
fixed arrays, 108-109

fixed-length string variables, 94
fixed-width string variables, 94
fixed-width text files
    creating, 386-390
    opening, 372-373, 376-379
Fixed1.txt fields, 372
fixes, application support, 708-709
Flag parameter (Navigate method), 542-543
flat files, 435
FlexGrid (MSFlexGrid) control, 183-184
FllForm event procedure, 290
floating-point numbers, 91
floppy disks, packaging applications, 683
Folder object, 508
folders
    Outlook, 512-516
    packaging applications, 683
Font property (Label control), 172
FontBold property, 132
FontItalic property, 132
FontName property, 132
fonts
    Code window, 59-60, 69
    properties, 132
FontSize property, 132
FontStrikeThru property, 132
FontTransparent property (Printer object), 333
FontUnderline property, 132
For Each statement
    Control collection, 301
    Forms collection, 299
For Each..Next statement, 299
For...Next statements, 77-78, 298
ForeColor property
    Control collection, 301-303
    Label control, 171
Format function, 331
formatting
    Code window, 69
    reports, 351-352
    text files, 365
        delimited, 366-367
        fixed width, 365-366
FormDescription object, 509
FormDescription property (Outlook), 522
FormMeths.vbp, 140-144

FormProp.vbp
    frmFonts, 132
    frmMain, 139
    frmTag, 137
forms, 18-20, 121
    adding, 125
    applications, 699-701
        About dialog box, 704-705
        organizing, 702-704
        whitespace, 701
    controls, 18-20, 29
        adding, 168
        aligning, 168-169
        attaching code, 30-32
        layout, 169-170
        properties, 29-30
    creating, 28, 123-124
    Design view, 56-57
    dialog boxes, 154
        Input box, 158
        Message box, 155-158
    events, 147-148
        Activate, 149
        Deactivate, 149
        GotFocus, 149
        Initialize, 148
        keyboard, 153-154
        Load, 148
        LostFocus, 149
        mouse, 150-153
        Paint, 150
        QueryUnload, 149
        Resize, 150
        Terminate, 149
        Unload, 149
    FllForm event procedure, 290
    instances, multiple, 161-162
    Jet DAO application, 443-446
    loading, 145-146
    MDI (Multiple-Document Interface) parent,
        159-160
        child forms, 160-161
        creating, 160
        startup forms, 161
    methods, 139
        Circle, 141
        Cls, 143

Hide, 145
Line, 141-142
Move, 140
Point, 143
PSet, 142-143
Refresh, 143
SetFocus, 144
Show, 144-145
TextHeight, 143
TextWidth, 143
ZOrder, 140
modal, 145
modeless, 145
practicing, 162-163
properties, 125-127
BackColor, 131
BorderStyle, 127-129
Caption, 129
changing, 126
ControlBox, 133
fonts, 132
Height, 134
Icon, 129-130
Left, 135
MaxButton, 134
MinButton, 134
Movable, 135
Name, 129
Picture, 130-131
referencing, 138-139
runtime changes, 139
ScaleHeight, 137
ScaleLeft, 138
ScaleMode, 137
ScaleWidth, 137
ShowInTaskbar, 136
StartupPosition, 134
Tag, 136-137
Top, 135
Width, 134
WindowState, 135-136
unloading, 146-147
see also windows
Forms collection, 296-298
properties, changing, 298-300
Formula command (Edit menu), 343
Formula Text window (Crystal Reports), 344

formulas
Crystal Reports, 343-344
Report Wizard, 349
Form_Load event, 270, 447
Forward method, 517
Frame control, 166, 178
frames
ADO databases, 581-583
headers, 583
FreeFile function, 371
FRM files, 24
frmAppInfo's Form_Load procedure
(Listing 25.14), 620
frmCars, *see* **Car example**
frmControls (Collect.vbp), 300-303
frmDeleteSetting (Registry.vbp), 652-653
frmDelim2, 379-382
frmDrawing (FormMeths.vbp), 140-144
frmFixed1, 373
frmFixed2, 376-379
frmFonts (FormProp.vbp), 132
frmForms, 297-298
frmGeneric (Listing 11.2), 279
frmGetAllSettings (Registry.vbp), 653-654
frmGetProfileSetting cmdGetValue_Click
(Listing 26.20), 669
frmGetProfileString (Registry.vbp), 668-669
frmGetSettings (Registry.vbp), 651
frmHdwInfo, 629-630
frmMain (FormProp.vbp), 139
frmRegQueryValue, 663
frmRomeo, 492-494
frmSaveSetting (Registry.vbp), 650
frmString, 85-87
frmTag (FormProp.vbp), 137
frmVolInfo, 635
frmWinInfo, 623
frmWritePrivateProfileString (Listing 26.23),
670
frmWriteProfileString (Registry.vbp), 667
FROM clause (SQL), 420
Fruit object (Listing 12.11), 310
FullName property (Internet Explorer), 547
FullScreen property (Internet Explorer), 546
FunctionName keyword, 610

functions, 51-52

aggregate functions (SQL), 423-424
apiGetComputerName, 630
apiGetVolumeInformation, 636
apiGetWindowsDirectory, 623-624
CDec, 112
ChangeCaption, 619
ConfirmDeletion, 221
Crystal Reports, 344
CVErr, 113
Dir, 393-394
EOF, 394-395
FileDateTime, 395
FileLen, 395
filter, 412
Format, 331
FreeFile, 371
GetAttr, 396-397
GetCaption, 617-618
GetCommand, 621
GetData, 440
GetOutlook, 514
GetPrivateProfileString, 602
InputBox, 158
InStr, 300
IsEmpty, 113
IsMissing, 117
IsNull, 113, 392
IsNull(), 72
Left, 392
Len(), 71
LOF (length of file), 396
Mid, 373, 378, 392
MsgBox, 155-158
RegisterUser, 661-662
Registry
    DeleteSetting, 648, 651-653
    GetAllSetting, 648, 653-654
    GetSetting, 648-651
    SaveSetting, 648-650
Registry.vbp
    GetValue, 663
    OpenKey, 659
Right, 392
SetAttr, 397-398
Spc, 330-331
String$(), 613

Tab, 330-331
trim, 94, 378
TypeName, 302
ValidatePassword, 77
variable value conversions, 106-107
VarType, 114
VerifyIdentity, 72
VerifyUser, 52
Win32 API upgrades, 608-609
WinAPI.vbp example, 615-616, 622-623,
    629-630
    GetClassNameA, 621-622
    GetCommandLineA, 620-621
    GetComputerNameA, 630
    GetDiskFreeSpaceA, 632-634
    GetDriveTypeA, 631-632
    GetParent, 619-620
    GetSystemDirectoryA, 624-625
    GetTempPath, 625-626
    GetUserNameA, 629
    GetVersionExA, 626-628
    GetVolumeInformationA, 634-637
    GetWindowsDirectoryA, 623-624
    GetWindowTextA, 616-618
    SetWindowTextA, 618-619
Windows API (application programming
    interface), 655
    declarations, 610-614
    INI files, 666-672
    RegCloseKey, 664
    RegCreateKeyEx, 656-659
    RegDeleteKey, 665
    RegDeleteValue, 664-665
    RegFlushKey, 662
    RegOpenKeyEx, 659-660
    RegQueryValueEx, 662-664
    RegSetValueEx, 660-662
    see also methods; procedures
Functions window (Crystal Reports), 344

G

generic class module (Listing 11.1), 278
generic referencing, 190-191
generic referencing controls (Listing 6.9), 190
**Get Data button on frmFixed1 (Listing 15.4),
    373**

Get property
deleting, 282
procedures, 273-275
GetAllSetting function, 648, 653-654
GetAttr function, 396-397
GetAttributes procedure, 397
GetCaption function, 617-618
GetClassName function, 622
GetClassNameA function, 621-622
GetCommand function, 621
GetCommandLine function, 621
GetCommandLineA function, 620-621
GetComputer function, 630
GetComputerNameA function, 630
GetData() function, 440
GetDiskFreeSpace function prototype, 632
GetDiskFreeSpaceA function, 632-634
GetDiskInfo wrapper subroutine, 632-634
GetDriveTypeA function, 631-632
GetFormattedDate function, 113
GetInspector property (Outlook), 522
GetOrderHistory.txt (Listing 18.3), 456
GetOutlook() function, 514
GetParent function, 619-620
GetPrivateProfileInt function, 666, 672
GetPrivateProfileSection function, 666
GetPrivateProfileString, 602, 666, 671-672
declaring, 605
Windows SDK, 605
GetProfileInt function, 666, 669
GetProfileSection function, 666
GetProfileString function, 666-669
GetSetting function, 648-651, 706
GetSystemDirectory function, 624-625
GetSystemDirectoryA function, 624-625
GetTempPath function, 625-626
GetUserName function, 628-629
GetUserNameA function, 629
GetValue function, 663
GetVersion function, 626-628
GetVersionExA function, 626-628
GetVolumeInformation function, 635
GetVolumeInformationA function, 634-637
GetWinDir function, 624
GetWindowsDirectory function, 623
GetWindowsDirectoryA function, 623-624
GetWindowTextA function, 616-618

GetWindowTextLengthA function, 617
global variables, 104, 439, 445
GoBack method (Internet Explorer), 545
GoForward method (Internet Explorer), 545
GoHome method (Internet Explorer), 546
GoSearch method (Internet Explorer), 546
GotFocus event, 149
Goto shortcut key, 202
GoTo statement, 250
Graph reports, 346
graphical user interfaces, *see* **GUI forms**
grids
alignment, 168-169
controls, 183-184
data grids, 453-456
GROUP BY clause (SQL), 424-425
GUI (graphical user interface) forms, 18-20, 121
adding, 125
applications, 699-701
About dialog box, 704-705
organizing, 702-704
whitespace, 701
controls, 18-20, 29
adding, 168
aligning, 168-169
attaching code, 30-32
layout, 169-170
properties, 29-30
creating, 28, 123-124
Design view, 56-57
dialog boxes, 154
Input box, 158
Message box, 155-158
events, 147-148
Activate, 149
Deactivate, 149
GotFocus, 149
Initialize, 148
keyboard, 153-154
Load, 148
LostFocus, 149
mouse, 150-153
Paint, 150
QueryUnload, 149
Resize, 150
Terminate, 149
Unload, 149

FllForm event procedure, 290
instances, multiple, 161-162
Jet DAO application, 443-446
loading, 145-146
MDI (Multiple-Document Interface) parent,
  159-160
    child forms, 160-161
    creating, 160
    startup forms, 161
methods, 139
    Circle, 141
    Cls, 143
    Hide, 145
    Line, 141-142
    Move, 140
    Point, 143
    PSet, 142-143
    Refresh, 143
    SetFocus, 144
    Show, 144-145
    TextHeight, 143
    TextWidth, 143
    ZOrder, 140
modal, 145
modeless, 145
practicing, 162-163
properties, 125-127
    BackColor, 131
    BorderStyle, 127-129
    Caption, 129
    changing, 126
    ControlBox, 133
    fonts, 132
    Height, 134
    Icon, 129-130
    Left, 135
    MaxButton, 134
    MinButton, 134
    Movable, 135
    Name, 129
    Picture, 130-131
    referencing, 138-139
    runtime changes, 139
    ScaleHeight, 137
    ScaleLeft, 138
    ScaleMode, 137
    ScaleWidth, 137

ShowInTaskbar, 136
StartupPosition, 134
Tag, 136-137
Top, 135
Width, 134
WindowState, 135-136
unloading, 146-147
see also toolbars; windows

H

handles, Windows API, 614-615
handling runtime errors, 247-248, 252-255
hard disk drives, WebBrowser control, 550
HAVING clause (SQL), 425
HEADER.HTM (Listing 24.2), 583
headers (frames), 583
**Headers parameter (Internet Explorer),
  544-545**
Height property, 134, 172
help
    applications
        documentation, 695
        online, 698
    Code window, 67-68
    Outlook VBA Help file, 511
    runtime error messages, creating, 246-248
    setting, 44-45
Help shortcut key, 203
HelpContextID parameter
    InputBox function, 158
    Menu Editor, 199
    MsgBox function, 156
HelpFile parameter
    InputBox function, 158
    MsgBox function, 156
helpful error messages (Listing 9.3), 247
Hide method, 145
hiding
    Internet Explorer, 541
    toolbars, 204
hierarchies
    ADO, 459-460
    Jet DAO, 437-438
    object models, 495-496
    Registry, 647

HKEY_CLASSES_ROOT (Registry), 641
HKEY_CURRENT_CONFIG (Registry), 641
HKEY_CURRENT_USER (Registry), 641
HKEY_DYN_DATA (Registry), 641
HKEY_LOCAL_MACHINE (Registry), 641
HKEY_USERS (Registry), 641
Home page (Internet Explorer), setting up, 545-546
Horizontal scrollbar control, 166
HTML (Hypertext Markup Language)
    ActiveX controls, 572-573
    scripting, 578-579
<HTML> tag (HTML), 573
Hungarian naming conventions, 726-727
    files, 733
    prefixes, 731-733
        arrays, 731
        indexes, 732
        scope, 732
    procedures, 731
    suffixes, 733
    tags, 727
        collections, 728
        constants, 728
        derived classes, 730
        enumerated data types, 729-730
        menus, 729
        properties, 728
        user-defined data types, 730
        variables, 727-728
hWnd parameter
    GetWindowTextA function, 617
    SetWindowTextA function, 618
hwnd prefix (API arguments), 606
Hypertext Markup Language (HTML)
    ActiveX controls, 572-573
    scripting, 578-579

I

Icon property, 129-130
icons
    changing, 208
    toolbars, 205
IDs, ADO databases, 588

If compiler directive, 81-82
If...Then compiler directive, 82
If...Then statements, 70-72
    If...Then...Else, 72-73, 589
    If...Then...Else If, 73-75
    If...Then...End If, 73-75
Image box control, 167
ImageList control, 208
ImageList property (Toolbar control), 207
Immediate window, 232-233
Immediate Window command (View menu), 440
implicit declaration (variables), 97
    bugs, 98
    explicit comparisons, 98-99
Importance property (Outlook), 522-523
indenting code, 59, 66
Index property
    control arrays, 188
    custom collections, 318
    Menu Editor, 199
Indexed Sequential Access Method (ISAM), 431
indexes
    Jet DAO (Data Access Objects), 432
    naming conventions, 732
IndexValue parameter (collections), 309-310
Indicator bar (Code window), 55
INI (initialization) files, 639-640, 665-666
    Win.ini, 668
    Win32 API upgrades, 609
    Windows API functions, 666-667
        GetPrivateProfileInt, 672
        GetPrivateProfileString, 671-672
        GetProfileInt, 669
        GetProfileString, 668-669
        WritePrivateProfileString, 669-671
        WriteProfileString, 667-672
Initialize event, 148, 278-279, 284-285
Initialize routine, 562
initializing classes, 277
Input mode, 370
Input statement, 383-385
InputBox function, 158
INSERT INTO statement (SQL), 416

installations

    ActiveX control installation files, creating, 568-571

    Package and Deployment Wizard, 676-677

        deploying applications, 682-684

        script management, 684-685

        starting, 677-682

        testing, 685

instances, 263

    Jet databases, 438

    multiple, 161-162

InStr function, 300

integer variables, 88-90

    boolean, 92

    coercion, 106

    long, 91

Intellisense, 267

interact with ActiveX controls (Listing 23.2), 574

interfaces, report-selection interfaces, 357-358

internal applications, 688

internal storage variables (Listing 10.9), 274

Internet, packaging applications, 683-684

Internet Explorer

    automation, 539

        referencing, 540-541

        shutting down, 541

        Visible property, 541

    cache, 543

    GoBack method, 545

    GoFoward method, 545

    Home page, setting up, 545-546

    Navigate method, 541-545

    properties

        appearance, 546-547

        Busy, 548-549

        documents, 547-548

        FullName, 547

    Search page, setting up, 546

    WebBrowser control, 549-552

        events, 552-558

Interval property (Timer control), 182

intrinsic constants, 515-516

invalid Car objects (Listing 12.18), 314

ISAM (Indexed Sequential Access Method), 431

IsEmpty function, 113

IsMissing function, 117

IsNull function, 72, 113, 392

Isolation Level property (Connection object), 463

italic font property, 132

Item method

    collections, 303, 309

    custom collections, 318

ItemData property (List Box control), 174

Items object, 509-510

J

Jet DAO (Data Access Objects), 242, 429-431

    application

        creating, 443-447

        records, 449-451

        starting, 447-449

    classes, 437

    collections, 437

    DDL (data definition language), 436-437

    DML (data manipulation language), 436-437, 441-443

    hierarchy, 437-438

    indexes, 432

    naming conventions, 735-738

    normalization, 435-436

    objects, 437

    opening databases, 438-441

    Package and Deployment Wizard, 679

    queries, 432

    relational databases, 432-435

    SQL (Standard Query Language), 451-452

        Data Bound Control, 452-453

        data grids, 453-456

    storage, 431

    tables, 431

Jet database connection using DAO (Listing 19.2), 461-462

JOIN statement (SQL), 419

joins, 347-348

JournalItem object, 509, 530-532

K

key method, 309

Key parameter (Add method), 306-307

keyboard events, 194-195

keyboard shortcuts, 60-62
keyboards
  ByVal, 115
  events, 153
    KeyDown, 153-154
    KeyPress, 154
    KeyUp, 153-154
  menu controls, 202
KeyCode parameter, 153-154
KeyDown event, 153-154, 194
KeyPress event, 154, 194
KeyPreview property, 153, 195
keys (Registry), 641
  adding, 645-647
  INI files, 639
  uninstalling, 647
KeyUp event, 153-154
keywords
  AliasName, 611
  ByVal, 612-613
  Call, 51
  DESC, 422
  Dim, 86, 102
  End, 51
  Forms, 297
  FunctionName, 610
  LibraryName, 610-611
  New, 263, 269, 305
  Nothing, 280
  Preserve keyword, 109
  Private, 50
  Public, 102
  Rem, 52
  Static, 104
  Sub, 50
  While, 80
  see also clauses; statements
Kill statement, 393
kill switch, 711
KillDoc method, 332

L

l prefix (API arguments), 606
Label control, 166
  procedure naming conventions, 731
  properties, 171-172

Landscape printing, 333
Last function (SQL), 423
Last suffix (naming conventions), 733
LastModificationTime property (Outlook),
  516, 522
late binding, *see* **DLLs (dyamic link libraries)**
laying out controls, 169-170
lCaptionSize paramter (GetWindowTextA
  function), 617
lData parameter (RegSetValueEx function),
  661
lDesired argument (RegCreateKeyEx function),
  657
lDesired parameter (RegOpenKeyEx function),
  660
lDisposition argument (RegCreateKeyEx func-
  tion), 657
Left function, 392
Left property, 135
legal issues, 709
  copyrights, 710
  trademarks, 709-710
Len() function, 71
Let property
  Color property, adding, 285-286
  deleting, 281-282
  Year property, adding, 286-287
Let property procedures, 273-275
libraries
  ADO (ActiveX Data Objects), 458-459
  DLLs (dynamic link libraries), 24, 600-602
    MSVBVM60.DLL, 24-25
    SHDOCVW.DLL, 539-540
    Win32 API upgrades, 608
    Windows API, 603-611
  msoutl8.olb, 511
LibraryName keyword, 610-611
LIKE predicate (SQL), 422
Lim suffix (naming conventions), 733
Line control, 167
Line Input statement, 383
Line method, 141-142
links, Report wizard, 347-348
list box AddItem method (Listing 6.1), 174
List Box control, 166, 173-175
list box Selected property (Listing 6.3), 175
LIST.ASP (Listing 24.3), 584

ListIndex property (Combo Box control), 175
listings
   Accelerate method, 268
   ACONFIRM.ASP, 588
   ADD.HTM, 586-587
   adding a new record with ADO, 472
   adding a new record with DAO, 471
   adding Color property, 286
   adding methods, 287-288
   adding property procedures, 285
   adding Year property, 286-287
   ADO Northwind database analysis, 468
   API function alias, 611
   apiGetVolumeInformation, 636
   applying routine conventions, 693-694
   Appointment items, Outlook, 527
   array demonstration, 109
   attach an object to an email item, 519
   Automation code, 493
   BadRead routine, 380-381
   BlueCount property, 321
   ByVal, 116
   ByVal keyword, 612
   Car collection Add method, 305-306
   Car example Color property, 292
   Cars collection object restrictions, 314
   ChangeCaption function, 619
   changing Control collection properties,
     301-302
   changing Forms collection by name, 299
   Circle method, 141
   class module property declarations, 267
   cmdDelete1_Click event procedure, 311
   cmdMethods control array, 270-271
   Color Property Let in clsCar, 320-321
   ColorCount property, 321-322
   contact items, Outlook, 525
   control arrays, 188
   control array constants, 188-189
   control collection errors, 302
   control's SetFocus method, 192
   Controls collection, 191
   converting string variable values, 105-106
   converting Word macros, 500-501
   Count property in collections, 307-308
   create notes in Outlook, 529
   CreateField.txt, 442

   CreateItem method, Outlook, 518
   CreateObject function, Outlook, 514
   creating and destroying Car objects, 291
   creating parameters with ADO, 480-481
   customized Northwind database connection,
     464
   DCONFIRM.ASP, 594
   decelerate method, 288
   decimal variant variables, 112
   Declare statement, 610
   declaring an ADO object, 461
   declaring array inventory, 119
   DEFAULT.ASP, 583
   DELETE.ASP, 593
   DeleteSetting statement, 652
   determining control types, 191
   Dir function, 394
   DiskInfo structure, 633
   displaying Outlook, 515
   displaying the invisible menus, 203
   ECONFIRM.ASP, 592
   EDIT.ASP, 591
   enabling and disabling custom navigational
     buttons, 554
   enumerate the Cars collection, 308
   enumerating the members of a collection, 298
   EOF function, 395
   Err.Number, 246
   error handling, 244
   error logging, 254-255
   event processing of a menu array, 200
   explicit declarations speed test, 99
   Explicit variables, 98
   fields in Fixed1.txt, 372
   FillForm procedure, 634
   filling frmVolInfo with mVolInfo structure, 637
   FlexGrid control, 183-184
   FllForm event procedure, 290
   Forms collection, 297
   Forms collection to change properties, 299
   Form_Load event procedure, 270
   FreeFile function, 371
   frmAppInfo's Form_Load procedure, 620
   frmGeneric, 279
   frmGetProfileSetting cmdGetValue_Click, 669
   frmString modules, 86
   frmWritePrivateProfileString, 670

Fruit object, 310
generic class module, 278
generic referencing controls, 190
Get Data button on frmFixed1, 373
GetAllSettings function, 653-654
GetAttributes procedure, 397
GetCaption function, 617
GetClassName API function prototype, 622
GetClassNameA API function prototype, 621
GetCommandLine API function, 621
GetCommandLineA API function prototype, 621
GetComputer function, 630
GetComputerNameA API function prototype, 630
GetDiskFreeSpace API function prototype, 632
GetDiskInfo wrapper subroutine, 633
GetDriveTypeA API function prototype, 631
GetDriveTypeA constants, 631
GetFormattedDate function, 113
GetOrderHistory.txt, 456
GetParent API function prototype, 620
GetPrivateProfileInt API function, 672
GetPrivateProfileString API function, 671
GetPrivateString function, 671-672
GetProfileInt API function declaration, 669
GetProfileString API function declaration, 668
GetSetting function, 651
GetSystemDirectory API function prototype, 624
GetSystemDirectory function, 625
GetTempPath API function, 625-626
GetUserName API function prototype, 628
GetUserName function, 628-629
GetVersion API calls, 627-628
GetVersion API constant declarations, 627
GetVersion function prototype, 626
GetVolumeInformation API function prototype, 635
GetWinDir function, 624
GetWindowsDirectory API function prototype, 623
GetWindowTextA API function prototype, 616
GetWindowTextLengthA API function prototype, 617
handling errors, 247-248, 255
HEADER.HTM, 583

helpful error messages, 247
Implicit variable bugs, 98
Implicit variables, 97
Input statement, 385
integer variable coercion, 106
interact with ActiveX controls, 574
internal storage variables, 274
invalid Car objects, 314
IsMissing function, 117
Jet database connection using DAO, 461-462
KeyDown event, 154
Kill statement, 393
Line method, 142
list box AddItem method, 174
list box Selected property, 175
LIST.ASP, 584
loading a document into Word, 497
macro produced by the Word macro recorder, 500
mColCars collection Add method, 318-319
mColCars collection Item method, 318
mColCars collection Paint method, 320
mColCars collection Remove method, 320
MeetingRequestItem, 528
MouseUp event, 152
MsgBox function, 157
multiple instances of forms, 162
multiresult set recordset with ADO, 483-484
mVolInfo data structure, 636
navigating the Data control recordset, 410
object calls to your ActiveX control, 572
object variables, 95
On Error GoTo statement, 252
opening a DAO recordset with a SQL statement, 475-476
opening the Employee table with ADO, 470
opening the Employee table with DAO, 469-470
optional arguments, 116
OSVERSIONINFO structure, 606-607
Outlook object variables are declared, 513
Outlook Task item, 532-533
Outlook's Journaling feature, 530-531
painting all the Car objects, 315
parameter-driven stored procedures with ADO, 482-483

parameter-driven stored procedures with DAO, 481-482
parsing delimited text data, 374-375
passing a control, 190
percentage progress of a download, 556
Picture property, 130
print routines, 329
Print statement output, 387-388
printer methods, 332
printer properties, 334-335
printing a Word document, 498
printing in fixed or variable columns, 329-330
private Collection object, 317
private constants and variables, 284-285
Property Get, 274
Property Get for the Count property, 317
property values, assigning, 272
PSet method, 142-143
read and display data, 378
read-only Clean check box, 292
Read-Only property, 281-282
reading all text file lines, 378-379
reading delimited text, 382
referencing button properties, 210
referencing items by ordinal value, 311
RegCloseKey API function declaration, 664
RegCreateKeyEx API function declaration, 656
RegCreateKeyEx function, 658-659
RegCreateKeyEx security constants, 658
RegDeleteKey API function declaration, 665
RegDeleteValue API function declaration, 665
RegFlushKey API function declaration, 662
RegisterUser function, 661-662
RegOpenKeyEx API function declaration, 659
RegOpenKeyEx OpenKey wrapper function, 660
RegQueryValueEx API function declaration, 662
RegSetValueEx API function declaration, 660
RegSetValueEx Constant values, 661
removing frmFixed2 text box references, 377
removing Word macro default arguments, 501
repeated object references, 312
Resume statement, 251
retrieving document information, 548
retrieving RegQueryValueEx, 663
retrieving values from the list box, 175

routine before applying coding standards, 692
SaveRecord.txt, 450-451
saving a document, 504
Send method, Outlook, 520
set Outlook variables to Nothing, 520
SetFocus method, 144
SetWindowTextA API function prototype, 618
SetWindowTextA function prototype, 619
simple child protection filter, 553
simple Web browser, 557-558
specifying a document template, 503
static procedure variables, 105
static variables, 104
tab locations in the Print statement, 389
Tag property, 137
Tag property to change Forms collection, 300
temporary tables with ADO, 474-475
temporary tables with DAO, 473-474
testing for objects, 281
trap errors in each procedure in a call stack, 253-254
update query with ADO, 466
update query with DAO, 465-466
user interface on frmFixed2, 376-377
user-defined types, 371
variant variable conversions, 111
VarType function, 114
Visual Basic declaration for GetPrivateProfileString, 605
Wash method, 267
Windows SDK reference for GetPrivateProfileString, 605
With block, 189
With statement, 312
Word document in Print Preview, 502
Write statement, 391
WriteProfileString API function declaration, 667

lKey argument
RegCreateKeyEx function, 657
RegQueryValueEx function, 663
RegSetValueEx function, 661
lLength parameter (GetCaption function), 618
Load event, 148
Load event procedure, 270
LOAD routine, 706
Load statement, 146

loading forms, 145-146

loading a document into Word (Listing 20.2),
497

local disk drives, WebBrowser control, 550

local variables, 102

locally handling runtime errors, 252-254

Locals window, 233-234

LocationName property (Internet Explorer),
547

LocationURL property (Internet Explorer),
548

LOF (length of file) function, 396

Logger subroutine, 254-255

logging runtime errors, 254-255

logical errors, 214-217

long integer variables, 91

Long variables, 88

loops, 69, 76
    Do...Loop, 79-81
    For Each, 299
    For Each..Next, 299
    For...Next, 77-78, 298

lOptions argument (RegCreateKeyEx function), 657

lOptions parameter (RegOpenKeyEx function),
660

LostFocus event, 149

lpsz prefixes, API arguments, 606

lReserved argument
    RegCreateKeyEx function, 657
    RegQueryValueEx function, 663
    RegSetValueEx function, 661

lResult argument
    RegCreateKeyEx function, 657
    RegOpenKeyEx function, 659-660

lReturnBuffer argument (GetSystemDirectory
function), 624

lRetVal variable, 234

lRetValue variable, 233

lSecurityAttributes argument
    (RegCreateKeyEx function), 657

lSize argument (RegQueryValueEx function),
663

Ltrim function, 94

lType parameter (RegSetValueEx function),
661

M

Macro command (Tools menu), 498

macros, Word macro recorder, 498-500

Macros dialog box, 499

Mail Label reports, 346

MailItem object, 509
    methods, 517-519
    properties, 516-519
    Send methods, 519-520

Make page (project properties), 45-46

Make Project dialog box, 34

margins, Code window, 69

market research, 688-689

marketing applications, 711-712

Max function (SQL), 423

Max suffix (naming conventions), 733

MaxButton property, 134

MaxLength property (Text Box control), 178

mColCars collection
    Add method, 318-319

mColCars collection
    Add method, 318-319
    Item method, 318
    Paint method, 320
    Remove method, 320

mconSize constant, 282

MDI (Multiple-Document Interface) parent
forms, 159-160
    child forms, creating, 160-161
    creating, 160
    startup forms, 161

MDIChild property, 160

MeetingRequestItem object, 509-510, 528

memory errors, 217

Menu and Toolbar Demo program, 211

Menu Editor command (Tools menu), 198

Menu Editor dialog box, 198

menus, 20, 197-198
    arrays, 200
    configuring, 203-204
    conventions, 200-201
        ellipses, 201
        keyboard controls, 202
        shortcut keys, 202-203
    Menu and Toolbar Demo program, 211

Menu Editor, 198-199
pop-up, 203
tags (naming conventions), 729
MenuTbar.vbp, 211
Message box 155-158, 215, 220-223
messages, Outlook
attaching objects, 519
creating, 516-519
sending, 519-520
methods, 264
ActiveDocument.SaveAs, 504
ActiveX controls, adding to, 564-566
Add, 519
collections, 303, 306
custom collections, 318-319
adding, 287
Accelerate, 288-289
Decelerate, 288
BOFAction property, 402-403
classes, adding, 267-268
Common Dialog control, 180
Connection object (ADO), 462-464
CreateQuerydef(), 455
Data controls, 193, 406-413
Data File, 338
defaults, 282-284
Display, 516
EOFAction property, 403
forms, 139
Circle, 141
Cls, 143
Hide, 145
Line, 141-142
Move, 140
Point, 143
PSet, 142-143
Refresh, 143
SetFocus, 144
Show, 144-145
TextHeight, 143
TextWidth, 143
ZOrder, 140
Internet Explorer
GoBack, 545
GoForward, 545
GoHome, 546
GoSearch, 546
Navigate, 541-545
Item
collections, 303, 309
custom collections, 318
key, 309
List Box control, 174
MailItem object, 517-519
MoveLast, 405
Name, 309
ordinal value, 309
Paint, 320-321
Parameter object (ADO), 477-479
Picture Box control, 179
Printer object, 329-332
Remove
collections, 303, 310-311
custom collections, 319-320
Send, 519-520
SQL/ODBC, 338
Update, 447
Microsoft
Data Bound Grid Control, 453-456
Jet DAO, *see* Jet DAO
Outlook, *see* Outlook
Word 97
commands, 498-501
object model, 496-497
opening documents, 497-498
Print Preview mode, 501-502
saving, 503-504
templates, creating, 503
Mid function, 373, 378, 392
Mileage property (Outlook), 522
Min function (SQL), 423
Min suffix (naming conventions), 733
MinButton property, 134
modal forms, 145
mode property (Connection object), 463
modeless forms, 145
Modify command (Edit menu), 644
modules, 49, 269-271, 278
Code window, 54
creating, 265-266
error handling, 219-220
opening, 57
procedures, 50

comments, 52-53
functions, 51-52
subroutines, 50-51
public, 22-23
variables, 104
Windows API, 602
mouse
events, 150, 195
Click, 151
DblClick, 151
MouseDown, 151-152
MouseMove, 153
MouseUp, 151-152
shortcuts, 62
MouseDown event, 151-152
MouseMove event, 153
MouseUp event, 151-152
Movable property, 135
Move method, 139-140, 409-411, 517
MoveFirst method, 402, 410
MoveLast method, 403, 405, 410
MoveNext method, 409
MovePrevious method, 409
moving toolbar buttons, 209
MSFlexGrid control, 183-184
MsgBox function, 155-158, 215, 220-223
msoutl8.olb, 511
MSVBVM60.DLL, 24-25
Multimedia control, 185
multiple instances of forms (Listing 5.10), 162
multiresult set recordset with ADO (Listing 19.18), 483-484
MultiSelect property (List Box control), 173-174
mVolInfo, 636

N

Nag dialog box, 711
name font property, 132
Name method, 309
Name property, 129
Command Button control, 172
Menu Editor, 199
Parameter object, 477
named arguments, 117-118

NameSpace object, 508-509, 512
naming conventions
arrays, 108
class modules, 265-266
controls, 29-31, 186
conventions, 101
files, 733
functions, 610
Hungarian, 726-727
objects
Access 97, 734-735
DAO 3.5, 735-738
VB 5, 738-739
prefixes, 731-733
arrays, 731
indexes, 732
scope, 732
procedures, 50, 731
Reddick, 725-726
suffixes, 733
tags, 727
collections, 728
common controls, 739-741
constants, 728
derived classes, 730
enumerated data types, 729-730
menus, 729
properties, 728
user-defined data types, 730
variables, 727-728
variables, 87, 99-100
Navigate method, 541-545
NavigateComplete2 event, 552, 555
navigating the Data control recordset (Listing 16.1), 410
navigation
Data controls, 408-413
Internet Explorer, 545
navNoHistory constant (Flag parameter), 542
navNoReadFromCache constant (Flag parameter), 542
navNoWriteToCache constant (Flag parameter), 542
navOpenInNewWindow constant (Flag parameter), 542
negative numbers, byte variables, 89
NegotiatePosition property (Menu Editor), 199

NetWindow2 event, 555
New Collection statement, 311-312
New keyword, 263, 269, 305
New Project command (File menu), 123
New Project dialog box, 123
New Report dialog box, 346
New shortcut key, 202
newline characters, 367
NewPage method, 331
NewWindow2 event, 552
Next (Resume statement), 250-251
NoAging property (Outlook), 522
normalization, 435-436
NoteItem object, 509, 528-529
Nothing keyword, 280, 311-312
Nothing value
    testing objects, 280-281
    variant variables, 113
null errors, 216
null values, 110, 113
Number property (Err object), 246
numbers
    floating-point, 91
    integer variables, 90
    string variables, 94
numeric fields, 367
Numeric variant variables, 111
NumericScale property (Parameter object), 477
NWind.mdb, 433
    customers, 434
    orders, 434-435

O

Object Browser, 292-293
object calls to your ActiveX control (Listing 23.1), 572
object linking and embedding (OLE), 182
object models, 495-496
    Outlook, 512
    Word 97, 496-498
        commands, 498-501
        Print Preview mode, 501-502
<OBJECT> tag (HTML), 573
Object variables, 88, 95-96
object-oriented programming, 15, 96

objects, 260-263
    ADO, 460
        Collection, 468
        Command, 477-479
        Connection, 461-467
        creating, 458
        Error, 467-468
        Parameter, 477-483
        Recordset, 469-477
    classes, 263
    Code window, 54
    creating, 290-291
    deleting, 290-291
    encapsulation, 260
    Err object, 245
        Err.Description property, 245-246
        Err.Number property, 246
        help messages, creating, 246-248
    EventID Request, 589
    Internet Explorer, Automation object, 540-541
    InternetExplorer, 540-541
    Jet DAO, see Jet DAO
    modules, 269-271
    naming conventions
        Access 97, 734-735
        arrays, 731
        DAO 3.5, 735-738
        indexes, 732
        scope, 732
        VB 5, 738-739
    Object Browser, 292-293
    Outlook
        AppointmentItem, 526-528
        attaching to messages, 519
        ContactItem, 524-526
        JournalItem, 530-532
        MailItem, 516-519
        NoteItem, 528-529
        properties, 521-523
        TaskItem, 532-535
    Print
        methods, 329-332
        properties, 333-334
    Printer, 327-328
        print routines, 329
        variables, 328

properties, 263-264
  adding, 266-267
testing for, 280-281
see also object models
OffLine property (Internet Explorer), 546
olAppointmentItem constant (Outlook), 521
olContactItem constant (Outlook), 521
OLE (object linking and embedding), 182
OLE Container control, 167, 182-183
OLE DB, 457-458
olJournalItem constant (Outlook), 521
olMailItem constant (Outlook), 521
olNoteItem constant (Outlook), 521
olTaskItem constant (Outlook), 521
Omega, 429
On Error statements, 243-245
  On Error GoTo statement, 252
  On Error Resume Next statement, 303, 318
OnFullScreen event, 552
online help, 698
OnStatusBar event, 552
OnTheaterMode event, 552
OnToolbar event, 552
OnVisible event, 552
Open shortcut key, 202
Open statement, 370, 383
opening
  Code window, 56-57
  DAO recordsets, 475-476
  documents, 497-498
  Jet DAO databases, 438-441
  modules, 57
  projects, 40
  tables
    ADO, 470
    DAO, 469-470
  text files, 369-371
    delimited, 374-375, 379-382
    fixed-width, 372-373, 376-379
OpenKey function (Registry.vbp), 659
OpenMode.vbp, 144-145
operators
  concatenation, 87
  TypeOf, 302
Operators window (Crystal Reports), 344

optimizing, 696
Option Button control, 166
  creating, 210
  properties, 177-178
Option Explicit statement, 100-101
optional arguments (variables), 116-117
Options dialog box, 66-69, 215, 219-220
ordinal value method, 309
organizing application forms, 702-704
Orientation property (Printer object), 333
OSVERSIONINFO data types, 606-607, 626-627
outdents, 58-59
Outlook, 507
  AppointmentItem object, 526-528
  automation
    constants, 521
    creating items, 521
    properties, 521-523
  closing, 520-521
  ContactItem object, 524-526
  controllers, 511-512
  displaying, 515-516
  folders, 512-513
  JournalItem object, 530-532
  MailItem object, 516
    Attachments property, 519
    methods, 517-519
    properties, 516-517
    Send method, 519-520
  NoteItem object, 528-529
  object model, 508-512
  TaskItem object, 532-535
  variables, creating, 513-515
  VBA Help file, 511
Outlook Services dialog box, 519
Outlook1.vbp, 512
OutlookInternalVersion property (Outlook), 522
OutlookVersion property (Outlook), 522
output, Print statement, 386
Output mode, 370
OwnerForm parameter (Show method), 145

P

<P> tag (HTML), 573
Package and Deployment Wizard, 675-677
  deploying applications, 682-684
  script management, 684-685
  starting, 677-682
  testing, 685
Page Footer section, Crystal Reports Design window, 341
Page Header section, Crystal Reports Design window, 341
Page property (Printer object), 333
Paint event, 150
Paint method, 320-321
Painting all the Car objects (Listing 12.19), 315
panes, Registry Editor, 643-644
PaperBin property (Printer object), 333
PaperSize property (Printer object), 333
Parameter object, 460, 477-483
  queries, 479-481
  stored procedures, 481-483
parameter-driven stored procedures
  ADO, 482-483
  DAO, 481-482
parameters
  Add method, 306-307
  CharacterPosition, 386
  Dir function, 394
  Error event, 408
  FileCopy statement, 395
  GetAttr function, 396
  GetCaption function, 618
  GetSetting function, 650
  GetSystemDirectory function, 624
  GetWindowTextA function, 617
  Index, 318
  IndexValue, 310
  InputBox function, 158
  Internet Explorer
    Headers, 544-545
    TargetFrameName, 544
  KeyCode, 153-154
  Line Input statement, 383
  MsgBox function, 155-158

  procedure naming conventions, 731
  RegOpenKeyEx function, 659-660
  RegSetValueEx function, 661
  SetWindowTextA function, 618
  Show method, 145
  SQL (Standard Query Language), 416
  text files, 370
  Validate event, 407
parent forms, 159-160
  child forms, creating, 160-161
  creating, 160
  startup forms, 161
Parent property (Outlook), 522
parsing delimited text data (Listing 15.5), 374-375
passing
  arguments
    by reference, 115
    by value, 115
    Windows API declarations, 612-613
  controls as arguments, 189-190
Paste shortcut key, 202
percentage progress of a download (Listing 22.4), 556
performance of applications, 695-698
personal applications, 688
Picture Box control, 167, 179
Picture property, 130-131, 179
Point method, 143
pop-up menus, 203
PopulateForm, 448
Portrait printing, 333
positioning
  controls, 29
  forms, 134
    Height property, 134
    Left property, 135
    Movable property, 135
    ShowInTaskbar property, 136
    StartupPosition property, 134
    Top property, 135
    Width property, 134
    WindowState property, 135-136
  toolbar buttons, 209
PostItem object, 510

Precision property (Parameter object), 477
predicates (SQL)
ALL, 421
DISTINCT, 421
DISTINCTROW, 421
LIKE, 422
prefixes
API arguments, 606
Hungarian naming conventions, 726, 731-733
arrays, 731
indexes, 732
scope, 732
Preserve keyword, 109
Preview window
Crystal Reports, 341-342
reports, 351-352
Print method, 329
Print Preview mode, 501-502
print routines, 329
Print shortcut key, 202
Print statement, 132
fixed-width text files, 386-390
output, 387-388
Print to File (Crystal Reports), 355
Print Window (Crystal Reports), 355
Printer (Crystal Reports), 355
Printer collection, 334-335
printer methods (Listing 13.3), 332
Printer object, 327-328
methods, 329-332
print routines, 329
properties, 333-334
variables, 328
printer properties (Listing 13.4), 335
printing
Debug.Print statements, 223-224
reports, 356
Word documents, 498
PrintOut method, 517
PrintQuality property (Printer object), 333
Print_Line variables, 329
private Collection object (Listing 12.20), 317
private constants
declaring, 284-285
Read-Only property, 282
Private keyword, 50
private scope, 102

private strYear variable, 287
private variables, declaring, 284-285
Problem button's Click event procedure
(Listing 10.7), 272
procedures, 22-23, 50
BadRead, 379-381
Call Stack, 237-239
Class_Initialize, 277-279, 284-285
Class_Terminate, 277-280
CloseFile, 379
cmdGo_Click, 90
cmdTestDecimal_Click, 112
cmdTestVariant_Click, 111
Code window, 54-55
comments, 52-53
DeleteRecord, 452
empty, 56
FllForm, 290
functions, 51-52
GetDiskInfo wrapper, 632-634
Hungarian naming conventions, 731
Initialize, 562
Load, 270, 706
Logger, 254-255
naming conventions, 31
property procedures, 271-275
adding, 285
Color, 285-286
invalid values, 275-276
Year, 286-287
PublicMessenger1, 248
RefreshForm, 447
separators, 68
SetCaption, 190
static, 105
subroutines, 50-51
Unload, 706
Windows API declarations, 610
see also functions; methods
professional applications, 687-688
programming, 12
classes, 263
creating, 23, 264-265
methods, 264, 267-268
modules, 265-266, 269-271
properties, 263-267
property procedures, 271-276

COM (Component Object Model), 260-261
comments, 52-53
controls, 29
    attaching code, 30-32
    properties, 29-30
creating applications, 26-27
debugging, 32-33
DOS, 13
event-driven, 20-22
functions, 51-52
object-oriented, 15
objects, 260-263
procedures, 22-23
runtime conversions, 33-34
subroutines, 50-51
Visual Basic, 17-18
Windows, 13-14
programs, *see* **applications; listings**
Progress Bar control, 185
ProgressChange event, 552, 555-556
Project Explorer, 40, 43
project life cycle (applications), 689
    coding, 690-694
    debugging, 694-695
    designing, 689-690
    documentation, 695
Project menu commands
    Add Class Module, 265
    Add Form, 125
    Add MDI Form, 160
    Components, 167, 353
    References, 495, 540
Project Properties dialog box, 45-47, 447
projects, 37-38
    choosing, 39
    Code window, 53
    components, 40-42
    customizing, 44-47
    multiple, 44
    opening, 40
    Project Explorer, 40, 43
Projects menu commands, Add Form, 452
Prompt parameter
    InputBox function, 158
    MsgBox function, 155

properties, 263-264
    ActiveX controls, adding to, 564-566
    App.Path, 377
    AutoRedraw, 150
    BlueCount, 321-322
    ButtonHeight, 210
    ButtonWidth, 210
    Caption, 262
        GetWindowTextA function, 616
        toolbar buttons, 210
    Checked, 203
    Crystal Reports, 354-355
        Action, 356
        runtime changes, 356-357
    classes, adding, 266-267
    Color, 291-292
    ColorCount, 322
    Connection object, 462-464
    ConnectString, 462
    Control collection, 301-303
    controls, 29-30, 170-171
        Check Box, 176-177
        Combo Box, 175-176
        Command Button, 172-173
        drag-and-drop, 193
        Frame control, 178
        Label, 171-172
        List Box, 173-175
        Option Button, 177-178
        Picture Box, 179
        Text Box control, 178
        Timer, 182
    Count, 303, 307-308
    CurrentX, 140
    CurrentY, 140
    Data controls, 192-193, 400-402
        BOFAction, 402-403
        DataField, 404
        DataSource, 403-404
        EOFAction, 402
    Data Mode, 454
    Data Source, 454
    defaults, 282-284
    Enabled, 204

Err object
    Err.Description, 245-246
    Err.Number, 246
    help messages, creating, 246-248
ForeColor, 301
forms, 125-127
    BackColor, 131
    BorderStyle, 127-129
    Caption, 129
    changing, 126
    ControlBox, 133
    fonts, 132
    Height, 134
    Icon, 129-130
    Left, 135
    MaxButton, 134
    MinButton, 134
    Movable, 135
    Name, 129
    Picture, 130-131
    referencing, 138-139
    runtime changes, 139
    ScaleHeight, 137
    ScaleLeft, 138
    ScaleMode, 137
    ScaleWidth, 137
    ShowInTaskbar, 136
    StartupPosition, 134
    Tag, 136-137
    Top, 135
    Width, 134
    WindowState, 135-136
Forms collection, 298-300
Get, 282
Index, 188
Internet Explorer
    appearance, 546-547
    Busy, 548-549
    documents, 547-548
    FullName, 547
KeyPreview, 153, 195
Let, 281-282
MDIChild, 160
Menu Editor, 199
Outlook, 521-523
    AppointmentItem object, 526-527
    Attachments, 519

ContactItem object, 524-525
JournalItem object, 531-532
MailItem object, 516-517
NoteItem object, 529
TaskItem object, 533-534
Parameter object (ADO), 477-479
Printer object, 333-334
Read-Only, 281-282
RecordCount, 475
RecordSource, 425
ReportFileName, 354
Shortcut, 202-203
TabIndex, 192
TabStop, 192
tags (naming conventions), 728
tbrButtonGroup, 210
tbrCheck, 209
Text, 32
toolbars
    AllowCustomize, 207
    BorderStyle, 207
    ImageList, 208
    ShowTips, 207
    ToolTipText, 207
Visible
    Internet Explorer, 541
    menus, 204
    pop-up menus, 203
Write-Only, 282
Properties window, 125-126
Properties Window command (View menu), 125
Property Get for the Count property (Listing 12.21), 317
Property Let (Listing 10.10), 274
Property object, 460
Property Pages dialog box, 354
property procedures, 271-275
    adding, 285
        Color, 285-286
        Year, 286-287
    arguments, 275
    invalid values, 275-276
PSet method, 142-143
public compiler constants, 83
Public keyword, 102
public modules, 22-23

public scope, 102
public variables, 102
   declaring, 266-267
   lifetimes, 103
PublicMessenger1 subroutine, 248

Q

queries
   Jet DAO (Data Access Objects), 432
   Parameter object (ADO), 479-481
   SQL (Structured Query Language), 415-417
      aggregate functions, 423-424
      AS clause, 420
      calculated fields, 419-421
      Data Control, 425
      filters, 421-423
      FROM clause, 420
      GROUP BY clause, 424-425
      HAVING clause, 425
      JOIN statement, 419
      multiple tables, accessing, 418-419
      SELECT statement, 417-418
      testing, 425-427
      WHERE clause, 419-422
QueryUnload event, 149
Quick Info, 67-68
Quick Watch command (Debug menu), 234
quotes ('), 52

R

radio buttons, 589
random file access method (text files), 367-369
Range objects, 495
read and display data (Listing 15.8), 378
read-only Clean check box (Listing 11.15), 292
Read-Only property
   check boxes, 292
   creating, 281-282
reading all text file lines (Listing 15.9), 378-379
reading delimited text (Listing 15.11), 382
ReceivedByName property (MailItem object), 516
ReceivedTime property (MailItem object), 516

Recipients object, 509
Recipients property
   MailItem object (Outlook), 517
   Outlook, 522
RecordCount property (ADO), 475
records, 364
   adding, 471-473
   ADO databases
      adding, 585-588
      deleting, 592-595
      editing, 588-592
   Data controls, 402-403
   Jet DAO application
      adding, 449
      saving, 449-451
   retrieving, 417
Recordset object, 460, 469
   creating, 469-470
   listing, 583-585
   records, adding, 471-473
   stored procedures, 483-484
   temporary tables, 473-477
recordsets property (Data controls), 402
RecordsetType property (Data controls), 402
RecordSource property
   Data control, 193
   Data controls, 400
   Find methods, 412
   SQL statements, 425
RecurrencePattern object, 509
Reddick VBA naming conventions, 101, 725-726
   see also Hungarian naming conventions
Redim statement, 108-109
redirecting program execution, 231-232, 243
References command (Project menu), 495, 540
References dialog box, 438, 495, 540
referencing
   automation servers, 494-495
   button properties, 210
   controls, 189-191
   Internet Explorer, 540-541
   items by ordinal value, 311
   properties, 138-139
Refresh command (View menu), 649
Refresh method, 143, 406
RefreshForm subroutine, 447

RegCloseKey function, 655, 664
RegConnectRegistry function, 655
RegCreateKey function, 655
RegCreateKeyEx function, 655-659
  arguments, 657
  constants, 657-658
RegDeleteKey function, 655, 665
RegDeleteValue function, 655, 664-665
REGEDIT editor, 642-644
  adding keys, 645-647
  panes, 643-644
  uninstalling keys, 647
  values, 644-645
RegEnumKey function, 655
RegEnumKeyEx function, 655
RegEnumValue function, 655
RegFlushKey function, 655, 662-664
RegGetKeySecurity function, 655
RegisterUser function, 661-662
registration, application requirements, 709
Registry, 640-642, 647
  applications, 705-706
  editors, 642-644
    panes, 643-644
    values, 644-645
  hierarchy, 647
  keys, 641
    adding, 645-647
    uninstalling, 647
  statements, 648
    DeleteSetting, 651-653
    GetAllSetting, 653-654
    GetSetting, 650-651
    SaveSetting, 649-650
  subkeys, 641
  values, 641
  Windows API, 654-656
    data types, 655
    RegCloseKey function, 664
    RegCreateKeyEx function, 656-659
    RegDeleteKey function, 665
    RegDeleteValue function, 664-665
    RegFlushKey function, 662
    RegOpenKeyEx function, 659-660
    RegQueryValueEx function, 662-664
    RegSetValueEx function, 660-662

Registry.vbp
  basPublics, 657
  frmDeleteSetting, 652-653
  frmGetAllSettings, 653-654
  frmGetProfileString, 668-669
  frmGetSettings, 651
  frmSaveSetting, 650
  frmWritePrivateProfileString, 670
  frmWriteProfileString, 667
  GetValue function, 663
  OpenKey function, 659
RegLoadKey function, 655
RegNotifyChangeKeyValue function, 655
RegOpenKey function, 655
RegOpenKeyEx function, 655, 659-660
RegQueryInfoKey function, 656
RegQueryValueEx function, 662, 656
RegReplaceKey function, 656
RegRestoreKey function, 656
RegSaveKey function, 656
RegSetKeySecurity function, 656
RegSetValue function, 656
RegSetValueEx function, 656, 660-662
RegUnLoadKey function, 656
REG_BINARY, 655
REG_DWORD, 655
REG_NONE, 655
REG_SZ, 655
relational databases, see databases
Rem keyword, 52
remote database configurations, 436
RemoteItem object, 510
Remove method
  collections, 303, 310-311
  custom collections, 319-320
removing frmFixed2 text box references
  (Listing 15.7), 377
removing Word macro default arguments
  (Listing 20.6), 501
repeated object references (Listing 12.15), 312
Replace shortcut key, 202
Reply method, 518
ReplyAll method, 518
Report menu commands
  Edit Group Selection Formula, 345
  Edit Record Selection Formula, 345

Select Groups, 345
Select Records, 345
Report Wizard, 346
    database tables, 347
    fields, 347-349
    formulas, 349
    linking data, 347-348
    previewing, 351-352
    sorting, 350
    styles, 351
    totals, 350-351
report-selection interfaces, 357-358
ReportFileName property, 354
ReportItem object, 510
reports, 345, 698
    Crystal Reports, 337-339
        Design window, 339-341
        formulas, 343-344
        functions, 344
        Preview window, 341-342
        selecting data, 344-345
        wizards, 342-343
    Custom control, 352-354
        printing, 356
        properties, 354-357
        ReportFileName property, 354
    database tables, 347
    fields, 347-349
    formatting, 351-352
    formulas, 349
    linking data, 347-348
    previewing, 351-352
    report-selection interfaces, 357-358
    sorting, 350
    styles, 346, 351
    totals, 350-351
Reposition event, 408
research marketing, 688-689
Resize event, 150
Response parameter (Error event), 408
restricting custom collection objects, 313-315
Resume statement, 245
    runtime errors, 249-252
RETAIL compiler constant, 81
Retrieving document information (Listing 22.1), 548

retrieving
    objects, 308-309
    records, 417-418
    RegQueryValueEx, 663
    values from list box, 175
return values, Windows API functions, 613-614
RichTextBox control, 185
Right function, 392
RollbackTrans, 465-467
routines, *see* **functions; methods; procedures**
Rtrim function, 94
runtime conversions, 33-34
runtime errors, 217, 242-243
    Bad DLL calling convention, 612
    Err object, 245
        Err.Description property, 245-246
        Err.Number property, 246
        help messages, creating, 246-248
    GoTo statement, 250
    handling, 245-254
    logging, 254-255
    On Error GoTo statement, 252
    redirecting programs, 245
    Resume statement, 249-252
        Label, 250
        Next, 250-251
    trapping, 243-245, 248-249
runtime properties, changing, 139, 356-357
RVBA (Reddick VBA) naming conventions, 725-726
    see also Hungarian naming conventions

S

Save method, 518-519
Save parameter (Validate event), 407
Save shortcut key, 202
SaveAs method, 518
Saved property (Outlook), 517, 522
SaveRecord.txt (Listing 18.2), 450-451
SaveSetting command, 706, 648-650
saving
    bookmarks, 64
    documents, 504
    records, 449-451
    Word 97, 503-504

Scale method, 332
ScaleHeight property, 137
ScaleLeft property, 138
ScaleMode property, 137
ScaleWidth property, 137
sCaption parameter
    GetCaption function, 618
    GetWindowTextA function, 617
    SetWindowTextA function, 618
schema, 436
sClass argument (RegCreateKeyEx function),
    657
scope
    naming conventions, 732
    variables, 102-103
<SCRIPT> tag (HTML), 573
scripting, 577-578
    ActiveX controls, 571-573
    ASPs (Active Server Pages), 579-580
    client-side, 578-579
    databases, 580-581
        adding records, 585-588
        deleting records, 592-595
        editing records, 588-592
        frames, 581-583
        listing events, 583-585
    Package and Deployment Wizard, 684-685
sData parameter, 655
    RegSetValueEx function, 661
    RegQueryValueEx function, 663
Search and Replace, 60
search page (Internet Explorer), setting up, 546
security, 658
Select All shortcut key, 202
Select Case statements, 75, 246
Select Groups command (Report menu), 345
Select Records command (Report menu), 345
SELECT statement (SQL), 416-418
Selected property (List Box controls), 175
selecting
    Crystal Reports data, 344-345, 355
    multiple controls, 169-170
Selection Formula dialog boxes, 345
SelectionFormula property (Crystal Reports),
    355
semicolon (;), 329
Send method, 518-520

Sensitivity property (Outlook), 522-523
SentOn property (MailItem object), 517
separators, 198
    Code window, 55
    procedures, 68
    see also delimiters
sequential access method (text files), 367
server-side scripting
    ASPs (Active Server Pages), 579-580
    client-side comparisons, 577-578
    databases, 580-581
        adding records, 585-588
        deleting records, 592-595
        editing records, 588-592
        frames, 581-583
        listing events, 583-585
servers
    automation (ActiveX), 491-492
        object models, 495-496
        Outlook, see Outlook
        referencing, 494-495
        Word 97, see Word 97
    Internet Explorer, 539-540
Set Next Statement command, 231-232
set Outlook variables to Nothing (Listing 21.7),
    520
Set property procedures, 273
Set statement, 540
SetAttr function, 397-398
SetCaption subroutine, 190
SetFocus method, 144, 191-192
Setup Wizard, 25-26
SetValue method, 565
SetWindowTextA function, 618-619
shareware, 711
SHDOCVW.DLL, 539-540
shift key, 152
short date format variables, 93
shortcut keys, 202-203
Shortcut property (Menu Editor), 199
shortcuts
    Code window
        keyboard, 60-62
        mouse, 62
    single-character, 606
Show method, 144-145
ShowColor method, 180

ShowFont method, 180
ShowHelp method, 180
showing
    Internet Explorer, 541
    Outlook, 515-516
    toolbars, 204
ShowInTaskbar property, 136
ShowOpen method, 180-181
ShowPrinter method, 180
ShowSave method, 180
ShowTips property (toolbars), 207
shutting down Internet Explorer, 541
simple child protection filter (Listing 22.2), 553
simple Web browser (Listing 22.5), 557-558
SimpleCalc
    compiling, 568
    creating, 560-562
        codes, adding, 562-564
        functionality, changing, 566-567
        methods, 564-566
        properties, 564-566
    Setup, creating, 568-571
    testing, 571-575
single data type variables, 88, 91
single-character shortcuts, 606
size font property, 132
Size property
    Get property, 282
    MailItem object (Outlook), 517
    Outlook, 522
    Parameter object, 478
sizing
    controls, 29
    fonts, 69
    prints, 333
    tabs, 68
Slider control, 185
Snap-to-Grid (Crystal Reports), 339
snapshot-type recordsets, 402, 453
sorting reports, 350
SourceFile parameter (FileCopy statement), 395
sPath argument (GetDiskFreeSpace function), 632
Spc function, 330-331
specifying a document template (Listing 20.8), 503

spreadsheets, 183-184
SQL (Structured Query Language), 415-417
    aggregate functions, 423-424
    clauses
        AS, 420
        FROM, 420
        GROUP BY, 424-425
        HAVING, 425
        WHERE, 419-422
    Data Control, 425
    fields, calculating, 419-421
    filters, 421-423
    Jet databases, 451-452
        Data Bound Control, 452-453
        data grids, 453-456
    JOIN statement, 419
    multiple tables, accessing, 418-419
    predicates
        ALL, 421
        DISTINCT, 421
        DISTINCTROW, 421
        LIKE, 422
        SELECT statement, 417-418
    testing, 425-427
SQL/ODBC method, 338
sReturnBuffer parameter (GetSystemDirectory function), 624
SSTab controls, 184-185
sSubKey argument (RegCreateKeyEx function), 657
Standard Setup package, Package and Deployment Wizard, 679
starting
    Jet DAO application, 447-449
    Package and Deployment Wizard, 677-682
startup forms, 124, 161
StartupPosition property, 134
statements
    Call, 51
    compiler directives, 81-83
    Debug.Print, 223-224
    Declare, 610
        arguments lists, 612
        ByVal keyword, 612-613
        functions, 610-614
        subroutines, 610
    Dim, 87

Do...Loop, 79-81
End Function, 318
End If, 71
Exit For, 77-78
Exit Function, 77
FileCopy, 395
For Each
    Control collection, 301
    Forms collection, 299
For Each..Next, 299
For...Next, 77-78, 298
GoTo, 250
If...Then, 70-72
    If...Then...Else, 72-73, 589
    If...Then...Else If, 73-75
    If...Then...End If, 73-75
Input, 383-385
InputBox, 158
JOIN, 419
Kill, 393
Line Input, 383
Load, 146
MsgBox, 155-158, 215, 220-223
New Collection, 311-312
Nothing, 280, 311-312
On Error, 243-245
    On Error GoTo, 252
    On Error Resume Next, 303, 318
Open, 370, 383
Option Explicit, 100-101
Preserve, 109
Print, 132, 386-390
procedures, 51
Redim, 108-109
Registry, 648
    DeleteSetting, 651-653
    GetAllSetting, 653-654
    GetSetting, 650-651
    SaveSetting, 649-650
Resume, 245, 249-252
    Label, 250
    Next, 250-251
SELECT, 417-418
Select Case, 75, 246
Set, 540
Stop, 228-229
Type, 119-120, 606

UnLoad, 146-147
With, 312-313
Write, 383, 390-391
    see also functions; methods; procedures
Static keyword, 104
static linking, 600
static procedures, 105
static variables, 104-105
Status Bar control, 185
StatusBar property (Internet Explorer), 546
StatusText property (Internet Explorer), 546
StDev function (SQL), 423
StDevP function (SQL), 423
stepping through code, 229-230
Stop statements, 228-229
storage
    Jet DAO (Data Access Objects), 431
    variables, 88, 110-112
stored procedures, 481-484
strColor argument, 286
strikethrough font property, 132
string functions, 392
string values (Registry), 655
string variables, 88, 94
    assigning values, 87
    converting values, 105-106
    fixed length, 94
    fixed width, 94
    passing arguments, 613
    variant variables, 111
String$() function, 613
Structured Query Language, *see* SQL
strYear variables, 287
style parameter (Show method), 145
Style property
    Check Box control, 176
    Combo Box control, 176
Subject property (MailItem object), 517
subkeys (Registry), 641
submenus, 197, 201
subroutines, *see* functions; methods; procedures
suffixes, Hungarian naming conventions, 726, 733
Sum function (SQL), 423
Summary reports, 346

Summary section, Crystal Reports Design window, 341
support, applications, 706-707
    access, 707-708
    tracking users, 708
    upgrades/fixes, 708-709
sValueName parameter
    RegQueryValueEx function, 663
    RegSetValueEx function, 661
syntax checks, 67
syntax errors, 214-216
system drivers, 679
System Information dialog box, 629
System Registry, *see* **Registry**
System.ini, 665

T

Tab control, 184-185
Tab function, 330-331
tab locations in the Print statement (Listing 15.14), 389
TabIndex property (controls), 192
table-type recordsets, 402
tables
    ADO (ActiveX Data Objects), creating, 473-477
    databases, *see* databases
    Jet DAO (Data Access Objects), 431
    SQL, accessing, 418-419
tabs, sizing, 68
TabStop property (controls), 192
TabStrip control, 184-185
Tag property, 136-137, 300
tags
    common controls, 739-741
    HTML (Hypertext Markup Language), 572-573
    Hungarian naming conventions, 726-727
        collections, 728
        constants, 728
        derived classes, 730
        enumerated data types, 729-730
        menus, 729
        properties, 728
        user-defined data types, 730
        variables, 727-728

objects
    Access 97, 734-735
    DAO (Data Access Objects) 3.5, 735-738
    VB 5, 738-739
TargetFrameName parameter (Internet Explorer), 544
TaskItem object, 510, 532-535
TaskRequestItem object, 510
tbrButtonGroup property, 210
tbrCheck property, 209
templates, Word 97, 503
temporary tables
    ADO (ActiveX Data Objects), 473-477
    DAO (Data Access Objects), 473-474
Terminate classes, 279-280
Terminate event, 149
terminating classes, 277
terminators, 51
testing
    ActiveX controls, 571-575
    applications, 32-33, 694-695
    objects, 280-281
    Package and Deployment Wizard, 685
    SQL (Standard Query Language), 425-427
Text Box control, 166, 178
text files, 361-362, 365
    accessing, 367
        binary method, 369
        random file method, 367-369
        sequential method, 367
    deleting, 393
    delimited, 366-367
        creating, 390-392
        opening, 374-375, 379-382
    Dir function, 393-394
    EOF function, 394-395
    FileCopy statement, 395
    FileDateTime function, 395
    FileLen function, 395
    fixed-width, 365-366
        creating, 386-390
        opening, 372-373, 376-379
    GetAttr function, 396-397
    Input statement, 383-385
    Line Input statement, 383
    LOF function, 396
    Open statement, 383

opening, 369-371
SetAttr function, 397-398
Text property, 32
TextHeight method, 143, 332
TextMatrix property (FlexGrid control), 183
TextWidth method, 143, 332
TheaterMode property (Internet Explorer), 546
Timer control, 166, 181-182
title case, 200
Title parameter
InputBox function, 158
MsgBox function, 156
Title section, Crystal Reports Design window, 341
<TITLE> tag (HTML), 573
TitleChange event, 552, 556-558
To property (MailItem object), 517
toggle buttons, creating, 209
toggling bookmarks, 63
Toobar property (Internet Explorer), 546
Toolbar Builder, 205-207
Toolbar control, 205-207
toolbars, 20, 204
buttons
adding, 209
captions, 210
deleting, 207
moving, 209
option controls, 210
toggle controls, 209
creating, 205-207
customizing, 207
Debug, 225
events, 210-211
icons, 205, 208
Menu and Toolbar Demo program, 211
runtime configurations, 210
ToolTips, 165-166, 207-208
Toolbars command (View menu), 225
toolbox, 165-167
Tools menu commands
Macro, 498
Menu Editor, 198
ToolTips, 165-166
changing, 207-208
ToolTipText property, 207
Top N reports, 346

Top property, 135
trademarks, 709-710
transaction commands, 465-467
transmitting data, 363
trap errors in each procedure in a call stack (Listing 9.8), 253-254
trapping runtime errors, 248-249
TreeView control, 185
Trim function, 94, 378
troubleshooting, 23-24, 32-33, 213-214, 224-225
breakpoints, 226-229
call stack, 237-239
Debug toolbar, 225
Debug.Print statements, 223-224
Immediate window, 232-233
Locals window, 233-234
logical errors, 214-217
modules, 219-220
MsgBox statements, 220-223
property procedures, 271-273, 275-276
runtime errors, 217, 242-243
Err object, 245-248
handling, 245
redirecting programs, 245
trapping, 243-245
stepping through code, 229-230
syntax errors, 214-216
variables, declaring, 218-219
watches, 234-237
year 2000, 93
tuning applications, 696
txtCount's caption property (ActiveX controls), 565
Type property
Internet Explorer, 548
Parameter object, 478-479
Type statement, 119-120, 606
TypeName function, 302
TypeOf operator, 302

U

UIs (user interfaces), *see* GUI (graphical user interface) forms
UIType (RegQueryValueEx function), 663
underlining font property, 132

Undo shortcut key, 203
unhandled errors, breaking, 220
Unicode, 608
uninstallations
    Package and Deployment Wizard, 676
    Registry keys, 647
unique indexes, 432
Unload event, 149, 706
UnLoad statement, 146-147
unloading forms, 146-147
UnRead property
    MailItem object (Outlook), 517
    Outlook, 522
Update method, 447
UPDATE statement (SQL), 416
UpdateControls method, 413
UpdateRecord method, 413
updating queries
    ADO, 466
    DAO, 465-466
upgrades, application support, 708-709
user interfaces, *see* GUI (graphical user
    interface) forms
user-defined data types, 371
    tags (naming conventions), 730
    text files, 367-369
UserProperties object, 509
UserProperties property (Outlook), 522

V

Validate event, 406-407
ValidatePassword function, 77
Value property
    ActiveX controls, 565
    Check Box control, 176
    Parameter object, 479
values
    GetSetting function, 650
    INI files, 639
    Nothing, 280-281
    null, 110
    passing arguments, 115
    property procedures, 275-276
    Registry, 641
        adding, 645-647
        editing, 644-645

tags (naming conventions), 727-728
variables
    converting, 105-107
    string variables, 87
    variant variables, 113-114
    Windows API functions, 613-614
Var function (SQL), 423
variable-length fields, 431
VariableName parameter (Line Input state-
    ment), 383
variables, 85
    arguments
        named, 117-118
        optional, 116-117
    arrays, 107
        bounds, 108
        declaring, 107-108
        dynamic, 108-109
        fixed, 108-109
        Preserve keyword, 109
        Redim statement, 108-109
    boolean, 92
    byte, 89-90
    Code window, 67-68
    constants, 118-119
    converting values, 105-107
    currency, 91-92
    Date, 92-93
    declaring, 97-98
        class modules, 266-267
        forcing, 100-101
        implicit/explicit comparisons, 98-99
    double, 91
    frmString example, 85-87
    global, 104
    Integer, 90
    Jet DAO, 439, 445
    lifetimes, 103-105
    long integers, 91
    lRetVal, 234
    lRetValue, 233
    modules, 104
    naming, 87, 99-101
    object, 95-96
    Outlook
        creating, 513-515
        Nothing, 520-521

passing to procedures, 114-116
Printer object, 328
Print_Line, 329
private
    declaring, 284-285
    strYear, 287
scope, 102-103
single, 91
static, 104-105
string, 94
    assigning values, 87
    fixed length, 94
    fixed width, 94
    passing arguments, 613
tags
    Access 97, 734-735
    DAO 3.5, 735-738
    VB 5, 738-739
Type statement, 119-120
variant, 88, 96-97, 109-110
    conversions, 111
    storage requirements, 110-112
    values, 113-114
watches, 234-237
wrd, 494
variant variables, 88, 96-97, 109-110
    storage requirements, 110-112
    values, 113-114
VarP function (SQL), 423
VarType function, 114
VBA (Visual Basic for Applications), 49
    Code window, 53-56
        automatic word completion, 65
        bookmarks, 62-64
        closing, 57
        color queuing, 59-60
        comment blocks, 65-66
        continuation characters, 57-58
        declarations, 67
        drag-and-drop editing, 68
        formatting, 69
        help, 67-68
        indents, 59, 66
        keyboard shortcuts, 60-62
        members lists, 67
        mouse shortcuts, 62
        opening, 56-57

outdents, 58-59
procedure seperators, 68
Search and Replace, 60
syntax checks, 67
tabs, sizing, 68
variables, 67-68
views, 68
compiler directives, 81-83
conditional branches, 70
    End If, 71
    If...Then, 70-72
    If...Then...Else, 72-73
    If...Then...Else If, 73-75
    If...Then...End If, 73-75
    Select Case, 75
loops, 69, 76
    Do, 79-81
    For...Next, 77-78
modules, 49
procedures, 50
    comments, 52-53
    functions, 51-52
    subroutines, 50-51
VBP files, 24
VerifyIdentity() function, 72
VerifyUser function, 52
Version value (GetSetting function), 650
Vertical scrollbar control, 166
View menu commands
    Call Stack, 237
    Code, 57
    Immediate window, 232, 440
    Properties Window, 125
    Refresh, 649
    Toolbars, 225
viewing Object Browser, 292-293
views
    Code window, 55, 68
    Registry Editor, 643-644
Visible property
    Internet Explorer, 541
    Menu Editor, 199
    menus, 204
    Picture Box control, 179
    pop-up menus, 203

W

w prefixes (API arguments), 606
Wall Data, 363
watches, 234-237
WebBrowser control events, 549-558
  BeforeNavigate2, 553
  CommandStateChange, 553-554
  DownloadBegin, 554
  DownloadComplete, 555
  NavigateComplete2, 555
  NetWindow2, 555
  ProgressChange, 555-556
  TitleChange, 556-558
WebPost, 683-684
WHERE clause (SQL), 419-422
While keyword, 80
whitespace, 701
Width property, 134, 172
Win.ini, see Windows API, INI files
Win32 API, upgrading to, 607-609
  functions, 608-609
  INI files, 609
WinAPI.vbp example, 615-616, 622-623, 629-630
  GetClassNameA function, 621-622
  GetCommandLineA function, 620-621
  GetComputerNameA function, 630
  GetDiskFreeSpaceA function, 632-634
  GetDriveTypeA function, 631-632
  GetParent function, 619-620
  GetSystemDirectoryA function, 624-625
  GetTempPath function, 625-626
  GetUserNameA function, 629
  GetVersionExA function, 626-628
  GetVolumeInformationA function, 634-637
  GetWindowsDirectoryA function, 623-624
  GetWindowTextA function, 616-618
  SetWindowTextA function, 618-619
windows, 121-123
  Crystal Reports
    Design window, 339-341
    Preview window, 341-342, 351-352
  Edit Formula dialog box, 344
  Immediate, 232-233
  Locals, 233-234

windows
  Project Explorer, 40
  Properties, 125-126
  see also forms
Windows 3.1, Win32 upgrades, 607-609
  functions, 608-609
  INI files, 609
Windows API (application programming interface), 599-600, 609-610
  compatibility, 603
  Declare statement, 610
    arguments lists, 612
    ByVal keyword, 612-613
    functions, 610-614
    subroutines, 610
  DLLs (dynamic link libraries), 600-603
    documentation, 603-607
  handles, 614-615
  INI file functions, 666-667
    GetPrivateProfileInt, 672
    GetPrivateProfileString, 671-672
    GetProfileInt, 669
    GetProfileString, 668-669
    WritePrivateProfileString, 669-671
    WriteProfileString, 667-668
  modules, 602
  pre-tested code, 602
  Registry, 654-656
    data types, 655
    RegCloseKey function, 664
    RegCreateKeyEx function, 656-659
    RegDeleteKey function, 665
    RegDeleteValue function, 664-665
    RegFlushKey function, 662
    RegOpenKeyEx function, 659-660
    RegQueryValueEx function, 662-664
    RegSetValueEx function, 660-662
  Win32 upgrades, 607-609
    functions, 608-609
    INI files, 609
  see also WinAPI.vbp example
Windows SDK reference for GetPrivateProfileString (Listing 25.1), 605
WindowState property, 135-136
With statement
  blocks, 189
  collections, 312-313

wizards

Crystal Reports, 342-343

Package and Deployment, 675-677

deploying applications, 682-684

script management, 684-685

starting, 677-682

testing, 685

Report Wizard, 346

database tables, 347

fields, 347-349

formulas, 349

linking data, 347-348

previewing, 351-352

sorting, 350

styles, 351

totals, 350-351

Toolbar Builder, 205-207

Word 97

documents, opening, 497-498

macro recorder, 498-499

object model, 496-497

commands, 498-501

Print Preview mode, 501-502

saving, 503-504

templates, creating, 503

word completion feature, 65

Word document in Print Preview (Listing 20.7), 502

Word Options dialog box, 122

word wrapping, 330

Word1.vbp, 492-494

Wordwrap property (Label control), 171

workarounds, 708

Worksheet objects, 495

wrapping words, 330

wrd object, 498

wrd variable, 494

Write statement, 383, 390-391

Write-Only properties, creating, 282

WritePrivateProfileSection function, 666

WritePrivateProfileString function, 666, 669-671

WriteProfileSection function, 666

WriteProfileString function, 666-668

X-Z

Xpos parameter (InputBox function), 158

year 2000 problem, troubleshooting, 93

Year property procedures, adding, 286-287

Ypos parameter (InputBox function), 158

Zoom property (Printer object), 333

ZOrder method, 140

Add to Your Sams Library Today with the Best Books for Programming, Operating Systems, and New Technologies

To order, visit our Web site at www.mcp.com or fax us at

1-800-835-3202

ISBN	Quantity	Description of Item	Unit Cost	Total Cost
0-672-31309-X		Visual Basic 6 Unleashed	$49.99	
0-672-31308-1		Sams Teach Yourself Database Programming with Visual Basic 6 in 21 Days	$45.00	
0-672-31299-9		Sams Teach Yourself OOP with Visual Basic in 21 Days	$39.99	
1-56276-577-9		Doing Objects in Visual Basic 6	$49.99	
0-672-31307-3		Sams Teach Yourself More Visual Basic 6 in 21 Days	$35.00	
1-56276-576-0		Dan Appleman's Developing COM/ActiveX Components with Visual Basic 6	$49.99	
0-672-31063-5		Roger Jennings' Database Developer's Guide with Visual Basic 6	$59.99	
1-57169-154-5		The Waite Group's Visual Basic 6 Client/Server How-To	$49.99	
		Shipping and Handling: See information below.		
		TOTAL		

Shipping and Handling

Standard	$5.00
2nd Day	$10.00
Next Day	$17.50
International	$40.00

201 W. 103rd Street, Indianapolis, Indiana 46290   1-800-835-3202 — Fax

Book ISBN 0-672-31054-6

Visual Basic 6 Unleashed

—Rob Thayer

Visual Basic 6 Unleashed provides comprehensive coverage of the most sought-after topics in Visual Basic programming. It provides a means for a casual-level Visual Basic programmer to quickly become productive with the new release of Visual Basic. This book provides you with a comprehensive reference to virtually all the topics used in today's leading-edge Visual Basic applications. You learn topics important to developers including creating and using ActiveX controls, creating wizards, adding and controlling RDO, tuning and optimization, and much more.

Price: $49.99 US/$71.95 CDN

ISBN: 0-672-31309-X

User Level: Advanced–Expert

1000 pages

Sams Teach Yourself Database Programming with Visual Basic 6 in 21 Days

—Curtis Smith

Sams Teach Yourself Database Programming with Visual Basic 6 in 21 Days is a tutorial that enables you to learn about working with databases in a set amount of time. The book offers a step-by-step approach to learning what can be a critical topic for developing applications. Each week focuses on a different aspect of database programming with Visual Basic. Learn about issues related to building simple database applications using the extensive collection of data controls available with Visual Basic. Concentrate on techniques for creating database applications using Visual Basic code. Study advanced topics such as SQL data definition and manipulation language and issues for multiuser applications such as locking schemes, database integrity, and application-level security.

Price: $45.00 US/$64.95 CDN

ISBN: 0-672-31308-1

User Level: Casual–Accomplished

900 pages

Sams Teach Yourself OOP with Visual Basic in 21 Days

—John Conley

In just 21 days, you'll have all the skills you need to get up and running efficiently with object-oriented programming with Visual Basic. With this complete tutorial you'll master the basics and then move on to the more advanced features and concepts. Master all the new and advanced features that object-oriented programming with Visual Basic offers. Learn how to effectively use the latest tools and features by following practical, real-world examples. Get expert tips from a leading authority on implementing object-oriented programming with Visual Basic in the corporate environment. This book is designed for the way you learn. Go chapter by chapter through the warranted, step-by-step lessons, or just choose those lessons that interest you the most.

Price: $39.99 US/$57.95 CDN

ISBN: 0-672-31299-9

User Level: Intermediate

600 pages

Doing Objects in Visual Basic 6

—Deborah Kurata

Doing Objects in Visual Basic 6 is an intermediate level tutorial that begins with the fundamentals of OOP. It advances to the technical aspects of using the Visual Basic IDE to create objects and interface with databases, Web sites, and Internet applications. This revised edition features more technical information than the last edition and specifically highlights the features of the new release of Visual Basic.

Price: $49.99 US/$46.18 CDN   *User Level: Intermediate–Expert*

ISBN: 1-56276-577-9   *560 pages*

Sams Teach Yourself More Visual Basic 6 in 21 Days

—Lowell Mauer

Sams Teach Yourself More Visual Basic 6 in 21 Days provides comprehensive, self-taught coverage of the most sought-after topics in Visual Basic programming. This book uses the step-by-step approach of the best-selling *Sams Teach Yourself* series to continue more detailed coverage of the latest version of Visual Basic. Learn about enhanced controls, collections, loops, MDI and SDI, database processing and designing a database application, Internet programming, ActiveX documents, building online help, and using Crystal Reports, including how to incorporate it into your applications.

Price: $35.00 US/$50.95 CDN   *User Level: Beginner–Intermediate*

ISBN: 0-672-31307-3   *700 pages*

Dan Appleman's Developing COM/ActiveX Components with Visual Basic 6

—Dan Appleman

Dan Appleman's Developing COM/ActiveX Components with Visual Basic 6 is a focused tutorial for learning component development. It teaches you the programming concepts and the technical steps needed to create ActiveX components. Dan Appleman is one of the foremost developers in the Visual Basic community and is the author that Visual Basic programmers recommend to their friends and colleagues. He consistently delivers on his promise to break through the confusion and hype surrounding Visual Basic and ActiveX and goes beyond the basics to show you common pitfalls and practical solutions for key problems.

Price: $49.99 US/$71.95 CDN   *User Level: Intermediate*

ISBN: 1-56276-576-0   *850 pages*

Roger Jennings' Database Developer's Guide with Visual Basic 6

—*Roger Jennings*

Roger Jennings' Database Developer's Guide with Visual Basic 6 offers complete coverage of Visual Basic 6, ActiveX controls, Microsoft's new Internet database technologies and Microsoft's newest client-server technology, Microsoft transaction server. You learn updated coverage of OLE DB and ADO data access objects and data-aware controls, database and query design concepts, an introduction to database front-end design, advanced programming for data access and automation, multiuser and client/server database front ends, intranets and the Internet, and enterprise-level development techniques.

Price: $59.99 US/$85.95 CDN

User Level: Accomplished— Expert

ISBN: 0-672-31063-5

1,100 pages

The Waite Group's Visual Basic 6 Client/Server How-To

—Noel Jerke, et al

Visual Basic 6 Client/Server How-To is a practical step-by-step guide to implementing three-tiered distributed client/server solutions using the tools provided in Microsoft's Visual Basic 6. It addresses the needs of programmers looking for answers to real-world questions and assures them that what they create really works. It also helps simplify the client/server development process by providing a framework for solution development. You save hundreds of hours of programming time by learning step-by-step solutions to more than 75 Visual Basic 6 client/server problems. This book covers topics such as OOP, ODBC, OLE, RDO, distributed computing, and three-tier client/server development and addresses the issues associated with deploying business rules on an intermediate, centralized server.

Price: $49.99 US/$71.95 CDN

User Level: Intermediate– Advanced

ISBN: 1-57169-154-5

1,000 pages

What's on the CD-ROM

The companion CD-ROM contains all the authors' source code and samples from the book and many third-party software products.

Windows 95/NT4 Installation Instructions

1. Insert the CD-ROM disc into your CD-ROM drive.

2. From the Windows 95 desktop, double-click the My Computer icon.

3. Double-click the icon representing your CD-ROM drive.

4. Double-click the icon titled SETUP.EXE to run the installation program.

5. Installation creates a program group named Peter Norton VB6. This group will contain icons to browse the CD-ROM.

Note: If Windows 95 is installed on your computer and you have the AutoPlay feature enabled, the SETUP.EXE program starts automatically whenever you insert the disc into your CD-ROM drive.